Hellenic Studies 11

VICTIM OF THE MUSES

VICTIM OF THE MUSES

POET AS SCAPEGOAT, WARRIOR, AND HERO IN GRECO-ROMAN AND INDO-EUROPEAN MYTH AND HISTORY

TODD M. COMPTON

CENTER FOR HELLENIC STUDIES
Trustees for Harvard University
Washington, DC
Distributed by Harvard University Press
Cambridge, Massachusetts, and London, England
2006

Victim of the muses: poet as scapegoat, warrior, and hero in Greco-Roman and
    Indo-European myth and history
    by Todd M. Compton
Copyright © 2006 Center for Hellenic Studies, Trustees for Harvard University
All Rights Reserved.
Published by Center for Hellenic Studies, Trustees for Harvard University,
    Washington, DC
Distributed by Harvard University Press, Cambridge, Massachusetts, and
    London, England
Volume Editor: Casey Dué
Production Editor: Ivy Livingston
Cover Design and Illustration: Joni Godlove

EDITORIAL TEAM:
Senior Advisors: W. Robert Connor, Gloria Ferrari Pinney, Albert Henrichs,
    James O'Donnell, Bernd Seidensticker
Editorial Board: Gregory Nagy (Editor-in-Chief), Christopher Blackwell,
    Christopher Dadian (Managing Editor), Casey Dué (Executive Editor),
    Mary Ebbott (Executive Editor), Olga Levaniouk, Anne Mahoney, Leonard
    Muellner, Ross Scaife
Production Editors: M. Zoie Lafis, Ivy Livingston, Jennifer Reilly
Web Producer: Mark Tomasko

LIBRARY OF CONGRESS CATALOGING-IN-PUBLICATION DATA

Compton, Todd Merlin.
Victim of the muses: poet as scapegoat, warrior, and hero in Greco-Roman and
    Indo-European myth and history / by Todd Merlin Compton.
        p. cm. — (Hellenic studies ; 11)
    Includes bibliographical references and index.
    ISBN 0-674-01958-X
1. Authors, Classical—Biography. 2 Poets, Greek—Biography. 2 Poets, Latin—
    Biography. 4 Scapegoat. I. Title. II. Series.
PA3005.C66 2006
809'.93352—dc22

                                    2006002331

Ex is, qui in porticibus spatiabantur, lapides in Eumolpum recitantem miserunt. At ille, qui plausum ingenii sui nouerat, operuit caput extraque templum profugit. Timui ego, ne me poetam uocaret.

Petronius Satyricon

Contents

Preface

THE FOLLOWING STUDY started out as an attempt to do for hero poets what Fontenrose had done for hero athletes. Thus, his methodology of theme comparison will be apparent in the following pages, and also an interest in hero cult. However, Aesop, Hipponax, and Sappho, especially, led me to the central theme of the *pharmakos*, and I became interested in the theme of the exclusion of the poet—by trial, exile, or execution/murder—of which the *pharmakos* theme is the ritual reflex. Though hero cult and the *pharmakos* complex are related, my focus shifted to the scapegoat.

However, this study's compass goes far beyond the classic Aesopic *pharmakos* pattern. Any time a poet-satirist is subjected to legal punishment, is exiled, or is executed or murdered, I have examined the story. Such themes are closely related to the *pharmakos* pattern, of course, for that unfortunate victim was sometimes chosen by trial, was forcibly expelled from his city, and, at least in legend, was killed. Expulsion is the key theme.

I have examined such stories whether they were legendary or historical—or, as was often the case, an ambiguous interface between the two. Thus my focus is quite different from the investigation of those who have been concerned with proving a story ahistorical. While they often seem to lose interest as soon as they have come to the conclusion that a story is not factually true, I became increasingly interested in persistent legendary patterns, which can be very archaic. Often, it is close to impossible to ascertain whether a story is historical or legendary, though one can make educated guesses one way or the other. There are undoubtedly ahistorical legends of exiled or murdered poets (most obvious when there is a miraculous or supernatural framework, as in the legend of Simonides in which the Dioscuri save the poet from death and punish a stingy, dishonest patron); but there are undoubtedly historical cases of exiled or executed poets. To complicate the issue, certainly historical cases often have legendary accretions. But, for my purposes, certainty on the question of historicity is not necessary, though, when possible, it is useful to have. A legendary pattern has its own significance and interest.

Thus, my analysis of these stories, and my central theme, led me to probe the meaning of the scapegoat in Greek, and other cultures, both in legend and history. I became especially interested in the positive aspects of the scapegoat—in the case of the poet, he is inspired; in legendary cases, often overtly consecrated by a theophany, thus sacred. Seemingly, much different from the deformed human *katharma*, refuse, stoned out of Greek cities. Of course, the scapegoat is ambiguous, even in ritual, and the effect of the scapegoat is always positive, according to the ideology of the ritual.

In addition, the connections of the scapegoat—and of our poets—with war led to related issues. Often the *pharmakoi* are excluded to deal with war or invasion as a crisis. And often, our poets had military vocations, partially or dominantly. Archilochus was a soldier, and was reportedly killed in battle, a death linked to a cultic legend. Tyrtaeus is a standard deformed, dim-witted, mad *pharmakos* figure, whom the Athenians have selected as their least desirable citizen, to expel from the city and give to the Spartans; he becomes the Spartans' general, poetic source of martial inspiration, and savior.

Furthermore, satirical poetry and language have often been compared to violent combat. A common denominator of poet and warrior is madness—or, more precisely, possession. The aggression of the satirist and the aggression of the warrior are both ambiguously focused toward the good of the community, and the warrior becomes as much a scapegoat as does the poet. The warrior wields a sword or spear; as does the satirist, verbally (though his poetry is often compared to the violence of the animal's bite, as well as to weapons).

After examining the Greek poets, I turn to a comparative perspective. In 1975, M. L. West criticized classicists for examining Greek culture in isolation, then showed how the myth of Helen in Greece had possible Indo-European roots.[1] Though there are certainly pitfalls and uncertainties in cross-cultural comparison, such comparison nevertheless often offers important insights. Greek etymology, for instance, without study of extra-Greek cognates, would be obviously uncritical. The study of extra-Greek mythical and cultural cognates is just as valuable for an understanding of Greek myth and culture. West referred to analysis of Helen, without its Indo-European context, as a "dereliction of knowledge,"[2] and wrote that in some (not all) areas of Greek studies, "it is necessary to view the Greeks in a larger spatio-temporal context

---

[1] West 1975.
[2] West 1975:15.

... We must not be afraid to cross boundaries ... I would hesitate to dismiss any branch of knowledge as having nothing to contribute to the rest."[3] Such study, like all other research, is subject to constant revision, but some solid progress has been made in this area. The studies of West, Georges Dumézil, Marcello Durante, Gregory Nagy, and Calvert Watkins on the prehistory of Indo-European poetics effectively show how breadth of perspective can contribute toward specialization. Watkins's *How to Kill a Dragon* (1995) is an exciting contribution both to comparative poetics and myth.[4]

Thus, in chapters 17 through 19, I examine poets and myths about poets chiefly in two European countries, Ireland and Germany. Many of the themes in Greek culture receive affirmation and illumination from these poets, especially in my analysis of the combination of aggression and possession in the archaic poet. Many Irish poets were warriors, and two of the chief warrior figures studied by Dumézil, Starkaðr and Suibhne, were leading poets in their cultures. I examine their poetic dimensions in chapter eighteen. In the following chapters I examine exiled or executed poets in Rome.

I should make a few preliminary points. First, my definition of the poet is broad: I look at any verbal artist or satirist. To me, the continuity of satirical language patterns and themes is more important than defining the poet strictly as a metrical practitioner. Thus, Aesop, Socrates, and Cicero are included as important examples of the pattern I discuss. I touch on the relationship of poetry, philosophy, and oratory in the Cicero chapter. In the Mythical Poets chapter, I include Marsyas and related figures, sometimes musicians, not poets by limited definition, largely because Aesop and Socrates were both explicitly compared to Marsyas. But poetry and music were not separate spheres in ancient Greece—for instance, we have the relationship of the word *mousikē* with Muse, *Mousa*, traditional consecrator of poets. The etymology of *poiētēs*, which has a base meaning of 'maker, creator', suggests the broad definition of poet I am working with in this study, (verbal) creative artist.[5] Bloomfield defines "early" poets as using "all forms of verbal art except conversation. It is difficult to find an accurate word to cover these forms in early societies because verbal art is so closely woven into its culture ... Some

---

[3] West 1975:15. West has dealt with Semitic parallels to Greek myth and philosophy extensively in his books (see now his vast *East Face of Helicon*, West 1997), more rarely with Indo-European parallels. But see the following note. Burkert has also dealt mostly with Semitic parallels in his comparative work, see Burkert 1992, 2004. Cf. Seaford 1994; Penglase 1994; Sergent 1998.

[4] See West 1973 and 1973b; Dumézil 1943; Durante 1958, 1962, and 1971; Nagy 1979; Bremmer 1987:2, with bibliography; Watkins 1995.

[5] See below, ch. 3.

'poetry' will of course include what we normally mean when we use 'prose' as opposed to 'poetry.'"[6]

Second, and paradoxically, though this study examines poets, it is chiefly a study in myth, legend, religion, and history, though it has obvious relevance to literary study, especially to archaic Greek poetry. Examination of the poet's poetry is frequent, though the life of the poet is examined first. Clearly, this is merely one way of looking at an issue, not a value judgment on a "right" or "wrong" way.

Third, much of the biographical evidence for poets is late, but this does not automatically mean that it could not be based on earlier traditions. K. J. Dover writes that, "to reject every historical proposition for which a writer of the Roman period fails to cite a Classical source by name . . . would be to turn the *ars nesciendi* into an obsession."[7] On the other hand, some late evidence will clearly not reflect early tradition; when this can be convincingly shown, it is obviously an advance in scholarship. But late does not automatically mean valueless. One of the most significant contributions of Timothy Gantz's magnum opus, *Early Greek Myth*, is its repeated demonstration that many myths not attested in the literary record until Hellenistic times or later were certainly pre-Hellenistic, because they are attested in art much earlier than in the fragmentary literary record. For example, Heracles' murder of Linus is not attested in the written record until Diodorus and Apollodorus; however, it is recorded in fifth-century BC red-figure pottery.[8] In fact, we should often regard the first attestation in the historical record as the end of a process (often including much variation in oral tradition and legend, especially in the heroizing narratives we will examine in this study) rather than the beginning.

Fourth, though I examine the lives of many of the most important Greek and Latin poets, I am by no means trying to deal with all major Greek or Latin poets. Still less am I trying to fit them all into the "scapegoat-exile" pattern. Many poets, in fact, even many satirists, are not in any way related to the pattern. Many seem to follow a different pattern, the bright mirror inversion of the dark scapegoat satirist, so to speak. This pattern would certainly be worthy of study, but is not examined in this book. Such poets do not seem to be embroiled in bitter quarrels; they often live peacefully in their home cities all

---

[6] Bloomfield and Dunn 1989:1n.

[7] Dover 1976:39. For the importance of "late" sources in the study of myth, see Henrichs 1987. Obviously, archaic material was often preserved in masses of Hellenistic and Imperial scholia and in collections of myth. Biographical traditions, historical or otherwise, also preserved some archaic data.

[8] Gantz 1993:378–379, cf. 411, 438, 459.

their lives; they perhaps have close, friendly ties with local political leaders. In genetic Indo-European terms, the poet often has mutually beneficial relations with his or her patron.[9] One thinks of Sophocles, Pindar, or Horace. However, the "dark" pattern is found frequently enough to be an important pattern.

II

All scholarship is based on the work of others. Many of my influences will be apparent; I am especially indebted to the work of Walter Burkert, J. Fontenrose, and Nagy, in the field of classics; in the field of Indo-European studies, Dumézil and Jaan Puhvel. Though I differ with Mary Lefkowitz occasionally, I owe much to her book on the Greek poets. I was fortunate in having Puhvel as head of my doctoral committee; his encouragement and polymathic expertise in philological and Dumézilian matters were invaluable. I owe Gregory Nagy special thanks for his willingness to foster comparative work like this book in the field of classics. In addition to his own pathbreaking and ever-stimulating work, he will leave a important legacy in the work of scholars whom he has generously "aided and abetted." I would also like to thank Casey Dué Hackney, Leonard Muellner, and M. Zoie Lafis for help in preparing this book for publication.

I am far from a specialist in Irish or Sanskrit, so I am grateful to my co-worker Randall Gordon for his help with those languages in my Indo-European chapters. In addition, I am grateful to Steven Lattimore, Ann Bergren, Kees Bolle, Donald Ward, Richard Janko, Jan Bremmer, Michael Haslam, and Leslie Myrick for reading parts or all of this manuscript; their criticisms and suggestions have improved my work immeasurably. All of the limitations in this book are entirely my own, however.

On a personal level, I would like to thank my parents and siblings for encouragement while this book was beginning. Thanks also to Dave and Mike, Terry, Stephen, Dan, Elbert, Kaz, Leslie, Martha, Jeff, Katy, Laurel, Robert, Becky, and Esther, for friendship and inspiration in the ongoing quest. I am indebted to Gene Wolfe, classicist and fantasist nonpareil, for patiently enduring early descriptions of the content of this book. However, this book is dedicated to Laura, who has shown the continued truth of *Odyssey* vi 182-185.

[9] Watkins 1995:70–84.

Abbreviations

ANET: *Ancient Near Eastern Texts* = Pritchard 1974

CHCL I: Easterling and Knox 1985

CHCL II: Kenney and Clausen 1982

DK: Diels, H. and Kranz, W., eds. 1934–1937. *Die Fragmente der Vorsokratiker.* 3 vols. 5th ed. Berlin

FGH: Jacoby, F., ed. 1923–1958. *Die Fragmente der griechischen Historiker.* 3 vols. Berlin

IG: *Inscriptiones Graecae*

ITS: *Irish Texts Society*

LCL: Loeb Classical Library

OCD: Hammond and Scullard 1970 (2nd ed.)

OCD³: Hornblower and Spawforth 1996

OLD: Glare, P. G. W., ed. 1982. *Oxford Latin Dictionary.* Oxford

PCG: Kassel and Austin 1983–

RE: Pauly, Wissowa, and Kroll 1893–

Part One

GREECE

1

The *Pharmakos* in Archaic Greece

THE GREEK RITUAL SCAPEGOAT, referred to as the *pharmakos*, provides an essential foundation for the study of legendary lives of the archaic Greek poets. The lives of Aesop, Hipponax, and Tyrtaeus are especially close to *pharmakos* themes and characteristics. The Greek ritual scapegoat is a complex religio-historical phenomenon, and aspects of it have been vigorously debated by scholars. Nevertheless, that the *pharmakos* complex existed in some form is undoubted.

Ritual

The *pharmakos*[1] was a human embodiment of evil who was expelled from the Greek city at moments of crisis and disaster. The name is probably, but problematically, connected with *pharmakon*, 'medicine, drug, poison'.[2] Both poison and drug were originally magical; so a *pharmakon* is a magical dose (Greek *dosis* 'gift, dose', cf. the German *Gift* 'poison') causing destruction or healing. *Pharmakos* then would be 'magic man, wizard' first, though the borderline

---

[1] On the *pharmakos* custom, the treatments I have used the most are Burkert 1979:59–77; Vernant 1981; Bremmer 1983b; and Burkert 1985:82–84. Other useful sources are Nilsson 1967 1:107–110; Gebhard 1926; Höfer 1884; Farnell 1896 4:268–284; Wiechers 1961:31–43; Guépin 1968:81–100; Deubner 1932:179–198; Frazer 1911 vol. IX, esp. 252–274; Harrison 1922:95–119; Murray 1934:13–16, 253–258; O'Connor-Visser 1987:211–232; Hughes 1991:139–165 (mainly concerned with the question of whether the *pharmakos* was killed); Parker 1983:257–280; Ogden 1997:15–23 (even including a few pages on Aesop and "scapegoat-poets," 38–40, 44–46) and passim; Faraone 1992:96–100. Two influential books that devote much attention to the *pharmakos* are Girard 1977:9, 94–98, 293–294, 298, 307, and Derrida 1981:128–134. For the literary *Nachleben* of the *pharmakos*, see Frye 1957: 41–48, 148–149 and Vickery 1972. Further bibliography can be found in Burkert 1985:379–380, 82–84; Derrida 1981:130n56; Höfer 1884:2276–2277. For Roman "rituals of exclusion," see Brelich 1949/50. "*Pharmakos* theory" has begun to be applied to political history, see Ogden 1997; Rosenbloom 2002.

[2] Lloyd 1979:44n184; Burkert 1979:65; Derrida 1981:132n59; 131 on the ambiguity of the concept of poison in Greece and Rome, quoting Aulus Gellius *Attic Nights* 12.9 and others.

3

between magic and religion is not easy to define; the early *pharmakos* might have been 'magic man' or he might have been 'sacred-man'. Then, presumably, he or she was 'healer, poisoner', then later, expiatory sacrifice for the city and rascal, off-scourings, and so on.[3] On the one hand, the *pharmakos* could be the medicine that heals the city (according to scholia on Aristophanes *Knights* 1136c, the *pharmakos* is used in order to obtain a *therapeia*—'service, tending, medical treatment'—for the prevailing disaster[4]); on the other, he could be the poison that had to be expelled from the system (he is often ugly or criminal). Thus these two interpretations are not exclusive.[5]

Sometimes the *pharmakos* crisis was real (such as a plague or famine),[6] as at Massilia ("for the Massilians, as often as they were suffering from the plague . . .")[7] and Colophon ("either famine or plague or another harm").[8] Sometimes it was a periodic calendrical moment of crisis, as in the Attic Thargelia, when the city had to be cleansed before the first fruits of the harvest could be stored up.[9]

Usually a criminal or a slave or an excessively ugly or deformed man[10] was chosen as *pharmakos*, a cast-off from society. Strabo wrote that the *pharmakos* was "one of those who were guilty," (at Leucas).[11] According to Plutarch,

---

[3] For *pharmakos* as a term of abuse in comedy, see Harrison 1922:97; but it is already a term of abuse in our earliest attestation, Hipponax, 5–10W.

[4] For *pharmakos* as *therapeia*, cf. *theraps, therapōn*, 'attendant, servant', which is probably, but not certainly, cognate with Hittite *tarpassa-, tarpa(na)lli-*, 'substitute victim'. Cf. Tischler 1993:27–32. Nagy and others have interpreted Patroclus as Achilles' substitute victim; see Nagy 1979:292–297; 33 and 1983:193–194; Lowenstam 1981:126–178. However, cf. Greenhalgh 1982:81–90. It is true that *therapōn* is nowhere found in Greek with the meaning, 'substitute victim'. But, as the Greek-Hittite cognate (if it is valid) shows, there can be a relationship between the concept of servant and the concept of substitute victim. Cf. the story of Tamun, "the Stump," in ch. 17.

[5] See also Dodds 1951:59n88; Harrison 1922:108. Cf. the principle, "he that wounds shall make whole," discussed in Fontenrose 1978:78–79; Puhvel 1987:134 and 1976:20–22.

[6] Cf. the Aenianes' myth of stoning their king because of a disastrous drought, Plutarch *Greek Questions* 297b–c, 294a; Burkert 1979:66; and Apollonius' stoning of a beggar during an Ephesian plague (Philostratus *Life of Apollonius* 4.10: "the plague fell upon the Ephesians, and nothing could protect them from it," ἡ νόσος τοῖς Ἐφησίοις ἐνέπεσε καὶ οὐδὲν ἦν πρὸς αὐτὴν αὔταρκες). For the connection between famine (*limos*) and plague (*loimos*), see Bremmer 1983b:301n17.

[7] Petronius fr. 1 *nam Massilienses quotiens pestilentia laborabant.*

[8] Tzetzes *Chiliades* ("Thousands") 5.728: εἴτ' οὖν λιμός, εἴτε λοιμός, εἴτε καὶ βλάβος ἄλλο.

[9] Harpocration, s.v. *pharmakos*; also at Abdera, Scholia in Ovid *Ibis* 467 (La Penna), *in uno quoque anno . . . in Kalendis Ianuarii*, "every year . . . at the Kalends of January"; and at Leucas, Strabo *Geography* 10.2.9, *kat' eniauton*, "every year." See Burkert 1979:65.

[10] Cf. Wiechers 1961:34–35; Bremmer 1983b:303; Garland 1995:23–26. Scholia on Aristophanes *Knights* 1136c: λίαν ἀγεννεῖς καὶ πένητας καὶ ἀχρήστους, "exceedingly low-born, penniless, and useless," following text in Koster 1969 ad loc.

[11] *Geography* 10.2.9, τινα τῶν ἐν αἰτίαις ὄντων. See also Ogden 1997:16nn20–21.

at Chaeronea he was a slave;[12] at Colophon he was excessively ugly, "the most deformed of all"[13] and at Athens, "the most unpleasant and mistreated by nature, maimed and lame man, such sort . . . they sacrificed."[14]

At Athens there was a *pharmakos* for males and one for females. "They would lead out two men to serve as a cleansing [*katharsia*] for the city in the Thargelia, one on behalf of the men, and one on behalf of the women."[15] Sometimes he was chosen by public vote.[16] In the case of a *pharmakos* as criminal, this public council would take the form of a trial, which must lie behind his selection.

He was called *pharmakos*, *katharma* ('that which is thrown away in cleansing: in plural, offscourings, refuse of a sacrifice . . . in plural, purification', LSJ), *perikatharma* (an intensification of *katharma* from *perikathairō*, 'cleanse on all sides, or completely'), *peripsēma* (from *peripsaō*, 'wipe all round, wipe clean',—so, 'anything wiped off, offscouring'[17]); at Chaeronea, an expelled slave was called *boulimos*, 'ravenous hunger'.[18] The whole expulsion process was called *katharsis*. For example, Callimachus tells us that "at Abdera a bought man (became) the purification [*katharsion*] of the city."[19] *Pharmakoi* were some-

---

[12] *Convivial Questions* 6.8.1 (693f); Burkert 1979:65. The rite at Chaeronea was not technically a *pharmakos* rite, but it was close to it; cf. Deubner 1932:195; Bremmer 1983b:302, "The Colophonian *pharmakos* ate slave's food" (Hipponax 8, 26.6, 115.8W), and Bremmer 1983b:305n41; Deubner 1932:182nn7, 8, 9.

[13] Tzetzes *Chiliades* 5.731, τὸν πάντων ἀμορφότερον.

[14] τὸν ἀηδέστατον καὶ παρὰ τῆς φύσεως ἐπιβεβουλευμένον πηρόν, χωλόν, τοὺς τοιούτους . . . ἔθυον, Scholia in Aeschylus *Seven Against Thebes* 680, cf. Deubner 1932:184; Scholia in Aristophanes *Frogs* 742: "vile men and those mistreated by nature," τοὺς γὰρ φαύλους καὶ παρὰ τῆς φύσεως ἐπιβεβουλευομένους.

[15] Harpocration, s.v. *pharmakos*, δύο ἄνδρας ἐξῆγον καθάρσια ἐσομένους τῆς πόλεως ἐν τοῖς Θαργηλίοις, ἕνα μὲν ὑπὲρ τῶν ἀνδρῶν, ἕνα δὲ ὑπὲρ τῶν γυναικῶν. Also, Hesychius s.v. *pharmakoi*: "Pharmakoi: those who cleanse, cleansing the cities thoroughly [*perikathairontes*], a man and a woman." φαρμακοί, καθαρτήριοι, περικαθαίροντες τὰς πόλεις, ἀνὴρ καὶ γυνή. This latter reference could be a misunderstanding of the first. Cf. Bremmer 1983b:301n12, Deubner 1932:179–180; Frazer 1911:254; Guépin 1968:89.

[16] E.g. Hipponax 128W, *psēphidi . . . boulēi dēmosiēi*, "stoned [?] . . . by public decree"; see Wiechers 1961:36. See below, ch. 4 (Hipponax). Cf. the name Polycrite, 'she who was chosen by many', or 'much chosen' or 'chosen out of many', discussed by Bremmer 1983b:305; Burkert 1979:73. Cf. Fontenrose 1968:78 (themes H, I), 92. Ostracism, involving a public vote, has been compared to the *pharmakos* custom, see Vernant 1981:205n66; Burkert 1985:83; Ranulf 1933:132–141.

[17] Cf. Frazer 1911:255n1; *1 Corinthians* 4.13.

[18] See Bremmer 1983b:302n18, and LSJ s.v.

[19] Callimachus *Aetia* fr. 90 (Pf.), *diēgēsis* II, Ἀβδήροις ὠνητὸς ἄνθρωπος καθάρσιον τῆς πόλεως. Also, Harpocration, s.v. *pharmakos*, quoting Ister: . . . to be purification [*katharsia*]of the city" καθάρσια ἐσομένους τῆς πόλεως ; ". . . pharmakoi, who indeed cleanse [*kathairousi*] the cities by their deaths"; . . . φαρμακούς, οἵπερ καθαίρουσι τὰς πόλεις τῷ ἑαυτῶν φόνῳ, Scholia on Aristophanes *Knights*, at 1136c; *Suda*, s.v. *katharma*: ". . . for the purification [*katharmou*] of the

times fed by the state, often for a considerable length of time (at Massilia for a year); sometimes, as at Colophon, they were fed immediately before expulsion. Bremmer notes that being kept by the state was usually reserved only for very important people.[20]

On the day of his departure, the *pharmakos* was dressed in "holy garments," *vestibus sacris*, and adorned with sprigs (at Massilia);[21] at Athens, the two *pharmakoi* wore black and white figs.[22] The holy garments show the "positive," sacral side of the scapegoat, which is also suggested by another name for *pharmakoi*, *sumbakkhoi*, 'fellow-possessed'.[23] This suggests that there was an ecstatic, perhaps Dionysiac, aspect of the *pharmakos*. Ogden writes that the name probably means that "scapegoats were held to be in some sort of divinely possessed, ecstatic and exceptionally powerful state at the point of their expulsion."[24]

After a procession and circumambulation, an important part of the rite,[25] the *pharmakoi* were driven from the city,[26] often chased away by stoning, a ritual that provides community solidarity (all who stone participate in the punishment), even as it extrudes its chosen object.[27]

At Colophon, the scapegoat was reportedly beaten around the genitals by figsprays and squills (large onions).[28] Outside the city, according to some accounts, whose reliability has been thoroughly debated, he was killed—by

---

city they killed a man who was adorned, whom they called *katharma*." Ὑπὲρ δὲ καθαρμοῦ πόλεως ἀνῄρουν ἐστολισμένον τινά, ὅν ἐκάλουν κάθαρμα. Also, Lysias 6.53; Tzetzes *Chiliades* 726, 730, 761. See Else 1957:224–232 and 421–431 for an introduction to the concept of *katharsis* in Greece; as *katharsis* is a key element in tragedy, it is not surprising that the *pharmakos* pattern has been analyzed in a number of Greek tragedies—see especially Vernant 1981:200–205 (Oedipus), Pucci 1990; Foley 1993 (Oedipus, analyzing the problem of the ending), also Segal 1981:141, 46–51 (Antigone, Ajax); Dodds 1953:196, 215 and Seaford 1994:313–318 (Pentheus). Cf. Vickers 1973:609–616; Parker 1983; Schmitt 1921.

[20] Bremmer 1983b:305; Burkert 1979:65. Cf. Plato *Apology* 36d–e, with notes by Dyer 1976:106.

[21] Petronius fr. 1, cf. Frazer 1911:253.

[22] Helladius *ad* Photius *Bibliotheca* 534a (Henry ed.); Bremmer 1983b:301.

[23] Helladius *ad* Photius *Bibliotheca* 534a (Henry ed.).

[24] Ogden 1997:21, cf. Seaford 1994:313–318.

[25] Petronius fr. 1; Callimachus fr. 90, *diēgēsis*, cf. Dio Chrysostom 8.14; Bremmer 1983b:313–314.

[26] Callimachus fr. 90, *diēgēsis*; Ister, in Harpocration, s.v. *pharmakos*; Murray 1934:326–331; Rotolo 1980. See Rowland's discussion of expulsion from a community, 1980:91–94.

[27] Hirzel 1909:244, cf. Lloyd-Jones 1968:136; Gras 1984:75–88; Steiner 1995. For stoning generally, Lactantius on Statius *Thebaid* 10.793, *saxis occidebatus a populo*, "he was killed by the people with stones"; Callimachus fr. 90, *diēgēsis* II 29–40; Burkert 1979:67; Rowland 1980:95–96; Visser 1982:404–405n5, 408–409; Pease 1918:5–18; Fehling 1974:59–80; Barkan 1979:41–53; Eitrem 1977:282–294; Schadewaldt 1936:29. See below on Hipponax, ch. 4.

[28] Hipponax 5–6W; Bremmer 1983b:300, 301; cf. Frazer 1911:257–258. For the importance of beating in the *pharmakos* rite, see Harrison 1922:100–101.

stoning, burning, or by being thrown over a cliff into the ocean.[29] At the very least, the reports of the *pharmakos'* death show society's desire for it; expulsion itself is a kind of symbolic death. There is some evidence, at least, that the death of the *pharmakos* was seen, ideologically, as a sacrifice, as a number of sources refer to the victim as being "killed" or "sacrificed." A scholiast writes, *victima . . . inmolatur.* "The victim . . . is sacrificed."[30] Murray rightly observes that these are late scholia, and that the earliest sources do not speak of killing or sacrificing a *pharmakos*. Even if this is accepted, it is indisputable that there was a *mimēma* of a death in the *pharmakos* pattern; Murray admits that this may show that "a *pharmakos*-sacrifice was known to have existed at some time somewhere." Vernant suggests that human sacrifice perhaps did take place, originally, but Bremmer is probably correct when he doubts the presence of actual human sacrifice connected with the *pharmakos* custom. In the legends connected with the *pharmakos*, however, execution was almost a requirement.

Pharmakos: Legendary *Aitia*

The *pharmakos* custom actually took place, though details of how it was practiced are not always certain. But these ritual occurrences were always tightly bound up with stories serving as *aitia* for them in Athenian tradition:

> ὅτι ἔθος ἦν ἐν Ἀθήναις φαρμακοὺς ἄγειν δύο . . . τὸ δὲ καθάρσιον τοῦτο λοιμικῶν νόσων ἀποτροπιασμὸς ἦν, λαβὸν τὴν ἀρχὴν ἀπὸ Ἀνδρόγεω τοῦ Κρητός, οὗ τεθνηκότος ἐν ταῖς Ἀθήναις παρανόμως τὴν λοιμικὴν ἐνόσησαν οἱ Ἀθηναῖοι νόσον, καὶ ἐκράτει τὸ ἔθος ἀεὶ καθαίρειν τὴν πόλιν τοῖς φαρμακοῖς.

> Because it was the custom at Athens to lead two *pharmakoi* . . . This cleansing served to ward off plagues of disease, and it took its beginning from Androgeus the Cretan [son of King Minos], because the Athenians were afflicted with a plague of disease when he died

---

[29] See the following note; Bremmer 1983b:315–317; Murray 1934:326–331; below, app. A. For precipitation over a cliff, often linked with stoning, Steiner 1995, cf. Barkan 1979:54–55. See also Frazer 1913 3:417, at 4.22.7.

[30] Scholiast on Ovid *Ibis* 467, b. Also, Scholia on Aristophanes *Knights* 1136c: *ethuon*: "they killed [or "sacrificed"]." Scholia on Aeschylus *Seven Against Thebes* 680, *ethuon* "they killed [or "sacrificed"]" as quoted in Wiechers 1961:34. Lactantius on Statius *Thebaid* X 793: *hostia humana* "human sacrifice"; Tzetzes *Chiliades* 5.731: *tēn thusian,* "the sacrifice." Murray 1934:328–329, cf. 32–35; Bremmer 1983b:315–318; Vernant 1981:200n41. Barkan notes that while some scholars (e.g. Hirzel) have suggested that stoning outside the city took place so that the victim might escape, the evidence does not support such an idea, 1979:52.

unjustly in Athens, and this custom began to be in force, to always cleanse the city with *pharmakoi*.

Helladius, in Photius *Bibliotheca* 279[31]

Androgeus is a figure who has not been given the attention he deserves, as *pharmakos* theorists have tended to focus on the ritual itself. It is significant that he was an athlete who had been victorious in the Panathenaic games: "defeating all the contestants in the games."[32] He is thus a type of youthful vigor and agonistic victory, rather than the deformed refuse one might expect as background for a *pharmakos* myth. In one variant of his death legend, he was killed by the men he had defeated. "He was waylaid and murdered by the jealous competitors."[33] Androgeus subsequently received hero cult at Kerameikos and Phalerum.[34] These data show an identification of the athlete-heroes of Fontenrose's important article on hero-cult, "The Athlete as Hero," with Androgeus, and, presumably to the *pharmakos*.[35] When Androgeus was murdered, he was on his way to Thebes to take part in Laius' funeral games.[36]

In an important variant, Aegeus, king of Athens, sends Androgeus out to face the bull of Marathon, but the hero is killed by the monster.[37] Thus he fits the champion or *therapōn* pattern, to a certain extent. Another important variant has him killed in battle.[38]

Most of the sources agree that Androgeus is killed unjustly while in a foreign land. Accordingly to Diodorus, he was "treacherously slain,"

---

[31] Other sources on Androgeus are Scholiast on Plato *Minos* 321a; Diodorus Siculus 4.60–61; Zenobius 4.6, in Leutsch and Schneidewin 1958–1961 1:85; Scholiast on Homer *Iliad* XVIII 590; Plutarch *Theseus* 15; Pausanias 1.27.9–10; Servius on Virgil *Aeneid* 6.14; and Lactantius on Statius *Achilleid* 192. For discussion see Gantz 1993:262; Gebhard 1926:18–19; Murray 1934:328; Toepffer 1893; Kerényi 1959:227; Frazer 1921 2:116.

[32] Diodorus Siculus 4.60: ἐν δὲ τοῖς ἀγῶσι νικήσας τοὺς ἀθλητὰς ἅπαντας.

[33] Apollodorus 3.15.7: πρὸς τῶν ἀγωνιστῶν ἐνεδρευθέντα διὰ φθόνον ἀπολέσθαι. Cf. Gantz 1993:262.

[34] Amelesagoras of Athens, FGH 330 F 2 (Kerameikos); Pausanias 1.1.4; Clement of Alexandria *Hortatory Address to the Greeks* 26A; Callimachus fr. 103 Pfeiffer; Toepffer 1893; Deubner 1932:181n3; Kearns 1989:149, 38–41. For hero cult generally, see Clay 2004; Ekroth 2002; Boehringer 2001; Hägg 1999; Larson 1995; Antonaccio 1995, 1993; Kearns 1989; Burkert 1985:203–208; Nagy 1979; Bremmer 1978; Coldstream 1976; Damon 1974; Fontenrose 1968; Brelich 1958; Hack 1929; Farnell 1921; Pfister 1909–1912.

[35] Fontenrose 1968. Heracles was a famous athlete, and exemplifies some of Fontenrose's crucial motifs (1968:86), cf. below, ch. 16. Fontenrose mentions neither Androgeus nor the *pharmakos* in his rich paper. See also Bohringer 1979; Kurke 1993. For connections between athletes and war (victorious athletes who became generals), Kurke 1993:136–137.

[36] Apollodorus 3.15.7; Diodorus Siculus 4.60.5.

[37] Apollodorus 3.15.7.

[38] Hyginus *Fables* 41; Frazer 1921 2:117n1. Cf. the story of Codrus, below, and the death of Archilochus, ch. 3.

edolophonēsen; the Homeric scholiast uses the same verb. Plutarch has him killed by *dolos*, deceit. Apollodorus describes him being ambushed, *enedreuthenta*, which suggests the irregularity of his death. Servius has him killed as a result of a plot between the Athenians and Megarians, *Atheniensibus et vicinis Megarensibus coniuratis occisus est.*

After the Athenians were afflicted with famine, pestilence, and war as a result of the murder of Androgeus, they consulted an oracle to find a means of deliverance. The oracle required satisfaction for Minos; so came about the familiar delivery of youths and maidens to the Minotaur every nine years.[39] Plutarch writes, "Now as to this tribute, most writers agree that because Androgeus was thought to have been treacherously killed within the confines of Attica, not only did Minos harass the inhabitants of that country greatly in war, but divinity [*to daimonion*] also laid it waste, for a terrible barrenness and pestilence fell upon it, and its rivers dried up."[40] This is a combination of all three disasters with which the *pharmakos* was associated. Here, though, instead of the plague before the expulsion of the *pharmakos*, the plague follows the expulsion/death of the *pharmakos*, whose athletic victory had created a "plague" of shame for the native Athenian athletes. The seven maids and youths are, as it were, compensatory scapegoats.

The story of Androgeus ends with the rebirth motif, in a list of famous healings in Propertius 2.1.61–62: "And the Epidaurian god [Asclepius] restored Androgeon to his father's home with Cressian herbs."[41] That this story is consistent with Cretan saga is shown by the resurrection of Androgeus' brother Glaucus by Polyidus, or by Asclepius in some variants.[42]

Istros, quoted in Harpocration, offers a different aetiology for the Greek scapegoat, the story of a man named Pharmakos:

ὅτι δὲ ὄνομα κύριόν ἐστιν ὁ Φαρμακός, ἱερὰς δὲ φιάλας τοῦ Ἀπόλλωνος κλέψας ἁλοὺς ὑπὸ τῶν περὶ τὸν Ἀχιλλέα κατελεύσθη, καὶ τὰ τοῖς Θαργηλίοις ἀγόμενα τούτων ἀπομιμήματά ἐστιν.

[39] Apollodorus 3.15.8. γενομένου δὲ τῇ πόλει λιμοῦ τε καὶ λοιμοῦ, "When the city was afflicted by famine and plague . . ."

[40] Plutarch *Theseus* 15.1, trans. Perrin, modified; ὅτι μὲν οὖν Ἀνδρόγεω περὶ τὴν Ἀττικὴν ἀποθανεῖν δόλῳ δόξαντος, ὅ τε Μίνως πολλὰ κακὰ πολεμῶν εἰργάζετο τοὺς ἀνθρώπους καὶ τὸ δαιμόνιον ἔφθειρε τὴν χώραν (ἀφορία τε γὰρ καὶ νόσος ἐνέσκηψε πολλὴ καὶ ἀνέδυσαν οἱ ποταμοί). For the motif of offering young men and women (who often give themselves up willingly) to allay disasters, see below on mythical scapegoat patterns, and Frazer 1921 2.118n1; 111n2.

[41] *Et deus exstinctum Cressis Epidaurius herbis / restituit patriis Androgeona focis.* Cf. Richardson 1977 ad loc.

[42] Apollodorus 3.3, 3.10.3–4, with Frazer's notes.

That the proper name is Pharmakos, who, having stolen the holy cups of Apollo, was captured by Achilles' men and stoned; and the things done at the Thargelia are re-enactments [*apomimēmata*] of these things. . . .

Istros FGH 334 F 50 = Harpocration 180, 19, s.v. *pharmakos*[43]

Thus mythical *aition* and rite, as always, relate in a subtle interchange. One need not enter the debate on myth/ritual priority here, but it is worth noting in passing that these passages have the rite repeating continually a primary myth.

Legendary scapegoats

There are a number of stories exhibiting a regular scapegoat pattern, involving mythical *pharmakoi*, which often have no overt connection to cult; but because of their close resemblance to the actual scapegoat customs, they deserve consideration, though they must be differentiated as forming an alternate, parallel pattern.[44] They often have kings or princes or princesses as scapegoats, thus providing a contrast to the polar opposite ritual *pharmakoi* (though Androgeus, explicitly linked to the *pharmakos* rite, is a prince). However, as Vernant's work on the ambiguity of Oedipus has shown, both ends of the pole are closely identified with their opposites.[45] But the legends have a different emphasis.

The story of Codrus, king of Attica, illustrates what is only hinted at in the *pharmakos* rituals: the identification of the preexpulsion scapegoat with a king or hero.[46] Codrus, when the Dorians are besieging Attica, receives an oracle predicting that the Dorians will never take Attica if they kill him. (The

---

[43] Cf. Gebhard 1926:16; Jackson 1994. For the theme of stealing temple cups, see on Aesop, ch. 2 below. Pharmakos may have ties to Thersites, whom Achilles also kills (but not for stealing Apollo's cups, and not by stoning). See ch. 16 below, on Achilles.

[44] See Burkert 1979:72–77; Larson 1995, chapters 5 and 6.

[45] Vernant 1981.

[46] Pherecydes FGH 3 F 154; Hellanicus FGH 323a F 23; Plato *Symposium* 208d; Lycurgus *Against Leocrates* 84; a vase dated ca. 430 BC, the name vase of the Codrus painter, Bologna PU 273. For discussion of Codrus, see Pease 1955 2:1083; Fontenrose 1978:374(L49); Burkert 1979:62–63; Robertson 1988:224–230; Kearns 1989:56, 178; Kearns 1990:328–329, 336; Sourvinou-Inwood 1990 (an interpretation of Bologna PU 273). See also the story of Leonidas and the oracle at Thermopylae, Herodotus 7.220.3–4; Fontenrose 1978:77(Q152); Mikalson 2003:64. In Fontenrose's view, here the oracle is a post eventum element brought into the tale to assimilate Leonidas to Codrus. For a mythical king stoned during a drought, see Plutarch *Greek Questions* 26 (297 b–c), 13 (294a).

oracle is a common motif in the mythical scapegoat tradition; the logical thing to do in the face of a disaster is to consult an oracle to find a cure for it.)[47] So Codrus dresses as a slave, goes out among the Dorians, and arranges for himself to get killed in a brawl. The Dorians, finding out what has happened, give up their Attic invasion.[48] In one variant, the king dies in battle,[49] which is reminiscent of the variant tradition of Androgeus killed in battle.

Here we have the disaster (invasion); the descent of the greatest man of the land down to the level of the common woodsman, the lowest element in society; his voluntary self-expulsion from his land; and his death, which saves his state from the disaster.

In these legendary patterns, the motif of the death of young maidens or youths, often royal, is common.[50] As Kearns notes, often these saviors of the city-state are marginal, coming from unexpected sources; sometimes they come from the center, the king, as in the case of Codrus. However, often there is a combination of the two social poles, as when princesses (women, thus marginal; of the royal family, thus central) are the saviors.[51] Death is often voluntary, an important theme, as in the case of Aglauros, daughter of Cecrops, the first king of Attica. According to one variant, when Athens is besieged, an oracle states that the only chance of victory is for someone to sacrifice himself

---

[47] Pausanias writes that when Heracles and the Thebans were preparing to engage in battle with the Orchomenians, "an oracle was delivered to them that success in the war would be theirs if their citizen of the most noble descent would consent to die by his own hand," 9.17.1, trans. W. H. S. Jones, λόγιόν σφισιν ἦλθεν ἔσεσθαι τοῦ πολέμου κράτος ἀποθανεῖν αὐτοχειρίᾳ θελήσαντος, ὃς ἂν τῶν ἀστῶν ἐπιφανέστατος κατὰ γένους ἀξίωμα ᾖ. (The daughters of the most genealogically distinguished man willingly consent to die, then receive hero cult.) In a similar story, a daughter of Heracles, Macaria, in response to an oracle, kills herself to give the Athenians victory in a war against Sparta, Pausanias 1.32.6, Kearns 1989:58; Larson 1995:101. Cf. the daughters of Antipoenus, Pausanias 9.17.1. The story of Oedipus is an obvious example of consulting an oracle in order to alleviate a plague, only to have it require the expulsion of a sinful pollutant from the city. Cf. Bremmer 1983b:305; Fontenrose 1968:92.

[48] For the scapegoat and war, see preceding note. In Pausanias 1.32.4–6, those killed in the battle of Marathon receive hero cult, cf. Kearns 1989:55, 183, Ekroth 2002:75–77. The dead at Plataea received similar honors, Thucydides 3.58.4, Plutarch *Aristides* 21.2–5, cf. Ekroth 2002:77–78, 94–96, 102, 124–126. For cult awarded to "war dead" generally, Ekroth 2002:204, 258–262, 339. See below ch. 11 (Tyrtaeus), and ch. 18. See also Rohde 1925 1:131; Stern 1991; Herodotus 7.134–144, 3.153–163, in which Zopyrus, a Persian noble, mutilates himself, cutting off nose and ears, to bring about Babylon's fall. How and Wells (1928 1.300) accept the story's possible historicity; Stern (1991:308n19) rejects this possibility.

[49] Cicero *Tusculan Disputations* 1.48.116. See below, ch. 3, on Archilochus; ch. 11, on Tyrtaeus.

[50] Polycrite is an example, see below and above, this chapter; Androgeus is a prince, see above. Cf. Burkert 1979:71n29; Bremmer 1983b:302–305; Loraux 1987a:31–48; Kearns 1989:56–58; Hughes 1991:71–138.

[51] Kearns 1990.

or herself on behalf of the city. Aglauros therefore commits suicide by jumping off the Acropolis. She is rewarded with an Aglaureion after death, where male ephebes later took their oath of allegiance in connection with their military service. (She is the first of eleven "gods" called as witnesses in this oath.) Once again, we find the scapegoat theme aligned with the military ethos.[52] The daughters of Erechtheus, sometimes called the Hyacinthides, offer a similar configuration of oracle-engineered self-sacrifice in time of war, hero cult, and use of cult for military purposes.[53]

There are elements of such a story in the actual *pharmakos* complex; invasion is a typical disaster, like plague or famine;[54] the preexpulsion *pharmakos* was often treated as an important person, not as the lowest of the low—he was fed well, clothed in holy garments, and adorned with symbols of fertility. According to one report, sometimes the acceptance of the scapegoat role was voluntary.[55] All victims in Greek sacrifice were ideologically voluntary. Bremmer writes, "People pretended the victim went up to the altar of its own accord, and even asked for its consent. Whenever the animal did not shake its head in agreement, wine or milk was poured over its head. When, subsequently, the animal tried to shake this off its head, this was interpreted as a sign of consent! . . . sometimes it was pretended that the animal had committed a crime . . ."[56]

As has been noted, even if the *pharmakos* was not actually killed, the city kills him ideologically. It seems likely that, if the Greeks went to such lengths to make it appear as if ordinary animal sacrifices were voluntary, the *pharmakos*—who may have been viewed as a sacrifice—might have been *always* at least symbolically voluntary. Though, as Bremmer notes, these scapegoat

---

[52] Philochorus FGH 328 F 105–106; Burkert 1983:67–68; Kearns 1989:139–140, 23–27, 57–63; Kearns 1990:330, 341; Larson 1995:40–41, 102. See also Herodotus 8.53; Demosthenes 19.303. For the more well-known tradition about Aglauros' death after disobediently opening the box enclosing the snake-guarded Erichthonius, which includes the leap off the cliff, but which gives no context for the ephebes' oath, or for the three sisters' subsequent reputation as nurturers of children, see Euripides *Ion* 270–274; Apollodorus 3.15.6, with Frazer's notes; Kron 1981 with bibliography; Burkert 1983:150–154; Gantz 1993:234–238. Larson (1995:40–41) concludes that Aglauros did not have close ties to the Erichthonius complex.

[53] Euripides *Erechtheus* fr. 370 K; Apollodorus 3.15.4; Kearns 1989:201–202, 59–63; Larson 1995:102; Ekroth 2002:258. The willing self-sacrifice is ambiguous, as often.

[54] In Greece and Rome it is a common *legendary* theme, see preceding notes. Burkert discusses the "invasion" theme in Hittite ritual, 1979:60–61; ANET 347; Gurney 1977:47–52.

[55] According to Petronius, fr. 1, this was the custom in Massilia, though the victim was poor and was fed for a year before expulsion. Other sources temper the willingness of the victim by speaking of rewards, e.g. Lactantius on Statius *Thebaid* 10.793.

[56] Bremmer 1983b:307–308. Cf. Schmitt 1921, O'Connor-Visser 1987, Burkert 1985:56, 1983:4, 1979:71; Girard 1986:63–67; see on Codrus above.

myths do not exactly reflect *pharmakos* ritual, there is an undeniable connection between the myths and the ritual.

Finally, there are examples of the legendary scapegoat receiving hero cult after he or she dies. This is the case with Codrus, who had a shrine in Athens.[57] The legend of Polycrite has close ties to the Thargelia ritual and the *pharmakos*. She was stoned oddly at the hands of her countrymen by "girdles, wreaths, and shawls" after saving her city from destruction (by being a fatal gift to the enemy), then died outside the city gate. Burkert writes, "The pelting with wreathes and clothes, as used in the parades of Olympic victors and their like, is equivalent to the stoning of the *pharmakos* and has the same effect. Polycrite must die outside the city."[58] Her tomb was honored by cult, and she was given sacrifices during the Thargelia festival.[59] The legendary scapegoat, the ritual *pharmakos*, and hero cult intersect here.[60]

Themes

Thus the following themes can be found in the *pharmakos* tradition (including both the actual custom and the aetiological myths of Pharmakos and Androgeus, as they are closely connected to the rite), listed following the methodology of Fontenrose.[61] This list will outline some important recurring ideas, starting with the background of the *pharmakos* situation (communal, ritual pollution), then defining the *pharmakos* himself, then outlining the process of his expulsion, ending with his cult. Miscellaneous related themes from legendary or athletic traditions will follow.

---

[57] IG II² 4258 (tomb at the foot of the Acropolis); IG I³ 84 (temenos of Codrus, Neleus, and Basile); Sokolowski 1969 no. 14, 418/417 BC; cf. Hooker 1960:115; Burkert 1979:62n14; Kearns 1989:178.

[58] 1979:73, cf. 173n1 for further references and discussion; Bremmer 1983b:303; Larson 1995:136. There is a comparable odd "clothes stoning" in the historical tradition: the death of Draco, see *Suda*, s.v. *Drakon*. "Draco, Athenian lawgiver. He came to Aegina to help with their legislation, and when he was acclaimed by the Aeginians in the theater they threw so many hats, coats and garments upon his head that he was smothered, and he was buried in that very theater." Δράκων, Ἀθηναῖος νομοθέτης. οὗτος εἰς Αἴγιναν ἐπὶ νομοθεσίαις εὐφημούμενος ὑπὸ τῶν Αἰγινητῶν ἐν τῷ θεάτρῳ ἐπιρριψάντων αὐτῷ ἐπὶ τὴν κεφαλὴν πετάσους πλείονας καὶ χιτῶνας καὶ ἱμάτια ἀπεπνίγη καὶ ἐν αὐτῷ ἐτάφη τῷ θεάτρῳ. Cf. Szegedy-Maszak 1978:207n42. The acclamation is a capital sentence. See below, ch. 7 on ironic, remarkable deaths.

[59] Parthenius 9.

[60] Cf. the daughters of Erechtheus, who after having died to save Athens from defeat in war, are, with Erechtheus their sacrificer, "reckoned among the gods at Athens," *in numero deorum sunt . . .*, Cicero *On the Nature of the Gods* 3.19.50; cf. Kearns 1989:59–60; van den Bruwaene 1970 3:89–90n175; Pease 1955 2:1084; Frazer 1921 2:111n2. Wineless sacrifices were awarded the daughters in Athens. (Scholia on Sophocles *Oedipus at Colonus* 100.)

[61] See Fontenrose 1968 and 1959. Such listings have been used less for ritual than for myth.

1. *Ritual pollution.* This may be the first in a series of imbalances that need to be righted in the course of ritual or event. This is often caused by a crime:

   1a. *Crime of hero, pharmakos,* as in the case of Pharmakos, killed by Achilles' friends.

       1a1. *Criminal impiety,* as in temple robbing.

           1a1a. *Theft of sacred things, hierosulia,* as when Pharmakos steals the sacred vessels of Apollo.

   1b. *Crime against hero,* as in the death of Androgeus the Cretan.

       1b1. *Inhospitality*—the crime is committed against a stranger, unjustly, as in the case of Androgeus.

       1b2. *Murder*—the stranger is murdered.

       1b3. *Deceit*—the stranger is murdered deceitfully (Androgeus is ambushed).

2. *Communal disaster.* This can be plague, famine, invasion, cyclic period of infertility, or any combination of the above.

   2a. This can cause the scapegoat's expulsion/death (as commonly in the ritual sequence). This can be a psychological "plague," a "plague of shame"; i.e. Androgeus had defeated the native Athenians in their games; they found this intolerable, so they killed him in retribution.

       2a1. *Plague.* Oedipus.

       2a2. *Famine.* Oedipus.

       2a3. *War.* Codrus. Aglauros.

   2b. This can be caused by the scapegoat's expulsion/death (as in the case of Androgeus). Again, it can be plague, famine, war, loss of fertility.

3. *Oracle.* Often an oracle can be involved in interpreting and prescribing a remedy for the disaster. Thus, an oracle follows Androgeus' death and the resulting plague/famine. Oracles are common in the legendary tradition.

4. *The Worst.* In ritual sources, the *pharmakos* is a beggar, slave, or criminal—the worst. (In legendary sources, a king may dress as a beggar to enact his role as scapegoat, as in the story of Codrus.)

4a. *Poor*—often the *pharmakos* is recruited from among the poor.

    4a1. *Beggar.*

    4a2. *Poor or scanty food.*

4b. *Slave.*[62]

4c. *Criminal* (see 1a–1c above).

4d. *Ugly/deformed.*

4e. *Foreigner.* For example, Androgeus at Athens.

4f. *Poison imagery.* (Drug, medicine.)

5. *The Best.* In ritual sources, he is dressed in beautiful clothes (not like a beggar), and is well fed, as if he were aristocracy. He symbolizes health and abundance before expulsion. In legend, royal victims, such as Androgeus, Codrus, and Aglauros.

    5a. *Sacred.* The *pharmakos*-hero is often holy. He is dressed in holy clothing in the ritual tradition.

    5b. *Salvation imagery.* The *pharmakos* is the salvation (*sōtēria*), the *therapeia* (service, medical treatment).[63]

    5c. *Victorious.* Androgeus has won the Panathenaic games, and thus is the best.

    5d. *Athlete.* Androgeus once again.

    5e. *Royal.* Androgeus is the son of King Minos. This is rare in the ritual tradition (even here we find it only in the *aition* for the rite), common in the legendary sources.

6. *Peripety.* The scapegoat can undergo a peripety from best to worst; the well-fed and clothed *pharmakos* suddenly finds himself a hated outcast. This theme is defined better in the legendary tradition because there is more emphasis on the best, as in the royal victim. King Codrus must dress in rags to be killed, becoming a beggar overnight.

7. *Selection by public meeting.* In the case of the criminal *pharmakos*, this public meeting could be in the nature of a trial.

---

[62] Cf. Wiechers 1961:35.
[63] *Sōtēria*: Photius, s.v. *peripsēma. Therapeia*, see above.

8. *Voluntary.* However, the *pharmakos* is sometimes voluntary. This is attested in the ritual tradition, but is almost de rigueur in the legendary tradition.

    8a. *Ambivalent volition.* The *pharmakos'* death was seen as both voluntary and involuntary.

9. *Procession.*

    9a. *Blows.* Cf. stoning below.

10. *Expulsion.* The *pharmakos* is always expelled from the city. (Often after procession.) This is perhaps the key theme.

    10a. *Exile.*

11. *Death.* Often the *pharmakos* dies, if only symbolically, especially by

    11a. *Stoning,* or

    11b. *Being thrown from cliff* into sea. This is almost a physical expression of peripety, falling from best to worst.

    11c. *Poisoning.*

    11d. *By sword or knife,* as in the case of Androgeus.

12. *Sacrifice.*

13. *Hero cult.* As in the case of Androgeus; furthermore, cult awarded to scapegoat heroes is found in the legendary tales, the stories of Codrus and Polycrite.

    13a. Thus, *immortality of hero,* as a usual concomitant of hero cult.[64]

23. *Hero is sacred, superhuman.*

    23d. *Resurrection of hero,* as in the case of Androgeus.

Though not every story or rite will have all of these themes, the presence of a number of these themes will show some identification with the *pharmakos* complex. Especially conclusive are the following: 2, communal disaster, 10, expulsion of hero, 4, "worstness" of hero (ambiguous) because of crime or ugliness, and 11a, stoning or 11b, ejection over a cliff. Through the balance of this study, the ejection of an ambiguously worst hero from a city or country (including historical exiles in the case of Sappho or Ovid), or a more final form of ejection, execution, will be considered the central motif of the complex.

It is true that some rituals or ritual types may share characteristics with this complex. The *pharmakos* comes under the broad classification of purifica-

---

[64] See e.g. Pausanias 6.6.4–10; Fontenrose 1968:81.

tion and sacrifice. Yet though the *pharmakos* will intersect with other rituals, it also has important idiosyncratic elements. For instance, sacrifice had a form of pelting with grain, but it was not an actual stoning. Stoning was not regularly used as a form of capital execution; it tended to be an extralegal action of enraged mobs. Thus its use on a selected day of the year, or as a premeditated means of averting a plague, differentiates the *pharmakos* idea. However, any stoning is a manifestation of communal desire for expulsion; the victim dies or leaves. The theme of expulsion is central; the *pharmakos* is only a striking example of this, on a ritual level, an important pattern in Greek culture.

In addition, some themes are especially characteristic of the legendary scapegoat. These are related to the ritual *pharmakos*, but are distinct in some ways. Cult and myth cannot be separated, for the aetiological *pharmakos* legends are included in the preceding list.

14. *Royal.* Often the legendary scapegoats are seen as royal, princes or princesses. See 5e.

15. *Virgin.* Often the scapegoat is female, young, sexually pure, voluntary, as in the case of Aglauros.

16. *Evil eye.* Often the hero's extraordinary nature (because he is best or worst) attracts attention or envy, the evil eye. Polycrite's tomb is called *baskanou taphos*, the tomb of the evil eye.[65]

17. *Fatal, saving gift.* The expelled hero is often a fatal gift to an enemy, salvation to his own people. This theme can appear at various points in the narrative. Codrus and Polycrite, for instance, "give" themselves to the enemy. As has been noted earlier, poison is a magical "gift," *dosis*, and the German word for poison is *Gift*,[66] so this then is closely related to 4f, poison imagery.

18. *Divine persecutor/patron.* Often the hero is persecuted, killed, and deified with cult by the same god.[67] Cf. the part played by the oracle in the scapegoat stories; they can require both the expulsion of the scapegoat (as in the case of Codrus) and his immortalization through cult.

---

[65] Plutarch On the *Virtues of Women* 17 (254e). Cf. Rowland 1980:45–46; Dundes 1980. Deformed men have been used to ward off the evil eye, Welsford 1936:61.

[66] Cf. Antiphon 1.18 (a *dosis pharmakou*, "dose [or "gift"] of poison"); Dioscorides *Medical Treatise* 2.171 (a *dosis* of medicine).

[67] Cf. Burkert 1983:77, Burkert 1966:102–104; Nagy 1979:121, 305–307; also Burkert 1983:133, 119, 177 (god/victim equation).

The hero-athletes studied by Fontenrose again are related, if distinct in some ways, and their stories add a few important themes. The fact that Androgeus, the *aition* for the Athenian *pharmakos*, was a hero athlete, and that many hero athletes were stoned, and that legendary *pharmakoi* received hero cult, make their consideration here useful. They will be an important comparand for the lives of the poets. Bohringer concludes that these legends were based on preexisting myth and cult and were used or revived when the heroes' cities faced specific crises. She sees a link between these tormented, violent yet "best" and saving figures and the figure of the warrior in Greek myth—both have a duality between "external action and internal rejection, belonging and marginality, defense of and defiance of the community."[68]

19. *Madness* of the hero, as in the case of Cleomedes of Asypalaia.[69]

20. *Murderer.* The hero's crime is murder (cf. 1b2 above).[70]

21. *Imprisonment* (Euthycles of Locri).[71]

To take a prominent legendary *pharmakos*, we may look at Oedipus. Here the crime of the hero (1a), the murder (1a3, 20) of his father, creates ritual pollution (1). This causes a communal disaster (2, 2a), plague and famine. Oedipus the king (14) sends to the Delphic oracle (3). Though there is no trial per se in the myth, there is a legal investigation (cf. 7), headed up by Oedipus himself, that eventually convicts him of the crime. Oedipus expels himself voluntarily (10, 10a, 8) from Thebes (eventually). He is the king, the best (5), but he turns out to be a patricide, the worst (4), undergoes a peripety (6), and is expelled from the city.[72] In Sophocles' *Oedipus at Colonus* (433–443) he wishes for stoning (11a); he is viewed as a sacrifice (12). He eventually receives hero cult (13),[73] and like Androgeus, becomes a revenant (23d).[74] This is a typical legendary *pharmakos* pattern, which is characterized by the bestness, the royalty, of the hero, his simultaneous worstness and encapsulation of worstness, the voluntary expulsion, and hero cult.[75]

---

[68] Bohringer 1979:18. See especially ch. 18 below.

[69] Pausanias 6.9.6–8; discussion and further references in Fontenrose 1968:73. Cf. below, ch. 8, on Sappho.

[70] See previous note.

[71] Callimachus fr. 84–85 Pf. with *diēgēsis*; Oenomaus at Eusebius *Preparation for the Gospel* 5.34, p. 232bc, quoted by Pfeiffer at Callimachus fr. 84–85; Fontenrose 1968:74.

[72] Famously, not at the end of the extant *Oedipus Rex*. See Hester 1984.

[73] For Oedipus' legend and cult, see Edmunds 1981; Gantz 1993:492–502 (many variants, including Oedipus dying in battle, *Iliad* XXIII 677–680).

[74] Euripides *Phoenician Women* 1540–1545; Edmunds 1981:230.

[75] See also for Oedipus as scapegoat Vernant 1981:200–205, Pucci 1990; Foley 1993; Seaford 1994:130–133. Griffith 1993 dissents.

2

Aesop: Satirist as *Pharmakos* in Archaic Greece

ESOP IS THE GREEK SATIRIST, by broad definition a poet,[1] who is most clearly and richly assimilated to the *pharmakos*. The myth of Aesop's death at Delphi under a false accusation was generally known by the time of Herodotus, according to whom the Delphians, commanded by the Delphic oracle, offered compensation for the life of Aesop, who had been a slave (2:134).[2] Aristophanes, *Wasps* 1446–1449, shows a knowledge of Aesop being falsely charged with stealing a temple cup.[3] A fifth-century Attic vase portrays him as ugly and deformed.[4] Thus, according to M. L. West, in "the latter part of the fifth century something like a coherent Aesop legend appears."[5] If one accepts that there was a coherent Aesop legend that had probably existed for

---

[1] As was explained in the preface, this book uses a broad definition of the poet as verbal artist, whether fabulist, orator, philosopher, or composer of metrical poems. However, Callimachus *Iambus* 2.15–17, fr. 192Pf (test. 23 Perry), speaks of Aesop "singing a tale," *aidonta muthon*: ταῦτα δ' A<ἴσω>πος / ὁ Σαρδιηνὸς εῖπεν, ὅντιν' οἱ Δελφοί / ᾄδοντα μῦθον οὐ καλῶς ἐδέξαντο. "Aesop of Sardis said this, whom the Delphians did not receive hospitably when he sang his tale." My trans. Herodotus 2:134 refers to him as a *logopoios*, "creator of fables." According to *Vita* W, he is *ho logomuthopoios* (1), which has about the same meaning. Parker refers to Aesop as a poet, 1983:274; West disagrees, 1985:94, apparently using strictly metrical criteria for classification. Yet Aesop certainly was a satirist who used figurative language, and as we have seen, Callimachus envisions him singing. In addition, Aesop receives a poetic consecration exactly parallel to those of Hesiod and Archilochus, see below. Both Aesop and Archilochus use fables satirically, sometimes the same fables; Archilochus merely puts them into meter, cf. ch. 3 below, also ch. 6 (Hesiod).

[2] Aesop was a Phrygian slave (G 1 and test. 4 Perry), which was a realistic touch, see DeVries 2000:340; Phrygians were the most common ethnic type of slaves in Attica in the fifth to fourth centuries. Cf. Hipponax 27W, and on Marsyas below.

[3] For Aristophanes' use of Aesop and his fables in *Wasps*, see the insightful article by K. Rothwell, Jr. 1995. See also Plato Comicus, fr. 68 Kock (test. 45 Perry) for an early tradition of Aesop receiving immortality.

[4] Kylix, in Rome, Vatican, 16552; Wiechers 1961:32; Garland 1995:111, plate 32; Lissarrague 2000:137 (who dates the vase to 450 BC).

[5] West 1984:105–136, esp. 119.

some time before Herodotus wrote (he treats it as a given, not a novelty), we should date it even further back. And, by Aristophanes' time, there may be a book of some sort on Aesop's life and wisdom.[6] The story of Aesop's death, with other incidents in the life of the fabulist, is retold in a remarkable Hellenistic prose novelette. This *Vita*, drawing on earlier written and oral traditions, was written down perhaps in the first century AD. It is extant in two main versions, G (the fullest) and W (somewhat abbreviated, but with some unique passages).[7] This novellette was for centuries treated with open contempt, as unhistorical, unsophisticated, and late. However, in our generation a number a scholars, such as Wiechers, Nagy, and Holzberg, have begun to evaluate and interpret this Aesop "novel" with new respect.[8] Holzberg's work has been particularly important in its narratological focus, interpreting the *Vita* as a carefully structured, cohesive whole in the picaresque tradition of the ancient novel. Holzberg is also significant for his emphasis on how the early parts of the *Vita* thematically prepare for and support the final episode, Aesop's death at Delphi.[9]

The following details are from *Vita* G, manuscript 397 of the Pierpont Morgan library, unless I note otherwise.[10]

Aesop was the worst of mankind. He was a slave (*doulos*, 1, and passim),[11] and furthermore, "worthless as a servant [*eis hupēresian sapros*, 1]"; and the ugliest of men: "loathsome to look at . . . potbellied, with a deformed head, flat-nosed, mute, dark-skinned, stunted, splay-footed, weasel-armed, squint-eyed, liver-lipped—a portentous blasphemy" (1).[12] An overseer, instructed to

[6] West 1984:121; Aristophanes *Birds* 471.

[7] Perry 1965: xlvi; Adrados 1979:93. Cf. Birch 1955. Another version, the work of thirteenth-century AD Maximus Planudes, is "an adaptation of *Vita* W, but with no fundamental changes." Holzberg 2002:73. The few extant papyrus fragments of the Aesop *Vita* support G at times, W at times. Perry 1936; Haslam 1986; Holzberg 2002:73.

[8] Examples are Wiechers 1961; Nagy 1979:280–290; Winkler 1985:279–291; Jedrkiewicz 1989; Compton 1990; Holzberg 1992; Hopkins 1993; van Dijk 1995; Papademetriou 1997; Holzberg 2002:76–83; Kurke 2003; Robertson 2003. See also the articles and bibliography in Holzberg 1999, 2002:93–94.

[9] However, my interpretation of Aesop's death differs from Holzberg's, see below.

[10] See Perry 1952:35–80; translations are by Daly 1961 unless noted otherwise. Daly has been reprinted in Hansen 1998. The W *Vita* can be found at Perry 1952:81–107. For new editions of G and W, see Papathomopoulos 1991 and 1999; Ferrari et al. 2002.

[11] For Aesop as slave, often outwitting his master, an academic philosopher, see Winkler 1985:279–291; Hopkins 1993; Hägg 1997; Konstantakos 2003.

[12] Κακοπινὴς τὸ ἰδέσθαι . . . προγάστωρ, προκέφαλος, σιμός, σόρδος, μέλας, κολοβός, βλαισός, γαλιάγκων, στρεβλός, μυστάκων, προσημαῖνον ἁμάρτημα, my trans. For textual variants, see Perry 1952. Cf. Himerius *Orations* 13.5 (test. 30 Perry). For a book which takes Aesop's ugliness as a central theme, see Papademetriou 1997. For the image of the belly and the satirical tradition,

sell the poet, laughs: "'Are you joking, master? Don't you know about his deformity? Who will want to buy him and have a doghead instead of a man?'" (11).[13] References to Aesop's ugliness are found virtually throughout his biography. He is called "refuse" (*perikatharma*, 14), "a completely misshapen pot" (*holos hamartēma khuseōn*, 21), "this awful thing" (*to . . . kakon touto*, 21), an "unearthly portent" (*teras*, 24, *Vita* W 98, G), "deformed" (*sapros*, 26, 27, 37), "trash" (*katharma*, 30, 31, 69, 77b [*Vita* W]), "riddle" (*ainigma*, 98), and "a temple thief and a blasphemer" (*hierosulon kai blasphēmon*, 132). The Samians, upon seeing the fabulist, exclaim, "Let another portent-interpreter be brought so that he may interpret this omen [*to sēmeion*]. How monstrous is his appearance! He's a frog, or a hedgehog, or a jar with a hump, or a captain of monkeys, or a little flask, or a cook's chest, or a dog in a bread-basket!" (87).[14] His name, etymologically, may mean 'uneven face'.[15] His subhuman, deformed nature is emphasized by his being dumb in the early episodes of the *Vita*. Our earliest visual evidence, the fifth-century vase portrayal of Aesop, shows him with a crutch.

However, Aesop was also the best of mankind: he is "the great benefactor of mankind" (*ho panta biōphelestatos*, 1), and his life presents frequent examples of his intelligence and courage. For instance, even though he is mute, he proves he is innocent of eating his master's figs by vomiting, and causing his master to make all the other slaves vomit (2–3). He also courageously stands up against an unjust and violent overseer (9). Later he fearlessly condemns the Delphians at Delphi (124–126).

He is also pious and holy (*ton eusebē*, 5): he receives his voice because of his hospitality and kindness to a priestess of Isis who had lost her way. Afterward the priestess, given a meal and redirected to her road, prays to Isis for Aesop, that she will pity "this workman, this sufferer, this pious one, because he was reverent, not to me, mistress, but to your majesty."[16]

---

see Svenbro 1976:50–59; Burnett 1983:59n17; Lefkowitz 1981:2; Nagy 1979:229–231. See below, ch. 4 (Hipponax); ch. 6 (Hesiod). For the ugliness of the poet, see below, chs. 4 (Hipponax); 7 (Simonides), 8 (Sappho); 11 (Tyrtaeus); 15 (Socrates); 17 (Ameirgein, Caillín); and 18 (Starkaðr).

[13] παίζεις, δέσποτα; οὐκ οἶδας αὐτοῦ τὴν ἀμορφίαν; τίς αὐτὸν θελήσει ἀγοράσαι καὶ κυνοκέφαλον ἀντὶ ἀνθρώπου ἔχειν;

[14] My trans. G 87. ἀχθήτω ἄλλος σημειολύτης, ἵνα τοῦτο τὸ <u>σημεῖον</u> διαλύσηται. τὸ τέρας τῆς ὄψεως αὐτοῦ! βάτροχός ἐστιν, ὗς τροχάζων, ἢ στάμνος κήλην ἔχων, ἢ πιθήκων πριμιπιλάριος, ἢ λαγυνίσκος εἰκαζόμενος, ἢ μαγείρου σκευοθήκη, ἢ κύων ἐν γυργάθῳ.

[15] Ogden 1997:39. For other possibilities, see Nagy 1979:315n.

[16] My trans. G 5. ". . . ἐλέησον τόνδε τὸν ἐργάτην, τὸν κακοπαθοῦντα, τὸν εὐσεβῆ, ἀνθ' ὧν εὐσέβησεν, οὐκ εἰς ἐμέ, δέσποινα, ἀλλ' εἰς τὸ σὸν σχῆμα."

As a result, Aesop, while sleeping in the woods, receives a theophany of Isis and the nine Muses.[17] Isis speaks to the Muses:

"ὁρᾶτε, θυγατέρες, [εὐσεβείας κατακάλλυμμα] τὸν ἄνθρωπον τοῦτον, πεπλασμένον μὲν ἀμόρφως, νικῶντα δὲ εἰς εὐσέβειαν πάντα ψόγον· οὗτός ποτε τὴν ἐμὴν διάκονον πεπλανημένην ὡδήγησεν· πάρειμι δὲ σὺν ὑμῖν ἀνταμείψασθαι τὸν ἄνθρωπον. ἐγὼ μὲν οὖν τὴν φωνὴν ἀποκαθίστημι, ὑμεῖς δὲ τῇ φωνῇ τὸν ἄριστον χαρίσασθε λόγον."

"Look, daughters, at this man, formed in a misshapen way, but who conquers every fault in his piety. This man set my servant on the right road when she had gone astray; I am here with you to reward him. Therefore, I will restore his voice, and you give him the best word for his voice."

Aesop *Vita*, G 7, my trans.

Then, the Muses confer on him "each something of her own endowment," and "with a prayer that he might achieve fame, the goddess went her way, and the Muses, when each had conferred her own gift, ascended to Mount Helicon."[18]

The parallels offered by the lives of Archilochus and Hesiod argue that Aesop's poetic consecration is an ancient tradition—heroizing legends of the poets tend to accumulate around the their consecrations and deaths.[19] If we accept that probability, we are left to assess which Greek deity was replaced by the Egyptian Isis in the late Aesop novel. There are two clear choices, both almost equally attractive. First, Nagy argues that the original deity was Apollo, called "the leader of the Muses" a number of times in the *Vita*.[20] This is an ancient association,[21] and would fit well with the traditions of Apollo as inspirer, rival, persecutor, and deifier of Aesop.

However, the second possibility is Mnemosyne 'Memory', known since Hesiod as the mother of the Muses (*Theogony* 53–62, 915–917). This would tie in nicely with G 100 (Perry text), where Aesop honors her with a statue. "Memory" would be especially important to a travelling performer, such as Aesop will

[17] In W, Tyche, 'Fortune', without the Muses, appears to him. However, he had just helped some priests of Isis find their way, and had given them food and drink, as in G. Clearly, W is using Tyche as a form of Isis.

[18] ἐκάστη<ν> τι τῆς ἰδίας δωρεᾶς χαρίσασθαι . . . κατευξαμένη δὲ ἡ θεὸς ὅπως ἔνδοξος γένηται, εἰς ἑαυτὴν ἐχώρησεν. καὶ αἱ Μοῦσαι δέ, ἑκάστη τὸ ἴδιον χαρισάμεναι, εἰς τὸ Ἑλικῶνα ἀνέβησαν ὄρος. For more on this episode, see Winkler 1985:285–296; Dillery 1999; Finkelpearl 2003; Robertson 2003.

[19] Robertson 1993:253–258 offers further arguments for the antiquity of the consecration story.

[20] Nagy 1979:291n.

[21] See Clay 2004:12–13; Nagy 1979:291.

become. Robertson, who accepts that Mnemosyne was the original inspirer in the Aesop legend, notes that in G, Isis refers to the Muses as her daughters.[22] The substitution of Isis for Mnemosyne would have been an easy transition.[23]

While Aesop was thus on good terms with the Muses (at Delphi he takes refuge in the shrine of the Muses, 134), he became an enemy of Apollo. At Samos, after the Samians honor the fabulist, dedicating an Aesopeum to him, "when he had sacrificed to the Muses, he then constructed a shrine for them, placing a Mnemosyne statue in their midst, not one of Apollo. Therefore, Apollo was enraged with him as he had been with Marsyas" (100, 127).[24] Earlier, Aesop had told a story that was uncomplimentary to Apollo: "Because the leader of the Muses [*prostatēs tōn Mousōn*, i.e. Apollo] asked, Zeus gave him the gift of prophecy so that he excelled everyone who practiced mantic arts. But the leader of the Muses, as he was marveled at by all men, thought it right to despise everyone else, and was too boastful in everything" (33). [25]

The awarding of the Samian shrine to Aesop took place as follows: when King Croesus required tribute from the citizens of Samos if they would stave off invasion, Aesop advised them not to give in. Croesus prepared to invade, but a counselor advised him that he would never be able to take the city while

---

[22] Robertson 1993:258 also points out that Mnemosyne was mentioned often in early poetry, but not in later poetry.

[23] For bibliography on the consecration theme in Greek literature (Hesiod, Aeschylus, Archilochus, etc.), see Rankin 1977:16; 111n63, 1974nn79–85; West 1966:158–161, cf. bibliography p. 151; Falter 1934:34–60 and passim; Kambylis 1965; Dodds 1951:117; 80–81; Burnett 1983:18n7; Walcot 1957; Evelyn-White 1917; Maehler 1963; Latte 1946; P. Murray 1981. See below ch. 3 (Archilochus); ch. 6 (Hesiod). For Aesop and the Muses, see Perry 1936:14–15. According to Perry, Aesop is associated with the "democratic" Muses, which opposes him to the "aristocratic," academic Apollo (cf. his conflict with the philosopher Xanthus). This seems over-schematized, and does not explain his paradoxically close connection with Apollo. For inspiration, possession, and poetry, see Pritchett 1979:5–6; Gil 1967; ch. 3 (Archilochus thunderstruck with wine) below.

[24] My trans. ὁ δὲ Αἴσωπος θύσας ταῖς Μούσαις ἱερὸν κατεσκεύασεν αὐταῖς, στήσας μέσον αὐτῶν Μνημοσύνην, οὐκ Ἀπόλλωνα. ὁ Ἀπόλλων ὀργισθεὶς αὐτῷ ὡς τῷ Μαρσύᾳ. Perry's text here (he emends μνημόσυνον to Μνημοσύνην) cannot be accepted as certain—he is doing the best he can to make sense of a corrupt passage. It is also possible that Aesop set up a statue to himself, as Papathamopoulos and Ferrari edit the text. However, in my view, the logic of the narrative in the rest of the Aesop novel (especially the poetic consecration and the Delphi episode) supports Perry's text. But too much weight should not be placed on either textual interpretation, given the corrupt nature of the text. See below on Holzberg's interpretation of Aesop at Delphi. For Aesop and Marsyas, see Perry 1936:15 and ch. 16 below; cf. the story of Dionysus and Orpheus, ch. 16. Marsyas was, like Aesop, a Phrygian, see DeVries 2000:354.

[25] My trans. δεομένῳ γὰρ τῷ προστάτῃ τῶν Μουσῶν ὁ Ζεὺς ἐχαρίσατο τὴν μαντικήν, ὥστε καὶ πάντας τοὺς ἐν τῷ χρησμῷ ὑπερέχειν. ὁ δὲ προστάτης τῶν Μουσῶν ὑπὸ πάντων θαυμαζόμενος ἀνθρώπων, τῶν ἄλλων ὑπερφρονεῖν πάντων νομίσας, ἀλαζονότερος ἦν ἐν τοῖς ἄλλοις ἅπασιν.

Aesop lived, so that he should require the inhabitants of the city to surrender Aesop in order to prevent their own destruction. He followed the advice, sent the adviser to Samos, and the adviser told the Samians that they had to give up Aesop to keep the friendship of the king. "At first the people shouted, 'Take him. Let the king have Aesop.'"[26] Though Aesop changed their minds through a fable, he then willingly returned to Croesus with the ambassador. He charmed Croesus, who granted him his life and any request. Aesop requested peace for the Samians and the king granted it. When Aesop returned to Samos, the Samians "named the place where he had been turned over the Aesopeum." (92–100).[27]

Here we have many typical scapegoat themes: the crisis (military threat); the offering of Aesop as propitiation by the voice of the people; the self-sacrificial offering of Aesop; his obtaining salvation for the city; the hero cult offered to the poet at the very place where he had been expelled by the people.

Later, at Babylon, Aesop became a great favorite of the king, Lukoros, who appointed him chamberlain. "After giving an exposition of his philosophy, he was acclaimed as a great man" (101).[28] Because Aesop could outdo anyone in any kingdom in riddle contests (problēmata philosophias), Lukoros' kingdom continually expanded, with Aesop acting as his intellectual warrior. "In those times, kings had the custom of collecting tribute from one another by means of valiant battle. They did not face one another in wars and military battles. For they wrote philosophical riddles in letters, and the one who couldn't solve a riddle paid tribute to the one who had sent it" (102). [29] Through Aesop, Babylon conquers most of the known world, by ancient standards (barbarian nations, most lands up to Greece).[30]

Aesop was certainly the best at this odd form of warfare, which relates to his identity as poet, for there was a close connection between the archaic

---

[26] καὶ τοσοῦτον οἱ ὄχλοι ἀνεφώνησαν· "ἀπάγαγε, λαμβανέτω ὁ βασιλεὺς τὸν Αἴσωπον."

[27] καὶ ἐκάλεσαν τὸν τόπον ἐκεῖνον Αἰσώπειον, ὅπου ἦν ἐνηλλαγμένος.

[28] ἐπιδειξάμενος δὲ αὐτοῦ τὴν φιλοσοφίαν μέγας παρὰ τοῖς Βαβυλωνίοις ἀνεδείχθη . . . G has King Lycurgus, but P. Berol. 11628 and P. Oxy. 3720 have King Lukoros.

[29] My trans. ἐπ' ἐκείνοις δὲ τοῖς καιροῖς ἔθος εἶχον οἱ βασιλεῖς παρ' ἀλλήλων φόρους λαμβάνειν διὰ τῆς ἐναρέτου μάχης· οὔτε γὰρ ἐν πολέμοις συνίσταντο οὔτε μάχαις· ἔγραφον γὰρ προβλήματα φιλοσοφίας δι' ἐπιστολῶν, καὶ ὁ μὴ εὑρίσκων διαλύσασθαι φόρους ἐτέλει τῷ πέμψαντι. The historian of Phoenicia, Dius, cited in Josephus Against Apion 1.111–115, records King Solomon and Hiram engaging in exactly this kind of contest. Cf. Levine 2002:143.

[30] For the relationship riddle = problēma, see Clearchus of Soli (at Athenaeus 10.448c), who defines a riddle (griphos) as "a problem [problēma] put in jest, requiring, by searching the mind, the answer to the problem to be given for a prize or forfeit," trans. Gulick. γρῖφος πρόβλημά ἐστι παιστικόν, προστακτικὸν τοῦ διὰ ζητήσεως εὑρεῖν τῇ διανοίᾳ τὸ προβληθὲν τιμῆς ἢ ἐπιζημίου χάριν εἰρημένον.

riddle contest and poetry. Huizinga writes, "Archaic poetry is barely distinguishable from the ancient riddle-contest." For the purposes of this discussion, it is valuable to see the riddle poem as contest/combat, thus demanding aggressive competition.[31] In fact, in archaic legend, these poetic riddle contests were deadly serious affairs, in which the loser often lost his head.

After Aesop "conquers" Egypt (112–123), Lukoros "ordered the erection of a golden statue of Aesop with the Muses, and he held a great celebration in honor of Aesop's wisdom."[32] Hence, both at Samos and at Babylon, cult was instituted in honor of Aesop and his preeminence among men, and because he had helped to save both Samos and Babylon (just as he had earlier saved his master Xanthus on the point of committing suicide because he could not interpret an omen to the Samians; this was particularly noble on Aesop's part because Xanthus had recently cheated Aesop of his freedom and a large sum of money [78–91]).

While at Babylon, Aesop adopted a son, named Ainos in *Vita* W (103-110); when his son almost succeeded in having him killed through a palace intrigue, Aesop sternly rebuked him, and the young man, stricken by guilt "at being tongue-lashed by" Aesop (*dia logōn memastigōsthai*), committed suicide.[33] In *Vita* W, Ainos jumped off a cliff, a standard *pharmakos* death. Thus the blame poet has power to cause the death of his own unjust son, who is made a *pharmakos* by the just man who is later to be made a *pharmakos* himself.[34] It is the poet's power to create victims that makes him a victim.

---

[31] Huizinga 1955:133, cf. 122. See also ch. 6 (the contest of Homer and Hesiod). For further on these riddle contests, cf. Calchas and Mopsus, Hesiod fr. 278 M-W; Euphorion fr. 97 in Powell 1925:47 (the contest is given a sacral setting, the sanctuary of Apollo at Gryneion); Apollodorus *Epitome* 6.3–4, with Frazer's note, Frazer 1921; the Sphinx, *Oedipus Rex* 1198. See also Huizinga 1955:115–118, 133, 146. On the poet as warrior, see ch. 3 (Archilochus); ch. 9 (Alcaeus); ch. 11 (Tyrtaeus); and ch. 18, on Indo-European warrior myths, nearly passim. Cf. Oedipus as riddle warrior, causing the death of the sphinx, who had learned her riddle from the Muses (Apollodorus 3.5.8). Also, R. Griffith 1990:98n7. Sophocles refers to the sphinx as a singer (*Oedipus Rex* 37, *sklēras aoidou*, "harsh singer"). For the riddle in Greece, see Schultz 1909–1912; M. Griffith 1990:192; West 1996:1317; Collins 2004:7, 129–132; for Mopsus, cf. Huxley 1969:58; Löffler 1963:47–50. For Indo-European background, see Huizinga 1955:105–114; Lindow 1975; Clover 1980 (flytings as an "exchange of verbal provocations between hostile speakers," p. 445); ch. 17 below (Irish poets engaging in riddle contests).

[32] ἐκέλευσεν οὖν ὁ Λυκοῦργος ἀνδριάντα χρυσοῦν ἀνατεθῆναι τῷ Αἰσώπῳ μετὰ καὶ τῶν Μουσῶν, καὶ ἐποίησεν ἑορτὴν μεγάλην ὁ βασιλεὺς ἐπὶ τῇ τοῦ Αἰσώπου σοφίᾳ, G 123. For the statue in hero cult, see Lattimore 1988; Clay 2004, with index. For another example of hero cult before death, see the story of Euthymos, Pliny *Natural History* 7.47.152.

[33] G 110. In G, the son is called Helios. Haslam 1986:152n1, suggests that both Ainos and Helios might be corruptions of Linos, though he agrees with Perry that Ainos could have been original. On variation in the manner of Ainos' death, see ibid. p. 170n on lines 99f. Cf. Nagy 1979:239n2.

[34] This story, of course, brings to mind the famous story of the death of Lycambes and his daughters in the Archilochus tradition (see ch. 3), with its echo in the Hipponax tradition (ch. 4). This

Finally, Aesop visited Delphi.[35] There he gave an exhibition,[36] as he had successfully at other cities, but at Delphi "the people enjoyed hearing him at first but gave him nothing."[37] He started to "jibe" at them: "When I was far off from your city, I was extremely impressed with you as men who were rich and generous, but now that I see you are less than other men in your ancestry and in your city, I know that I was wrong" (125).[38] After referring to them as "slaves of all the Greeks" (Hellēnōn <douloi>), he prepared to leave. But the city officials, "seeing how abusive he was," felt they could not allow him to leave—"If we let him go away," they said, "he'll go around to other cities and damage our reputation" (127).[39] Aesop, as blame poet, is about to commit the unforgivable

---

is one of many points of continuity between Aesop and Archilochus (the use of fables and the consecration theme are also obvious comparands). Burnett (1983:58, 97) acutely notes that Archilochus makes his victim like a *pharmakos*. Hipponax would also assimilate an enemy to the *pharmakos*, then become one himself.

[35] Here my interpretation parts company with Holzberg, who believes the author emphasized Aesop's great hubris (Holzberg 2002:83), while I interpet the *Vita* (and the legend behind the *Vita*) as emphasizing Aesop's blamelessness and the Delphians' wickedness. Certainly, there is ambiguity in Aesop's inimical bond with Apollo, but I follow Burkert and Nagy in analyzing a hero's paradoxical relationship with a patronizing/persecuting deity. In addition, one of the cornerstones of Holzberg's hubris argument (that Aesop arrogantly erected a statue to himself in the Samos episode, G 100) is based on a reading of the text by Papathomopoulos which is not certain. The received text is corrupt, and both Perry and Papathomopoulos must emend to try to make sense of it. For the relative merits of the Perry and Papathomopoulos editions of G, see Haslam 1992.

[36] This seems to be the motivation for Aesop's visit: performance; note that later Aesop emphasizes that he had heard of the Delphians' generosity, another hint of the motivation. Thus Robertson (2003:258) is not quite correct when he says that in G there is no motive at all for Aesop's visiting Delphi. However, a variant tradition found in Plutarch (*On the Delays of Divine Vengeance* 12 [556f]) has him go there as an agent for Croesus to distribute money to the Delphians, but he does not distribute it because he feels they are unworthy. Robertson argues for this as the original story (2003:259), but having Aesop as the messenger of Croesus feels as though the Croesus legend were trying to bring Aesop within its orbit.

[37] οἱ δὲ ὄχλοι ἡδέως μὲν αὐτοῦ ἠκροῶντο τὸ καταρχάς, οὐδὲν δὲ αὐτῷ παρεῖχον, G 124. This is in stark contrast to the poor slave Aesop's hospitality to the servant(s) of Isis.

[38] My trans. <ἔτι δὲ καὶ αὐτοῖς προσκρούσας ἔφη . . .> "κἀγὼ πόρρωθεν ὑπάρχων τῆς πόλεως ὑμῶν κατεπλησσόμην ὑμᾶς <ὡς> πλουσίους καὶ μεγάλους ταῖς ψυχαῖς ὄντας, ἰδὼν δὲ ὑμᾶς τῶν ἄλλων ἀνθρώπων ἥττονας καὶ γένει καὶ πόλει πεπλάνημαι. Aesop is not admitting to a moral wrong, as Holzberg argues. He was merely misinformed.

[39] οἱ δὲ ἄρχοντες ἰδόντες αὐτοῦ τὸ κακόλογον ἐλογίζοντο· "ἐὰν αὐτὸν ἀφῶμεν ἀποδημῆσαι, περιελθὼν εἰς τὰς ἑτέρας πόλεις πλεῖον ἀτιμοτέρους ἡμᾶς ποιήσει." O'Leary remarks on the fact that much of the power of the archaic satiric poet came from his ability to travel. His effectiveness came through his "almost instinctive sense of the anomalous and risible [which] was magnified by an ability to express his revelations and condemnations in a singularly memorable (and often memorizable) fashion, and by a mobility which enabled him to carry such verse denunciations to every corner of the island [of Ireland] and into Gaelic Scotland." O'Leary 1991:26. See below on the legendary Homer as blind, itinerant poet, ch. 5.

crime in a culture in which shame is a prominent component.[40] The thought of being shamed publicly in all of Greece is not tolerable for the Delphians. So "because Apollo was angry at how Aesop had dishonored him on Samos, when he had not set up his statue along with those of the Muses, the Delphians . . . devised a villainy." (127)[41]

They placed a golden temple cup in his baggage, then arrested him outside the city the next day, and told him, "You have stolen treasure from the temple." Aesop, whose conscience was clear, said with tears in his eyes, "I am ready to die if I am found guilty of such a thing" (128).[42] However, they brought Aesop back to the city and imprisoned him.

Temple thievery was among the most weighty of accusations in ancient Greece. Barkan, after describing the seriousness of general charges of impiety in Athens, which often brought a capital punishment, writes, "Sacrilege in the form of temple-robbery (*hierosulia*) was a most flagrant act of *asebeia*. The Athenian legislators of the fifth century placed temple-robbing in juxtaposition with high treason. And the penalty in both cases was death, denial of interment on Attic soil, and confiscation of property."[43] The torture applied to an apprehended temple thief was so feared that, according to Plutarch, the thief would sometimes take hemlock before the robbery so he could die quickly if caught; if he was successful, he would take the antidote (wine).[44]

Having thus prepared at least an accusation that merited death, "The Delphians came in to Aesop and said, 'You must be thrown from the cliff today, for thus we voted [*epsēphisamen*] to execute you—since you have earned it as a temple thief and a blasphemer [*blasphēmon*]—so that you would not merit burial. Prepare yourself'" (132).[45]

---

[40] See below, this chapter, on shame and guilt in archaic cultures. For praise and blame in archaic Greece, see "Le Memoire du poete," Detienne 1973:18–27; Nagy 1979:211–275; below, ch. 22 (Cicero).

[41] My trans. καὶ τοῦ Ἀπόλλωνος μηνίοντος διὰ τὴν ἐν Σάμῳ ἀτιμίαν, ἐπεὶ σὺν ταῖς Μούσαις ἑαυτὸν οὐ καθίδρυσεν, μὴ ἔχοντες εὔλογον αἰτίαν ἐμηχανήσαντό τι πανοῦργον . . . Daly's "with the connivance" does not render the genitive absolute adequately. It is not so much a matter of Apollo plotting along with the Delphians as it is Apollo influencing the Delphians in their plot.

[42] "χρήματα ἔκλεψας ἐκ τοῦ ἱεροῦ." ὁ δὲ Αἴσωπος μηδὲν ἑαυτῷ συνειδὼς κλαίων ἔφησεν "ἀπολέσθαι θέλω, ἐάν τι τοιοῦτον εὑρεθῇ εἰς ἐμέ."

[43] Barkan 1979:26. For bibliography on this stereotypical crime, see Wiechers 1961:31n1. Cf. Xenophon *Hellenica* 1.7.22; Demosthenes *Against Aristocrates* 23.26, 57.64; Antiphon 5.10; Plato *Laws* 857A.

[44] Plutarch *On Loquacity* 14 (509E). For further on Aesop as *hierosulos*, see the following testimonia from Perry: 21, 24 (Aesop is thrown from the cliff reserved for the punishment of *hierosuloi*), 22, 20.

[45] My trans. Οἱ δὲ Δέλφιοι εἰσελθόντες πρὸς τὸν Αἴσωπον ἔφησαν "ἀπὸ κρημνοῦ σε δεῖ βληθῆναι σήμερον· οὕτως γάρ σε <u>ἐψηφίσαμεν</u> ἀνελεῖν, ἄξιον ὄντα <ὡς ἱερόσυλον> καὶ <u>βλάσφημον</u>, ἵνα

After Aesop recounts a fable in which a mouse is murdered by a frog, but in turn causes the death of the frog, he told them, "If I die, I will be your doom. The Lydians, the Babylonians, and practically the whole of Greece will reap the harvest of my death" (133).[46] As the Delphians led the poet to the cliff, he managed to take refuge in "the shrine of the Muses [*en tōi hierōi tōn Mousōn*]" (134). Though Aesop warned them not to dishonor the small shrine and told them they should "reverence Zeus, the god of strangers and Olympus,"[47] they dragged him away. Paradoxically (or so it would seem), in *Vita* W (134), Aesop takes refuge in the shrine of Apollo.

On the brink of the cliff Aesop managed to tell two last fables, both extremely insulting to the Delphians. Then

> Αἴσωπος καταρασάμενος αὐτούς, καὶ τὸν προστάτην τῶν Μουσῶν μάρτυρα προσκαλούμενος, ὅπως ἐπακούσῃ αὐτοῦ ἀδίκως ἀπολλυμένου, ἔρριψεν ἑαυτὸν ἀπὸ τοῦ κρημνοῦ κάτω. καὶ οὕτω τὸν βίον μετήλλαξεν.
>
> λοιμῷ δὲ κατασχεθέντες οἱ Δέλφιοι χρησμὸν ἔλαβον παρὰ τοῦ Διὸς ἐξιλάσκεσθαι <τὸν> τοῦ Αἰσώπου μόρον. μετὰ ταῦτα, ἀκούσαντες οἱ ἀπὸ τῆς Ἑλλάδος καὶ οἱ ἀπὸ Βαβυλῶνος καὶ <οἱ> Σάμιοι, ἐξεδίκησαν τὸν τοῦ Αἰσώπου θάνατον.

Aesop, after cursing them and calling on the leader of the Muses [*ton prostatēn tōn Mousōn*] as his witness so that he would hear him as he died unjustly [*adikōs*], threw himself down from the cliff. And thus he ended his life.

When the Delphians were oppressed with famine, they received an oracle from Zeus telling them to expiate the death of Aesop. Later, when the people of Greece, and of Babylon, and the Samians heard, they avenged Aesop's death.

Aesop Vita G 142, my trans.

Thus Aesop, whose unjust death had been engineered by Apollo, calls on "the leader [*prostatēs*] of the Muses" at the moment of his death to witness its

---

μηδὲ ταφῆς ἀξιωθῇς. ἑτοίμασαι σεαυτόν." Cf. ch. 3 for Archilochus as a *blasphēmos*. Here we have the theme of the public vote against the fabulist: cf. Himerius *Orations* 13.5–6 (test. 30 Perry), which speaks of the Delphians bringing an unjust vote (*psēphon adikon*) against Aesop.

[46] "ὁμοίως κἀγώ, ἄνδρες, ἀποθανὼν ὑμῖν μόρος ἔσομαι· καὶ γὰρ Λύδιοι, Βαβυλώνιοι, καὶ σχεδὸν ἡ Ἑλλὰς ὅλη τὸν ἐμὸν καρπίσονται θάνατον." For Aesop's use of fables in his accusing speeches to the Delphians, see van Dijk 1994:141–149.

[47] αἰδέσθητε Δία Ξένιον καὶ Ὀλύμπιον, G 139. Robertson (2003:264–265) notes that there was an actual shrine to the Muses at Delphi. Cf. ch. 6 (Hesiod).

injustice. But, as the *Vita* tells us earlier (33), Apollo is *prostatēs tōn Mousōn*.[48] As a further complication, another reference to Aesop cult hints at his identification with Apollo. Apollo had been angry when he, the leader of the Muses, had not been awarded a statue along with the Muses in the Samian Aesopeum; in Babylon, Lukoros erects a statue of Aesop with the Muses and institutes a great festival (*heortēn megalēn*) in honor of Aesop's wisdom (123). As in the case of Marsyas, Apollo is antagonistic to Aesop because he is so much like himself in his mantic wisdom. It is striking that Aesop warns the Delphians to honor Apollo in *Vita* W.[49] Libanius speaks of Apollo raging because of the death of Aesop.[50] According to Zenobius, it is Apollo's prophetess, the Pythia, who commands the Delphians to make recompense for the pollution of Aesop's death.[51]

Other manuscripts of the *Vita* add important details. In some versions of the *Life*, Aesop is stoned to death.[52] In *P. Oxy.* 1800 (Perry test. 25), "They stoned him and pushed him off a cliff." *P. Oxy.* 1800 also tells us of hero cult established for Aesop at Delphi, and gives another reason for Aesop's satire:

ἔστ]ιν δ' αἰτία τοια[ύτη] εἰρ[η]μένη· ἐπὰν [εἰσέ]λθῃ τ[ις] τῷ θεῷ
θυσιάσ[ων ο]ἱ Δελφ[ο]ὶ περ[ι]εστήκασι τὸν βωμ[ὸ]ν ὑφ' ἑαυτοῖς
μαχαίρας κ[ο]μίζοντες, σφαγιασαμένου δὲ τοῦ ἱερείου καὶ δείραντος
τὸ ἱερεῖον καὶ τὰ σπλάγχνα περιεξελομένου, οἱ περιεστῶτες ἕκαστος

---

[48] And also "the superior of the Muses [*ho meizōn tōn Mousōn*]," 33. Kurke 2003, limiting her interpretive focus mainly to G, reads the story of Aesop in Delphi as a thoroughgoing attack on Apollo and Delphi. While her view of Aesop and the Delphians is valuable, she underplays complexities in the relationship of Aesop and Apollo. Early traditions show a continuity with Apollo after Aesop's death (see following text). Though an oracle of Zeus requires cult for Aesop in G, in *P. Oxy.* 1800, the context of the narrative clearly has Apollo at Delphi prescribing cult for the fabulist. Furthermore, in G Aesop receives his poetic consecration from the Muses, who are closely connected with Apollo (often called the "leader of the Muses" in the *Vita*). Aesop's and Apollo's ties with Marsyas in G (100, 127) are also notable; he is another rival and victim of Apollo who has continuity with him after death. (See ch. 16.) The Aesopic fables attacked the Delphians, but praised Apollo, Lissarrague 2000:144. Finally, the papyrus record shows that there were elements of both G and W in our earliest extant texts.

[49] 139: ἄνδρες Δελφοί, μὴ ἀτιμάσητε τὸν θεὸν τοῦτον ... αἰδέσθητε τὸν Ἀπόλλωνα. Cf. ch. 15 (Socrates).

[50] Libanius *On the Apology of Socrates* 181 (test. 29 Perry). "Once this very god, raging, surrounded his own priests with evils because of Aesop." τοὺς αὐτοῦ ποθ' ἱερεῖς οὗτος αὐτὸς ὁ θεὸς ὑπὲρ Αἰσώπου χαλεπαίνων περιέβαλε κακοῖς.

[51] Zenobius 1.47 (test. 27 Perry). "They say that the Pythia told them to atone for the pollution [*musos*] perpetrated against Aesop." τὴν Πυθίαν φασὶν ἀνῃρηκέναι αὐτοῖς ἱλάσκεσθαι τὸ ἐπὶ Αἰσώπῳ μύσος. For Aesop's solidarity with and antagonism to Apollo, see Nagy 1979:289–292.

[52] Scholia on Callimachus, Pfeiffer 1949 I:165, line 25 (test. 26 Perry): οἱ δὲ λιθόλευστον ποιῆσαί [φασιν?] Cf. Wiechers 1961:33; Nagy 1979:281.

ἦν ἂν ἰσχύσῃ μοῖραν ἀποτεμνόμενος ἄπεισιν, ὡς πολλάκις τὸν
θυσιάσαντα αὐτὸν ἄμοιρ[ο]ν απι[έ]ναι. τοῦτο οὖν Αἴ[σ]ωπ[ο]ς Δελ-
φοὺς ὀνιδ[ί]ζων ἐπέσκωψεν, ἐφ᾽ οἷς διοργισθέντες οἱ πολλοὶ λίθοις
αὐτὸν βάλλοντες κατὰ κρημνοῦ ἔωσαν. μετ᾽ οὐ πολὺ δὲ λοιμικὸν
πάθος ἐπέσκηψε τῇ πόλει, χρηστηριαζομένοις δ᾽ αὐτοῖς ὁ θεὸς
ἀνεῖπεν οὐ πρότερον [λήξ]ειν τὴν νόσ[ον μέ]χρις [ἂν Α]ἴσωπον
ἐξι[λάσκωντ]αι. οἱ δὲ περιτει[χίσ]αντες τὸν τόπον [ἐν ᾧ κ]ατέπεσεν
βωμὸ[ν θ᾽ ἱ]δ[ρυσά]μενοι λυτηρ[ί]ο[υς] τῆς νόσου, ὡς ἥρῳ θ[υσίας]
προ[σ]ήνεγκαν.

The cause is said to be this: When someone goes in for the purpose
of initiating sacrifice to the god, the Delphians stand around the
altar carrying concealed daggers. And after the priest has slaugh-
tered and flayed the sacrificial victim and after he has apportioned
the innards, those who have been standing around cut off whatever
portion of meat each of them is able to cut off and then depart, with
the result that the one who initiated the sacrifice oftentimes departs
without having a portion himself. Now Aesop reproached and ridi-
culed [onid[i]zōn epeskōpsen] the Delphians for this, which made the
people angry. They stoned him and pushed him off a cliff. Not much
later, a pestilence fell upon the city, and when they consulted the
Oracle, the god revealed that the disease would not cease until they
propitiated Aesop. So they built a wall around the place where he
fell, set up an altar as an antidote to the disease, and sacrificed to
him as a hero.[53]

This attests to the paradox of hero cult for Aesop at Delphi, also found in
W 142, the last paragraph of the *Vita* :

"... καταρῶμαι οὖν ὑμῶν τὴν πατρίδα καὶ θεοὺς μαρτύρομαι, οἳ
ἐπακούσουσί μου ἀδίκως ἀπολλυμένου καὶ ἐκδικήσουσί με." οἱ δὲ
ὠθήσαντες ἔρριψαν αὐτὸν κατὰ τοῦ κρημνοῦ, καὶ οὕτως ἀπέθανε.
λοιμῷ οὖν καὶ συνοχῇ ἰσχυρᾷ κατασχεθέντες οἱ Δελφοὶ χρησμὸν
ἔλαβον ἐξιλεώσασθαι τὸν τοῦ Αἰσώπου μόρον. ἐτύπτοντο γὰρ ὑπὸ
τῆς συνειδήσεως δολοφονήσαντες τὸν Αἴσωπον. ναοποιήσαντες οὖν
ἔστησαν αὐτῷ στήλην. μετὰ δὲ ταῦτα ἀκούσαντες οἱ τῆς Ἑλλάδος
ἔξαρχοι καὶ οἱ λοιποὶ διδάσκαλοι τὸ εἰς τὸν Αἴσωπον πραχθέν,

---

[53] Test. 25 Perry. Trans. Nagy 1979:285. On the theme of meat division, see Nagy 1990:269–275.
See below, ch. 7 (Simonides given an inadequate share at a feast). For the verb, *skōptō*, see Nagy
1979:245, 288, 303; ch. 3 (Archilochus' *Dichterweihe*).

παραγενόμενοι ἐν Δελφοῖς καὶ συζήτησιν ποιησάμενοι ἐξεδίκησαν τὸν τοῦ Αἰσώπου μόρον.

"I curse [*katarōmai*] your fatherland and I call as witness the gods, who will hear me as I perish unjustly and will avenge me." But they pushed him and cast him down the cliff, and so he died. Therefore they were burdened by a plague and a heavy affliction, and received an oracle that they should make propitiation for the death of Aesop. For they were struck by guilt at having killed Aesop deceitfully. Therefore, they built a shrine and placed a stele in it. After this, the lords of Greece and the other teachers heard what had been done to Aesop, and gathered at Delphi. After making an investigation, they avenged Aesop's death.[54]

In G and W, Aesop's death caused a war directed against the Delphians. Wiechers suggests that Aesop's labeling the Delphians as slaves (G, W 126) provides a context for linking his death to the First Sacred War. In the *Vita* tradition, Aesop's death causes the war, which the gods (especially, perhaps, Apollo, in G) send to the Delphians as punishment. But the result of the war was favorable for the Delphians, adding Cirrha/Crisa to their territory, making "all Delphi . . . sacred to Apollo."[55] And the institutions that Aesop mocks—sending tithes of slaves and other things to Delphi, and priests eating all sacrificial meat, leaving none for the provider of the animal—came into being after the First Sacred War. Thus, Aesop's mocking of ritual customs serves as an *aition* for their existence, and his death serves to further the holiness of Delphi—in fact, "an entire conglomeration of institutions sacred to Apollo—the very essence of Delphi after the First Sacred War."[56] The ambiguity of Aesop's relationship with Apollo has taken its last turn, bringing us into a complex interface between ritual, history, and story. Aesop, critic of Delphic practice and killed at inhospitable Delphi because of Apollo's enmity, is sacred to Apollo, is Apollo's servant, and is an *aition* for Delphic practice.[57]

---

[54] 142, my trans. The hero cult theme is an example of how the papyrus tradition sometimes supports W. The ending of G seems somewhat abrupt.

[55] Nagy 1979:286.

[56] Nagy 1979:284. My discussion of this question is dependent on pp. 283–284. Kurke (2003:87) suggests that bringing tithes of slaves to Delphi need not be limited to the time of the First Sacred War. However, it was certainly done at that time.

[57] For Aesop's cult at Delphi, see Clay 204:127.

Aesop as *Pharmakos*

Wiechers shows convincingly that the Aesop story is closely connected to the *pharmakos* complex:

1. The *pharmakoi* are the most worthless people, they are *aēdestatoi, akhrēstoi, eutelestatoi, agenneis,* and *phauloi*—Aesop comes from the lowliest class of society, the slave class; he is repulsively ugly and entirely misshapen, and he is designated in the *Vita* as a *katharma*, a word that is commonly used as a synonym for *pharmakos*.

2. The *pharmakoi* were led through the city before execution, then led out of it, so that they could meet their end at a designated, well-known place—Aesop experiences the same thing. He is also dragged for a long way to the place of execution, after he is fetched from prison; he also thereupon is led out of the city, so that he can finally be executed at the designated place of execution.

3. The *pharmakoi* meet their death by stoning, or by being thrown over a cliff—Aesop is executed in just this way; either he is thrown down from cliffs, or he is killed by being thrown over a cliff linked with stoning.

4. The *pharmakoi* were killed following a decision of the people (*boulēi dēmosiēi*, Hipponax 128W) by a crowd representing the whole people—Aesop comes up against a similar decision among the Delphians (*ebouleusanto . . . anelein*, G 127; they explain: . . . *se epsēphisamen anelein*, G 132) and is therefore killed by the entire people.

5. The *Pharmakos* named by Istros has stolen a golden cup out of the temple treasure—Aesop is reproached for the same fault.

6. The *pharmakoi* were offered in the Thargelia, performed for the service of Apollo; the *pharmakos* named by Istros commits an offense against this god and is destroyed by him. In the case of Aesop, Apollo also plays an important role; he also helps in the plot directed against Aesop. So the *pharmakoi*, as also Aesop, lose their lives because of Apollo.[58]

---

[58] Wiechers 1961:35–36. See also Parker 1983:260, 270, 274; Adrados 1979; Jedrkiewicz 1989; Ogden 1997:38–40. To the best of my knowledge, Aesop is never explicitly called *pharmakos*, but his ugliness, his alleged temple theft, and stoning/cliff execution make the identification with the *pharmakos* pattern convincing.

Wiechers also adduces Androgeus as an important parallel to the story of Aesop (the unjust murder of a stranger-guest, followed by the wrath of god, plague, and ritual purification).[59] Robertson compares Aesop's execution by the Delphians to the archaic festival of Charila at Delphi, in which an effigy (of a poor orphan girl, begging, who has been kicked and excluded by the Basileus, then hangs herself in legend, resulting in the standard plague, oracle, and cult) is kicked, then taken away, strangled, and buried.[60]

The traditions of Aesop's life parallel the following list of *pharmakos* themes:

1. *Ritual pollution.* Aesop's supposed theft of temple treasure causes a supposed pollution that his death must expiate. In actuality, the unjust death of Aesop causes a ritual pollution at Delphi.

    1a. *Crime of hero.* This is a false accusation, but the theme is still there.

    1a1. *Criminal impiety.*

    1a2. *Theft of sacred things.* Here the parallel of *pharmakos* and Aesop is exact: The theme of the theft of a golden cup is found in both stories. Aesop is accused of being a "temple-thief" (*hierosulon*, *Vita* W 132). Yet the Delphians are actually guilty of desecrating a temple as they drag Aesop away from a shrine of the Muses, or shrine of Apollo in *Vita* W (134), where he has taken refuge, on the way to his execution.

    1b. *Crime against hero.* This is actual.

    1b1. *Inhospitality.* Aesop is a visitor at Delphi, as was Androgeus at Athens.

    1b2. *Murder.* Aesop is killed.

    1b3. *Deceit.* Aesop is killed deceitfully (*ebouleusanto ... anelein dolōi*, G 127; *dolophonēsantes*, "killing by ruse," *Vita* W 142).

2. *Communal disaster.* In the case of the Delphians, both plague[61] and invasion.[62]

    2a. *Communal disaster causes hero's expulsion or death*, e.g. "plague" of shame. Aesop's mockery of the Delphians creates a psychological climate that they cannot tolerate—as it were, a plague of shame.

---

[59] Wiechers 1961:42.

[60] Plutarch *Greek Questions* 12 (293b–f). Robertson 2003:260–262. Cf. the hanging women in ch. 3 (Archolochus) and app. A (Iambe).

[61] *P. Oxy.* 1800 (test. 25 Perry), "... *loimikon pathos.*" *Vita* W 142, cf. G 142.

[62] *Vita* G, W 142.

This is the real reason they must kill him, to keep his satiric criticisms from shaming them in front of the rest of the Greeks, as the *Vita* makes clear (G 127). (A literal plague overtakes the Delphians after they kill him.)

2b. *Communal disaster caused by hero's death or expulsion.* This calamity was caused by Aesop's expulsion/death.

3. *Oracle.* As in the myth of Androgeus, an oracle (here the Delphic oracle) instructs the plague-ridden Delphians to expiate the death of Aesop. It is significant that the scene of Aesop's death is laid at Delphi, the most holy oracle of Greece.

4. *The Worst.* Aesop is the worst of men, the most valueless of slaves (at two points in the *Vita*, his seller almost has to give him away to be rid of him [G 15, 27—here, his owner sells him at cost]), ugly, completely deformed.

4b. *Slave.*

4c. *Criminal.* This is imputed to Aesop.

4d. *Ugly.*

4e. *Foreigner.*

5. *The Best.* Aesop is the best of men, courageous, surpassing all men in wisdom and cleverness, conquering the world for Lukoros through his "intellectual warfare." He is moreover sacral: holy, pious, given special gifts from the Muses; while living, he is offered cult by the Samians and Lukoros. Moreover, he has a salvific aspect, saving his unworthy master Xanthus from death, saving the Samians from Croesus, and saving Lykoros from being defeated by Egypt.[63]

5a. *Sacred.*[64]

5b. *Salvation imagery.*

5c. *Victorious.* Aesop is supreme in his intellectual warfare.

6. *Peripety.* Aesop, after having conquered most of the known world through his superior wit, suffers a peripety at Delphi, where he is killed as an accursed temple thief.

---

[63] According to Photius, s.v. "*peripsēma*," the *pharmakos* is a *sōtēria.*

[64] Cf. also Zenobius 1.27 (test. 27 Perry), where Aesop is referred to as "beloved by god" (*theophilēs*). The context of the passage clearly points to Apollo as the god who loves Aesop.

7. *Trial, unjust. Selection by public meeting.* Aesop receives his death sentence by legal decree of the people of Delphi.

8. *Voluntary (exile or death).* At first sight, Aesop seems an utterly involuntary scapegoat, like most *pharmakoi* (apparently); in fact, he dies cursing the Delphians for killing him unjustly. However, he has certain unmistakable voluntary traits: in *Vita G*, after he is taken to the place of execution, he finally throws himself off the cliff. Earlier, at Samos, when the Samians decide not to deliver him to Croesus, Aesop unexpectedly leaves Samos voluntarily with Croesus' ambassador.

8a. *Ambivalent volition.*

9. *[Procession?]* Wiechers interprets this theme in the Aesop novel.[65] However, though Aesop is made a source of public display, he is not explicitly led in a procession. After the cup is found in Aesop's luggage, and before he is imprisoned, the Delphians "loudly and violently made a spectacle [*paradeigmatizontes*] of him."[66] Nevertheless, there was an implicit collective movement of Delphians and Aesop to the cliff.

10. *Expulsion.* Aesop is expelled because of the inhospitality of the Delphians. They only arrest and imprison him in order to kill him, which is a more final expulsion. At that time, Aesop is taken from the prison to the cliff of execution outside the city. As was noted earlier, the ejection from the cliff is usually an expulsion from land to sea, into another element. Though in Delphi an expulsion into the sea is not possible,[67] in the death of Aesop, he does have the experience of being pushed from cliff to air, a liminal experience marking boundaries between land and nothingness, life and death.

11. *Death.* Aesop is executed.

11a. *Stoning.*

11b. *Being thrown from cliff.* Most sources mention this as the method of execution.

11f. *The death is unjust,* as in the case of Androgeus.

---

[65] Wiechers 1961:36.

[66] G 128: μετὰ βίας καὶ θορύβου παραδειγματίζοντες αὐτόν. Aesop becomes a paradigm, as it were.

[67] Cf. *P. Oxy.* 1800 (test. 25 Perry), see above. "So they built a wall around the place where he fell."

12. *Sacrifice imagery.* Though Aesop's death isn't referred to as a sacrifice, in *P. Oxy.* 1800, his blame poetry, death, and hero cult are connected with sacrifice. Aesop mocks the Delphians for how they practice sacrificial ritual at Delphi (the Delphians, with concealed knives, get pieces of meat while the one who initiates the sacrifice often goes without); this makes the Delphians angry, and they stone him and push him over a cliff; after they are afflicted by a plague, they set up an altar at the place where he fell "and sacrificed to him as a hero."

13. *Hero cult.* Aesop thus is given hero cult.

16. *Evil eye.* Aesop's ugliness is so great that his fellow slaves think it will attract the evil eye (G 16). The master bought the deformed man "to use him as a horror to protect the market from the evil eye."[68]

18. *Divine persecutor/patron.* Aesop is persecuted by Apollo, who later orders his hero cult. Aesop insults Apollo, is killed because Apollo motivates the Delphians to kill him; Aesop rebukes the Delphians, telling them to honor Apollo, and calls on Apollo to witness his unjust death; then Apollo (presumably) sends the plague to Delphi, and tells the Delphians they must expiate it through setting up hero cult to Aesop. Aesop's death causes a war that avenges his death and extends Delphi's sacred boundaries. Aesop's mocking of Delphic institutions serves as a charter for their continuance. Though this relationship is paradoxical, it is typical of Greek myth, as the relationship of Hera and Heracles shows.[69]

21. *Imprisonment.*

23. *Hero is sacred, superhuman.*

23d. *Resurrection.* There is an odd, but early, tradition that Aesop was resurrected. Zenobius writes, "For Aesop was so dear to the gods that the story is told of him that he was resurrected, like Tyndareos and Heracles and Glaucus."[70]

---

[68] ἵνα αὐτὸν προσβάσκανον τοῦ σωματεμπορίου ποιήσῃ.

[69] See chs. 16 and 18 below.

[70] οὕτω γὰρ θεοφιλὴς ἐγένετο ὁ Αἴσωπος ὡς μυθεύεται αὐτὸν ἀναβιῶναι, ὡς Τυνδάρεων καὶ Ἡρακλῆν καὶ Γλαῦκον. Zenobius 1.47 (test. 27 Perry). Glaucus was the brother of Androgeus. See also test. 45–48 Perry (the earliest attestation is the comic poet Plato, *circa* 400 BC); Wiechers 1961:41; Nagy 1979:316; above, on Androgeus; below, chs. 6 (Hesiod) and 16 (Empedocles).

Aesop as Satirist

So, in the Aesop *Vita*, there is a full, complex story that is closely identified with the *pharmakos* pattern. But more importantly for our purposes, this *pharmakos* is a satirist, a verbal artist, a blame poet in the archaic tradition delineated by Donald Ward, Nagy, and others, and his blame poetry has been a crucial element that places him into the scapegoat situation. In *Vita* G, Aesop blames the Delphians for their inhospitality and lack of generosity, a typical archaic occasion for blame. Ward, for example, writes, of the target of the typical Indo-European satirist, "Not until the intended victim had become guilty of some shameful deed, such as greed, inhospitality, or above all, the refusal to make a gift of any treasured object to a friend, guest, or relative who admired it, could he be attacked in song."[71] Nagy, in an analysis of the diction of epic blame poetry, finds that generosity or lack of it is a central theme.[72] In the *Odyssey*, "When a man is blameless himself, and his thoughts are blameless, the friends [*xeinoi*] he has entertained carry his fame [*kleos*] widely to all mankind, and many are they who call him excellent."[73] It is the *xeinoi*, the guest-friends, who spread the praise of the blameless man; it is presumably they who will spread the blame of the ungenerous man. In Pindar, the poet is the guest-friend of his patron, whom he praises. "I am a guest-friend [*xeinos*]; keeping away dark blame [*psogon*], leading true fame [*kleos*] to a dear man like waves of water, I will praise him [*ainesō*]."[74] It is significant that Aesop is a stranger, a foreigner at Delphi; there he should have been able to rely on the values of hospitality to protect him.

This criticism of the Delphians brings about Aesop's arrest, imprisonment, and execution. The Delphians fear that his blame of them will spread throughout Greece if he is allowed to depart and live, which would create a situation intolerable for them. This is the plague of shame that Aesop's death must prevent. Aesop is not just a poet, but he is a very powerful poet—in fact, "the best" man living with regard to his wits, powers of intellectual warfare,

---

[71] Ward 1982:133. Watkins emphasizes the sacred bond of gift exchange between poet and patron in Indo-European traditions. Watkins 1995:70–75.

[72] Nagy 1979:224–236.

[73] *Odyssey* xix 332–334, trans. Lattimore. ὃς δ' ἀμύμων αὐτὸς ἔῃ καὶ ἀμύμονα εἰδῇ, / τοῦ μέν τε κλέος εὐρὺ διὰ ξεῖνοι φορέουσι / πάντας ἐπ' ἀνθρώπους, πολλοί τέ μιν ἐσθλὸν ἔειπον. Cf. Nagy 1979:257, 253–264, 281.

[74] *Nemean Odes* 7.61–63: ξεῖνός εἰμι· σκοτεινὸν ἀπέχων ψόγον, / ὕδατος ὥτε ῥοὰς φίλον ἐς ἄνδρ' ἄγων / κλέος ἐτήτυμον αἰνέσω. For the institution of guest-friendship in archaic Greece, see bibliography in Bremmer 1983b:303n27; Finley 1978:99–103; cf. Benveniste 1973:278.

and supernatural insight. It is the poet's power to broadcast blame throughout society that is feared, that causes his assimilation to the *pharmakos* theme. Furthermore, it is Aesop's very mobility that makes the Delphians fear him—he travels through Greece like a rhapsode, performing for his survival, dependant on hospitality.[75] It is significant that in *Vita* G (139), Aesop, after telling the pointed fable of the tumblebug, hare, and eagle, warns the Delphians to reverence Zeus Xenios, Zeus of strangers, guest-friends.[76]

In *P. Oxy.* 1800, again Aesop blames and mocks the greed of the Delphians (*onid[i]zōn epeskōpsen*) as they carry out the ritual of sacrifice. This provokes them to anger, and they execute him. This incident is particularly noteworthy because it seems to be an *aition* for ritual practice.

Though I have concentrated mostly on Aesop at Delphi to show his satiric speech, his use of blame is evident throughout his biography. For example, immediately after the pastoral and moving scene in which Aesop receives poetic inspiration from Isis and the Muses, as well as his voice, the first time he uses his voice to communicate with his fellow man, he verbally attacks his overseer for mistreating and beating another slave unjustly (G 9). The overseer immediately runs to his master, accuses Aesop of saying "monstrously slanderous things" (μεγάλως βλασφημεῖ) against the master, so the master quickly directs the overseer to sell the deformed slave (G 10).

The Aesop biography allows us to add some important themes to our list:

22. *Blame poet* as scapegoat hero.

22a. *Killing through blame*, satire. The blame Aesop directs at his son Ainos causes him to commit suicide.

22c. *Animal fables* used for blame.[77]

23. *Poet is sacred.*

23a. *Consecration of poet.* (Cf. 5a.)

24. *Conflict with political leader(s)*. It is the Delphian "officials" (*hoi ... arkhontes)* who first decide that Aesop cannot be allowed to leave Delphi alive (G 127).

---

[75] For rhapsodes, see especially ch. 5 (Homer), cf. ch. 7 (Simonides). Narratives of divine punishment falling on those who are inhospitable to traveling poets, rhapsodes, riddlers, or seers, especially if they are marginal, perhaps blind, would be the kinds of stories that rhapsodes would tell. Cf. the mirroring tales of Cridenbél and Cairbre in McCone 1989:123–124.

[76] Cf. Perry 1936:16.

[77] See e.g. *Vita* G 133–142, in which Aesop tells three fables blaming the Delphians and defending himself before he is executed.

So the blame poet is assimilated completely and richly to the Greek socio-religious scapegoat pattern,[78] a phenomenon that raises many questions. To answer these questions, we must explore the ambiguous place of the poet in archaic Greek culture. The poet is, like the *pharmakos*, the worst and the best in his society—the filth, *katharma*, and yet so holy as to be the object of sacrifice after death.[79] Poets in a culture where shame is a dominant component are especially powerful, focal points for broadcasting shame and honor, and so especially vulnerable to punitive action when they offend a community and its political leader(s) (as they often do). A culture informed by shame values would be a culture in which public loss of reputation and honor would count for more than inner guilt. Ruth Benedict writes that "shame cultures" "rely on external sanctions for good behavior, not, as true guilt cultures do, on an internalized conviction of sin. Shame is a reaction to other people's criticism. A man is shamed . . . by being openly ridiculed."[80]

Archaic Greece cannot be interpreted as a "pure" shame culture (if such ever existed); H. Lloyd-Jones, Dover, and Douglas L. Cairns, rejecting the evolutionary view of E. R. Dodds, note that shame and guilt are found in both archaic and later Greek culture.[81] However, this still leaves the question of whether one or the other is predominant, and how the balance may shift through time. Cairns tends to flatly reject the concepts of shame and guilt cultures, but writes, "This is not to say that there are not significant differences between

---

[78] Or, perhaps, the sacral poet helping to define such a pattern. Cf. chs. 16 and 18 especially, which suggest that myths of poets form a background for the Aesop/Archilochus/etc. poet-scapegoat-hero story structure. We might say that the historical blame poet is assimilated to the mythical poet-victim. Certainly, however, Aesop was assimilated to the *pharmakos* persona.

[79] For hero cult awarded to the poet in ancient Greece, see below, nearly all of chapters 3–16, and Clay 2004.

[80] Benedict 1946:223. I prefer terms less absolutist than "shame culture" or "guilt culture," see below. See also Radin 1927:50–51 (fear of ridicule as social motive); "Interpretative Statement," Mead 1937:493–495. Cf. below, ch. 17 (death of Luaine; blisters of "shame" on face).

[81] Within the parameters of the story of Aesop, the Delphians kill Aesop so he will not publicly shame them; however, after his death, they are struck by guilt (in W). A similar interweaving of shame and guilt can be found in the story of Nede and Caier in ch. 17. For Greece and shame, see Dodds 1951:28–63; Dover 1975:236–243, "causes and effects of shame," 26–33, abuse among orators or comedians; 220n3; Lloyd-Jones 1990; Cairns 1993. See also Bloomfield and Dunn 1989:7; Friedrich 1973; Peristiany 1966; Hallberg 1962:100–104. On the power of verbal mockery in Greek culture, see Halliwell 1991b:286–287. As he notes, Aristotle *Nicomachean Ethics* 5.2 (1131a9) and *Politics* 2.4 (1262a27), classes defamation and abuse as acts of violence, with assault, murder and robbery; cf. the frequent description of derision as *hubris*, e.g. Sophocles *Ajax* 196–169, 955–960; Demosthenes 9.60, 22.63; Aristotles *Rhetoric* 2.2 (1379a29–30). Greek laughter, of course, could also be friendly and playful, e.g. Plutarch *Lycurgus* 12, 14, 25, see Halliwell 1991b:283–284, 292.

our society and that of ancient Greece which may be usefully explained in terms of tendencies to emphasize shame rather than guilt."[82] Striking characteristics of extraordinary emphasis on shame can be found in Greek legend and history, and in many archaic cultures.[83]

Leaders in such a culture, even kings, inevitably must use force to combat powerful blame poets' psychological power. In fact, if kings do not do so, they sometimes have no choice but to abdicate. But if the inimical blame poet is intolerable to the king, the friendly praise poet is indispensable to him (though the blame poet and praise poet often cannot be strictly separated).[84]

In addition, the poet is, in archaic Greek society, *hieros anēr*[85]—sacred man, and so he shares in all the ambiguity of the essential concept of the sacred in archaic culture. The sacred man or woman is both accursed and blessed, polluted and pure, polluting and cleansing, despised *pharmakos* and revered hero receiving cult. The blameless Aesop is killed because the Delphians are inhospitable; as a skillful satirist, his presence cannot be tolerated. The weapon of the poet's verbal aggression has great power in a culture based on reputation. (Aesop is a warrior, on a verbal level, conquering territory for a king; the poet embodies verbal violence.) Because of this weapon, the poet will be feared, despised, and revered.

---

[82] Cairns 1993:44.

[83] See ch. 17 below; cf. Ward 1973; O'Leary 1991:24–25, 15.

[84] Watkins 1995:70–84.

[85] See Rowland 1980, a valuable analysis of the sacred man in ancient Greek myth, which treats at least one major poet, Archilochus.

3

Archilochus: Sacred Obscenity and Judgment

THE *VITA* OF AESOP is something of a prototype, both in its fullness and in its ringing the changes on the "sacred" scapegoat theme. The lives of many Greek poets include similar themes. They will be surveyed in this and subsequent chapters, concentrating on poets whose *vitae* have been assimilated to the scapegoat in some way, or who have been exiled, executed, or adversely tried. These *vitae* are sometimes clearly legendary, though there will be historical elements woven into some *vitae*, and some may be almost entirely historical. The patterns in archaic Greece will be considered first; then remnants of the same patterns will appear in later times, as traditions grow up around an author's reputation in the centuries after his death. The ahistoricity of a *vita* will not prevent it from being mythically valuable. As we will see, archaic themes will attach themselves to historical, or quasi-historical, or perhaps nonhistorical, poets. Documents from the Hellenistic age or late antiquity may reflect early tradition; in fact, colorful *vitae* of later poets derive in part from the mythical *vitae* of earlier poets.

Lefkowitz and others have pursued the theory that lives of poets derive from learned extrapolation from the received poetic corpus; this phenomenon clearly took place, but traditional legends of poets and heroes were also applied to prominent poets, sometimes no doubt by early oral tradition. Hero cult also served to solidify the poet's reputation and legacy; thus we often find an extraordinary emphasis on the poet's death in the legends.

The life of Archilochus, as has been noted, shares a number of themes with the life of Aesop.[1] An examination of the scattered but telling details from his biographical tradition will show that his *vita* sometimes fits closely into the pattern found in Aesop's life, that of the sacral blame poet who is rejected by society. The case of Archilochus is especially interesting because we are

---

[1] For Archilochus' poetry, see West 1989; poetry and testimonia in Tarditi 1968, Treu 1959; Gerber 1999b.

dealing here with a biographical tradition of putative historicity; debate concerning the historical reliability of many details of his life still continues.[2] As a boy, Archilochus receives his commission from the Muses, according to the inscription at Archilochus' shrine in Paros:[3]

> Λέγουσι γὰρ Ἀρχίλοχον ἔτι νεώτερον
> ὄντα πεμφθέντα ὑπὸ τοῦ πατρὸς Τελεσικλέους
> εἰ]ς ἀγρόν, εἰς τὸν δῆμον, ὃς καλεῖται Λειμῶνες,
> ὥ]στε βοῦν καταγαγεῖν εἰς πρᾶσιν, ἀναστάντα
> π]ρωΐτερον τῆς νυκτός, σελήνης λαμπρούσης,
> ἄγ]ειν τὴμ βοῦν εἰς πόλιν· ὡς δ᾽ ἐγένετο κατὰ τὸν
> τ]όπον, ὃς καλεῖται Λισσίδες, δόξαι γυναῖκας
> ἰδ]εῖν ἀθρόας· νομίσαντα δ᾽ ἀπὸ τῶν ἔργων ἀπιέναι
> αὐτὰς εἰς πόλιν προσελθόντα σκώπτειν, τὰς δὲ
> δέξασθαι αὐτὸν μετὰ παιδιᾶς καὶ γέλωτος καὶ
> ἐ]περωτῆσαι, εἰ πωλήσων ἄγει τὴμ βοῦν· φήσαντος δέ,
> εἰ]πεῖν ὅτι αὐταὶ δώσουσιν αὐτῶι τιμὴν ἀξίαν·
> ῥη]θέντων δὲ τούτων αὐτὰς μὲν οὐδὲ τὴμ βοῦν οὐκέτι
> φα]νερὰς εἶναι, πρὸ τῶν ποδῶν δὲ λύραν ὁρᾶν αὐτόν·
> κα]ταπλαγέντα δὲ καὶ μετά τινα χρόνον ἔννουν
> γεν]όμενον ὑπολαβεῖν τὰς Μούσας εἶναι τὰς φανείσας
> καὶ] τὴν λύραν αὐτῶι δωρησαμένας· καὶ ἀνελό-
> με]νον αὐτὴν πορεύεσθαι εἰς πόλιν καὶ τῶι πατρὶ
> τὰ γ]ενόμενα δηλῶσαι . . .

They recount that Archilochus, when he was still a young man, was sent by his father Telesicles to the fields, to the district called the Meadows, to bring a heifer down for sale. He got up at night before sunrise, while the moon was still bright, to lead the heifer to the city. As he came to the place called Slippery Rocks, they say that he thought he saw a group of women. And, since he thought that they were leaving work for the city, he approached them and made

---

[2] Rankin 1977 would see a real poet in the Archilochus fragments rather than just a poetic persona. West (1974:33–39) and Nagy (1979:243–252) tend to see in Archilochus' invective the stock "characters" (such as Lycambes or Enipo) who function as ritualized personifications or types. For the Archilochus cult legend as found in fragmentary form on the Archilocheion, see Müller 1985; Clay 2004. Cf. Rösler 1985; Burnett 1983:29n43; below, ch. 8 (Sappho).

[3] For the Archilocheion, see test. 4T; Treu 1959:40–54. On the dating of the legends found on the Archilocheion, see Müller 1985:141–146; Kontoleon 1964:60. It appears that they derive from archaic (sixth- or fifth-century) Paros tradition.

fun of them [*skōptein*].[4] But they greeted him with good humor and laughter [*meta paidias kai gelōtos*], and asked him if he intended to sell the cow he had in tow. When he answered that he did, they said that they would give him a good price. But, once they had said this, neither they nor the heifer could be seen, but lying before his feet he saw a lyre [*luran*]. He was dumbfounded and, after he had the time to regain his wits, he realized that the women who had appeared to him were the Muses and that it was they who had given him the gift of the lyre. And he picked up the lyre and went to the city and told his father what had happened.

Archilocheion E1 col. II (test. 4T)[5]

As in the poetic initiation of Hesiod (*Theogony* 22ff.), the poet receives a theophany of the Muses while engaged in tending animals; the goddesses mock him gently (perhaps a charter for the poet's future mockery), and give him a physical token of their inspiration and his future poetic gifts.[6]

Telesicles travels to Delphi and asks about the missing cow. He receives an answer to the effect that the first of his children who will greet him when he reaches home will be "immortal [*athanatos*] among men and famous in song [*aoidimos*]."[7] Though the inscription breaks off before the story is completed, it is obvious that Archilochus is the child referred to. In another source, Apollo at Delphi tells the poet's father that he will engender a child who will be immortal.[8]

Though the association of god and blame poet may seem odd at first, considering the negative associations of the blame poet generally and

---

[4] For this key word for blame poetics, see above, ch. 2 (Aesop at Delphi).

[5] Trans. Clay 2004:109. Text from Tarditi 1968:5. Cf. Clay 2004:14–16; Nagy 1979:303–304. For the consecration theme in Greek literature, see above, ch. 2 (Aesop); Kambylis 1963; Miralles and Portulas 1983:61–80. For the association of the lyre with satire, see the *Hymn to Hermes* 54–56, where Hermes, as soon as he invents the lyre, begins to sing satirically (*kertomeousin*)—see Burnett 1983:56n8; Miralles and Portulas 1983:81–126. Cf. the oracular associations of the lyre, *Hymn to Apollo*, 131–141, 514–519, *Hymn to Hermes* 471–474; Bergren 1982:91, 94, 97. For this association of blame poetry and the mantic, we may compare the persistent associations of Aesop and Archilochus with Delphi—for Aesop, see ch. 2; for Archilochus, cf. text below and Rankin 1977:111n69; Burnett 1983:19; Podlecki 1974:12.

[6] Cf. Breitenstein 1971. Also, below, ch. 17, the poet gains inspiration by supernatural food or drink, then receives a gift, e.g. Finn.

[7] E1 col. II 50 (test. 4T). Ἀθά]νατός σοι παῖς καὶ ἀοίδιμος, ὦ Τελεσίκλεις, / ἔ]σται ἐν ἀνθρώποισιν.

[8] Dio Chrysostom 33.11–12 (test. 50T), trans. Edmonds, "He proclaimed to the poet's father when he came to consult the oracle before the birth that his son would become immortal [*athanaton*]" (Τῷ πατρὶ δὲ αὐτοῦ χρωμένῳ πρὸ τῆς γενέσεως ἀθάνατόν οἱ παῖδα γενήσεσθαι προεῖπεν). Cf. Archilocheion E1 col. II.50 (test. 4T); *Palatine Anthology* 14.113 (test. 9T); Oenomaus *ap.* Eusebius *Preparation for the Gospel* 5.32–39.9 (test. 115T); Theodoretus *Remedy for the Diseases of the Greeks* 10.36 (141) (test. 179T). Cf. below, ch. 13 (Euripides).

Archilochus specifically, we must remember that the "good" archaic blame poet was *homo sacer*, expressing the will of the gods to a corrupt audience.[9] This sacral side of Archilochus is reflected in several of his poems. He writes,

εἰμὶ δ' ἐγὼ <u>θεράπων</u> μὲν Ἐνυαλίοιο ἄνακτος
καὶ Μουσέων ἐρατὸν δῶρον ἐπιστάμενος.

I am a servant [*therapōn*] of lord Ares[10]
and of the Muses, and am skillful in their lovely gift.

1W/1T

These lines may not be paradoxical, as some have interpreted them;[11] Archilochus may be referring to an archaic commonplace, the complementary duality of war and poetry in archaic Greece and related cultures.[12] Archilochus was also known as "servant of the Muses" (*Mousōn therapōn*) in his death legend, in which he dies in battle.[13] Archilochus' name means 'leader of a company'. This "may simply be an aristocratic assumption of warrior caste," or it may express the father's expectations for the son.[14] Both poetry and war are concerned with a kind of frenzy, poetic inspiration and battle fury.[15]

---

[9] For moral and immoral blame poets, see Elliott 1960:11; Snell 1953:54–55; Jaeger 1945 1.121–124; Hendrickson 1925b:114–115. The theme of the poet punishing the oath breaker is important, if the Strassburg epode (193T/Hipponax fr. 115W) is Archilochean, though it is probably by Hipponax—cf. 174W; see below. For the poet punishing the oath breaker, see below, chs. 4 (Hipponax), 8 (Sappho), 9 (Alcaeus), 10 (Theognis); ch. 17, the ambiguous poet as upholder of law.

[10] Literally, Enyalios.

[11] Burnett 1983:33–34.

[12] See further chapters and below, this chapter.

[13] Dio Chrysostom 33 (test. 50T); Müller 1985:135; see below, on Archilochus' death. For *therapōn* as ritual substitute, see ch. 1, on *pharmakos* as *therapeia*; ch. 17 (Tamun and DoDera), and chs. 18 and 27, the warrior as substitute for king.

[14] Rankin 1977:15.

[15] See Guépin 1968:20; Mattes 1970; cf. the following note and ch. 17 (Cuchulainn's battle frenzy), ch. 18 (Starkaðr's battle frenzy). For the association of the spheres of Dionysos (see following note) and of Ares, see Hutchinson 1985:124 (on Aeschylus *Seven Against Thebes*, lines 497f.); 99 (on lines 343f.); Dodds 1953:109 (on Euripides *Bacchae*, line 302), 170 (on lines 761–764); Plutarch *Table Talk* 7.10.2 (715E), the *Seven Against Thebes* brimming with Ares (see Aristophanes *Frogs* 1021) and with Dionysos; Guépin 1968:43–45. Cf. the epitaph of Aeschylus, which reputedly mentioned his role in the battle of Marathon, but not his poetry (Pausanias 1.14.5; see below, ch. 12); and on other poets in this chapter, Alcaeus, ch. 9; Socrates, ch. 15; Tyrtaeus and Solon, in ch. 11. Eratosthenes (*Constellations* 24) tells us that Thracians used to go to war drunk. Cf. ch. 16 below, on Orpheus' death.

For Archilochus's poetry that has been interpreted as protreptic, see the Sosthenes inscription A col. 1, line 3–4 (Treu 1959:54, test. 5T); 93W/120T 94W/121T; Burnett 1983:34; Jaeger

In another famous poem, Archilochus stakes a claim to other aspects of archaic spirituality. He states,

ὡς Διωνύσου ἄνακτος καλὸν ἐξάρξαι μέλος
οἶδα διθύραμβον οἴνωι συγκεραυνωθεὶς φρένας.

Thus I know how to lead off the dithyramb, fair song of lord
Dionysos,
when my wits are thunderstruck with wine.

120W/117T

In this mere couplet, Archilochus touches on a number of interrelated themes: Dionysiac religion and rite, the call and response of archaic musical and poetic performance, art and madness, art and (literal and spiritual) intoxication, even the sacrality of the thunderbolt.[16]

Leonidas asserts that "Indeed, the Muses and the Delian Apollo loved him [Archilochus]." "Longinus" describes Archilochus' poetry as carrying much ill-arranged matter in its flood, but as having an "outburst of the divine spirit" (τῆς ἐκβολῆς τοῦ δαιμονίου πνεύματος) which gives it its greatness, hard as the outburst is to control.[17] Like Aesop, Archilochus was known, at least by some, as pious.[18] He referred to himself once as a prophet, though the context for this fragment is difficult to ascertain.[19]

1945 1.121 (the satirically critical and paraenetic are often identical); Martin 1983:48. For Archilochus and war generally, Rankin 1977:80–82; Podlecki 1974:9 and Podlecki 1969; West 1985a:10–13; Burnett 1983:33–54; Parke 1933:4; Graham 2001:188–210; Clay 2004:23–24. Cf. ch. 17 below on Ireland's warrior-satirists.

[16] For the Dionysiac context of iambic poetry, see West 1974:23–25. Drunkenness may here be a metaphor for poetic inspiration (cf. Murray 1940:147, on the testimonia that report Aeschylus as composing in a state of drunkenness), though actual drinking need not be ruled out. See also Scheinberg 1979:19–23. See below, ch. 8 (Sappho); Gil 1967:170–173; Coffey 1976:25 for Ennius, Horace, and wine. On the sacral nature of the thunderstruck person, cf. Artemidorus 2.9, p. 94, 26, "he who has been struck by lightning is honored [*timatai*] as a god" (ὁ κεραυνωθεὶς ὡς θεὸς τιμᾶται), my trans.; Rohde 1925 2:581–582; Guépin 1968:93; 47–51; Nagy 1979:190; Mendelsohn 1992. For the madness of the poet, see previous note; see below, ch. 11 (Tyrtaeus); ch. 16 (Thamyris); ch. 17 (Dubthach Chafertongue; Séafra O'Donnchú); and ch. 18 (Starkathr's rage; Suibhne).

[17] Leonidas, in *Palatine Anthology* 7.664, trans. Edmonds. ἦ ῥά νιν αἱ Μοῦσαι καὶ ὁ Δάλιος ἠγάπευν' Ἀπόλλων . . . "Longinus" *On the Sublime* 33.5, my trans. Cf. Mattes 1970:39.

[18] "Demeas [wrote] an account not only of [the fame of others, but of the virtues of] our fellow citizen Archilochus, [his outstanding] piety [*eusebeias*], the love he bore to his country, Paros . . ." Sosthenes Incription, A col. 1, lines 1–4 (test. 5T). ἀναγέγραφεν] δ[' ὁ Δ]ημέας οὐ μόνον περὶ τ[ῆς Πάρου / ἀλλὰ ∗ ∗]σιλυ.π.λλλ πολίτης Ἀρχίλο[χο / [∗ ∗]εὐσ<εβ>είας καὶ τῆς περὶ τὴν πατ[ρίδα σπου-]/δῆς. Edmonds's translation is based on supplying different words in the lacunae in the inscription.

[19] See 25W/55T, "*mantis.*" See below, chs. 6, 16, on poet as prophet.

Archilochus was also a blame poet par excellence, the first great Greek satirist. Pindar writes of him,

> . . . ἐμὲ δὲ χρεὼν
> φεύγειν <u>δάκος</u> ἀδινὸν <u>κακαγοριᾶν</u>.
> εἶδον γὰρ ἑκὰς ἐὼν τὰ πόλλ' ἐν <u>ἀμαχανίᾳ</u>
> <u>ψογερὸν</u> Ἀρχίλοχον βαρυλόγοις ἔχθεσιν
> πιαινόμενον . . .

But I must flee the deep bite [*dakos*] of evil-speaking [*kakagorian*]. For though I am far, I have seen Archilochus, full of blame [*psogeron*], very much in want [*amaxaniai*], fattening himself on grimly worded hatreds.

Pythian Odes 2.54–56[20]

A poem from the *Palatine Anthology*, a supposed tomb inscription, speaks of Archilochus wielding a poisonous art; it also associates him with wasps. "This tomb by the sea is the grave of Archilochus, who first dipped a bitter Muse [*pikrēn Mousan*] in snake-venom [*ekhidnaiōi . . . kholōi*] and stained gentle Helicon with blood. Lycambes knows it, mourning the hanging of his three daughters. Pass by quietly, wayfarer, or you'll arouse the wasps that settle on his tomb."[21] Horace writes of him that "Rage [*rabies*] armed Archilochus with her own iambic."[22] Plutarch speaks of Archilochus' "bitter" or "spiteful" art.[23] Lucian says that Archilochus "did not hesitate at all to use insulting language

---

[20] My trans. For commentary, see Kurke (1991:100), who translates *amaxaniai* as "resourcessness." Oddly enough, in this *recusatio* of blame poetry, Pindar is blaming Archilochus. Cf. *Nemean Odes* 8.37–39. For further on Pindar and blame, see Kirkwood 1984; Nagy 1979:222-228. For the belly and blame, Burnett 1983:59n17; and above, ch. 2, potbellied Aesop.

[21] Gaetulicus (first century AD), in *Palatine Anthology* 7.71 (test. 66T), trans. W. R. Paton, modified (σῆμα τόδ' Ἀρχιλόχου παραπόντιον, ὅς ποτε <u>πικρήν / μοῦσαν</u> ἐχιδναίῳ πρῶτος ἔβαψε χόλῳ / αἱμάξας Ἑλικῶνα τὸν ἥμερον. Οἶδε Λυκάμβης / μυρόμενος τρισσῶν ἅμματα θυγατέρων. Ἠρέμα δὴ παράμειψον, ὁδοιπόρε, μή ποτε τοῦδε / κινήσῃς τύμβῳ σφῆκας ἐφεζομένους). Eustathius (*Commentary on the Iliad and Odyssey* 851.53) speaks of "scorpion-tongued Archilochus" (ὁ σκορπιώδης τὴν γλῶσσαν Ἀρχίλοχος).

[22] *Ars Poetica* 79 (trans. Edmonds): "*Archilochum proprio rabies armavit iambo.*" Cf. *Epode* 6:13 (trans. Edmonds): "Beware, beware! For I'm an extremely harsh man, and I bear horns ready for wicked men, like [Archilochus] . . ." (*Cave, cave; namque in malos asperrimus/ parata tollo cornua,/ qualis* [Archilochus] . . .) Cf. Apostolius *Proverbs*, 4.2 (test. 17T); Diogenianus *Proverbs* 2.95 (test. 56T), who refers to the poet as one of those who revile, "*tōn loidorountōn.*" However, Horace's statement bears witness to a tradition of the blame poet as righteous, attacking only those who are wicked. See below, app. B; also on oath-breaking, both in this chapter and Hipponax, ch. 4.

[23] *Cato Minor* 7.2, 762e (test. 139T). An angry man writes insulting iambic verse, "employing the venom [*pikrōi*] of Archilochus . . ." τῷ πικρῷ προσχρησάμενος τοῦ Ἀρχιλόχου.

[*oneidizein*], no matter how much pain he was going to inflict upon the victims of the bitterness [*kholēi*] of his iambics."[24]

The archaic genre of the curse, with its religious and magical overtones, is found in Archilochus' poetry.[25] Rankin would remove Archilochus' blame from the sphere of magic: "Greek poetry that is known to us has none of this true primitive magic about it. It has been secularized of magic ... We cannot deny that there may have been earlier more magical forms, but they are not available to us."[26] Rankin argues from assumptions that need to be carefully considered: for example, "magic" is "primitive"; a piece of culture, literary or otherwise, can be purely secular or purely magico-religious, with no gradations in between; the "magico-religious" use of the poetic formula cannot be a work of literary art. Actually, magic can shade imperceptibly into religion, which is not necessarily primitive. Thomas writes, "Anthropologists today are unsympathetic to the view that magic is simply bad science. They stress its symbolic and expressive role rather than its practical one."[27] Early Greek poetry—and nearly all Greek poetry and philosophy—combines the secular and the sacred.[28] The "magical" formula, even when used for blame, can be part of a sophisticated religious and literary tradition. The curse is a form of prayer, and has important ethical dimensions. Watson writes that "perhaps

---

[24] *The Liar* 1–2 (test. 101T), trans. A. M. Harmon, modified: ... μηδὲν ὀκνοῦντα ὀνειδίζειν, εἰ καὶ ὅτι μάλιστα λυπήσειν ἔμελλε τοὺς περιπετεῖς ἐσομένους τῇ χολῇ τῶν ἰάμβων αὐτοῦ. The supposed mother of Archilochus is the slave woman Enipo (Critias 88 B 44 (test. 46T)), and this name means 'abuse'. One remembers Ainos, the son of Aesop, see ch. 2. For the fable as weapon of the slave, see below and ch. 24 (Phaedrus), and Aesop as slave in ch. 2. Müller, 1985:106, argues that the Enipo detail derives from the legend; Lefkowitz 1981:26, typically would have it a late invention. Cf. Nagy 1979:247; Burnett 1983:28n34.

[25] E.g. 26W/30T; cf. 107W/101T; 108W/115T; 329W (spuria)/170T; 177W.4/174T; 200W/194T. 193T = Hipponax 115W/194Dg is possibly by Hipponax, possibly by Archilochus, see Treu 1959:224–228; Kirkwood 1961; Koenen 1977; Rankin 1977:106n1; Watson 1991:60; further bibliography in Degani 1983 *ad loc.* The directness and immediacy of 193T make it tempting to consider it Archilochean, but it will be discussed in the Hipponax section. See further Rankin 1977:50; Elliott 1960:8–9; Hendrickson 1925b:104, 112, 115–117; Watson 1991:63; Gerber 1995.

For the curse and satire generally, Elliott 1960:285–292, 294 s.v. "curse"; Watson 1991:46–47. For Aristophanes' use of the curse, Elliott 1960:93, Watson 1991:140–141; for Horace and the curse, Rankin 1977:50; Watson 1991:154–155. The poetess Moiro (born ca. 300 BC) wrote a poem called *Curses, Arai*, see Powell 1925:22; Hendrickson 1925b:109; Watson 1991:90, 167, as did Euphorion of Chalcis (born ca. 276/275 BC), see Powell 1925:8; Lesky 1966:757; Watson 1991:83, 223. Watson's *Arae: the Curse Poetry of Antiquity* (1991) provides a good general introduction to the curse in antiquity, and is especially good on Hellenistic curse poems. Cf. chs. 4 (Hipponax); 9 (Alcaeus); 10 (Theognis).

[26] 1977:52n36: See also Rankin 1974, "Archilochus was no magician."

[27] Thomas 1971:667.

[28] See Easterling 1985, cf. Robertson 1985.

the most constant motive for pronouncing a curse was the attaining of δίκη 'justice'."[29]

An element of Archilochus' blame that links him closely to Aesop is his tendency to use fables. "The animal tale was in fact one of Archilochus' favorite weapons when he wished to be abusive," writes Anne Pippin Burnett.[30] Just as the legendary Aesop told animal fables denouncing his Delphic persecutors before his death (G 132–142), so Archilochus used animal fables to accuse his archenemy, Lycambes.[31] Fragments 172–181W/166–174T, directed against Lycambes, retell a fable that is shared with Aesop (1 Perry), the fable of the fox and the eagle, in which a fox is victimized by an oath-breaking eagle, curses it, and gains revenge.[32]

Archilochus' most famous poetic victims were the previously mentioned Lycambes and his daughters, all of whom were said to have committed suicide after having been satirized by the poet. Archilochus wrote his poem after Lycambes had promised him his daughter, then broke his word. Thus satire, like the curse, is used to avenge broken oaths.[33] Horace speaks of Archilochus as the "son-in-law spurned by faithless Lycambes" (*Lycambae spretus infido gener*, *Epode* 6.11). A scholiast comments:

> Lycambes habuit filiam Neobulen; hanc cum Archilochus in matrimonium postulasset, promissa nec data est a patre. Hinc iratus Archilochus in eum maledicum carmen scripsit, quo Lycambes tanto est dolore compulsus, ut cum filia vitam laqueo finiret.

> Lycambes had a daughter, Neobule; when Archilochus had asked

---

[29] Watson 1991:38, cf. Gager 1992:175–199. For the curse in prayer, Pulleyn 1997:70–95. It is also worth noting that Archilochus had apparent associations with the priesthood of Demeter, see below. Cf. ch. 17, for the "magical" power of the word in folkore.

[30] Burnett 1983:60; cf. 59n18; 61n25; West 1984:107–108; West 1974:132n4; Nagy 1979:238–239; Holzberg 2002:12.

[31] For the *luk*- root in this name, cf. the symbolism of the wolf discussed at 2.7 (Alcaeus). For the possible ritual significance of the names in this narrative, see above, on the historicity or ahistoricity of Archilochus.

[32] For this fable, Irwin 1998, in the Lefkowitz school of biography interpretation. See also 185–187W/188–189T and Aesop 81 Perry, cf. Aristophanes *Birds* 651–653. In Julian *Orations* 7.207C, (test. 58 Perry) Aesop, as a slave, had no free speech (*parrēsia*), so had "to shadow forth his wise counsels" (ἐσκιαγραφημένας τὰς συμβουλὰς); Philostratus *Images* 1.3 (test. 131T, cf. West 1989:172). See below ch. 24 (Phaedrus), and app. A. Lasserre 1984:63–64, counts six certain and eight probable fables in Archilochus. For the cricket, see below, this chapter; and app. B. Also, Callimachus *Aetia* prologue, fr. 1.29ff. Boedeker 1984:81–83, discusses the poet as cicada in Greece, and the cicada's association with the Muses.

[33] Cf. 173W/179T: "And have you turned your back on a great oath made by salt and table?" (ὅρκον δ' ἐνοσφίσθης μέγαν / ἅλας τε καὶ τράπεζαν).

for her hand in marriage, she was promised to him by her father, but was not given. Therefore, Archilochus was enraged [*iratus*], and wrote an abusive poem [*maledicum carmen*] against him, by which Lycambes was driven to such great agony that he ended his life with a noose, and his daughter did the same with him.

"Acro" *ad Epode* 6[34]

Horace also knows the story of the fiancée hanging herself because of Archilochus' invective.[35] He speaks of Archilochus's "words attacking Lycambes" (*agentia verba Lycamben*) and points out that Alcaeus "does not seek a father-in-law whom he may besmear [or "pollute"—*oblinat*] with black verse neither does he tie a noose for his fiancée with an infamous song" (*nec socerum quaerit quem versibus oblinat atris, / nec sponsae laqueum famoso carmine nectit*). Here we see the blame poet as a polluter, as well as a killer.

Scholars continue to debate the possible historicity or ahistoricity of this story.[36] I am inclined to see a mythic/legendary development of a historical incident, with an admixture of ritual. But the story should not be automatically rejected as impossible. In a culture in which shame is a dominant value, suicide is an entirely reasonable (so to speak) reaction to public humiliation.[37] In some cultures, shame is used "as a principal external sanction." "Among

---

[34] Quoted in Lasserre and Bonnard 1968:cix, test. 18, my trans. See other scholiast references, test. 154–160T. Ovid, in his own curse poem, *Ibis* 53 (test. 119T), speaks of *tincta Lycambeo sanguine tela*, "arrows imbued with the blood of Lycambes," which *liber iambus*, "free iambic," will give to him for attacking his foe. Fragments of Archilochus' attacks on Lycambes are collected in fr. 172–181W/166–175T; 172/166T: "Father Lycambes . . . now you appear a big laugh to your fellow citizens," my trans., πάτερ Λυκάμβα . . . νῦν δὲ δὴ πολὺς / ἀστοῖσι φαίνεαι γέλως. For further references and discussion, Lasserre 1950:28–52; Rankin 1977:47–56; Burnett 1983:19–23; Rose 1960a:90n23; Hendrickson 1925b. For the theme of hanging, see below; ch. 6 (Hesiod); ch. 9 (Alcaeus).

[35] *Epistle* 1.19. The Cologne papyrus (196aW) offers us an example of the abuse directed at Neoboule, who is named, line 25. Cf. 118W/111T; Gentili 1988:185–188; Miralles and Portulas 1983:127–157; Aloni 1981:18–28. For all the daughters hanging themselves, Gaetulicus, in *Palatine Anthology* 7.71 (test. 66T): "Lycambes . . . mourning the hanging of his three daughters," text quoted above. Also, Eustathius, *Commentary on the Odyssey*, 11.277, 1684.45 (test. 64T): "It should be noted that literature has many cases of self-hanging for grief, and this was the death, according to the old story, of the daughters of Lycambes, who could not withstand the onslaught of the satires [*skōmmatōn*] of Archilochus," trans. Edmonds (ἰστέον δὲ ὅτι πολλῶν προσώπων ἀψαμένων βρόχους ἐπὶ λύπαις ἔπαθον οὕτω κατὰ τὴν παλαιὰν ἱστορίαν καὶ αἱ Λυκαμβίδαι ἐπὶ τοῖς Ἀρχιλόχου ποιήμασι, μὴ φέρουσαι τὴν ἐπιφορὰν τῶν ἐκείνου <u>σκωμμάτων</u>). See also Julianus Aegyptius, in *Palatine Anthology* 7.70 (test. 89T). For the theme of the broken engagement, see below, ch. 4 (Hipponax); ch. 16 (Philip of Croton); this is a standard topos for misery. For the broken oath, see below, ch. 4 (Hipponax); ch. 9 (Alcaeus).

[36] See bibliography in Rankin 1977:131. For the possible historicity of the story, see Carey 1986.

[37] See Mead 1937:494; O'Leary 1991:24.

the cultures with a strong development of the ego, the exercise of the sanction may result in suicide." Probably no culture is completely a shame or guilt culture, but some cultures certainly have a pronounced "shame" component.[38] It should be kept in mind that such sophisticated cultures as the modern Japanese can have a significant "shame" component.

Lycambes was evidently an official of some sort, and Archilochus' attack on him may have had political overtones, just as Lycambes' rejection of the poet may have had a political dimension. The comic dramatist Cratinas speaks of a Lycambean magistracy.[39]

Critias tells us that Archilochus left his native Paros because of financial difficulties (*dia penian kai aporian*[40]), went to Thasos, then quarreled with the Thasians when he got there.[41] A scholiast tells us that Archilochus "was sent into exile because of the wickedness of his speech."[42] His financial difficulties may have been caused by his free speech,[43] which would neatly harmonize the two traditions.

An Ovid scholiast describes a persecution following Archilochus' attack on Lycambes, carried out by Lycambes' friends; the poet responds by killing

---

[38] See the discussion of Aesop as satirist, ch. 2.

[39] Fr. 138 K-A/130 Kock (test. 45T); cf. Gentili 1988:192; Rankin 1977:50.

[40] See also Oenomaus, *ap.* Eusebius *Preparation for the Gospel* 5.31 (test. 114T)—Archilochus consults with the Delphic oracle because he has thrown away his possessions "in political foolishness," ἐν πολιτικῇ φλυαρίᾳ. Cf. Wiechers 1961:35. This motive for exile (poverty) also appears in other biographical traditions, see below, this chapter; chs. 4 (Hipponax); 5 (Homer); 6 (Hesiod).

[41] Critias fr. 44 *ap.* Aelian *Historical Miscellanies* 10.13 (test. 46T), trans. Edmonds: ". . . if Archilochus had not slandered himself in his poems, we wouldn't have known that he was the son of the slave-woman Enipo, nor that through poverty and perplexity [*aporian*] he left Paros for Thasos, nor that when he arrived there he quarrelled with the inhabitants; . . . and more, we should not know, had he not told us himself, that he was an adulterer, nor lecherous and wantonly violent . . ." (οὐκ ἂν ἐπυθόμεθα ἡμεῖς οὔτε ὅτι Ἐνιποῦς υἱὸς ἦν τῆς δούλης, οὔθ' ὅτι καταλιπὼν Πάρον διὰ πενίαν καὶ ἀπορίαν ἦλθεν ἐς Θάσον, οὔθ' ὅτι ἐλθὼν τοῖς ἐνταῦθα ἐχθρὸς ἐγένετο . . . οὔτε ὅτι μοιχὸς ἦν, ἤδειμεν ἄν, εἰ μὴ παρ' αὐτοῦ μαθόντες, οὔτε ὅτι λάγνος καὶ ὑβριστής . . .). On the theme of exile, see fr. 185W/188T, where an ape is banished by his fellow animals; Burnett 1983:62. Cf. this chapter, below, "worst." For Archilochus' mother, Enipo, see above, this chapter.

[42] *Archilochus inuentor iambi, propter linguae suae prauitatem, missus est in exilium, ad Ibis* 521, C (test. 160T). (My trans.) Cf. for the exile, Ellis 1881:151. In Plutarch *On the Ancient Customs of the Spartans* 34 (239b) (test. 143T) we find a strange account of the Spartans expelling Archilochus because they thought the shield poem disgraceful. Ἀρχίλοχον τὸν ποιητὴν ἐν Λακεδαίμονι γενόμενον αὐτῆς ὥρας ἐδίωξαν. "Archilochus the poet, when he arrived in Sparta, they ordered to depart that very instant . . ." trans. Babbitt. Cf. a Spartan expulsion of the poet's books "because he had attacked a home he hated with obscene curses," *quia domum sibi invisam obscenis maledictis laceraverat*, Valerius Maximus 6.3 ext. 1 (test. 182T), trans. Ellis 1881:151; cf. Hendrickson 1925b:122n31; Rankin 1977:42n49.

[43] This is the suggestion of Gentili 1988:193.

himself.[44] The persecution by Lycambes' friends is notable, and this might have contributed to Archilochus' misfortunes and exile if these two notes can be understood together. However, they are probably reporting divergent traditions.

A fragmented passage in the Mnesiepes inscription tells a more complex story that places Archilochus directly in the Aesopic tradition of sacral blame poet, societal rejection, oracle, and cult, and may also supply the background for an exile. I follow the reconstruction and translation of Treu.[45] There is a festival (*tei d' heor[tei*, E1.III.17, test. 4T) at which Archilochus improvises (*auto]skhedias[anta*, 19–20) on traditional themes (*paradedom[ena*, 23). An obscene song to Dionysus,[46] mentioning barley groats, unripe grapes, figs, and a Screwer (*oipholiōi*, 35, perhaps a cult title for Dionysus), is quoted. Despite the obscenity, the religious, cultic setting of this performance is clear.[47] The inscription continues:

Λεχθέντων [δὲ τούτων . . .
ὡς κακῶς ἀκ[ουσα . . .
ἰαμβικώτερο[ν

* * *

ἐν τεῖ κρίσει· Μ[ετὰ δὲ . . .
χρόνον γίνεσθ[αι   ἀσθενεῖς]
εἰς τὰ αἰδοῖα . . .

---

[44] Scholia *ad* Ovid *Ibis* 521 (test. 160T). "Archilochus . . . after he had forced Lycambes to hang himself, was persecuted by Lycambes' friends and killed himself," my trans., *Archilochus* . . . *postquam Lycamben coegerat ad suspendium, ab amicis eius persecutus se ipsum interfecit.*

[45] See also Clay 2004:16–23.

[46] Cf. on Dionysus above, this chapter. For possible connections of Archilochus and his iambics with the cult of Demeter, see Pausanias 10.28.3 (test. 121T) (Archilochus' grandfather, Tellis, is pictured by Polygnotus in a boat in the underworld with a woman who first introduced the rites of Demeter to Thasos); Paros is listed immediately after Eleusis as a cult center of Demeter in the *Homeric Hymn to Demeter* (491), see Richardson 1974 *ad loc.*; cf. Stephanus of Byzantium, s.v. Paros; Clay 2004:18; Rankin 1977:111n74; 17; 57; Nagy 1979:248 #7n2; Miralles and Portulas 1983:72; Burnett 1983:25; 56–57n9. West 1974:24 shows that the cults of Dionysus and Demeter can be related, connects Lycambes with Demeter cult, and sees cultic significance in the name of Archilochus' father.

These facts may be important for an understanding of the origins of archaic Greek satire, which appears to stem, in part at least, from forms of ritual license. See app. A. Cf. Iambe "the eponymous heroine of iambic verse," who "as an inspiration to her poets . . . was said to have hanged herself" as did the Lycambids, Burnett 1983:20n10; Scholiast on Hephaestion, 281/154T, Olender 1985. The woman hanging herself has definite cultic associations—see below, ch. 6 (Hesiod); Plutarch *Theseus* 20.1; Burkert 1983:64n26; 82n40; Lefkowitz 1981:4n10; Loraux 1987a:13–17; Loraux 1984; Clader 1976:70; Dietrich 1961; King 1983:118–124; Guépin 1968:97; Foley 1994: 45–46, 65–75. See below, this chapter, on Erigone.

[47] For cultic obscenity, aischrologia, see Collins 2004:225–230 and app. A below.

When these things had been recited . . . [they thought] /that it had been said evilly [concerning the god, and that Archilochus had composed these verses] / too satirically [*iambikōtero[n*, 38] . . . [On the following day they arraigned him before the court and condemned him] / in the legal proceedings [*en tei krisei*, 42]. [Because of god's wrath, not much] / time elapsed . . . [the men became weak] / in the genitals.

They send to Delphi to discover the cause for this ailment and find a remedy; the Pythia accuses the Parians of having judged unjustly (*Tipte dikais an[omois*, 47), and tells them there will be no [healing] until they [honour] Archilochus. Perhaps a new form of Dionysiac worship (*Dion[us-*, 55) is then introduced.

There is a close parallel to this story in a cultic tale found in scholia on Aristophanes:[48] the Athenians, not honoring the introduction of a statue of Dionysus, are afflicted by a plague "in the genitals" (*eis ta aidoia*, the same phrase found in the Mnesiepes inscription), and must seek an alleviation of the plague through oracle consultation and phallic cult awarded to the god. Both this and the Archilochus story are in the genre of Dionysiac vengeance myth.[49] Also in the genre is the story of Icarius and Erigone.[50] Icarius acts as a wine-apostle for the god, but then is clubbed to death by Attic shepherds inebriated for the first time, as they fear that the drink is a *malum medicamentum* (according to Hyginus). When his daughter, Erigone, hangs herself in grief,[51] the enraged wine god causes the daughters of the Athenians to die in the same way; the townspeople consult Delphi and a cult centered around Erigone is prescribed to allay the curse.[52] It is easy to see how close the poet's biographical tradition is to such "pure" myth.

---

[48] Scholia on Aristophanes *Acharnians* 243.

[49] See McGinty 1978.

[50] Callimachus *Aetia* fr. 178.3–4, Hyginus *Fables* 130; Apollodorus *Library* 3.14.7; Scholiast on *Iliad* XXII 29; Aelian *Nature of Animals* 7.28; Hesychius s.v. *Aiōra, Alētis*.

[51] Cf. the Lycambids, above, this chapter. They remind one of the father-daughter combination in Larson's pattern of father-daughter cult links, Larson 1995:99.

[52] Athenaeus 14.618E. Cf. Kearns 1989:167, 172; Larson 1995:99. See also the cult of Charila at Delphi. An orphan girl, she pleaded for food from the king during a famine, but he kicked her then threw a shoe at her. She hanged herself from shame and when the famine continued, an oracle prescribed cult for her. Plutarch *Greek Questions* 293cf; *Suda* s.v. *eidōlon*; Harrison 1922:106–107 (who sees this as a *pharmakos* rite); Larson 1995:140. Larson regards hanging as "a particularly feminine form of death in the Greek mind." The children in Caphyae, on the other hand, pretend to hang a statue of Artemis, and are stoned by the angered townspeople. But when the women of the town are struck with miscarriages, and Delphi is consulted, the Pythia prescribes cult sacrifice to the children. Pausanias 8.23.6–7.

Archilochus' association with Dionysiac cult myth reminds one of the possible Dionysiac associations of the *pharmakoi*, their name *sumbakkhoi*, and their apparent possession by divinity at the moment of expulsion.[53] This leads one to view 120W/117T as a poem that might fit into the *pharmakos* context somewhat.

H. D. Rankin connects the trial described here with the poet's exile;[54] this is an entirely reasonable possibility—it fits neatly with the Ovid scholiast who saw the wickedness of the poet's speech as the cause of an exile. Be that as it may, we see that Archilochus, despite his blasphemous tendencies, ended up with cult honors on his native island, as the Archilocheion itself shows.[55] Alcidamus, quoted by Aristotle, tells us that "The Parians honored [*tetimēkasin*] Archilochus, even though he was a slanderer [*blasphēmon*]."[56]

In the story of Archilochus' death we have a similar gathering of motifs: crime, oracles, propitiation, and hero cult.[57] A man named Calondas, but nicknamed Corax (the Crow) kills the poet in war;[58] he repairs to the Delphic oracle (for an unspecified reason, but one may suppose that he had been struck by some misfortune, perhaps a disease, and went to the oracle to find out why this had happened), and though he protests that he killed Archilochus in war, in a fair fight, and is innocent of guilt, the priestess, or Apollo in one account, drives him from the temple,[59] as he has slain "a man holy to the Muses" or

---

[53] See above, ch. 1.

[54] Rankin 1977:119n25; his main evidence is the scholiast on Ovid's *Ibis* 521, quoted above. For further on the Archilochean trial story, cf. Treu 1959:46–49 (text), 208–209; Müller 1985:123; West 1974:25; Webster in Pickard-Cambridge 1962:10; Rankin 1977:5; Rowland 1980:33–34. *Iambikōtero[n* (lit., 'too iambically') may be interpreted as "too satirically." See Rankin 1977:119n25.

[55] Mnesiepes Inscription E1 col.II 16–19 (test. 4T). Cf. Clay 2004; Nagy 1979:304, 308; Rowland 1980:34.

[56] See Aristotle *Rhetoric* 2.23, 1398b (test. 6T), trans. Edmonds: Πάριοι γοῦν Ἀρχίλοχον καίπερ βλάσφημον ὄντα τετιμήκασι . . . Alcidamas was a fourth-century BC rhetorician. The same word was applied to Aesop, *Vita G* 132, see above ch. 2, at Aesop's death. Cf. Rankin 1977:50. For the relationship of the word *timē* to cult, heroic or divine, see *Hymn to Demeter* 311, 261–263 (cf. Richardson 1974 *ad loc.*); Herodotus 1.168; 1.118.2; Rudhardt 1970:6–7; Ekroth 2002:199–206; below, ch. 8 (Sappho); ch. 11 (Tyrtaeus).

[57] Sources: Heraclides *On Politics* 8 (test. 73T); Plutarch *On the Delays of Divine Vengeance* 17 (560e) (test. 141T); Dio Chrysostom *Orations* 33.11 (test. 50T); *Suda* s.v. Archilochus I (test. 170T); Oenomaus *ap.* Eusebius *Preparation for the Gospel* 5.32–39 (test. 115T); Pliny *Natural History* 7.29 (test. 136T); Libanius *Orations* 1.74 (test. 95T); Aristides *Orations* 46.293–294 (test. 21T). See also Fontenrose 1978:287; Clay 2004:25–26.

[58] For Archilochus' "historical" death, see the Sosthenes inscription, C Vb, Clay 2004:117.

[59] Dio Chrysostom: τὸν . . . ὁ Ἀπόλλων ἐξελαύνων ἐκ τοῦ νεώ. For the theme of death in war, see above, ch. 1 (Codrus, Androgeus); below ch. 9 (Alcaeus); ch. 17 (Bleddyn Fardd); ch. 18.

the "servant [*therapōn*] of the Muses."[60] But "he was instructed to travel to the dwelling of the cricket [*tettix*] to propitiate the spirit of Archilochus."[61] The connections between Corax, Apollo, the Muses, and Archilochus here are complex: first, Corax, "the crow" can perhaps be identified with Apollo.[62] If this association is correct, "Apollo," through Corax, kills Archilochus, a poet whom he had patronized,[63] blames Corax for killing a sacred poet, and prescribes hero cult for the poet to propitiate his spirit. Furthermore, Archilochus in his own poetry had likened himself to a cricket being tortured by a human.[64]

Another Aesopian fable (470) explicitly links the cicadas with the Muses. Plato (*Phaedrus* 262d) tells us that crickets are "prophets of the Muses" (*tōn Mousōn prophētai*). Apollo is known as the "leader of the Muses" (*Mousarkhos* or *Mousagetēs*); the first major gods listed on the Paros inscription are the Muses, Apollo Mousagetes, and Mnemosyne.[65] Thus Archilochus, *therapōn* of the Muses, is tied even more closely to Apollo as patron, who must be viewed virtually as part of the group of the Muses.[66] As in the case of Aesop, the god Apollo ordains the poet's future fame and immortality; gives him his poetic commission; kills him (perhaps) by means of a human or humans; sends a plague to punish his killers; and ordains his hero cult as a means of allaying the plague. We remember Apollo engineering Aesop's death, then ordering his cult.

As we turn to Archilochus' poetry, we find an important theme that perhaps shows us that Archilochus himself—or his poetic persona—felt like a victim. In 223W/167T, Archilochus is a cricket whose wing is pulled, which

[60] E.g. Dio Chrysostom: *Mousōn theraponta* (also in Aristides and Origen *Against Celsus* 3.25 [test. 117T]). Plutarch *On the Delay of Divine Vengeance* 17 (560e) (test. 141T): *hieron andra tōn Mousōn*.

[61] Plutarch *On the Delay of Divine Vengeance* 17 (560e) (test. 141T), trans. Edmonds: ἐκελεύσθη πορευθεὶς ἐπὶ τὴν τοῦ Τέττιγος οἴκησιν ἱλάσασθαι τὴν τοῦ Ἀρχιλόχου ψυχήν. Also, *Suda* s.v. Archilochus. For the cricket, see above, this chapter.

[62] See Nagy 1979:302, who cites Aesopic fables. One (323, Perry) seems somewhat ambiguous in this context, but in other fables (125, 236) the crow is explicitly associated with prophecy. He "gave men omens, foretold the future to them, and was therefore consulted by them as an authority" (ἐπὶ τῷ διὰ οἰωνῶν μαντεύεσθαι ἀνθρώποις καὶ τὸ μέλλον προφαίνειν καὶ διὰ τοῦτο ὑπ' αὐτῶν μαρτυρεῖσθαι . . . [125]) In Herodotus 4.15, Aristeas accompanies Apollo in the form of a crow. The crow often helps fulfill mantic purposes in Delphic oracles, see Plutarch *On the Failure of Oracles* 5 (412c); Pausanias 9.38.3–4; Fontenrose 1978: 330 (Q191), cf. p. 73. Cf. Fürtwangler 1884 1.1, 444; Williams 1978:64; Bremmer 1983a:35; Burnett 1983:19n9; Keel 1977:79–91.

[63] We remember that the Delphic oracle, an Apolline institution, predicted the poet's immortality to his father, Dio Chrysostomus 33.

[64] 223W/167T = Lucian *The Liar* 1. This is probably part of the Lycambes invective fragments, Lasserre 1950:28–32.

[65] Archilocheion, E1 col. 1.3–4 (test. 4T) (Μούσαις καὶ Ἀπόλλ[ω]ν[ι / Μουσαγέται καὶ Μνημοσύνει); fr. *adesp.* 941 Page; Hesiod *Theogony* 94–95; further references in Nagy 1979:291.

[66] Cf. Nagy 1979:304. For the relationship of Archilochus with Delphi, see above.

forces him to retaliate by singing louder.[67] The fable of the fox and the eagle (174W/168T; (177W/174T) is exactly parallel in theme. In Archilochus' eyes, society, those who attack him, are sadistic—like the kind of person who would torture a beautiful singer—perhaps an archetypal image of the poet's relationship with society. The punishment of the poet's persecutors, through the poet's blame poetry, is just and moral (as Archilochus the cricket becomes Archilochus the wasp or poisonous snake). Most importantly, for our purposes, we see the persona of the poet as victim—weak, tortured, hated, and outraged by injustice—expressed in this passage, a fragment of the fearsome invective directed against Lycambes. The legend of the poetic victim and the victimizing as a poetic theme are closely connected.[68]

From the typology in chapter 1, we find the following themes in the life of Archilochus:

1a1. *Impiety of hero*: offensive verbalizing (introducing obscene phallic worship to Paros, he is called a *blasphēmos*).

2. *Communal disaster* (plague after dishonoring of the poet).

3. *Oracle* (telling how to remove plague through cult for the poet).

4. *The Worst*. Critias accuses him of being "an adulterer," "lecherous," "wantonly violent"—and "worst of all" he deserted his shield.[69]

4a. He is penurious; he leaves Paros because of lack of resources.[70]

4b. He is the son of a slavewoman.

4c. He is judged to be a criminal in his trial.

4f. *Poison/medicine imagery*. Archilochus' blame poetry is compared to snake venom, to the sting of a wasp.

5. *The Best*. Archilochus is preeminent as a satiric poet. He was frequently associated with Homer and Hesiod (e.g. Plato *Ion* 531a) as one of the "great originators who founded the Greek poetic tradition."[71] Plato

---

[67] See above, this chapter. For "defensive" satire, see below, ch. 4 (Hipponax); ch. 17 (Séafra O'Donnchú); ch. 18 (Starkaðr mocked); ch. 22 (Cicero); app. B.

[68] For a fuller discussion of this theme, with a very limited survey of its literary *Nachleben*, see app. B.

[69] *Ap.* Aelian *Historical Miscellanies* 10.13 (test. 46T), see quotation above. For the positive and negative lines of Archilochus' reputation in antiquity, see Rosen 1988c:12–13.

[70] Critias, *dia penian kai aporian*; Pindar (*Pythian Odes* 2.54) sees Archilochus *en amakhaniai*, in helplessness, want of means, hardship, cf. LSJ s.v. Lesky 1966:113 treats the theme of helplessness in archaic lyric.

[71] See Rankin 1977:2nn5–7.

has a character refer to him as "most wise" (*sophōtatos, Republic* 365c). Horace writes that he is following the meter and spirit of Archilochus, as did Sappho and Alcaeus; Quintilian judges him the best of the iambic poets. According to the Paros cult myth, Delphi tells the poet's father that Archilochus will be "famous in song among men" and "deathless."[72] This evidence, while not contemporary, shows that a strong tradition of the poet surpassing other satirists followed after him.

 5a. *Sacred.* Archilochus is closely identified with the Muses (cf. the consecration motif), Apollo, and Dionysus; he is *therapōn* of the Muses; he writes with divine inspiration. See on his death.

7. *Public meeting.* Archilochus is judged guilty at a trial.

 10a. *Exile.* We know that Archilochus left Paros "because of poverty and helplessness." However, his satiric, obscene poetry also caused the exile, according to some traditions. Perhaps the two traditions are related.

11. *Death.* The poet is killed by a warrior who is possibly associated with Apollo.

13. *Hero cult.* This is richly attested, especially by the Mnesiepes inscription, and also in Archilochus' death legend. Now Diskin Clay's recent book, *Archilochus Heros: The Cult of the Poets in the Greek Polis*, provides exhaustive documentation for and insightful discussion of this theme.[73]

 13a. *Immortality through hero cult*; also through poetry, as the oracle to the poet's father promised.

18. *Divine persecutor-patron.* We possibly have a version of the divine persecutor/patron theme in the story of Corax.

22. *Blame poet.*

 22a. *Killing through blame.* Archilochus is, of course, famous for this theme.

 22c. *Animal fables used for blame.*

 22e. *Curse as theme.*

---

[72] Cf. Horace *Epistles* 1.19.23ff. (test. 86T); Quintilian 10.1.59.

[73] Clay 2004. Cf. Alcidamas, above; Konteleon 1964:44–54; Treu 1959:40–63; Nagy 1970 ch. 18n1; Nagy 1990b:47–51.

23. *Poet is sacred*, superhuman.

23a. *Consecration of poet.*

23e. *Immortality through poetry.*

Though Archilochus' *vita* is more fragmentary than Aesop's, it still contains a convincing configuration of *pharmakos* / hero cult themes. The hero cult is, of course, clear, and the important theme of the trial for ritual pollution (along with the striking cicada fable) sets it firmly in the sphere of the *pharmakos*, even if stoning or ejection from a cliff are absent. It is significant that, as in the case of Aesop, it is Archilochus' poetry, Dionysiac iambs (the standard medium for blame poetry), that sets in motion the ritual mechanism of arrest, trial by the people, punishment, exile (perhaps), plague upon the people, and hero cult for the punished hero.

One is struck by the similarities to the life of Aesop. In some way, it is as if one life is being used for two men (just as some of Archilochus' blame fables appear in the Aesop tradition). We have a consecration at the start of the poet's career; killing through blame; animal fable used for blame; a poet brought to trial for his satire, and convicted; the people punished by god after his conviction; and ritual institutionalized as recompense. After the poet is killed, his killer(s) (associated somewhat with Apollo) are instructed by the Delphic oracle to help found the poet's cult.

Archilochus adds an important new theme to our list:

26. *Poet as warrior.* Archilochus, though certainly not living by any Homeric military ethic, was a soldier, and took war as an important theme in his poetry.[74] It is true that nearly every well-to-do Greek man was also a soldier, but not every poet wrote as much about war as did Archilochus. Pindar is a point of comparison. Many modern poets are an even more stark comparison—it is hard to think of Keats, Wordsworth, Yeats, or Robert Frost as soldiers, though war has been a theme of some poets of the first rank in the twentieth century.

Furthermore, Archilochus as soldier is part of his legend; he is killed in battle.

Thus the combination "follower of Dionysus/Muses/Ares" (as evidenced in the fragments of his poetry) is basic for Archilochus. A man used to handling weapons (2W/2T) also used his word as a weapon. Aggression would drive both

[74] See above, and many well-known fragments: 1W, 3W, 5W, 6W; also 114W, 110W, 111W, 91W, 93W, 94W, 96W, 98W.

skills. A madness/possession is also a common denominator for Dionysus/ Muses/Ares. Somewhat comparable is the riddle warfare of Aesop, theme 25. We also remember that Aesop is surrendered to an invading army to save a city.

26a. *Martial paraenesis* is one of Archilochus' poetic themes, as some critics interpret his poetry.

In addition, Oemomaus, quoted by Eusebius, lists two main targets of the poet, one of whom is, not surprisingly, Lycambes—but curiously, Lycambes is mentioned second. The Sapaeans, the Thracian tribe who fought with the poet and the Parians when they settled Thasos, are listed first. "For surely there is no lack even now of Sapaeans or Lycambes ready to be caricatured."[75] Thus in some of Archilochus' lost poems he apparently made his actual warring opponents his satirical targets—combining verbal and physical attack.[76]

---

[75] Oenomaus *The Detection of Impostors, ap.* Eusebius *Preparation for the Gospel* 5.33, tr. E. H. Gifford: οὐ γὰρ δὴ οὐκ εἰσὶ καὶ νῦν ἕτοιμοι κωμῳδεῖσθαι καὶ Σαβαῖοι καὶ Λυκάμβαι . . . For Sapaeans, see the "robber Sapaeans" (λῃστὰς Σάπας) in the Sosthenes inscription, A1 51 (test. 5T); fr. 5W; Strabo 12.550.

[76] For Archilochus in Thasos, see Graham 2001:188–222; Tsantsanoglou 2003.

4

Hipponax: Creating the *Pharmakos*

IPPONAX WAS AN IAMBIC SATIRIST second only to Archilochus in fame, and his traditional life shares important themes with Archilochus' (for example, causing death through satire).[1] Like Archilochus, he is an exiled poet. Hipponax is of special interest because he is the earliest extant witness for the *pharmakos* rite. It is striking that an exiled, death-dealing blame poet should be our earliest source for the *pharmakos* ritual; this poetic *pharmakos* uses the scapegoat custom in order to practice blame, to make someone else a *pharmakos*.

Hipponax was a satirist whose abuse was, if anything, even more extreme than that of Archilochus.[2] One poem is a perfect verbal mirroring of physical aggression: "Take my clothes, I'll punch Bupalus in the eye. For I'm ambidextrous, and I don't miss when I hit."[3] As is often the case for blame poets, the curse plays a prominent part in his work:

> κύμ[ατι] πλα[ζόμ]ενος·
> κἀν Σαλμυδ[ησσ]ῶι γυμνὸν εὐφρόνε. [
>   Θρήϊκες ἀκρό[κ]ομοι
> λάβοιεν—ἔνθα πόλλ᾽ ἀναπλήσαι κακὰ
>   δούλιον ἄρτον ἔδων—
> ῥίγει πεπηγότ᾽ αὐτόν· ἐκ δὲ τοῦ χνόου
>   φυκία πόλλ᾽ ἐπέχοι,
> κροτέοι δ᾽ ὀδόντας, ὡς [κ]ύων ἐπὶ στόμα
>   κείμενος ἀκρασίηι

---

[1] For his poetry, see West 1989; for his poetry and testimonia, see Degani 1983; Gerber 1999b.

[2] Cf. Rosen 1988a:296; Burnett 1983:99–100; more generally, Degani 1984:161–226; West 1974:29; Miralles and Pòrtulas 1988. For his blame directed against women, Burnett 1983:100, and see below, this chapter. All translation are by Knox 1946, unless otherwise noted.

[3] My trans. Fr. 120–121W: λάβετέ μεο ταἰμάτια, κόψω Βουπάλωι τὸν ὀφθαλμόν. / ἀμφιδέξιος γάρ εἰμι κοὐκ ἁμαρτάνω κόπτων.

ἄκρον παρὰ ῥηγμῖνα κυμα.... δου·
ταῦτ᾽ ἐθέλοιμ᾽ ἂν ἰδεῖν,
ὅς μ᾽ ἠδίκησε, λ[ὰ]ξ δ᾽ ἐπ᾽ ὁρκίοις ἔβη,
τὸ πρὶν ἑταῖρος [ἐ]ών.

... beaten by the waves.
In Salmydessus let "well-meaning"
   top-knot Thracians
seize his naked body (he can get his fill of evil
   eating slavish bread)
rigid from cold! Let seaweed
   rise from scum and bind him!
Let him grind his teeth, lying
   spent and muzzle down,
dog-fashion in the surf ...!
These things I long to see
because he wronged me [ēdikēse], walked upon his oaths
   [horkiois],
   who was once my friend [hetairos].

   115W/194Dg[4]

Leonidas wrote:

ἀτρέμα τὸν τύμβον παραμείβετε, μὴ τὸν ἐν ὕπνῳ
πικρὸν ἐγείρητε σφῆκ᾽ ἀναπαυόμενον·
ἄρτι γὰρ Ἱππώνακτος ὁ καὶ τοκεῶνε βαΰξας,
ἄρτι κεκοίμηται θυμὸς ἐν ἡσυχίῃ.
ἀλλὰ προμηθήσασθε, τὰ γὰρ πεπυρωμένα κείνου
ῥήματα πημαίνειν οἶδε καὶ εἰν Ἀΐδῃ.

Quietly pass by the tomb lest you rouse
   the bitter wasp [pikron ... sphēk'] that rests there.
For but lately has rest been found and quiet

---

[4] Trans. Burnett 1983:100–101. For authorship of this poem, see above, ch. 3. For the curse in Hipponax, 114aW/133Dg, 128W/126Dg; Rosen 1988a:295; ch. 3 above. Cf. the theme of broken oath in Archilochus fr. 173W, and below, chs. 7 (Simonides) and 9 (Alcaeus). Cf. Masson 1951:435; Burnett 1983:100n15. For the "slavish bread," we may note the custom, attested by Hipponax himself, of feeding the *pharmakos* badly: "And in his grip take barley-cakes, dried figs / and cheese, such cheese as scapegoats may feed on" (κἀφῆι παρέξειν ἰσχάδας τε καὶ μᾶζαν / καὶ τυρόν, οἷον ἐσθίουσι φαρμακοί [fr. 8W/28Dg.]) Cf. Bremmer 1983b:305. For the seashore death, a frequent theme in actual curses, Watson 1991:59, cf. 128W/126Dg; 118W E/130Dg; 103W.7/106Dg; 115W/194Dg.

for the soul of Hipponax that barked even at his parents.[5]
But beware: even in Hades
his fiery words can injure.

Palatine Anthology 7.408 (test. 16Dg), trans. Knox, modified

However, the view of Hipponax as dispenser of amoral, malevolent abuse should be rejected. Even in Hipponax's colloquial satire, with all its idiosyncrasies and verbal aggression, there is an undercurrent of ethical judgment. According to Theocritus, if you are a scoundrel, you should avoid his tomb, but if you are honest, you need not fear it.[6] If this had not been the case, Hughes argues, Callimachus would not have taken Hipponax as a model.[7]

According to the *Suda*, Hipponax was a native of Ephesus,[8] but was banished by the tyrants Athenagoras and Comas; he then lived in Clazomenae.[9] So we have the theme of political exile of a satirist, perhaps historical.[10]

The poet became involved in a deadly feud that is probably legendary. He was reputed to be ugly and deformed, an Aesop figure. This feels like a folkloric detail. "Hipponax . . . was a most eloquent poet, but ugly and deformed of face," writes a scholiast.[11] His ugliness was satirized by insulting portraits by the brothers Bupalus and Athenis. "He was despised for his deformity . . . [Bupalus] painted Hipponax, a certain deformed poet, for a laugh."[12] In return the poet satirized them through his poetry, and they hanged themselves in shame.[13] Pliny writes, "Hipponax had a remarkable facial ugliness; because of which, they [Bupalus and Athenis], out of wantonness, exhibited a mocking

---

[5] The poetic attack on his parents is otherwise unknown.

[6] Theocritus *Epigram* 19 Gow (test. 18Dg).

[7] Hughes 1997:205. For a similar ethical view of the satire in Old Comedy, Horace *Satires* 1.4.1–5.

[8] Callimachus *Iambs*, 203.12; Strabo 14.1.25 (642).

[9] *Suda*, s.v. Hipponax (test. 7Dg): ὑπὸ τῶν τυράννων Ἀθηναγόρα καὶ Κωμᾶ ἐξελαθείς. Cf. Picard 1922:611; Huxley 1966:111; Seibert 1979:284; Knox 1946:xiin3.

[10] Cf. fr. 34.36W/24 b.29Dg.

[11] "Acro" ad Horace *Epodes* 6.11ff (test 9bDg), my trans., *Hipponax . . . qui poeta erat eloquentissimus, foeda et vitiosa facie.* Aelian *Historical Miscellanies* 10.6 (test. 19aDg), my trans.: "They say that Hipponax the poet not only had a little, ugly [*aiskhron*] body, but he was also thin" (λέγουσι δὲ καὶ Ἱππώνακτα τὸν ποιητὴν οὐ μόνον γενέσθαι μικρὸ τὸ σῶμα καὶ αἰσχρόν, ἀλλὰ καὶ λεπτόν). See also Rosen 1988a and 1988b; Davies 1981.

[12] "Acro" ad Horace *Epodes* 6.11ff (test. 9aDg), my trans.: *pro deformitate contemptus est . . . [Bupalus] Hipponactem quendam poetam deformem pro risu pinxit.* See below, ch. 11 (Tyrtaeus).

[13] See Callimachus fr. 191.1–4 (test 13Dg); Philippus Thessalonicus, in *Palatine Anthology* 7.405.1–3 (test. 15Dg); Pliny *Natural History* 36.11 (test. 2Dg); Lucian *The Liar* 2 (test. 14Dg); "Acro" ad Horace *Epodes* 6.14 (test. 9Dg, a–e) (Horace describes Hipponax as "*acer hostis Bupalo*," "bitter enemy of Bupalus"); *Suda* s.v. Hipponax (test 7Dg). These can also be found in West 1989:109–110. Cf. Burnett 1983:98. For the theme of hanging, see above, ch. 3 (Archilochus).

statue of him to crowds of laughing people. Therefore Hipponax, outraged, unleashed[14] bitterness of songs to such an extent that it is believed by some that he forced them to the noose."[15]

A scholiast on Horace adds an Archilochean touch: "[Hipponax] sought to wed the daughter of Bupalus, but was despised for his deformity."[16] This replication of the Archilochus–Lycambes relationship appears to be a wandering theme. It is possible that there was a historic component to the Archilochus story, but it is very unlikely that there is any truth to it here. There is likewise no early attestation for the story in Hipponax.

Though these events are almost certainly legendary, one must not forget that it is certain that Hipponax did have preferred poetic victims in Bupalus and Athenis, for many of his fragments list Bupalus by name. One at least names Athenis.[17] And unlike Lycambes, Bupalus is known as a historical figure, a sculptor, outside of Hipponax.[18]

There are frequent references to the *pharmakos* in Hipponax's poetry; they are always associated with blame poetry. These show how the poet assimilates his enemies to the *pharmakos*, and also how he assimilates himself (the two processes are related; the satirist who drives others out of the city may eventually be driven out).[19] The following is the locus classicus for the *pharmakos* (5–10W/26–30Dg; 6Dg):

---

[14] *Destrinxit*, 'unsheathe', or even 'injure (by criticism, censure)' OLD, cf. Ovid *Tristia* 2.466.

[15] Pliny *Natural History* 36.12 (test. 8Dg = West, test., p. 109), my trans., *Hipponacti notabilis foeditas vultus erat; quamobrem imaginem eius lascivia iocosam hi proposuere ridentium circulis. quod Hipponax indignatus destrinxit amaritudinem carminum in tantum ut credatur aliquis ad laqueum eos compulisse.*

[16] Scholiast on Horace *Epodes* 6.11ff. (test. 9aDg), my trans.: "[Hipponax] ... who sought to marry the daughter of Bupalus and was despised because of his deformity ... [Bupalus] painted Hipponax, a certain deformed poet, to get a laugh; because of which, the latter, beside himself with rage, attacked him with such an [abusive] song that he hung himself by a noose" (*[Hipponax] qui Bupali filiam nuptum petiit et pro deformitate contemptus est ... hic [Bupalus] Hipponactem quendam poetam deformem pro risu pinxit; quo ille furore commotus tali eum carmine perculit ut se laqueo suspenderet*). Also, "Bupalus the painter exhibited [Hipponax] painted in the Panathenaea so that he might move the people to laughter. He, enraged, so harassed him [Bupalus] with iambs that he put an end to his life by hanging. And he attacked his father-in-law with songs, after he was defrauded." Scholiast on Horaces *Epodes* 6.11f. (test. 9bDg), my trans.: *hunc Bupalus pictor in Panathenaeis pictum proposuit ut risum moveret populo. ille iratus iambis eum ita fatigavit ut vitam suspendio finiret. etiam iste socerum suum, postquam se fraudavit, carminibus petiit.* See also scholiasts on Ovid *Ibis* 54 and 521 (Degani test. 11–12a).

[17] 1W/17Dg, 15W/18Dg, 95aW/19Dg, 12W/20Dg, 84W/86.18Dg; 120W, cf. Rosen 1988a:292. For Athenis, 70.11W/70.1Dg, cf. Rosen 1988a 294n16, and below, this chapter.

[18] Pliny *Natural History* 36.5.11–13; Pausanias 9.35.6.

[19] See ch. 9 (Alcaeus).

πόλιν καθαίρειν καὶ κράδηισι βάλλεσθαι.

βάλλοντες ἐν χειμῶνι καὶ ῥαπίζοντες
κράδηισι καὶ σκίλλησιν ὥσπερ φαρμακόν.

δεῖ δ' αὐτὸν ἐς φάρμακον ἐκποιήσασθαι.

κἀφῆι παρέξειν ἰσχάδας τε καὶ μᾶζαν
καὶ τυρόν, οἷον ἐσθίουσι φαρμακοί.

πάλαι γὰρ αὐτοὺς προσδέκονται χάσκοντες
κράδας ἔχοντες ὡς ἔχουσι φαρμακοῖς.

λιμῶι γένηται ξηρός· ἐν δὲ τῶι θύμωι
φαρμακὸς ἀχθεὶς ἑπτάκις ῥαπισθείη.

Must cleanse the city [*polin kathairein*], and with twigs pelted.

Pelting him in the meadow[20] and beating
With twigs and squills like a scapegoat [*pharmakon*].

He must be chosen from among you [*ekpoiēsasthai*] as a scape-
goat.

And in his grip take barely-cakes, dried figs
And cheese, such cheese as scapegoats may feed on.

For long have they awaited them gaping
armed with fig-branches like they have for scapegoats.[21]

That he be parched with famine and, led out
A scapegoat, seven times on his piece beaten.[22]

There is a persistent association of the blame poet, often himself exiled, with scapegoat phenomena. For instance, Ovid's *Ibis*, with its scholia, is a central source for *pharmakos* data; it is a curse poem Ovid wrote in exile. Phaedrus, the Roman versifier of Aesop, himself punished by Sejanus for his satire, wrote an important fable on a military scapegoat. Aristophanes, with his scholia, is another central source for *pharmakos* references. He was possibly exiled, certainly subjected to legal persecution.[23]

[20] West translates this "in winter."
[21] I use West's translation for this line.
[22] Trans. Knox, modified, except as noted. For Hipponax and *pharmakos*, cf. Miralles and Portulas 1988:13–29; Masson 1949; Slings 1987.
[23] Ovid *Ibis* 467 with scholia, see below, this chapter, also ch. 24. For Aristophanes, see ch. 14,

There are other, less well-known, *pharmakos* passages in Hipponax:

ὁ δ' ἐξολισθὼν ἱκέτευε τὴν κράμβην
τὴν ἑπτάφυλλον, ἣν θύεσκε Πανδώρηι
Ταργηλίοισιν ἔγκυθρον πρὸ φαρμακοῦ.

Slipping, he implored the seven-leafed cabbage
he used to offer potted[24] to Pandora
at the Thargelia, before the scapegoat.

104W/107Dg, trans. West[25]

West remarks on the difficulty of understanding the meaning of this fragment. However, we seem to have the context of blame ("The particular cabbage is specified in a parenthesis designed to stress the low-class character of the man concerned") and clear reference to the *pharmakos* custom (*Targēlioisin*, *pharmakou*). West translates the last phrase, with some uncertainty, "before the *pharmakos* event."[26]

Hipponax is our source for the tune played by flutes "when the *pharmakoi* were being led out" (τοῖς ἐκπεμπομένοις φαρμακοῖς, 152–153W/146Dg).

Another poem combines stoning and the curse:

Μοῦσά μοι Εὐρυμεδοντιάδεα τὴν ποντοχάρυβδιν,
τὴν ἐν γαστρὶ μάχαιραν, ὃς ἐσθίει οὐ κατὰ κόσμον,
ἔννεφ', ὅπως ψηφῖδι <κακῆι> κακὸν οἶτον ὀλεῖται
βουλῆι δημοσίηι παρὰ θῖν' ἁλὸς ἀτρυγέτοιο.

Eurymedontiades his wife with knife in her belly,[27]
Gulf of all food, sing Muse, and of all her disorderly eating:
Sing that by public vote at the side of the unharvested ocean
Pebbled with stones she may die, an evil death to the evil.

128W/126Dg[28]

---

below. See also ch. 25, on Petronius, an executed satirist who preserves an important *pharmakos* fragment.

[24] "Cooked in a pot," following West's *egkuthron* rather than the received *egkhuton* ("poured-in," a cake). Cf. Hesychius s.v. *pharmakē*. "*Pharmakē*, the pot [*khutra*] they prepared for those cleansing the cities" (φαρμακή. ἡ χύτρα, ἣν ἡτοίμαζον τοῖς καθαίρουσι τὰς πόλεις). See Parker 1983:258n8; Degani 1984:269.

[25] This is preceded and followed by fragmentary lines.

[26] West 1974:145–146. For numerous other possible translations, see Degani 1983 *ad loc.* and Degani 1984:269–270.

[27] Apparently, she wolfs down her food without chewing it, so it has to be cut up in her belly; see Knox 1946:61n3.

[28] Trans. Knox; with a slightly different text, West 1974:148. Degani supplies <*kakēi*> from Mus-

In this poem, the target for poetic attack, a woman, is assimilated to the *pharmakos*: she is stoned or mistreated by order of a public vote.[29] Her seaside punishment links her to the seaside death of 115W/194Dg;[30] both poems are curse poems.[31]

The poem (128W) makes the belly a focal point for abuse, reminding us of imagery previously noted. Aesop, as part of his remarkable ugliness, has a pronounced belly;[32] the Muses attack the class of shepherds, which Hesiod belongs to, as "bellies only."[33] The wife of Eurymedontiades bolts her food; she is the gulf of all food; she eats beyond that which is decent. Thus she becomes worthy of a *pharmakos* death, by public decree.

We have also seen that Pindar viewed Archilochus as "fattening" himself on his hatreds. Blame is seen as something monstrous (*ou kata kosmon*).[34] So Hipponax's target here is a *pharmakos* (according to some traditions, fed with inadequate, bad food),[35] yet also an insatiable glutton. Both the satirist and the satirist's *pharmakos* victim are seen as fattening themselves in a revolting way. In an intriguing interpretation of this poem, Christopher Faraone sees it as using "hexametrical chants or incantations" designed to expel harmful famine demons or to escort human scapegoats from the city. The poem may have a political dimension, in the tradition of invective-curse that views political opponents "as rapacious pests who threaten to gobble up the commonwealth of the city and who therefore must be expelled from the community, precisely like a famine-demon."[36]

In these poems, Hipponax uses the theme of the *pharmakos* in order to abuse others. Yet we also have a short, important fragment that shows the

---

urus. West notes that "death on the seashore . . . and the mistreatment of the *pharmakos* are favourite motifs of Hipponax." On *psēphis*, cf. Degani 1983:130; 1984:199–202; Bremmer 1983b:301, 316. Some interpret this word as an "evil vote," not a stoning, but even if this reading were accepted, the "public council" still shows that Hipponax is dealing with the *pharmakos*, or a comparable phenomenon, here. Slings notes that the sea is "the natural receptacle of filth," in Bremer et al. 1987:92. Cf. 118eW/130Dg. Hughes argues against a *pharmakos* interpretation, but the theme of the adverse vote leading to the "evil fate" shows a clear scapegoat context (1991:145). In addition, the *pharmakos* was sometimes kept at the public expense, and thus the word *dēmosios* was sometimes applied to the *pharmakos*—see Scholia on Aristophanes *Knights* 1136a; and above, ch. 1.

[29] Cf. the Sapphic theme of woman as *pharmakos*, see below ch. 8.
[30] See on 115W above.
[31] See Degani 1983:168; Wünsch 1912; Faraone 2004.
[32] See above chs. 2, 3 (Pindar on Archilochus).
[33] See below, ch. 6 (Hesiod).
[34] See above ch. 3.
[35] See on 115W above, on Hipponax's death, below, cf. 10W/30Dg.
[36] Faraone 2004:245, cf. ch. 9 (Alcaeus and Pittacus, use of word *daptō*) below.

poet overtly viewing himself as the abused one, the *pharmakos*. "He ordered them to throw and cast stones at Hipponax."[37] Someone orders a group of people (a mob? Bupalus and Athenis and friends?) to stone Hipponax, as the poet himself bitterly reports. Perhaps the stoning is here a metaphor for literary reprisals against his attacks, though he feels that those attacks have been justified.[38]

So, after assimilating many others to the *pharmakos*, Hipponax himself is assimilated to the pattern. As has been noted previously, the powers of abuse and expulsion are ambiguously interchangeable. Furthermore, according to Ovid, Hipponax died "hated, by failure of food." As we have seen, bad food or starvation is sometimes linked to the *pharmakos*-death.[39] Hipponax's poetry portrays him as afflicted by poverty, which may be the result of exile.[40]

It is significant that Hipponax reportedly attacked Bupalus and Athenis only after they had attacked him; this detail enables us to view the poet as a justified blame poet, as in the case of Archilochus and the oath-breaking Lycambes—it brings to mind Archilochus as tortured cicada, Hesiod's nightingale in the claws of the eagle. It is also curious that Hipponax is attacking fellow artists, if artists working in a different medium. Blame is often used for internecine artistic warfare. It is entirely natural for rival artists to attack each other; the literary feud is an archaic phenomenon in the history of literature.[41] It brings to mind the myth of the poetic *agōn*, where two chief poets vie for

---

[37] 37W/46Dg, my trans., ἐκέλευε βάλλειν καὶ λεύειν Ἱππώνακτα. Cf. Masson 1949:317; and Masson 1962:127; Hughes 1991:146. Hughes argues that this does not necessarily refer to *pharmakos* ritual, but could be an example of stoning as mob justice. However, such a reference to stoning in the few existing fragments of a poet who was very interested in the *pharmakos* strongly suggests that Hipponax was thinking in terms of the *pharmakos*. Cf. Miralles and Portulas 1983:47, 57.

[38] Vox 1977:87–89, argues that the "I" of 41W, καὶ νῦν ἀρειᾶι σύκινόν με ποιῆσαι, is a *pharmakos*. "And now he threatens to make me a worthless fellow." Trans. West.

[39] Ovid *Ibis* 523 (test. 12Dg) trans. Knox, modified, "And like he who attacked Athenis in choliambic metre may you perish, hated, by failure of food" (*Utque parum stabili qui carmine laesit Athenin, / Invisus pereas deficiente cibo*). This is probably a reference to Hipponax, though "Athenin" is a conjecture; "Athenas" is found in the manuscripts, and the scholiasts on this passage did not look to Hipponax as the poet referred to. See Degani 1984:61–62; Rosen 1988a. For the bad food / starvation and the *pharmakos*, see above; and the poem quoted in the text (5–10W): "such cheese as scapegoats may feed on"; "parched with famine."

Accounts of Hipponax hanging himself are apparently confused scholiastic replications of the deaths of the poet's victims: Scholia on Ovid *Ibis* 447 (Degani test. 10a–f). Cf. Scholia on Horace *Epode* 6.14; Knox 1946:xiii; Rosen 1988a:292. On absurdities in the Hipponactian biographical tradition, see Degani 1984:20–24.

[40] See 32W, 36W, cf. 26, 26aW; the themes of miserable poverty and exile are also prominent in Theognis' poetry, ch. 10; cf. chs. 3 (Archilochus); 6 (Hesiod).

[41] E.g. Sappho and her poetic rivals, see ch. 8; Callimachus, see following notes.

supremacy; and behind that, the riddle contest of seers, in which the loser dies.[42]

On the other hand, this theme looks ahead to literary vendettas in the Hellenistic world, Callimachus being the best example of a satirist whose main targets were fellow poets. In the introduction to the *Aetia* (fr. 1 Pfeiffer), he attacks the "telchines," mischievous hobgoblins, his rival poets, who have abused him because of his refusal to write epic (thus he responds in a typically defensive rhetorical posture). Callimachus' most famous poem of abuse is the *Ibis*, which was directed, according to ancient testimonia, against Apollonius of Rhodes.[43] In this poem, the object of the attack is likened to the ibis because it is an unclean and destructive bird (Strabo 17.823). A scholiast tells us that Callimachus' invective caused his target's death—an Archilochean biographical conceit. "The intention of Ovid in [his] work is to imitate Callimachus, because just as Callimachus made invective against his enemy and led him to death, so this one . . ."[44]

Callimachus felt a special bond to Hipponax. In *Iamb* 1 (191Pf) he brings Hipponax up from the underworld; as Trypanis notes, Callimachus sees himself as a Hipponax redivivus.[45]

So, once again, Hipponax, the blame poet, is a *pharmakos*—as well as our primary early source for the *pharmakos*, for he uses *pharmakos* imagery to attack his poetic targets, as Aristophanes would do later. Yet the poet himself is reportedly ugly and deformed. He is a blame poet who in legend kills through his satire after he himself is unjustly satirized; he uses the curse liberally in his poetry. He is exiled after conflict with political leaders; and in a poem he portrays himself as a *pharmakos* who is stoned. There is no cultic drama here,[46]

---

[42] See ch. 6 (Hesiod); for the riddle contest, ch. 2 (Aesop as riddle warrior); ch. 16, the *agōn* in the Marysas, Thamyris narratives; ch. 17, *agōn* section.

[43] *Suda*, s.v. Callimachus, cf. Lefkowitz 1981:117; see also bibliography in Lesky 1966:717n1; Pfeiffer 1968 1.144; Williams 1978: 2. Cameron somewhat unconvincingly argues for no specific persons as Callimachus' targets (1995:228, 230). Pfeiffer 1949 1:307, *ap.* fr. 382 (5), concludes, "This name [Apollonius] has neither less nor more authority than the names of the Telchines . . . it is not a Byzantine conjecture, but an ancient grammatical teaching." For further discussion of Callimachus, see below, app. B.

[44] *Intentio Ouidii est in hoc opere imitari Callimachum, quia sicut Callimachus fecit invectivam contra imimicum suum et ipsum duxit ad mortem, ita iste . . .* Scholiast on Ovid *Ibis*, Ellis 1881:43, ms. P, cf. Hendrickson 1925b:111; Elliott 1960:128.

[45] Trypanis 1958:104n. See also Ardizzoni 1960; Degani 1984:44–50; Hughes 1997; Edmunds 2001. Like Hipponax, Callimachus turned his attention to the scapegoat phenomenon: *Aetia* IV fr. 90, with *diēgēsis*.

[46] However, Rosen has argued that there are the elements of a poetic initiation scene in test. 21Dg, with Iambe as inspiring goddess, Rosen 1988d. See also Brown 1988. Certainly, this seems to have a parodic tone, but an underlying seriousness may be present.

and no attested hero cult; but the poet is nevertheless steeped in scapegoat imagery and legend.[47]

---

[47] Thus the following themes are represented in Hipponax's *vita*: 4a2. Poor or scanty food is eaten (both by the poet and his victims). This is related to 4a1 and 4b, Beggar, slave. It is possibly a *pharmakos* theme. 4d, The hero is ugly or deformed. 10a, He is exiled. 11a, He is stoned. 22, He is a blame poet. 22a, He kills through blame. 22a1, His enemies hang themselves. 22e, He uses the curse against his enemies. 23a, Possible consecration of poet (through theophany). 24, He comes into conflict with political leaders.

5

Homer: The Trial of the Rhapsode

NOT SURPRISINGLY, considering the overwhelming prestige of the *Iliad* and the *Odyssey*, a heroizing body of legend attached itself to a person regarded as the author of those poems. The legend of Homer follows the pattern under consideration in important ways: the poet is a wanderer, like Aesop; he is exiled from inhospitable cities; and there is a dramatic treatment of the trial theme we found in Aesop and Archilochus. This legend, preserved in the Hellenistic biography by "Herodotus," is based on earlier Ionic traditions, and contains epigrams that probably date from the seventh or sixth centuries BC.[1] The legend of Homer's death is referred to as early as Heraclitus, which dates it to the end of the 6th century at the latest.[2] A treatment of Homer's death is also found in the *Contest of Homer and Hesiod*.[3] Homer is the best poet: "the wisest of all the Greeks" and "the sweetest singer."[4] He is

---

[1] The pseudo-Herodotean *Vita* is found in Allen 1919 5:192-218, also in von Wilamowitz-Moellendorff 1916b. There are English translations in Lefkowitz 1981:139-155 and West 2003:354-403; translations in this section are from Lefkowitz, unless noted otherwise. This document is dated by West, in its present form, to the "late second or early first century B.C.," (West 1984:125), but is based on earlier Ionic traditions that were perhaps made into a written text by the fifth century BC (ibid., cf. West 1999:378). In Isocrates *Helen* 65, the Homeridae have stories of Homer's life. The Homeric epigrams found in the biography—one of which, the fourth, reflects the trial theme—can be comfortably dated to the seventh or sixth century BC, see Markwald 1986:281n7 for further bibliography on dating of the text. On the legend, see Schadewaldt 1959a; Schadewaldt 1959b:54-130; Brelich 1958:320-321; Wade-Gery 1952; Jacoby 1933; von Wilamowitz-Moellendorff 1916a:356-366, 396-413 (on the *Contest of Homer and Hesiod*), 413-439 (on the pseudo-Herodotean Life); older literature in Jacoby 1933:9n2; Schadewaldt 1959a:69-71. Schadewaldt, p. 41, reasonably concludes that the legend of Homer was developed by rhapsodes in the sixth century BC.

[2] DK 22 B 56, cf. "Herodotus" *Vita* §35 (492ff.); Markwald 1986:16.

[3] 15 Wil. / 254-339 Allen. For dating of the *Contest*, see below, ch. 6 (Hesiod).

[4] On Homer's wisdom, see below. Sweetness: *anēr hēdistos aoidōn* (*Homeric Hymn to Apollo*, 169). This description of a blind poet was applied to Homer at least by the time of Thucydides 3.104.5.

holy,[5] the son of a Muse and Apollo.[6] His epitaph refers to "the sacred head of divine Homer."[7]

Like Aesop, Hesiod, and Archilochus, Homer receives a supernatural vision as inspiration for his poetry: Helen appears to him in a dream and demands that he write the *Iliad*.[8] Another story of supernatural inspiration links Homer with the Muses. Praying at the tomb of Achilles, he becomes blinded by a vision of the warrior in full armor, and receives poetic skill from Thetis and the Muses as compensation. This compensation/inspiration theme shows how close the poet is to the seer in archaic Greece.[9] The idea of a blind singer is actually traditional; in his discussion of Eastern European oral singers, Milman Parry notes that, while the blind are not always the best singers, a number of prestigious oral singers were blind.[10]

After Homer has learned his poetic craft, he becomes a wanderer; in the pseudo-Herodotean biography, he is forced to leave three cities (Smyrna, Neon Teichos, and Cyme) in succession before he finally finds a home in Chios. He leaves Smyrna because "he had no means of support [ἄπορος ἐὼν τοῦ βίου, §9]," then departs from Neon Teichos because he was "hard up [*aporos*] and finding it difficult to feed himself."[11] The emphasis on the word *aporos* recalls Archilochus, who left Paros "because of poverty and lack of resources [*dia penian kai aporian*]."

This portrait of wandering insecurity would seem to be a realistic, historical touch. The traveling *aoidos* or rhapsode must have led an uncertain, dependent life, continually visiting more or less hospitable cities. In Plato (*Republic*

---

[5] Cf. Falter 1934:78. See below.

[6] *Suda*, p. 256 Allen. For association of Homer with Apollo, cf. the Hesiodic fragment that has Homer, with Hesiod, starting off his bardic career in Delos, composing a hymn to Apollo, fr. 357 M-W. Cf. the blind singer in the *Homeric Hymn to Apollo*, 165–178; see Nagy 1979:297n7, also *Contest of Homer and Hesiod* 14 Wil. / 271–274 Allen; 18 Wil. / 318 Allen.

[7] *Contest of Homer and Hesiod* 18W (337–338); *Vita* VI p. 253 Allen. τὴν ἱερὴν κεφαλὴν . . . θεῖον Ὅμηρον.

[8] *Vita* VI, p. 252 Allen; Isocrates *Helen* 65; cf. Falter 1934:80. In an entirely fitting eventuality, Homer himself would later achieve divine status, and appear to Ennius in a dream to inspire him to write the *Annals*, see fr. ii–x of that book, Skutsch 1985:147–153; Falter 82–84; West 1966:159. Cf. following note.

[9] *Vita* VI p. 252 Allen. For the mythical reflex of the pattern: Euenius, blinded, is given divination as a recompense, Herodotus 9.92–94 (cf. Parker 1983:274), just as Demodocus is deprived of sight, but given inspired song at the same time (*Odyssey* viii 63–64, cf. *Iliad* II 599–600). Tiresias is the most famous mantic example (Hesiod fr. 275; Apollodorus 3.6.7; Callimachus *Hymn* 5, "The Baths of Pallas"). See also Buxton 1980; Loraux 1987b; Halliday 1967:77–79, 72; P. Murray 1983:8, 9; below, ch. 16 (Demodocus, Tiresias); ch. 17 (Cridenbel, Lugaid, Dallán).

[10] Lord 1960:18–20. Contra: Wilamowitz 1916a:421.

[11] Trans. West. ἀπόρως κείμενος καὶ μόλις τὴν τροφὴν ἔχων, §11.

600d, cf. *Ion*), Homer and Hesiod are said to have been so little valued that no city wanted to have them stay. Herodotus (5.67) describes a tyrant repressing rhapsodes.[12] Thus I agree that legends of Homer and similar poets encapsulate rhapsodic experiences over generations.[13] We can accordingly posit an oral tradition for stories of Homer—legends, folk tales, developed from preexisting legends of mythical seers and heroes—long before these stories began to be written down.

In the case of Cyme, we have a fleshed-out episode with Aesopic resonances. The poet approaches Cyme with high hopes for righteousness and hospitality; he composes the following epigram: "May my feet bring me straight to a city of righteous men; their hearts are generous and their intentions best."[14] In the same way, Aesop had looked to Delphi for righteous and hospitable men.[15] As in the case of Aesop, Homer is well received at first, but then receives no hospitality.[16] He proposes that the city give him support in return for his poetic performances and is told to present his case to the town senate. The senate is initially sympathetic to his proposal, but a powerful senator opposes him, arguing that if all blind men (called *homēroi*, 'hostages', by the Cymeans) were supported by the state, they would have to shelter a huge crowd of useless individuals (and so Homer, previously called Melesigenes, received his second, more famous name).[17] The unsympathetic senator sways the senate, and they vote against supporting Homer, which in effect exiles him. The inimical senator goes outside and announces the decision to Homer; Homer pronounces a curse on the town to the effect that no famous poets will bring it glory. He recites the fourth epigram, surprisingly beginning with theological meditations:

οἵη μ' αἴσῃ δῶκε πατὴρ Ζεὺς κύρμα γενέσθαι,
νήπιον αἰδοίης ἐπὶ γούνασι μητρὸς ἀτάλλων.

---

[12] Cf. Foley 1998:161–162 (Ćor Huso Husković, blind legendary singer in Montenegro and Serbia); Kirk 1962:312–315; P. Murray 1983; Lord 1960:19 (accounts of historical modern oral singers who were blind beggars, professional wandering singers); Sealey 1957:312; Lesky 1966:15; Chadwick and Chadwick 1932 1:568–634. On rhapsodes generally, Nagy 1990b:21–28, 1996:60–77.

[13] See Nagy 1996a; Foley 1998:163, who writes that the archaic poetic hero "lives on the cusp of real-life bardic practice and the alternate reality of legend."

[14] *Epigram 2* ("Herodotus" *Vita* §11). αἶψα πόδες με φέροιεν ἐς αἰδοίων πόλιν ἀνδρῶν· / τῶν γὰρ καὶ θυμὸς πρόφρων καὶ μῆτις ἀρίστη.

[15] See *Vita* G 125: "When I was far away from your city, I was impressed with you as men of wealth and generosity."

[16] *Vita* G 124; "Herodotus" *Vita* §12: "By his words, he brought joy to his listeners" (ἐν τοῖς λόγοις ἔτερπε τοὺς ἀκούοντας).

[17] On Homer's name, see Durante 1957:94; Nagy 1979:296–300, 1996:75; West 1999:366, 373–376.

ἥν ποτ' ἐπύργωσαν βουλῇ Διὸς αἰγιόχοιο
λαοὶ Φρίκωνος, μάργων ἐπιβήτορες ἵππων,
ὁπλότεροι μαλεροῖο πυρὸς κρίνοντες Ἄρηα,
Αἰολίδα Σμύρνην ἁλιγείτονα ποντοτίνακτον
ἥν τε δι' ἀγλαὸν εἶσιν ὕδωρ ἱεροῖο Μέλητος·
ἔνθεν ἀπορνύμεναι κοῦραι Διός, ἀγλαὰ τέκνα,
ἠθελέτην κλῆσαι δῖαν χθόνα καὶ πόλιν ἀνδρῶν,
οἱ δ' <u>ἀπανηνάσθην</u> ἱερὴν ὄπα, φῆμιν, ἀοιδήν.
<u>ἀφραδίῃ</u> τῶν μέν τε παθών τις φράσσεται αὖθις,
ὅς σφιν <u>ὀνείδεσσιν</u> τὸν <u>ἐμὸν διεμήσατο πότμον</u>.
κῆρα δ' ἐγὼ τήν μοι θεὸς ὤπασε γεινομένῳ περ
τλήσομαι ἀκράαντα φέρων τετληότι θυμῷ.
οὐδέ τι μοι φίλα γυῖα μένειν ἱεραῖς ἐν ἀγυιαῖς
Κύμης ὁρμαίνουσι, μέγας δέ με θυμὸς ἐπείγει
δῆμον ἐς ἀλλοδαπῶν ἰέναι ὀλίγον περ ἐόντα.[18]

To what a fate did Father Zeus deliver me as a prey [*kurma*], even while he nourished me as a child, at my revered mother's knees! By the will of aegis-holding Zeus, the people of Phricon, riders of wanton horses, more active than raging fire in the test of war, once built the towers of Aeolian Smyrna, wave-shaken neighbour to the sea, through which glides the splendid water of sacred Meles; from here the daughters of Zeus, glorious children, arose, and desired to make that fair country, and its populous city, famous. But in their folly [*aphradiēi*] those men scorned [*apanēnasthēn*] the divine voice and renown of song, and one of them will suffer and remember this afterwards—he who directed scornful words [*oneidessin*] to them and plotted my fate [*emon diemēsato potmon*]. Yet I will endure the doom which heaven gave me even at my birth, bearing my disappointment with a patient heart. My limbs no longer yearn to remain in the sacred streets of Cyme, but rather my great heart urges me to go to another country, small though I am.

"Herodotus" *Vita* §14[19]

Here Homer associates himself with the Muses (who will later arrange his death); like Aesop, before his departure he pronounces a curse on the city

---

[18] West 2003:370 emends the last three words to ὀλιγηπελέοντα, "in my debility."

[19] Trans. Evelyn-White, adapted. On this epigram see Markwald 1986:84–94; Peppmüller 1895. Markwald, at p. 286, notes that it is closely connected with the *Vita*.

that exiles him, and thus he enters the sphere of the poet who harms through words.[20] Twice he mentions the fate he has received from Zeus; a god has engineered his misery, his poetic vocation.[21]

So we have the theme of rejection of the poet by an inhospitable city; a public vote against the poet; in addition, there is the theme of the conflict of the poet and a powerful individual political figure, who has taunted or mocked Homer somehow (*oneidessin*).[22] There is a hint of a similar story set in Athens. Heraclides Ponticus tells us that Homer was fined fifty drachmas by the Athenians for insanity![23]

Homer is also seen as a "harmful" poet in the fourteenth epigram, the "Kiln Poem," a kind of begging song, in which the poet curses potters who may be dishonest and ungenerous to him. "Come also you daughter of the Sun, witch Circe: mix your wild drugs, and harm [*kakou*] them and their work . . . may . . . the kiln collapse, and the men groaning watch the work of destruction." In Lindsay Watson's interpretation, Homer, in an inhospitable world, suspects that the potters intend to cheat him of payment.[24] In *Epigram 6*, the poet also asks for divine vengeance against an inhospitable, dishonest patron. Once again, one senses that a wandering rhapsode was often at the mercy of ungracious hosts.[25]

Homer's death, like Hesiod's, is linked to an oracle and his failure to understand the answer to a riddle. Though he does not die because he could

---

[20] For Homer as satirist, reputed author of the *Margites*, see Rankin 1974:15; West 2003:225–228, 240–253. Cf. "Herodotus" *Vita* §15, *eparēsamenos*. See below on the kiln poem.

[21] For divinity creating the poet's miserable vocation, see below, chs. 7 (Ibycus); 15 (Socrates); 23 (Ovid).

[22] Cf. Diogenes Laertius 2.46 (Socrates): Homer was assailed [*ephiloneikei*] by Syagrus in his lifetime. Perhaps Syagrus is this Cymaean burger.

[23] *ap.* Diogenes Laertius 2.43. Plato (see above) supports this detail.

[24] δεῦρο καὶ Ἡελίου θύγατερ, πολυφάμακε Κίρκη, / ἄγρια φάρμακα βάλλε, κάκου δ' αὐτούς τε καὶ ἔργα. . . . πίπτοι δὲ κάμινος· / αὐτοὶ δ' οἰμώζοντες ὁρῷατο ἔργα πονηρά, trans. West, cf. Watson 1991:69–74. See, in addition to Markwald 1986:219–229, Schönberger 1912; Cook 1948:55–57, Cook 1951:9; Milne 1965; Gager 1992:153–154 (who notes that half a millennium after the Homer epigram, in Pliny *Natural History* 28.4.19, potters believe that curses can shatter their wares); Faraone 2001. Watson sees a comparatively playful tone in this poem that leads to "literary" Hellenistic curse poems. In fact, some portions of the poem may be Hellenistic, see Markwald 1986:29–41, Milne 1965, Faraone 2001, but the body of the poem is archaic.

[25] *Epigram 6*, lines 7–8 (17/241–242). See above, ch. 2 (Aesop at Delphi); ch. 3 (Archilochus); ch. 4 (Hipponax); below ch. 9 (Alcaeus); ch. 23 (Ovid). For another notable "begging song" among the Homeric epigrams, see *Epigram 15* (33/467–480), an Eiresione, the song used in the Thargelia, the festival in which the *pharmakos* was driven out of Athens. The song was associated with Samos, so Homer had to visit the island to compose it. For the Eiresione, see Toepffer 1888:142–145; Nilsson 1972:36–39; Harrison 1922:79–82.

not answer the riddle, he can only die after he fails to answer it—perhaps an attenuation of the original theme of riddle contest and death of loser.[26] The Delphic oracle tells the poet he will die in his mother's country, and that he should beware of the riddle of young children.[27] Much later, in Ios, children who have been fishing tell him: "All that we caught we left behind, and carry away all that we did not catch." Homer does not understand that they are talking of lice, not fish, and when he learns the answer, he remembers the oracle, then soon after slips on his side and dies.[28] A Hellenistic epigram adds the detail that the children were inspired by the Muses to ask the riddle, "In Ios the boys, weaving a riddle at the bidding of the Muses, vexed to death Homer the singer of the heroes,"[29] which leads us to the theme of Muses engineering the death of someone they have particularly inspired.[30] Without this theological dimension, the death of Homer makes little sense; it would hardly be a heroizing tale such as rhapsodes would repeat continually.

Homer receives hero cult. In the *Contest of Homer and Hesiod*, after the poet visiting Argos praises the ancestors of the Argives, they "set up a brazen statue to him, decreeing that sacrifice [*thusian*] should be offered to Homer daily, monthly, and yearly; and that another sacrifice should be sent to Chios every five years."[31] On the statue, they inscribe that they serve him ("divine [*theios*] Homer") "with the honors of the deathless gods [*timais amphepei athanatōn*]."[32] Outside of legend, rite and honor awarded Homer is widely attested in many places, including the full gamut of poetic cult: dedication of temples to the poet, sacrifice, statues, coins, and even ascription of a month to Homer on Ios, where he died.[33] His poetic immortalization continues.

Thus Homer is the best of poets, a sacred figure, who is reduced to wandering and beggary. He is marginal, blind. He suffers inhospitality where

---

[26] See above, ch. 2, for riddle warfare in the life of Aesop; also the riddle poem contest of Homer and Hesiod, ch. 6.

[27] *Contest of Homer and Hesiod* 5 Wil. / 59–60 Allen. Translations of the *Contest* are by Evelyn-White, modified, unless otherwise noted.

[28] *Contest of Homer and Hesiod* 18 Wil. / 334–335 Allen. Ὅσσ' ἔλομεν λιπόμεσθα, ὅσ' οὐχ ἔλομεν φερόμεσθα. For Homer's death in the *Contest*, see O'Sullivan 1992:104; Janko 1982:259–260; West 1999:378; Levine 2002 (valuable, but missing the "theology" of Homer's death).

[29] Alcaeus of Messene, in *Palatine Anthology* 7.1. ἡρώων τὸν ἀοιδὸν Ἴῳ ἔνι παῖδες Ὅμηρον / ἤκαχον ἐκ Μουσέων γρῖφον ὑφηνάμενοι.

[30] See ch. 16 below (Marsyas and Thamyris); ch. 2 above, the death of Aesop.

[31] εἰκόνα δὲ χαλκῆν ἀναστήσαντες ἐψηφίσαντο θυσίαν ἐπιτελεῖν Ὁμήρῳ καθ' ἡμέραν καὶ κατὰ μῆνα καὶ κατ' ἐνιαυτὸν <καὶ> ἄλλην θυσίαν πενταετηρίδα εἰς Χίον ἀποστέλλειν.

[32] *Contest of Homer and Hesiod* 17 Wil. / 304–314 Allen.

[33] Clay 2004:75–76, 136–143, discussion of the pan-Hellenic nature of Homer's cult, as opposed to the local cult of Hesiod. For further on Homer's cult, Farnell 1921:367, 425n304.

he had expected support; offending a powerful political figure, he is exiled by a political meeting; he curses the town prophetically, so that they are afflicted with poetic sterility from that time on. He looks on the god who inspired him as his persecutor. The Muses set up his death after he fails to understand a riddle. He then receives hero cult. Once again, we see familiar shadows, Aesop and Archilochus, behind a poetic *vita*: the wandering performer, the inhospitality, the trial, the curse, the disaster, and the poet's hero cult.[34]

---

[34] Thus we find the following themes in the *vita* of Homer: 1b, crime against hero; 1b1, inhospitality; 2b, communal disaster caused by the poet's expulsion (curse); 4a1, beggar; 5, best; 5a, sacred; 7, selection by public meeting; 10a, exile; 13, hero cult; 18, divine persecutor-patron; 22e, curse; 23a, consecration; 24, conflict with political leader or leaders; 25, contest theme; 25a, riddle/poetry contest.

6

Hesiod: Consecrate Murder

IN HESIOD'S *VITA*, we find a substantial set of the familiar legendary themes we have encountered so far—consecration, victory in riddle contest, oracle-related death, and cult. Hesiod's *vita* is clearly moving in the same orbit as those of Aesop and Archilochus, ringing the changes on the standard story of the sacral poet's life and death. A. Brelich, in his study of hero cult, makes Hesiod a prime example of the poet assimilated to hero cult and cult myth.[1]

Hesiod is, by some accounts, the best of poets. On his tombstone it is written that Hesiod's renown "is greatest among men of all who are judged by the test of wit."[2] In the *Contest of Homer and Hesiod*, the two poets engage in a riddle/poetry contest (*amphibolous gnōmas*, 102–103), in which they battle to a standoff, and finally read passages of poetry in competition. The prize for best poet is given to Hesiod, if only because the judge values peace more than war—the audience's applause had gone mostly to Homer. The poet dedicates his victory tripod to the Muses with the inscription, "Hesiod dedicated this tripod to the Muses of Helicon after he had conquered divine Homer at Chalcis through song."[3] The riddle contest itself brings Aesop to mind.[4]

---

[1] "*Hesiodos ha assunto quasi completamente la forma tradizionale dell'eroe,*" 1958:321. Brelich makes no *pharmakos* association, but the *pharmakos* is largely absent from *Gli Eroi Greci*. For the heroization of Hesiod, see also Nagy 1982; Beaulieu 2004.

[2] *Contest of Homer and Hesiod* 252–253 Allen. τοῦ πλεῖστον ἐν ἀνθρώποις κλέος ἐστὶν / ἀνδρῶν κρινομένων ἐν βασάνῳ σοφίης.

[3] *Contest of Homer and Hesiod* 213–214 Allen. Ἡσίοδος Μούσαις Ἑλικωνίσι τόνδ' ἀνέθηκεν / ὕμνῳ νικήσας ἐν Χαλκίδι θεῖον Ὅμηρον.

[4] *Contest of Homer and Hesiod*, 13 Wil. / 213–214 Allen. Texts of the *Contest of Hesiod and Homer* can be found in Allen 1919:225–238 and von Wilamowitz-Moellendorff 1916. Again, translations in this chapter are quoted, with adaptations, from Evelyn-White 1967:565–598 unless otherwise noted. See also a text and translation by M. L. West, 2003:318–353. Cf. Schadewaldt 1959a; Weiler 1974:118–119; West 1967; Heldmann 1982, with further bibliography, pp. 94–104; Richardson 1981; Kakridis 1983; M. Griffith 1990:192; Collins 2004:177, 184–191; Ford 2002:274–

The consecration theme, showing the sacrality of the poet, is found in the famous passage at the beginning of the *Theogony* (22–34):

αἵ νύ ποθ' Ἡσίοδον καλὴν ἐδίδαξαν ἀοιδήν,
ἄρνας ποιμαίνονθ' Ἑλικῶνος ὑπὸ ζαθέοιο.
τόνδε δέ με πρώτιστα θεαὶ πρὸς μῦθον ἔειπον,
Μοῦσαι Ὀλυμπιάδες, κοῦραι Διὸς αἰγιόχοιο:
ποιμένες ἄγραυλοι, <u>κάκ' ἐλέγχεα</u>, γαστέρες οἶον,
ἴδμεν ψεύδεα πολλὰ λέγειν ἐτύμοισιν ὁμοῖα,
ἴδμεν δ', εὖτ' ἐθέλωμεν, ἀληθέα γηρύσασθαι.
ὣς ἔφασαν κοῦραι μεγάλου Διὸς ἀρτιέπειαι:
καί μοι <u>σκῆπτρον</u> ἔδον δάφνης ἐριθηλέος ὄζον
δρέψασαι, θηητόν: ἐνέπνευσαν δέ μοι αὐδὴν
θέσπιν, ἵνα <u>κλείοιμι</u> τά τ' ἐσσόμενα πρό τ' ἐόντα.
καί με κέλονθ' ὑμνεῖν μακάρων γένος αἰὲν ἐόντων,
σφᾶς δ' αὐτὰς πρῶτόν τε καὶ ὕστατον αἰὲν ἀείδειν.

And once they [the Muses] taught Hesiod lovely song while he was shepherding his lambs below holy Helicon, and the goddesses spoke this word to me first—the Muses of Olympus, daughters of aegis-holding Zeus:

"Rustic shepherds, evil reproaches [*kak' elegkhea*], mere bellies, we know how to speak many false things that are similar to real things; but we [also] know how to utter true things, when we want to."

So spoke the ready-voiced daughters of great Zeus, and they plucked and gave me a rod [*skēptron*], a shoot of flourishing laurel, a marvelous thing,[5] and breathed into me a divine voice so that I could

---

277. For the contest more generally, see Weiler 1974; Brelich 1961; Nagy 2002:37; Collins 2004.

There is continued discussion on the antiquity of different parts of the *Contest*, a Hellenistic document using archaic traditions. A version of the *Contest* dates to Alcidamas (fourth century BC) at least. For Alcidamas, see O'Sullivan 1992; Clay 2004:75. The most important element of the *Contest* for the purposes of this study, Hesiod's murder, is attested as early as Thucydides 3.96.1 and Aristotle fr. 565 (Rose). For the contest theme, cf. "Hesiod" fr. 357 M-W; Plutarch *The Dinner of the Seven Wise Men* 153f. Richardson (1981:1) dates the story to at least the sixth century BC. On the riddle contest theme, cf. Hesiod's *Melampodia*, fr. 270–279, M-W; the battle of seer Calchas and Mopsus, see ch. 16; the contest of epic poets Lesches and Arctinus (Phaenias, fr. 33 Wehrli); Aesop as riddle warrior, in ch. 2. In Plutarch, a riddle, not poetry, decides the contest, cf. West 1967:438–439. It seems likely that this was the earliest version of the story, see Richardson 1981:2.

[5] This *skēptron* relates Hesiod the poet to kings (*Iliad* I 279), priests (*Iliad* I 15, 28), prophets (*Odyssey* xi 90), heralds (*Iliad* VII 277), speakers in assemblies (*Iliad* III 218). Nagy suggests that the rod gives Hesiod primacy among poets (1990:52). See Fisher 1997 for the Indo-European

celebrate [*kleioimi*] things that will be and things that have been; and they commanded me to sing of the race of the blessed gods who are eternal, and to sing of them, both first and last, always. [6]

Pausanias (9.31.5), reporting a local Boeotian tradition, tells us explicitly that Hesiod was concerned with the mantic: "These same Boeotians say that Hesiod learned seercraft [*mantikēn*] from the Acarnanians, and there are extant a poem called *Mantica* (*Seercraft*), which I myself have read, and interpretations of portents." [7] He was also the author of a poem on the seer Melampus, a few fragments of which are extant (270–279 M-W). The poet's consecrational gift of knowledge of things in the future and present (*Theogony* 32) is also a mantic theme. [8]

As in the case of Archilochus, blame is an important component of the message the Muses give to the poet. [9] In the case of Archilochus, blame is a key element of his own poetry. There is also an important satirical component in Hesiod's poetry, [10] a blame that is sometimes directed against unjust and violent

---

dimensions of the staff. The Greek *skēptron* is usually a "badge of authority," a long, wooden staff. The related Indo-European staff is an emblem of royal, judicial, priestly, and prophetic authority.

[6] My trans. For an introduction to the literature on this passage, see West 1966:151, 158–161; he includes a typology of the poetic consecration experience, 159–160. See also Kambylis 1965:31–68; Falter 1934:12–17; Walcot 1957; Latte 1946; Müller 1985:102–104; Williams 1971; Choite and Latacz 1981:85–95; Pascal 1985; Calame 1996:51–56. For Hesiod's consecration as a dream, see Kambylis 1965:55–59; cf. Falter 1934:79–88; Müller 1985:102–103.

[7] Trans. Jones, adapted, οἱ δὲ αὐτοὶ οὗτοι λέγουσι καὶ ὡς μαντικὴν Ἡσίοδος διδαχθείη παρὰ Ἀκαρνάνων· καὶ ἔστιν ἔπη Μαντικά, ὁπόσα τε ἐπελεξάμεθα καὶ ἡμεῖς, καὶ ἐξηγήσεις ἐπὶ τέρασιν. See Delgado 1986. For the Acarnanian mantic tradition, Apollodorus 3.7.6; Herodotus 1.62.4 (cf. How and Wells 1928 *ad loc.*); 7.221; Huxley 1969:54; Löffler 1963.

[8] Cf. *Iliad* I 70 (the seer Calchas); West 1966, at line 32; Van Unnik 1962:86–94; ch. 11 (Tyrtaeus); ch. 17 (knowledge and poetic *agōn*); ch. 19 (Odin's knowledge and kingship). For the connection of knowledge with poetry and prophecy, see Chadwick 1952:2–3; Dodds 1951:100n118. For the connection of poetry and prophecy generally, see Chadwick 1952; Durante 1971–1974 2:167–169; Kugel 1990 (including Semitic examples, and literary *Nachleben*); ch. 17, below, section 2, on Irish poets, and ch. 19, Germanic traditions. It is also worth noting that Hesiod had mantic ancestry: he is a grandson of Apollo (*Contest* 46A; 4W) on his father's side and mother's side; he is also a descendant of Orpheus (Hellanicus FGH 4 F 5). In Hesiod's view, the poet is *therapōn* of the Muses, *Theogony* 99–101; Nagy 1990:48. Cf. Brelich 1958:321; Lefkowitz 1981:7.

[9] Cf., in West's typology, #4: "The god who appears (or the prophet inspired by him) addresses mankind in strongly derogatory terms," (1966:160). See also Svenbro 1976:50–59 for a treatment of "belly" as diction of blame. Cf. Tucker 1987; Katz and Volk 2000 (unconvincing). See above, ch. 2, for Aesop's belly.

[10] As Rankin (1977:52n44) notes, Hesiod repeatedly attacked unjust judges: *Works and Days* 39, 221, 264. See also Hunt 1981; Nagy 1979:312–314. Both Nagy and Hunt note that the blame poet's themes are reflexes of the mythology of strife, see Hunt, esp. 32. For Hesiod's blame directed against women, see Marquardt 1982; Arrighetti 1981.

political leaders. The portrait Hesiod paints of Perses,[11] his brother, is also not complimentary (he accuses him of cheating him out of his fortune),[12] and his brother is linked to corrupt judges: "For we had already divided our inheritance, but you seized the greater share and carried it off, greatly swelling the glory of our bribe-swallowing lords who love to judge such a cause as this" (*Works and Days* 37–39).[13]

Russell Hunt notes that Hesiod, like Aesop, is a "justified" blame poet;[14] like Aesop and Archilochus he uses the fable for blame directed at violent leaders. In *Works and Days* (202–212) a hawk grips a nightingale in his cruel talons—and the persecuted creature is a "singer," *aoidon*:[15]

> Νῦν δ' αἶνον βασιλεῦσιν ἐρέω φρονέουσι καὶ αὐτοῖς·
> ὧδ' ἴρηξ προσέειπεν ἀηδόνα ποικιλόδειρον . . .
> ἣ δ' ἐλεόν, γναμπτοῖσι πεπαρμένη ἀμφ' ὀνύχεσσι
> μύρετο· τὴν ὅ γ' ἐπικρατέως πρὸς μῦθον ἔειπεν·
> "δαιμονίη, τί λέληκας; ἔχει νύ σε πολλὸν ἀρείων
> τῇ δ' εἶς ᾗ σ' ἂν ἐγώ περ ἄγω καὶ <u>ἀοιδὸν</u> ἐοῦσαν."

And now I will tell a fable for lords who are capable of understanding. Thus said the hawk to the nightingale with speckled neck . . . and she, pierced by his crooked talons, cried pitifully. To her he spoke disdainfully: "Fool, why do you cry out? One who is far stronger than you holds you fast, and you must go wherever I take you, singer [*aoidon*] though you may be."

The fable brings the imagery of Archilochus as tortured cricket-singer strongly to mind.[16] Thus, the familiar situation of just poet striking out at unjust political leaders through fable, combined with the persecution of the poet by the leaders, is not absent in the case of Hesiod.

---

[11] This name may be related to Hecate, whom Hesiod (and his father) apparently worshipped, *Theogony* 411–452, cf. *Theogony* 377, 409–411, *Works and Days* 10; West 1966:278; Burkert 1983:210. Hunt would like to link it to *perthō/portheō* ('ravage', 'waste', 'destroy'), as a descriptive name, a traditional element of blame (1981:33).

[12] Hunt 1981:34. Perses is a *mega nēpios* (633, 286), "great fool."

[13] ἤδη μὲν γὰρ κλῆρον ἐδασσάμεθ', ἄλλα τε πολλὰ / ἁρπάζων ἐφόρεις μέγα κυδαίνων βασιλῆας / δωροφάγους, οἳ τήνδε δίκην ἐθέλουσι δίκασσαι. Hunt discusses the theme, so important for blame poetry, of strife arising from improper division, 1981:32.

[14] Hunt 1981:31–32.

[15] Cf. Hunt 1981:36; Nagy 1979:312–314.

[16] See above, ch. 3. Cf. Diogenes Laertius 2.46 (Socrates), "Hesiod was criticized in his lifetime by Cercops" (ἐφιλονείκει . . . καὶ Κέρκωψ Ἡσιόδῳ ζῶντι . . .).

Hesiod came from poor parents; Hesiod's family leaves Cyme because of their poverty. Hesiod's pastoral occupation perhaps also shows his poverty. In *Works and Days* 633–640,[17] he writes, "Your father and mine, great fool Perses, used to sail in ships because he lacked sufficient livelihood . . . he left Aeolian Cyme in a black ship and fled, not from riches and substance, but from wretched poverty which Zeus gives to men, and he settled near Helicon in a miserable hamlet, Ascra, which is bad in winter, hot in summer, and good at no time."[18]

ὥς περ ἐμός τε πατὴρ καὶ σός, μέγα νήπιε Πέρση,
πλωίζεσκ᾽ ἐν νηυσί, βίου κεχρημένος ἐσθλοῦ·
ὅς ποτε καὶ τεῖδ᾽ ἦλθε, πολὺν διὰ πόντον ἀνύσσας,
Κύμην Αἰολίδα προλιπών, ἐν νηὶ μελαίνῃ,
οὐκ ἄφενος φεύγων οὐδὲ πλοῦτόν τε καὶ ὄλβον,
ἀλλὰ κακὴν πενίην, τὴν Ζεὺς ἄνδρεσσι δίδωσιν.
νάσσατο δ᾽ ἄγχ᾽ Ἑλικῶνος ὀιζυρῇ ἐνὶ κώμῃ,
Ἄσκρῃ, χεῖμα κακῇ, θέρει ἀργαλέῃ, οὐδέ ποτ᾽ ἐσθλῇ.

This is somewhat in the tradition of geographical blame that Archilochus used in describing Thasos (fr. 21W). As Plutarch notes, Archilochus "slandered the island [*diebale tēn nēson*]," for Thasos had corn fields and vineyards.[19] Perhaps the abuse of the new land is related to the longing for the homeland; this geographical blame is inextricably connected to the theme of the exile of the poet.[20]

In a striking parallel to the Archilochus *vita*, the Tzetzes life of Hesiod tells us that Hesiod's family left Cyme "because of helplessness and need" (διὰ τὸ ἄπορον καὶ τὰ χρέα).[21] The lives of archaic Greek poets are full of wandering motifs such as this.

Hesiod's death, about which we know more than we do about his life, is a typical cultic tragedy.[22] Our earliest witness is Thucydides: "Demosthenes, after locating his army in the precinct of Nemean Zeus—in which Hesiod the poet is said to have been killed by those living there, as it had been foretold

---

[17] See also Tzetzes *Vita*, p. 2 Solmsen; p. 47W; this derives, through Tzetzes, from Proclus, who used Plutarch; see West 1978:68.

[18] Trans. Evelyn-White, modified. Another tradition has Hesiod's father leave Kyme because he had killed a relative, see Ephorus, FGH 70 F 100.

[19] Plutarch *On Exile* 12 (604c), quoted in fr. 21W.

[20] Cf. Lefkowitz 1981:1 for further references.

[21] For the theme of helplessness and poverty in archaic Greece, see Martin 1983:57–59 and passim.

[22] Cf. Lefkowitz 1981:8: "Pausanias too [as well as Plutarch] devotes twice as much space to Hesiod's death as to his life and works."

to him in an oracle that he would suffer this in Nemea—set out for Aetolia at dawn."²³ Thucydides seems to have Hesiod killed by a group; but perhaps he merely meant he had been killed "by locals," even if that was only two men as in other versions.

According to the *Contest of Homer and Hesiod*, which gives a fuller version, the Delphic oracle warns the poet to stay away from the grove of Nemean Zeus. As often happens with warning oracles, the recipient's efforts to avoid the oracular doom (by wandering far from the most famous grove of Nemean Zeus) lead him to fulfill it:

... εἰς δὲ Οἰνόην τῆς Λοκρίδος ἐλθὼν καταλύει παρ' Ἀμφιφάνει καὶ Γανύκτορι, τοῖς Φηγέως παισίν, ἀγνοήσας τὸ μαντεῖον. ὁ γὰρ τόπος οὗτος ἅπας ἐκαλεῖτο Διὸς Νεμείου ἱερόν. διατριβῆς δὲ αὐτῷ πλείονος γενομένης ἐν τοῖς Οἰνοεῦσιν ὑπονοήσαντες οἱ νεανίσκοι τὴν ἀδελφὴν αὐτῶν μοιχεύειν τὸν Ἡσίοδον, ἀποκτείναντες εἰς τὸ μεταξὺ τῆς Εὐβοίας καὶ τῆς Λοκρίδος πέλαγος κατεπόντισαν. τοῦ δὲ νεκροῦ τριταίου πρὸς τὴν γῆν ὑπὸ δελφίνων προσενεχθέντος ἑορτῆς τινος ἐπιχωρίου παρ' αὐτοῖς οὔσης Ἀριαδνείας πάντες ἐπὶ τὸν αἰγιαλὸν ἔδραμον καὶ τὸ σῶμα γνωρίσαντες ἐκεῖνο μὲν <u>πενθήσαντες ἔθαψαν</u>, τοὺς δὲ φονεῖς ἀνεζήτουν. οἱ δὲ φοβηθέντες τὴν τῶν πολιτῶν ὀργὴν κατασπάσαντες ἁλιευτικὸν σκάφος διέπλευσαν εἰς Κρήτην. οὓς κατὰ μέσον τὸν πλοῦν ὁ Ζεὺς κεραυνώσας κατεπόντωσεν, ὥς φησιν Ἀλκιδάμας ἐν Μουσείῳ. Ἐρατοσθένης δέ φησιν ἐν †ἐνηπόδῳ† Κτίμενον καὶ Ἄντιφον τοὺς Γανύκτορος ἐπὶ τῇ προειρημένῃ αἰτίᾳ ἀνελόντας σφαγιασθῆναι θεοῖς τοῖς ξενίοις ὑπ' Εὐρυκλέους τοῦ μάντεως. τὴν μέντοι παρθένον τὴν ἀδελφὴν τῶν προειρημένων μετὰ τὴν φθορὰν ἑαυτὴν ἀναρτῆσαι, φθαρῆναι δὲ ὑπό τινος ξένου συνόδου τοῦ Ἡσιόδου Δημώδους ὄνομα· ὃν καὶ αὐτὸν ἀναιρεθῆναι ὑπὸ τῶν αὐτῶν φησιν.

And he came to Oenoe in Locris and stayed with Amphiphanes and Ganyctor, the sons of Phegeus, which shows that he did not understand the oracle; for all that region was called the sacred place of Nemean Zeus. After he had stayed a rather long time at Oenoe, some young men, suspecting that Hesiod had seduced their sister, killed him and cast his body into the sea which separates Euboea

---

²³ Thucydides 3.96.1, my trans., αὐλισάμενος δὲ τῷ στρατῷ ἐν τοῦ Διὸς τοῦ Νεμείου τῷ ἱερῷ, ἐν ᾧ Ἡσίοδος ὁ ποιητὴς λέγεται ὑπὸ τῶν ταύτῃ ἀποθανεῖν, χρησθὲν αὐτῷ ἐν Νεμέᾳ τοῦτο παθεῖν, ἅμα τῇ ἕῳ ἄρας ἐπορεύετο ἐς τὴν Αἰτωλίαν.

and Locris.[24] On the third day, however, his body was brought to land by dolphins while a certain local feast of Ariadne[25] was being held. Everyone hurried to the shore, and recognizing the body, lamented over it and buried it [*penthēsantes ethapsan*], and then began to look for the murderers. But fearing the anger of their countrymen, the murderers launched a fishing boat, and put out to sea for Crete. They had finished half their voyage when Zeus sank them with a thunderbolt, as Alcidamas states in his *Museum*. Eratosthenes, however, says in his *Hesiod*[26] that Ctimenus and Antiphus, sons of Ganyctor, killed him for the reason already stated, and were sacrificed by Eurycles the seer to the gods of hospitality.[27] He adds that the girl, sister of the above-named, hanged herself after she had been seduced, and that she was seduced by a certain stranger, named Demodes, who was travelling with Hesiod, and who was also killed by the brothers.[28]

Contest of Homer and Heisod 234–235A, 14W

Directed by an oracle, the men of Orchomenus remove his body to their land, and erect a tomb for it. Like Oedipus and Homer, Hesiod is a man of special divine inspiration who cannot interpret a divine oracle correctly; a riddle master who cannot decipher the meaning of a riddling oracle.

Especially noteworthy in this legend is the help of the dolphins, which gives us the theme of animal helper, a hint that the poet is semidivine.[29] Here the animal helps avenge the hero's death and bring the murderers to justice.

---

[24] A mistake by the compiler; this is not eastern Locris, but Ozolian Locris, see Thucydides 3.95.3 (who calls the town Oineon) and West 2003:343.

[25] Who, according to one tradition, hanged herself: Plutarch *Theseus* 20.1; cf. Burkert 1983:64n26.

[26] A conjecture by Göttling.

[27] The "gods of hospitality" are otherwise unknown; Lefkowitz 1981:6, suggests that they may refer to Zeus, the usual protector of hospitality, but the plural is still somewhat puzzling. Cf. the theme of hospitality in the death of Aesop, ch. 2; in the life of Homer the rhapsode, ch. 5; ch. 17, the *Vision of MacConglinne*.

[28] Trans. Evelyn-White, modified. Pausanias 9.31.6 tells us that, according to some, Hesiod actually did seduce the sister of his hosts, but this will be a secondary accretion, despite O'Sullivan's argument (1992:98–99) that this was the older version of the story. In terms of heroic legend (not purported history), Hesiod as seducer would justify Hesiod's murderers and give no reason for the divine intervention through dophin and dog that brings the murderers to justice, to say nothing of Zeus striking the murderers dead with a thunderbolt (a detail explicitly from Alcidamas). Cf. Plutarch *Dinner of the Seven Sages* 19 (162c–d).

[29] For the animal helper theme, cf. Beaulieu 2004:106–108, who notes that the animals are the servants of god in this kind of story, who thus "change" the recipient and heroize him. For the cultic resonances of the dolphin, Burkert 1983:196–204; Lefkowitz 1981:7n22. See below, ch. 7, the lives of Ibycus and Arion. Cf. Somville 1984; Fontenrose 1978:73.

In a variant from Plutarch, Hesiod's dog barks and rushes at the murderers, pointing them out.[30] The Hesiodic tradition offers a number of variants on the story as found in the *Contest*. Plutarch adds a suggestive detail: "The girl's brothers killed him, lying in wait for him [*enedreusantes*] near the temple of Nemean Zeus in Locris."[31] This is the same way Androgeos the Cretan died—a guest entitled to the rights of hospitality, he is killed by his hosts lying in ambush; and, as in the case of Aesop, he is killed unjustly, on a false charge. In fact, in Apollodorus' version of Androgeus's death, the same verb is used: *enedreuō*.

The cultic associations of Hesiod's death are numerous: his death is predicted, and, in fact, caused, by the Delphic oracle; he is killed in or near a temple precinct; his body is discovered by the Locrians during a feast of Ariadne, and given lamentation and burial.[32] He is buried near the same precinct in which he was killed. In one account, Hesiod's murderers are sacrificed ("to the gods of hospitality") by a seer. M. P. Nilsson suggests that the narrative of Hesiod's death "is an aetiological myth for the Locrian ritual, which may have involved mourning and a representation of hanging, like the festival of Ariadne at Crete."[33]

The familiar theme of plague averted by propitiation of dead hero is found, applied to Hesiod, in Pausanias: "They say that they [the Orchomenians] thus recovered the bones of Hesiod. A pestilence fell on men and beasts, so that they sent envoys to the god. To these, it is said, the Pythian priestess made answer that to bring the bones of Hesiod from the land of Naupactus to the land of Orchomenus was their one and only remedy [*iama*]."[34] The theme of

---

[30] Plutarch *On the Intelligence of Animals* 13 (969e), 36 (984d); Pollux *Onomasticon* 5.42.

[31] Plutarch *Dinner of the Seven Sages* 19 (162d), trans. Babbitt, modified, ἀπέκτειναν γὰρ αὐτὸν οἱ τῆς παιδίσκης ἀδελφοὶ περὶ τὸ Λοκρικὸν Νέμειον <u>ἐνεδρεύσαντες</u>. Thucydides 3.96.1 places the poet's murder in the precinct/temple [*en ... tōi hierōi*] of Nemean Zeus, see above. For the theme of pollution caused by murder on holy ground see Parker 1983:273; 182–185; Rowland 1980:38–72.

[32] Plutarch gives a somewhat different story: Hesiod is discovered while the Locrians were celebrating their "Rhian sacrifice and festal gathering [ἡ τῶν Ῥίων καθεστῶσα θυσία καὶ πανήγυρις]." He is buried where he was killed, at the temple of Nemean Zeus (*pros tōi Nemeiōi*); despite the efforts of the Orchomenians, they never transferred the body. *Dinner of the Seven Sages* 19 (162d–e).

[33] Cf. Nilsson 1906:383–384; Burkert 1983:203–204; Lefkowitz 1981:4. Burkert places Hesiod's death myth in the sphere of Dionysus (Ariadne, the Dolphins) and Poseidon (Pausanias 10.11.6 has the festival of the Locrians dedicated to Poseidon; cf. Burkert 1983:203n37). In the Archilochus *vita*, see above, ch. 3; the associations of blame poetry and hanging women, especially Iambe and the Lycambids, have been noted.

[34] Pausanius 9.38.3, trans. Jones. καταδέξασθαι δέ φασιν οὕτω τοῦ Ἡσιόδου τὰ ὀστᾶ. νόσου καταλαμβανούσης λοιμώδους καὶ ἀνθρώπους καὶ τὰ βοσκήματα ἀποστέλλουσι θεωροὺς παρὰ

the transferral of bones to avert disaster is commonly associated with heroes and hero cult.[35] According to a Hellenistic epigram, nymphs wash his body, build his tomb, and goatherds pour libations of milk and honey on it.[36] Clay contrasts the limited status of Hesiod's cult at Orchomenus[37] with Homer's panhellenic honors, but Homer is extraordinary; typically, hero cult is limited to one or a few locations, often the grave of the hero.[38] There was also a statue of Hesiod at the grove of the Muses at Helicon. Claude Calame argues that the place of Hesiod's poetic consecration was also a focus for the poet's heroization, which would neatly parallel Clay's suggestions that the Archilocheion was localized near the place of Archilochus' consecration.[39]

Finally, as in the case of Androgeus and Aesop, we have the theme of double birth, two lives, applied to Hesiod, attested by Pindar and Aristotle. Tzetzes states that one of the epigraphs on Hesiod's tomb in Orchomenus, attributed to Pindar, was "Hail, you who have twice been a youth, and who have twice met with a tomb, / Hesiod, you who possess the (highest) measure of wisdom among men."[40] Interpretation of this theme is extremely varied, ranging from simple tomb transfer to reincarnation to mythical rejuvenation and resurrection.[41] Through this theme, Ruth Scodel links Hesiod with other typical Greek shamanistic wonder workers. For this study, it suffices to note

---

τὸν θεόν. τούτοις δὲ ἀποκρίνασθαι λέγουσι τὴν Πυθίαν, Ἡσιόδου τὰ ὀστᾶ ἐκ τῆς Ναυπακτίας ἀγαγοῦσιν ἐς τὴν Ὀρχομενίαν, ἄλλο δὲ εἶναί σφισιν οὐδὲν ἴαμα.

[35] E.g. Orestes (Pausanias 3.3.6), Theseus (Pausanias 3.3.7), Hector (Pausanias 9.18.5), Pelops (Pausanias 5.13.4–6); further references in Parker 1983:272; Rohde 1925:122; see below, ch. 16, the bones of Linus. Cf. Pfister 1909:230–240; Wallace 1985; Boedeker 1993, on the politics of bone transfer.

[36] Alcaeus (of Mytilene or Messene), in *Palatine Anthology* 7.55; cf. Gabathuler 1937:91–2; Lefkowitz 1981:10 (who refers to the nymphs as Muses).

[37] Clay 2004:136, 75. See Thucydides 3.96.1 (murder at cult site); Aristotle fr. 565 (Rose) and Plutarch (Sandbach 1969:182) = *ap.* Schol. (Proclus) in Hesiod *Works and Days* 639–640 (bone transferral); Aristotle *Constitution of the Orchomenians*, fr. 565 Rose (double burial, *gēras* of a double life); *Contest of Homer and Hesiod* 236A/14W (lamentation, burial, bone transferral); Plutarch *Dinner of the Seven Sages* 19 (162e–f) (secret burial near cult site, bone transferral sought); Pausanias 9.38.3 (plague, oracle, bones, plague stayed); cf. Nagy 1990a:50.

[38] Ekroth 2002:21.

[39] Pausanias 9.30.3. Calame 1996:53; Clay 2004:37.

[40] Tzetzes *Life of Hesiod* p. 51.9–10 Wil., Solmsen et al. 1983:3, my trans., χαῖρε δὶς ἡβήσας καὶ δὶς τάφου ἀντιβολήσας, / Ἡσίοδ', ἀνθρώποις μέτρον ἔχων σοφίης. Aristotle fr. 565 (Rose). The *Suda* (at *to Hēsiodeion gēras*) also attributes the poem to Pindar. Cf. Scholia Bernensia at Virgil *Eclogues* 6.65; Sarpedon and Tiresias, at Apollodorus 3.1.2; 3.6.7, Frazer 1921 1.364–365n. See discussions by Beaulieu 2004:114–115; Scodel 1980:301–320; Brelich 1958:321; MacKay 1959. See above, chs. 1, 2, on Androgeus' and Aesop's resurrection; below, ch. 16, on Epimenides.

[41] See Scodel 1980, passim.

the parallel with Androgeus and Aesop, and the mythical resonance of the theme, whatever its exact interpretation.

Thus Hesiod is the best poet; victorious over Homer in bardic *agōn*; sacred; and he receives divine consecration in his poetic mission. He is also a blame poet, and uses animal fables for blame, criticizing political leaders through them; exile is a theme in his poetry; and his family was once exiled. He dies far from home, after receiving hospitality from a friend, and is unjustly murdered by his hosts (his murderers are later punished under the auspices of the "gods of hospitality"). This theme links him to the murder of Androgeus, the *aition* for the Attic *pharmakos*, as both men are killed by ambush. Hesiod is killed at a temple, which turns his death into a sort of sacrifice. His death has been "arranged" by Apollo (the Delphic oracle), who also arranges his hero cult; thus we have the divine persecutor-patron. Familiar hero cult themes surround the recovery of the poet's body: lamentation, transferral of bones, in addition to the familiar plague and oracle consultation. He finally, like Aesop, receives some kind of second life.

A numerical listing of the themes in Hesiod's *vita* includes:

1. *Ritual pollution* involving poet.

   1a. *Crime of hero* (imputed).

      1a1. Seduction of host's daughter (imputed); or

   1b. *Crime against hero* (falsely accused of seduction).

      1b1. Inhospitality of hosts.

      1b2. Murder.

      1b3. By deceit.

         1b2a. False accusation.

         1b2b. Ambush.

2. *Communal disaster*.

   2b. Communal disaster caused by hero's death.

3. *Oracle.* remedy for disaster.

5. *Best.*

   5a. Sacred.

   5c. Victorious.

11. *Death.*

12. *Sacrifice* (he is killed at a temple).

13. *Hero cult.*

   13a. Immortality of hero.

18. *Divine persecutor-patron* (Apollo "arranges" Hesiod's death, and his hero cult).

22. *Blame poetry.*

    22a1. Hanging.

   22c. Animal fables for blame.

23. *Poet is sacred.*

   23a. Consecration of poet (by theophany).

   23d. Resurrection.

24. *Conflict with political leaders.*

   25a. Riddle contest.

27. *Exile as poetic theme.*

This is an impressive dossier. Hesiod adds themes to the list: 23c, animal helper (related to sacrality of poet); 12a, death at a cultic place (though compare Aesop at Delphi); 13b, bones transfer.

There are many continuities with Aesop—animal fable used for blame, death far from home caused by those who should have given him hospitality; execution because of a falsely imputed crime. However, Hesiod differs on an important point. Aesop suffered a legal execution, with imprisonment and trial engineered by political leaders; Hesiod is killed by stealth, by private individuals. Thus we have parallel, related themes with divergent outcomes. The trial outcome would continue in Plato's account of Socrates' death, and gain great influence through Plato's literary skill; but the Androgeus–Hesiod apolitical outcome is no less related to the theme of the unjust murder of the *pharmakos.*

7

Shadows of Hesiod:
Divine Protection and Lonely Death

THE LIVES OF IBYCUS, ARION, STESICHORUS, AND SIMONIDES echo Hesiod's *vita* in their themes of divine protection, often through animals, and lonely, violent death. Therefore it will be useful to consider them in close proximity to Hesiod.

Ibycus

Ibycus[1] was born in Rhegium, Italy, and left there, for Samos, rejecting a chance to reign as a tyrant.[2] Like Hesiod, he was murdered far from home, killed on a deserted beach where he had just landed, near Corinth. "Robbers killed you, Ibycus, the day you left ship to land on a pathless desert shore . . ."[3]

However, like Hesiod, Ibycus was avenged miraculously. As he died he called on some cranes to avenge him; later, the murderers were overheard laughing about the statement when they saw some cranes, and were brought to justice.[4] According to one source, the very clamor of the cranes seemed to

---

[1] On his life, see testimonia in Davies 1991:236–239; Campbell 1991:209–213. All references to testimonia in Ibycus and Stesichorus refer to Davies. Translations in this chapter are by Edmonds, adapted, unless otherwise noted.

[2] Diogenianus *Proverbs* 2.71 (test. 4D): "Ibycus, when he might have reigned as a tyrant over his fellow-citizens, went away to live in Ionia" (Ἴβυκος γὰρ τυραννεύειν πολιτῶν δυνάμενος ἀπεδήμησεν εἰς Ἰωνίαν).

[3] Antipater, in *Palatine Anthology* 7.745.2 (test. 5D): Ἴβυκε, λῃσταί σε κατέκτανον ἔκ ποτε νηὸς / βάντ᾽ ἐς ἐρημαίην ἄστιβον ἠϊόνα . . . Cf. *Suda* (test. 1D). "Falling one day among robbers in a deserted spot he was killed exclaiming that the very cranes which flew over at the moment would prove his avengers" (trans. Edmonds), συλληφθεὶς δὲ ὑπὸ λῃστῶν ἐπὶ ἐρημίας ἔφη, κἂν τὰς γεράνους ἃς ἔτυχεν ὑπερίπτασθαι ἐκδίκους γενέσθαι.

[4] Antipater of Sidon, in *Palatine Anthology* 7.745 (test. 5D); Plutarch *On Loquacity* 14 (509e–f) (test. 6D); Statius *Silvae* 5.3.152–3 (test. 8D); *Suda* s.v. Ibycus (test. 1D).

avenge the murder.[5] This theme of the poet aided, in life or death, by animals, appears to be an example of miraculous, hence divine, protection awarded to the specially sacred individual. Antipater exclaims, "Alas, you greedy robbers! why do you not fear the wrath of the gods?"[6]

Iamblichus (*Life of Pythagoras* 126) wisely doubts the historicity of this tale, since he heard it told of many other people. This may be a good example of how poets' lives were constructed from already existing myths, oral traditions, and folk motifs.[7]

This pattern of the remarkable death is perhaps an attenuation of the sacred death, a kind of folkloric secularization, with an atmosphere of the uncanny lingering around it.[8] "Sotades" writes, "All who wanted to make a great discovery or an artful poem or a clever bit of learning, all these have come to a bad end in their deaths and have suffered at the hands of the world's creator."[9] "Sotades" then lists tragic poets' and philosophers' deaths, putting them in a religious context.

Another example of the remarkable death is Ibycus' companion in amatory verse, Anacreon, who died when a "grape-stone" stuck in his mouth— a fittingly ironic death for a man who had continually lauded the fruit of the vine.[10]

Arion

Arion, another poetic recipient of miraculous bestial aid, is, like Ibycus, attacked by murderous robbers, but in his case the animal preserves his life rather than avenges his death. In the well-known story from Herodotus, a crew of Corinthians, attracted by Arion's wealth which he has amassed in Sicily,

---

[5] Antipater, in *Palatine Anthology* 7.745: "because of their cries an avenging Fury avenged your murder" (τῶνδε διὰ κλαγγὴν τίσατο σεῖο φόνον). Cf. Lefkowitz 1981:37.

[6] ἰὼ φιλοκερδέα φῦλα / ληιστέων, τί θεῶν οὐ πεφόβησθε χόλον; *Palatine Anthology* 7.745; cf. Thompson 1955 s.v. "cranes of Ibycus," N 271.3 (with extra-Greek references); Fairweather 1974:271; 272n215; Lefkowitz 1981:37.

[7] Cf. Wilamowitz 1956:244; Falter 1934:95; Lefkowitz 1981:37. Further literature at test. 9D.

[8] Cf. Bell 1978:31n7; Szegedy-Maszak 1978:206–208; Fairweather 1974:260n149; 269n192; Fairweather 1973; Lefkowitz 1981:96n43; Martin 1993:110; the deaths of Aeschylus, Euripides, see below in chs. 12 and 13. For the extraordinary death, often ironic, in the athlete hero myth, see Fontenrose 1968:87–89.

[9] "Sotades" 15.5–8 (see Powell 1925:243), as quoted by Lefkowitz 1981:96n43. ὅτι πάντες ὅσοι περισσὸν ἠθέλησαν εὑρεῖν / ἢ μηχανικὸν ποίημ᾽ ἢ σοφὸν μάθημα, / οὗτοι κακὸν εἰς τὸν θάνατον τέλος ἐποίησαν / ὑπὸ τοῦ γεννήτορος κόσμου κακῶς παθόντες.

[10] For Anacreon's *vita*, see Rosenmeyer 1992:12–15. For Anacreon as satirist, cf. fr. 43 LP.

conspire to murder him. Arion, after singing one last song, jumps overboard, and is succored by a dolphin, which he rides to land; the poet is later able to bring the evil sailors to justice.[11] The theme of the protection of the gods is here underlined by the dolphin's strong association with Apollo.[12] In Hyginus, Apollo actually sends Arion a dream directing his actions—this would explain his willingness to jump into the sea, fully clothed, after a last song (which attracted a musically inclined dolphin).[13] In the elaborately crafted Plutarch narrative, the poet is divinely inspired to dress ceremonially and sing his last song, and in it invokes the gods of the sea.[14]

An important aspect of this theme, and another link to the story of Hesiod, is that Arion (like Ibycus) is attacked far from home, when he should have been able to rely on the rights of guest-friendship. This motif of death far from home (as in the case of Homer, Hesiod, and Ibycus) surfaces repeatedly in the lives of the poets. This may be an example of a poet's *vita* being developed from underlying mythical motifs, for the theme "salvation by dolphin" is well attested in myth, as Bowra shows. However, there are documented cases of men riding dolphins to safety. As often, history can mirror myth.[15]

Stesichorus

Stesichorus presents a scattering of our familiar themes.[16] He was also killed by robbers, one more innocent poet killed unjustly far from home. He used the animal fable for political blame, to oppose the power of a general or tyrant.[17] The fable argued against awarding the already powerful general a bodyguard.

---

[11] Herodotus 1.23; Plutarch *Dinner of the Seven Sages* 18 (160e–162b); Aelian *On Animals* 12.45; Bowra 1963 (which discusses Aelian at length); Csapo 2003:91–92. For the theme of poet as protected by the gods, see Falter 1934:94. The theme is explicit in Plutarch. "He fully realized that his rescue had been guided by God's hand" (162a, trans. Babbitt), παντάπασιν αἰθέσθαι θεοῦ κυβερνήσει γεγονέναι τὴν κομιδήν.

[12] Falter 1934:94.

[13] *Fables* 194, cf. Falter 1934:94.

[14] For hero cult awarded Arion, see Herodotus 1.23 (statue); Clay 2004:130.

[15] Bowra 1963:131–132 lists example of men saved by dolphins who help to establish cult, which brings Hesiod to mind. Historical examples on p. 131. Bowra believes that Arion's story is connected with cult in some way, p. 133, perhaps in his association with dithyrambic performance.

[16] On his life, testimonia in Davies 1991:134; Campbell 1991:39–43; see also Maas 1929:2459–2460; Vürtheim 1919; West 1971; Lefkowitz 1981:31–35. The dates for his life are separated by centuries, and some conclude that there were two (or three) poets named Stesichorus.

[17] For the general, Phalaris, see Aristotle *Rhetoric* 2.1393b (test. 8D); for the tyrant, Gelon, see Conon FGH 26 F1.42 (test. 10D). Cf. Demetrius *On Style* 99.

A horse, whose pasturage is destroyed by a deer, asks a human for help. The man offers help provided he can mount the horse; the horse agrees, the man mounts, and the horse finds he has received slavery instead of deliverance. This took place at Himera, Stesichorus' home, in Sicily; thus there is a hint of tension with his native city.[18]

There was also tension with Pallantium in Arcadia, from which he was exiled. "Others say that he went to Catana when banished from Pallantium in Arcadia, and there died."[19]

The occasion of his famous palinode to Helen was his abuse of Helen: "They say that for writing abuse [*psogon*] of Helen he was struck blind, but received his sight again on writing an encomium of her, the palinode, in obedience to a dream."[20] This is a peculiar mixture of themes: the blindness of the poet; the consecration of the poet through dream; blame as productive of consecration and praise. Pausanias, on the other hand, tells us that Helen sent Stesichorus the message explaining his blindness from an isle of heroes (a "white island") through a warrior who had been wounded and had come to the isle to be healed by Ajax on the instructions of Delphi.[21] Burkert connects this story with the legends of the Greek pre-Socratic wonder-working shaman philosophers.[22]

Stesichorus' poems, though lyric, were largely concerned with "great wars and famous chieftains."[23] His power as a poet is attested by the story that through his poetry he pacified a civil strife.[24] He was killed, along with a flute player named Aeschylus, by a professional robber named Hicanus.[25] He had a substantial tomb near a gate at Catana, which was named after him, a detail characteristic of hero cult.[26] Emily Kearns writes that "the hero at the gate," is typical of the "protector hero"—"No doubt the sacred guardianship of gates

---

[18] Cf. West 1971:302–303.

[19] *Suda* s.v. Stesichorus (test. 19D): οἱ δὲ ἀπὸ Παλλαντίου τῆς Ἀρκαδίας φυγόντα αὐτὸν ἐλθεῖν φασιν εἰς Κατάνην κἀκεῖ τελευτῆσαι.

[20] *Suda* s.v. Stesichorus: φασὶ δὲ αὐτὸν γράψαντα ψόγον Ἑλένης τυφλωθῆναι, πάλιν δὲ γράψαντα Ἑλένης ἐγκώμιον ἐξ ὀνείρου, τὴν παλινῳδίαν, ἀναβλέψαι. See also Plato *Phaedrus* 243a–b. Plato refers to the Palinode as "an ancient mode of purification [*katharmos arkhaios*]."

[21] Pausanias 3.19.12–13 (test. 40D); cf. West 1971: 303; Conon FGH 26 F1.18 (test. 41D); Hermias on Plato *Phaedrus* 243a (test. 42D). Cf. Detienne 1957:141.

[22] Burkert 1972:153n182.

[23] Quintilian 10.1.62: *maxima bella et clarissimos canentem duces.*

[24] Diogenes Babylonius fr. 84 *ap.* Philodemus *On Music* 18 Kemke (test. 12D); Wilamowitz-Moellendorff 1956:235; Huxley 1962:64, 71; West 1971:303. Cf. below on Thaletas, ch. 16.

[25] *Suda* s.v. *epitēdeuma* (test. 44D). He is identified as a *kitharōidos*, one who sings to the lyre.

[26] *Suda* s.v. Stesichorus; Pollux 9.100; Clay 2004:152. Heroes at the gate: see below on Simonides, this chapter; and on Solon, ch. 11.

has much to do with 'goings out and comings in,' with the special qualities of boundaries."[27] Mythical figures such as Oedipus, Amphion, and Zethus also received cult at gates; as did the soldiers who fell at Plataea.[28] It is difficult to understand why a poet should be viewed as a protector important enough as to receive such cult; but militaristic, savior poets such as Tyrtaeus or Solon would fit the logic of the phenomenon neatly.

So we have, once again, a blame poet in conflict with a strong political leader; he is exiled at some point in his career; he uses animal fables for blame. He is murdered far from home by a robber, and receives a special form of hero cult. This life is notable in that there is very little in his poetry that seems to have anything to do with it.

Simonides

Simonides is another example of a poet protected from death by the gods.[29] Callimachus has Simonides say, "nor yet had he [a general who pulls down Simonides' tombstone] any fear of you brethren, O Polydeuces, who made me, alone of all the guests, pass out before the roof fell, when the house at Crannon came down alas! upon the mighty Scopadae."

> οὐδ' ὑμέας, Πολύδευκες, ὑπέτρεσεν, οἵ με μελάθρου
> μέλλοντος πίπτειν ἐκτὸς ἔθεσθέ κοτε
> δαιτυμόνων ἄπο μοῦνον, ὅτε Κραννώνιος αἰαῖ
> ὤλισθεν μεγάλους οἶκος ἐπὶ Σκοπάδας.

> Callimachus *Aetia* fr. 64.11–14Pf, trans. Edmonds

Cicero tells the complete story:

> gratiamque habeo Simonidi illi Ceo, quem primum ferunt artem memoriae protulisse. dicunt enim, cum cenaret Crannone in Thessalia Simonides apud Scopam fortunatum hominem et nobilem cecinissetque id carmen quod in eum scripsisset, in quo multa ornandi causa poetarum more in Castorem scripta et Pollucem fuissent, nimis illum sordide Simonidi dixisse se dimidium eius ei, quod pactus esset, pro illo carmine daturum; reliquum a suis Tyndaridis quos aeque laudasset peteret si ei videretur. paulo

---

[27] Kearns 1989:54.
[28] See Clay's discussion at 2004:96.
[29] For his life, see testimonia in Campbell 1991:344ff, 375–379; Molyneux 1992.

post esse ferunt nuntiatum Simonidi ut prodiret; iuvenes stare ad
ianuam duo quosdam, qui eum magno opere evocarent; surrex-
isse illum, prodisse, vidisse neminem. hoc interim spatio conclave
illud ubi epularetur Scopas concidisse; ea ruina ipsum cum cognatis
oppressum suis interisse.

I thank that Cean Simonides, whom they say first excelled in the
art of memory. For they say that when Simonides was dining with
Scopas, a wealthy and noble man, at Crannon in Thessaly, and the
poet had sung a song which he had written about him, and in which,
for the sake of embellishing in the manner of poets, much had
been written as if to Castor and Pollux, Scopas said in a very stingy
fashion [*nimis ... sordide*] that he would give half of that which
had been agreed upon [*quod pactus esset*] for that poem; Simonides
should ask the rest from his Tyndarides, if he didn't mind, whom he
had praised equally. Not long afterward they say it was announced
to Simonides that he should go forth, as a certain two youths were
standing at the door, who called him out in a vehement way. He
arose, went out, and saw no one. Meanwhile, during this interval,
that chamber where Scopas was dining fell down, and, flattened by
the wreckage, he died, along with his friends.

Cicero On Oratory 3.86[30]

In a gruesome twist, all of the corpses are so crushed as to be unrecognizable,
but Simonides is able to identify them because he remembered exactly where
each person had been placed at the feast.

This story fits into the pattern of divine protection of the poet, and
vengeance against his enemies. But more importantly, the archaic theme of
the niggardly patron is combined with it.[31] The vengeance of the gods is swift:
the patron who reneges on full payment of his fees is summarily executed. The
theme of oath breaking, as in the lives of Archilochus, Hipponax and Alcaeus,
is also here. This is the type of story poets might tell to protect their own
interests. And in fact, there is a purely mythical antecedent to this theme, the

---

[30] My trans. Cf. Quintilian 11.2.11; Ovid *Ibis* 511; Valerius Maximus 1.8. ext.7 (following Cicero, see
Oates 1932:3); Phaedrus 4.25 (following Quintilian); Aelian. fr. 63 H. = *Suda* s.v. Simonides; Oates
1932:2–4; 7–12; Falter 1934:94–95; Page 1962:510, 242–244; Molyneux 1971:197–205 (further
bibliography, ancient and modern, 197–198); Slater 1972:232–240 (who dates the story to at
least the school of Aristotle, 238); Lefkowitz 1981:55–56; Molyneux 1992:121–126.

[31] See above, ch. 2 (Aesop); below, ch. 26 (Juvenal); ch. 17, on the poets Cridenbel and Aniér
MacConglinne.

story of the seer Melampus, who is imprisoned and treated cruelly by a female guard. He divines that his jail is going to collapse by supernatural means (he overhears two woodworms discussing the weakness of a roofbeam), prevails on his captors to remove him from the building, which collapses, killing the cruel guard. (So we have themes of the mantis applied to the poet, himself mantislike, or perhaps a seer in his own right.)[32]

Though Lefkowitz characteristically derives the story of Simonides and Scopas from misinterpreted allusions in Simonides' own poetry, it is more likely that it was a common, archaic story that was applied to Simonides. Also of interest in the story is the tension between poet and political leader. At other periods of Simonides' life, he worked in harmony with rich patrons such as the tyrant Hipparchus in Athens.[33]

Another Simonidean story of tension between poet and patron again feels archaic. Here Simonides complains because he is not given a share of roast hare as were the other guests of the tyrant Hieron.[34] In Homer, a proper feast is an equal, just division.[35] The feast defines social standing and justice; the feast may logically be the occasion for excluding the poet from justice, just as in the Scopas story.

---

[32] Pherekydes FGH 3 F33. Further parallels and examples of houses caving in may be found in Slater 1972:238. As happens so often, this theme is shared with the athlete-heroes' lives, see Fontenrose 1968:102. Both may have inherited the theme from mantic mythology. It is possible that Simonides referred to this incident in his poetry, or to something like it, see Quintilian 11.2.11, who discusses variations in the details of the Scopas story, and supports one variant by citing Simonides himself: "as Simonides himself seems to indicate in a certain passage" (trans. Gerber), *ut ipse quodam loco significare Simonides videtur*. But this appears to be an allusion, not a retelling of the story by the poet. Cf. Oates 1932:10.

[33] "Plato" *Hipparchus* 228c; Molyneaux 1992:65–80.

[34] Chamaeleon, at Athenaeus 14.656c–d = fr. 33 of Wehrli 1969; cf. *Thebaid* fr. 3, in Allen 1912 5.113; West 2003b:46; Bell 1978:30.

[35] *Odyssey* iii 66; *Iliad* XIX 179–180, cf. above, ch. 2, for sacrificial aspects of the feast in the Aesop *vita*; Burkert 1983:37–38; Nagy 1979:125–141. The theme of the poet demanding a correct portion of a feast has archaic dimensions. For instance, the bad poet Cridenbel always demands the best portions of his patron's feast, see below chapter 17; cf. above on Hesiod, ch. 6; Nagy 1979:231. Significantly, Chamaeleon (see previous note) has no sympathy for Simonides: the poet was "a skinflint and sordidly greedy of gain" (κίμβιξ . . . καὶ αἰσχροκερδής). Again, the justice of the poet's cause may depend on the point of view of the narrative. Cf. Plato *Republic* 1.331e, where Simonides is referred to as a "wise and divine man," σοφὸς γὰρ καὶ θεῖος ἀνήρ, and Cicero *The Nature of the Gods* 1.22, "Simonides, of whom tradition speaks not only as a delightful poet but in all respects a learned and wise man" (*Simonidem . . . [non enim poeta solum suavis, verum etiam ceteroqui doctus sapiensque traditur]*); cf. Bell 1978:77. We seem to have parallel negative and positive traditions, a common phenomenon in poetic biography. Cf. above on Archilochus, ch. 3; and below, ch. 17, on Aithirne and other ambiguously malevolent poets.

Still another story of supernatural protection explains how the poet avoids a shipwreck. He finds an anonymous, unburied corpse on the seashore, and piously gives it its last rites. The body's ghost, out of gratitude, warns the poet against embarking on a sea voyage he had planned. Simonides heeds the warning, and tries (unsuccessfully) to convince his fellow passengers to stay behind also. Not surpisingly, there is a tremendous storm, a shipwreck, and all of the ship's passengers die. The poet then writes an epitaph for his unknown savior.[36]

Again—like Aesop, Sappho, Socrates, and Hipponax—Simonides was reputed to be ugly.[37] He also, like Aesop, Homer, and Hesiod, was associated with riddles.[38] Like Stesichorus, he was reputed to have prevented a war by reconciling inimical rulers.[39] There is an emphasis on his tomb in the literature—which according to Callimachus, speaking in the poet's voice, "the citizens of Acragas threw up for me before their city in awe of Zeus the Hospitable." This suggests hero cult,[40] and attributes of deity protecting hospitality are especially appropriate for cult awarded to poets.[41]

---

[36] *Palatine Anthology* 7.77; scholia to Aristides, 3.533 (Dindorf = p. 201 Frommel); Cicero *On Divination* 1.27.56–57, 2.66.135, Libanius 8.42 (Foerster); Tzetzes *Chiliades* 1.619–639; Valerius Maximus 1.7.ext. 3. See also Wilamowitz-Moellendorff 1893:7–8; Oates 1932:4–6; Pease 1963:194.

[37] Plutarch *Themistocles* 5.

[38] Chamaeleon fr. 34 Wehrli/Athenaeus 14.456c (see above), cf. Bell 1978:59n118; Lefkowitz 1981:54.

[39] Timaeus (*ca.* 356–260 BC), quoted by a scholiast on Pindar *Olympic Odes* 2.29d; Molyneaux 1992:224.

[40] Callimachus *Aetia* fr. 64: ἐμόν κοτε σῆμα, τό μοι πρὸ πόληος ἔχ[ευ]αν / Ζῆν'] Ἀκραγαντῖνοι Ξείνι[ο]ν ἁζόμενοι. Clay 2004:152 insightfully suggests that this might have been a "tomb at the gate," see on Stesichorus above. According to the *Suda*, a general tears down the tomb to fortify the city (which suggests that it was a substantial structure), and it is at that spot that the city is taken.

[41] Cf. the "gods of hospitality" in the story of Hesiod's death.

8

Sappho: The Barbed Rose

O NE WOULD NOT EXPECT SAPPHO, who was associated largely with delicate love poetry, to have a *vita* that would resemble the patterns followed by the Aesop and Archilochus *vitae*. Yet, though she does not have as full a dossier of the scapegoat hero cult themes as do Aesop and Archilochus, and her life is not as (folklorically) well documented as theirs, even so, certain themes in her *vita* link her to the familiar pattern. Though the greater part of her poetry dealt with exquisitely evoked love, yet there was a definite current of blame running through her poetic corpus. And Archilochus shows that the satiric muse is not necessarily divorced from poetic sophistication. The poet can take the archaic categories of praise and blame and exploit them with high artistic skill. Love can obviously inspire praise poetry,[1] but since it often produces such emotions as loss, betrayal, and bitterness, it can also inspire blame. (Archilochus' Lycambid poetry resulted from "failed love," a broken engagement.) Perhaps praise is always balanced by blame in the structure of the archaic mind. Archilochus writes, "I know how to love my friend, but I also know how to hate [and revile?] my enemy."[2] The transposition of this ethical formulation to the field of poetry is praise and blame, love poetry and hate poetry: one would expect Sappho to be a satirist part of the time if she had enemies, as she did. A similar dualistic formulation is found in her fr. 5V.6–7, where Sappho prays that her brother be a joy to his friends, a [grief] to his enemies.

---

[1] See e.g. 23V, 34V (with test. III), 16.17–20. Texts of Sappho and Alcaeus are from Voight 1971, unless otherwise noted. Translations are from Campbell 1982, unless otherwise noted. Themistius 13 p. 170d speaks of Sappho and Anacreon giving unbounded praise to their lovers, cf. Dover 1978:174; Naafs-Wilstra 1987:276–277. Sappho could also praise patron divinities, notably Aphrodite (1V).

[2] ἐπ]ίσταμαί τοι τὸν φιλ[έο]ν[τα] μὲν φ[ι]λεῖν[, / τὸ]ν δ' ἐχθρὸν ἐχθαίρειν τε [κα]ὶ κακο[(23W.14–15). Archilochus can also write, "And I know one big thing, how to return terrible evils upon the man who treats me badly" (ἒν δ' ἐπίσταμαι μέγα, / τὸν κακῶς <μ'> ἔρδοντα δεινοῖς ἀνταμείβεσθαι κακοῖς, 126W). Cf. 201W: "The fox knows many things, but the porcupine one big thing" (πόλλ' οἶδ' ἀλώπηξ, ἀλλ' ἐχῖνος ἓν μέγα). See Campbell 1983:120–121.

Sappho and Blame

The extent of the blame found in Sappho is at first glance surprising, as is her ability to express such themes with her characteristic delicacy and sensitivity. Sappho's satirical side has not gone unnoticed, but it will be useful to view it as a totality, noting continuities with the larger blame tradition, before considering her *vita*.[3]

According to the *Suda*, Sappho wrote iambics, unfortunately not extant.[4] This implies satirical subject matter—as West remarks, "Invective was clearly regarded as the outstanding feature of the genre." We recognize iambus "in explicitly sexual poems, in invective which goes beyond the witty banter we found in elegy, and in certain other forms of vulgarity."[5] Philodemus informs us that Sappho writes some poems "satirically" or "iambically" (*iambikōs*).[6] One hopes that someday some of Sappho's iambics may be discovered on papyrus.

Sappho's extant blame poetry divides itself neatly into four categories. First, there are three sets of victims: her wayward brother, Charaxus, and his lover, the courtesan, Doricha; Sappho's rivals, especially Gorgo and Andromeda; and her pupils/lovers/friends who have deserted her. Then there are traditional abuse elements in her epithalamia.

One of the earliest historical references to Sappho deals with her, Charaxus, and Doricha (Rhodopis), and it portrays Sappho as a satirist. After telling a folkloric tale of Rhodopis erecting a pyramid by plying her trade, Herodotus tells us that she "was ransomed for a vast sum by Charaxus, a Mytilenaean . . . brother of Sappho the poetess . . . Charaxus, after ransoming Rhodopis, returned to Mytilene, and Sappho in her poetry [*en meleï*] thoroughly mocked [*polla katekertomēse*] him."[7] LSJ defines *katakertomeō* as 'rail violently'. This captures the strength of the word, with its intensifying *kata-*, but as Page notes, the more exact meaning is 'mock, taunt, jeer at'. Thus, this verb, with *polla* added, is very strong: "Sappho mocked him violently."

---

[3] See Page 1955:131–138 (a somewhat unsympathetic treatment), Burnett 1983:212.

[4] *Suda* s.v. Sappho (test. 236V).

[5] West 1974:25.

[6] *On Poems* 2 fr. 29 (p. 252 Hausrath). As Burnett notes, this statement refers to "temper," not "meter," Burnett 1983:211n11.

[7] Herodotus 2.135 (test. 254aV): ἐλύθη χρημάτων μεγάλων ὑπὸ ἀνδρὸς Μυτιληναίου Χαράξου . . . ἀδελφεοῦ δὲ Σαπφοῦς τῆς μουσοποιοῦ . . . Χάραξος δὲ ὡς λυσάμενος Ῥοδῶπιν ἀπενόστησε ἐς Μυτιλήνην, ἐν μέλεϊ Σαπφὼ πολλὰ κατεκερτόμησέ μιν. Curiously enough, this is the same passage in which Herodotus witnesses to Aesop's slave parentage and his being killed by the Delphians. According to Herodotus, Rhodopis was "a fellow-slave of Aesop the story-writer" (σύνδουλος δὲ Αἰσώπου τοῦ λογοποιοῦ).

Charaxus seems to have resented his sister's poetry, at least according to later biographical tradition. Sappho is a moral preceptress in one of Ovid's *Heroines* (15.63–68), where the Ovidian Sapphic persona grieves over her ne'er-do-well brother: "My idle brother burned, captured by the love of a harlot, and he has suffered losses, mixed with foul shame . . . And he hates me because I have admonished him well and faithfully many times."[8] Later in the poem, Charaxus rejoices when Sappho suffers unrequited passion for Phaon (15.117–120). If these elements reflect Sapphic poetry, they show how poetry can serve to broadcast shame (*turpi . . . pudore*), and how blame poetry can exist on a high moral plane—Sappho is, in essence, calling her brother to repentance.[9] Though, unfortunately, the poems in which Sappho mocked Charaxus are not extant, there are some Sapphic poems that reflect the strained relationship and contain elements of blame. In 5V, Sappho prays for her brother's safe homecoming, and mentions his former sins, which she hopes he will atone for: "may he atone for all the things which he formerly did wrong" (ὄσσα δὲ πρ]όσθ' ἄμβροτε πάντα λῦσα[ι). She also hopes, in line 9, that he will give her honor, which hints that he has not treated her well. This is not mocking satire, but rather moralizing blame, putting the sins of a brother in public view.

Not surprisingly, Sappho seems to have attacked Doricha also. Athenaeus speaks of the courtesan, "whom fair Sappho attacked [*diaballei*] with her poetry . . . when she became the lover of Sappho's brother, Charaxus and caused him to lose much wealth."[10] In 15V, Sappho prays that Doricha "find you, Cypris, very harsh" (Κύ]πρι κα[ί σ]ε πι[κροτάτ]αν ἐπεύρ[οι), and that she may not boast of having made Charaxus fall in love with her again.

Fragments 5V and 15V give valuable confirmation to the situation described by Herodotus and Ovid. Charaxus is a fairly close parallel to Hesiod's Perses: both men have become impoverished after possessing substantial sums of money;[11] both are lazy.[12] Perhaps a wayward brother is a conventional

---

[8] *arsit inops frater meretricis captus amore / mixtaque cum turpi damna pudore tulit. . . . me quoque, quod monui bene multa fideliter, odit.*

[9] She speaks with *pia lingua* (*Heroines* 15.68) in admonishing him. For other moralizing Sapphic poetry, cf. 158V. For the moral force of archaic Greek satire, see Jaeger 1945 1.121–124; Elliott 1960:11n20; above, chs. 3 and 4 on Archilochus and Hipponax.

[10] See 13 (596b–c) (test. 254cV): ἦν ἡ καλὴ Σαπφὼ ἐρωμένην γενομένην Χαράξου . . . διὰ τῆς ποιήσεως διαβάλλει, ὡς πολλὰ τοῦ Χαράξου νοσφισαμένην.

[11] Perses seized the greater part of the inheritance, *Works and Days* 37–38, but later is reduced to begging, 394–404. Charaxus is "made poor" (*factus inops*) by Doricha, Ovid *Heroines* 15.65, after he "evilly cast away" his money, 15.66.

[12] Charaxus is *iners* (*Heroines* 15.63); Perses is inclined to waste his time lounging around the law courts, *Works and Days* 27–29.

poetic theme.[13] It would be odd for a family member to broadcast the sins and foolishness of a family member under normal circumstances.

It is notable that there is another brother whom Sappho praises. Sappho "often praises" (*pollakhou . . . epainei*) Larichus because he pours wine in the Mytilenean prytaneum.[14] The two brothers form a neatly symmetrical symbolic range for Sappho's praise and blame.

The last two categories of Sappho's blame poetry, her rivals and "students," place us firmly in the middle of a fascinating and intricate culture we still know too little about, a world of women, poets, surrounded by groups of young women, living separately, it seems, from normal walks of life. Beyond this, and even in this, there are many points of controversy. One wonders how religious these organizations were, to what extent the relationships between the leaders of the groups and the younger women were spiritual or sexual, if these groups were finishing schools or poetry appreciation groups. I will not try to solve such problems here, but for convenience I will use a teacher-student frame of reference,[15] though there were obviously sexual and religious dimensions to whatever the Sapphic circle, whether it was formal or informal, might have been. The poems we will examine show that the emotions involved in the culture—feelings between leader and follower, animosity between rival leaders—were very intense.

Maximus of Tyre compares Sappho to Socrates: "What the rival craftsmen [*hoi antitekhnoi*] Prodicus and Gorgias and Thrasymachus and Protagoras were to Socrates, Gorgo and Andromeda were to Sappho. Sometimes she censures [*epitimai*] them, at other times she cross-examines [*elegkhei*] them, and she uses irony [*eirōneuetai*] in the same way that Socrates did."[16] Sappho's frag-

---

[13] See Hunt 1981:32–33; Nagy 1979:312. For further on Charaxus, see Benedetto 1982.

[14] Athenaeus 10.425a = 203aV.

[15] Lesky 1966:144–147 gives an overview of these controversies. For the groups as educational *thiasoi*, see Fraenkel 1975:175; Lesky only partially agrees (146). For Wilamowitz's view of the groups as schools, see Lesky 1966:144; Page strongly disagrees (1955:128), but new evidence inclines Dover (1978:174–175) to regard Sappho as leader of a school of music and poetry, preparing young women for choral performance in festivals. Burnett (1983:15) accepts the school scenario. See also Calame 1977:62, 367–372; 368n17; 420–438. Gentili (1988:72–89), following Calame, sees Sappho's circle as a kind of female homosexual *thiasos* worshipping Aphrodite and the Muses with song and ritual, including a kind of initiatory marriage ritual. Parker (1996) insists that there was no formal teacher–student relationship between Sappho and her circle, though he agrees that Sappho taught music performance to members of her group. Parker is entirely successful in dispelling modern "schoolmistress" ideas of Sappho, but less successful in arguing against possible ancient ideas of educational relationships. He argues for a *hetairia* setting for Sappho's poetry; it is hard to imagine a poet of Sappho's gifts not being the leader of the group.

[16] Maximus of Tyre 18.9 (test. 219V): καὶ ὅ τι περ Σωκράτει οἱ ἀντίτεχνοι Πρόδικος καὶ Γοργίας καὶ

ments, scanty as they are, support Maximus' evaluation. Athenaeus, quoting 57V, writes, "Sappho derides [*skōptei*] Andromeda":

> τίς δ' ἀγροΐωτις θέλγει νόον . . .
> ἀγροΐωτιν ἐπεμμένα στόλαν . . .
> οὐκ ἐπισταμένα τὰ βράκε' ἔλκην ἐπὶ τῶν σψύρων;

> And what farm-girl bewitches your heart . . .
> Clothed in rustic garb . . .
> Not knowing how to draw her robe over her ankles?[17]

Here, Sappho derides a farm-girl directly; she attacks Andromeda indirectly by satirizing her lover, a technique used in later satire, as by Catullus (*Odes* 6), who mocks Flavius by imagining what diseased prostitute (*quid febriculosi scorti*) he must be sleeping with secretly. Sappho is much more restrained and delicate, but the same theme is here.

Andromeda is mentioned in two other fragments. In one (131V), Sappho reproaches Atthis for flying off to Andromeda; in the other (133V), there is a note of gloating irony: "Andromeda has a lovely recompense" (Ἔχει μὲν Ἀνδρομέδα κάλαν ἀμοίβαν . . .). One can imagine something bad happening to Andromeda (a favorite's departure?) and Sappho needling her over the failure.

We have a few scant lines of poetry remaining that were dedicated to Gorgo, Sappho's other chief opponent. Page describes them as "unfriendly."[18] In one, 213V, a woman, Archeanassa, is called "wife" or "yoke-mate" (*sundugos*) of Gorgo. Oddly enough, given Sappho's later reputation, this could be a negative reference to a homosexual relationship.[19] Fragment 144V tells us of people "who have thoroughly had their fill of Gorgo" (μάλα δὴ κεκορημένοις / Γόργως . . .).

Perhaps the unnamed rival of fr. 55V is either Gorgo or Andromeda; all we know of her is that she was wealthy, uncultured, and ignorant, in Sappho's eyes:[20]

> κατθάνοισα δὲ κείσηι οὐδέ ποτα μναμοσύνα σέθεν
> ἔσσετ' οὐδὲ †ποκ'† ὔστερον· οὐ γὰρ πεδέχηις βρόδων

Θρασύμαχος καὶ Πρωταγόρας, τοῦτο τῇ Σαπφοῖ Γοργὼ καὶ Ἀνδρομέδα· νῦν μὲν ἐπιτιμᾷ ταύταις, νῦν δὲ ἐλέγχει καὶ εἰρωνεύεται αὐτὰ ἐκεῖνα τὰ Σωκράτους.

[17] Athenaeus 1.21b–c, see further testimonia in Voigt 1971.

[18] Page 1955:134.

[19] For Sappho and homosexuality, see Dover 1978:174–179; Snyder 1997, and see below, this chapter. For a different interpretation of this word, see Gentili 1988:76.

[20] According to Plutarch *Table Talk* 3.2 (646E); *Advice to Bride and Groom* 145f–146a, probably reflecting Sappho.

τὼν ἐκ Πιερίας, ἀλλ᾽ ἀφάνης κἀν Ἀίδα δόμωι
φοιτάσηις πεδ᾽ ἀμαύρων νεκύων ἐκπεποταμένα.

But after you have died, you will lie there, neither will there
be any remembrance of you,
neither desire for you afterwards. For you have no part in the
roses
of Pieria, but unseen, in the house of Hades,
you will wander among the dim dead, having flown away
from us.

This is almost equivalent to a curse, though expressed in Sappho's exquisite language; it predicts the worst possible fate for a poet, oblivion; Hipponax 115W similarly wishes the worst fate possible for Hipponax's enemy, though here the fate precedes death.[21] The emphasis on the memory of the rival totally disappearing is notable; she will also be invisible, *aphanēs*. Marcel Detienne has shown how blame is connected with forgetfulness in the structure of Greek thought; this poem is a clear example of that thesis, with obscurity (parallel to forgetfulness in Detienne's list of linked opposites) thrown in for good measure.[22]

Finally, some of Sappho's poetry is turned against former students/ lovers. As was noted previously, the deep emotions of love can be transformed into feelings of hurt, betrayal, or hatred when a relationship is severed; in Archilochus, the poetic response to such feelings is savage blame. The poetic response in Sappho is also blame, but expressed more delicately than in Archilochus. In fact, the theme of betrayal and suffering after friendship and love is a central theme in both poets' work. Sappho's two most complete poems, 1 and 31, are both grieving responses to loss of a loved one. In 1.19– 23, a lost lover "wrongs" Sappho, will not accept her gifts, and does not love Sappho anymore: "Who wrongs you, O Sappho?" (τίς σ᾽, ὦ / Ψά]πφ᾽, ἀδικήει;). Such an accusation of injustice is squarely in the blame tradition; in Hipponax 115W/194Dg, the poet wishes the worst on his enemy, then explains that "he wronged me" (*hos m᾽ ēdikēse*). Also related to the satiric tradition is the poet's chronicling of his/her sufferings.[23] In fr. 31V, Sappho apparently agonizes as

---

[21] For the incantatory quality of Sappho's poetry, cf. Segal 1947; Portulas 1983.

[22] Detienne refers briefly to this poem, 1973:23n78. Sappho also boasts that, blessed by the Muses, "there would be no forgetfulness [*lēthē*] of her when she was dead" (οὐδ᾽ ἀποθανούσης ἔσται λήθη). Aristides *Orations* 28.51 (test. IV *ad* 55V, cf. 32V = 193 LP).

[23] See e.g. Archilochus 223W, where the poet must show how much he has been hurt before he retaliates with poetry. For the concept of injustice in Sappho's poem, see Rivier 1967. Cf. also

she watches her former lover linked to a male husband/lover. The parting takes a terrible toll on her, and the famous physical symptoms described in the poem are a result.[24] Archilochus' treatments of the agonies of love, 191W and 193W, are somewhat comparable to Sappho 1 and 31 in their use of physical symptoms to express suffering. Some of the diction is similar: *khalepēisi . . . oduneîsin*, cf. *khalepan . . . ek merimnan* (193W.2/1V.25–26); *kardiēn . . . stētheōn*, cf. *kardian en stēthesin* (191W.1,3/31V.6). In both poets, love causes blindness (31V.111/191W.2); there is psychic dislocation, madness (191W.3/1V.18).[25]

A number of other Sapphic fragments describe the departure of beloved companions to rival camps, 16V.15–16; 130.3–4V, 49V. In 130V, Atthis has flown off to the Sappho's archrival, Andromeda; in 49V, Sappho refers to Atthis as graceless, *akharis*, when a child. This could be affectionate reminiscing, or it could be bitter in tone, reminding Atthis what Sappho had done for her, how ignorant and untalented she had been before meeting her teacher. A fragment addressed to Mica (71V) has invective that puts it firmly in the satirical tradition: "Mica . . . but I will not allow you . . . you chose the friendship of the women of the house of Penthilus[26] . . . you wicked person [*ka[ko]trop'*]" ( ]μισσε Μίκα /]ελα[. . ἀλ]λά σ' ἔγωὐκ ἐάσω /]ν φιλότ[ατ'] ἤλεο Πενθιλήαν[/]δα κα[κό]τροπ'). Fragment 155V evidently contains irony directed at a lover, though whether it is a farewell or a greeting is uncertain.[27]

Finally, there are elements of traditional mockery in Sappho's epithalamia.[28] Demetrius, commenting on 110–111V, explains that Sappho "mocks [*skōptei*] . . . the boorish bridegroom and doorkeeper."[29]

Sappho's complaint that those to whom she has done good sin most against her, 26 LP, cf. Campbell 1982:76. For the broken oath in Sappho, cf. Calame 1977:368–369; chs. 3 and 4 above (Archolochus and Hipponax); and ch. 9 below (Alcaeus). For interpretations of the ritual background of this poem see Calame 1977 and Nagy 1996:98–99.

[24] On this poem, see Segal 1974; a survey of interpretation in Burnett 1983:232.

[25] Cf. Snell 1953:52–54, for other Archilochean–Sapphic parallels.

[26] This is the house into which Pittacus, Alcaeus' opponent (70V, 75V) married. There is some evidence that Sappho was in exile at the same time Alcaeus was, thus possibly allied with him politically, see Campbell 1982:xv. Cf. fr. 98V.

[27] The source of the fragment, Maximus of Tyre 18.9, specifically describes this line as ironic; Page interprets it as a farewell, but cf. possible evidence for the fragment as a greeting, 1955:135n11.

[28] See 103–117V; 31V; 44V; T 234V, cf. Catullus 61, 62, 64.323–381; Fraenkel 1975:173; Burnett 1983:216–224. Killeen (1973:197) suggests that there is an ithyphallic bridegroom in the last line of 111.

[29] *On Style* 167 (test. III at 110V): σκώπτει . . . τὸν ἄγροικον νυμφίον καὶ τὸν θυρωρὸν.

The *Vita*

Thus, satire, mockery, even invective were not at all foreign to Sappho. Such a poetess, compared in antiquity to Socrates for her verbal admonitions and irony, could very easily incur the enmity of Lesbian high society, just as Socrates gained the enmity of certain prominent Athenians.

And in many ways, Sappho follows the pattern for blame poets we have already seen. She was the worst. She was reported to be very ugly, as were Aesop and Hipponax: "In appearance she seems to have been contemptible [[eu]kataphronētos] and quite ugly [duseidestatē[n]], being dark in complexion and of very small stature."[30] Her homosexuality was reportedly also a cause for recrimination.[31]

She was also the best: she was judged to be the best of women poets. "I know of no woman who even came close to rivalling her as a poet," writes Strabo.[32] She was sacred, and boasts that "the Muses had made her truly blessed and enviable";[33] she describes herself as one who serves the Muses: "For it is not right that there should be lamentation in the house of those who

---

[30] *P. Oxy.* 1800, fr. 1¹ (test. 252V): τὴν δὲ μορφὴν [εὐ]καταφρόνητος δοκεῖ γε[γον]ένα[ι κα]ὶ δυσειδεστάτη[[ν]], [τ]ὴν μὲν γὰρ ὄψιν φαιώδης [ὑ]πῆρχεν, τὸ δὲ μέγεθος μικρὰ παντελῶς. Cf. bibliography in Campbell 1982:3n5; Maximus of Tyre 18.7, Ovid *Heroines* 15.31–36.

[31] *P. Oxy.* 1800 (see preceding note): "She has been accused by some of being irregular in her ways and a woman-lover"(κ[α]τηγόρηται δ᾿ ὑπ᾿ ἐν[ί]ω[ν] ὡς ἄτακτος οὖ[σα] τὸν τρόπον καὶ γυναικε[ράσ]τρια). *Suda* s.v. Sappho (test. 253V): "She had three companions and friends . . . and she got a bad name for her impure friendship with them" (ἑταῖραι δὲ αὐτῆς καὶ φίλαι γεγόνασι τρεῖς . . . πρὸς ἃς καὶ διαβολὴν ἔσχεν αἰσχρᾶς φιλίας). Cf. Porphyrio *On the Epistles of Horace* 1.19.28 (test. 260V): "she is maligned as having been a tribad" (*tribas diffamatur fuisse*), and Seneca, *Epistles* 88.37 (test. 244V), on Sappho as a prostitute. As Dover remarks, none of this tradition precedes Hellenistic times (1978:174); he concludes, though, that Sappho and her circle practiced homosexual love (182). Was Sappho blamed for it? We know she was blamed by Hellenistic times, by other cities and cultures. For different attitudes, disapproving and tolerant, toward homosexuality in Greece, see 185–195. Surprisingly, Plato, in the *Laws*, 636ab, has an Athenian embarrass a Spartan by saying that the sexual pleasure shared by males with males, or females with females, "seems to be contrary to nature, a crime of the first order, committed through inability to control the desire for pleasure," as quoted by Dover 1978:186. The fact that Plato specifies female homosexuality is worthy of note. Dover (1978:190) suggests that this passage seems to contradict the *Symposium*. Apparently, respectable Spartan women had accepted homosexual relationships with young girls (1978:173). Female homosexuality was somewhat of a taboo subject in Greek culture, but see ibid. See also, Calame 1977:62, 367–372; 368n17; 420–438.

[32] Strabo 13.2.3 (test. 264V), cf. Scholiast O on Aeschylus *Persians* 883; Eusebius *Chronicles*, Olympiad 45.1. (test. 249V); Antipater, in *Palatine Anthology* 7.15, quoted in Campbell 1982:47; Sappho fr. 106V.

[33] Aristides *Orations* 28.51 (test. IV at 55V): αὐτὴν αἱ Μοῦσαι τῷ ὄντι ὀλβίαν τε καὶ ζηλωτήν.

serve the Muses. That would not be fitting for us."[34] She is frequently associated with the Muses, and was in fact called the tenth Muse.[35] As a writer of love poetry, she is, of course, strongly associated with Aphrodite;[36] Alcaeus perhaps calls her "holy [*agna*]."[37]

Sappho was exiled, living for a while in Sicily, according to the *Parian Marble*: "From when Sappho sailed away in exile from Mytilene to Sicily." The reasons for the exile are obscure, but political tensions with the house of Penthilus could reasonably have caused it. As Andromeda and Gorgo were linked to the Penthilidae, tensions with her rivals might have been related to the political problems.[38]

Like Aesop and Hipponax, Sappho is ugly; like Hipponax, she is at one point exiled. Finally, Sappho's legendary death assimilates her even more closely to the *pharmakos*, as she dies voluntarily, like Aesop, throwing herself from a cliff. Strabo writes, of the white cliff of Leucas:

ἔχει δὲ τὸ τοῦ Λευκάτα Ἀπόλλωνος ἱερὸν καὶ τὸ ἅλμα, τὸ τοὺς ἔρωτας παύειν πεπιστευμένον· οὗ δὴ λέγεται πρώτη Σαπφώ, ὥς φησιν ὁ Μένανδρος, τὸν ὑπέρκομπον θηρῶσα Φάων', / οἰστρῶντι πόθῳ ῥῖψαι πέτρας / ἀπὸ τηλεφανοῦς ἅλμα κατ' εὐχήν / σήν, δέσποτ' ἄναξ. ... ἦν δὲ καὶ πάτριον τοῖς Λευκαδίοις κατ' ἐνιαυτὸν ἐν τῇ θυσίᾳ τοῦ Ἀπόλλωνος ἀπὸ τῆς σκοπῆς ῥιπτεῖσθαί τινα τῶν ἐν αἰτίαις ὄντων ἀποτροπῆς χάριν.

It contains the temple of Apollo Leucatas, and also the "Leap," which was believed to put an end to the longings of love. "Where Sappho is said to have been the first," as Menander says, "when through frantic longing she was chasing proud Phaon, to fling herself with a leap from the far-seen rock, calling upon thee in prayer, O lord and

---

[34] 150V: οὐ γὰρ θέμις ἐν μοισοπόλων <δόμωι> / θρῆνον ἔμμεν' <......> οὔ κ' ἄμμι πρέποι τάδε. Cf. fr. 32V.

[35] Plato, in *Palatine Anthology* 9.506, Catullus 35.16, cf. Campbell 1982:49n1.

[36] E.g. frr. 1, 2, 5, 15, 22, 33V. Cf. Segal 1974:159. See also Page 1955:126–128; Nagy 1973:175–177.

[37] Fr. 384V, see Crit. app. Cf. Ferrari 1940:33–53; Gentili, "Holy Sappho," in Gentili 1988:216–222: "the greeting presents itself as a reverent tribute to the sacral dignity of the poetess as ministrant of Aphrodite" (222); Burnett 1983:276n130.

[38] *Parian Marble*, ep. 36 (Jacoby 1904:12) (test. 251V): ἀφ' οὗ Σαπφὼ ἐγ Μυτιλήνης εἰς Σικελίαν ἔπλευσε φυγοῦσα. Cicero tells us that a statue of Sappho stood in the Syracusan town hall, *Against Verres* 2.4.125–127. See also, for the exile, fr. 98V(b), Campbell 1982:125; 71V. Cf. Bauer 1963; Seibert 1979:283; Gentili 1988:81; Campbell 1982:xi, xv. Either Andromeda or Gorgo was a Penthilid: 71V.3, see above; Gentili 1988:261n42. Page remarks on the scantiness of political allusions in Sappho's poetry (1955:131); 71 and 98 contain nearly the sum total of the politics in Sappho's extant verse.

master." . . . It was an ancestral custom among the Leucadians, every year at the sacrifice performed in honor of Apollo, for some criminal to be flung from this rocky look-out for the sake of averting evil [though he was saved from drowning by boats waiting below].

Strabo 10.2.8–9 (test. 211V), trans. H. Lloyd-Jones[39]

So Sappho killed herself in a fashion characteristic of the *pharmakos*,[40] and in a cult site in which criminal *pharmakoi* were expelled from land to sea. She dies calling upon Apollo (apparently), as did Aesop. As in the case of the death legends of Aesop and Hesiod, this death legend could be an *aition* for ritual practice.

Sappho was often honored with coins and statues after her death. In addition, Alcidamas wrote that the Mytilenaeans honored [*tetimēkasi*] Sappho, even though she was a woman, which in the context of the passage probably refers to hero cult.[41]

There may be hints of the divine persecutor-patron theme in Sappho's relationship with Aphrodite, for she prays to her frequently,[42] yet in the Leucas legend dies of unrequited love, presumably a product of Aphrodite.[43] The theme of madness is also in Sappho's *vita*, for Sappho is driven to her death leap by "goading desire" (*oistrōnti pothōi*), according to Menander.[44]

---

[39] Cited more fully in Campbell 1982:23. Cf. Anacreon 376; Euripides *Cyclops* 166–167; *Suda* s.v. Sappho, second notice (test. 211aV); Ovid *Heroines* 15, esp. 160ff.; Segal 1974; Burnett 1983:272 (further bibliography, 272n117); Campbell 1982:22n1. Cf. Nagy 1973 (to the best of my knowledge, Nagy nowhere mentions the *pharmakos* aspects of the Sappho's death; he sees Indo-European myth behind Phaon); Houbaux 1923. In Anacreon 376, we have another form of drunkenness to place beside war drunkenness and mantic drunkenness: love drunkenness (*methuōn erōti*); see also Ibycus fr. 6 Page. Cf. Sappho 1V.18.

[40] As Gernet notes, "the victim of the Leap from Leukas . . . can be considered a *pharmakos*" (1981:133). See also Hughes 1991:160–161.

[41] Aristotle *Rhetoric* 1398b, cf. Clay 2004:150–151. See also Farnell 1921:367; 421–426; Sappho seated in shrine, see Wroth 1975–1983, pl. 39.11; pp. 200, lxx–lxxi. Julius Polydeukes, in Pollux 9.84 (the Mytilenaeans put Sappho on their coins); Aristides *Orations* 12.85; Cicero *Against Verres* 2.4.125f., a bronze statue of Sappho by Silanion (mid-fourth century BC) in the prytaneion at Syracuse; Campbell 1982:13n1; Richter 1965 1.70–72; Heintze 1966.

[42] See above on fr. 1.

[43] For love/Aphrodite as persecutor-patron in Latin poetry, see below, ch. 23 (Ovid).

[44] Fr. 258, in Strabo *Geography* 10.2.9 (test. 211aV), cf. *oistraō* LSJ s.v.: "sting, sting to madness; go mad, rage." See also Mattes 1970:105, 110. This word is used by Plato in his discussion of madness, *Phaedrus* 251d, cf. *Republic* 573e; *Theaetetus* 179e. For the symbolism of the goad used in a description of madness and prophetic possession, see Virgil *Aeneid* VI 78–80, 100–101. Cf. the symptoms of fr. 31V, discussed in McEvelley 1978; Tsagarakis 1986, 1979; Privitera 1969; Manieri 1972; Burnett 1983:239–241; 1V.18; Ovid *Heroines* 15.176.

Though Sappho's *vita* is unfortunately fragmentary, important pieces of the puzzle are still there to fit her into the legendary pattern of the poet as scapegoat—most significantly, the *pharmakos* death.[45] Then, the ugliness fits into the pattern, and her sacrality, her partial satirical/blame poetry function, her exile, and (probably) hero cult.[46]

---

[45] There was a tradition that a woman *pharmakos* was expelled in Athens, Hesychius s.v. *pharmakoi*. Legendary scapegoats, such as Aglauros, were often young women.

[46] So the following themes can be found in the life of Sappho: 4, she is the worst, 4d, ugly, 4c, a sinner; 5, she is also the best, 5a, sacred; 8, her death is voluntary; 10a, she is exiled; 11, she dies, 11b, leaping from a cliff; 13, she subsequently receives hero cult (perhaps); 18, she may have a divine persecutor-patron, Aphrodite; 19, she suffers madness; 22, her poetry has a satirical/blame component, including the themes of 22d, artist satirizing artist and 22e, the curse.

9

Alcaeus: Poetry, Politics, Exile

LCAEUS IS AN IMPORTANT TRANSITIONAL FIGURE in this study, because with
the *vita* of Alcaeus we seem to leave legend or legend-embroidered
history and enter firmly into history. The events in his life, as reflected
in his poetry, even though they concern jockeyings for power among rival
clans and tyrants in a relatively unimportant island, still have the feeling of
authenticity, the ring of sordid, unromanticized truth.[1] Perhaps as a result,
Alcaeus' *vita* lacks the rich cultic associations we found in the lives of Aesop,
Archilochus, and Hesiod (unjust death, pollution, hero cult, and so on).

Yet a number of the important themes found in the other poets' lives
can still be found in Alcaeus'. The essential combination—a poet using abusive
language, then punished, excluded from the community—is there. This may
serve as a warning not to regard the lives of Archilochus or even of Aesop as
entirely nonhistorical. The myths may be elaborations on the social realities;
but the social realities may have also helped shape the myths. The social mech-
anism that drives satirical poets into exile is ancient, powerful and recurrent.

Alcaeus, though he did not have the reputation of being primarily a sati-
rist, as did Archilochus, used satirical attacks as a significant part of his poetic
language. This abuse was directed largely at two tyrants of Mytilene, Myrsilus
and Pittacus.[2] Strabo writes, "Alcaeus abused [*eloidoreito*] him [Pittacus] and the
rest alike, Myrsilus and Melanchrus and the Cleanactids and others."[3] Aristotle,
as cited by Diogenes Laertius, concurs: "Pittacus was assailed [*ephiloneikei*] by

---

[1] See Podlecki 1984; Snell 1961:29–34; though compare Page 1955:159. For the historical back-
ground of Alcaeus, see Page 1955:149–159; Berve 1967; Andrewes 1956; Rösler 1980:26–33;
Boruhovi 1981.

[2] Quintilian *Training in Oratory* 10.1.63 (test. 21C); cf. *Palatine Anthology* 9.184.7f., Maximus of Tyre
37.5. For tyrants in the ancient Greek world, see Berve 1967 (91–95 on Lesbos); Andrewes 1956
(92–99 on Lesbos); Fileni 1983. Further bibliography in Rösler 1980:26.

[3] Strabo 13.2.3 (test. 468V): Ἀλκαῖος μὲν οὖν ὁμοίως ἐλοιδορεῖτο καὶ τούτῳ καὶ τοῖς ἄλλοις,
Μυρσίλῳ καὶ Μελάγχρῳ καὶ τοῖς Κλεανακτίδαις καὶ ἄλλοις τισίν.

... Antimenidas and Alcaeus."[4] According to Diodorus Siculus, Alcaeus "had been his [Pittacus'] confirmed enemy and had reviled him most bitterly [*pikrotata leloidorēkota*] by means of his poems."[5] Julian reports that Alcaeus, like Archilochus, used invective to alleviate his hardships.[6] Even the "ship of state" allegorical poems can be classified as attacks on tyrants, for Alcaeus compares the oppressive evils of the tyrants to storms at sea.[7]

There is an interesting tradition that Alcaeus' abusive poetry was so powerful that it caused his targets to leave Mytilene. A scholiast on Horace, commenting on Horace's reference to Alcaeus' "threatening songs" (*Alcaei minaces . . . Camenae, Odes*, 4.9.7) writes, "The songs of Alcaeus are called 'threatening' because he was so bitter that he drove many people from the state by the harshness [*austeritate*] of his poetry."[8] Another Horatian scholiast reports that Alcaeus actually drove Pittacus from Mytilene at one time: "He waged wars against tyrants, and drove out Mytilenaen Pittacus, after Pittacus had been conquered."[9] Though this is obviously late evidence, it is still an interesting example of the theme of the poet's ability to create exiles, to make scapegoats. Fragment 298V, which discusses how the Greeks, who were on the point of stoning the sacrilegious Locrian Ajax, erred in not killing him,[10] evidently suggests that Pittacus be hanged and stoned, like a *pharmakos*. "[Best] fasten a noose around his neck / and finish him with stones!"[11] One thinks of Archilochus' victims hanging themselves; and of the principle we suggested earlier, that a poet becomes a scapegoat through his power for making others scapegoats. To wish stoning upon a powerful enemy may bring it upon oneself.

The curse, the usual concomitant of blame poetry, makes a passionate appearance in Alcaeus' poetry:

---

[4] Diogenes Laertius 2.46 (test. 471V): ἐφιλονείκει . . . Πιττακῷ Ἀντιμενίδας καὶ Ἀλκαῖος.

[5] Diodorus Siculus 9.12.3 (test. 8C): ἐχθρότατον αὐτοῦ γεγενημένον καὶ διὰ τῶν ποιημάτων πικρότατα λελοιδορηκότα . . .

[6] Julian *Beard-Hater* 337ab. Cf. Davies 1985; Fraenkel 1975:192–193; Burnett 1983:156–181. See also 429V, and passim in this section for other poetic abuse of Pittacus.

[7] Heraclitus *Allegories* 5 (test. I *ad* 208V). See also fr. 6V; and below on Theognis, ch. 10.

[8] Porphyrio *ad* Horace *Odes* 4.9.5–8 (test. 23C). *minaces autem Alcaei Camenae dicuntur, quonium adeo amarus fuit ut austeritate carminis sui multos civitate eiecerit.*

[9] "Acro" on Horace *Odes* 1.32.5, cf. Keller 1967:116. *Hic etiam res bellicas aduersus tyrannos gessit et Pittacum Mytileneum uictum expulit.* My trans.

[10] For mythology as a source of abuse, see Davies 1985:37; cf. Tarditi 1969:96.

[11]]ην δὲ περβάλον[τ᾽ ἀν]άγκα<ι> / αὔ]χενι λαβολίωι π . [. .]αν· (298V); see the interpretation of Lloyd-Jones 1968; Rösler 1980:204–221; Gallavotti 1970; Burnett 1983:198. For stoning, see also 68V; Rösler 1980:214n248; and above, ch. 1. For hanging, cf. above on Archilochus, ch. 3.

… ἄ[γι]τ' εὔνοον
θῦμον σκέθοντες ἀμμετέρα[ς] ἄρας
ἀκούσατ', ἐκ δὲ τῶν[δ]ε μόχθων
ἀργαλέας τε φύγας ῥ[ύεσθε·

τὸν Ὕρραον δὲ πα[ῖδ]α πεδελθέτω
κήνων Ἐ[ρίννυ]ς ὥς ποτ' ἀπώμνυμεν
τόμοντες ἄ [
μηδάμα μηδ' ἔνα τὼν ἑταίρων

* * *

κήνων ὁ φύσγων οὐ διελέξατο
πρὸς θῦμον ἀλλὰ βραϊδίως πόσιν
ἔ]μβαις ἐπ ὀρκίοισι δάπτει
τὰν πόλιν ἄμμι…

Come, with gracious spirit hear our prayers [*aras*], and rescue us
from these hardships and from grievous exile [*phugas*]; and let their
Avenger pursue the son of Hyrrhas [Pittacus], since once we swore
[*apōmnumen*], cutting … never (to abandon?) any of our comrades
… but Pot-belly [Pittacus] did not talk to their hearts; he recklessly
trampled the oaths underfoot and devours [*daptei*] our city.

129V.9–16, 22–24[12]

This poem, which shows how the Greek word *ara* can mean both prayer and
curse,[13] exhibits Alcaeus defending the sanctity of the oath, a common theme
(and there are clear echoes of Hipponax here).[14] It also gives us an example of
invective targeting Pittacus.[15]

The verb *daptō*, 'devour', is used only of animals in Homer (lions, jackals,
wolves, dogs); elsewhere (296aV.8) Pittacus is a lion, certainly not for the

[12] Trans. Campbell. Cf. 112V; Rösler 1980:191–204; Burnett 1983:150, 158, 160–161.

[13] Cf. Rösler 1980:194; and above, ch. 3.

[14] For the theme of oath breaking, cf. ch. 3; Davies 1985:37 (parallels from oratory, e.g. Dinarchus
1.47; Demosthenes 19.126, 191). For the importance of the oath in the *hetaireia*, see Plescia
1970:78. Often these groups were called *sunōmosiai*. For religious sanctions on oath breaking,
86. Of course, oaths generally included invocation of a god and a curse if the oath was broken,
11–12; Herodotus 6.86. For curses repaying oath breaking, Watson 1991:57; chs. 3 and 4 above
(Archilochus and Hipponax).

[15] For Pittacus as "pot-belly," see Diogenes Laertius 1.81, quoted in Campbell 1982:428. According
to Alcaeus, Pittacus was also "drag-foot," "chap-foot," "prancer," "big-belly," "dusky-diner,"
(because he did not light a lamp at dinner) and "well-swept" (per Diogenes, "because he was
slovenly and dirty").

modern heroic qualities of the lion.[16] Though Alcaeus' blame does not explicitly use fables, as did Aesop and Archilochus, animal imagery is frequent in his abusive characterizations. In 69V.6–7, Pittacus (probably) is a "wily fox" (*alōpa*[/ *poik*[*i*]*lophrōn*).

However, the poet's abusive language was also directed, in a milder, friendly form, against the fellow *sumpotai* of the *hetaireia* 'drinking club, oath-bound political faction, *Männerbund*' he was associated with. In an important book, Wolfgang Rösler suggests that Alcaeus' poetry was written entirely for this audience.[17]

Thus, Alcaeus was a satirist, in part, attacking important political figures, which often leads to exile. The fragments of biography we have refer to a series of exiles undergone by the poet. Alcaeus spends a "first exile" in Pyrrha.[18] *P. Oxy.* 2506 refers to a second exile and perhaps a third.[19] We know that Alcaeus went to Egypt at some time.[20] Aristotle writes that "the Mytilenaeans once chose Pittacus to act against the exiles led by Antimenidas and the poet Alcaeus."[21]

It is uncertain what role the poet's abusive poetry may have played in these exiles. It seems reasonable to assume that it would have been a contributing factor; membership in unsuccessful political factions obviously would also be a factor. As we have seen, the Horace scholiast, at least, reported that Alcaeus was "so bitter that he drove many people from the state by the harshness of his poetry."[22] Another scholiast tells us that the poet "had been driven out [*pulsus esset*] by Pittacus, the tyrant of his city, because he was exhorting

---

[16] For this type of abuse generally, see Koster 1980 Index s.v. *Tiervergleich*; for its use in Alcaeus, see Davies 1985:36; Burnett 1983:163; 165n18; 162n10. Cf. the use of animals in the misogynist blame poetry of Semonides, for which, see Jaeger 1945 1.122; Nagy 1979:315n6. Aesop is described with animal features, see ch. 2. This type of abuse is found in Homer, see Faust 1970:25; Faust 1969:69, 109n204.

[17] See Rösler 1980; Bremmer 1990; Burnett 1983:141–143; Nagy 1996:85. "Blame of this loving and ironical sort was easily practiced and easily accepted because it was an intra-mural sport in which satirist and satirized might change places at any moment" (Burnett 1983:143).

[18] Scholia *ad* 114V, see Campbell 1982:286: "in the first exile" (κατὰ τὴν φυγὴν πρώτην), Alcaeus and his friends, after plotting against Myrsilus, were discovered, and to avoid prosecution, escaped to Pyrrha.

[19] 306A e, V. This papyrus, a commentary on Alcaeus, is dated to the first or second century AD.

[20] Strabo 1.2.30, 432C.

[21] *Politics* 1285a, 470V (trans. Campbell): εἵλοντό ποτε Μυτιληναῖοι Πιττακὸν πρὸς τοὺς φυγάδας, ὧν προειστήκεσαν Ἀντιμενίδης καὶ Ἀλκαῖος ὁ ποιητής. See also "Acro" *ad* Horace *Odes* 2.13.28 (Alcaeus gathers an army and wins a battle against the Mytileaneans); *P. Oxy.* 2506, 306V, e.4–5, 12–13. Burnett 1983:113–115; see Campbell's notes to T 4C and 9C.

[22] Porphyrio *ad* Horace *Odes* 4.9.7 (Alcaeus' poems are menacing, *minaces*) (p. 152 Holder), T 23C. Cf. Horace *Epistles* 1.19.28–33, where Horace denies that Alcaeus would commit poetic murder like Archilochus.

the Mytilenaeans to the love of liberty."[23] This was possibly, in part, poetic exhortation, political protreptic poetry, such as Tyrtaeus or Solon used, and if it preached liberation from a tyrant, it must have attacked the tyrant, and so it is reasonable to connect this reference to Alcaeus' abuse of specific tyrants. Thus a reasonable supposition, supported by some late evidence (and scholiastic evidence can never be automatically discounted), allows us to tentatively suggest that Alcaeus may have been exiled in part for his poetic attacks on tyrants.

Alcaeus' exiles and their misery formed a major theme in his poetic corpus. Horace identifies a major Alcaeic theme as "the evil hardships of exile [*dura fugae mala*]."[24] In fr. 129.11–12V, quoted above, Alcaeus prays to his gods: "rescue us from these hardships and from grievous exile." In a poem entirely about exile and its misery (130Va,b), he laments:

> . . . ὀ τάλαις ἔγω
> ζώω μοῖραν ἔχων ἀγροϊωτίκαν
> ἰμέρρων ἀγόρας ἄκουσαι
> καρυ[ζο]μένας ὦ (Ἀ)γεσιλαΐδα
>
> καὶ β[ό]λλας· τὰ πάτηρ καὶ πάτερος πάτηρ
> κα<γ>γ[ε]γήρασ' ἔχοντες πεδὰ τωνδέων
> τὼν [ἀ]λλαλοκάκων πολίταν
> ἔγ[ω ἀ]πὺ τούτων ἀπελήλαμαι
>
> <u>φεύγων</u> ἐσχατίαισ', ὡς δ' Ὀνυμακλέης
> ἔνθα[δ'] οἶος ἐοίκησα λυκαιμίαις[25]
>]ον [π]όλεμον . . .

---

[23] "Acro" ad Horace *Odes* 2.13.28 (i 179 Keller), T 7C, *a Pittaco tyranno civitatis suae pulsus esset, eo quod Mytilenensibus amorem libertatis suaderet.*

[24] *Odes* 2.13.28. Cf. Favorinus, *On Exile* 9.2 (test. 452V).

[25] For this word, Page suggests 'wolf-thicket man'. According to Haslam (1986:123), the correct reading is -*aikhm*-. This would translate as something like 'wolf man', 'wolf-spearman' (nominative), or 'wolf battles' (dative or accusative plural), which Haslam prefers. He is followed by Lefkowitz and Lloyd-Jones 1987. The word could refer to the loneliness of the wolf, or to his trickiness in battle (Lefkowitz and Lloyd-Jones, cf. Euripides *Rhesus* 208–248), depending on reading and interpretation. Relying purely on context, wolf as lone exile would be preferable, though in line 11, the word [*p*]*olemon* is found. Whichever interpretation is correct, the *luk*-'wolf' element of the word is not in doubt. If the word refers to the wolf in a war context, it could also refer to his ferocity, cf. the Homeric word for battle fury, *lussa*, which probably is connected to *lukos* 'wolf' (Ernout 1949). Cf. for another interpretation of the etymology, de la Vega 1952. See *Iliad* XVI 158–163, 352–355 with Janko's notes *ad loc.*, 1992:338, cf. 361–362.

See also Rösler 1980:280n392; Page 1955:205; Burzacchini 1976: 47; Latte 1947:142; Burzacchini 1986.

I, poor wretch, live with the lot of a rustic, longing to hear the assembly being summoned, Agesilaidas, and the council: the property in possession of which my father and my father's father have grown old among these mutually destructive citizens, from it I have been driven, an exile [*pheugōn*] at the back of beyond . . ., and like Onomacles I settled here alone in the wolf-thickets (?) (leaving the?) war.[26]

In line 10, Alcaeus refers to himself as wolflike in his exiled state. The wolf is a common symbol for the exile, the loner, the outcast, and has strong links with the *Männerbund* and initiate—often the initiate is required to undergo a period of exclusion (as in the Spartan Crypteia), in which he lives like an animal in the wilderness, sometimes even "becoming" a wolf.[27]

Louis Gernet attempts an association of the Greek *pharmakos* with wolf symbolism, with some success.[28] The criminal Hero, who can be linked to the *pharmakos* complex (like Aesop, he is both stoned and then receives cult from his killers)[29] is portrayed as wearing the skin of a wolf, and is called

---

[26] Trans. Campbell. Cf. 130aV, 131V, 132V, 148V.

[27] For further on the wolf as liminal, an exile, scapegoat, initiate, see Burkert 1983 sect. II, "Werewolves Around the Tripod Kettle," 83–134, esp. 90–91; 88n26; Buxton 1987:63–64; Page 1955:206; Bremmer 1982:141n35; 144; Gerstein 1974; Schmidt 1927 13.2 col. 2228. For the Krypteia, see Jeanmaire 1939:550–569; Burkert 1985:262nn16–17; Kershaw 2000. See also, on wolves and wolf symbolism: Mainoldi 1984; Eliade 1975:81–83, 72, 109, bibliog. 156; Burnett 1983:53; Nagy 1979:83; Bremmer and Horsfall 1987:31, 41, 43; Gershenson 1991.

In view of the persistent connection of the *pharmakos* with Apollo and Delphi, the associations of the wolf with Delphi are worth noting. See Gershenson 1991:1–23. Aelian (*On the Characteristics of Animals* 12.40) wrote that the Delphians "honor/worship [*timōsi*]" the wolf, cf. Burkert 1983:120. According to a legend in Aelian, a wolf tracked down sacred gold of Delphi that had been stolen; because of this, a bronze statue of a wolf was shown at Delphi, Pausanias 10.14.7. The Delphians came from Lykoreia, 'wolf-mountain' (10.6.2); cf. Callimachus, fr. 62Pf.; *Hymn* 2.18–20; Strabo 9.418.3; Apollonius *Argonautica* 4.1490; *Parian Marble*, FGH 239 A 2,4; Euphorion fr. 80.3 in Powell 1925:44. For Leto as a she-wolf, Aristotle *History of Animals* 6.35, 580A; Aelian *On the Characteristics of Animals* 4.4. Why the wolf is connected with the mantic is a matter of much speculation; Burkert has an interpretation involving sacrifice. However, it is possible that, once again, the wolf may be a symbol of madness, which is related to mantic madness, cf. Eliade 1975:72: "The Scandinavian berserker 'heats' himself in his initiatory combat, shares in the sacred frenzy or *furor* (*Wut*), behaves at once like a beast of prey and a shaman . . . To behave like a beast of prey—wolf, bear, leopard—betokens that one has ceased to be a man, that one incarnates a higher religious force, that one has in some sort become a god." For further on the wolf, including the connections between wolf, männerbund, and warrior, see below, ch. 17, on Finn as poet and outlaw; ch. 18, on the wolflike appearance of poet-warrior Starkaðr, and Suibhne living among wolves; ch. 19, on the berserker phenomenon.

[28] Gernet 1981:132n81; 133n86. See also Ogden 1997:41–42.

[29] For stoning, Pausanias 6.6.7; *Suda* s.v. *Euthumos*. Miralles and Portulas, 1988:134 and 1983:53–63, link the *pharmakos* with the cult of Lycian Zeus.

Lycas.[30] The Athenian hero Lycus became a wolf, as did the athlete-hero Damarchos.[31]

Thus, we have our central pattern, moreover in a fairly solid historical, nonlegendary manifestation: an eloquent political satirist is exiled, in part at least (so it appears) for his abuse of a powerful political figure. One could argue that he was exiled for purely political reasons; but this would probably betray a modern view of the separation of poetry and politics. In archaic Greece, the poem could act as campaign speech and newspaper editorial.[32] If we have an ancient Greek politician who abuses his political enemies in poetry, it is difficult to separate poetic and political factors.

Like Archilochus, Alcaeus was known as a soldier.[33] Horace speaks of him as "brave in war" (*ferox bello*), and he sang of Dionysus, the Muses, and Aphrodite even "still amid the fighting" (*tamen inter arma*).[34] War was a major theme in his poetry.[35] Athenaeus describes the poet as "excessively warlike" (*mallon tou deontos polemikos*).[36] Fragment 140V glorifies the armor and weapons hanging in an ancestral hall, and Athenaeus, quoting the poem, tells us that, even though Alcaeus was thoroughly "devoted to the Muses if ever anyone was, [he] puts manly achievements before poetic achievements, since he was warlike to a fault."[37] Fragment 400V tells us that it "is a fair thing to die for Lord Ares" (τὸ γὰρ / Ἄρευι κατθάνην κάλον). The *hetaireiai* that Alcaeus celebrated were essentially drinking clubs that created solidarity of the warrior group.[38] Alcaeus, like Archilochus, is the realistic sort of soldier who will run from his armor in battle to save himself.[39] There is a tradition that Alcaeus died in battle.[40]

---

[30] Pausanias 6.6.11. Cf. Rohde 1925 1:153–154.

[31] Harpocration, *dekazōn*; Pausanias 6.8.2, cf. Fontenrose 1968:89, for whom this transformation represents the "madness of the hero" theme.

[32] See below on Solon, ch. 11; Anhalt 1993:135–139; Fraenkel 1975:218, an elegy by Solon "is therefore a substitute for a speech in the popular assembly."

[33] See 6V.1, 12–14 for paraenesis in Alcaeus' poetry.

[34] *Odes* 1.32.4. For this association of Dionysus and war, see above on Archilochus, ch. 3.

[35] Horace *Odes* 2.13: *dura fugae mala, dura belli.*

[36] Athenaeus 14.627a–b, cf. 140C.

[37] Ἀλκαῖος ... εἴ τις καὶ ἄλλος μουσικώτατος γενόμενος, πρότερα τῶν κατὰ ποιητικὴν τὰ κατὰ τὴν ἀνδρείαν τίθεται, μᾶλλον τοῦ δέοντος πολεμικὸς γενόμενος. Athenaeus 14.627a–b.

[38] Another association of war and Dionysos. See Rösler 1980; Burnett 1983:110n14; 121. Cf. fr. 140V, where we have singing in a hall of weapons; Bremmer 1982; Benveniste 1973:270; Trumpf 1973.

[39] 401B(V); Herodotus 5.95.

[40] 306A.e(V) = *P. Oxy.* 2506 fr. 98; cf. Lefkowitz 1981:37. Further on Alcaeus as soldier: Podlecki 1969.

Thus, Alcaeus was an exiled poet who expressed the theme of the misery of exile in his poetry. Like Archilochus he was, partially at least, a virulent satirist, and like Archilochus, he was also a soldier. Like Aesop and Archilochus, he came into conflict with political leaders. Like Archilochus, he used the curse in his poetry. The standard mythology of the poet, consecration, ritual death, and so on, is absent here, but the exile of the poet still remains. However often we come upon the poet's exile in the lives of the poets, we cannot automatically discount it as ahistorical: it may be the kernel of history which myth and folklore have been attracted to.

Thus, while it is possible to see the lives of the poets as almost entirely mythical, in the sense of nonhistorical,[41] it is also possible that there was an Aesop and an Archilochus, dominant figures in oral poetic tradition, who lived historical lives of exclusion, came into conflict with authority, then had these lives "heightened" by standard, traditional cult myth—as a tribute to their poetry, and because poet and poetry were seen as sacred in ancient Greece. Alcaeus was not awarded cult myth (at least none is attested), but the exclusion and conflict with authority remain.[42]

---

[41] Cf. Nagy 1982:52, 67.

[42] Themes: 10, Expulsion. 10a, Exile. 11a, Stoning is found in Alcaeus' poetry. 22, Satirical, blame themes. 22a1, Hanging is found in Alcaeus' poetry. 22b, Exiling through blame. 24, Conflict with political leaders. 26, Poet as soldier. 26a, Martial parainesis as poetic theme. 27, Exile as poetic theme. 28, Wolf imagery, linked to exile. Compared to earlier poets, a scanty list; but the satiric poet exiled is still here.

10

Theognis: Faceless Exile

THEOGNIS OF MEGARA is a shadowy figure whose poetry offers us some evocative hints about his life; one can only wonder if it is a real life or a stereotypical poet's life.[1] As early as Plato, we read of the "poet ... Theognis, a citizen of Megara in Sicily" (ποιητὴν ... Θέογνιν, πολίτην τῶν ἐν Σικελίᾳ Μεγαρέων, *Laws* 1.630a). Thus, we see that Theognis' poetry was well known in Plato's day, but that already Plato is wrong about an important detail of his life, as it is certain that the Theognidean corpus often refers to the mainland Megara.[2] It is possible that the Sicilian Megara was claiming Theognis when Plato visited Sicily. And, of course, the Theognidean corpus may have started with a single poet, Theognis perhaps, but then received later editings and additions, including possible Sicilian accretions to the Theognidea.

As usual, certainty about the historical validity of many details in the poet's life is impossible; the similarities to the life of Alcaeus are striking, almost suspicious. When such close similarities are found, one often suspects wandering themes.

However, despite these difficulties, we seem to find in the corpus a typical poetic situation: dissatisfaction with leaders, including poetic attacks on them, followed by the exile of the poet. There is tension between the poet and his native city: "And not yet have I been able to please all my townsmen" (24).[3] So he criticizes his town's political leaders:[4]

---

[1] See the scant testimonia on his life in Gerber 1999:166–175.

[2] See scholiast on the *Laws* passage. The *Suda* places Theognis in 544–541 BC, which is probably about one hundred years late, cf. Cobb-Stevens, Figueira and Nagy 1985:1; Figueira 1985:298; Oost 1973. For Theognis' native land and dubious historicity, see Figueira and Nagy 1985 passim; older studies, Hudson-Williams 1910:4–12, a useful gathering of the ancient data; Harrison 1902:268–305; Trever 1925:129n1. For Plato and Theognis, see Figueira 1985:112–158, 124–127. For the weak biographical tradition on Theognis, see ibid., 121–124.

[3] ἀστοῖσιν δ' οὔπω πᾶσιν ἁδεῖν δύναμαι.

[4] Cf. Okin 1985:17.

Κύρνε, κύει πόλις ἥδε, δέδοικα δὲ μὴ τέκηι ἄνδρα
   εὐθυντῆρα κακῆς ὕβριος ἡμετέρης.
ἀστοὶ μὲν γὰρ ἔθ' οἵδε σαόφρονες, ἡγεμόνες δὲ
   τετράφαται πολλὴν εἰς κακότητα πεσεῖν.
οὐδεμίαν πω Κύρν' ἀγαθοὶ πόλιν ὤλεσαν ἄνδρες·
   ἀλλ' ὅταν ὑβρίζειν τοῖσι κακοῖσιν ἅδηι,
δῆμόν τε φθείρωσι δίκας τ' ἀδίκοισι διδῶσιν
   οἰκείων κερδέων εἵνεκα καὶ κράτεος,
ἔλπεο μὴ δηρὸν κείνην πόλιν ἀτρεμίεσθαι
   μηδ' εἰ νῦν κεῖται πολλῆι ἐν ἡσυχίηι,
εὖτ' ἂν τοῖσι κακοῖσι φίλ' ἀνδράσι ταῦτα γένηται
   κέρδεα δημοσίωι σὺν κακῶι ἐρχόμενα.
ἐκ τῶν γὰρ στάσιές τε καὶ ἔμφυλοι φόνοι ἀνδρῶν
   μούναρχοί τε· πόλει μήποτε τῆιδε ἅδοι.

Kurnos, this city is pregnant, and I fear lest it bear a man
   to be a chastiser of our evil outrage.[5]
For these citizens are still wise, but the leaders
   have been turned to fall into much evil.
Men who are noble men have never destroyed a city, Kurnos;
   but when it pleases base men to commit outrages,
and they destroy the people and give judgments to the unjust
   for their own gain and power,
do not expect that city to be quiet for a long time,
   even though it remains in complete quiet now,
when to these evil men these things become dear,
   gains accompanied by public evil.
For from these things come conflicts and internecine murders
   and dictators. May such things never please this city.

                                                            39–52W

οὕνεκα νῦν φερόμεσθα καθ' ἱστία λευκὰ βαλόντες
   Μηλίου ἐκ πόντου νύκτα διὰ δνοφερήν,
ἀντλεῖν δ' οὐκ ἐθέλουσιν, ὑπερβάλλει δὲ θάλασσα
   ἀμφοτέρων τοίχων· ἦ μάλα τις χαλεπῶς
σώιζεται, οἷ' ἔρδουσι· κυβερνήτην μὲν ἔπαυσαν

---

[5] Verses 1081–1082B are very similar, but the second line changes: "Kurnos, this city is preg-
nant, and I fear lest it bears a man / who is violent [*hubristēn*], a leader of a harsh faction. / For
these citizens are still wise, but the leaders / have been turned to fall into much evil." Cf. Cerri
1968:8; Dovatus 1972; Trever 1925:127–128.

ἐσθλόν, ὅτις φυλακὴν εἶχεν ἐπισταμένως·
χρήματα δ' ἁρπάζουσι βίηι, κόσμος δ' ἀπόλωλεν,
δασμὸς δ' οὐκέτ' ἴσος γίνεται ἐς τὸ μέσον·
φορτηγοὶ δ' ἄρχουσι, κακοὶ δ' ἀγαθῶν καθύπερθεν.
δειμαίνω, μή πως ναῦν κατὰ κῦμα πίηι.

... because now we are borne along, throwing down white sails,
from the Melian sea through the dark night,
and they don't want to bale out water, and the sea is thrown up
above both sides of the ship. Indeed, a man
would only be saved with great difficulty, such things they do.
They stopped
the good steersman, who kept watch knowledgeably;
and they seize goods by violence, and order is lost,
and there is no equal division toward the common good;
and porters rule, base men above the noble.
I fear, lest somehow a wave swallow the ship.

671–680W

This use of ship and storm imagery to blame leaders is, of course, reminiscent of Alcaeus.[6]

Theognis attacks the Corinthian tyrants, the Cypselids, who ruled from 655 to 625 BC, ending the extant poem (891–894) with a curse:[7]

ὤ μοι ἀναλκίης· ἀπὸ μὲν Κήρινθος ὄλωλεν,
Ληλάντου δ' αγαθὸν κείρεται οἰνόπεδον·
οἱ δ' ἀγαθοὶ <u>φεύγουσι</u>, πόλιν δὲ κακοὶ διέπουσιν.
ὡς δὴ Κυψελιδῶν Ζεὺς ὀλέσειε γένος.

O defenseless me! Kerinthos has perished,
the fair plain of Lelantos is ravaged;
noble men are exiled [*pheugousi*], and base men run the city.
That Zeus might destroy the race of Cypselids!

Evidently Theognis was exiled himself: "I am Aithon by birth, and I have an abode [*oikō*] in well-walled Thebes since I have been exiled from my native

---

[6] See also 257–260; 291–292; 797–798; 855–856; 1081–1082b; 1203–1206. For Alcaeus' use of ship and storm allegory to criticize leaders, see above, ch. 9.

[7] For the curse, see above on Archilochus, ch. 3. For the historical background of this poem, cf. Figueira 1985:289–290. For the curse in Theognis, Watson 1991:66–69. Other curses in Theognis: 600–602, 869–872, 1087–1090, 341–350.

land" (1209–1210).[8] Nagy argues that *oikō* is burial, hero-cult diction, suggesting that Theognis/Aithon is "buried in Thebes as an exile from Megara."[9] This is a suggestive interpretation, though not yet certain. The misery of exile is a theme in Theognis' poetry: "Surely there is no friend and faithful comrade to an exile; and this is more painful than the exile itself" (209–210).[10] Poverty is a recurring Theognidean motif.[11] The poet's financial degradation may have been brought about by his exile—as has been pointed out previously,[12] poverty is often linked to the exile in archaic poetry.[13]

Theognis is not precisely a satirical poet, but he is moralizing, and uses blame as a tool.[14] Verses 600–602 constitute another curse poem: "[You were] stealing my friendship. Go to hell [*erre*], hated by the gods and faithless among men, you chill and clever snake that I nurtured in my bosom."[15]

> . . . κλέπτων ἡμετέρην φιλίην.
> ἔρρε θεοῖσιν <τ'> ἐχθρὲ καὶ ἀνθρώποισιν ἄπιστε,
> ψυχρὸν ὃν ἐν κόλπωι ποικίλον εἶχον ὄφιν.

Verses 341–350 form a curse poem that reminds one of Alcaeus, including appeal to divinity and prayer for vengeance:[16]

> ἀλλὰ Ζεῦ τέλεσόν μοι Ὀλύμπιε καίριον εὐχήν·
> δὸς δέ μοι ἀντὶ κακῶν καί τι παθεῖν ἀγαθόν·
> τεθναίην δ', εἰ μή τι κακῶν ἄμπαυμα μεριμνέων
> εὑροίμην. δοίην δ' ἀντ' ἀνιῶν ἀνίας·

---

[8] Trans. Nagy, in Figueira and Nagy 1985:76, Αἴθων μὲν γένος εἰμί, πόλιν δ' εὐτείχεα Θήβην / οἰκῶ, πατρῴας γῆς ἀπερυκόμενος. Nagy interprets Aithon as meaning 'burning [with hunger]', "an epithet suitable to characters primarily known for their ravenous hunger" (123).

[9] Nagy 1985:78. For the theme of the grave of the hero found far from his homeland, see above, Ibycus and Stesichorus, ch. 7; ch. 2 (Aesop) and ch. 6 (Hesiod).

[10] οὐδείς τοι φεύγοντι φίλος καὶ πιστὸς ἑταῖρος / τῆς δὲ φυγῆς ἐστιν τοῦτ' ἀνιηρότερον. Theognis 332a-b repeats this, changing it slightly. Having no reliable friend is "the most painful aspect of exile" (my emphasis): τῆς δὲ φυγῆς ἐστιν τοῦτ' ἀνιηρότατον. Theognis also instructs Cyrnus never to befriend an exile (333–334)!

[11] See 173–178; 181–182; 267–270; 277–278; 351–354; 383–392 (poverty is *mēter' amēkhaniēs* 'mother of perplexity', 385; *amēkhaniē* is a constant theme in these passages); 393–398; 523–526; 619–620; 649–652; 667–668; 683–686; 750–752; 903–930; 1062; 1114A–1114B; 1129.

[12] See above, ch. 3, Archilochus and ch. 6, Hesiod.

[13] See West 1974:69, who accepts Theognis and his poems as historical; he notes the similarity of the Theognis story, as derived from the poems, to the Alcaeus *vita*, 1974:71. For the experience of exile as expressed in Theognis' poetry, see Doblhofer 1987:24; cf. Seibert 1979:285–286.

[14] Cf. 1271–1272. On praise and blame in Theognis, see Cobb-Stevens 1985:173–174; cf. Theognis 873–876.

[15] Reading *hon* and *eikhon*, Sintenis; mss.: *hos* and *eikhes*. Cf. 894.

[16] Watson 1991:69.

αἶσα γὰρ οὕτως ἐστί, τίσις δ᾽ οὐ φαίνεται ἡμῖν
ἀνδρῶν οἳ τἀμὰ χρήματ᾽ ἔχουσι βίηι
συλήσαντες· . . .

* * *

τῶν εἴη μέλαν αἷμα πιεῖν· ἐπί τ᾽ ἐσθλὸς ὄροιτο
δαίμων ὃς κατ᾽ ἐμὸν νοῦν τελέσειε τάδε.

But fulfill my proper prayer, Zeus of Olympus;
and allow me to experience some good instead of evils.
May I die, if I do not find some rest from these evil
cares. May I give sorrows in return for sorrows.
For it is my allotted right that it should be thus, but I have
no vengeance
upon the men who own my wealth, after plundering it
by violence . . .
May I drink their dark blood, and may some good divinity arise
to accomplish these things as I desire them.

There may be influence here; on the other hand, both Alcaeus and Theognis may simply be following the ritual typology of the curse.[17]

We also find in Theognis such standard archaic and Alcaeic themes as military paraenesis[18] and a concern with the wickedness of oath breaking.[19] Theognis' poetry also shows an interest in the Muses and Apollo.[20]

West sums up what we can know of Theognis' purported life: "When we survey the whole evidence of the Cyrnus poems, Theognis takes on the colours of an Alcaeus: aristocratic witness of a demotic revolution, betrayed conspirator, and embittered exile."[21] On the other hand, it is possible that no "Theognis" ever existed, and that the Theognidean corpus was modeled on a typical poetic life. Whichever is true, once more, the poet, whether he be historical or legendary, is exiled.[22]

---

[17] Cf. Alcaeus 129V, see above, ch. 9; Murray 1965; Nagy 1985:81; Watson 1991:66. Seibert links this with the theme of exile (1979:285). The poem also has obvious echoes of Sappho 1, another impassioned prayer for redress.

[18] See 1003–1006; 865–868. Cf. *Suda* s.v. Theognis, which reports that Theognis wrote paraenetic poems, *parainetikas*; also Stephanus of Byzantium *Lexicon*, s.v. Megara; Dio Chrysostom 2.18.

[19] See 1139; 1195; cf. 811, 600–602; West 1974:69; see above on Archilochus, ch. 3.

[20] Muses: 15–18 (an invocation); 237–250; 769–770; 1055–1056. Apollo: 1–10. See Edmunds 1985α:96–111, 100–101.

[21] West 1974:71.

[22] Thus we have the following themes in Theognis' life: 10a, exile. 10b, death in a far country? 13, hero cult? 22, blame themes in poetry; 24, conflict with political leaders; 22e, curse as poetic theme; 26a, martial paraenesis as poetic theme. For such a shadowy *vita*, this is a fuller list than might be expected.

11

Tyrtaeus: The Lame General

VIRTUALLY ALL CRITICS AGREE that the story of Tyrtaeus, in which the lame Athenian schoolmaster is sent to the Spartans as a joke, only to become their general in the Second Messenian War, is unhistorical—a piece of Attic propaganda, perhaps, to account for the fact that the Spartans even produced a poet.[1] H. J. Rose is typical: "No attention need be paid to the absurd Athenian story . . . that he was an Athenian, still less to the absurder one . . . that he was lame Athenian schoolmaster."[2] But if the deceptively simple and amusing story of Tyrtaeus' Cinderella-type military career may seem trivial at first glance, we nevertheless find underlying it an almost classic expression of the radical exclusion of the poet—just as the Ionic *pharmakos* is driven out of the city because he is deformed and despised, so Tyrtaeus is excluded from Athens because he is lame, stupid, of low birth, and mad; he is in fact given to Sparta as a joke. While thus far, Tyrtaeus' assimilation to the scapegoat repeats an Aesopic, Hipponactian pattern, his assimilation to victorious warrior adds a unique twist to the pattern, linking him somewhat to Archilochus, Alcaeus, and Solon, and reflecting parallel aspects of the poet and warrior in archaic Greece.

The idea that Tyrtaeus was an Athenian was well known by the time of Plato. The kernel of the story is found in the *Laws* 1 (629a): "Let us cite Tyrtaeus

---

[1] For the Second Messenian War, with its accretions of legend, see now Ogden 2004. For the earliest sources on the war (starting with the received corpus of Tyrtaeus poetry), Ogden 2004:177–189. Much of our information on the war comes from Pausanias, who used historians and poets such as Callisthenes, Aristotle's nephew, executed by Alexander; Ephorus (ca. 405–330 BC); Philochorus (born before 340 BC); Myron of Priene (mid-third century BC?); and Rhianus (later third century BC?), author of a *Messeniaca*. The chronology of the war is problematic, but the most generally accepted hypotheses date the war in the mid or later seventh century BC, Ogden 2004:132. Some scholars have attempted to place Tyrtaeus in the fifth century BC, notably, Schwartz 1899. For the failure of such attempts, see Den Boer 1954:70n, cf. Ogden 2004:180. The acmes of the *Suda* and Jerome both place the poet in the 640–630 BC decade, test. 2–3, Gentili and Prato 1979.

[2] Rose 1960a:84n7.

as an authority, who was an Athenian by birth, but who became a citizen of the Lacedaemonians."[3] Lycurgus, speaking not much later, refers to the Tyrtaeus legend as being widespread among the Greeks: "For who of the Hellenes does not know that they [the Spartans] took Tyrtaeus as general from our city, with whom they conquered their enemies, and they organized the young men in military order, not only for the danger they were facing, but for all time, counseling well?"[4] If the story of Tyrtaeus as Athenian-born Spartan general is known by all the Greeks (not just the Athenians) by the time of Lycurgus, speaking in the fourth century, it obviously had a prehistory as an oral tale in at least the fifth century BC, and probably earlier.[5]

C. M. Bowra's suggestion that Plato invented the tale (which then was further embellished by Rhianus) thus seems untenable.[6] Even Plato's Athenian speaks as if the story is already well known. It is much more likely that the story started as an oral tradition which aligned neatly with the tendency for Sparta to import poets.[7]

Pausanias (4.15.6) gives a fuller account of the legend:

Ἐγένετο δὲ καὶ Λακεδαιμονίοις μάντευμα ἐκ Δελφῶν τὸν Ἀθηναῖον ἐπάγεσθαι σύμβουλον. ἀποστέλλουσιν οὖν παρὰ τοὺς Ἀθηναίους τόν τε χρησμὸν ἀπαγγελοῦντας καὶ ἄνδρα αἰτοῦντας παραινέσοντα ἃ χρὴ σφισιν. Ἀθηναῖοι δὲ οὐδέτερα θέλοντες, οὔτε Λακεδαιμονίους ἄνευ μεγάλων κινδύνων προσλαβεῖν μοῖραν τῶν ἐν Πελοποννήσῳ τὴν ἀρίστην οὔτε αὐτοὶ παρακοῦσαι τοῦ θεοῦ, πρὸς ταῦτα ἐξευρίσκουσι· καὶ ἦν γὰρ Τυρταῖος διδάσκαλος γραμμάτων νοῦν τε ἥκιστα ἔχειν δοκῶν καὶ τὸν ἕτερον τῶν ποδῶν χωλός, τοῦτον ἀποστέλλουσιν ἐς Σπάρτην. ὁ δὲ ἀφικόμενος ἰδίᾳ τε τοῖς ἐν τέλει καὶ συνάγων ὁπόσους τύχοι καὶ τὰ ἐλεγεῖα καὶ τὰ ἔπη σφίσι τὰ ἀνάπαιστα ᾖδεν.

There was an oracle from Delphi to the Lacedaemonians that they should bring in "the Athenian" as advisor. Therefore they sent messengers to the Athenians announcing the oracle and asking for a man to advise them in what they should do. But the Athenians, not desiring either of these things, that the Lacedaemonians should

---

[3] Προστησώμεθα γοῦν Τυρταῖον, τὸν φύσει μὲν Ἀθηναῖον, τῶνδε δὲ πολίτην γενόμενον.

[4] τίς γὰρ οὐκ οἶδε τῶν Ἑλλήνων ὅτι Τυρταῖον στρατηγὸν ἔλαβον παρὰ τῆς πόλεως, μεθ' οὗ καὶ τῶν πολεμίων ἐκράτησαν καὶ τὴν περὶ τοὺς νέους ἐπιμέλειαν συνετάξαντο, οὐ μόνον εἰς τὸν παρόντα κίνδυνον ἀλλ' εἰς ἅπαντα τὸν αἰῶνα βουλευσάμενοι καλῶς; Lycurgus died ca. 323 BC.

[5] Cf. Lefkowitz 1981:38.

[6] Bowra 1960:41.

[7] Aelian *Historical Miscellanies* 12.50; cf. Herodotus 9.33.3 (a seer imported because of an oracle); Jacoby 1918:10n.; Weil 1900:203; Fontenrose 1978:121.

capture the best part of the lands in the Peloponnese without great dangers, or, on the other hand, that they should disobey the god, in response sought a solution. Since Tyrtaeus was a teacher of letters who seemed to have very little intelligence and was lame in one foot, they sent him to Sparta. He, when he had arrived, gathered together as many as he came upon, both officially and in private, and sang his elegies and anapests to them.[8]

Tyrtaeus is later crucial in persuading (*metepeithen*) the Spartans not to give up the war after the battle of the Boar's Tomb, by "reciting his poems" (*elegeia aidōn*) and bringing helots into the Spartan army (4.16.6).

Most accept Athens as the source of the tale; for instance, Lefkowitz interprets the story as showing that Sparta's "most important cultural legacy, the elegies of Tyrtaeus, were the result of *Athenian* talent and training."[9] On the other hand, the story portrays the Delphic oracle helping the Spartans in their imperialism, and exhibits the Athenians in an uncomplimentary light, furthering the Spartan cause while trying to play a joke on them. When the joke is on the Athenians, finally, it is a fitting punishment for trying to subvert

---

[8] Similar accounts including the oracle and the lame Tyrtaeus can be found in a Platonic scholiast (ap. *Laws* 1.629a–630d (301s Greene); *Suda* s.v. Tyrtaeus; "Acro" on Horace *Ars Poetica* 402; Porphyrio ad ibid.; Justinus/Trogus 3.5.4; Ampelius *Memory Book* 14 (27 Assman). See testimonia 43–64 in Gentili and Prato 1979, Gerber 1999:24–35. The story of the oracle is found in Callisthenes (FGH 124 F 24 = Strabo 8.4.10). Philochorus holds that Tyrtaeus was an Athenian (FGH 328 F 215 = Strabo 8.4.10), and became the Spartan general (FGH 328 F 216 = Athenaeus 14.630f). See also Isocrates *Orations* 6.31; Philodemus *On Music* 17.3 (28 Kemke); Diodorus Siculus 8.27.1; Aelian *Historical Miscellanies* 12.50; Themistius *Orations* 15.196c–198a. Cf. Fontenrose 1978:121, Q18; Giarratano 1906; Wilamowitz-Moellendorff 1900:116; Otto 1955:365–398; Blumenthal 1948:1943–1945; Verrall 1896, and 1897; Macan 1897; Bates 1897. The kernel of the Tyrtaeus story can thus be traced back to Plato, Lycurgus, Callisthenes, and Philochorus. How far the *elaborated* story can be traced back is uncertain. It is possible that if Plato had told the story in more depth he would have told the story of the lame schoolmaster chosen by the oracle; or this story might have been a later development, an elaboration (perhaps Delphic or anti-Attic, see below) on the Attic tale of an Athenian becoming a Spartan poet-general. One might guess, however, that if the idea of such an anomaly became widespread early (as the Lycurgus reference shows), reasons for such an anomaly, a narrative aetiology, would develop either contemporaneously or not long after. Thus it seems likely that the story of Tyrtaeus as lame oracle-called schoolmaster was told in the fifth century BC or earlier. Niese 1891:26 argues that Xenophon would have introduced such a story in *Hellenica* 6.5.33 if he had known it, but it is possible that the laconizing historian would have simply ignored such an anecdote, with its Athenian general winning a Spartan battle. For Xenophon's Spartan leanings, see Tigerstedt 1965:159–178, esp. 166n517, 167, 169n534; Rawson 1969:33–34. Cf. Higgins 1977:65–76 and Proietti 1987:XIIIn8, whose arguments cannot remove the historian's pro-Spartan tendencies, though he convincingly show that there were certainly ambiguities in his attitudes toward Sparta.

[9] Lefkowitz 1981:38; see also Tigerstedt 1965 I.46n295; Campbell 1967:170; Pearson 1962:400.

the oracle. The outwitting of those who are trying to persecute the underdog, here the lame poet, is a common folktale motif,[10] another hint that the legend started as an oral story. Schwartz argues that the tale (coming to Athens around 370 BC as part of a book of Tyrtaeus' poems) had a Spartan origin, serving as propaganda for Sparta's right to possess Messenia, recently taken from them after Leuctra.[11] But this interpretation would have the Spartans flattering the Athenians, while the story portrays the Athenians as would-be oracle subverters who are outwitted—a theme that would be quite tactless if intended as propaganda—not, in fact, a *"klug ausgedachte ... Manöver."*[12] Thomas Figueira suggests a complex scenario for the tale, including three original sources and two stages: propaganda by fifth-century Spartans, "self-proclaimed Messenians," and Attic Laconizers (in which Tyrtaeus is a friendly general from Athens); then this propaganda has to be counteracted by taking the received story and making Tyrtaeus lame and an Athenian mistake.[13] This is attractive, but I continue to be impressed by how germane the lame general is to the story, and how it gives point to an amusing oral tale.

Using all of the ancient variants, we may create a composite account of the lame Tyrtaeus, emphasizing elements of special interest. The poet is by all accounts the worst possible human being, both physically and psychically. He is lame (Pausanias, *Suda*, Iustinus [*claudo pede*], Porphyrio [*clodum*], "Acro" [*claudum*]). Porphyrio intensifies this: Tyrtaeus is one-eyed (*luscum*) and "wholly deformed in his limbs" (*omni parte membrorum deformis*); "Acro" adds that he is frail in body (*corpore ... debilis*). He is of mean birth (*euteles ten tukhen*, Platonic Scholiast), and mentally impaired—he has the "least" wits of any Athenian (Pausanias); Diogenes Laertius even speaks of him as "mad" (*parakoptein*, 2.43).[14] There is perhaps an association of simplemindedness in his profession, schoolteacher (*didaskalos grammatōn*, Pausanias; *grammatistēs*, Platonic Scholiast), for the teacher of *grammata* teaches the simplest lessons, reading and writing, to the youngest children. The stereotype of the simple-minded schoolmaster survived into American folklore in the figure of Irving's Ichabod Crane. Apparently, the typical Athenian schoolmaster was poorly paid, thus adding poverty to the picture of Tyrtaeus' degraded state in Athens.

---

[10] See Thompson 1955 L400–499, pride brought low; L300–399, triumph of the weak; cf. L100–199, unpromising hero/heroine, L160, success of unpromising hero/heroine. See also the main pattern studied in Ogden 1997.

[11] Schwartz 1956:211.

[12] Schwartz 1956:211. See also Kroymann 1937:XII.

[13] Figueira 1999:230–231.

[14] Cf. Visser 1982:415n39; Brelich 1958:264. See above, ch. 3 (Archilochus).

Demosthenes taunts Aeschines with his life of utter poverty when his father was a teacher's assistant.[15]

As a result of these mean origins, deformity, dimwittedness, insanity, and poverty, Tyrtaeus is thoroughly despised by all—*kataphronoumenos en Athēnais* (Platonic Scholiast). His fellow townsmen mock him for his deformity, *quem deformem riderent* (Porphyrio).[16] In some sources, Tyrtaeus seems to have been known as a poet already in Athens.[17]

Meanwhile, the Spartans have reached their wits' end in the Second Messenian War, and are thoroughly demoralized; they apply to Delphi for advice. Apollo (Platonic Scholiast) tells them they must take, as general (*stratēgos*, Lycurgus, *Suda*; *hēgemona*, Diodorus Siculus 8.27.1; 15.66.3; *dux*, Ampelius, Orosius, "Acro"), ally (*summakhian*, Themistius; cf. Porphyrio, *auxilio*), or advisor (*sumboulon*, Pausanias, Platonic Scholiast), an Athenian, or the Athenian (Pausanias), or perhaps Tyrtaeus was mentioned specifically by the oracle (Platonic Scholiast). Messengers are sent to Athens with the news; the Athenians, not wanting to help Sparta, but not wanting to disobey the oracle, search through their population to find (*exeuriskousi*, Pausanias) the man least likely to succeed in helping the Spartans. Tyrtaeus is chosen—the worst of the Athenians, as it were. He is "given" to the Spartans as their leader (ἡγεμὼν ἐδόθη τοῖς Σπαρτιάταις, Diodorus Siculus). Thus the worst, the most deformed and insane, is excluded from the community; in effect Tyrtaeus is exiled. He is sent to Sparta as a joke—*per ludibrium missus* (Ampelius), as an insult to the Spartans, an emblem of hatred, *in contemptum Spartanorum* (Iustinus), *in contumeliam* ("Acro").[18]

But "the oracles did not deceive in what they had promised" (*sed oracula, quae promiserant, non frustrata sunt*, "Acro")—perhaps a central theme of this story.[19] In offering Tyrtaeus, the Athenians are not mocking the Spartans alone; they are also mocking Delphi, trying to subvert the response of the oracle. Tyrtaeus is a doubly ambiguous gift. While the Athenians give him to the Spartans as the negative image of what the Lacedaemonians want, a deformed joke in human form, the oracular god will invert this image into an authentic Spartan savior—turning him into something of a joke on the Athenians. The

---

[15] *On the Crown* 258; cf. Flaceliere 1965:95.

[16] For deformity as a source of humor, cf. the two chief objects of laughter in the *Iliad*, Hephaestus and Thersites, both lame, *Iliad* II 211–277, I 599–600, XVIII 410–411. For Thersites, a specialist in verbal abuse, see below, ch. 17.

[17] Iustinus; Themistius; Porphyrio; Orosius *History Against the Pagans* 1.21.7; *Suda*.

[18] Cf. Themistius, who inverts the Athenians' motivations: "being wise," the Athenians knew that a poet to motivate the Spartans would help them more than military aid.

[19] Thus Delphi might be considered as a source for this tale.

Spartans conquer the Messenians through Tyrtaeus' influence—either through his military leadership[20] or through his paraenetic poetry, or through a combination of the two. Arriving at Sparta, the poet "becomes inspired" (*epipnous genomenos*, Platonic Scholiast), and is able to transmit this inspiration to others—Plutarch says of the young men of Sparta that "being filled with divine fury [*enthousiasmou*] by his poems, they rushed into any danger."[21] The Spartans are "spurred forward" (*protrapentes*) by Tyrtaeus, and eagerly turn to military discipline (Diodorus Siculus 8.27). The kings are on the point of reducing the army when Tyrtaeus intervenes, and infuses the soldiers with such great ardor that they think no longer of survival, but of burial.[22] Thus the poet is mad before coming to Sparta, becomes "inspired" when he arrives there, and infuses (martial) inspiration into soldiers. He is involved with heightened emotion bordering on madness on both a poetic and a martial plane; in fact, poetic and martial madness are combined in him. Luginbill describes the paraenetic message in the Tyrtaean corpus (especially poems 12 and 10) as "fame versus shame." Courageous warfare brings honor; retreat brings dishonor.[23]

We know little else about the legendary Tyrtaeus, after the defeat of the Messenians. Philodemus only tells us that he was preeminently honored by the Spartans for his poetry (προτετιμ[ηκέ]ναι διὰ μουσικὴν).[24]

We might tentatively suggest at this point a possible background for the rise of the Tyrtaeus legend as we have it. If we rule out the idea that Tyrtaeus really was Athenian, then this kernel of the story might come from Athens; but

---

[20] Cf. above in text, numerous references to Tyrtaeus as general; Pausanias shows Tyrtaeus in a battle, urging troops on at the rear of the army (4.16.2). Legend aside, there is some indication that Tyrtaeus was a general—see Strabo 8.4.10 (C 362); Wilamowitz 1900:109–119; Bowra 1960:40–41, cf. Campbell 1967:169; most reject the idea, notably Jaeger 1966:117n; also Jacoby 1918:2–10 and Tigerstedt 1965:346n297.

[21] Plutarch *Cleomenes* 2.3 (805d): ἐμπιπλάμενοι γὰρ ὑπὸ τῶν ποιημάτων ἐνθουσιασμοῦ παρὰ τὰς μάχας ἠφείδουν ἑαυτῶν. On the concept of enthousiasmos in Greek religion, see Democritus B 17, 18 (DK 2:146): "And Democritus in the same way [as Plato]: As much as a poet writes with madness [*enthousiasmou*] and holy spirit [*hierou pneumatos*] is wonderfully beautiful" (καὶ ὁ Δημόκριτος ὁμοίως [as Plato *Ion* 534b] 'ποιητὴς δὲ ἄσσα μὲν ἂν γράφηι μετ᾽ ἐνθουσιασμοῦ καὶ ἱεροῦ πνεύματος, καλὰ κάρτα ἐστίν . . .); Plato *Phaedrus* 245A; Cicero *On Oratory* 2.46.194; Cicero *On Divination* 1.38.80; Horace *Ars Poetica* 295; Mattes 1970:39; Delatte 1934; Burkert 1985:109–111; Cornford 1952:65–73; Tigerstedt 1970 (hyperskeptical). See above, ch. 3 (Archilochus); below, ch. 17, the poet Lugh.

[22] Iustinus; the story of the Spartans writing their names on sticks attached to their hands follows (see also Diodorus Siculus 8.27.1; Polyaenus 1.17).

[23] Luginbill 2002:410.

[24] Actually, Philodemus states (apparently) that this was not recorded, because it did not need to be recorded. The sense is that it was general knowledge. See Gerber 1999:29. For cultic associations of *timaō*, see above, ch. 3 (Archilochus), and below, this chapter.

it could also come from a source antagonistic to Sparta which saw Athens as a logical homeland for a poet. The rest of the story—Tyrtaeus as stupid, deformed schoolteacher, sent to Sparta as a joke, to subvert the Delphic oracle—is probably not Athenian, for it portrays the Athenians as irreverent and foolish. If the kernel of the story is Athenian, this is a countertradition, possibly from Sparta, that attached itself to the original idea to subvert it. But the whole tradition could easily come from one anti-Spartan source, which had no great respect for Athens either. So we would have a small, provincial city thumbing its nose amusingly at Greece's two superpowers through this tale.

Messenia is a logical candidate for such a small state. It is well established that Messenia is the source of much of the legendary history of the Second Messenian War, with its Messenian hero Aristomenes. Messenian legend, with its anti-Spartan bias, was a prime source for Callisthenes, who influenced Ephorus, who influenced later historiographers, including Rhianus, who composed a verse epic on the Second Messenian War. This was summarized in prose, and used by Pausanias. Though this legendary history may have received a powerful impetus from the revived Messenia after Leuctra, it certainly was not concocted at that time. It probably developed and spread as oral tradition through the sixth and fifth centuries till it appeared in the written record.

Thus the Tyrtaeus tale might be whole-cloth anti-Spartan and anti-Athenian, with a Messenian source, though a more complex narrative development (an Athenian tale with anti-Athenian accretions?) cannot be ruled out. At some point, typical heroizing themes attached to Tyrtaeus—his exploits in battle, as general or poet; scapegoat themes. The resulting amusing and striking folk tale gained a wide popularity and currency in Greece, and eventually found its way into Plato, Lycurgus, and the Hellenistic written record.

The first part of Tyrtaeus' tale is a somewhat typical assimilation of the poet to scapegoat—the poet is revolting and despised, and must be gotten rid of. Aesop, as we have noted, is likewise ugly and misshapen, as was the Ionic *pharmakos*. Like the *pharmakos*, Tyrtaeus was of low status and impoverished. Like the *pharmakos*, he is chosen carefully (*exeuriskousi*, Pausanias) as the very worst of the community. He is despised by all (*kataphroumenos*), and the community, after it has singled him out, mocks him with laughter.[25] He is sent out of the city as a joke—the worst when the Spartans had asked for a general, the best.

---

[25] Girard discusses this theme (1977:254): "Derision of one form or another plays a large part in the negative feelings that find expression in the course of the ritual sacrifice and that are finally purified and purged by it." This exclusion is a reciprocal reflex of the satirist's ability to exile others through the power of his mockery. Directly comparable is Bupalus' and Athenis' mockery of Hipponax; they ridicule Hipponax's deformities in a painting. See above, ch. 4.

When Tyrtaeus becomes the best, the Spartan general-counselor, we have a reversal of the Oedipal scapegoat pattern studied by Vernant,[26] in which Oedipus, king and savior of Thebes, is found to be incestuous and a patricide, and therefore must be excluded from the city by decree of Delphi. Tyrtaeus, on the other hand, starts as the least, lame and mad, and, by decree of Delphi, becomes a victorious general and powerful paraenetic poet, the savior of Sparta. Despite the inversion, Oedipus and Tyrtaeus both embody stark contradictions.[27]

One of the poles of contradictions mediated in the person of Tyrtaeus is the warrior; he is deformed, excluded, insane, least; a poet; and a Spartan general. This suggests an important theme, the scapegoat excluded in a context of war—often sent as a fatal gift to the enemy in response to an invasion or hopeless battle. In the case of the Roman *devotio*,[28] the scapegoat is a warrior, originally the general, whose attack, which must end in the general's death, spreads panic through the opposing army. The legendary Athenian king, Codrus, when he throws himself, disguised as a beggar (an Oedipus-like peripety), against enemy swords, is a useful comparison.[29]

A similar story contains a close parallel to the Tyrtaeus legend. Cnopus makes war against the "Cretan" Erythrae in Asia Minor. An oracle instructs him to take a Thessalian priestess as his general; when she arrives, she arranges to have a bull adorned and given a drug. This turns the bull mad, and he runs to the enemy, who sacrifice him and are themselves driven mad, thus enabling Cnopus to conquer them easily.[30] Here we have the Tyrtaean theme of oracle selecting an unlikely general (in this case, marginal in her womanhood), who brings the army success. The bull is clearly an extension of the general (the priestess, named Chrysame, covers the bull with gold);[31] and the parallel to the *devotio* is striking. In both cases, the scapegoat, sent to the enemy forces, causes madness and panic among them.

---

[26] Vernant 1981.

[27] For the special power and sacrality of the marginal person, the deformed, the criminal, the exile, the female, the youth, and paradoxically, the king, see Bremmer 1980; on Medon, who was, like Tyrtaeus, lame in one foot, Pausanias 7.2.1. Cf. a sentence that could be applied to the Tyrtaeus legend: "Society seemingly took recourse to its marginals in times of great confusion" (Bremmer 1980:74n45). See also Bremmer 1983b:303–304 and passim; Kearns 1990; Ogden 1997.

[28] A famous example is Decius Mus, Livy 8.9f.; cf. Burkert 1979:63.

[29] See above, ch. 1.

[30] Polyaenus 8.43; Burkert 1979:59–60.

[31] See below, ch. 27. Polycrite, like Tyrtaeus, is "given," excluded, by her native people. Tarpeia inverts this pattern by betraying her people to the invading general whom she was fallen in love with. Burkert 1979:72–73; 76–77.

Thus scapegoat-warrior-savior is a frequent combination in folkloric history, myth, and related ritual and martial practice. The soldier is always, in a way, a scapegoat and a savior, sent by a society to conquer the enemy and sacrifice himself for the society's good.[32] And, if poets tend to become scapegoats, the poet can also become a warrior-general-savior, as in Tyrtaeus' case. The poet-warrior conjunction makes sense in some important ways; both figures are ambiguous, dangerous to society, yet prized by society;[33] both figures specialize in a kind of madness. In a paraenetic poet like Tyrtaeus, there is a congruence of lunacies. The poetic exaltation is focused toward instilling martial madness that will bring victory to Sparta.

Solon's *vita* has some themes that are directly comparable to the warrior-poet themes that we find in Tyrtaeus' *vita*. When the Athenians had given up on fighting the Megarians for Salamis, they passed a law threatening death to anyone who proposed further hostilities. Solon wrote a paraenetic poem, memorized it, pretended sickness and madness, and ran out in his sickclothes to deliver the poem to a large crowd. Fortunately for Solon, this poetry had the desired effect; the war was started again, and, instead of being executed, Solon became general of the Athenian operation.[34] Like Tyrtaeus, Solon comes to the fore in a period when his city is demoralized after persistent defeat in a war carried on for possession of desirable nearby territory.[35] Like Tyrtaeus, he uses paraenetic poetry to stir up his people, and becomes general. He is perceived as mad (*mainesthai*, Diogenes Laertius 1.46) and this madness is linked with his poetry. The theme of exclusion of the poet-lawgiver is also found in Solon's *vita*, as he goes into exile after the *seisachtheia*.[36] He becomes a "hero at the

---

[32] For the concept of warrior as scapegoat, see the Phaedrus fable discussed in ch. 24, below. Oedipus, before he is revealed as the incestuous parricide who must be expelled from Thebes to allay a plague, saves Thebes from the murderous sphinx in single riddle combat with that monster, see Sophocles *Oedipus Rex* 48; 507–511; ch. 1.

[33] For the warrior's ambiguity, see Dumézil 1983, *The Stakes of the Warrior*. Starkaðr, perhaps the most archaic of the figures Dumézil studies, is a passionate supporter of kingship, yet also a serial regicide. See also Dumézil 1970b:43, 63; below, ch. 18.

[34] Plutarch *Solon* 8.1–3 = 1W, cf. further bibliography there, also Gerber 1999b:106–111. Diogenes Laertius 1.46–56; Cicero *On Duties* 1.30, 108; Demosthenes 19.252 (and schol.); Philodemus *On Music* 20.18; Justinus 2.7ff.; Aristides *Oration* 37, vol. 1, p. 708 Dindorf and *Oration* 46, vol. 2, p. 361 Dindorf; Polyaenus *Strategems* 1.20; Pausanias 1.40.5; Porphyrius, *ad Iliad* II 183. See Linforth 1919:40. For Solon's poetry, Anhalt 1993.

[35] And we thus find, in the poetry of both poets, the theme of geographical praise of the desired territory, Solon 1, 3W; Tyrtaeus 5.2–3W. Cf. Solon 4.23–25W; Tyrtaeus 6W. For a discussion of the historical context of the latter poem, see Den Boer 1954:74. Further parallels in the poetry of the two poets are discussed in Jaeger 1966:120, 131; Tigerstedt 1965:349n331; 345n281; Anhalt 1993:74.

[36] See Plutarch *Solon* 16.3, cf. fr. 34W. For discussion of this, along with similar examples from other legendary lawgivers, see Szegedy-Maszak 1978:205–207; cf. Linforth 1919:93–103.

gate" after death, in one tradition, thus receiving hero cult.[37] The similarities with Tyrtaeus are so close that one wonders if either story was influenced by the other. Thus the Solon story, in some of its aspects, might be as fictitious as is Tyrtaeus' (probably). If it is historical, it is a surprising witness to the historical feasibility of some aspects, at least, of the Tyrtaeus legend.

The Archilochus legend has a few comparable themes. This poet is condemned by his native community (as a blasphemer), is exiled; like Tyrtaeus writes paraenetic martial poetry, and is so much a soldier that he dies in battle.[38] Thus, once again, we have a paraenetic warrior poet; and his heroic nature has again attracted the expulsion theme. The parallel with Solon is closer; but Archilochus is an exiled poet given adverse trial by society, and he is also a thoroughgoing soldier-poet. The motif of death in battle perhaps links the heroization as poet and the heroization as warrior.[39]

Even closer to the stories of war scapegoats referred to above is the incident from the Aesopic *vita* in which the Samians are prepared to give up Aesop to ward off destruction from the invading Croesus. "At first the people shouted, 'Take him. Let the king have Aesop.'" Thus the people are willing to exclude the monstrously ugly fabulist to escape invasion. Aesop goes willingly, and a shrine to him is built where he gives himself up.

Here we have many typical themes: the crisis (military threat); the offering of Aesop as propitiation by the voice of the people; the self-sacrificial volition of Aesop; his saving the city; the hero cult given to the poet at the very place where he had been expelled by the people. (Thus heroization of the poet through his acting as sacrificial warrior.) Tyrtaeus is likewise monstrously ugly, excluded by his people during a military crisis, and the savior of a people. But his story has been adapted so as to make him save a different city than his own.

Tyrtaeus' poetry attests to the theme of the heroization of the warrior. He writes of the soldier:

> τὸν δ᾽ ὀλοφύρονται μὲν ὁμῶς νέοι ἠδὲ γέροντες
> ἀργαλέωι δὲ πόθωι πᾶσα κέκηδε πόλις,
> καὶ τύμβος καὶ παῖδες ἐν ἀνθρώποις ἀρίσημοι
> καὶ παίδων παῖδες καὶ γένος ἐξοπίσω·
> οὐδέ ποτε <u>κλέος</u> ἐσθλὸν ἀπόλλυται οὐδ᾽ ὄνομ᾽ αὐτοῦ,

---

[37] Aelian *Historical Miscellanies* 16, cf. Kearns 1989:54. In other traditions, his ashes are scattered over Salamis.

[38] See above, ch. 3.

[39] See below, ch. 18; for Heracles and Achilles as poets, ch. 16.

ἀλλ᾽ ὑπὸ γῆς περ ἐὼν γίνεται <u>ἀθάνατος</u>,
ὅντιν᾽ ἀριστεύοντα μένοντά τε μαρνάμενόν τε
γῆς πέρι καὶ παίδων θοῦρος Ἄρης ὀλέσηι.

They lament him, young and old alike,
and the whole city mourns him with bitter longing,
and his tomb and his children are famous among men,
and his children's children and his descendants thereafter.
Neither does his noble fame [*kleos*] or his name ever perish,
but even though he is beneath the earth he becomes
    immortal [*athanatos*]—
whoever distinguishes himself in bravery by standing stead-
    fast and fighting
for the sake of his land and children, and is destroyed by
    furious Ares.

                                                    12.27–34W

This passage contains many details that could be easily linked to hero cult: polis-wide lamentation; emphasis on the tomb; immortality "even though he is beneath the earth." All this because he has sacrificed himself on behalf of his land and children.[40]

Though we do not have overt testimony that Tyrtaeus received cult honors, it is likely that he did, judging from the Philodemus passage cited above, and from the parallels of other poets. However, he is certainly heroized by the legend of his generalship in the Second Messenian War. Thus the Tyrtaeus legend, however unhistorical it may be, still reflects ancient narrative patterns, and offers us valuable insight into how the poet was sometimes perceived in archaic Greek culture—marginal, disabled,[41] yet valued as an adjunct to war in a martial society. It is perhaps appropriate that the poet who heroized death in battle should himself be a paraenetic poet-general, excluded as least, but heroized in legend by martial success.[42]

---

[40] Cf. hero cult awarded to Strategos, the hero general, Kearns 1989:198; and to the Marathon dead, Kearns 1989:183. See also Ekroth 2002:159, 262n232, 338–339; above, ch. 1, on Codrus, Aglauros, and Androgeus; and the tomb of Aeschylus, ch. 12 below.

[41] On the theme of the blind poet and prophet, see above on Homer, ch. 5.

[42] See Fuqua 1981; Otto 1955:365–398. We find the following themes in Tyrtaeus' *vita*: 3, oracle, often prescribing remedy for disaster; 4, worst; 4a, poor; 4d, ugly, deformed; 5, best; 5c, victorious (in war); 10, expulsion; 10a, exile; 13, hero cult? 26, poet as soldier; 26a, martial paraenesis as poetic theme.

12

Aeschylus: Little Ugly One

A S WE TURN TO THE MAJOR ATHENIAN DRAMATISTS, we find that three of the four fit into our pattern somewhat; Aeschylus suffers an adverse trial against his poetry and bitterly leaves Athens; Euripides is attacked by the Athenians and leaves Athens, only to be torn to pieces by comic poets or women; Aristophanes attacks Cleon, and is subjected to trial and punished as a result. Only Sophocles lives a peaceful life and receives a peaceful death, an example of the Pindaric line of development in poetic *vitae*, the positive life.[1]

Aeschylus offers a rich clustering of motifs. His name means 'Little Ugly One', which is a curious coincidence, given the strong tradition for poetic ugliness.[2] He was renowned as a soldier: according to his *Vita*, which describes him as "noble" (*gennaion*), he served in all three of the major battles of the Persian

---

[1] Sophocles had a peculiarly pious reputation. He was visited by Heracles in a dream and was enabled to recover a stolen crown of gold, *Vita* 12 (in Pearson 1957:xviii–xxi; translation in Lefkowitz 1981:75–87); after his death Dionysus appeared to a Spartan commander to make the dramatist's proper burial possible (*Vita* 15; Pausanias 1.21.1); his epitaph called him "a most sacred person" (*Vita* 16: *skhēma to semnotaton*). He was a priest of Halon, a hero associated with Asclepius (*Vita* 11); he received the title Dexion because he received Asclepius in his house (Plutarch *Numa* 3; *Etymologicum Magnum* s.v. Dexion), see Connolly 1998. He led a *thiasos* devoted to the Muses (*Vita* 6). Like Aeschylus, and most Athenians, he was a soldier; he was elected general twice. (*Vita* 9; Plutarch *Pericles* 8; Plutarch *Nicias* 15.)

There are a number of deaths to choose from, but none of them fits the exiled poet pattern. Like Anacreon he died choking on a grape pip; or he died straining his voice in a rehearsal of *Antigone*; or, perhaps most fittingly, he died of joy when awarded first prize for the *Antigone* (all *Vita* 14.) For the Cleobis and Biton theme—ecstatic death—cf. Fairweather 1974:269–270. For "literary" death, cf. Theophrastus, who dies of exhaustion after writing too many books, *Suda* s.v. Theophrastus. All of these qualify as extraordinary deaths, but are not otherwise remarkable.

Sophocles received hero cult after death (*Vita* 17): "Istros says that the Athenians voted to sacrifice [*thuein*] to him every year because of his *aretēn* [bravery or excellence]" (Ἴστρος δέ φησιν Ἀθηναίους διὰ τὴν τοῦ ἀνδρὸς ἀρετὴν καὶ ψήφισμα πεποιηκέναι κατ' ἔτος αὐτῷ θύειν). Cf. *Vita* 15–16; Pausanias 1.21.1; Clay 2004:78–79, 151–152.

[2] Cf. Aesop's "deformed" name.

War.[3] His epitaph, perhaps composed by the poet himself, is well known; it does not even mention poetry:

Αἰσχύλον Εὐφορίωνος Ἀθηναῖον τόδε κεύθει
μνῆμα καταφθίμενον πυροφόροιο Γέλας·
ἀλκὴν δ' εὐδόκιμον Μαραθώνιον ἄλσος ἂν εἴποι
καὶ βαθυχαιτήεις Μῆδος ἐπιστάμενος.

This tomb in grainbearing Gela covers an Athenian, Aeschylus son of Euphorion, who died here. The famous grove of Marathon could tell of his courage and the longhaired Mede knew it well.[4]

This martial background found some expression in Aeschylus' art, especially in the *Seven Against Thebes*, which Aristophanes described as "brimming with Ares,"[5] and impelling the Athenians to battle.

Plutarch, commenting on Aristophanes' observation, wrote that the *Seven* was brimming with Dionysus more than Ares, as were all Aeschylus' plays.[6] The dramatist Aeschylus was clearly moving in a Dionysian sphere of influence; interesting in this regard is the statement, widely reported, that Aeschylus wrote his plays while drunk.[7] This phrase, "obviously figurative," as Gilbert Murray remarks, points to the poet possessed by the divine, the inspired, slightly mad poet. He was widely acknowledged to be the best writer of satyr plays, whose Dionysiac, archaic character is clear.[8]

Aeschylus was so closely associated with Dionysus that this god presides over a typical consecration scene in the poet's biographical tradition: "Aeschylus said that once when he was a youth he went to sleep while watching grapes in a field, and that Dionysus appeared and commanded him to write tragedy. And when it was day, since he wished to be obedient, he made

---

[3] *Vita* 4. This document can be found in Radt 1985 test. 1, whose paragraph notation, following Wilamowitz, I use. It is also in Page 1972:331–333 and in Wilamowitz-Moellendorff 1914. Translation in Lefkowitz 1981:157–160 (from which translations in this section are quoted, with modifications, unless noted otherwise), cf. 68–70.

[4] *Vita* 11 (test. 162R), Pausanias 1.14.5; Athenaeus 14.627d; Plutarch *On Exile* 13–15 (604–606) (test. 88R). Pausanias and Athenaeus have Aeschylus write this epitaph; the *Vita* has the people of Gela write it, and later quotes another epitaph (17) related to his death. Cf. Dioscorides in *Palatine Anthology* 7.411; Antipater of Thessalonica in *Palatine Anthology* 7.39; Diodorus in *Palatine Anthology* 7.40 (test. 162–165R). For bibliography on scholars who have accepted or rejected this epitaph as Aeschylean, see Radt 1985:106–107.

[5] *Frogs* 1021: *Areōs meston*. Cf. above, ch. 3 (Archilochus).

[6] *Table Talk* 7.10.2 (715E) (test. 188R).

[7] Athenaeus: "*methuōn*," 10.428f (test. 117aR), with further references at test. 117b–gR. See also Murray 1940:147. Cf. Cratinus fr. 199K, at Athenaeus 2.39c. See above, on Archilochus, ch. 3.

[8] See Seaford 1984; Pausanias 2.13.6 (test. 125bR); Diogenes Laertius 2.133 (test. 125aR).

an attempt and hereafter found composing tragedy quite easy. He himself would tell this story."⁹

As in the cases of Hesiod and Archilochus, the poetic theophany takes place in nature, in the fields, in a setting of pasturage and cultivation (tending either animals or plants). Here, appropriately, the plant is the grape. As in the case of Archilochus, the poet is given his visitation while a youth. Judging the antiquity of this story is difficult; the scholia referring to the poet writing drunk would easily encourage such an anecdotal elaboration, in the tradition of Hesiod. On the other hand, Pausanias mentions twice that Aeschylus is the source of the tale; the imperfect, *elegen*, perhaps emphasizes that he would tell the story frequently. This kind of emphasis is impressive, though putting an apocryphal tale in the mouth of a hero is standard strategy in pseudepigraphy.

Though Aeschylus is chosen by a god and inspired by him—or perhaps because he is chosen—he ends his life in defeat and ambiguously voluntary exile (after a humiliating public defeat), which places him securely in the tradition we have been analyzing. He leaves Athens out of shame or anger after losing a poetic competition—either with the young Sophocles, in a tragic competition, or with Simonides, after Aeschylus and the lyric poet have each composed an elegy for the dead at Marathon.¹⁰

Plutarch tells us that an unusual jury of the most prestigious men of Athens, Cimon and his fellow generals, was pressed into duty to decide the contest with Sophocles. "The contest caused unusual rivalry because of the high reputation of the judges. When the victory was at last awarded to Sophocles, they say that Aeschylus, becoming overwrought and taking it hard, did not stay long in Athens, and went in anger to Sicily, where he died, and was buried near the city of Gela."¹¹

This theme has parallels in myth; Ajax feels he has been unjustly denied the prize in the contest for the arms of Achilles, and he descends to madness, attempted murder, and death. Heracles, after winning a marriage contest, is

---

⁹ Pausanias 1.21.2 (test. 111R), trans. Jones, modified, ἔφη δὲ Αἰσχύλος μειράκιον ὢν καθεύδειν ἐν ἀγρῷ φυλάσσων σταφυλάς, καί οἱ Διόνυσον ἐπιστάντα κελεῦσαι τραγῳδίαν ποιεῖν· ὡς δὲ ἦν ἡμέρα—πείθεσθαι γὰρ ἐθέλειν—ῥᾷστα ἤδη πειρώμενος ποιεῖν. οὗτος μὲν ταῦτα ἔλεγεν. For the dream theophany of Dionysus, cf. Dionysus' appearance to Spartans after the death of Sophocles, instructing them to honor his tomb, Pausanias 1.21.1; Sophocles *Vita* 15–16.

¹⁰ *Vita* 8: ἡσσηθεὶς νέῳ ὄντι τῷ Σοφοκλεῖ . . . ἡσσηθεὶς Σιμωνίδη.

¹¹ Plutarch *Cimon* 8 (test. 57R), trans. Clough, modified, ὁ μὲν οὖν ἀγὼν καὶ διὰ τὸ τῶν κριτῶν ἀξίωμα τὴν φιλοτιμίαν ὑπερέβαλε. νικήσαντος δὲ τοῦ Σοποκλέους λέγεται τὸν Αἰσχύλον περιπαθῆ γενόμενον καὶ βαρέως ἐνεγκόντα χρόνον οὐ πολὺν Ἀθήνησι διαγαγεῖν, εἶτ᾽ οἴχεσθαι δι᾽ ὀργὴν εἰς Σικελίαν, ὅπου καὶ τελευτήσας περὶ Γέλαν τέθαπται.

unjustly denied his bride, and also descends to madness that results in his death. Fontenrose finds this same reflex in his hero-athlete tales, as the hero-athlete (Cleomedes, Euthycles) goes mad after an athletic council denies him what he feels is his due prize.[12]

The *Vita* adds that he "was criticized [*kataspoudastheis*; perhaps 'oppressed'] by the Athenians."[13] So we have the familiar themes of poetic contest (as with Homer and Hesiod, here we have two prominent poets) and rejection by a jury, combined with popular criticism and voluntary exile (ambiguous, in that the jury and people have already rejected him).

If this story is true, it is a remarkable example of how reality may follow myth; it is also possible that it is myth itself, modeled on the *vitae* of Homer, Hesiod, and Aesop. When Aeschylus was invited to Hieron's court, lured away from Athens by promise of great reward, later generations—perhaps, as in the case of Plato, his immediate students and friends—molded the life to the already existent myth(s). It was a way of honoring the greatness of a poet, giving him the literary equivalent of hero cult; or perhaps, a way of filling up an otherwise incomplete or relatively uneventful biography.[14]

This story of great poet losing a poetic contest is remarkably similar to the story of Homer (both poets leave a city after prominent citizens vote against them). Aeschylus' death is equally similar: a riddling oracle leads to an odd death that fulfills the oracle in a distant land. The oracle has told him that something thrown from the sky will kill him; in Sicily, as an eagle tries to break a tortoise by dropping it on rocks, it hits Aeschylus' bald head instead and brings about his death.[15] This is a classic example of the extraordinary or miraculous death discussed earlier; it perhaps has a note of sacralization about it.[16]

---

[12] See Fontenrose 1968:86, 73–77. The trial theme is also found in the stories of Aeschylus revealing the mysteries in his plays (Scholia on Aristotle *Nicomachaean Ethics* 3.2.1111a8 (test. 93bR), cf. further references in test. 93-94), and in the story that he terrified the audience by the appearance of the Eumenides in the play of the same name, Apsines *The Art of Rhetoric* 2 p. 229.14 Spengel-Hammer (test. 95R).

[13] *Vita* 8: ὑπὸ Ἀθηναίων κατασπουδασθείς.

[14] Cf. Lefkowitz 1981:72, who characteristically opts for the prosaic idea that Aeschylus was invited to Sicily, and was paid well to go there. There is another variant of the aetiology of Aeschylus' departure: the *Suda* (test. 2R) tells us that "he went into exile [*phugōn*] in Sicily because the stage fell down when he was putting on a performance" (φυγὼν δ' εἰς Σικελίαν διὰ τὸ πεσεῖν τὰ ἰκρία ἐπιδεικνυμένου αὐτοῦ).

[15] *Vita* 10; cf. Wilamowitz 1958 #32 p. 11, citing Valerius Maximus 9.12. extract 2 (test. 96R); Sotades, in Stobaeus *Anthology* 98.9 Mein.; Pliny *History of Animals* 10.7 (test. 97R); Aelian *On the Characteristics of Animals* 7.16 (test. 98R).

[16] See above, ch. 7; Piccolomini 1888.

After Aeschylus' death he was given hero cult: "The people of Gela buried him lavishly in the city's cemetery and honoured [*etimēsan*] him magnificently [by the epitaph quoted above]. All who made their living by performing tragedies went to his tomb, offered sacrifices [*enēgizon*] and performed his plays there."[17] *Enagizō* is a standard word used to denote sacrifices to the dead in cult, as opposed to divine sacrifices; the importance of elaborate ritual connected with the gravestone, documented here in Aeschylus' funeral rites, is also an important aspect of hero cult.[18] However, it is striking that his tomb, though the focus of hero cult awarded to a poet, has an inscription that heroized him by remembering his bravery in battle. One remembers the Archilocheion celebrating Archilochus' bravery in war.

Predictably, the Athenians who earlier had "criticized" Aeschylus now "liked him so much that they voted after his death to award a golden crown to whoever was willing to put on one of his dramas . . . He won quite a few victories after his death."[19] The heroizing vote after death complements the rejecting vote in life.[20]

---

[17] *Vita* 11, my trans., ἀποθανόντα δὲ Γελῶιοι πολυτελῶς ἐν τοῖς δημοσίοις μνήμασι θάψαντες ἐτίμησαν μεγαλοπρεπῶς . . . εἰς τὸ μνῆμα δὲ φοιτῶντες ὅσοις ἐν τραγωιδίαις ἦν ὁ βίος ἐνήγιζόν τε καὶ τὰ δράματα ὑπεκρίνοντο. For Aeschylus' hero cult, see Clay 2004:127.

[18] See Burkert 1985:194, 200. For *enagizein*, 194n46. However, the *enagizein/thuein*, hero/god dichotomy can be overschematized, see Kearns 1989:4; Ekroth 2002:74–128; Clay 2004:94–95.

[19] *Vita* 13, trans. Lefkowitz, Ἀθηναῖοι δὲ τοσοῦτον ἠγάπησαν Αἰσχύλον ὡς ψηφίσασθαι μετὰ <τὸν> θάνατον αὐτοῦ τὸν βουλόμενον διδάσκειν τὰ Αἰσχύλου χρυσὸν λαμβάνειν . . . οὐκ ὀλίγας δὲ μετὰ τελευτὴν νίκας ἀπηνέγκατο.

[20] Thus we find the following themes in the Aeschylean tradition: 1a1, criminal impiety (revealing the mysteries in his plays); 3, oracle; 4d, ugly (at least, in his name); 5a, sacred; 7, adverse judgment by public meeting; 8, ambiguously voluntary (exile); 10a. exile; 13, hero cult; 19, madness; 23a, consecration theophany; 25a, poetry contest; 26, poet as soldier. 26a, military paraenesis as poetic theme.

13

Euripides: *Sparagmos* of an Iconoclast

URIPIDES WAS CLOSER than either of the other two major tragedians to a blame poet, so it is not surprising that his *vita* conforms to the exclusion pattern quite closely.[1] His plays had satirical aspects: he was especially noted for his critique of war (*The Trojan Women*) and for his attacks on women.[2] According to the *Vita*, he was *misogunēs*, "a hater of . . . women" (23). Influenced by his first wife's promiscuity, he wrote "*Hippolytus*, in which he loudly proclaims the shamelessness of women" (24). When Euripides' second wife is unchaste "he became all the readier to speak ill of women. But the women wanted to kill him . . ." (24–25).[3]

He "jeered at [*eskōpte*] women in his poems" (29).[4] "Because of his mockery [*dia tous psogous*]" the women at the Thesmophoria plot to kill him, but give up the plot out of respect for the Muses (30). This is certainly an elaboration from Aristophanes' *Thesmophoriazusae*. Hermesianax tells us that "he won the hatred [*misos*] of all men by his barking concerning all women."[5]

---

[1] For Euripides' *Vita*, see Kovacs 1994, test. 1; Meridier 1925:1–5. For translations, see Paley 1872: lx–lxii (*Vita* 1–44); Lefkowitz 1981:163–169 and Kovacs 1994 (whose translation I use, unless noted otherwise). Satyrus *The Life of Euripides* in *P. Oxy.* 9.1176 (1912) (test. 4K), is quite early, a manuscript from the third century BC; see Arrighetti 1964, but cf. a review by S. West 1966; von Arnim 1913:3–13; Stevens 1956. See also *Suda* s.v. Euripides (test. 2K), Arrighetti 1964:97; Westermann 1845:141; a life by Thomas Magister (test. 3K), Westermann 1845:139–140; Aulus Gellius *Attic Nights* 15.20 (test. 5K); Hermesianax 7.61–68 (test. 64K), in Powell 1925:105, *ad* Athenaeus 13.598d–e. Also Piccolomini 1888:116–121; Delcourt 1933; Stevens 1956; Goossens 1962:660–662; Dover 1976:29, 42–46; Lefkowitz 1981:88–104; Lefkowitz 1984; Franco 1986.

[2] *Vita* 29–30; 23–25. See also Hermesianax 7.61–68. See above, ch. 6 (Hesiod), Semonides fr. 7, for misogynist blame.

[3] Ἱππόλυτον, ἐν ᾧ τὴν ἀναισχυντίαν θριαμβεύει τῶν γυναικῶν. . . . εἰς τὴν κατὰ τῶν γυναικῶν βλασφημίαν ἐθρασύνετο. αἱ δὲ γυναῖκες ἐβουλήθησαν αὐτὸν κτεῖναι . . .

[4] ἔσκωπτε δὲ τὰς γυναῖκας διὰ τῶν ποιημάτων.

[5] καὶ πάντων μῖσος κτώμενον ἐκ συνοχῶν / πάσας ἀμφὶ γυναῖκας . . . Trans. Gulick, using Headlam's "by his barking" (*ex hulakōn*). Kovacs prefers *ex onukhōn*, Jacobs's suggestion, thus, "full to his fingertips of hatred against all women."

Satyrus describes him as "simply disdaining everything that was not high and lofty."[6] When the musician Timotheus is rejected by the Athenians, Euripides "ridicules" (*katagelasai*) the audience for their lack of taste, and saves Timotheus from suicidal depression.[7] Thus his *Vita* portrays him as unpopular: "he was treated with ill-will [*ephthoneito*] by the Athenians," though a favorite of foreigners.[8] Satyrus writes: "Everyone became his enemy [*apēkhthont'*], the men because he was so unpleasant to talk to, the women because of his abuse [*psogous*] of them in his poetry. He ran into great danger from both sexes."[9] We have already seen that Athenian women reportedly plotted to kill him, though they relented out of respect for the Muses, and because he promised to stop his attacks. He was also a favorite target of the comic poets. "The comic poets too attacked him and tore him to pieces [*diasurontes*] in their envy" (*Vita* 35).[10] Their animalistic, artistic violence presages his eventual death.

There are traditions that he was subjected to legal harassment. Aristotle tells us that a Hygiaenon opposed the dramatist in a trial for an exchange of properties, and accused him of impiety, in that Euripides had allegedly recommended perjury in a play.

ὥσπερ Εὐριπίδης πρὸς Ὑγιαίνοντα ἐν τῇ ἀντιδόσει κατηγοροῦντα ὡς ἀσεβής, ὅς γ' ἐποίησε κελεύων ἐπιορκεῖν "ἡ γλῶσσ' ὀμώμοχ', ἡ δὲ φρὴν ἀνώμοτος." ἔφη γὰρ αὐτὸν ἀδικεῖν τὰς ἐκ τοῦ Διονυσιακοῦ ἀγῶνος κρίσεις εἰς τὰ δικαστήρια ἄγοντα· ἐκεῖ γὰρ αὐτῶν δεδωκέναι λόγον, ἢ δώσειν εἰ βούλεται κατηγορεῖν.

So with Euripides' reply to Hygiaenon, who, in the action for an exchange of properties, accused him of impiety in having written a line encouraging perjury—[*Hippolytus* 612] "My tongue has sworn: my heart is unsworn." Euripides said that his opponent himself was guilty in bringing into the law-courts cases whose decision belonged to the Dionysiac contests. "If I have not already answered

---

[6] Fr. 39.IX: ἁπλῶς ἅπαν εἴ τι μὴ μεγαλεῖον ἢ σεμνὸν ἠ[τι]μακώς. Cf. Lefkowitz 1981:166n7.

[7] Satyrus fr. 39.XXII, cf. Stevens 1956:90.

[8] *Vita* 27: ὑπὸ γὰρ Ἀθηναίων ἐφθονεῖτο.

[9] Satyrus fr. 39.X: <u>ἀπήχθοντ'</u> αὐτῶι πάντες, οἱ μὲν ἄνδρε[ς] διὰ τὴν δυ[σ]ομιλίαν, α[ἱ δὲ] γυναῖκε[ς δ]ιὰ τοὺς <u>ψ[ό]γους</u> τοὺς ἐν τοῖς ποιήμασιν. Cf. Lefkowitz 1981:168n12; Franco 1986:115.

[10] Trans. Lefkowitz, Ἐπέκειντο δὲ καὶ οἱ κωμικοὶ φθόνῳ αὐτὸν <u>διασύροντες</u>. Aristophanes' *Frogs* is the most famous example. Cf. *Vita* 32: "The poets of Old Comedy derided him for being the son of a vegetable-seller" (τοῦτο οἱ τῆς ἀρχαίας κωμῳδίας ποιηταὶ ὡς λαχανοπώλιδος υἱὸν κωμῳδοῦσι). According to Lesky, he is "the chief object of the indignation and ridicule of the conservatives . . . Comedy is full of it" (1966:361). See Prato 1955.

for my words there, I am ready to do so if you choose to prosecute
me there."

Aristotle *Rhetoric* 3.15 (1416a3) (test. 59K),

trans. W. Roberts, modified

This is early, quite sober evidence, though one wonders what *asebeia* had to
do with *antidosis*, whether it was actually part of the charge, or whether it was
supportive character defamation. But it is significant that the charge haunts
Euripides in a law case. Lefkowitz characteristically argues against the histo-
ricity of this reference, suggesting that such stories resulted from emphasis
on Plato's trial, or from Old Comedy.[11] But Aristotle was born only twenty-two
years after Euripides' death; one wonders if the philosopher, himself a shrewd
and sober critic, would be susceptible to complete fantasy after such a short
period of time.

According to a third-century AD papyrus, Euripides is also brought
to trial once by Cleon because he portrayed the madness of Heracles;[12] and
once by Cleon for general impiety, according to Satyrus (39.X).[13] In favor of
the possible historicity of this event, Dover lists, 1, that there were elements
in Euripides' plays that could give rise to the charge of impiety, and 2, that if
anyone was capable of prosecuting a dramatist, Cleon was, as the prosecution
of Aristophanes by Cleon after the *Babylonians* showed. We might add 3, the
comparative earliness of Satyrus' biography, and 4, the parallel from Aristotle.
Against the historicity of this event, Dover argues that Satyrus is "an extremely
disreputable source," because he reported the attack on Euripides by women
at the Thesmophoria as history. This argument has some weight, but it would
be strengthened if he could suggest a similar source for the Cleon story.

Euripides' response to this unpopularity was withdrawal, both physical
and psychological. "He was rather proud and pardonably stood aloof from the
majority, showing no ambition as regards his audience" (34). He is described
as looking "sullen and pensive and stern, a hater of laughter ..." (23). "He
wore a long beard and had moles on his face" (12).[14] These details add up to

---

[11] Lefkowitz 1987. Cf. Momigliano 1971:66–77.

[12] *P. Oxy.* 2400, a list of subjects for rhetorical exercises (test. 60K), cf. Dover 1976:29; Stevens
1956:88. Stevens (who dates the papyrus in the second century AD) incorrectly suggests that
the three events on the list are purely imaginary. As Dover notes, "The other two items ... of
this list refer to historical events, and the author of the list probably regarded the prosecution
of Euripides also as historical."

[13] Cf. Dover 1976 on the Cleon prosecution; also Stevens 1956:88; Lefkowitz 1981:110; Lefkowitz
1987.

[14] Trans. Lefkowitz, πλέον τι φρονήσας εἰκότως περιίστατο τῶν πολλῶν, οὐδεμίαν φιλοτιμίαν

a kind of ugliness. Once "a boorish lad said out of ill-will that Euripides had foul-smelling breath." This, surprisingly, is paralleled by an early source. In Aristotle we find Euripides scourging a Dechamnichus: "for the poet had been irritated at some remark made by Dechamnichus on the foulness of his breath."[15] Again, the earliness of this tradition prevents us from immediately dismissing it as ahistorical. Euripides is one of the few figures in the classical tradition noted for bad breath.[16] Whether Aristotle's reference has historicity or not, the fact that such a story would be promulgated shows that the dramatist had enemies, and that they had a sympathetic audience.

The poet leaves the city, lives in a "grim and gloomy cavern" (*speluncam ... taetram et horridam*),[17] in Salamis, "fleeing the crowd," φεύγοντα τὸν ὄχλον (22), and writes his tragedies there (22; 25).[18]

One wonders how much, if any, historical validity there is in all of this. While one must subject this *vita* to a thorough skeptical critique, one should also allow for the presence of occasional kernels of historicity embedded in it. Euripides, though he was certainly popular on the whole,[19] may have had bitter moments of disfavor and unpopularity; he may have been sullen in appearance, or he may have grown sullen; and he may have withdrawn from his public. The withdrawal and the unpopularity would have encouraged each other. His marriages may have been disillusioning failures. All of these elements are common among writers and thespians throughout history. Often artists fall out of fashion after successful careers, which makes comparative neglect all the more difficult to accept. P. T. Stevens, who rejects most of the romantic aspects of the *vita*, allows the possibility that Euripides "was much less successful, less sociable, and less popular than Sophocles, and by comparison showed a certain aloofness and reserve of manner" and that "like most well-known men, he had his ups and downs in popular favour."[20] The contemporary attacks by Aristophanes show that Euripides, if judged one of the three best tragedians, was still a popular target;[21] and the traditions of unpopularity

---

περὶ τὰ θέατρα ποιούμενος. . . . σκυθρωπὸς δὲ καὶ σύννους καὶ αὐστηρὸς ἐφαίνετο καὶ μισόγελως . . . ἐλέγετο δὲ καὶ βαθὺν <τὸν> πώγωνα θρέψαι καὶ ἐπὶ τῆς ὄψεως φακοὺς ἐσχηκέναι.

[15] *Vita* 28: μειρακίου δέ τινος ἀπαιδευτοτέρου στόμα δυσῶδες ἔχειν ὑπὸ φθόνου . . . Aristotle *Politics* V.10 (1311b30f) (test. 61K): ὁ δ' Εὐριπίδης ἐχαλέπαινεν εἰπόντος τι αὐτοῦ εἰς δυσωδίαν τοῦ στόματος.

[16] See also Satyrus fr. 39.XX; Stobaeus, *Anthology* 41.6.

[17] Philochorus, fourth century BC, *ad* Aulus Gellius *Attic Nights* 15.20.5 (test. 5K); cf. Satyrus fr. 39.IX.

[18] For the cave as a stereotypical feature in the lives of thinkers, see Stevens 1956:88n9.

[19] See Stevens 1956:91–92; Lefkowitz 1987:151; Franco 1986:119.

[20] Stevens 1956:93.

[21] Cf. Prato 1955.

and harassment are found as early as Aristotle, which suggests that we should be very cautious about rejecting them entirely.

If some of these elements are historical, the biographers would have heightened them through the idiom of well-worn anecdote shading into archaic legend, taking cues from his writings or from Aristophanes on occasion. Lefkowitz writes an insightful chapter on Euripides, pursuing the thesis that his *vita* was derived from the tragic hero of his plays. This is convincing in some ways, though she probably goes too far, especially when we examine his violent death. However, by my thesis, the Euripidean tragic hero and the Euripidean *vita* would have derived, in part, from the same mythical source. The Euripidean heroes and heroines have a tendency toward self-sacrifice, and Bremmer and Burkert treat them in the context of the legendary scapegoat (in which young princes or princesses sacrifice themselves for the good of the community);[22] Euripides' *vita* was merely a poetic outcome of the scapegoat—as it were, the Aesopic line of development. Here again there is nothing to prevent separate development with contamination, that is, the Euripidean biographical traditions deriving from myth, but also being influenced by the Euripidean tragic hero.

Euripides completed his withdrawal by leaving Attica altogether, like Aeschylus, an interesting parallel (and perhaps a wandering theme). Murray calls it a "voluntary exile."[23] When the dramatist was attacked by the comic poets and his audience, "he ignored it all and departed to Macedonia and the court of King Archelaus" (ὑπεριδὼν δὲ πάντα εἰς Μακεδόνας ἀπῆρε πρὸς Ἀρχέλαον τὸν βασιλέα ... , 35). According to Satyrus (39.XV.25), the "native ill-will" of his fellow-Athenians (ἐπιχωρίωι φθόνωι τῶν πολιτῶν), as well as attacks by other dramatists, grieves the poet, and, though there is a gap in the text, this probably is a reason for his leaving Athens. A statement by Philodemus, probably applicable to Euripides, suggests this: "in grief, because almost all Athenians were rejoicing over him, he departed to Archelaus."[24]

In Macedonia the playwright suffers his violent, odd, ironic death: "Some time later he was taking his rest in a grove that stands before the city. When Archelaus went out for a hunt and the young hounds, let loose by the huntsmen, came upon Euripides, the poet was torn in pieces [*diesparakhthē*]

---

[22] Bremmer 1983b:307n43; Burkert 1979:71n29; Larson 1995. Cf. the legendary scapegoats in ch. 1, above.

[23] Murray 1913:166.

[24] *On Vices* X, col. XIII (in Jensen 1911:22): ἀχθόμενον αὐτὸν ἐπὶ τῶι σχεδὸν πάντας ἐπιχαίρειν πρὸς Ἀρχέλαον [ἀπ]ελθεῖν.

and devoured and eaten [*katabrōtheis*]."[25] This is a literal, physical expression of the line from the *Vita*: "The comic poets too attacked him and tore him to pieces [*diasurontes*] in their envy." As Lefkowitz points out, this is also how a Euripidean hero would die.[26] One significant variant of this story has two envious poets bribe the keeper of the king's dogs to set them loose on the dramatist.[27] Euripides being torn apart by poets (literally: poet-directed dogs) is just that much closer to literal expression of his victimization by the comedians. In another significant variant, the king's servant hates Euripides because the dramatist had slandered (*ek tinōn diabolōn*) his master.[28] So, if only in folkloric elaboration, Euripides is killed expressly because of his abusive proclivities.

The mythical resonances of the *sparagmos* death are obvious: Orpheus, Dionysus, Pentheus, and Actaeon are all torn to pieces. Actaeon, of course, is even torn apart by dogs.[29] In Hyginus, furthermore, Euripides' death is sacralized by taking place in a temple of Artemis. Ovid further tells us that a "crowd of dogs, guardians of Diana" tear Euripides apart.[30]

---

[25] *Vita* 21: χρόνῳ δὲ ὕστερον Εὐριπίδης ἐν ἄλσει τινὶ πρὸ τῆς πόλεως ἠρέμει. Ἀρχελάου δὲ ἐπὶ κυνηγέσιον ἐξελθόντος, τῶν σκυλάκων ἀπολυθέντων ὑπὸ τῶν κυνηγῶν καὶ περιτυχόντων Εὐριπίδῃ, διεσπαράχθη καταβρωθεὶς ὁ ποιητής.

[26] *Vita* 35, see above. Lefkowitz 1981:96. This is true to an extent; Pentheus suffers the sparagmos, for instance. But other details of Euripides' death find no parallel in his writings. There is no trace of the "freewill" theme, so common in Euripides' writings (see below), in his death legend. The earliest reference to this death is the third-century BC Hermesianax, writing perhaps a century and a half after Euripides' actual death. See also Diodorus 13.103.5, *diaspasthēnai*. On various versions of the dog death, see Arrighetti 1964:146–147.

[27] *Suda* s.v. Euripides. "Arrhibaeus of Macedon and Crateuas of Thessaly, who were poets and hostile to him" (ἐτελεύτησε δὲ ὑπὸ ἐπιβουλῆς Ἀρριβαίου τοῦ Μακεδόνος καὶ Κρατεύα τοῦ Θετταλοῦ, ποιητῶν ὄντων καὶ φθονησάντων αὐτῷ . . .). Another, less significant, detail has Euripides pursuing the king's housekeeper when he is overtaken by the dogs (*Suda*; Hermesianax 7.61–68).

[28] "Plutarch" *Alexandrine Proverbs* (at Leutsch and Schneidewin 1961 Suppl., IIIa, p. 14n26, Crusius), quoted in Arrighetti 1964:146.

[29] The story of Actaeon is attested as early as Hesiod's *Ehoiai*, fr. 217A M-W, see Gantz 1991:478–481. A version of the tale in Euripides' *Bacchae* (337–340) has Actaeon destroyed by Artemis because he boasts that he is the best hunter, which reminds us of Marsyas and Thamyris, see ch. 16 below. On a more "historical" level, Lucian (see *Suda* s.v., cf. Lefkowitz 1981:90n12) and Heraclitus (see Diogenes Laertius 9.3–5; Fairweather 1973) were purportedly torn apart by dogs. Diogenes the Cynic dies after being severely bitten by dogs, an ironic death (Diogenes Laertius 6.77; *Suda* s.v. Diogenes, cf. Fairweather 1973:235). Cf. Pausanias 9.38.4 and Visser 1982:409n21 for Actaeon in hero cult myth.

[30] Hyginus *Fables* 247: "Euripides, author of tragedies, was destroyed in a temple" (*Euripides tragoediarum scriptor in templo consumptus est*); Ovid *Ibis* 595, cf. La Penna 1957 *ad loc*. "And as a crowd of vigilant dogs, guardians of [the temple of] Diana, did to the tragic bard, so may they tear you to pieces also" (*Utque coturnatum vatem, tutela Dianae, / Dilaniet vigilum te quoque turba canum*). See above, on Hesiod, ch. 6, for the death localized at a temple.

The attacks Euripides suffered from women are expressed in another detail from the *Vita*: the poet is killed by the children of a female dog who had been sacrificed by villagers; Euripides prevented the villagers from paying reparation to the king for the crime (21). But in another version of the death found in the *Suda*, Euripides is actually torn apart by women: ὑπὸ γυναικῶν νύκτωρ διασπασθῆναι.[31] This provides a link to Orpheus, as well as being appropriate to his misogynist reputation.

There is no chance of historicity in any of these deaths, as his murderers are too closely related to his traditional critics in life, whose attacks probably have some realistic basis (as Aristophanes' attacks show). But Euripides' *sparagmos* still has a significant mythic power, as its widespread popularity shows.

Euripides, predictably, is given great honor after his death: Sophocles appears at the theater dressed in black and has his actors perform crownless; and now the Athenians weep (20). The dramatist is given a cenotaph at Athens and a tomb in Macedonia, and both are struck by lightning (19). The motif of two monuments to a hero being struck by lightning is strikingly mirrored in hero cult: the athlete Euthymos has two of his statues struck by lightning on the same day, which occasions a Delphic consultation and hero cult offered to the living man as a result.[32] The cenotaph is also found in hero cult.[33] It seems odd that the great religious iconoclast[34] should end up a semideity of sorts, receiving cultic honor, but perhaps he earned this distinction by his *sparagmos*.

As has been noted previously, poets whose lives have attracted the special themes of this study (judgment, exile, execution) often are interested in the ideology of the scapegoat. This is also true of Euripides—the theme of free-will sacrifice for the community is a repeated motif in Euripides' plays.[35] These scapegoats are following the "legendary" pattern, with princes and princesses giving themselves up to death willingly. Often these sacrifices are prescribed by divine injunction.

Thus, in Euripides' life we find the ugliness of the poet, his satiric attacks on women and war, his persecution by his native townsmen and fellow drama-

---

[31] *Suda* s.v. Euripides (test. 2K). Cf. Nestle 1898, esp. 135, 138–142.

[32] Callimachus fr. 99 Pf., at Pliny *Natural History* 7.47.152; Pausanias 6.6.4–6; Aelian *Historical Miscellanies* 8.18; Fontenrose 1968:79; Clay 2004:134–135. For the more general theme of sacrality and lightning, see above, ch. 3 (Archilochus). For Euripides' monuments struck by lightning, see also Anonymous, in *Palatine Anthology* 7.48.

[33] Pausanias 6.23.3.

[34] The question of Euripides' religious views is, of course, extremely complex. See Rohde 1925 II:459.

[35] Schmitt 1921; Roussel explicitly compares Euripides' heroes to the *pharmakos* (1922: 225–240); Nancy 1983; Foley 1985; O'Connor-Visser 1987, with further literature, pp. 5–18.

tists; he is brought to trial, and finally leaves Athens in a sort of "voluntary exile" to escape these troubles. In Macedonia, he dies a cultic death, and receives hero cult.[36] We can see the Aesopic-Archilochean pattern behind the tragedian's *vita*.[37]

---

[36] There is at least a hint of the consecration motif in Euripides' biography, for an oracle prophesied to his father that his boy would win at a contest which awarded crowns. As often happens, the oracle was misunderstood, and Euripides was trained to be an athlete before he found his dramatic vocation (*Vita* 3; Aulus Gellius *Attic Nights* 15.20.2). The oracle to the father of the poet prophesying a poetic vocation for the son is of course an Archilochean theme. See above, ch. 3.

[37] Thus we find the following themes in Euripides' biographical traditions: 4, worst; 4d, ugly; 7, trial; 10a, exile (with 8a, ambivalent volition); 10b, death in far country; 12a, death at cult site; 22, blame poetry/satirical (attacks on women and militarists); 24, conflict with political leaders.

14

Aristophanes: Satirist versus Politician

RISTOPHANES AND THE OTHER COMIC POETS INHERITED, as part of their comic art, the iambic abuse of Archilochus and Hipponax.[1] Perhaps the hallmark of Old Comedy was political satire; it is not surprising therefore that the poet in conflict with politician is constantly in evidence in the history of Old Comedy.[2]

For example, Cratinus, known as the "emulator of Archilochus," took Pericles as his favorite target;[3] Teleclides often attacked politicians,[4] as did the militantly satirical Hermippus, who went beyond the bounds of poetry and brought Pericles' mistress Aspasia to court for impiety and immorality (a curious inversion of the poet being haled to court by the unsympathetic politician).[5] Plato (Comicus) wrote comedies named after the politicians he attacked: *Hyperbolus, Pisander, Cleophon*.[6] Eupolis attacked Pericles (in *Prospaltians*), Hyperbolus (in *Marikas*), and Alcibiades (in *Baptai*).[7] According to one patently

---

[1] See Rosen 1988c:25 and passim; Degani 1988; West 1974:35; de la Torre 1987; cf. Lesky 1966:233–240. In view of the importance of phallic cult in the ancestry of comedy (Aristotle *Poetics* 1449a10; Semus, *ad* Athenaeus 14.622c–d; West 1974:36–37; Rosen 1988c:4; Giangrande 1963), we may remember the importance of Archilochus' possible advocacy of some kind of phallic cult in his cult legend and its close parallels. The tragedians also wrote satyr plays, which apparently always had satirical, obscene aspects, cf. Seaford 1984.

[2] For Aristophanes' blame, see Harriott 1985:46–67, who discusses both praise and blame in the comic poet. Also Kraus 1985; Halliwell 1984a:86–87 and Halliwell 1984b (who would argue for a lack of "personal authorial commitment" in Aristophanes' satire; I tend to disagree, see below); Carey 1994; Degani 1993. For Old Comedy apart from Aristophanes, Harvey and Wilkins 2000.

[3] See relevant fragments from *Nemesis; Dionysalexandros; Chirones*, and especially *Thracian Women* in PCG. Cf. Plutarch *Pericles* 13, 3; Lesky 1966:419–420; Storey 1998n1.

[4] See fr. 44, 45 PCG, attacks on Nicias and Pericles.

[5] On the Aspasia story, Plutarch *Pericles* 32; Gilula 2000:76. See *Bread-Sellers*, which attacked Hyperbolus, scholia on Aristophanes, *Clouds* 551.

[6] See PCG 7, fragments s.v. those titles; cf. Lesky 1966:421–422.

[7] PCG 5.448, test. 260; scholia on Aristophanes *Frogs* 569 = PCG 5.400; Aristophanes *Clouds* 551; for Alcibiades, see following note.

unhistorical but revealing anecdote, the angry Alcibiades threw Eupolis over-board on a voyage to Sicily, drowning him.[8]

Of course, the victims of the comedians were not limited to politicians: any public figure, a philosopher, Sophist, a tragic poet, or a fellow comic poet, could offer a legitimate target for the comedian, as Aristophanes' *Clouds* and *Frogs* show us. This leads to the theme of poet attacking poet; we have already seen comic poets involved in the legendary death of Euripides.[9]

Aristophanes' most prominent political target is the demagogue Cleon. The comedian's conflicts with Cleon have become the subject of ongoing debate, with some critics believing that in the ritual environment of Old Comedy, the poet's attacks and Cleon's responses were not taken seriously, and the poet was subjected to no serious legal danger. Other scholars argue that Aristophanes was subjected to serious legal harassment by a powerful politician, who deeply resented the poet's insults. Some have taken a middle ground between the two positions.[10] We can do no more than survey some of the basic evidence here. In the *Acharnians* (377–382), Aristophanes wrote:

αὐτός τ' ἐμαυτὸν ὑπὸ Κλέωνος ἅπαθον
ἐπίσταμαι διὰ τὴν πέρυσι κωμῳδίαν.
εἰσελκύσας γάρ μ' ἐς τὸ βουλευτήριον
διέβαλλε καὶ ψευδῆ κατεγλώττιζέ μου
κἀκυκλοβόρει κἄπλυνεν, ὥστ' ὀλίγου πάνυ
ἀπωλόμην μολυνοπραγμονούμενος.

And Kleon. Him I know from—shall we say?—personal experience. Last year's comedy provoked him. To say the least. He dragged me into the Senate House, sued me, and opened the sluicegates. Slander and lies gushed from his tongue in torrents, and down the arroyo of his mind there roared a flash flood of abuse. To purge me, he purged

---

[8] 151 Tzetzes, *Prooemium* I (*Prolegomena*) line 87; Koster and Wilson 1975 1a:27, also in PCG 5.332, test. iv.; see other testimonia, ibid. Eratosthenes, FGH 241 F 19 = Cicero *Epistles to Atticus* 6.1.18 = Eupolis test. 3, PCG 5.295.

[9] See Luppe 2000, for a conflict between prominent comic poets.

[10] See Gelzer 1970, esp. 1398–1399; Rosen 1988c:63 (summarizing the position that the attack is historically accurate), 61n4 (taking the position that insult in Old Comedy was ritualistic and was not taken seriously, thus holding that the attack on Cleon is not historical). Halliwell (2004:139–140) holds to the same general perspective, arguing that the cultic setting of aischrology in Old Comedy prevented significant retaliation against poets. Arguing for real animus, bitter resentment, and dangerous legal harassment in Old Comedy are Henderson 1990 (p. 304: "Kleon's subsequent lawsuit—no doubt another *graphē*—looks like a serious response to serious abuse rather than merely an oversensitive reaction to harmless ridicule"); Atkinson 1992; Sommerstein 2004. This is only a selective list that will introduce the reader to the issue.

himself—and in the offal, filth and fetor of his verbal diarrhea, I nearly smothered, mortally immerded.[11]

Later (502–503), Aristophanes writes, "A year ago, Kleon charged [*diabalei*] that I had slandered the State [*tēn polin kakōs legō*] in the presence of strangers, by presenting my play, *The Babylonians*, at our Great Festival of Dionysos."[12] Earlier in the play, he wrote of the "happy glow in my stomach when I saw Cleon fairly caught in that comedy by Aristophanes, compelled to belch up those five talents."[13] Aristophanes' *Vita* outlines a feud between the dramatist and the demagogue, in which the comic poet was evidently brought to trial three times; Aristophanes finally triumphs over Cleon when he gains his citizenship.[14]

After *Acharnians*, Aristophanes would attack Cleon in *Knights* and *Wasps* (1284–1291).[15] The latter passage probably reflects a second trial of Aristophanes by Cleon after the *Knights*:[16]

εἰσί τινες οἵ μ' ἔλεγον ὡς καταδιηλλάγην,
ἡνίκα Κλέων μ' ὑπετάραττεν ἐπικείμενος
†καί με κακίσταις† [κακίσας, Briel] ἔκνισε· κᾆθ' ὅτ' ἀπεδειρόμην
οὑκτὸς ἐγέλων μέγα κεκραγότα θεώμενοι,
οὐδὲν ἄρ' ἐμοῦ μέλον, ὅσον δὲ μόνον εἰδέναι
σκωμμάτιον εἴποτέ τι θλιβόμενος ἐκβαλῶ.
ταῦτα κατιδὼν ὑπό τι μικρὸν ἐπιθήκισα·
εἶτα νῦν ἐξηπάτησεν ἡ χάραξ τὴν ἄμπελον.

To rectify the record: Rumor has it that I, the author, have kissed and made up with Kleon. It alleges that he scratched and badgered until I buried the hatchet. A canard. Here are the facts: I found I

---

[11] Trans. Parker. Cf. MacDowell 1971:299; Foley 1996; Olson 2002:173–174.

[12] οὐ γάρ με νῦν γε διαβαλεῖ Κλέων ὅτι / ξένων παρόντων τὴν πόλιν κακῶς λέγω. For a more literal translation, cf. Henderson's: "Besides, Cleon shall not be able to accuse me of attacking Athens before strangers." See Olson 2002:201–202. He concludes, "there was a real (and perhaps continuing) dispute between the two men somehow sparked by [Kleon's reaction to *Babylonians*]" (Olson 2002:xxx).

[13] *Acharnians* 6: ἐγᾦδ' ἐφ' ᾧ γε τὸ κέαρ ηὐφράνθην ἰδών, / τοῖς πέντε ταλάντοις οἷς Κλέων ἐξήμεσεν. For the talents, see Carawan 1990.

[14] The information in 502–503 is echoed by scholia on Aristophanes, *Acharnians* 503, 378; Koster and Wilson 1975 1b:59, 70; and *Vita* 20 (see following note). See also *Acharnians* 300, 659. For the *Vita*, see Koster and Wilson 1975 1a:133–150; Cantarella 1949 I:135–144; translation in Lefkowitz 1981:169–172.

[15] Cf. Edmunds 1987:51–57; Körte 1921:1233–1236; Gelzer 1970:1398–1399.

[16] Sommerstein 1980:32–33, 1983:233–234; Storey 1995. However, this, like every detail of Aristophanes' conflict with Cleon, is disputed, see Storey 1995:8.

was fighting alone. When the Tanner [Cleon] dragged me to court, I expected popular support from the folks who flocked to the case. And what did I get? Laughs. He peeled my skin off in strips; I howled—and the spectators roared. Dimly, I saw that my backing was only a comedian's claque, political voyeurs assembled to see me prodded until I produced some tasty billingsgate. Faced with such odds, I changed my tactics—played the ape, flattered Kleon a bit. But what does he think today, now that this docile doormat is pulling the rug from under him? (trans. Parker)

Thus, Aristophanes was apparently brought to court again, and his popular backing deserted him; he was, metaphorically, flayed alive by the Tanner. He was forced to some kind of truce with Cleon, which he later rejected at the time of *Wasps*.

According to scholiasts, there were consistent attempts to muzzle the comic poets. In 440/439 an act against comic poets was passed, but was repealed three years later.[17] In 426, after Aristophanes attacked Cleon in *The Babylonians*, a bill against using names in comedy may have been passed.[18] In 415/414 Syracosius is said to have sponsored the same kind of bill.[19] In 387 it was decreed that the poets could ridicule no one by name.[20] Lefkowitz casts doubt on the historicity of these references because "there appears to be no reference to legal censorship outside commentaries on old comedy."[21] But a bill proposed by Diopeithes in 434 against atheists and philosophers is attested outside the scholia.[22] C. Carey argues that the 440/439 law "seems certain, since the source . . . introduces it tangentially; it is therefore not based on conjectural attempts to make sense of the text of Aristophanes."[23] The historicity of the Syracosius decree has been defended by A. Sommerstein.[24] It is

---

[17] Scholia on *Acharnians* 67; Koster and Wilson 1975 1b:17.

[18] Scholia on Aristides *Orations* 3.8 (Eupolis *Baptae* test. 3, PCG). See Halliwell 1991a:55; Lefkowitz 1981:106.

[19] Scholia on *Birds* 1297, citing a fragment of Phrynichos. Koster and Wilson 1991 2.3:192.

[20] Cf. *Vita* 51–52; Platonius *On Comedy*, lines 23–29, Koster and Wilson 1975 1a:4. Also, Plutarch *On the Glory of the Athenians* 5 (348b–c); "Xenophon" *The Constitution of the Athenians* 2.18, commentary by Frisch 1942:277–281.

[21] Lefkowitz 1981:106.

[22] Plutarch *Pericles* 32. Cf. Rudhardt 1960:92; Finley 1973:91; Nilsson 1972:121–122. Dover rejects this (1976:39–40), cf. Derenne 1930:223, 237f. But Dover's argument that Plutarch should be rejected because one would have expected his data to appear somewhere else is not convincing: history and textual criticism are full of examples of important data surviving in only one line of tradition. See Bauman's convincing argument in favor of the historicity of the *psēphisma* (1990:39).

[23] Carey 1994:71.

[24] Sommerstein 1986, but cf. Carey 1994:71 and Sommerstein 2004.

attested by a scholiast, but the scholiast quotes the comic poet Phrynichos as his source.[25] Albin Lesky also argues that the 438 (440) and 414 (415) bills must be considered historical.[26] Richard Bauman, approaching the problem from the perspective of legal history, suggests that "Cleon's approach to the Boule against Aristophanes [after *The Babylonians*] may have been preceded, then, by a *psēphisma* . . ."[27] This would support the scholiastic evidence for the 426 bill.

The debate on the historicity of these laws continues; certainly there is some relevant scholiastic evidence that is patently nonhistorical.[28] But one cannot simply discount scholiastic evidence whole cloth—it often preserves authentically ancient data. The scholiastic references that are fictitious, however, show how the myth-making literary mind created an atmosphere of persecution and censorship for its heroes.[29]

At least one scholar has suggested that Aristophanes was exiled by Cleon, which would be a valuable datum if it could be substantiated.[30] But even without an exile, Aristophanes fits our pattern; he mocked and criticized Cleon, and was subjected to some kind of legal harassment by that powerful politician. This is reflected in the *Acharnians* and *Wasps*, and the event is probably historical. To this core we may add the scholiastic and biographical material, selecting and rejecting according to our taste.

Ralph Rosen has taken Aristophanes' portrait of Socrates in the *Clouds* as a parallel to argue that Aristophanes actually had no real quarrel with Cleon; that the quarrel mentioned in the *Acharnians* is as unfactual as is the quarrel with Socrates; that the comic poet, in treating Cleon was merely directing traditional invective themes against a prominent figure; and that these themes had little relationship with historical fact. Rosen follows Lefkowitz in deriving the scholiastic accounts of a quarrel from misunderstood interpretation of the plays themselves.

Despite Rosen's arguments, I am inclined to accord the quarrel and legal battles historicity. First of all, aspects of the Socrates and *Clouds* case seem to me to argue for it. However much the *Clouds* is misleading, exagger-

---

[25] Scholia on *Birds* 1297 = fr. 27 of Phrynichos (active as playwright 429–405 BC). Though there are many ways to interpret this passage (and certainly the scholiast might have misunderstood Phrynichos), one cannot categorically reject Phrynichos as a reliable source.

[26] Lesky 1966:420.

[27] Bauman 1990:55.

[28] See Halliwell 1991:55 and passim.

[29] See further Edmunds 1987:60; Halliwell 1984a:86–87; Atkinson 1992; Storey 1998; Halliwell 2004; Sommerstein 2004.

[30] Leeuwen 1888, cf. Whitman 1964:307n2; Steffen 1954.

ated, offering stereotypes instead of facts,[31] Plato's Socrates still feels that it has shaped public opinion against him in a powerful way, and feels some resentment toward it. Before the actual accusers of the *Apology* were earlier accusers: "more formidable" (*deinoteroi*, 18b, e) than the later ones; they are authentically "my dangerous accusers" (οἱ δεινοί εἰσίν μου κατήγοροι, 18c). And Socrates emphasizes that his later accusers are certainly "formidable enough" (*kai toutous deinous*, 18b).

They seem to be maliciously, consciously telling untruths; they "tried to fill your minds with untrue accusations against me" (κατηγόρουν ἐμοῦ μᾶλλον οὐδὲν ἀληθές, *Apology* 18b). These people "tried to set you against me out of envy and love of slander" (φθόνῳ καὶ διαβολῇ χρώμενοι ὑμᾶς ἀνέπειθον, 18d). Moreover, this lying is done to children who cannot easily tell truth from lies; Socrates seems to find this lying to minors especially reprehensible, and he emphasizes it by mentioning it twice (18b, c). The only person singled out among these earlier accusers is "a playwright" (18c), who is later specified as Aristophanes (19c).

The tone here is not that of genial amusement, tolerant allowance of festive high spirits and the fantasy of *Clouds*, with its traditional satirizing that everyone understood had no relationship with reality. On the contrary, by Socrates' account, most of the Athenians have believed Aristophanes and those like him. The philosopher, being tried for his life, singles out Aristophanes by name and speaks of malicious "envy and slander." Socrates blames Aristophanes and his allies more than his actual accusers.

Rosen quotes a scholiast who reports that Aristophanes did not write the *Clouds* out of enmity. Yet this is effectively countered by this passage from the *Apology*, obviously much earlier than the scholiast, and written by a close friend of Socrates.[32]

Rosen might also adduce an interesting passage in Plutarch, in which Socrates reports that he was not offended by *Clouds*. This deserves a close reading:

---

[31] See Dover 1972:118–119; Erbse 1954.

[32] Scholia on *Clouds* 96. When one assesses these late sources in conjunction with the *Apology*, perhaps the earliest Platonic writing, probably written not too long after Socrates' death, the *Apology* has much greater weight. One might bring up the Socratic question, certainly; it is not proven that Socrates spoke these words. But they are certainly Platonic, and are possibly somewhat Socratic, as the dialogue was written during Plato's most "Socratic" period. Brickhouse and Smith 1989 argue for the general historical reliability of the *Apology*. I would agree that the framework of the *Apology* is historical, while Plato's literary allusiveness gives mythological resonance to Socrates' trial. See ch. 15 below.

Ἀριστοφάνους δέ, ὅτε τὰς Νεφέλας ἐξέφερε, παντοίως πᾶσαν ὕβριν αὐτοῦ κατασκεδαννύντος, καί τινος τῶν παρόντων "κᾆτα τοιαῦτα κωμῳδούμενος οὐκ ἀγανακτεῖς" εἰπόντος "ὦ Σώκρατες;" "Μὰ Δί' οὐκ ἔγωγε" ἔφησεν· "ὡς γὰρ ἐν συμποσίῳ μεγάλῳ τῷ θεάτρῳ σκώπτομαι."

And when Aristophanes brought out *Clouds* and heaped all manner of abuse upon Socrates, in every possible way, one of those who had been present said to Socrates, "Are you not indignant, Socrates, that he used you as he did in the play?" "No indeed," he replied, "when they break a jest upon me in the theatre I feel as if I were at a big party."

On Educating Children 14 (10c)

This does portray a Socrates unruffled by Aristophanes' play. But it also portrays a friend of Socrates who is clearly shocked at the extent of the abuse ("all manner of abuse ... in every possible way") directed at his friend. In addition, this fits into the familiar genre of Socratic stories in which he is seen as an extraordinarily wise man (it is prefaced by an explanation that wise men can control their anger, 10b). The point of the story is that one would expect Socrates to be upset, but he reacts with wisdom, self-control, and urbanity. If Old Comedy were a place where verbal attacks could not sting, the story and the characterization would be pointless.

As of yet, I have not disputed one of Rosen's central points: that the Socrates of the *Clouds* is often far removed from the historical Socrates.[33] But the *Apology* passage shows that many Athenians accepted Aristophanes' Socrates as true, and that Socrates (or the Platonic Socrates) seriously resented that portrait, which he characterized as lying, slanderous, and created out of envy.

In another book on Aristophanes, Malcolm Heath argues with Rosen that the Aristophanic portrait of Socrates was not meant with any animus or seriousness. He gives an interpretation of the *Apology* passage along these lines, and supports it with a discussion of Aristophanes in the *Symposium*. His interpretation of the *Apology* passage is problematic: he argues that the comic poet of 18d1-2 is "implicitly" distinguished from Socrates' remote malicious accusers.[34] Yet the whole section, 18a-24b, deals with his first accusers. In

---

[33] For those who see at least some elements of the historic Socrates in *Clouds*, see Nussbaum 1980:43–47 (summary of the problem); Schmid 1948:222; Stark 1953:77–89; Edmunds 1987:60n9; Edmunds 1985b:209–230.

[34] Heath 1987:9.

18d1–2, Socrates says that none of accusers can be named, *except* for a playwright, who is later specified as Aristophanes. Thus the comic playwright is emphatically part of the earlier, malicious accusers.[35] Heath further proposes that Socrates' argument is that the earlier charges came from comedy, thus should not be taken seriously, as everyone realizes that comic portraiture has no relationship with reality.[36] Yet Plato's point is that the earlier accusers, among whom Aristophanes is a ringleader, were very much believed; they were the more dangerous accusers.[37]

Thus, the *Apology* passage is far from "inconclusive." Heath's discussion of *Symposium* is more persuasive. Socrates and Aristophanes are apparently on friendly terms in the banquet, and at one point Alcibiades designates everyone there, including Aristophanes by name, among those who have "shared in the madness [*manias*] and ravings [*bakkheias*] of philosophy" (218a7–b4),[38] which in context perhaps means Socratic philosophical discussions, though this is not explicit.

This has been a traditional aporia, and has not yet been conclusively solved. As G. Daux notes, there is really no hatred of Aristophanes expressed in the *Symposium*.[39] Dover writes that "a satisfactory reconstruction of the history of Plato's feelings towards the real Aristophanes continues to elude us."[40]

One method of dealing with the conflict between *Apology* and *Symposium* in this matter is simply to pronounce that *Symposium* outweighs the *Apology*.[41] Yet, from a historical perspective, the *Apology*, though undoubtedly containing its idealizing mythopoeic dimensions, was written much earlier than the *Symposium*, and in a much more "Socratic" period of Plato's career.[42] And its subject matter is certainly as deeply felt and serious as is the *Symposium's*.

If one reads both dialogues carefully, it is possible to see the *Symposium* in the light of *Apology*, instead of vice versa. It is significant that, as Dover points out, Aristophanes' tale in the *Symposium* differs from all the other banquet

---

[35] Brickhouse and Smith also include Aristophanes among those early accusers. *Clouds* is "the very paradigm of the 'first' accusations" (1989:63–64).

[36] Heath 1987:10.

[37] Cf. Edmunds 1987:60.

[38] After Alcibiades mentions that he has been bitten in the heart or mind by Socrates' philosophy, he names everyone present, including Aristophanes: πάντες γὰρ κεκοινωνήκατε τῆς φιλοσόφου μανίας τε καὶ βακχείας . . .

[39] Daux 1942.

[40] Dover 1966:50.

[41] As does e.g. Murray 1933:143.

[42] Dover, in fact, suggests that the elaborate frame Plato gives the *Symposium* reflects its mythical, fictional nature (1980:9).

offerings in celebrating a concrete love. Again, alone of all the offerings, it receives a direct refutation from Diotima/Socrates/Plato.[43] It was composed "by Plato, as a target for Diotima's fire."[44] Aristophanes—brilliant and amusing as he is—is the jarring note in the banquet devoted to spiritual love. And in this perspective, *Symposium* begins to make dramatic sense as an *agōn* like the *Republic* or *Gorgias*, where a most dangerous opponent of Socrates speaks last or near to the last, only to be vanquished by the master.

This interpretation of Aristophanes as a vanquished opponent of Socrates is confirmed by the end of the dialogue, where Socrates argues with Aristophanes and Agathon through the night. In an elegant double motif, defining Socrates' superhuman nature by his sleeplessness, Socrates clinches his argument at dawn, as the two dramatists begin to nod. "First Aristophanes fell off to sleep, and then Agathon, as day was breaking" (223d).[45] Socrates conquers in argument and in sleeplessness. Thus, *Symposium* can be read as a critique of Aristophanes, subtle, urbane, but serious. If its tone is different from the *Apology* passage (the dramatic situations are very different), thematically it is not entirely dissimilar.[46]

Thus, even if Aristophanes' portrait of Cleon is entirely untrue—which is not certain—the politician might have resented it as much as the Platonic Socrates did his own portrait, or more, for as a politician and militarist, he was likely to have been a much less self-controlled and genial man than was Socrates. And a politician's natural tool for retaliation would have been the law court.

Furthermore, as William Arrowsmith notes, Aristophanes' portrait of Cleon was much more savage than was his portrait of Socrates.[47] Thus it is likely that Cleon responded to Aristophanes more violently than did Socrates, first with verbal abuse, then perhaps with legal harassment. Since he was much more powerful than Socrates, this is not at all unlikely.

A second major argument used by Rosen is the implication that since Aristophanes used traditional elements in his attacks on Cleon (which Rosen shows skillfully), they had no basis in fact, were meant with no animus on Aristophanes' part, and were not resented by Cleon. Aside from the question of how deeply Aristophanes felt about his pacificism—for his attack on Cleon was to a certain extent an attack on militarism—it seems that this dichotomy

---

[43] *Symposium* 205d.10–e.7; 212c.4–6, cf. Dover 1966:48.
[44] Dover 1966:50.
[45] καὶ πρότερον μὲν καταδαρθεῖν τὸν Ἀριστοφάνη, ἤδη δὲ ἡμέρας γιγνομένης τὸν Ἀγάθωνα.
[46] See Sommerstein 2004:158.
[47] Arrowsmith, *Clouds* 1969:6.

between traditional themes and sincere involvement with the people and issues of his time is too extreme. A poet can use traditional poetic techniques, even formulae, for his own idiosyncratic, deeply-felt purposes, and to communicate with his own milieu.[48]

Thus, the feud between Cleon and Aristophanes (and the prosecutions against the comic dramatist) were probably historical. According to Cedric Whitman, *Knights* is "a monument, and a vigorous one, to the personal animosity of Aristophanes," the only play of that playwright where he abandons himself "fully to the luxury of sheer hate."[49]

Many aspects of Aristophanes' art continue archaic blame traditions.[50] The curse is found in Aristophanes' arsenal of verbal weapons.[51] The animal fable of Aesop has at least a relative in the animal choruses of comedy, one of the most archaic aspects of the genre, and still prominent in Aristophanes.[52] Animal imagery, common in the iambic satirical tradition, was also frequent in comedy.[53] The poetical *agōn*, so important in the *vitae* of Homer, Hesiod, Simonides, Aeschylus, and others, is the centerpiece of Aristophanes' *Frogs*, where Aeschylus and Euripides compete in the underworld.

Aristophanes is also a satirist who makes a *pharmakos* of his target, for he, like Hipponax, is a primary source for the word *pharmakos*, which he uses as a strong term of abuse.[54] Though the poet has the power of creating *pharmakoi*, this power makes him the victim, by harassment in the courts, of the political leader, Cleon.

Stoning is occasionally found in Aristophanes' plays.[55] The *Acharnians'* Dicaeopolis is made, as it were, a righteous *pharmakos* when he concludes a private peace with the Spartans and is stoned by the reactionary war party of Athens (285–344). Just before the stoners arrive, Dicaeopolis had been organizing his family in a Dionysiac procession, including phallus in basket and phallic song to Phales (260–279). Connecting this scene with Aristotle *Poetics*

---

[48] Cf. Cicero's use of tradition invective *topoi*, which nevertheless brought about his exiles and death. See below, ch. 22.

[49] Whitman 1964:80–81. Edmunds points out a background of "deme-centered animosities" in the feud (1987:61).

[50] For Old Comedy's background in lyric iambus, see Henderson 1975:18–24.

[51] *Acharnians* 1150–1160, cf. Rosen 1988c:72; Watson 1991:140–141, 238.

[52] Cf. Lesky 1966:237, 418; Rothwell 1995.

[53] See Lilja 1979; cf. Moulton, "The Lyric of Insult and Abuse," in Moulton 1981:18–47. See above, ch. 9 (Alcaeus); Rosen 1988c:32–33.

[54] See *Knights* 1402–1405; *Frogs* 730–733; fr. 655KA; Gebhard 1926: test. 1–12 Athens (pp. 11–15); Harrison 1922:97; Rosen 1988c:21–24.

[55] E.g. *Acharnians* 280–295; 319; 341–346; 331. Cf. ch. 1; Barkan 1927:47.

1449a, Lowell Edmunds describes Dicaeopolis as a "proto-poet."[56] As Martha Nussbaum notes, commenting on this passage, "The danger that the audience will not tolerate the poet's freedom, or hear his truths, is a recurrent theme in Aristophanic Comedy."[57] Thus, in the *Acharnians*, we have a proto-poet practicing phallic ritual stoned for his pacifist political views. In Sutton's view, Dicaeopolis and Aristophanes are closely connected.[58]

So Aristophanes, the dominant comic dramatist of his day, repeatedly attacked the dominant politician of his day, Cleon; Cleon apparently brought him to trial more than once in retaliation. One scholar suggests that his punishment was exile. But the punishment was only temporary, and Aristophanes eventually survived the law courts and continued his satirical attacks. In his work, Aristophanes becomes a key source for knowledge of the *pharmakos*. Ironically, he also was involved in intra-poetical, intra-intellectual satirical attacks, and helped make a victim of Euripides, our previous subject, and Socrates, our next, and culminating (for Greece), subject.[59]

---

[56] Edmunds 1980:6. We remember the association of Archilochus' legendary crime (phallic singing?) with phallic cult, see above, ch. 3. Cf. app. A, below.

[57] Nussbaum 1980:61. See *Acharnians* 318, *Frogs* 384–394; *Clouds* 518.

[58] Sutton 1988.

[59] We find the following themes in the Aristophanes biographical traditions and plays: 1a, crime of hero (by Cleon's accusation). 7, trial of poet, unjustly accused; 10a, exile (possible); 11a, stoning (as theme in poetry); 22, satirical themes; 22d, artist satirizing artist; 22e, curse as poetic theme; 24, conflict with political leaders.

15

Socrates: The New Aesop

I N MANY WAYS, the Platonic Socrates fits into the pattern of Aesop, the mythical blame poet who is moral, called by god, yet rejected by a corrupt society.

Socrates, like Aesop, was seen as the best of men. Thus, in the ending of the *Phaedo*: "Such, Echecrates, was the end of our comrade, who was, we may fairly say, of all those whom we knew in our time, the best [*aristou*] and also the wisest and most upright man."[1] The jailer in *Phaedo* refers to Socrates as "the noblest and gentlest and best [*ariston*] of all the men that have ever come here."[2] In Xenophon's *Apology*, Socrates reports that, after Chaerephon consulted Delphi concerning him, "in the presence of many people, Apollo answered that no man was more free than I, or more just, or more prudent . . . Apollo did not compare me to a god; he did, however, judge that I far excelled the rest of mankind."[3]

Socrates receives a divine commission, a consecration, and thus is sacred. He was given his obligation to cross-examine and unmask the pseudo-wise "in obedience to God's commands given in oracles and dreams and in every other way that any other divine dispensation has ever impressed a duty upon

---

[1] *Phaedo* 118: Ἥδε ἡ τελευτή, ὦ Ἐχέκρατες, τοῦ ἑταίρου ἡμῖν ἐγένετο, ἀνδρός, ὡς ἡμεῖς φαῖμεν ἄν, τῶν τότε ὧν ἐπειράθημεν <u>ἀρίστου</u> καὶ ἄλλως φρονιμωτάτου καὶ δικαιοτάτου. Cf. *Seventh Letter* 324d: Socrates is "the justest [*dikaiotaton*] man of his time" (<u>δικαιότατον</u> εἶναι τῶν τότε). Xenophon (*Memorabilia* 4.8.11) calls him "the best and happiest man" (ἄριστός τε ἀνὴρ καὶ εὐδαιμονέστατος). See Koch 1960:237, on the perfection of the Platonic Socrates; Zeller 1962:73–74. (All translations of Plato in this chapter are from Hamilton and Cairns 1961, unless otherwise noted.)

[2] *Phaedo* 116c: γενναιότατον καὶ πρᾳότατον καὶ <u>ἄριστον</u> ἄνδρα ὄντα τῶν πώποτε δεῦρο ἀφικομένων.

[3] *Apology* 14–15 (trans. O. J. Todd): πολλῶν παρόντων ἀνεῖλεν ὁ Ἀπόλλων μηδένα εἶναι ἀνθρώπων ἐμοῦ μήτε ἐλευθεριώτερον μήτε δικαιότερον μήτε σωφρονέστερον . . . ἐμὲ δὲ θεῷ μὲν οὐκ εἴκασεν, ἀνθρώπων δὲ πολλῷ προέκρινεν ὑπερφέρειν. As Chroust notes, this contradicts the Platonic Socrates (1957:31). Cf. below.

man."[4] Socrates' mission "is what my God commands."[5] He claims that "God has specially appointed me to this city."[6] Socrates describes himself as given (*dedosthai*) to Athens by god.[7] He is, in fact, the "gift of God," *theou dosin*, to Athens (*Apology* 30d)—or, perhaps, god's dose of medicine or dose of poison. Like Aesop and Archilochus, Socrates had a close connection with Delphi,[8] which was, as it were, the instrument of his consecration. In the *Apology*, he calls on "the god at Delphi" to be witness on his behalf, an Aesopic theme.[9]

Like Aesop, Socrates uses an animal quasi-fable (the gadfly and the horse) in his last statement to his accusers that, among other things, defends his divine mission, and includes a prophecy of his death. It is also somewhat insulting to his listeners, and allegorizes his satirical role. Socrates describes the fable as sounding "rather comical [*geloioteron*]"; it is itself in the satirical tradition.

ἀτεχνῶς—εἰ καὶ γελοιότερον εἰπεῖν—προσκείμενον τῇ πόλει ὑπὸ
τοῦ θεοῦ ὥσπερ ἵππῳ μεγάλῳ μὲν καὶ γενναίῳ, ὑπὸ μεγέθους δὲ
νωθεστέρῳ καὶ δεομένῳ ἐγείρεσθαι ὑπὸ μύωπός τινος, οἷον δή μοι
δοκεῖ ὁ θεὸς ἐμὲ τῇ πόλει προστεθηκέναι τοιοῦτόν τινα, ὃς ὑμᾶς
<u>ἐγείρων καὶ πείθων καὶ ὀνειδίζων</u> ἕνα ἕκαστον οὐδὲν παύομαι τὴν
ἡμέραν ὅλην πανταχοῦ προσκαθίζων. τοιοῦτος οὖν ἄλλος οὐ ῥᾳδίως
ὑμῖν γενήσεται, ὦ ἄνδρες, ἀλλ' ἐὰν ἐμοὶ πείθησθε, φείσεσθέ μου·
ὑμεῖς δ' ἴσως τάχ' ἂν ἀχθόμενοι, ὥσπερ οἱ νυστάζοντες ἐγειρόμενοι,
κρούσαντες ἄν με, πειθόμενοι Ἀνύτῳ, ῥᾳδίως ἂν ἀποκτείναιτε, εἶτα
τὸν λοιπὸν βίον καθεύδοντες διατελοῖτε ἄν, εἰ μή τινα ἄλλον ὁ θεὸς
ὑμῖν ἐπιπέμψειεν κηδόμενος ὑμῶν.

It is literally true, even if it sounds rather comical, that God has specially appointed me to this city, as though it were a large thor-

---

[4] *Apology* 33c: ἐμοὶ δὲ τοῦτο, ὡς ἐγώ φημι, προστέτακται ὑπὸ τοῦ θεοῦ πράττειν καὶ ἐκ μαντείων καὶ ἐξ ἐνυπνίων καὶ παντὶ τρόπῳ ᾧπέρ τίς ποτε καὶ ἄλλη θεία μοῖρα ἀνθρώπῳ καὶ ὁτιοῦν προσέταξε πράττειν.

[5] *Apology* 30a: ταῦτα γὰρ κελεύει ὁ θεός.

[6] *Apology* 30e: προσκείμενον τῇ πόλει ὑπὸ τοῦ θεοῦ.

[7] *Apology* 31a–b. So we come to the complex of gift/poison/medicine, including my theme 17. Cf. 23b: "My service to God has reduced me to extreme poverty" (ἐν πενίᾳ μυρίᾳ εἰμὶ διὰ τὴν τοῦ θεοῦ λατρείαν). For Socrates as one specially favored by god, Chroust 1957:238n140; Xenophon *Memorabilia* 4.3.12. For Socrates and the state religion, see Meijer 1981:249; Zeller 1962:77. For Socrates' inspiration, Zeller 1962:82–83. Brickhouse and Smith 1989 insist on the historicity of the Delphian oracle account (96–100). On the historicity of the *Apology*, cf. Chroust 1957:245n209. I would caution that only the basic stories, the stories in outline, might be historical.

[8] See e.g. *Apology* 20e–23b; Chroust 1957:30–33.

[9] *Apology* 20e–23b: τὸν θεὸν τὸν ἐν Δελφοῖς.

oughbred horse which because of its great size is inclined to be lazy and needs the stimulation of some stinging fly. It seems to me that God has attached me to this city to perform the office of such a fly, and all day long I never cease to settle here, there, and everywhere, rousing, persuading, reproving [*egeirōn kai peithōn kai oneidizōn*] every one of you. You will not easily find another like me, gentlemen, and if you take my advice you will spare my life. I suspect, however, that before long you will awake from your drowsing, and in your annoyance you will take Anytus' advice and finish me off with a single slap, and then you will go on sleeping till the end of your days, unless God in his care for you sends someone to take my place.

Apology 30e–31a

Like many of the poets we have studied, Socrates was a soldier on occasion. This would not be especially worthy of note, except that Alcibiades, in the *Symposium*, used the military theme, Socrates' heroism in battle, to heroize his master.[10] Socrates' soldiering is part of his persona as best of men.

Socrates was also seen as the worst of men in some ways. He was poverty-stricken,[11] and most importantly, was accused of criminal impiety, for which crime he was executed.[12] Late evidence (Josephus) denies that he was a temple thief,[13] which may or may not imply that there was such a tradition extant.

Significantly, as in the case of Aesop, as in the case of Sappho and Hipponax and Tyrtaeus, we also have a strong tradition that Socrates was ugly. According to Xenophon, he had protruding eyes, which seemed to want to see round the back of his head, and a snub nose[14] with wide nostrils.[15] Alcibiades in the Platonic *Symposium* likens Socrates to a Silenus, particularly to the satyr Marsyas; these creatures were proverbially coarse featured, bestial, and ugly.[16]

---

[10] See *Apology* 28e; *Symposium* 219e–220e; *Laches* 181b; *Charmides* i; Zeller 1962:67n2. Cf. ch. 3 (Archilochus).

[11] See *Apology* 23b, 31b–c; Dio Chrysostom, *Orations* 55.9; Chroust 1957:249nn283–285; 271n658; Zeller 1962:62–65; Montuori 1981:182; Socrates is always starving, ibid. 183. See above, ch. 4 (Hipponax).

[12] On the charge of *asebeia* 'impiety', see Finley 1977:65–66; Chroust 1957:311n1294; Ferguson 1913. See Brickhouse and Smith 1989, who are inclined to see the *Apology* as more historical than myth. Cf. the tradition of poet as *blasphēmos*, see above on Archilochus, ch. 3.

[13] Josephus *Against Apion* 2.263; Chroust 1957:244n197.

[14] Cf. *Theaetetus* 209.

[15] Xenophon *Banquet* 5.5–6; cf. Cross 1970:37.

[16] *Symposium* 215a–b, e; 216c–d; 221d–e; cf. 222d. For sileni and satyrs, see Euripides *Cyclops*; Ovid *Metamorphoses* 11.89–101; Sophocles, *Trackers*; Kuhnert 1884 IV.444–453; Rose 1959:156–157; Kerényi 1974.179; Seaford 1984:5–10; Lissarrague 1990; Hedreen 1992; Gantz 1993:135–139. For Aesop and satyrs, see above, ch. 2.

Xenophon's *Banquet* (4.16–19) shows that satyrs were seen as ugly, and that Socrates resembled a satyr. *Banquet* chapter 5 is Socrates' self-defense of his ugly features. Here again he argues that he is a silenus. The comparison with the sileni is apt, for these creatures were artistic, Muse-inspired (they were pipers), and mantic (they prophesied when captured).[17] The explicit identification of Socrates with Marsyas ("this latter day Marsyas," *Symposium* 215e, τουτουῒ τοῦ Μαρσύου) is also richly suggestive, for in addition to being a surpassingly sweet piper (215b–d), Marsyas is a mythological poet whom Apollo kills.[18] Plato is once more mythologizing his master and his upcoming death.[19]

Plato emphasizes the magical nature of Marsyas' playing; it "bewitches mankind" (ἐκήλει τοὺς ἀνθρώπους), and his tunes "have a magic power" (μόνα κατέχεσθαι ποιεῖ, 215c). The grotesquely ugly, animalistic satyr's tunes are also holy: "Because they are divine they reveal those men who need the gods and initiation."[20]

As we have seen, Socrates freely satirized his fellow citizens. The allegory of the horse and gadfly, a brilliantly satirical *ainos*, shows Socrates "rousing, persuading, reproving"; the drowsy horse is annoyed enough by this to slap the fly dead. Expressed more directly, the Athenians have found his "discussions and conversation" to be "too irksome and irritating" so they try to "get rid of them" (*Apology* 37c–d).[21] Socrates' historian was even seen to be in the iambic tradition. Gorgias, reading Plato's *Gorgias*, reportedly said, "How well Plato knows the art of producing iambs [*iambizein*]," and Gorgias even referred to him as a new Archilochus.[22]

As in the case of Aesop, Socrates' greatest occasion of blame is his farewell speech before death. "When I leave this court I shall go away condemned by you to death, but they [his accusers] will go away convicted by truth herself of wickedness and injustice [*mokhthērian kai adikian*]" (*Apology* 39b).[23] This opposition of true and false wickedness is an important theme in the story of Aesop's death.

---

[17] Herodotus 8.138; Aristotle fr. 40 (V. Rose), quoted by "Plutarch" *Consolation to Apollonius* 115b; Virgil *Eclogue* 6; H. Rose 1959:163n62; Clay 2000:74.

[18] See ch. 16, below.

[19] See Clay 2000:52–53, 69–76.

[20] *Symposium* 215c (my trans.): δηλοῖ τοὺς τῶν θεῶν τε καὶ τελετῶν δεομένους διὰ τὸ θεῖα εἶναι.

[21] ... ὑμεῖς μὲν ὄντες πολῖταί μου οὐχ οἷοί τε ἐγένεσθε ἐνεγκεῖν τὰς ἐμὰς διατριβὰς καὶ τοὺς λόγους, ἀλλ' ὑμῖν βαρύτεραι γεγόνασιν καὶ ἐπιφθονώτεραι, ὥστε ζητεῖτε αὐτῶν νυνὶ ἀπαλλαγῆναι.

[22] Athenaeus 11.505d–e: ὡς καλῶς οἶδε Πλάτων ἰαμβίζειν (Archilochus test. 76T). Athenaeus fully sympathizes with those that Plato satirized, portraying him as an unjust and nonhistorical satirist. See also Gentili 1988:192; Tracy 1937:153–162.

[23] καὶ νῦν ἐγὼ μὲν ἄπειμι ὑφ' ὑμῶν θανάτου δίκην ὀφλών, οὗτοι δ' ὑπὸ τῆς ἀληθείας ὠφληκότες μοχθηρίαν καὶ ἀδικίαν.

Yet Socrates was often an urbane satirist. "All his life he spends . . . practicing irony and mocking people [*eirōneuomenos de kai paizōn*]" (*Symposium* 216dff.).[24] At one point, Socrates is about to tell a friend, "One must, o Hippothales, converse with a beloved friend in such a way as will bring down his pride and humble him [*tapeinounta kai sustellonta*], but not, as you, make him more blown up and conceited."[25]

Puncturing blown-up pride obviously does not ingratiate a person with the conceited, who are by nature indisposed to receive criticism. Thus Socrates made enemies among some prominent citizens of Athens. In particular, Socrates criticized Anytus, his main accuser, a politician, for making his son a tanner.[26] Because of this, this politician brought suit against him. The *Seventh Letter* says Socrates was brought to trial by "some of those in authority" (*dunasteuontes tines*).[27] His blame is explicitly a cause for the charge being brought against him.[28]

After being condemned (unjustly)[29] by a public meeting, a trial, and a vote,[30] he was imprisoned.[31] All these are Aesopic themes, developed with consummate skill by Plato. Moses Finley writes of the different versions of Socrates' trial, "These versions do not agree with each other, and in places they are quite contradictory. Here before our eyes is the mythmaking process at work."[32]

After the condemnation, his acceptance of death seems voluntary, for he refuses to go into exile,[33] and takes his poison without any cowardice or

---

[24] εἰρωνευόμενος δὲ καὶ παίζων πάντα τὸν βίον πρὸς τοὺς ἀνθρώπους διατελεῖ.

[25] *Lysis* 210e. As quoted in Friedländer 1969:140. χρή, ὦ Ἱππόθαλες, τοῖς παιδικοῖς διαλέγεσθαι, ταπεινοῦντα καὶ συστέλλοντα, ἀλλὰ μὴ ὥσπερ σὺ χαυνοῦντα καὶ διαθρύπτοντα.

[26] Xenophon *Apology* 29. Socrates was also attacked by the comic poets—Aristophanes' *Clouds* is the most famous example of such an attack. This is another example of the Hipponactian theme of artist attacking artist—here poet attacking poet-philosopher. See above, ch. 14. Cf. Finley 1977:71: "[Aristophanes] . . . must bear a heavy responsibility . . . for the eventual trial and execution of Socrates." Aristophanes, Cratinus, Ameipsias, and Eupolis all satirized Socrates; Chroust 1957:192; Montuori 1981:3n3.

[27] *Seventh Letter* 325b. For political dimensions of this trial, see Chroust 1957:164–196; Finley 1977:60–73, with bibliography, 202–203; Brickhouse and Smith 1989:69–71, 80.

[28] Cf. Brickhouse and Smith 1989:198.

[29] *Seventh Letter* 325b–c; also, the *Apology* passim; Xenophon *Apology* 28.

[30] This is, of course, described in the *Apology*. For the theme of the frustration of the philosopher in court, see Chroust 1957:234n92.

[31] Both *Crito* and *Phaedo* take place in prison.

[32] Finley 1977:62.

[33] *Apology* 37c–38b. This passage suggests that the court's original intention was to merely exile Socrates. The philosopher makes it clear that he prefers death. "Or shall I suggest banishment? . . . I should have to be desperately in love with life to do that, gentlemen" (ἀλλὰ δὴ φυγῆς τιμήσωμαι; . . . πολλὴ μεντἂν με φιλοψυχία ἔχοι, ὦ ἄνδρες Ἀθηναῖοι, εἰ οὕτως ἀλόγιστός εἰμι). Socrates makes it clear that he would be banished from any city he lived in: "A fine life I should have if I left this country at my age and spent the rest of my days

delay.[34] Plato emphasizes this point: Socrates takes the cup of poison "cheerfully" (*Phaedo* 117b, *mala hileōs*) and drinks the poison "with no sign of distaste" (117c, *eukolōs*). This serenity is probably an idealization, to some extent.[35]

Oddly enough, or perhaps naturally enough, in the days before he drank the hemlock, Socrates occupied his time in versifying Aesop's fables (*Phaedo* 60c–61b).[36] While one cannot disallow the possibility that this is historical, it is also possible that it is purely Platonic. In any case, Plato was enough of a conscious artist that he was using this detail for more than incidental meaning. Before Socrates mentions his versifying of Aesop, he discusses pain and pleasure and makes up a fable about them (they are like quarreling men joined at the head by god) that he describes as Aesopic—"I am sure that if Aesop had thought of it he would have made up a fable about them, something like this" (60c).[37] Socrates makes up Aesopic fables and (re-)writes Aesop's fables (almost as Pierre Menard rewrites the *Quixote* in Borges's story); he is being assimilated to Aesop by Plato, and surely Aesop's death is being echoed here, in the *Phaedo*, the dialogue of Socrates' death. The story of Aesop's unjust execution was already a commonplace in Athens, since Herodotus and Aristophanes refer to it.[38] Diogenes Laertius even preserves a purported excerpt from one of these poems:

> Αἴσωπός ποτ' ἔλεξε Κορίνθιον ἄστυ νέμουσι,
> μὴ κρίνειν ἀρετὴν λαοδίκῳ σοφίῃ.

---

trying one city after another and being turned out [*exelaunomenōi*] every time!" (καλὸς οὖν ἄν μοι ὁ βίος εἴη ἐξελθόντι τηλικῷδε ἀνθρώπῳ ἄλλην ἐξ ἄλλης πόλεως ἀμειβομένῳ καὶ ἐξελαυνομένῳ ζῆν). Socrates will always talk to the youth, and their "fathers and other relatives" (πατέρες δὲ καὶ οἰκεῖοι) will always drive him out. Cf. Chroust 1957:311n1296; Montuori 1981:197. For the volition of the sacrificial victim, see above, ch. 1; and below, ch. 22 (Cicero).

[34] See *Phaedo* 116c; 116d–117a for the grace and willingness with which Socrates takes the poison.

[35] Barkan 1979:76 and Gill 1973:25–28 write that a person who died of hemlock usually thrashed around in convulsions. But see now Sullivan (2001), who concludes that certain strains of hemlock produced more peaceful deaths.

[36] For Socrates and Aesop, see Jedrkiewicz 1989; Compton 1990; Schauer and Merkle 1992; Lissarrague 2000:136. Schauer's and Merkle's argument that Plato in the *Phaedo* introduces Aesop in an unfavorable light, as a negative contrast to Socrates, is not compelling, and seems to me to misread Plato's seriocomic tone here (*Phaedo* 60b–61c). Furthermore, Schauer and Merkle have not taken into consideration how Plato assimilated Socrates to other mythical victims of unjust trials, Ajax or Palamedes, *Apology* 41b (see below). In addition, their antithesis of the "voluntary" death of Plato and the "involuntary" execution of Aesop ignores the "voluntary" motif in Aesop's death and "involuntary" aspects of Socrates' death. They recast Socrates' death as a sort of suicide, while Socrates in the *Phaedo* explicitly rejects straightforward suicide (61c–62c). Both Aesop and Socrates die as the result of unjust trials, see the *Crito*. However, Plato's point is that, after receiving such an unjust verdict, a good man is prepared to die.

[37] καί μοι δοκεῖ, ἔφη, εἰ ἐνενόησεν αὐτὰ Αἴσωπος, μῦθον ἂν συνθεῖναι ὡς . . .

[38] *Phaedo* 60c–61b, and see above, ch. 2.

> Aesop once said to those living in the city of Corinth
> that they should not judge virtue by the wisdom of a jury-court.
>
> Diogenes Laertius 2.42, my trans.

Even if this is not authentic, it shows that Socrates is being assimilated to Aesop because of Aesop's unjust death.

Versifying Aesop explicitly makes Socrates a poet,[39] though his philosophical pursuits and verbal artistry would have qualified him as a poet in a less technical sense; as we have seen, Alcibiades refers to him as a Marsyas, a maker of supernaturally beguiling music. He is specifically a blame poet, a satirist, and a moral critic, to a significant degree.

These Aesopic allusions are closely connected with the cult of Apollo, for Socrates is working on adapting the Aesopic fables and is composing a hymn to Apollo at the same time; and he is doing both of them in response to dreams encouraging him to "practice and cultivate the arts [*mousikēn*]."[40] Socrates makes poems by "versifying the tales of Aesop and the hymn to Apollo."[41] Socrates works at these poems during a festival to Apollo that is delaying his death—in fact the hymn is written in honor of that festival and its god.[42] And perhaps we are to understand that Apollo has inspired the dreams—if so, Apollo himself is extending the link from Aesop to Socrates, in Plato's elaborate system of correspondences.

Socrates' daimon has engineered his death;[43] but, as Socrates makes clear, death is not a bad thing for a just man,[44] so the daimon is his patron, working for his good. This is a clear expression of the notion of divinity as beneficent executioner that lies behind so many of these lives of poets.

Like Aesop and Homer, Socrates prophesies serious consequences arising from his unjust execution:

---

[39] See also Socrates as Marsyas, the magical musician (*Symposium* 215 b–c), above, this chapter; for Aesop compared to Marsyas, see ch. 2.

[40] *Phaedo* 60c–61b. 60e: "Ὦ Σώκρατες," ἔφη, "μουσικὴν ποίει καὶ ἐργάζου." For the meaning of *mousikē*, see ch. 16, on Marsyas.

[41] *Phaedo* 60c–d: περὶ γάρ τοι τῶν ποιημάτων ὧν πεποίηκας ἐντείνας τοὺς τοῦ Αἰσώπου λόγους καὶ τὸ εἰς τὸν Ἀπόλλω προοίμιον ... For the meaning of *enteinō* here, see Plato *Hipparchus* 228d; LSJ v.2; Burnet 1911:15–16; Hackforth 1955:33n4; Rowe 1993:120.

[42] On this festival, see *Phaedo* 58a–c; 59e; 60d–61b (the hymn to Apollo composed in honor of the festival to Apollo). Curiously, this festival is linked to Androgeus the Cretan, whose death set off the chain of imbalances that ended in the yearly ship to Delos. "They have a law that as soon as this mission begins the city must be kept pure" (ἐπειδὰν οὖν ἄρξωνται τῆς θεωρίας, νόμος ἐστὶν αὐτοῖς ἐν τῷ χρόνῳ τούτῳ καθαρεύειν τὴν πόλιν ..., 58b). The mission begins when the priest of Apollo garlands the stern of the ship.

[43] *Apology* 40a–c.

[44] *Apology* 40a–42. Cf. Chroust 1957:235n108.

Τὸ δὲ δὴ μετὰ τοῦτο ἐπιθυμῶ ὑμῖν χρησμῳδῆσαι, ὦ καταψηφισάμενοί μου· καὶ γάρ εἰμι ἤδη ἐνταῦθα ἐν ᾧ μάλιστα ἄνθρωποι χρησμῳδοῦσιν, ὅταν μέλλωσιν ἀποθανεῖσθαι. φημὶ γάρ, ὦ ἄνδρες οἳ ἐμὲ ἀπεκτόνατε, τιμωρίαν ὑμῖν ἥξειν εὐθὺς μετὰ τὸν ἐμὸν θάνατον πολὺ χαλεπωτέραν νὴ Δία ἢ οἵαν ἐμὲ ἀπεκτόνατε· νῦν γὰρ τοῦτο εἴργασθε οἰόμενοι μὲν ἀπαλλάξεσθαι τοῦ διδόναι ἔλεγχον τοῦ βίου, τὸ δὲ ὑμῖν πολὺ ἐναντίον ἀποβήσεται, ὡς ἐγώ φημι. πλείους ἔσονται ὑμᾶς οἱ ἐλέγχοντες ... καὶ χαλεπώτεροι ἔσονται ὅσῳ νεώτεροί εἰσιν, καὶ ὑμεῖς μᾶλλον ἀγανακτήσετε.

I feel moved to prophesy to you who have given your vote against me, for I am now at that point where the gift of prophecy comes most readily to men—at the point of death.[45] I tell you, my executioners, that as soon as I am dead, vengeance shall fall upon you with a punishment far more painful than your killing of me. You have brought about my death in the belief that through it you will be delivered from submitting your conduct to criticism, but I say that the result will be just the opposite. You will have more critics ... and being younger they will be harsher to you and will cause you more annoyance.

Apology 39c–d

So there will be a moral, rhetorical plague (more, harsher critics) following Socrates' death. This is to a certain extent a departure from the earlier prophecies. Aesop warns of plague and war, and Homer prophesies a shortage of poets for Cyme, a plague of poetic sterility, as it were, but Plato prophesies more and harsher satirist philosophers, an inversion of the Homeric plague. However, Socrates' prophecy perhaps by implication predicts a dearth of moderate philosophers and thus continues the Homeric tradition.[46] Thus this theme shows us three outcomes: the cultic, the literary, and the literary/philosophical. The cultic reality continues in literary trappings; we have a literary cult hero and a literary cult myth. We have the echo of cultic honors to Socrates: not long after his death ("immediately," *euthus*), the Athenians feel

[45] Cf. Xenophon *Apology* 30. For parallels to this idea, Homer *Iliad* XVI 851–861; XXII 358–368; Xenophon *The Education of Cyrus* 8.7.21; Artemon of Miletus, quoted by Eustathius in *Iliad* p. 1089; Cicero *On Divination* 1.30, 36; Vergil *Aeneid* 10.739; Burnet 1924:164; Chroust 1957:284n870; Dyer 1976:107; Janko 1992:420.

[46] The immediate consequence of Socrates' death is the departure of his disciples to Megara—according to Diogenes Laertius, because they feared the cruelty of the political leaders (Diogenes Laertius 2.10.106).

such remorse that they put Meletus to death and exile other prominent accusers. Then "they honoured [*etimēsan*] Socrates with a bronze statue [*eikoni*], the work of Lysippus, which they placed in the hall of procession."[47]

The Xenophonic *Apology* has a different prophecy: Anytus's son will not continue in the servile profession that his father forced him into, and "through want of a worthy adviser he will fall into some disgraceful propensity and will surely go far in the career of vice" (30). As it turns out, this prophecy is later fulfilled when the son becomes an alcoholic.[48] Anytus himself suffers exile, misery, and finally stoning.[49]

There is another curious coincidence in Socrates' biographical tradition. According to Apollodorus, Socrates was born on the sixth day of the month Thargelion,[50] the day on which the *pharmakos* ritual was carried out, the first of two days of the Thargelia. If this were factual, it would be an interesting coincidence; but it is more likely that it is once again an example of mythical elaboration. According to Greek tradition, this was also the day on which Troy fell; the day of the Greek victories at Marathon and Plataea; and the date of the victory of Alexander over Darius. "Evidently," writes Bremmer, "the expulsion of evil was felt so intensely that this seemed to be the appropriate day to celebrate these victories."[51] It also seemed right, evidently, that Socrates should be born on such a mythically charged ritual day.

Poison is a major theme in the *Phaedo*.[52] To Socrates, poison, the means of death, is really the means of achieving life, for in the Platonic scheme of things, this body is a tomb[53] or a prison.[54] Separating the soul from the body

---

[47] Diogenes Laertius 2.43: Σωκράτην δὲ χαλκῇ εἰκόνι ἐτίμησαν, ἣν ἔθεσαν ἐν τῷ πομπείῳ, Λυσίππου ταύτην ἐργασαμένου. For the importance of statues in hero cult, see Clay 2004:88–89; ch. 2 (Lykoros honors Aesop); ch. 5 (Homer), ch. 13 (Euripides) above. On Lysippus' statue, cf. Clay 2000:69–70.

[48] διὰ δὲ τὸ μηδένα ἔχειν σπουδαῖον ἐπιμελητὴν προσπεσεῖσθαί τινι αἰσχρᾷ ἐπιθυμίᾳ καὶ προβήσεσθαι μέντοι πόρρω μοχθηρίας.

[49] Xenophon *Apology* 31; Themistius 520, p. 293 Dindorf; Diogenes Laertius 2.43, 6.10; Chroust 1957:232n72. Cf. Plato's description of Meletus, another accuser, *Gorgias* 521c, "an utterly bad and worthless creature" (μοχθηροῦ ἀνθρώπου καὶ φαύλου). Though Meletus is not mentioned by name, this is clearly a reference to him. He is eventually executed (Diogenes Laertius 6.10). See also *Euthyphro* 2b; *Apology* 26b, 26e; Chroust 1957:240n169.

[50] Cited in Diogenes Laertius, 2.44. "He was born . . . on the sixth day of the month of Thargelion, when the Athenians purify their city, which according to the Delians is the birthday of Artemis," trans. Hicks, Ἐγεννήθη δέ . . . Θαργηλιῶνος ἕκτῃ, ὅτε καθαίρουσιν Ἀθηναῖοι τὴν πόλιν καὶ τὴν Ἄρτεμιν Δήλιοι γενέσθαι φασίν. Cf. Derrida 1981:134; Zeller 1962:54n1.

[51] 1983b:318; see also Burkert 1979:169n12.

[52] See 63d–e; 115a–118.

[53] *Gorgias* 493.

[54] *Cratylus* 400c.

is called "catharsis—purification."[55] And "true philosophers make dying their profession."[56] Socrates says, in his famous last words: "Crito, we ought to offer a cock to Asclepius. See to it and don't forget."[57] Though this is a much-disputed problem, one certainty is that Asclepius was a god of healing. A reasonable interpretation of these last words is that Socrates is being healed by the poison that is bringing about his death. The poison is his medicine, just as he is the dose of healing poison administered to Athens.

Thus, Socrates, as portrayed by his disciples, is the best of men, and sacred—he is commissioned by god to deliver his message—he was closely connected with Apollo and Delphi. He was also the worst—poor, accused of criminal impiety, and remarkably ugly. He was a blame "poet," occasionally using the animal fable to attack the Athenians, and his fellow citizens found his teachings intolerable. He was condemned in a trial, imprisoned, and sentenced to death—in actuality, a practical sentence of exile. But he chose obedient death over exile. He felt that the situation of his trial was directed by god—so his patron deity engineered his death—and he calls upon Apollo as his witness during his last speech. His condemnation was followed by disastrous consequences for Athens, but it was also followed by the influence of his teachings in the hands of such disciples as Plato.

It is entirely possible, as many scholars have argued, that Plato especially shaped Socrates' *vita* into the form of such a myth. Montuori argues that the *Apology* is not a faithful account of Socrates' defense at his trial, or even a mixture of truth and fiction; it is "above all an apologia for Plato and of Socrates' disciples." To portray Socrates' relentless cross-examining as beneficial, not corrupting, Plato must invent the oracle to Chaerephon, which transforms Socrates into something of a prophet, an Apolline gift to Athens.[58] Though Montuori is generally correct on Plato's skillful mythologizing, the oracle to Chaerophon is in Xenophon (*Apology* 14), so cannot have been a purely Platonic invention.

In the generation after Socrates' death, a literature of polemic grew up attacking and defending Socrates—Polycrates, Plato, Xenophon, and Isocrates began "a vast literary movement by which the followers of Socrates" rehabilitated the relationship of the philosopher and Alcibiades. This "vast liter-

---

[55] *Phaedo* 67c.

[56] *Phaedo* 67e: οἱ ὀρθῶς φιλοσοφοῦντες ἀποθνῄσκειν μελετῶσι.

[57] *Phaedo* 118: Ὦ Κρίτων, ἔφη, τῷ Ἀσκληπιῷ ὀφείλομεν ἀλεκτρυόνα· ἀλλὰ ἀπόδοτε καὶ μὴ ἀμελήσητε. There is an extensive literature on these words. See Carafides 1971.

[58] The Chaerophon invention is "at the root of Plato's transfiguration of the Socratic personality" (Montuori 1981:220; 221); see 225n151 for bibliography on Socrates as Delphic missionary.

ary movement" eventually was reduced to one powerful myth, the Platonic Socrates, *die Sokratesdichtung*, as Olof Gigon expresses it.[59] Gigon is the radical skeptic, for whom the Platonic life of Socrates is a poem that has nothing to do with history.[60] It is possible that the Socratic myth is dependent for its genesis on an anti-myth, of which we have especially the *Clouds* remaining.

Many of the features highlighted above are paralleled in the Aesop biographical traditions, and these similarities are cemented by the Platonic Socrates versifying Aesop in his last days, because of a divine directive, during a festival of Apollo. Aesop is the mythological poet-*pharmakos*, and Socrates is the new Aesop.[61] Plato would assimilate Socrates to Aesop chiefly because of the blatant injustice of what amounted to a political murder in both cases. And in assimilating Socrates to Aesop, he also calls on archaic resonances of the *pharmakos*, who was selected for execution "by a public vote"— *psēphidi . . . boulēi dēmosiēi*, to deepen his narrative. In the cases of Aesop, Archilochus, and Socrates, the community uses the selection process to unwittingly select itself as polluted, and doomed to a certain extent. As the group of citizens isolates the poet as a sinner, the lone pseudocriminal, both holy and animalistic filth, is able to invert and reciprocally broadcast the judgment through his expulsion or execution. The poet is, as it were, the unwanted moral mirror of the community, and the trial is the moment of mirroring, of ambiguous moral reciprocity.

That these suggestions of Aesop and *pharmakos* are a conscious strategy on Plato's part is suggested by the fact that in the *Apology*, he also skillfully compared Socrates to other mythical figures who were victims of injustice, as Socrates wishes to speak to Palamedes and Ajax in the underworld. "It would be a specially interesting experience for me to join them there, to meet Palamedes and Ajax, the son of Telamon, and any other heroes of the old days who met their death through an unfair trial [*krisin adikon*], and to compare my

---

[59] Gigon 1947:69–178

[60] For an overview of the conflict between skeptics and historicists in this century's Platonic scholarship, see Montuori 1981:42–53; for a shrewd critique of Gigon, see Friedländer 1969:361n6. For the *Nachleben* of the Socrates myth through Western civilization, see Montuori 1981:3–56.

[61] Socrates would seem to be part of a new line of development in our mythical theme, the execution or exclusion of the philosopher. Of course, Aristotle was tried for impiety in Athens, and so withdrew to Calchis, where he died (Diogenes Laertius 5.5–6); cf. below, ch. 25 (Seneca and Cornutus), Epilogue. Cato the Censor and his friends banished Greek philosophers—Suetonius *On Rhetoricians* 1; Athenaeus (12.547a–b) lists other examples of expelled philosophers. Cf. the death of the Cynic Homeromastix Zoilos, who was stoned and crucified by different accounts (Vitruvius *On Architecture* Praefat. to VII, #9); another Homeromastix, Daphitas, was crucified for mocking kings in poetry (Strabo 14.1.39); *Suda* s.v. Daphitas; Cicero *On Fate* 3—cf. Gärtner 1978:1535–1536.

fortunes with theirs—it would be rather amusing, I think."[62] Palamedes was killed by stoning on a false accusation of treason because of false evidence planted by Odysseus and Diomedes in his tent. As a result of this death, Palamedes' father, Nauplius, caused a great number of the Greek ships to be shipwrecked. Here we have Plato skillfully assimilating Socrates to a mythological model who was stoned after a *krisin adikon* based on falsely planted evidence, and whose death caused a disaster to the perpetrators.[63]

Yet many other aspects of Aesop would be suggestive—his ugliness (which certainly makes him a more sympathetic figure), the punishment that descends upon the city that has killed him, his satirical bent. Most important would be the suggestion of the poet's ambiguity—though he is ugly and hated by the community for his just satire, which is his real "crime," he is also the best, sent by the gods, protected by the gods, and will always be famous. One wonders how far Plato took the comparison; perhaps he saw Aesop's death as part of a divine mechanism, and wanted to show the same mechanism operative in Socrates' death. It was an attempt on his part to construct a theodicy for what was still a traumatic, chaotic event; to create meaning from his master's death. Socrates' "voice" does not dissuade him from speaking at his trial, or keep him from escaping execution by leaving Athens; the philosopher learns to die; his death is prepared by the god.[64]

Thus the poet is ambiguous, enigmatic. To Vernant, Oedipus is "a man in the form of a riddle."[65] Aesop is even referred to as a riddle, *ainigma* (G 98). Yet Aesop is also referred to as a sign, *sēmeion* (G 87),[66] and if he is a *teras*, "monster," *teras* can also mean "sign." The ambiguity of the poet, so well captured in the myth of his trial, points to meaning. The trial of the poet, especially as expressed in Plato's *Apology*, is one of the most meaningful myths in ancient Greece.

---

[62] *Apology* 41b: ἐπεὶ ἔμοιγε καὶ αὐτῷ θαυμαστὴ ἂν εἴη ἡ διατριβὴ αὐτόθι, ὁπότε ἐντύχοιμι Παλαμήδει καὶ Αἴαντι τῷ Τελαμῶνος καὶ εἴ τις ἄλλος τῶν παλαιῶν διὰ <u>κρίσιν ἄδικον</u> τέθνηκεν, ἀντιπαραβάλλοντι τὰ ἐμαυτοῦ πάθη πρὸς τὰ ἐκείνων—ὡς ἐγὼ οἶμαι, οὐκ ἂν ἀηδὲς εἴη. Cf. notes of Burnet 1924 *ad loc.*; also, Brenk 1975:44–46. For Plato's assimilation of Socrates to such heroes as Odysseus, Achilles, and Heracles, see Loraux 1985:93–105; Clay 1972; Clay 2000:56–57.

[63] See also Xenophon *Apology* 26.

[64] Thus we find the following themes in the life of Socrates: 1a1, criminal impiety (imputed); 2b, communal disaster caused by hero's expulsion or death; 3, oracle; 4, worst; 4d, ugly; 4f, poison imagery; 5, best; 5a, sacred; 7, selection by public meeting; 10a, (exile); 11, death; 18, divine persecutor-patron; 21, imprisonment; 22, blame poet; 22c, animal fables for blame; 23a, (consecration of poet); 24, conflict with political leaders; 26, poet as soldier.

[65] Vernant 1981:208.

[66] "Let another portent-interpreter be brought so that he may interpret this *sēmeion*," say the Samians, on catching sight of him. See ch. 2.

16

Victim of the Muses: Mythical Poets

A
S HAS BEEN SHOWN PREVIOUSLY, the lives of the poets are often composed of legendary and mythical elements, side by side with historical elements. We will now approach the problem from the other side, looking at selected mythical poets, testing these myths for attestations of the same patterns. A more complete survey of mythical poets can be found in Jeno Platthy's odd book, *The Mythical Poets of Greece*.

The Musical *Agōn*

Both Plato and the Aesop Romance assimilated their heroes to Marsyas, the satyr, so he is a logical starting point. Though he is not a poet per se, he is a musician, and poetry and music (separated by modern definitions) were always closely associated in archaic Greece.[1] Furthermore, the structure of his story offers a close parallel to the stories of poetic *agōnes* we have found in stories of ancient poets, in the cases of Homer, Hesiod, and Aeschylus. Thus Marsyas is an important mythical antecedent to the legends of the Greek poets. In his myth, and in related stories, the hero is explicitly victim of the Muses.[2]

We first hear of Marsyas in Herodotus: "Here, too [at Celaenae, near Phrygia, in Asia Minor], the skin of Marsyas the Silenus is exhibited; according to the Phrygian legend Apollo flayed Marsyas and hung the skin up here in the marketplace."[3] The oldest reference to an *agōn* is in Xenophon: "Here it is

---

[1] Originally, *mousikē* included poetry, music, and dancing, Gentili 1988:24. The music was combined with poetry at first; later, solo music developed, "Plutarch" *On Music* 30 (1141d); Gentili 1988:26–28. Finally, in the Hellenistic era, music dominated completely, with the words "accompanying" the music. Gentili 1988:30; Koller 1963; Nagy 1990b:24–26; Nagy 2002:36; Murray and Wilson 2004.

[2] For myths relating to music, see Murray and Wilson 2004:2, with further bibliography. Much valuable information on the Muses, Mnemosyne, and Apollo can also be found in this book.

[3] Trans. Selincourt, Herodotus 7.26: ἐν τῇ καὶ ὁ τοῦ Σιληνοῦ Μαρσύεω ἀσκὸς [ἐν τῇ πόλι] ἀνακρέμαται, τὸν ὑπὸ Φρυγῶν λόγος ἔχει ὑπὸ Ἀπόλλωνος ἐκδαρέντα ἀνακρεμασθῆναι. See

said that Apollo flayed Marsyas, having conquered him when he was striving [*erizonta*] with him concerning skillfulness."[4] There are other early references in Plato, as Alcibiades compares Socrates to Marsyas and emphasizes the sacral sweetness of his music, in contrast to his (and Socrates') satyrlike, bestial ugliness.[5] Apollodorus gives a standard exposition of the complete story:

Ἀπέκτεινε δὲ Ἀπόλλων καὶ τὸν Ὀλύμπου παῖδα Μαρσύαν. οὗτος γὰρ εὑρὼν αὐλούς, οὓς ἔρριψεν Ἀθηνᾶ διὰ τὸ τὴν ὄψιν αὐτῆς ποιεῖν ἄμορφον, ἦλθεν εἰς <u>ἔριν περὶ μουσικῆς</u> Ἀπόλλωνι. συνθεμένων δὲ αὐτῶν ἵνα ὁ νικήσας ὃ βούλεται διαθῇ τὸν ἡττημένον, τῆς κρίσεως γινομένης τὴν κιθάραν στρέψας <u>ἠγωνίζετο</u> ὁ Ἀπόλλων, καὶ ταὐτὸ ποιεῖν ἐκέλευσε τὸν Μαρσύαν· τοῦ δὲ ἀδυνατοῦντος εὑρεθεὶς κρείσσων ὁ Ἀπόλλων, κρεμάσας τὸν Μαρσύαν ἔκ τινος ὑπερτενοῦς πίτυος, ἐκτεμὼν τὸ δέρμα οὕτως διέφθειρεν.

Apollo also killed Marsyas, the son of Olympus. For Marsyas, having found the pipes which Athena had thrown away because they disfigured her face,[6] engaged in a musical contest [*erin peri mousikēs*] with Apollo. They agreed that the victor should work his will on the vanquished, and when the trial took place Apollo turned his lyre upside down in the competition [*ēgonizeto*] and bade Marsyas do the same. But Marsyas could not, so Apollo was judged the victor and killed Marsyas by hanging him on a tall pine tree and stripping off his skin.

1.4.2, trans. Frazer, adapted[7]

In other variants, it is made explicit that the Muses were the judges of the competition.[8]

---

also Plutarch *Alcibiades* 2.5ff. (192E); Pausanias 1.24.1; Ovid *Metamorphoses* 6.382ff.; Vogel 1964:34–56; further references in Weiler 1974:37. For fifth-century BC artistic representations of Marsyas, see Gantz 1993:95.

[4] Xenophon *Anabasis* 1.2.8: ἐνταῦθα λέγεται Ἀπόλλων ἐκδεῖραι Μαρσύαν νικήσας <u>ἐρίζοντά</u> οἱ περὶ σοφίας.

[5] See ch. 15; *Symposium* 215a–b, e; 216c–d; 221d–e; cf. 222d. Also, Xenophon *Banquet* 4.16–19.

[6] When Athena had thrown them away, she had laid a curse on whoever should play them.

[7] Weiler (1974:37–59) surveys the variants, including Diodorus Siculus 3.59.2; *Scriptores Rerum Mythicarum* ("Writers on Mythical Subjects") 2.115; in other versions, the two agonists perform in rounds, and Marsyas wins the first round, forcing Apollo to stoop to trickery to come off victor. In artistic representations, Marsyas is sometimes shown playing a kithara, like Apollo (Weiler 1974:51). For the theme of hanging, see ch. 3 (Archilochus).

[8] See Hyginus *Fables* CLXV 4; Diodorus Siculus 3.59.2; *Scriptores Rerum Mythicarum* 2.115; cf. Weiler 1974:49–50.

Ovid tells us that the lamentations of the fauns, satyrs, nymphs, shepherds, and rustics produced such an enormous amount of tears that the river Marsyas resulted.[9] Later, we learn from Pausanias, Phrygians "repelled the army of the Gauls by the aid of Marsyas, who defended them against the barbarians by the water from the river and by the music of his flute."[10] Both these details strongly suggest hero cult awarded to the satyr.

Though Apollo remained inimical to the pipe because of Marsyas for some time, Pausanias tells us that a Pythian flute tune was played at Delphi;[11] and that Marsyas' pipes were eventually possessed by Apollo. The river Marsyas carried them to the Maeander, which took them to the Asopus, then they were washed ashore in the Sicyonian territory, and a shepherd gave them to Apollo.[12] Thus, according to the formulation of Burkert, enmity in myth entails unity in cult.

Here we see familiar themes. There is a poetic consecration, of sorts; in a comic story playing on Athena's puffed-out cheeks and vanity, Marsyas receives his instrument from a goddess, just as Archilochus had received a lyre. (Our earliest iconographic evidence for Marsyas, the statue by Myron, portrays the satyr at this moment.[13]) The poet-musician is subhuman, animalistic, yet rivalling Apollo himself in making beautiful music. The musical contest amounts to a trial (*krisis*) with the poet's life at stake; he is bested unfairly perhaps, thus making the judgment against the poet unjust (perhaps). The death of the poet-musician follows; he is explicitly killed by the god, seconded by the Muses (with the theme of hanging). But the god eventually possesses the pipes that had originally caused the enmity. Finally, the musician receives hero cult, and gives victory in battle.

As has been mentioned, both Aesop and Socrates are explicitly linked to Marsyas in their *vitae*. The Aesopic parallel is above all linked to the ambivalent enmity with Apollo; the animalistic marginality in appearance is also comparable. The explicit Socratic parallels are the physical animalism, but also the mantic musicality of Socrates' speech.

Similar stories are told of other figures in Greek myth. Pan also competed with Apollo in a musical contest, pitting rustic pipes against Apollo's lyre,

---

[9] *Metamorphoses* 6.390–400. For the lament and hero cult, see Nagy 1979:114–117 and ch. 6, "Lamentation and the Hero."

[10] Trans. Jones, Pausanias 10.30.9: φασὶ δὲ ὡς καὶ τὴν Γαλατῶν ἀπώσαιντο στρατείαν τοῦ Μαρσύου σφίσιν ἐπὶ τοὺς βαρβάρους ὕδατί τε ἐκ τοῦ ποταμοῦ καὶ μέλει τῶν αὐλῶν ἀμύναντος.

[11] Pausanias 2.22.8,9. A flute player, Sacadas, was supposed to have assuaged Apollo's wrath, probably a secondary aetiological detail.

[12] Pausanias 2.7.9. Cf. association of Aesop with the river Aesop, Adrados 1979:104.

[13] See Gantz 1993:86; Melanippides of Melos, Page 1962 # 758.

and the arbitrant, King Tmolus, awarded the victory to Apollo.[14] Interestingly, Apollo learned the gift of prophecy from Pan,[15] and so we have identification of victor with vanquished once again.

Thamyris engaged in a similar foolhardy contest, which is attested as early as the *Iliad*:

> ... Δώριον, ἔνθα τε Μοῦσαι
> ἀντόμεναι Θάμυριν τὸν Θρήϊκα παῦσαν ἀοιδῆς,
> Οἰχαλίηθεν ἰόντα παρ' Εὐρύτου Οἰχαλιῆος·
> στεῦτο γὰρ εὐχόμενος νικησέμεν, εἴ περ ἂν αὐταὶ
> Μοῦσαι ἀείδοιεν, κοῦραι Διὸς αἰγιόχοιο·
> αἱ δὲ χολωσάμεναι πηρὸν θέσαν, αὐτὰρ ἀοιδὴν
> θεσπεσίην ἀφέλοντο καὶ ἐκλέλαθον κιθαριστύν.

> ... Dorion, where the Muses
> encountering Thamyris the Thracian stopped him from
> singing
> as he came from Oichalia and Oichalian Eurytos;
> for he boasted that he would surpass, if the very Muses,
> daughters of Zeus who holds the aegis, were singing against
> him,
> and these in their anger struck him maimed, and the voice of
> wonder
> they took away, and made him a singer without memory ...

> *Iliad* II 594–600, trans. Lattimore

According to Apollodorus, "Thamyris, who excelled in beauty[16] and in lyre-singing, engaged in a musical contest with the Muses, the agreement being that, if he won, he should enjoy them all, but that if he should be vanquished he should be bereft of what they would. So the Muses got the

---

[14] Ovid *Metamorphoses* 11.146–173; cf. *Homeric Hymn* 19; Gantz 1993:110–111.

[15] Apollodorus 1.4.1: Ἀπόλλων δὲ τὴν μαντικὴν μαθὼν παρὰ Πανὸς ... Cf. Hyginus *Fables* 191.

[16] Cf. Robert 1920 1.414n5; on the whole Thamyris episode, ibid. pp. 413–416; Gantz 1993:55. On the madness of the poet, Hesychius s.v. Thamyris; Robert 1920 1:416n2. See Pausanias 10.7.2; and above ch. 3 (Archilochus). For possible iconographic evidence that Thamyris was also a favorite of the Muses, see Robert 1920 1:414n5. However, this interpretation is not certain, see Roscher 1884 5.478, which includes a drawing of the vase in question. Lucian tells us that Thamyris received his gift of singing from the Muses, *Fisherman* 6. In Polygnotus' famous painting of the underworld, the blinded Thamyris is shown with a broken lyre at his feet, Pausanias 10.30.8.

better of him and bereft him both of his eyes and of his lyre-singing."[17] The blinding is attested as early as Hesiod, apparently.[18] The theme of the blinding of the poet, evidenced most memorably in the Homer *vita*, returns again. Demodocus was another poet who was blinded by a Muse, but was given the gift of song as recompense.[19] One thinks in this connection of Tiresias, the seer, who had his eyesight taken away by Hera, as punishment for taking Zeus' side in the two gods' famous quarrel as to which of the sexes experiences most satisfaction in love making; in recompense, Zeus gave him the power of prophecy.[20] Here we have a clearly parallel motif shared by poet and prophet. Thamyris, of course, does not fit this mantic pattern, for he loses both his eyesight and his poetic gifts simultaneously. But his musical gifts cause his blindness.

Thamyris seems a somewhat unsympathetic failure, disastrously punished by the Muses in his hubris; he nevertheless received a statue, in the grove of the Muses at Helicon.[21]

The Linus who was the forefather of the Linus killed by Heracles (according to Pausanias), fits into this category of poets. The son of a Muse, Urania, he " won a reputation for music greater than that of any contemporary or predecessor, and ... Apollo killed him for equalling him in singing [*exisoumenon kata tēn ōidēn*]."[22] After his death the whole world mourns (which seemingly puts Apollo in an unsympathetic light); even in Egypt there was a

---

[17] Trans. Frazer, modified, Apollodorus 1.3.3: Θάμυρις δὲ κάλλει διενεγκὼν καὶ κιθαρῳδίᾳ περὶ μουσικῆς ἤρισε Μούσαις, συνθέμενος, ἂν μὲν κρείττων εὑρεθῇ, πλησιάσειν πάσαις, ἐὰν δὲ ἡττηθῇ στερηθήσεσθαι οὗ ἂν ἐκεῖναι θέλωσι. καθυπέρτεραι δὲ αἱ Μοῦσαι γενόμεναι καὶ τῶν ὀμμάτων αὐτὸν καὶ τῆς κιθαρῳδίας ἐστέρησαν. For a Freudian interpretation of Thamyris, see Devereux 1987.

[18] Hesiod fr. 65 M-W, from the *Ehoiai*.

[19] *Odyssey* viii 63–73. "And the herald came near, leading the worthy singer, whom the Muse loved, and gave him both good and evil; she deprived him of his eyes, but gave him sweet song" (Κῆρυξ δ' ἐγγύθεν ἦλθεν ἄγων ἐρίηρον ἀοιδόν / τὸν πέρι Μοῦσ' ἐφίλησε, δίδου δ' ἀγαθόν τε κακόν τε· / ὀφθαλμῶν μὲν ἄμερσε, δίδου δ' ἡδεῖαν ἀοιδήν ...). Cf. Dodds 1951:80. The ambiguity of the bardic calling is well expressed here; in the same way, Cassandra is given good and evil by Apollo: she is awarded the gift of prophecy, but no one will believe her; see Apollodorus 3.12.5, with further bibliography in Frazer's edition, 48n2; Halliday 1967:77, 69, 72. Euenius has divination as recompense for blindness, Herodotus 9.92–94. Cf. above, ch. 5 (Homer); ch. 17 below, on Cridenbel and other blind poets.

[20] See Hesiod *Melampodia* fr. 275–276 M-W; Pausanias 3.7.1; further references in Gantz 1993:528–529; Halliday 1967:84. Cf. Löffler 1963.

[21] Pausanias 9.30.1.

[22] Trans. Jones, Pausanias 9.29.6–9: μεγίστην δὲ τῶν τε ἐφ' αὑτοῦ καὶ ὅσοι πρότερον ἐγένοντο λάβοι δόξαν ἐπὶ μουσικῇ, καὶ ὡς Ἀπόλλων ἀποκτείνειεν αὐτὸν ἐξισούμενον κατὰ τὴν ᾠδήν. Cf. *Iliad* XVIII 569.

Linus lament. Here the poet is almost assimilated to the dying god of Frazer and the ancient Near East. As in the case of Hesiod, there is a significant emphasis on the placement of bones after death: "The Thebans assert that Linus was buried among them, and that after the Greek defeat at Chaeronia, Philip the son of Amyntas, in obedience to a vision in a dream, took up the bones of Linus and conveyed them to Macedonia; other visions induced him to send the bones of Linus back to Thebes." Also in the grove of the Muses at Helicon is a rock sculpture of Linus: "To Linus every year they sacrifice [*enagizousi*] as to a hero before they sacrifice to the Muses."[23]

Here we have familiar patterns: close association with the Muses or Apollo, including cultic association after death; the bestness of the poet; enmity with Apollo—*agōn* and execution by the god; lamentation, emphasis on the bones and grave of hero, and hero cult. We are moving in the same world as the *vitae* of Aesop, Archilochus, and Hesiod.

Poet as *Mantis*/Shaman

The recurrent association of these *agōn* myths with Apollo leads us repeatedly to think of Delphi, the site of the Aesopic cult myth. Burkert writes, "Music was the primary mode of experiencing the Delphic god's epiphany, and the musical *agōn* was the most important at Delphi."[24] This musical *agōn* appears faithfully in these myths of poets, as it does in the story of the contest of Homer and Hesiod,[25] because of the close connection between seers and poets. Here one recalls the riddle contest between seers, as in the story of Calchas and Mopsus, where the seer who loses the contest dies of grief or through suicide.[26]

---

[23] Pausanias 9.29.6–9: τούτῳ [Linus] κατὰ ἔτος ἕκαστον πρὸ τῆς θυσίας τῶν Μουσῶν ἐναγίζουσι ... Θηβαῖοι δὲ λέγουσι παρὰ σφίσι ταφῆναι τὸν Λίνον, καὶ ὡς μετὰ τὸ πταῖσμα τὸ ἐν Χαιρωνείᾳ τὸ Ἑλληνικὸν Φίλιππος ὁ Ἀμύντου κατὰ δή τινα ὄψιν ὀνείρατος τὰ ὀστᾶ ἀνελόμενος τοῦ Λίνου κομίσειεν ἐς Μακεδονίαν· ἐκεῖνον μὲν δὴ αὖθις ἐξ ἐνυπνίων ἄλλων ὀπίσω τοῦ Λίνου τὰ ὀστᾶ ἐς Θήβας ἀποστεῖλαι. For bones in hero cult, see ch. 6 (Hesiod). Cf. West 1983:56–67; Clay 2004:143.

[24] Burkert 1983:130.

[25] See above ch. 2, the story of Aesop and Ainos. For the agonistic spirit in Greece, see Huizinga 1955:64, 73; Collins 2004.

[26] Apollodorus *Library, Epitome* 6.2–4, Frazer 1921 2.242–243. This story probably is referred to by Hesiod in *Melampodia* fr. 278 M-W. See Gantz 1993:702; Halliday 1967:73–74. For Indo-European background, Lindow 1975:319 (the Contest of Wisdom tale, often between a god and a mortal or giant); Clover 1980, on flytings, ritualized exchanges of aggressive verbal attacks, with many examples on p. 446. These are related to the genre of "wisdom dialogue."

Shamanistic themes begin to be repeatedly associated with all these themes.[27] After pathbreaking studies by K. Meuli and Dodds, Burkert, and Bremmer have urged caution in speaking of Greek shamanism. For the purposes of this study, it is less important to determine whether actual extra-Greek shamanism influenced Greece than it is to isolate authentic shamanic themes that appear there. Furthermore, it is clear that shamanism can be broadly or narrowly defined.

The shaman was focused on ecstasy. Eliade defines the shaman as "the great master of ecstasy" who experiences "a trance during which his soul is believed to leave his body and ascend to the sky or descend to the underworld." Animals often act as helpers. In its pure form, shamanism is found in Central and North Asia.[28]

Often the shaman was a healer.[29] In a similar way, the archaic Greek poet sometimes functioned as healer—Aelian writes, "If ever the Spartans required the aid of the Muses on occasion of general sickness of body or mind or any like public affliction, their custom was to send for foreigners at the bidding of the Delphic oracle, to act as healers and purifiers. For instance they summoned Terpander, Thales [= Thaletas], Tyrtaeus, Nymphaeus of Cydonia, and Alcman."[30] This links the archaic Greek poet closely to the wandering seer/wise man such as Epimenides, who was a healer and purifier.

[27] For shamanism in general, see Eliade 1964 and 1961; Lewis 1971. For shamanism in Greece, see Meuli 1935; Dodds 1951:140–142; 80–82; Burkert 1972:163–165, 1992:56; Bolton 1962:125–146; Bremmer 1983a:25–51; West 1983:144–150; Eliade 1972:40–42, with further bibliography. For Indo-European shamanism, Miller 2000:298–303. See on Orpheus, below, this chapter. For shamans engaging in contests, Halliday 1967:74.

[28] Eliade 1964:4–5. Eliade's definition has been criticized as too broad, Burkert 1972:164n244. However, an anthropological authority, Lewis, also emphasizes the ecstatic, possession qualities of the shaman (1971).

[29] See below on Epimenides and Orpheus. For purification in archaic Greece, see Burkert 1992:55–64. The Thracian followers of Zalmoxis used *epōidai* (spells, charms, cf. the later poetic genre, the epode) to "heal the soul," Plato *Charmides* 156d–157a: "And the cure of the soul, my dear youth, has to be effected by the use of certain charms, and these charms are fair words," trans. Jowett, Θεραπεύεσθαι δὲ τὴν ψυχὴν ἔφη, ὦ μακάριε, ἐπῳδαῖς τισιν, τὰς δ' ἐπῳδὰς ταύτας τοὺς λόγους εἶναι τοὺς καλούς. Cf. Burkert 1972:164. One cannot escape thinking of the Aristotelian catharsis in this context, *Poetics* 1449b, 6.2. If we view the poet as scapegoat, *katharma*, we have the person who sometimes serves as the expelled societal purification dispensing medical purification to the individual in the form of poetry (spells). One wonders if the magical-medical purification worked through the expulsion of evil, perhaps evil spirits. See also Parker 1983:212n25 on the healing paean; Boyancé 1937:100–115.

[30] Aelian *Historical Miscellanies* 12.50 (trans. Edmonds 1927 3:610, 1:27): εἰ δέ ποτε ἐδεήθησαν τῆς ἐκ Μουσῶν ἐπικουρίας ἢ νοσήσαντες ἢ παραφρονήσαντες ἢ ἄλλο τι τοιοῦτον δημοσίᾳ παθόντες, μετεπέμποντο ξένους ἄνδρας οἷον ἰατροὺς ἢ καθαρτὰς κατὰ πυθόχρηστον. μετεπέμψαντό γε μὴν Τέρπανδρον καὶ Θάλητα καὶ Τυρταῖον καὶ τὸν Κυδωνιάτην Νυμφαῖον καὶ Ἀλκμᾶνα. Cf. Elliott 1960:10n16; see below, this chapter, on Epimenides and Thaletas.

Often the shaman used music (chanting and dancing, accompanied by sacred drums) to induce ecstasy and healing.[31] Thus, Dodds writes, "Out of the north came Abaris, riding, it was said, upon an arrow, as souls, it appears, still do in Siberia ... he banished pestilences, predicted earthquakes, composed religious poems, and taught the worship of his northern god, whom the Greeks called the Hyperborean Apollo."[32] In such a figure, we have the healer, the prophet, the poet. And we have seen that ecstasy is an important aspect of poetic creativity (as in the consecration epiphanies of Aesop, Archilochus, Hesiod, and Aeschylus; Archilochus sings the Dionysiac dithyramb when thunderstruck with wine) and of poetic communication (Tyrtaeus instilled *enthousiasmos*, a state of divine possession, into the Spartan warriors).

Since we have seen the persistent association of poet as cult hero with Delphi, it is worth noting that the poet Olen, a Hyperborean, was one of the founders of Delphi; he became Apollo's first prophet, and the inventor of hexameter poetry.[33] Thus poetry and prophecy are explicitly associated at the beginning of the Delphic tradition.[34] The Hyperborean background of Olen brings shamanism to mind.[35] Strabo tells us that Delphi kept a staff of poets who versified the oracles.[36] M. L. West notes that, from northern Thrace, "it is not far to Pieria, the region north and east of Mount Olympus" and that in shamanism there is the tradition of a sky god with "seven or nine 'sons' or 'daughters.'" There was an early cult of the Muses at Delphi.[37] The first Delphic

---

[31] See Eliade 1964:175: "musical magic" determined "the shamanic function of the drum." "The trance, as among the Siberian shamans, is induced by dancing to the magical melody of the *kobuz* [a stringed instrument]. The dance, as we shall see more fully later, reproduces the shaman's ecstatic journey to the sky." Cf. Lewis 1971:134: "Here [among the Veddas of Ceylon], as so widely elsewhere, the shaman's controlled possession trance is achieved by means of dancing and singing which becomes increasingly frenetic as he works himself up to the point of ecstasy." See also Nagy 1990b:29–46.

[32] Dodds 1951:141. Cf. Burkert 1972:150; Bremmer 1983a:45n85 (who challenges the arrow-riding parallel, cf. below on Orpheus and tattooing); Eliade 1964:388. For more on arrows, Eliade 1968.

[33] Boio, *ad* Pausanias 10.5.7–8; Herodotus 4.35; cf. Fontenrose 1978:215–216; West 1983:53.

[34] The combination of poetry and prophecy is a commonplace in world literature; see Chadwick 1952; Kugel 1990; Leavitt 1997, cf. Dodds 1951:100n118; 80–81. Strabo VII fr. 19, "In olden times prophets were wont to practice the art of music ... ," as quoted in Harrison 1922:469, Ὅτι τὸ παλαίον οἱ μάντεις καὶ μουσικὴν εἰργάζοντο. The Roman word *vates* meant both poet and prophet, see Thieme 1968; Watkins 1995:117–118; chs. 18 and 19, on Odin; ch. 23 (Ovid) below.

[35] Herodotus 4.36.

[36] Strabo 9.3.5, p. 419; Plutarch *The Oracles at Delphi No Longer Given in Verse* 25 (407b); both cited by Fontenrose (1978:213), who is skeptical of their validity; cf. Edmonds 1927 3:593.

[37] West 1983:146, quoting Eliade 1964:9. See *Homeric Hymn* 27.15; Plutarch *Table Talk* 9.14 (744c, 745a); Sperduti 1950:218n39. The Muses instructed Aristaeus in the arts of healing and prophecy, Apollonius 2.512. It is possible that *Mousa* is etymologically related to *mania*

Sibyl was reared by the Muses at Helicon, and the Muses were associated with the Castalian spring, close to Delphi.[38]

Epimenides of Crete

Epimenides is firmly in the tradition of poet-prophet, and is curiously half-mythical, half-historic[39]—a philosopher and a seer with shamanic characteristics. I consider him here for his many parallels with Hesiod, for his blame fragment, and for his associations with purification. Huxley remarks that the seers "Melampous and his family stand out, by reason of their skill and percipience, as the true intellectual ancestors of the philosophical pioneers of early Ionia." Thus Greek philosophy and poetry had their roots in the mantic in archaic Greece.[40] Greek philosophy was never entirely separated from the mantic.[41]

Like Hesiod, Epimenides receives a divine consecration, and like Hesiod, he was a shepherd, and there is a pastoral setting for the supernatural event that gave him his mantic vocation. "One day he was sent into the country by his father to look for a stray sheep,[42] and at noon he turned aside out of the way, and went to sleep in a cave, where he slept for fifty-seven years . . . so he became famous throughout Greece and was believed to be a special favorite of heaven."[43] His fifty-seven-year-long dream taught him divine wisdom.[44] Like Hesiod, he wrote a *Theogony*;[45] he also wrote an *Oracles*, just as Hesiod wrote a *Mantika*.[46] Like Hesiod and Aesop, he was reborn after death.[47]

'madness' and *mantis* 'prophet', cf. *mainomai*, Bie 1884–1937:3238. Aesop takes refuge in a shrine of the Muses at Delphi, above, ch. 2.

[38] Plutarch *On the Pythian Oracle* 8 (398C); Pausanias 10.8.9–10.

[39] For his apparent historicity, see Dodds 1951:162n40. Burkert, on the other hand, puts the seer in "the main line of specifically Cretan cult and myth" (1972:150). Parker (1983:209) sees Epimenides as transitional between "shadowy or legendary figures" (i.e. Bacis, Thaletas, and Abaris) and those having "firm historical reality" (i.e. Empedocles). For further on the legendary seers, see Parker 209n11; Culianu 1980; Cornford 1952:62–124; Burkert 1992:41–87.

[40] 1969:59. See below, app. A, on phallic cult and Melampus.

[41] See Pfeffer 1976.

[42] Archilochus is also sent by his father on a pastoral errand when he receives his consecration, see above, ch. 3.

[43] Diogenes Laertius 1.109–110 (trans. Hicks): οὗτός ποτε πεμφθεὶς παρὰ τοῦ πατρὸς εἰς ἀγρὸν ἐπὶ πρόβατον, τῆς ὁδοῦ κατὰ μεσημβρίαν ἐκκλίνας ὑπ' ἄντρῳ τινὶ κατεκοιμήθη ἑπτὰ καὶ πεντήκοντα ἔτη . . . γνωσθεὶς δὲ παρὰ τοῖς Ἕλλησι θεοφιλέστατος εἶναι ὑπελήφθη. This cave sleep was known as early as the sixth century, Xenophanes B20 DK.

[44] FGH 457 F 2.

[45] Diogenes Laertius 1.111.

[46] FGH 457 test. 8a; for Hesiod, see above, ch. 6. Abaris and Aristeas also wrote poems entitled *Theogony*, *Suda* s.v. Abaris and Aristeas; West 1983:54.

[47] Diogenes Laertius 1.114, *pollakis anabebiōkenai*. See above, ch. 2, the rebirth of Aesop; the same

We know, on the basis of one fragment, that he was a blame poet: he wrote, "Cretans, always liars, evil beasts, idle bellies."[48] Aside from the echoes of Hesiod and the early blame tradition here,[49] the fragment is interesting for the tension it expresses between the poet and his native land. According to West's interpretation, this is part of the poetic/mantic initiation theophany (as the Hesiodic a parallel would support)—after Epimenides' long cave sleep, "Truth and Justice" (attributes of Zeus?) visit him and speak these words.[50]

There is perhaps a hint of the consecration theme in the tradition that he "was never seen to eat" because he had received special food from the nymphs.[51] It is tempting to see these nymphs as Muses,[52] but this is not explicit. Later, Epimenides starts to build a temple to the nymphs, but a heavenly voice advises a temple to Zeus instead.[53]

Thus we have a blame poet critical of his native country receiving the patronage of the nymphs; he receives wisdom from supernatural sources. This poet was also a famous seer; Plato calls him a "divine man" (*anēr theios*) and describes how he foretold events in the Persian wars.[54] However, according to Aristotle, an important part of his seership involved looking into the past.[55] This would be an important aspect of his function as a famous purifier; in order to purify a city or a person, one had to look into the past and diagnose the cause of the pollution. According to Aristotle, Diogenes, and others, Epimenides was brought to Athens to allay a plague; he diagnosed it as deriving from the murder of Cylon's associates, who had taken refuge at the altar of Athena. Accordingly, he "purified [*ekathēren*] the city and stopped the pestilence" (ἐκάθηρεν αὐτῶν τὴν πόλιν καὶ ἔπαυσε τὸν λοιμὸν)—by sacrifices of sheep, according to one account, and of two young men, by another, undoubtedly fictional, account.[56] Epimenides is also said "to have been the

---

verb is used there. So this is possibly a "shamanic" theme applied to Aesop and Hesiod.

[48] FGH 457 F2, from *Oracles*. Quoted by Paul (*Epistle to Titus* 1.12): Κρῆτες ἀεὶ ψεῦσται, κακὰ θηρία, γαστέρες ἀργαί.

[49] I.e. the derogatory reference to "bellies," as in Hesiod, see above, ch. 6. For animal symbolism in blame, see above on Alcaeus, ch. 9.

[50] Cf. West 1983:47; FGH 457 F2; test. 8a; test. 4f.

[51] Demetrius (probably of Phaleron, born about 350 BC), quoted by Diogenes Laertius 1.114: φησὶ δὲ Δημήτριος . . . ὡς λάβοι παρὰ Νυμφῶν ἔδεσμά τι . . . μηδὲ ὀφθῆναί ποτε ἐσθίων.

[52] Lefkowitz 1981:2n2. The Muses were probably mountain nymphs originally. Cf. Dodds 1951:99n111.

[53] Theopompus (probably of Chios) *Marvels*, as quoted in Diogenes Laertius 1.115.

[54] *Laws* 642d–e. Cf. Theopompus, FGH 115 F 67.

[55] Aristotle *Rhetoric* 1418a 23–26; see also Dodds 1951:143n52. Cf. the Hesiodic knowledge of things in the past and future, above at ch. 6 (Hesiod), with its mantic parallels.

[56] Diogenes Laertius 1.110, cf. FGH test. 4b, Aristotle *Constitution of Athens* 1 (ἐκάθηρε τὴν πόλιν).

first who purified houses and fields, and the first who founded temples."[57] The prophet also cured individuals: "He professed to purify people by rite from any damaging influence whatever, physical or mental, and to state its cause."[58] It is possible that Epimenides used music, poetry, and spells in his healing; another Cretan seer or poet, Thaletas, used music to combat a Spartan plague,[59] a theme that has been found in the life of Stesichorus.[60]

Epimenides' *vita* has a number of themes that are arguably shamanic: long departure from his body; cave initiation; tattooing; withdrawal into a cave; prophecy, healing; and reincarnation: "Tradition assimilated him to the type of the northern shaman."[61] Plutarch writes that he was "wise in divine things related to possession [*enthousiastikēn*] and initiation lore [*telestikēn sophian*]."[62]

Finally, Epimenides was given hero cult. He was worshipped by the Cretans after his death. "The Cretans sacrifice to him as a god; for they say that he had superhuman foresight." But "The Lacedaemonians guard his body

---

For the sacrifice of the two young men, Diogenes Laertius 1.110; Neanthes of Cyzicus, 84 FGH F 16 at Athenaeus 13.602c–d; Parker 1983:259. This version of the story is a thoroughgoing inversion of the pattern of this study: the poet-prophet is summoned to the city to allay the plague, not exiled or killed; while there, he has others killed in atonement. He is the purifier, not the *katharma*.

[57] Diogenes Laertius 1.112 (trans. Hicks): λέγεται δὲ καὶ πρῶτος οἰκίας καὶ ἀγροὺς καθῆραι καὶ ἱερὰ ἱδρύσασθαι. Cf. Culianu 1980:292.

[58] FGH 457, test. 4e: οὗτος Κρὴς μὲν ἦν τὸ γένος, ἱερεὺς Διὸς καὶ Ῥέας, [καὶ] καθαίρειν ἐπαγγελλόμενος παντὸς οὑτινοσοῦν βλαπτικοῦ, εἴτε περὶ σῶμα εἴτε περὶ ψυχήν, τελεταῖς τισι καὶ τὸ αἴτιον εἰπεῖν. Cf. Parker, who emphasizes the backward vision implied in the diagnosis of the disease (1983:210n17). Like Empedocles, Epimenides wrote a book called *Purifications* (*Katharmoi*), FGH 457 test. 7. Evidently, Empedocles also practiced as a healer, B111 DK; cf. Lloyd 1979:34–37; Parker 1983:208n9. Diogenes Laertius (1.112) describes Epimenides gathering herbs instead of sleeping. On the "healer-seer" (*iatromantis*), see Parker 1983:208–211, bibliography, 209n11, Burkert 1992:41; for Epimenides as *iatromantis*, ibid., 210nn17, 18; for military prophecy, 210n21; Pritchett 1979 3:47–90; for seers as outstanding warriors, 57–58.

[59] Pratinas, in Page 1962 #713 (iii) = "Plutarch" *On Music* 42 (1146b); Pausanias 1.14.4; Plutarch *Lycurgus* 4 (where Thaletas has characteristics of the Greek lawgiver, cf. Solon as poet-lawgiver); Aelian *Historical Miscellanies* 12.50; Edmonds 1927 1:34–37. See above, where Spartans use historical Greek poets to offset pestilence, another striking evidence for the close correlation of seer and poet in archaic Greece.

[60] See above, ch. 7.

[61] Dodds 1951:141, 143. See also Burkert 1972:150–152; Eliade 1964:389.

[62] Plutarch *Solon* 12.4: ἐδόκει δέ τις εἶναι θεοφιλὴς καὶ σοφὸς περὶ τὰ θεῖα τὴν <u>ἐνθουσιαστικὴν</u> καὶ <u>τελεστικὴν σοφίαν</u>. Graf (1987), who interprets elements of the Orpheus myth as a reflection of initiation and *Männerbund* cult, would probably be able to find data for a similar interpretation here. However, shamanism and war initiation are not exclusive spheres. Obviously, there is elaborate ritual for shamanic initiation; furthermore, madness, enthusiasm, and possession are important attributes for the archaic military *Männerbund*. See above, ch. 11 (Tyrtaeus).

in their own keeping in obedience to a certain oracle."[63] Just so, Hesiod's body is kept at a certain town because of an oracle.[64]

Orpheus

A key poet-prophet figure with shamanic resonances is Orpheus.[65] There is an extensive literature on him and on "Orphism," so one must be selective in any treatment of him. His associations with music and poetry were proverbial; he was also a magical healer. Pausanias writes, "Orpheus excelled . . . in the beauty of his verse, and reached a high degree of power because he was believed to have discovered mysteries, purification from sins [*ergōn anosiōn katharmous*], cures of diseases and means of averting divine wrath."[66] By his singing, he causes rocks and trees to move; animals are captivated by his singing; his music convinces Hades to allow Eurydice to live again.[67] He was the son of a Muse;[68] by one account, he was the son of Apollo.[69] The god gave him personal lessons in lyre-playing in the woods.[70]

After Orpheus' visit to the underworld, he suffered a violent death. According to one early account, Dionysus, angered by Orpheus' tendency to honor the sun over him, had his maenads tear him to pieces. Aeschylus writes, "He [Orpheus] did not honour Dionysos, but accounted Helios the greatest of the gods, whom also he called Apollo . . . Therefore Dionysos was enraged [*orgistheis*]."[71] This leads us back to the theme of divine rage in the story of

---

[63] Diogenes Laertius 1.114–115: Κρῆτες αὐτῷ θύουσιν ὡς θεῷ· φασὶ γὰρ καὶ <προ>γνωστικώτατον γεγονέναι . . . καὶ τὸ σῶμα αὐτοῦ φυλάττουσι Λακεδαιμόνιοι παρ' ἑαυτοῖς κατά τι λόγιον.

[64] See above, ch. 6.

[65] For shamanism in the Orpheus myth, see Dodds 1951:147; Eliade 1964:391. Cf. Graf 1987; Burkert 1962b and 1972:63; Freiert 1991:43–45; West 1983:3. For the Orpheus myth generally, an introduction in Gantz 1993:721–725.

[66] Pausanias 9.30.4: ὁ δὲ Ὀρφεὺς . . . ὑπερεβάλετο ἐπῶν κόσμῳ τοὺς πρὸ αὐτοῦ καὶ ἐπὶ μέγα ἦλθεν ἰσχύος οἷα πιστευόμενος εὑρηκέναι τελετὰς θεῶν καὶ ἔργων ἀνοσίων καθαρμοὺς νόσων τε ἰάματα καὶ τροπὰς μηνιμάτων θείων. See also Coman 1938:146 for music; for poetry, 153; for medicine, 157. Cf. Eliade 1964:391; Harrison 1922:455–460.

[67] Simonides fr. 567 Page; Aeschylus *Agamemnon* 1629–1631; Euripides *Bacchae* 650; Graf 1987:84; Frazer 1921 1.17n6; Dodds 1951:147, with shamanistic parallels; for the underworld singing, Ovid *Metamorphoses* 10.16. See Freirert 1991:32–35; Robert 1 1920:398–399.

[68] See Apollodorus 1.3.2, with Frazer's note.

[69] Scholia in Pindar *Pythian Odes* 4.313.

[70] Hyginus *On Astronomy* 2.7.

[71] Aeschylus, in Eratosthenes *Constellations* 24, see Radt 1985 3.138 = (as quoted in Harrison 1922:461): τὸν μὲν Διόνυσον οὐκ ἐτίμα, τὸν δὲ Ἥλιον μέγιστον τῶν θεῶν ἐνόμιζεν εἶναι, ὃν καὶ Ἀπόλλωνα προσηγόρευσεν . . . ὅθεν ὁ Διόνυσος ὀργισθεὶς . . . This theme can be dated at least to 490 BC, West 1983:4n6. See also Plato *Symposium* 179d; *Republic* 620a; Pausanias 9.30.5; further references in Apollodorus 1.3.2, Frazer's note.

Aesop and Apollo. Since Orphic cult was closely linked to a similar death of Dionysus,[72] we have once again enmity in myth entailing cultic unity.[73] Furthermore, the head of Orpheus is finally enshrined in a shrine of Dionysus, the Bakkheion, at Lesbos.[74] On the other hand, Orpheus' lyre is preserved in a temple of Apollo.[75] The roles of Apollo and Dionysus in Orpheus' life recall the beneficent and ambivalently maleficent/beneficent roles of the Muses and Apollo in the life of Aesop.

Orpheus' death has variants. Pausanias has Orpheus struck dead by a Zeus-thrown thunderbolt (*keraunōthēnai*).[76] Ovid describes him being stoned to death.[77]

After Orpheus' death, a plague ensues; the oracle enjoins the burial of the poet's head,[78] and he receives hero cult. At first, Orpheus' head is in a hero shrine, but later it becomes a full-fledged divine shrine, and he receives sacrifices typical of the Olympian gods.[79] According to one account, the Muses gather his limbs and bury them.[80] After he was torn to pieces, his head, still singing, floated out the Hebrus, into the ocean, and to the isle of Lesbos, where it was enshrined and delivered oracles. The singing, oracular head has been identified as a shamanic motif.[81]

---

[72] Proclus (*ad* Plato *Republic* p. 398, as quoted in Harrison 1922:461) says this explicitly: "Orpheus, because he was the leader in the rites of Dionysos, is said to have suffered the like fate to his god" (Ὀρφεὺς ἅτε τῶν Διονύσου τελετῶν ἡγεμὼν γενόμενος τὰ ὅμοια παθεῖν λέγεται τῷ σφετέρῳ θεῷ). In another variant, Aphrodite was responsible for Orpheus' death, Robert 1 1920:405–406.

[73] The death of the child Dionysus, torn apart by the Titans, was the central cult myth of "Orphism," Linforth 1941:315–325. For the death of Orpheus, cf. Harrison 1922:460–464.

[74] Faraone 2004; Gantz 1993:724–725; J. Nagy 1990. The first full literary source is Philostratus *On Heroes* 5.3, 28.7–12, see Maclean and Aitken 2002, cf. Rohde 1925:556–557, but there are portrayals of Orpheus' head as oracle in classical Attic iconography. See also Philostratus *Life of Apollonius* 4.14; Lucian *Against Ignorance* 11–12.

[75] Lucian *Against Ignorance* 11–12.

[76] Pausanias 9.30.5; Alcidamas *Odysseus* 24.

[77] Ovid *Metamorphoses* 11.18–19; Visser 1982:409. Further references on Orpheus' death in Graf 1987:103n16; Robert 1 1920:406.

[78] Conon FGH 26 F 1.45, cf. Harrison 1922:468; a similar story in Pausanias 9.30.9–12 (when the grave of Orpheus is disturbed, a plague afflicts the land).

[79] Conon FGH 26 F 1.45. Cf. Kerényi 1959:285, Harrison 1922:464–471. The emphasis on the grave(s) is central to hero cult, Kerényi 1959:286. For Orpheus as hero, see also Freiert 1991:38–43.

[80] Eratosthenes *Constellations* 24; cf. Robert 1 1920:408n8; for Orpheus raised in Pieria, the Muses' country, see Kerényi 1959:280n917. Harrison attempts to show that the Maenads and the Muses are connected, though her evidence is not entirely convincing (1922:463–464). For the association of Muses and hero cult, cf. on Achilles below.

[81] See Faraone 2004; Dodds 1951:147; Eliade 1964:391; Kerényi 1959:286. See below, ch. 17, the poet as prophet (mantic heads); ch. 19 (Mimir's head).

Fritz Graf has offered an important interpretation of Orpheus that emphasizes his connections with the warrior and *Männerbund*, discounting the ties with shamanism.[82] But shamanism may be a component of the myth without being its guiding principle, and parallels with archaic Greek poets incline me to accept shamanistic themes in archaic poet-seer miracle-workers.

Graf's insight into Orpheus' links with the warrior are still valuable, and provide another example of the ties of warrior with poet. In the Conon narrative, Orpheus is killed while initiating armed warriors in a hall of mysteries from which women are excluded. While celebrating the rituals, the men have to leave their weapons outside, and women, angered at being excluded, seize the weapons, enter the building, kill all the men who oppose them, and tear Orpheus to pieces, throwing his body parts into the ocean. The typical cultic denouement (plague, oracle, and cult for body of wronged hero) follows.[83]

In Pausanias (9.30.5) Orpheus' death is associated with drunkenness and war: "The women of the Thracians plotted his death, because he had persuaded their husbands to accompany him in his wanderings ... flushed with wine, however, they dared the deed, and hereafter the custom of their men has been to march to battle drunk."[84] The story of the men warriors following the example of the wine-addled murderers of Orpheus is very curious. The death of Orpheus seems to be a charter myth for warriors, though why women are used as charter heroes is not immediately obvious.

The tattooing of the Thracian female killers of Orpheus also suggests warrior initiation. A cylix dated near 500 BC shows a Thracian maenad with a tattoo on her right arm killing Orpheus.[85] According to Plutarch, Thracian men tattoo their wives as *punishment* for the murder of Orpheus.[86] One would expect that Thracian warriors would tattoo themselves, not their wives, as tattooing is a common feature of initiation.[87] And in fact, Herodotus tells us that "Tattooing is judged to be a mark of high birth" among Thracian men, whose highest values are war and plunder.[88]

---

[82] See Graf 1987; Kershaw 2000.

[83] Cf. Graf 1987:89.

[84] Trans. Jones, τὰς δὲ γυναῖκάς φασι τῶν Θρᾳκῶν ἐπιβουλεύειν μὲν αὐτῷ θάνατον, ὅτι σφῶν τοὺς ἄνδρας ἀκολουθεῖν ἔπεισεν αὐτῷ πλανωμένῳ ... ὡς δὲ ἐνεφορήσαντο οἴνου, ἐξεργάζονται τὸ τόλμημα, καὶ τοῖς ἀνδράσιν ἀπὸ τούτου κατέστη μεθυσκομένους ἐς τὰς μάχας χωρεῖν. See above, ch. 3 (Archilochus).

[85] Harrison 1888, 1922:463.

[86] Plutarch *On the Delays of Divine Vengeance* 12 (557D); Phanocles, in Powell 1925:106–108, v. 13.

[87] Van Gennep 1960:84 (in a warrior and plundering society, candidates are tattooed differently as they pass from level to level); Eliade 1975:18, 31, 43. See also Bremmer 1978.

[88] Herodotus 5.6.2: τὸ μὲν ἐστίχθαι εὐγενὲς κέκριται. "To make a living from war and plunder is considered best" (τὸ ζῆν ἀπὸ πολέμου καὶ λῃστύος κάλλιστον).

Furthermore, Epimenides, parallel to Orpheus in some ways, was found to be covered with tattoos when he died. And Zalmoxis, whom Graf finds close to Orpheus in initiation and *Männerbund* themes,[89] had a tattoo on his forehead.[90] It appears that the killing of Orpheus (by tattooed women) again provides a charter for a warrior-initiation practice.

Dodds identifies tattooing as a shamanic practice, and he is probably right, though he does not prove that the practice was characteristically shamanic.[91] Here again we find an ambiguity, if we choose shamanism or *Männerbund* initiation on a either/or basis. But if we see shamanism (possession) and warrior initiation as intersecting at times, there is no necessity for exclusive interpretation.

Though the female/male shift remains obscure,[92] perhaps a key to these issues may be found in the fact that the archaic religious leader gained his prestige by being a leader of warriors, and was also a master of magic, spells, poetry, related ecstatic states, initiation ritual, and *Kampfwut*.[93] One thinks of Archilochus as servant of Ares, living by his spear, yet also the servant of the Muses, and leading off the dithyramb of Dionysus, "thunderstruck with wine." (And in addition wielding invective as potent as a warrior's sword.) Just so, Orpheus has obvious ties with the Muses and Dionysus, but, as Graf has emphasized, he has links with war also. To the archaic mind, these categories created a unity; to the modern mind, the connections are not so comfortable.

The Singing Warrior

The two dominant heroes in Greek myth, Heracles and Achilles, each have some association with poetry. In view of the importance of Heracles for chapter 18, "The Stakes of the Poet," it will be useful to evaluate the importance of his poetic aspects here. Achilles and his men killed the mythical Pharmakos; he also killed the prototypical blame poet and scapegoat Thersites. Because

---

[89] Graf 1987:91.

[90] Dionysophanes, in Porphyry *Life of Pythagoras* 15; Dodds 1951:163n44.

[91] Dodds 1951:163n44. Some examples of shamanic tattooing in Hambly 1925:131. The arrow is one of the common tattooed symbols among some North American Indians, cf. Abaris above, this chapter. Often the guardian spirit/animal is tattooed on the shaman. For archaic Europe, see Hambly 1925:285–287. Cf. Wolters 1903.

[92] Perhaps Orpheus had to be killed by Dionysus, his tutelary god, through his servants; and his characteristic servants were simply Maenads, possessed women. Cf. Henrichs 1984.

[93] See Lewis 1971 passim, but e.g. 151, "competition for power within Macha society is couched in the idiom of possession"; Culianu 1980. Cf. James 1955:27, on "the prestige of supernatural power."

persecutors are often identified with their victims, he is worth looking at for that reason alone.

Achilles, the greatest hero of the Trojan war,[94] sings to himself in his moments of leisure:

> τὸν δ' εὗρον φρένα τερπόμενον φόρμιγγι λιγείῃ,
> καλῇ δαιδαλέῃ, ἐπὶ δ' ἀργύρεον ζυγὸν ἦεν,
> τὴν ἄρετ' ἐξ ἐνάρων πόλιν Ἠετίωνος ὀλέσσας·
> τῇ ὅ γε θυμὸν ἔτερπεν, <u>ἄειδε</u> δ' ἄρα <u>κλέα</u> ἀνδρῶν.

> . . . and they found Achilleus delighting his heart in a lyre, clear-sounding,
> splendid and carefully wrought, with a bridge of silver upon it,
> which he won out of the spoils when he ruined Eëtion's city.
> With this he was pleasuring his heart, and singing [*aeide*] of men's fame [*klea*].[95]
> *Iliad* IX 186–189, trans. Lattimore

Katherine Callen King writes, "Achilles is not the only man in the *Iliad* to sing . . . But he is the only one to sing individually." Achilles had gotten his lyre as war plunder: "There is no opposition between lyre and battle here."[96] In archaic Greece, every aristocratic man was a warrior; and perhaps every aristocratic man learned the basics of singing. But as King points out, it is worth noting that there is no opposition between the two phenomena in archaic Greece culture and ethos. One is hard put to think of a major modern poet who is also a mercenary soldier or for whom war is a central poetic theme.

Later tradition adds to the portrait. Achilles played the "first" lyre.[97] Philostratus gives the warrior poet a poetic theophany, in the tradition of Hesiod:

> ἐπεὶ δὲ θυμοῦ ἥττων ἐφαίνετο, μουσικὴν αὐτὸν ὁ Χείρων
> ἐδιδάξατο, μουσικὴ γὰρ ἱκανὴ πραΰνειν τὸ ἕτοιμόν τε καὶ ἀνεστηκὸς

---

[94] For an introduction to Achilles, see King 1987. For the broader context of epic heroes, see Dumézil 1973b; von See 1978; Nagy 1979; Honko 1990; Reichert and Zimmermann 1990; Miller 2000 (a splendid and insightful survey).

[95] For the significance of this word, see *Iliad* XXII 303–305, cf. VII 87–91, IX 413; Nagy 1979:28–29, 184n2, 175–189; King 1987:10–11. See below, ch. 17 on Cuchulainn-Achilles parallels.

[96] See King 1987:10–11. See also Frontisi-Ducroux 1986; Rocchi 1980; Notopoulos 1952; Bloomfield and Dunn 1989:18, 19.

[97] Scholia on *Iliad* IX 188; Eustathius p. 745.55; Aelian *Historical Miscellanies* 14.23; Athenaeus 14.624a. Cf. Diodorus Siculus 5.49.1, 4.

τῆς γνώμης, ὁ δὲ οὐδενὶ πόνῳ τάς τε ἁρμονίας ἐξέμαθε καὶ πρὸς
λύραν ᾖσεν. ᾖδε δὲ τοὺς ἀρχαίους ἥλικας ... οὐκ ἀδακρυτὶ ταῦτα
ᾖδεν. ἤκουσα δὲ κἀκεῖνα, θύειν μὲν αὐτὸν τῇ Καλλιόπῃ μουσικὴν
αἰτοῦντα καὶ τὸ ἐν ποιήσει κράτος, τὴν θεὸν δὲ ἐπιστῆναι καθεύδοντι
καὶ "ὦ παῖ", φάναι "μουσικῆς μὲν καὶ ποιητικῆς δίδωμί σοι τὸ
ἀποχρῶν, ὡς ἡδίους μὲν τὰς δαῖτας ἐργάζοιο, κοιμίζοις δὲ τὰς λύπας
...

When he appeared to yield to anger, Kheiron taught him [Achilles]
music. Music was enough to tame the readiness and rising of his
disposition. Without exertion, he thoroughly learned the musical
modes, and he sang to the accompaniment of a lyre. He used
to sing of the ancient comrades [Hyacinth, Narcissus, Adonis,
Hylla, Abderus] ... not without tears did he sing of these matters.

I also heard the following things: that he sacrificed to Calliope
asking for musical skill and mastery of poetic composition, and that
the goddess appeared to him in his sleep and said, "Child, I give you
enough musical and poetic skill that you might make banquets more
pleasant and lay sufferings to rest ..." [But he should practice war
as well.][98]

On Heroes 45

These details are clearly elaborated from the Iliadic picture of the lyre-playing
Achilles, but they show that the fascination with the poetic/musical side of the
warrior continued. Ovid would write that the centaur Cheiron taught Achilles
the art of the lyre: "He is believed to have employed, in strumming the lyre,
those hands which were one day to send Hector to death."[99]

Cheiron, according to some traditions, invented the art of the lyre, and
he was also a preeminent healer and *mantis*.[100] Achilles functions as a healer
on occasion.[101] So Achilles has something of the poet-healer persona, even as
early as the *Iliad*.

---

[98] Trans. from Maclean and Aitken 2001:137. Cf. Platthy 1985:43. For hero cult in Philostratus, see
Dué and Nagy 2004.

[99] *Fasti* 5.385: *ille manus olim missuras Hectora leto / creditur in lyricis detinuisse modis.* Eustathius
2:463, 33.

[100] *Iliad* IV 219; XI 841; *Orphic Argonautica* 370–380, cf. Platthy 1985:65. Cheiron, the wisest being in
the world, gives up his immortality to Prometheus so he can die and gain relief from a poisoned
wound (Apollodorus 2.5.4). He receives hero cult after death.

[101] *Iliad* XI 830–832; *Cypria*, see Proclus *Chrestomathy*, in Allen 1919 5.104.9–11; West 2003b:72;
Apollodorus *Epitome* 3.20; Hyginus *Fables* 101; King 1987:8–9; Kerényi 1959:340. A vase painting
by Sosias shows Achilles treating the wounded Patroclus, cf. Kerényi 1959:340, 1945:33.

His death is voluntary; he chooses to die young, avenging Patroclus, rather than live to a ripe old age.[102] And Apollo, the inimical god whom he resembles so closely, guides the arrow that kills the hero.[103] Pindar represents Achilles' hero cult as connected with the Muses:

τὸν μὲν οὐδὲ θανόντ' ἀοιδαί τι λίπον,
ἀλλά οἱ παρά τε πυρὰν τάφον θ' Ἑλικώνιαι παρθένοι
στάν, ἐπὶ θρῆνόν τε πολύφαμον ἔχεαν.
ἔδοξ' ἄρα καὶ ἀθανάτοις,
ἐσλόν γε φῶτα καὶ φθίμενον ὕμνοις θεᾶν διδόμεν.

Even in death, songs [*aoidai*] did not leave him,
but, standing beside his pyre and his grave, the maidens
of Helikon let fall upon him their abundant dirge [*thrēnon*].
Even the immortals were pleased to bestow on a brave
[*eslon*] man, though he was dead, the song [*humnois*] of
goddesses.[104]

Isthmians 8.62–66, trans. Lattimore

According to the *Odyssey*, "All nine Muses answering each other lamented [*thrēneon*] with their fair voices. Then you would not have seen any of the Argives tearless. For the clear-voiced Muse moved them to such an extent."[105] Thus, lamentation by the grave, hero cult through immortalizing song, is bestowed upon a poet-warrior by the Muses. He is given the standard *timē* of hero cult.[106] But he is given poetic immortality in the *Iliad*. The motif of Apollo murdering the poet connected in cult with the Muses is Aesopic.

It is curious that Achilles and his men killed the original Pharmakos. They also kill Thersites, a sort of epic *pharmakos*. Thersites' function is "to make strife against kings" (ἐριζέμεναι βασιλεῦσιν, *Iliad* II 214); he is the worst (*ekhthistos*, "most hated," II 220; *aiskhistos*, "most base," II 216) of the Achaeans;

---

[102] *Iliad* IX 413; Kerényi 1959:351; see below, ch. 17 (DoDera and Lugard MacCon).

[103] *Iliad* XXI 277ff.; XXII 359; XIX 404–417; Arctinus *Aethiopis*, in Proclus *Chrestomathy* 2, see Allen 1919 5:106.7–10; West 2003b:112; further references with variants in Frazer 1921 2:214–215. For the enmity of Apollo and Achilles, see *Iliad* XXIV 42; cf. Burkert 1985:147, who comments on the near identity of god and victim; Colombo 1977; Nagy 1979:62, 1990a:12.

[104] Cf. Nagy 1979:176.

[105] My trans. *Odyssey* xxiv 60: Μοῦσαι δ' ἐννέα πᾶσαι ἀμειβόμεναι ὀπὶ καλῇ / θρήνεον· ἔνθα κεν οὔ τιν' ἀδάκρυτόν γ' ἐνόησας / Ἀργείων· τοῖον γὰρ ὑπώρορε Μοῦσα λίγεια.

[106] *Odyssey* xxiv 80–84; Herodotus 5.94; Pliny *Natural History* 5.125; Diogenes Laertius 1.74; Philostratus *On Heroes* 53.8–18; Diodorus Siculus 17.17.3. At Elis, we find a cenotaph, and annual lamentation by women, Pausanias 6.23.3. Cf. Hedreen 1991:314; Escher-Bürkli 1894:222–223; Farnell 1921:284, 340–342; cf. Hommel 1980; Hooker1988; Nagy 1979:118.

he is repulsively ugly and deformed, II 217–219; he reproaches the king, Agamemnon, II 225–242; he is beaten by Odysseus, II 265–268; later he blames Achilles with a sexual taunt, and Achilles himself kills this proto-satirist poet. This killing causes strife in the army, and Achilles must travel to Lesbos for purification, where he sacrifices to Apollo, Artemis, and Leto.[107]

Thus, though Achilles offers a valuable example of hero persecuted by a god he has close ties to, and though he seems to have some kind of connection with the *pharmakos* cult myth (perhaps because the Thersites myth was primary, and then Pharmakos was assimilated to his story), his ties with poetry are not extensive, though they are intriguing. Singing is at least a part of his persona; the Muses lament him after death; and he is associated with the centaur Cheiron, a healer and singer.

Such hints are even more scanty in the case of Heracles. There was a tradition that linked him with the Muses. He was called *mousikos anēr* [a man of the Muses—or musical man], *Hercules Musarum* [Hercules of the Muses]. This was a Roman tradition, but it had its roots in Greece.[108] On black-figure Attic vases, Heracles is frequently pictured playing the kithara, like Apollo.[109] Pausanias saw a statue group of Apollo, the Muses, and Heracles by Damophon of Messene.[110]

According to Theocritus, Heracles was taught to sing by Eumolpus: he "made of him a singer [*aoidon*] and shaped his hand to the box-wood lyre."[111] Other accounts make Linus, a descendant of the earlier Linus,[112] his teacher;

---

[107] *Aithiopis*, Proclus summary, in Allen 1919 5.105–106; West 2003b:110. For interpretation of Thersites as *pharmakos*, see Wiechers 1961:44n2; cf. Gebhard 1926:58–60; Thalmann 1988; Nagy 1979:260–262, 279. Obviously, there is no question of viewing Thersites as a righteous blame poet like Aesop, though Garland notes that he has a certain clear-sighted view of the psychic problems facing the Greeks that was lacking elsewhere (1995:80–81). See ch. 17 on ambiguously malevolent poets in Ireland. Curiously, at one point, Achilles is threatened with stoning, when he refuses to return to battle, Aeschylus fr. 132c Radt. Perhaps this reflects the aggression of the *Männerbund* directed against members of their own group when they are perceived as less than adequate.

[108] Cf. Gratwick 1982:63; Robert 1 1920:622n2; cf. Roscher 1884 1:2189–2190, 2184 line 43 (a Hellenistic Attic votive relief shows Heracles eating at table with Apollo and the Muses); Dumézil 1983:137.

[109] Roscher 1884 1.2189. Gantz 1993:379.

[110] Pausanias 4.31.10.

[111] Theocritus 24.109 (trans. Edmonds): αὐτὰρ ἀοιδὸν ἔθηκε καὶ ἄμφω χεῖρας ἔπλασσε / πυξίνᾳ ἐν φόρμιγγι Φιλαμμονίδας Εὔμολπος. This is admittedly Hellenistic evidence. Cf. Lucian *Herodotus* 3, in which Heracles/Ogmios drags a number of men tethered by their ears with straps connected to his tongue.

[112] Apollodorus 2.4.9 (Frazer 1921 1:177n2); cf. Pausanias 9.29.6–9; Diodorus Siculus 3.67.2; Kerényi 1959:135. He was also the brother of Orpheus, Apollodorus 2.4.9. One account has Orpheus as Heracles' teacher, Robert 1920 1:408n7.

he misadvisedly hit Heracles, and the young hero struck back with his lyre and killed him—a musical homicide.[113] Here he seems almost an anti-poet.

Though we think of Heracles as a man of the labors, he also had obvious warrior associations. He is taught chariotry by his father Amphitryon, but Castor taught him the skills of fighting:

> δούρατι δὲ προβολαίῳ ὑπ' ἀσπίδι νῶτον ἔχοντα
> ἀνδρὸς ὀρέξασθαι ξιφέων τ' ἀνέχεσθαι ἀμυχμόν,
> κοσμῆσαί τε φάλαγγα λόχον τ' ἀναμετρήσασθαι
> δυσμενέων ἐπιόντα καὶ ἱππήεσσι κελεῦσαι
> Κάστωρ ἱππελάτας δέδαεν . . .
> Κάστορι δ' οὔτις ὁμοῖος ἐν ἡμιθέοις πολεμιστὴς
> ἄλλος ἔην πρὶν γῆρας ἀποτρῖψαι νεότητα.

> And how to abide the cut and thrust of the sword
> or to lunge lance in rest and shield swung over back,
> how to marshal a company, measure
> an advancing squadron of the foe, or give the word to a troop
>   of horse—
> all such lore had he of horseman Castor . . .
> till such time as age had worn away his youth,
> Castor had no equal in war among all the demigods.

Theocritus 24.125–133, trans. Edmonds[114]

Heracles shares with the other figures in this book a certain persecuted, wronged nature, and dies a horrible death before achieving an extraordinary heroization/deification.

In a theme that links him with athlete-heroes and Archilochus, he is denied a promised wife, an event that leads to his death. After winning the marriage contests for Iole, her father and brothers deny him her hand. He eventually kills them and obtains Iole, but the action is fatal, for then the jealous Deianeira gives him the poisoned robe.[115]

Thus, Heracles' poetic aspects are not strong, though the pattern of his heroic career offers a few parallels to poetic heroes. It is impossible to tell

---

[113] Apollodorus 2.4.9. Pausanias (9.29.6–9) speaks of two Linus figures. Though this story is found late in literature, it is quite widely attested by fifth-century art, Gantz 1993:379.

[114] See also Robert 1 1920:2.644n4. Castor is closely associated with poetry, war poetry in particular: Theocritus 22.215–220 (all singers are dear to the divine twins and to the heroes of the Trojan war); Pausanias 3.16.1–2. Cf. Plato *Laws* 796b; Burkert 1985:212nn6,7. For the comparative background of the Dioscuri, see Ward 1968; West 1975; and Burkert 1985:433n2.

[115] See Apollodorus 2.6.1; 2.7.7; Sophocles *Trachinian Women* 248ff., cf. Jebb 1893 *ad loc.*

whether his poetic associations are late embroidery or decayed remnants of a previously stronger tradition.[116]

Thus the myths of Marsyas, Thamyris, Pan, Linus, and Orpheus share important themes with the *vitae* of Aesop, Hesiod, Archilochus, and the other poets. Often the poet is the earthly champion in his skill; there is enmity between Apollo and the poet, which is sometimes contrasted by the poet's close alliance to the Muses; there is the *agōn*, which brings about the poet's death; after the death of the poet there is lamentation, hero cult, and emphasis on the placement of the hero's bones. In the cases of Marsyas and Orpheus, the cult of the hero killed by Apollo is identified with Apollo. After the death of Orpheus, a plague results, which can only be assuaged by hero cult paid to the poet.

If we assume the primacy of these myths over the lives of the poets, then, we can reasonably look to them as important sources (at least partially) for the poets' legendary *vitae*. These myths gave a framework on which many biographies could have been based.

Such a hypothesis is in no way absolute—it does not rule out other components in the biographies, including an authentic historical nucleus to a biography. Lefkowitz's thesis that the lives of the poets derive from mistaken interpretation of the poet's writings is not excluded either, though such accretion would be merely a component of the biographical tradition. Lefkowitz's method of explaining biography is by no means exclusive of mythical explanation. The biographer combs the extant text of the poet for biographical details; he misunderstands and misinterprets many details, but traditional themes from "the poetic biography" (Marsyas; Pharmakos; Aesop; Archilochus; Socrates) condition his misunderstanding, flesh out his biographical guesses. In fact, the scholiast may look for details in the corpus that fit the mythical "poetic biography."

However, the historical nucleus of these seemingly mythical tales should not be underrated: the myths were applied to the poets because poets' lives somewhat fit the structures of the already-existing myths. Poets were seen as sacred and powerful, inspired by god; poets came into conflict with elements of society, political or religious, or a combination of the two (Delphi, for instance, was a powerful political institution); poets were killed or exiled. So in the cases of poets such as Hesiod and Archilochus, no doubt their *vitae* are mixtures of history and myth; even a late figure such as Socrates, we have seen, has a biog-

---

[116] Heracles is also the weak link in the warrior triptych studied by Dumézil in *Stakes of the Warrior*. See below, ch. 18.

raphy self-consciously filled with mythical themes (Socrates is both Marsyas and Aesop; Aesop earlier had been Marsyas); but he certainly lived and was certainly tried by the Athenians, even if his trial may not have had all of the mythical power captured in Plato's *Apology*.

A revealing study in the ambiguous intersection of history, myth, and cult in Greek antiquity is the story of Philip of Croton, found in Herodotus (5.47), and ostensibly historical. Philip is the best—"the handsomest [*kallistos*] Greek of his day";[117] he is also an Olympic victor, which puts him in the sphere of Fontenrose's athlete-heroes. Like Archilochus, he is betrothed, and his betrothal is broken off, causing him great depression.[118] Like many of the poets we have studied, he is exiled, from Croton. Finally, like Archilochus, he is killed in battle. After his death, he is given hero cult by the Egestaeans (whom he had died fighting)[119] because of his beauty; they build a hero shrine for him upon his tomb and worship him with sacrifices.[120] In interpreting this story, we are faced with at least two options: it is historically reliable, and cult was awarded this singularly handsome, but singularly unfortunate man. The other option is that it is simply a traditional hero biography applied to a remarkably handsome Olympic victor to expedite his heroization/deification. A study of the lives of heroes, athletic and otherwise, shows the pattern that heroes must be exceedingly miserable before death.[121] In this case, Philip may have received a similar biography by exactly the same process.

Thus if poets were seen as heroes, superhuman, linked to the divine, they had to submit to the mechanism for heroization (exile; broken engagements; god-induced deaths; foreign deaths; unsympathetic trials[122]) standard in Greek myth. If we find such themes both in athlete-hero tales and poet-hero tales, it is likely that they came from the same source (mythical hero tale patterns). And of course, athlete-hero tales did not derive from learned conjecture out of the athletes' writings.

---

[117] κάλλιστος Ἑλλήνων τῶν κατ' ἑωυτόν. Cf. Thamyris, "who excelled in beauty," above, this chapter.

[118] Fontenrose 1968:86. The theme is found on a more obviously mythical plane in the story of Heracles, see above.

[119] Thus qualifying him for inclusion in Visser's "Worship Your Enemy," 1982:410.

[120] See Ekroth 2002:197–198.

[121] Fontenrose 1968:76–77.

[122] The trial theme is important in the athlete-hero tales, see Fontenrose 1968:76–77: the Hellanodicai deny the boxer Cleomedes his deserved victor crown because he killed his opponent; Theagenes is fined two talents; the sprinter Euthycles is unjustly convicted of bribery and betrayal of his city, and dies in prison. Oibotas is denied his proper honor by the Achaeans. Ajax, when denied (unjustly, he feels) the arms of Achilles after a contest (see Sophocles *Ajax* 442–449) is perhaps comparable.

If we have the hero tale pattern applied to athlete, and poet, it is not surprising that we also find it applied to seer, in the case of Carnos, whose military murder becomes an *aition* for a Doric festival. Apollodorus describes a regular cultic drama in a military context. The Heraclids are attacking the Peloponnese:

ἐφάνη γὰρ αὐτοῖς μάντις χρησμοὺς λέγων καὶ ἐνθεάζων, ὃν ἐνόμισαν μάγον εἶναι ἐπὶ λύμη τοῦ στρατοῦ πρὸς Πελοποννησίων ἀπεσταλμένον. τοῦτον βαλὼν ἀκοντίῳ Ἱππότης . . . τυχὼν ἀπέκτεινεν. οὕτως δὲ γενομένου τούτου τὸ μὲν ναυτικὸν διαφθαρεισῶν τῶν νεῶν ἀπώλετο, τὸ δὲ πεζὸν ἠτύχησε λιμῷ, καὶ διελύθη τὸ στράτευμα.

There appeared to them [the army at Naupactus] a prophet [*mantis*] reciting oracles in a fine frenzy [*entheazōn*], whom they took for a magician sent by the Peloponnesians to be the ruin of the army. So Hippotes . . . threw a javelin at him, and hit and killed him. In consequence of that, the naval force perished with the destruction of the fleet, and the land force suffered from famine, and the army disbanded.

Apollodorus 2.8.3[123]

The Dorians then gave cult to the enemy prophet after his death.

Fontenrose wrote perceptively of the application of hero myth to historical athletes:

The hero-athlete tale . . . belongs to a wider type of hero legend . . . the legend type tended to attach itself to famous athletes and shape them into legendary heroes; and then the subtype of hero-athlete tale, once it had been formed, sometimes converted legendary heroes into early Olympic athletes . . . History may be converted into legend, and myth and legend into pseudo-history.[124]

In the same way, the hero myth would attach itself to prominent Greek poets—Aesop, Archilochus, Hesiod, Homer. Thus we have such a curious life of a poet as that of Archilochus': combining overtly mythical themes (consecration by the Muses) with some solidly historical facts, along with some themes that could be history and could be myth. The fact that many of these themes are shared by other poets and heroes leads one to view many such ambiguous themes as legend, not history. The poet leading a life of disappointment,

---

[123] Pausanias 3.13.3, trans. Jones; Gebhard 1926:19, cf. Roscher 1884 2.967, s.v. Karnos.
[124] Fontenrose 1968:87.

wandering, and exile, and dying an unjust, divinely engineered death may be the traditional hero myth applied to the poet.

But, as has been noted, we should not underestimate the capacity for reality to imitate myth, since myths reflect cultural reality. A great poet can easily live a life of wandering, exile, and disappointment. There is, as it were, a mythical reality. To compound the problem, such a myth-imitating life would only attract mythical tailoring in the re-telling. In the ancient world, as in the modern, making an exact separation of myth from reality is impossible.

Part Two

INDO-EUROPEAN CONTEXT

17

Kissing the Leper:
The Excluded Poet in Irish Myth

I N 1596, EDMUND SPENSER WROTE,

There is amongst the Irish a certaine kind of people, called Bardes, which are to them insteed of Poets, whose profession is to set foorth the praises or dispraises of men in their poems or rymes, the which are had in so high regard and estimation amongst them, that none dare displease them for feare to runne into reproach thorough their offence, and to be made infamous in the mouthes of all men. For their verses are taken up with a generall applause, and usually sung at all feasts and meetings, by certaine other persons, whose proper function that is, who also receive for the same great rewards and reputation amongst them.[1]

Ireland has a rich dossier of the themes we have been considering so far; in fact, when parallels for Archilochus and the Lycambids are sought, the most striking comparanda have been found in Ireland, whose myth and folklore are full of powerful poets causing death, exile, and regal abdication through their satirical poetry, curses, and spells.[2] What has received less attention is the question of what happens to such powerful figures in Irish society. Again, the same social mechanisms seem to be in effect: the blame poet in Ireland often cannot be tolerated by society. Irish satirists are often imprisoned, killed, and exiled by political leaders and warriors; there seems to be a continual tension between king (or powerful political figure) and satirical poet, just as there

---

[1] *View of the State of Ireland.* 1810:119. He goes on to criticize the Irish poets for siding with the cause of the Irish against the English and fomenting rebellion.

[2] See e.g. Hendrickson 1925; Ward 1973; cf. Rankin 1974. For general surveys of Irish satirists and satire, Robinson 1912; Elliott 1960:8–48; McCone 1989; O'Leary 1991; for Irish poets, Caerwyn Williams 1972; Bloomfield and Dunn 1989:30–54; Breatnach 1996:76–77 (for satire, p. 115 with commentary).

is a mutually enriching bond between the king and poet who specializes in praise. In addition, important ancillary themes we have seen in the Aesop, Archilochus, and related traditions are in evidence here also: for instance, the poet as prophet; the poet as warrior; the poet as victim of inhospitality; and legislation directed against the satirist. If Ireland has a strong note of individuality that it infuses into these themes, it is the note of poetic malevolence. As has been noted earlier, the theme of the unsympathetic blame poet is also found in Greece (notably in the figure of Thersites).[3]

However, as has also been noted earlier, the moral standing of the poet is not absolute, but is often in the eye of the beholder. The documentary record for the malevolence of the Irish poet is a complex cultural and textual phenomenon, and one must at least try to arrive at a more ancient palimpsest of culture. John Rhys gives an example of tribal tension possibly causing animus against a famous poet, Aithirne from Ulster: the poet's story, in which he is seen as a most malevolent and amoral satirist, "comes to us from the *Book of Leinster*, written by the scribes of the hereditary foes of Ulster."[4]

But another, more widespread reason for the poet's unsavory reputation in Ireland could be the tension between the druid (priest, with poetic aspects) and *fili* (poet, *filid* plural) and the Christian priest and monk. For example, St. Patrick forbids poetic and mantic practices.[5] Scribes would of course tend to be Christian or Christianized, but according to the Chadwicks, the druid, unlike the *fili*, could not coexist with Christianity at all.[6] Robin Flower writes, "In the lives of the saints the poets are usually represented in a somewhat unfavourable light. They are called "mimes and histrions" (*mimi et histriones*) or *jongleurs* (*joculatores*) and they constantly appear extorting gifts under the threat of a satire."[7] However, as Flower notes, there may also have been some cooperation between the two groups, as St. Columba at one point saves the poets of Ireland from exile.[8] But this may merely symbolize the saint's dominance over the weakened poets. The church could "co-opt" poets by becoming their patron.[9] Christian scribes apparently were especially disapproving of Irish poets who specialized in satire.[10]

---

[3] See above, ch. 16. He represents Greece's major parallel to many unsympathetic Irish poets, though the Irish poets are more powerful and feared.

[4] Rhys 1979:326. See e.g. "The Siege of Howth," Stokes 1887.

[5] Stokes 1893:156, cf. Elliott 1960:29; Chadwick 1934:99, 129.

[6] Chadwick and Chadwick 1932 1:613.

[7] Flower 1947:75.

[8] Geoffrey Keating, *History of Ireland*, in Comyn and Dineen 1908 3:78ff.

[9] Breatnach 1987:89.

[10] McCone 1989:128.

In the same way, a tale that is "one long riotous attack on the poets and their ways," the *Proceedings of the Great Bardic Institution*, has a saint save the chief poet Senchán, whose satire on the chief cat of Ireland, Irusan, has gone awry, and who is about to be killed by the violent beast.[11] The tale satirizes the satirist and points up his subservience to the Christian saint. Though the saints are not exempted from the power of the satirists, "in general, when the satirists confront the saints, their sorcery is forced to succumb to a higher power."[12]

Interestingly, in an Irish document that is a miscellany about poets in Ireland, there is a tradition that views Aithirne in a sympathetic, moral light; the poet is the enforcer of moral law where the legal law cannot extend; [13] Aithirne the Importunate is quoted as prescribing "to poets a high standard of conduct."[14] Such a hint of a possible earlier tradition of the moral blame poet in Ireland is tantalizing.[15] In legislation relating to Irish poetry, there is a sense of moral and immoral satire,[16] and some stories support the necessary morality of the blame poet. The poet Dallán satirizes a king with flagrant injustice, and though he leaves the palace exulting, three days later he is dead.[17] In the ceremony for the famous Irish satire genre, *glám-dichenn*, the poets (who have been denied proper payment for a poem)[18] pray that "if it were they that were in the wrong, the earth of the hill would swallow them up."[19] This emphasis on the punishment of unlawful satire again is evidence for a strong tradition of moral blame.[20]

The moral issues of "justified" satire in Ireland are further complicated by legalistic interpretations of justification. The story of the poet Nede and the ruler Caier is a good example of the lengths the poet will go to find a "just"

---

[11] See Connellan 1860:111–119, cf. Joynt 1931; Mercier 1962:219–221.

[12] Robinson 1912:123–124, who collects further tales showing tension between saints and satirists.

[13] For the Irish poet as upholder of the law, see Mac Airt 1958:140–141; 145–146; Murphy 1940:201n4; Caerwyn Williams 1972:118; Meid 1974; Robinson 1912:107–108. Cf. Catullus 12 and 42, in which Catullus uses the threat of satire as a weapon to get stolen goods returned. For poet as avenger of oath breaking, see above, ch. 3 (Archilochus), ch. 4 (Hipponax), ch. 9 (Alcaeus). See also below, this chapter, last note, the poet as protector of the community.

[14] Gwynn 1940:3.

[15] See also Ó hÓgáin 1979:54 (the poet must have a pure heart).

[16] Robinson 1912:105.

[17] *Proceedings of the Great Bardic Institution*, in Connellan 1860:31–33.

[18] Cf. Simonides in ch. 7.

[19] *diamad iatson bad chintach ann talumh na tulchi dia slugadh*. Translation from *Book of Ballymote*, in Stokes 1891:119–120; cf. Robinson 1912:109; O'Curry 1873 2:216–226.

[20] See also O'Leary 1991:26 for the poets' responsibility to "judge" warriors and "reprove" them if necessary. He notes that in the Welsh tradition, the emphasis is on the poet praising good warriors and kings, while in the Irish tradition, the emphasis is on poets blaming. Cf. O'Leary 1991:21n31, for praise "washing" away dishonor in Irish texts.

pretext for his satire. Through Caier's wife, Nede learns that Caier has a knife that he has been forbidden by a *geis* (taboo) to part with. When Nede asks for the knife as a present and Caier is unable to give it, the king lays himself open to "just" satire through his apparent lack of generosity. This seems to be the moral casuistry of culture in which shame is a dominant component.[21]

Despite these ambiguities, the malevolent power of the Irish poets is most striking. Their lethal skill is exhaustively documented in Fred N. Robinson's classic essay, "Satirists and Enchanters in Early Irish Literature."[22] The poet Senchán kills ten mice through a satire;[23] a poetic curse ceremony provides that a stingy, oath-breaking regal patron will be swallowed up by the earth, along with his family and possessions.[24] Caier, after being dethroned by the satire of the poet Nede, flees from his kingdom, but dies of shame when the guilt-driven Nede seeks him out and he sees the poet face to face.[25] Though technically the poet's satire only causes the king's abdication, it effectively causes the shame that eventually kills him also. In much the same way, Aithirne and his sons, repulsed in their amatory advances by Luaine, the beautiful fiancée of King Conchobar, satirize her three times, leaving the customary blotches of Shame, Blemish, and Disgrace on her face, and she dies of shame. While there has probably never been a "pure" shame culture, clearly shame was a major component of this milieu, at least as reflected in such texts as these.[26]

Ferdiad, the friend of Cuchulainn, is threatened with death by satire, so prefers death in battle instead.[27] The woman Maistiu is satirized to death by

---

[21] For the power of mockery, dishonor, and shame in Ireland, see O'Leary 1991 and below. But the end of this story (see below) increases its moral complexity, as it shows Nede suffering from guilt, and finally dying as a result of it. Robinson 1912:113. Cf. Elliott 1960:31n33. See ch. 2, summary paragraphs at end of chapter; Ward 1973; also cf. Ward 1982; Elliott 1960:67–77.

[22] Robinson 1912.

[23] *Proceedings of the Great Bardic Institution*, in Connellan 1860:79. It should always be borne in mind that this is a Christian source prejudiced against the pre-Christian poet; however, it clearly preserves archaic traditions. Cf. Robinson 1912:96.

[24] *Book of Ballymote*, in Stokes 1891:119–120.

[25] *Cormac's Glossary* in the *Yellow Book of Lecan*, Codex B, in Stokes 1862:xxvi–xxx; xxxix–xl; also Meyer 1912:58–60, §698. A condensed translation available in Robinson 1912:113. For an introduction to Cormac, see Russell 1988.

[26] "The Wooing of Luaine and Death of Athirne," see Stokes 1903b; cf. Breatnach 1980; Robinson 1912:117–118. For the blotches, see below.

[27] *Táin* BL 2609–2619; translation in Kinsella 1969:168. Discussion of this passage in Miller (2000:237) who regards it as an example of how the warror can be controlled by satire, and behind that, threat of public shaming (despite the "magical" element in Irish satire). The *Táin Bó Cúalnge* is found in three major manuscripts, LU, YBL, and BL. The *Lebor na hUidre* (LU), "Book of the Dun Cow," dates from the twelfth century, and contains a flawed, mutilated, partial text. The *Yellow Book of Lecan* (YBL), dated to the late fourteenth century, also

a female satirist, Gris.[28] Another female satirist, Dub, finding out that she is married to a polygamist, kills her rival wife through a "sea-spell."[29] The Welsh Dafydd ap Gwilym is a historical figure, nearly contemporary with Chaucer, who was reputed to have killed through satirical poetry. He wrote a satire on a rival poet, Rhys Meigen; when Rhys heard it read, he reportedly fell dead on the spot.[30] The druids had the same lethal power as the later poets: according to the Dindsenchas of Laigen, "the druids of Ireland nearly exterminated by their songs the tribe of the Gaileoin."[31] There are two apparently historic instances from Ireland: the poet Hugh O'Higgins and his son kill through poetry an Englishman, John Stanley, in the fifteenth century. This is a just poetic execution: Stanley mercilessly persecuted churchmen, laymen, and scholars, driving them to homelessness and starvation. After being satirized, he lived only five weeks, then "died of the virulence of the lampoons."[32] Egan O'Rahilly, in the eighteenth century, kills a man through poetry and barely survives a poetic attack himself.[33]

---

includes a partial, flawed text. However, the language of these manuscripts dates from the eighth century, and some of the verse is dated to the sixth century. This has been referred to as Recension I. These manuscripts are the basis of Kinsella 1969. Text and translation in O'Rahilly 1976. The *Book of Leinster* (BL), dated to twelfth century with language dated at the same time, has the complete *Táin* (Recension II). See O'Rahilly 1967, text with English translation. Cf. Windisch 1905; Kinsella 1969:ix–x; O'Rahilly 1967:xiv–xvi.

[28] *Rennes Dindsenchas*, see Stokes 1894:334–336; cf. Robinson 1912:121; Cross et al. 1969:596–599.

[29] *Rennes Dindsenchas*, in Stokes 1894:326 (Cross et al. 1969:598), whence the name Dublind, from Dub-lind (*lind*, 'pool'), corrupted to Dublin. As Robinson notes, the boundaries between incantation and satire are often very difficult to define in this literature (1912:98–99 and passim). For the magical power of the word in archaic Indo-European culture, cf. the spell used by the brahmanic caste (Puhvel 1987:45), and also evidenced in the mythology of Varuṇa (1987:48–49), and associated gods (1987:54, 135). For a comparison of the Celtic poet and druid with the Indic brahman, see Dillon 1947:262, 259–264. See below, ch. 22 (Cicero), the enchanting power of the word in oratory.

[30] See Loomis 1982:85–88, poem 21. This poem is a rich compendium of traditional invective themes: Rhys is compared to various animals; we have the emphasis on the belly (43, 59); the vomiting/animal topos (he is compared to a "a noisy pig when he vomited," *Banw chweidwrw ban chwydai*, 46); he is a bad poet (31), and a cowardly warrior (54). This savage poem is a response to an obscenely insulting poem by Rhys, see p. 85. See also Stern 1910:25–26; Parry 1952:lxix–lxxii, also Carr 1973, for discussion of how the poet thought of himself as an outcast; and Bromwich 1967:12.

[31] Robinson 1912:122; Stokes 1894:299. See also O'Leary 1991:24.

[32] *fuair bás do neiṁ na naor*. *Annals of the Kingdom of Ireland*, by the Four Masters, see O'Donovan 1856 4:819; Elliott 1960:34. As O'Donovan notes, "An *aoir* is a poem in which the subject is not only lampooned, but imprecated and cursed."

[33] Dinneen 1900:xxxi. This passage was dropped from the second edition. Dineen gives no source. Cf. poem XXXVIII, a savage satire; here, as often, defensive, a reply to the attack of a rival poet. See also O'Donovan 1846:180n.

The poet's destructive power was often less than lethal, but still dreaded. Irish poets traditionally disfigured their victims with three blisters on the face, variously named with allegorical words of shame and defilement. In the story of Nede and Caier, they are "Stain, Blemish, and Defect" (*on, anim,* and *easbaidh*) and are red, green, and white.[34] One poet melts his enemies through his reviling.[35] One proposed victim of satire, when he cannot remove a ring the satirist Aithirne has asked for, hacks off the finger to avoid the attack;[36] a king, the one-eyed Eochaid, plucks out his eye and gives it to Aithirne to avoid a similar attack.[37] Kings surrender their wives to the demands of the same satirist.[38] The blame of Irish poets can even attack nature, the productivity of the land: in the story of Niall, Echu, and Laidchenn, Laidchenn's satires cause the trees and grains of Leinster to become barren; the poet Ferchertne causes a lake to rise or fall by praise or blame; the poet Forgoll threatens to curse waters to be barren of fish, woods to lack fruit, and plains to lack grain.[39] The poet can also attack the productivity of the land indirectly, by attacking the king, blemishing him.[40] But the poet can attack the king because he does not provide the required prosperity.[41]

---

[34] *Cormac's Glossary,* in Stokes 1862:xxxviii. In the story of Aithirne, the malevolent satirist, and Luaine (see "The Wooing of Luaine," Stokes 1903b:279, cf. Breatnach 1980), they are "Shame, Blemish and Disgrace," (*On 7 Ainim 7 Aithis*) and are black, red, and white. In the story of Ferdiad in the *Táin,* they are "Shame, Blemish, and Disgrace," *ail 7 anim 7 athis, Táin* BL 2624; in "The Bodleian Amra Choluimb Chille," appendix, Stokes 1899:421–422, they are Shame, Blemish, and Defect, (*On 7 Anim 7 Esbaid*), and are referred to as "poisonous ulcers (*cnuic nemi*)." Their effect on the victim is that he or she is "recognizable" to every one. Cf. Fafne, in Stokes 1894:306–307; Robinson 1912:114. For the range of meaning applicable to these shame/defect words, see O'Leary 1991:23–25. In Theocritus 12.24, *pseudea,* 'lies' are 'spots, pimples' on the nose, cf. LSJ s.v.; *scholia* and Gow 1965 *ad loc.* Conversely, the poet who satirized unjustly was subject to the same blemishes, Stokes 1891–1894:421–422.

[35] Laidchenn, in the story of Niall, Laidchenn and Echu, Meyer 1900; Robinson 1912:119; O'Curry 1873 2:70.

[36] See O'Grady 1857:297, who discusses a panegyrical poem on the Clannt-Suibhne, or Mac Sweeny's, by Red Owen Mac Ward (a famous Ulster poet hanged by the Earl of Thomond in 1672). The victim who loses his finger is one of the Mac Sweeny ancestors.

[37] "The Siege of Howth," Stokes 1887:49; cf. Elliott 1960:30; Ward 1973:134.

[38] "The Siege of Howth," Stokes 1887:49, 53; "A Story From which it is inferred that Mongán was Find mac Cumaill . . . ," in Meyer and Nutt 1972 1:49.

[39] For Laidchenn, see above; Ferchertne, see the *Táin,* in Windisch 1905 p. 789 (a late passage); Forgol, see "A Story From which it is inferred that Mongán was Find mac Cumaill . . . ," in Meyer and Nutt 1972 1:49; Robinson 1912:119.

[40] For the king as source of prosperity, see *Odyssey* xix 110; Ammianus Marcellinus 28.5.14; "The Birth of Cormac," in O'Grady 1970 2:288–289; Caerwyn Williams 1972:129; Dillon 1946–1947:138–139; Maier 1989:16; Dumézil 1943:64; Bremmer 1980:74–75.

[41] Dumézil 1943:230–240, discussing the avaricious Bres; *The Second Battle of Moytura,* Gray 1982:33–

As has been noted before, this kind of power will inevitably lead to friction with persons in high places, notably the king, and our central theme, the poet's exile or death, results. On the other hand, sometimes the Irish satirist is so powerful that the obverse of our theme, the satire-induced exile of the king, results (as in the remarkable story of Nede and Caier). As in Greece, it is the poet's ability to shame and exile his or her enemy (often the king or equivalent) that drives him or her into the persona of the *pharmakos* and practical exile. The agony of the poet-scapegoat is the obverse of the shame and agony he or she has caused (even if he or she has caused it with full justification).[42]

There were four different occasions when poets as a group were exiled from Ireland. In each case, a powerful protector (the first three times in Ulster) saved them from their fate. The first time (when they numbered twelve hundred), they were protected by King Conchobar of Ulster; the second time they (Eochaid, king-poet, and his seven hundred) were protected by King Fiachna mac Baedan, and the third time they (including Eochaid, Dallán, and Senchán) were saved by King Maelcobha mac Deamain. King Aed mac Ainmiri tried once more to exile them at the assembly of Drumceat, but now they were protected by a Christian saint, Columba, who did, however, limit their numbers.[43] These stories are curious in that they involve the themes of tension between poet and king, and unity of poet and king at the same time (one king exiles; another king saves).

In the case of the dreaded satirist Aithirne the Importunate, a kind of preventative exile is practiced; the men of Leinster meet the poet on the borders of their land and offer him jewels and treasures so that he will stay away. (The poet subsequently levies a tax of women and cattle, and a war results.)[44]

---

35. See also the poem by MacDaire to O'Brien, of the Elizabethan era, listing the destructive powers of the Irish poet—if he is attacked, O'Donovan 1846:21.

[42] As Burnett notes, the poet can create a *pharmakos*, 1983:58, 97. Ironically, this power is what leads him to become a *pharmakos*. There are two patterns, in which the poet is just (Aesop) and unjust (Thersites).

[43] See Keating, *History of Ireland*, in Comyn and Dineen 3:78–97. Cf. Flower 1947:3; Robinson 1912:124.

[44] "The Siege of Howth" in Stokes 1887:53, 55. For the theme of the poet as cause of wars, see Robinson 1912:118–119, cf. above on Niall's poet Laidchenn, who causes the strife that results in Niall's death. The tree musician Fer Fí sows strife among a group of warriors, *The Battle of Mag Mucrama* in O'Daly 1975:40; Dillon 1946:163; O Daly 1962:81–86; J. Nagy 1985:281n35. Randolph notes: "It is also significant that the Morrigu in her function as a female satirist foments the Cattle-Raid of Cooley, since stirring up desired quarrels between powerful chieftains and tribes was a major occupation among the male satirists" (1942:81). See also Randolph 1941:190n21. Cf.

Laws passed in Ireland often legislated against the poet[45] and sometimes they provided for his exile. A law passed in 1579 provided that a seneschal of O Byrnes county should "make proclamation that no idle person, vagabond or masterless man, bard, rymor, or other notorious malefactor, remain within the district on pain of whipping after eight days, and of death after twenty days."[46] Here we have the exile theme combined with an evaluation of the poet as the worst, ranked with tramps and "notorious malefactors." Similar evaluations are found in other Irish laws: "Thus satirists are classed among the men for whom no one may go surety; and woman-satirists, along with thieves, liars, and bush-strumpets,[47] are said to have no claim to an honor-price. Similarly, the son of a woman-satirist, like the son of a bondmaid, is declared to be ineligible to chieftaincy."[48]

The implications of these and numerous other laws regulating satire are numerous. The blame poet will be punished for practicing his art, either by fine, loss of rights, corporal punishment (such as whipping), exile, imprisonment, or death. Sometimes the poet's tongue was even cut out of his mouth.[49] Moreover, these laws were presumably produced either by powerful political leaders or by bodies of legislators representing their society. They imply the theme of selection and condemnation (of the poetic class) in a public meeting.

Leaving the theme of exile proper, we also find the theme of the violent killing of the poet to be common in Irish mythical tradition. In one case, satirists accuse a tribe, the Cenel Fhiachach, of being lowborn; in retaliation, the Cenel Fhiachach murder the poets.[50] Cuchulainn on three occasions was confronted by satirists; on all three occasions the poets died. In one case, the

---

Thersites' function, "to make strife against kings," see above; for the blame poet and the mythology of strife, see ch. 6 (Hesiod).

[45] Robinson 1912:103–108.

[46] Walsh 1933:186 (this was part of the English attempts to suppress Irish culture); cf. Caerwyn Williams 1972:133.

[47] Cf. Robinson 1912:107n51; Elliott 1960:25; ch. 8 (Sappho). On Irish woman satirists, see Randolph 1942; Chadwick 1934:111–112, where mantic inspiration in the Cuchulainn Cycle is seen to be "the special métier of women." An example would be the prophet-poet Fedelm in *Táin* BL 220–275, R1 29–112; Kinsella 1969:60–61. For an interpretation of the supernatural as feminine, see J. Nagy 1982–1983:58. The goddess Brig(it), who was a poet herself, was the special patron of poets, and was associated with wailing women, *The Second Battle of Mag Tuired*, Gray 1982:119. Curiously, she is associated with two anti-poetic figures, Bres and the Dagda (of whom she is wife and daughter, respectively). See also on Morrigan, below, this chapter.

[48] Robinson 1912:107; *Ancient Laws of Ireland* 1865–1901 5:456.

[49] See Stokes 1894:297 (if poet = *druid*); Ó hÓgáin 1979:51.

[50] O'Donovan 1846:180, citing *Leabhar Breac* fol. 35,b; O'Daly 1852:17n; Robinson 1912:108. Aesop also accused the Delphians of being lowborn, G 125, a standard topos, see Davies 1985:33.

satirist Redg, king Ailill's jester (*cainte*), is sent against Cuchulainn. He asks for the hero's spear, and when he is refused, threatens to take away the hero's honor through satire. Then Cuchulainn throws the spear through the back of Redg's head, a seemingly cowardly act. "'Now, that is a stunning gift,' the satirist cried," presumably immediately before he died.[51]

In another case, Riches, a female satirist, attacks Cuchulainn because he has killed her son. She assaults him by exposing herself, causing Cuchulainn to turn his head in shame, leaving him open to attack from her fosterling nearby. But Cuchulainn's charioteer levels Riches by slinging a stone at her and breaking her back. This allows Cuchulainn to regain his self-possession and kill the fosterling.[52] In both these stories, the psychological advantage of the satirist is obliterated by the brute force of the warrior. Cuchulainn kills three more satirists, much as he killed Redg, before his death.[53] However, in the story of Cuchulainn's death, in which three satirists demand his spear, and he "gives" it to them in the head, the "giving" of the spear eventually lays him open to a lethal return cast of the spear; the satirists, though they have died themselves, have helped cause his death.

Exactly parallel to these Cuchulainn stories is the story of Laidchenn's death, for this satirist is killed by a "champion's stone" hurled at him by Echu, when Laidchenn is melting the hero through satire.[54]

A classic poet–king conflict brings about the death of the poet Fafne.[55] Fafne's sister is transformed into a fawn by enemies and then is killed by the king's men. In retaliation, Fafne satirizes the king, blemishing him in the customary way. In return, Fafne is arrested and executed. This story is noteworthy not only for its paradigmatic clarity,[56] but for its sympathetic poet, who blemishes the king only because his sister has been murdered, and who then is killed for this just satire.

---

[51] *Táin Bó Cúalnge*, Kinsella 1969:126; *Táin* R1 1510–1520; the spear through the back of the head is found only in the Book of Leinster version, 1803–1815. *Ocus ní tharnaic úad acht a rád: 'Is sólom dún in sét sa.'* O'Rahilly translates: "Quickly did we get this treasure" (1967:188). Cf. Robinson 1912:120; Cross et al. 1969:335–337.

[52] *Mesca Ulad (Drunkenness of the Ulstermen)* in Cross et al. 1969:237; cf. Randolph 1942:76–77; J. Nagy 1985:285.

[53] See Cross et al. 1969:335–337; Elliott 1960:33.

[54] For Laidchenn, see above.

[55] Stokes 1894:306–308; Cross et al. 1969:597.

[56] Cf. the story of poet Thorleif, who is also wronged by the king and then satirizes him, discussed in Ward 1973:136–137.

Divine vengeance overtakes three poets who threaten to satirize St. Laisren; they are swallowed up by the earth.[57] This kind of death is found also in the legendary scapegoat tales of Greece.[58]

The poet Gris's destruction of Maistiu has been referred to above; Maistiu's lover then killed the poet, breaking her head with a rock.[59] Dub, also referred to above, is another lethal female satirist who is killed violently in revenge for a murderous chant.[60]

Aithirne's destruction of Luaine through satire has been referred to above.[61] The aftermath of this tragedy was the destruction of the poet and his family: King Conchobar and his Ulstermen trap the poet and his sons in their fortress, wall them in, kill the poet's two daughters, and burn down the structure. Again, despite the power of the poet, the power of force prevails, though the story ends with a prophecy of woe for the murderers delivered by other poets.

Another extraordinary satirist, the blind Cridenbel ("whose mouth was out of his breast"), is also murdered. When he demands the best three portions of his host's meals, and when his host, the Dagdae, begins to lose his health as a result, the Dagdae puts three golden coins in his food and gives these three bits to the insatiable lampooner, who dies of the golden dose.[62] Again, the story is set up so the unsympathetic poet receives his just deserts; but once again the poet is murdered—here in the house of his host, and by stealth. Though Cridenbel and Hesiod are far apart in character, they share this theme: the poet, perceived as criminal, is murdered by his host, by stealth, in a house where he should have received hospitality.[63]

A similar configuration of themes occurs in *Vision of MacConglinne*.[64] The scholar Aniér MacConglinne turns poet, and makes his first journey as a poet to receive a king's hospitality in Munster (8). But on the way he stays in a guesthouse in Cork; it turns out to be dirty and verminous (10). The abbot

---

[57] "*Acta Sancti Lasriani*," in de Smedt and de Backer 1888:11, col. 796. Cf. Robinson 1912:124.

[58] E.g. the story of Anchurus, who rides into a cleft in the ground opened up by Zeus Idaeus, pseudo-Callisthenes, FGH 124 F 56; Trophonius is also swallowed up by the earth, Pausanias 9.37.7.

[59] See above; cf. Stokes 1894:334–336; Elliott 1960:33n36; Randolph 1942:78.

[60] See above; cf. Stokes 1894:334–336; Cross et al. 1969:598; Randolph 1942:78; like Gris, she is killed by a hurled stone.

[61] Cf. Stokes 1903b; Breatnach 1980.

[62] Gray 1982:28–31; Stokes 1891:64–68, cf. McCone 1989, who suggests that a Christian overlay heightens Cridenbel's villainy.

[63] Cf. Androgeos and Aesop, in chs. 1 and 2 above.

[64] Page numbers are from Meyer 1892; the story is also in Cross et al. 1969:551–587.

in charge of it, Manchín, sends out meager ration of food, and MacConglinne, when he sees it, refuses the meal and sings bitter satirical quatrains about it. The servant boy memorizes the verses and repeats them to the abbot. Manchín is concerned that unless the wandering poet is punished, other little boys will sing the same verses (16). He subsequently accuses the poet of attacking the Church verbally (18). Accordingly, MacConglinne is stripped, scourged until his skin separates from his bones, immersed in the river Lee, and kept prisoner in the guesthouse in preparation for his crucifixion the next day. There is a curious trial, in which the abbot and monks accuse the poet unjustly (20). He in turns abuses them freely: "Ye curs and robbers and dung-hounds, ye monks of Cork!" (22).[65] He is tied all night to a pillar-stone, but it is at this point, when he has been reduced to his lowest ebb of misery, that he receives a vision from an angel (30); he puts it into rhyme, recites it to Manchín, and the abbot reluctantly is forced to spare the poet's life.

There are parallels to Aesop in this tale; the poet is inhospitably received, and satirizes his ungenerous hosts, who worry about the effect of the satire; so he is unjustly tried and sentenced to death. As an ironic reversal, the Christian monks sentence the poet to crucifixion. The archaic theme of the poet inhospitably received lies behind the Christian overlay.

The story in the *Táin* of the death of the jester, Tamun, "the Stump,"[66] has a king subject his "camp fool" to military murder; since the king dresses Tamun as himself, this murder has *therapōn*, ritual substitute resonances.[67] While Cuchulainn is holding off the Connacht army in his famous solitary defense of Ulster, King Ailill sends Tamun, made up to look like him and with a king's crown on his head, to try to deceitfully distract the hero from his defense. But when Cuchulainn hears Tamun's voice, he "knew by the man's speech that he was the camp fool. He shot a sling-stone from his hand and pierced the fool's head and knocked out his brains."[68]

Another fool, DoDera, dies as his master's champion. Foreseeing defeat for his master, Lugaid Mac Con, he volunteers to go against Eogan "with

---

[65] *a matadu ocus a latrannu ocus a c[h]onu cacca .i. a muinter C[h]orccaige!*

[66] Perhaps a reference to a deformity.

[67] See above, ch. 1 (on *therapōn* as ritual substitute); ch. 3 (Archilochus).

[68] *Ecmaic atgeóin-sium for erlabrai ind fir combo drúth. Srethis liic telma boí ina láim fair con sescaind ina c[h]end co tuc a inc[h]ind ass. Táin* R1 1580ff., 2480ff.; Kinsella 1969:140–141, cf. 271; *Táin* BL 2461–2472. For the theme of champion as scapegoat, *Táin* R1 2495ff. = Kinsella 1969:164. Soon after, Cuchulainn asks for someone to meet him in battle; the Connachtmen reply, "No scapegoat [*cimbid*] is owed by my people" (*Ní dlegar cimbid dom chenéol*). O'Rahilly 1967:207. *Cimbid* (*cimmid*), means 'victim, captive, someone to be killed, sacrifice', used of Jesus in the Irish Bible, Vendryes 1987:C-100.

your diadem on my head and wearing your battle-dress."[69] "The jester was exactly like Mac Con in form and appearance."[70] (Interestingly, the first mention of DoDera describes him as *drúid*, though this is probably simply an error for *drúth*). Eogan kills the fool after seeing through the disguise. This is a striking example, with a "fool" as the martial victim.[71] In Hittite ritual, there is emphasis on the ritual substitute victim's dressing like the king, being anointed with regal oil, and being given the king's crown. Then bad fortune is told to attack this substitute.[72]

The parallel with Achilles and Patroclus is obvious;[73] in both situations a man of high status, king or hero, sends a servant dressed as himself to face the greatest hero of the enemy's forces, and the servant is killed. Here the *therapōn* explicitly moves in the sphere of the satirist, for a number of passages in Irish literature show that the satirist and the fool are closely associated,[74] though such an association would seem natural even without such evidence.[75] Also significant is the fact that the poet is substituted for a king.

The story of Nede and King Caier, referred to briefly above, also ends with the poet's death. Nede, King Caier's nephew and adopted son, at the urging of Caier's wife, has caused the abdication and exile of the king through satire that is only technically justified, leaving the king's face blemished. "Caier fled thence that none might see the disgrace, until he was in Dun Cermnai" (*Atloi caieur as arnach nacedh nech fond aithis combœ in dun cermnai . . .*). This is a classic

---

[69] Lines 67–70: *ocus do mind-su for mo chind 7 t'erred immum.*

[70] Lines 63–64: *Comchosmail crotha 7 delba in drúth fri Mac Con.*

[71] *The Battle of Mag Mucrama*, see O Daly 1975:41–43. Cf. Stokes 1892; Dillon 1948:78–79; Carney 1959. I am indebted to Leslie Myrick for these references.

[72] See Gurney 1977:56; Kümmel 1967:10–11. The prisoner is not killed, but is led back to his own city. The word for the ritual substitute here is *tar-pa-al-li.*

[73] For Patroclus as *therapōn*, see above, ch. 1; G. Nagy 1979:292–295. For other parallels between the two epics, see Murphy 1966:117; Watkins 1976:271; Clader 1976:9n12; Melia 1979:255–261; Sergent 1998:126–127. Cuchulainn, like Achilles, chooses short life and glory over long life without it—*Táin* BL, 929ff.; *Iliad* XVIII 94–126, discussion in Miller 2000:129–132, 332. For the Hittite scapegoat, see Kümmel 1967, with plentiful bibliography, 19–21; 36; for *tarpassa*, van Brock 1959:117–146; Gurney 1977:52–58.

[74] The list of undesirables quoted below lists jesters immediately after satirists; in the lives of the saints, the *fili* is referred to as *joculator* (see above); in the *Second Battle of Moytura* 36 (Gray 1982:33), Bres is condemned for not providing poets, bards, satirists, musicians, jugglers, or fools in his household. In Mercier 1962:113, the "'touch of satire' is attributed to the saintly fool Mac Dá Cherda." Cf. O'Keefe 1911. The *crosan* is 'juggler, buffoon, satirist', Meyer 1906, under *crosan*; Todd 1848:182; Robinson 1912:104. Cf. another murdered fool (*druth*) in Stokes 1893:176, s.v. *orc treith*, (a talking head story; the poet is murdered after loyally telling Finn, his master, that Finn's wife has been unfaithful to him); Chadwick 1934:118; also Redg, a satirist and jester (see above), another casualty of Cuchulainn's battle prowess.

[75] For a seriously satirical fool, cf. *King Lear.*

case of the poet creating a regal *pharmakos.* Nede ascends the throne and marries the former king's wife. But after a year, a remarkable thing happens. Nede feels guilt or pity for the exiled king: "Grievous unto him was Caier's torment" (*Ba haithrech lais cradh caier*). Thus, even in archaic Irish myth, guilt seems to obtrude into a culture in which shame and dishonor are dominant motivating forces. Nede travels to the fort where Caier is receiving hospitality; he drives Caier's chariot, and is accompanied by Caier's wife and greyhound. When Caier sees them he inflicts another exile on himself: "Caier fled from them out of the house, till he was on the flagstone behind the fort." After entering the fort, Nede evidently pursues Caier with his dogs, who track him to the flagstone, under which he is hiding. When Nede approaches, "Caier died for shame on seeing Nede. The rock flamed at Caier's death, and a fragment of the rock flew up under Nede's eye, and pierced into his head."[76]

This story is remarkable for the humanizing of the previously ruthless poet. Driven by guilt and pity, he follows Caier into exile. There his own death complements the death of the king, which he unintentionally causes; paradoxically, the king seems to unintentionally cause Nede's death also, though there is a supernatural force involved. Like Caier, Nede exiles himself and suffers death far from his home. It would be hard to imagine a more symbiotic relationship of persecutor and victim; both men end up as exiled *pharmakoi*, and each destroys the other.[77]

These legendary accounts of the persecution of poets are paralleled by some historical accounts. In 1572, the Earl of Thomond hanged three poets whom he found offensive, for which offense against the bards he was satirized himself.[78] During the reign of James I, a poet named Teige Dall O'Higgin had his tongue cut out, and his wife and child were murdered, by the O'Haras, the recipients of one of his lampoons, who had abused his hospitality.[79]

---

[76] Trans. Stokes 1861:xxxvi–xl. *consela caier uaidib astigh corraba forsind liic iar cúl in duine . . . Atbad caier ar fele la aicsin nede. Rosich 7 rolassai innail la ec caier 7 rosescaind blog dind ailig fo suil nede co ro imid ina cend.*

[77] It is almost as if Nede destroys himself. But, in the parameters of the story, Nede is not the original moving force for the crime. Just as Eve gives Adam the apple, here Caier's wife has given Nede a silver apple for his love (see Robinson 1912:114n73), and led him to usurp the kingdom. Cf. the Oresteia myth, where a male seduces the queen and leads her to murder the king: D'Armes and Hulley 1946; Davies 1969. In addition to the dossier of murdered poets listed above, there is also Suibhne, who will be dealt with more fully in chapter 18; Oircbél/ Cethern, in "The Boyhood Deeds of Finn," trans. in J. Nagy 1985:216, cf. 166, 171; Casmáel, in Gray 1982:119.

[78] *Annals of the Kingdom of Ireland,* see O'Donovan 1856: 1572 AD, p. 1657.

[79] O'Donovan 1846:180; O'Reilly 1820:clxx.

Thus, we see that, on the one hand, the poet is one of the most important members of Irish society, whose power rivals that of the king on occasion; but, on the other hand, as blame poet, he is often intolerable to the king and society, and must be expelled, exiled or killed (as the cases of Redg, Riches, Laidchenn, Fafne, Aithirne, Dub, and Gris show us). This aspect of the poet—his inability to fit into society, his marginality, his criminality—is expressed in the law discussed above, where the poet is grouped with tramps and the lowest criminals. Thus, in a description of a "Demon-Banquet," poets are ranked among the offscourings of society again: this is a banquet "forfeited" to a demon which is awarded to "sons of death and bad men, i.e. to lewd persons and satirists [*caintib*] and jesters [*oblairaib*], and buffoons, and mountebanks, and outlaws [*merlechaib*], and heathens, and harlots and bad people in general . . ."[80] It is the satirist, not the eulogist, who is ranked with the worst of society. A similar estimation is given another satirist, the avaricious Fland, "the first professional poet of Ireland." *The Yellow Book of Lecan* describes three chief bards: "There were three learned poets of Connaught, Mac Liac and Mac Coise and Fland mac Lonain, that is, the son of God, the son of man and the son of the demon. Fland mac Lonain was called the son of the demon, for his covetousness and surliness; for he never entered a house without causing loss therein."[81]

The association of poet with outlaw in Ireland has been well documented in Joseph Nagy's *The Wisdom of the Outlaw*.[82] This theme is, of course, intimately related to the theme of poetic exile. In fact, the outlaw, *fénnid*, "is frequently an exile."[83] He becomes an outlaw "when his rights have been violated . . . having lost his social status, the new *fénnid* can find a life and identity in the world of fellow *fénnidi* and *fíana*."[84] The central figure of Nagy's book, Finn, is both *fili* 'poet' and *fénnid* 'outlaw'; both highly honored and an outcast at the same time. Another poet-outcast is the hermit Marbhán, also a swineherd,

---

[80] *Ancient Laws of Ireland* 1865–1901 III.24–25. *do macaib bais ocus drochdainaib .i. do druthaib, ocus caintib, ocus oblairaib, ocus bruidiraib, ocus fuirseoraib, ocus merlechaib, ocus geintaib, ocus merdrechaib, ocus drochdainaib arcena . . .*

[81] *Tri hollamain Chondacht .i. mac Liacc 7 mac Coisi 7 Fland mac Lonain .i. mac De 7 mac duine 7 mac deamain. Fland mac Lonain, mac deamain side ara geri 7 ara duilgi, uair ni deachaid a tig riam cen easba aire do denum and.* Gwynn 1991 3:532. Cf. Flower 1947:68–69. We are told that Fland went to a hell, but a contradictory account places him in heaven, a nice encapsulation of the dual reputation of many satiric poets.

[82] See especially ch. 1, "Finn, Poet and Outsider" (1985:17–40).

[83] J. Nagy 1985:19.

[84] J. Nagy 1985:20. For associations of Finn and the *fénnid* with the redg, see pp. 44, 245n22. For the wolf and its symbolism in Ireland and Indo-European countries, see McCone 1986, 1987, 1985, and 1984; Reinhard and Hull 1936; Puhvel 1986; Przyluski 1940; Lincoln 1975a:98–105; Gershenson 1991. See above, ch. 9 (Alceaus).

who wins a poetic knowledge contest with the assembled poets of Ireland, and sends them off on a quest for the *Táin Bó Cúalnge*.[85]

Also marginal is the physically disfigured person. We find a number of blind poets in Ireland, notably Cridenbel,[86] but also Lugaid, who divines the destruction of a naval expedition when he is brought the skull of the captain's pet dog.[87] Dallán, who satirizes King Hugh unjustly, is also blind.[88] Amairgein, chief poet of King Conchobar, has a loathsome appearance. After going fourteen years without speaking, Amairgein is described as follows: "His belly grew then until it was the vast size of a big house ... And the mucus ran out of his nose into his mouth. His skin was black ... his face was pallid ... His feet had crooked toes ... Knobby, bony, scabby his back. And so he was not handsome."[89] When Amairgein's first statement is a subtle riddle, the chief poet Aithirne tries to kill him out of jealousy. When he fails, he is obliged to take the loathsome, but brilliant teenager in fosterage.[90] The loathsome, clever Amairgein reminds one of Aesop.

But most significant are two stories of leprous poets who act as champions for their poetic companions. First is St. Caillín, who joins, under the persona of a leper, the expedition of poets and musicians, led by Senchán, seeking for the tale of the Cattle Raid of Cúalnge. When the poets seek to land on the Isle of Man, they are refused harbor until they can finish a group of half-quatrains called out to them. Only Caillín is able to finish the verses, enabling the poets to complete their quest. Thus the lowest, the diseased, is also the best, and the means of the group's salvation.[91] Earlier in the narrative Senchán is required to kiss the leper, a powerful expression of the ambiguous nature of the poetic vocation.[92]

---

[85] *Proceedings of the Great Bardic Institution*, in Connellan 1860:103. For Marbán as poet, see *Proceedings of the Great Bardic Institution* 89; *Colloquy of the Two Sages*, in Stokes 1905:50; Elliott 1960:22; cf. J. Nagy 1985:29, 31 (the swineherd "is both exile and *fili* extraordinaire"), 32, 36. For the mantic status of the swineherd in Irish legend, see Ní Chatháin 1979:200–211.

[86] See above; on blind poets, see above, ch. 16, on Thamyris, Demodocus and Tiresias; ch. 5 (Homer).

[87] See Flower 1947:7.

[88] *Proceedings of the Great Bardic Institution*, in Connellan 1860:31; cf. Randolph 1941:189; Thurneysen 1921:65. See also Ford 1990, who links the blindness to the poet's mantic propensities and to mantic rites such as *imbas forosnai*, where the poet composes in the dark.

[89] *Ro ás a brú iarum combo méit adbul teig móir. ... 7 a smucli asa śróin inna beolu. Ba dub a chroccend. ... Ba glasbán a aged. ... Batir laebladracha a thraigid. ... ba mellach cnámach carrgarb a druim. Nibó cáemduine samlaid.*

[90] Trans. from Ford 1990:28–30. See also Best et al. 1954–1983 2.435, lines 13565–13617; Amairgein means "born of *amar* 'singing, lamentation, wailing'."

[91] Connellan 1860:111–119.

[92] Connellan 1860:113. J. Nagy 1985:32, notes that the poet's name, "Little Wood," may refer to his eremitic, exiled way of life.

A story with the same structure is told of a leprous boy in ragged clothes who accompanies Senchán on another quest.

> gilldae écuisc[93] ... Intan, cetamus, do[m]bered nech amer fora etan nothéged athoesc digur brén [tria chluasaib] foradichulaid ... Ata lanech assidcid batar caib ahinchindi romebdatar trea chlocenn ... duibithir écc [a drech:] luaithidir fiamuin [a fégad]; buidithir ór rinn a fiacla, glassidir bun cuilinn ambun ... Dia tallta de inceirt bui imbi níbu decmaing di techt forimirghi a hoenur, manifuirmithe cloch fuirri, arimbud amíl.

> A foul-faced gillie ... when any one would put his finger on his forehead, a gush of putrid matter would come [through his ears] on his poll ... It seemed to every one who looked at him that the layers of his brain had broken through his skull ... blacker than death his face; swifter than a fox his glance; yellower than gold the points of his teeth; greener than holly their base ... If the rag that was round him were stript off, it would not be hard for it to go on a flitting alone, unless a stone were put upon it, because of the abundance of its lice.[94]

The company, after some initial hesitation, accepts him in their group. When they reach their destination, a hag starts quatrains and demands that Senchán finish them. But only the diseased boy is able to meet the challenge. When the *ollam* and the boy return home, the latter turns into a handsome blonde hero in royal clothing, then vanishes. He was "the spirit of poetry." *Dubium itaque non est quod ille poematis erat spiritus*, our text explains, slipping into Latin.[95] Thus this supernatural poet, the spirit of poetry itself, is diseased, leprous, the worst, then experiences an upward peripety, conquers an evil being in a poetic *agōn*, and becomes Senchán's savior and a beautiful, royal youth; he encompasses polar opposites. These two stories are worthy of note for their depictions of benevolent, if revolting, poets—benign bards seem rare in Ireland.[96]

Thus Ireland has no paucity of exempla for our central themes: the exiled blame poet, the killing of the poet by king or society, the poet as worst. The

---

[93] Literally, "a boy of appearance." Variant texts have *gillae ecuisc anindustae/ anindustai*, "a boy of ill-conditioned appearance." I am indebted to Randall Gordon for this insight.

[94] Stokes 1893:181–185; cf. Ford 1990:32; Elliott 1960:22.

[95] Stokes 1893:184. Senchán was named Senchán Torpéist after this *péist* 'monster' (183). Cf. *Sanais Cormaic*, in Meyer 1912 vol. 4 #1059; J. Nagy 1985:32; 239n39. Thomas Mann frequently equated poetic gifts with disease, cf. Hoffmann 1965; Politzer 1961.

[96] On benign poets, see above, on the ambiguity of Irish poets.

poet is too dangerous, or powerful, morally just or unjust, or unclean, to be endured.

Poet as Prophet

Despite the Irish poet's malevolent reputation, he nevertheless clearly had a sacral side. As in Greece, the Irish poet was to a great extent mantic. Nora Chadwick writes, of early Celtic literature, "Probably no other literature offers such a wealth of material for differentiating between various types of manticism, and various classes of mantic persons, such as the *druid, fili, geilt, awenyddion* . . . among the early Celtic peoples the inculcation of poetic inspiration and the entire mantic art were developed and elaborated to a degree for which we know no parallel."[97]

Indeed, the chief difficulty in dealing with the Celtic poet is the profusion and complexity of data available on the subject. Simply unraveling the names of the different kinds of poets, prophets, and priests is a confusing task.[98] But for our present purposes, we need merely emphasize that the poet (*fili, vates, bardos*) developed from the seer, and inherited many of the mantic and hieratic functions of the druid. The most common name for poet, *fili*, derives from a root meaning 'to see'.[99] Gerard Murphy writes that "*filid* [poets] and *fátha* [prophets] were originally the same."[100]

Interestingly, to my knowledge, in Ireland there are no elaborate theophanic poetic consecration scenes comparable to those of Greece; however, we find a comparable theme in later Irish folklore, where the poet

---

[97] Chadwick 1952:5–6; see also Ó hÓgáin 1979; cf. J. Nagy 1985:23–27; 137–138, 155–161, 234n4; also O'Rahilly 1946:318–340; Chadwick 1934.

[98] See Caerwyn Williams 1972:101, 113; Chadwick and Chadwick 1932 1:606, 612–614; Rees and Rees 1967:141; Murphy 1940:200–207; Mac Airt 1958:139–152; J. Nagy 1985:237n26, with bibliography cited there; Breatnach 1987. For shamanic themes in Celtic poetics, see Closs 1968:298–299; J. Nagy 1985:25 and J. Nagy 1982–1983; Chadwick 1952:58; Ó hÓgáin 1979; Eliade 1964:179; Benesch 1961; Chadwick 1934:120–126; Kittredge 1916:177–187 (the latter two references deal with Irish mantic heads); Dodds on mantic heads in Ireland (1951:147); Harrison 1922:468; J. Nagy 1990. Curiously, Eliade simply ignores Ireland in his survey of shamanism in the Indo-European traditions; Closs gives it a scant couple of paragraphs. For shamanic themes in Greek legend, and for Orpheus' mantic head, see above, ch. 16.

[99] Cf. Welsh *gwel* 'see'; Murphy 1940:200; Caerwyn Williams 1972:113; J. Nagy 1985:24. The word *druí* (druid) may come from a root meaning 'to know', Rees and Rees 1967:111; cf. Chadwick and Chadwick 1932: 1.611n1, also 606; Ní Chatháin 1979:210–211. The prophetess of the Bructeri is "Veleda," Tacitus *Histories* 4.61.

[100] Murphy 1940:200, who gives examples of *filid* who are referred to as *fátha*. The Welsh word for 'poetry' (later 'mockery', see Robinson 1912:102n24), *gwawd*, is related to the Irish *fáith*. See also Wagner (1970), whose main theories, however, are not convincing; Kershaw 2000:69, 77.

receives inspiration only after a first-hand experience with the fairies or old gods of Ireland.[101] The related theme of receiving inspiration through eating a supernatural food or drink is very common in Irish myth, however. Finn, for instance, receives wisdom by drinking at the otherworld well.[102] In one account, he drinks the liquor of inspiration.[103] In another account, Finn gets wisdom by eating the "Salmon of Wisdom," at which time his name changes from Demne to Finn. In a kindred Welsh motif, Gwion Bach, an earlier incarnation of Taliesin, receives drops from a magical cauldron of inspiration and immediately foresees the future in its totality.[104]

In a parallel to Aeschylus, some Irish poets gain knowledge while sleeping. Often poets receive a concrete symbol of their poetic consecration after such experiences—Dermot O'Shea receives a book from a mermaid, for instance. This parallels the consecrations of Hesiod, Archilochus, and Marsyas. Another poet sleeps, then finds beside him a sword, bagpipes, and a book.[105] The unsacralized person does not become a poet.

Poet as Warrior

The mantic ecstasy that the poet experiences has led some scholars to associate the Irish poet with the warrior in his war fury. "The preoccupation of *vates* (and probably of *filid*) with inspiration . . . seems to connect them with the function of the warrior—*débordant*, berserk . . ." write the Rees brothers.[106] The medieval Irish court poet often went on campaigns with his chieftain.[107] As has been mentioned, the hero Finn is both *fennid* 'warrior, hunter, outlaw' and *fili*; his poetic mentor is named Cethern mac Fintain; Cethern probably derives from *ce(i)thern* 'band of fighting men, warrior'.[108] This kind of dual identity is not uncommon in Ireland and other Celtic cultures, just as it was widespread in

---

[101] See Ó hÓgáin 1979:57.

[102] O'Rahilly 1946:326–340.

[103] O'Rahilly 1946:328.

[104] O'Rahilly 1946:329, 331. See also Ó hÓgáin 1979:56–58 and 1985:229; Henry 1979–1980; Ní Chatháin 1979:210–211; J. Nagy 1985:291n83; 290n81; 279n30; and J. Nagy 1981–1982. For drinking of liquor in a poetic ritual, see ibid., 137. For the mantic ritual of composing in the dark, Ó hÓgáin 1985:230–231.

[105] Ó hÓgáin 1985:229.

[106] Rees and Rees 1967:141; J. Nagy 1985:293, with cross-references: "The otherworldly 'fire' and power of martial valor parallels the otherworldly 'fire' and power of poetic inspiration." Just as the *mantis* was consulted before battle in Greece, so in the *Táin*, a female prophet is consulted before battle, see above. On the poet's mantic ecstasy, cf. Ó hÓgáin 1985:232.

[107] Caerwyn Williams 1972:132n5.

[108] J. Nagy 1985:164; text of "Boyhood Deeds of Finn," 209–218, also in Cross et al. 1969:360–370.

Greece (Archilochus, Alcaeus, Aeschylus, Tyrtaeus, and Socrates come quickly to mind).[109] The Irish warrior-poet Suibhne Geilt, cursed vagabond, madman, dweller in trees, is another example.[110] A number of the poets referred to above were also warriors; Cridenbel, for instance,[111] and Casmáel.[112]

The Irish goddess of war, Morrigan, appears to Cuchulainn in the persona of a satirist, riding in a chariot, clad in red, and with red eyebrows. A henchman drives a cow in front of her. "I am a female satirist" (*Am banchainti-sea em*) she tells Cuchulainn, after evading his questions for a time.[113] A description of an Ulster warrior-satirist, Dubthach Chafertongue, shows the paradoxical duality of the martial poet:

> Ell n-áilgen issin dara hóil dó, cubur fola fordeirggi issind óil aile dó .i. frecra mín munterda in dara fecht 7 frecra andíaraid in fecht aile . . . Sleg mór míleta ra aird a gúaland . . . Cairi dubfhola da lind adúathmar aidchi remi . . . cu fobairthea cend na slegi sin issind lind nemi sin in tráth na thiced a grith slegi.

> An expression of gentleness in one of his eyes; foam of crimson blood in the other eye; that is, at one time a gentle, friendly aspect, at another time a fierce expression . . . A large warrior-like spear to the height of his shoulder . . . A blood-black cauldron of horrid, noxious liquid before him . . . And the head of the spear was plunged in that poisonous liquid when its spear-ardor came.[114]

This description captures the essential ambiguity of both the warrior and the poet. The state depends upon the warrior's talent for mayhem, yet it is

---

[109] See "Warriors and Poets in Thirteenth-Century Ireland," ch. 2 in Murphy 1948.

[110] See Cohen 1977. For Suibhne as warrior, see 118n21; for Suibhne as poet-shaman, see 116n12; Benesch 1961. Suibhne will be a chief character in chapter 18, below.

[111] As a member of the Túatha Dé Danann, he prepares for a battle in the *Second Battle of Moytura*, and is one of the four Túatha Dé Danann chosen to fight Carmun and her sons, Gray 1982:120. He fights them with poetry, though: see Stokes 1894:311; Robinson 1912:122. Cf. ch. 19.

[112] Gray 1982:119.

[113] "The Cattle-Raid of Regamna," text in Stokes and Windisch 1887:242–244. Gray 1982:129–130; Randolph 1942:79; cf. Gulermovich Epstein 1997; Hennessy 1870. One of the Morrigan's functions is to "incite warriors to battle by performing poety," Gulermovich Epstein (1997:120).

[114] *The Intoxication of the Ulstermen*, in Cross et al. 1969:229–230. Irish text from Hennessy 1889:32–33. We may compare the well-known *furor heroicus* of Cuchulainn, in which we have similar emphasis on abnormal, dissimilar eyes, blood, and supernatural light (fiery particles burst around Chafertongue's spear). See *Táin*, rec. 1:428–434; Henry 1982. For supernatural light as a symbol of poetic inspiration, see J. Nagy 1985:293. Cf. Miller 2000:219, 305, 287, who includes Dubtach in a section on the "red knight," with red signifying "the destructively heated potentiality of the warrior." See below, ch. 18, on Śiśupāla in battle.

endangered by it, and finds it difficult to control. A good example is the well-known story in which Cuchulainn, in the grip of battle fury, nearly turns on his own army.[115] This is one of the primary themes of Dumézil's investigations into the warrior function in Indo-European traditions.[116] The poet, especially the satirist who uses words as weapons, is equally dangerous and valued.

The Welsh court poets, *pencerdd* and *bardd teulu* 'bard of the troop or royal retinue', were customarily warriors,[117] and the *bardd teulu* would sing paraenetic poetry to the army before it went to war. An elegy on the poet Bleddyn Fardd extols his prowess in battle: "The terror of warriors, in valor irresistible, ever leading, savage as a wolf was Bleddyn Fardd." Like Archilochus, he was killed in battle: "Bearing death-dealing blades, in his blue-enamelled armor the lion was slain."[118] A number of legendary Welsh and British poets were also warriors: Taliesin, and "Three Red-Speared Bards of the Island of Britain," Tristfardd, Dygynnelw, and Afan Ferddig.[119]

Just as Greece has famous warrior-heroes who are secondarily poets (Achilles, Heracles), so Ireland has a dominant warrior such as Lugh, who, in his mastery of all arts, is also a poet. Lugh is first described as "A handsome, well-built warrior with a king's diadem."[120] Later he enables the Tuatha De to win the second battle of Moytura by slinging a stone at the giant evil eye of Balor and turning it against the Fomorian forces (Gray, #135). Yet in the first doorway interview with Lugh, he describes himself as a poet (*file*, #62), harper, sorcerer, and historian (#60, 63, 62). He is also a smith, a wright, a champion, a hero, a cupbearer, a brazier, and a leech (#56–68).[121]

Indeed, the power of poetry was so great in Irish myth that satirists were sometimes used, *as poets*, in war. In the *Second Battle of Moytura*, Carpre, in a battle muster, offers his services in battle: "I will make a *glám dícinn* against them, and I will satirize them and shame them so that through the spell of my art they will offer no resistance to warriors."[122] Kings employed bands of

---

[115] *Táin*, Kinsella 1969:92, see discussions in McCone 1984:15, Sharpe 1979:82–87; J. Nagy 1984:27 and Lowe 2000.

[116] See e.g. Dumézil 1970b:43, 63; cf. ch. 18 below.

[117] Lloyd-Jones 1948:169–170.

[118] *blawt glyw glewyd diwahart / blaengar bleituar bletynt uart. y dan llafnawr lleith wotew / y dan llassar glas llas llew.* Morris-Jones et al. 1971:177. Quoted in Lloyd-Jones 1948:169. The Irish poet DonnBo was also killed in battle, *Battle of Allen*, in Stokes 1903b:53 (#11); Chadwick 1934:123. See above, ch. 3; and below, ch. 18 (the poet Suibhne killed in battle of Mag Rath in a variant tradition).

[119] Bromwich 1961:11. Morganwg and Probert 1977 #73; 40.

[120] Gray 1982:39, #53. *Óglǽch cóem cruthach co n-imscigg ríog . . .*

[121] Cf. O'Rahilly 1946:326; Mac Airt 1958:140.

[122] Gray 1982:#115. *Degén-sai gláim ndícind dóuib, 7 nusóerub 7 nus-anfíalub cona gébat frie hócu trie bricht mo dána-sa.*

satirists.[123] Mebd uses "druids and satirists and hard-attackers" (*na drúith & na glámma & na crúadgressa*) to force Ferdiad into battle.[124] Though this may seem to merely precipitate the combat, there is a fine line between the attack of satire and the attack of weapons. In the second battle of Moytura, Lugh uses a curious mixture of paraenesis and sorcery in battle: "Lug was urging the men of Ireland to fight the battle fiercely so they should not be in bondage any longer, because it was better for them to find death while protecting their fatherland than to be in bondage and under tribute as they had been. Then Lug chanted the spell which follows, going around the men of Ireland on one foot and with one eye closed."[125]

Yet the two actions are more closely related if the spell is a satire. O'Davoran's Glossary tells us that the satirical spell, the *glám dícenn*, is made on one foot, with one eye open.[126] The close association of the spell with the paraenesis shows their parallelism: through his command of reputation, shame and honor, the poet had almost a magical power.

The use of shame language on the battlefield recalls Tyrtaeus or Agamemnon in Greece. Agamemnon would exhort the courageous soldiers, but he would "reproach very bitterly," "in words of anger" those who were avoiding the battle.[127] He cries out, "Argives, you arrow-fighters, have you no shame, you abuses?" (Ἀργεῖοι ἰόμωροι, ἐλεγχέες, οὔ νυ σέβεσθε;) and then uses an animal simile, comparing the skulkers to fawns.[128] The war goddess (scald-crow) Badb mocks the boy Cuchulainn, after a setback on a battle field, as "a poor sort of warrior" (*olc damnae laích*), which inspires Cuchulainn to renewed effort.[129]

---

[123] "The Destruction of Dá Derga's Hostel," in Stokes 1901:294. Unfortunately, the text of this tale in Cross et al. 1969 is abridged. Cf. Robinson 1912:121.

[124] See above; also Robinson 1912:120, 121.

[125] Gray 1982:#129, cf. Gray's notes and bibliography, p. 106. *Boí Lug og nertad fer n-Érenn co rofer-dais go dícra an cath fo dégh ná beidis a ndoíri ní bod sírie. Ar ba ferr dúoib bás d'fhogáil oc díden a n-athardho indás beith fo doíri 7 fou cís amal rouhátar. Conid and rocan Lug an cétal-so síos, for lethcois 7 letsúil timchell fer n-Érenn.*

[126] Guyonvarćh 1964, 1965:441–446; 143–144, #82. See also de Vries 1958; Gray 1982:106. For further on Irish military paraenesis as a poetic theme, see Mac Airt 1944:143, Poem 35; Caerwyn Williams 1972:130, 95–96; Stokes 1903a:44–45 (Fergal's army will not go into battle without the poet Dunnbo). Cf. Chadwick 1942:131. For the *glám dícenn*, see above.

[127] *Iliad* IV 241, trans. Lattimore: τοὺς μάλα νεικείεσκε χολωτοῖσιν ἐπέεσσιν.

[128] Cf. ch. 9, above, on Alcaeus.

[129] *Táin*, Rec. 1, 500; Kinsella 1969:80. Cf. Hennessy 1870. See Jullian 1902:321, for the use of invective in battle among the Celtic tribes.

The Poetic *Agōn*

The poet as warrior is related to the theme of the poetic *agōn* as we have encountered it in the lives of Aesop, Homer, and Hesiod, at least to the extent that participants in the *agōn* are fighting against each other. (And we remember that losers in mythical riddle contests often lost their heads). The poetic *agōn* is also a persistent theme in lives of the Irish poets. We have already mentioned the diseased supernatural poet who saves Senchán twice through his prowess in a poetic quatrain contest.[130] One thinks of Aesop's salvific nature and mastery of riddles. Aithirne the Importunate, consuming a pig and mead alone in miserly fashion, has it taken from him when a fellow poet recites a line of poetry and Aithirne cannot make a rhyme to it.[131] In the *Proceedings of the Great Bardic Institution*, the poet-hermit Marbhán defeats all of the burdensome poets in riddle contests, and forces them to go off on a quest for the *Táin*.[132] One Irish text, "Colloquy of the Two Sages," has two prominent poets compete in a riddle contest for the office of chief poet of Ulster.[133] One is reminded of the two chief poets of Greece, Homer and Hesiod, meeting to decide ultimate precedence.[134]

Dáithí Ó hÓgáin notes that there are many examples of the poetic *agōn* in modern folklore, some involving riddles.[135] There is, of course, a continuum between poetry and riddle, and a range of enigmatic poetry and speech in the middle.[136] Huizinga notes the connection of *ainos* 'tale, praise', and *ainigma* 'enigma, riddle'.[137] The poet must be the person of knowledge, often otherworldly knowledge,[138] which brings to mind the almost encyclopedic tone of Hesiod's two extant poems.[139]

---

[130] See above, on Caillín and Senchán.

[131] *Book of Leinster* 117a–b, translated in Rhys 1979:332. Cf. Robinson 1912:116–117, with bibliography on verse-capping; Gummere 1901: 287–297, 396–405.

[132] Connellan 1860:93.

[133] "The Colloquy of Two Sages," in Stokes 1905; cf. Ó hÓgáin 1979:46.

[134] Cf. Taliesen's besting of the court poets in the *Tale of Gwion Bach and the Tale of Taliesin*, in Ford 1977:171. On the need for deciding precedence in Irish society, where the exact hierarchical station is a matter of intense importance for one's honor or shame, see O'Leary 1984; Gray 1982:94; Bromwich 1967:13–16.

[135] Ó hÓgáin 1979:47, see also Ó hÓgáin 1985:224–228.

[136] See Ó hÓgáin 1979:46–47; Dillon 1947:262; Lloyd-Jones 1948:173; Gonda 1950:57–61.

[137] Huizinga 1955:110; cf. 122–123.

[138] Ó hÓgáin 1979:46–47, Henry 1979–1980:117, 126; MacAirt 1958:152n1. For the knowledge of the satirist specifically, see Amaigren's poem, quoted in Chadwick 1934:108; cf. Macalister and MacNeill 1916:262f.; Macalister 1938–1956 5:110–113; Rees and Rees 1967:98.

[139] Furthermore, in archaic Vedic ritual, the riddles involved cosmogony or theogony. Huizinga 1955:106.

The archaic riddle contest is an Indo-European theme, strongly attested in India, Greece, and other Indo-European countries. "The function of . . . ritual riddle solving competitions is shown at its clearest in Vedic lore," writes Huizinga, who collects examples of the theme of the riddle contest with death as the stake from India (Yājñavalkya), Greece (Mopsus and Calchas) and Germany (Odin and the giant Vafthrúdnir).[140]

A tale from modern folklore offers a complex network of important themes: the poetic *agōn*; satire as a defensive weapon; art as an aggressive response to aggression; the poet satirizing poet; the poet as possessed:

> The nobleman-poet Séafra O'Donnchú was reputed to have given up composing, something which caused no small anxiety and disappointment to the rest of the poetic communion.[141] Aogán O'Rathaille solved the problem, for when he met Séafra one day he recited a satiric verse concerning Séafra himself and his family. Losing himself in a fit of frenzied anger, Séafra retaliated with an even more bitter satiric verse on Aogán.[142]

In the same way, Archilochus, the beautifully singing cicada, responded with bitter satire, the defensive satire of righteous indignation, when he was maliciously tortured; and Hipponax retaliated similarly when an artist lampooned him. This person-to-person artistic combat recalls the earlier combat of Irish poets explicitly in war, Cridenbel trading spells with enemy enchanters.[143] But the satirist is, as it were, always a warrior. The persistent use of terms implying aggressive blows or weapons to refer to satire is entirely in keeping with this aspect of the satirist's vocation. In a text on the diction of poetry collected in Robinson we find a number of weapon terms, especially *rindad* 'cutting'.[144] *Ail*, one of the three blemishes raised by satire, is the same as *ail* 'stone' "in the sense of a bump caused by a blow or metaphorically by a slur," writes Howard Meroney.[145] A poem on satire reads, "It's extempore bane that will stab in the face anybody it's flung at! / Not long is the respite from

---

[140] Huizinga, 1955:105, 108–110. See Davidson 1983; Kuiper 1960; Gaster 1981 2:495. Cf. ch. 6 (Hesiod); ch. 18, on Suibhne as agonic poet; ch. 2 (Aesop as riddle warrior).

[141] Thus he is somewhat comparable to the Hollywood cliché of the gunfighter who has given up his former profession and is trying to live peaceably, often incognito.

[142] Ó hÓgáin 1979:58; Ó Duilearga 1961:107–108. Cf. Ó hÓgáin 1985:233 for a very similar story with different characters.

[143] The comparison between poetic *agōn* and hand-to-hand combat is made by Caerwyn Williams 1972:91, with reference to Scandinavian *flytings*. See also Clover 1980.

[144] Robinson 1912:103–106.

[145] Meroney 1949–1950:207.

slaughter with spears of injurious gibing!"[146] *Glám* of *glám dícind* means 'attack, gibe', "the basic idea being to nab or nip—an action of fangs or fingers."[147] The poet Nede describes his profession as *rind feola*, "piercing flesh," and a glossator adds, "*faebur a aire hi feoil amail*, 'the edge of his satire like a point in flesh'."[148] Thus the poet is a warrior wielding razor-sharp weaponry; but he is also a predator whose tooth and claw can be lethal. Poets' tongues were widely thought of as "sharp" and "keen."[149] A folk etymology for *cáinte* 'satirist' is from dog, "for the satirist has a dog's head in barking, and alike is the profession they follow."[150] The most common word of laughter in early Irish literature, *tibid*, "combines the sense of 'laughter' with that of 'striking' or 'shoving'."[151]

The Poisonous Poet

Another metaphor for destructive, lethal poetry is that of poison, and the image of poetry as poison is common in the Irish tradition. A folk etymology derives *fili* 'poet' from *fi* 'poison' (satire) and *li* 'praise'.[152] The blemishes the poet produces on his victim's face are referred to as "poisonous ulcers [*cnuicc nemed*]."[153] A poem on satire speaks of the "venom of verse."[154] Weapon and poison imagery are combined in the poem's phrase "shaft of poison" (*gai fi*).[155]

---

[146] Meroney 1949–1950:99, 107 (#50). *As reicne nguin, gaífi forgnúis cáich gus·mbrogad; / ní móranad ní[th]o co [n]gaíbh gláime gonadh!*

[147] Meroney 1949–1950:217.

[148] Meroney 1949–1950:217. For other examples of satire as cutting weapon or defensive weapon (spear, point of spear or sword, shield), see O'Leary 1991:26n59.

[149] Ó hÓgáin 1979:50.

[150] *ar iscend con forincáinte ocamastraig. 7 isinand dán fogníít.* Cormac's Glossary, in Stokes 1862; Robinson 1912:110.

[151] O'Leary 1991:22, with a number of examples of satire and laughter words meaning an attack or blow.

[152] *Cormac's Glossary*, in Stokes 1862; cf. Meroney 1949–1950:118, 224; Robinson 1912:110. For further on the duality of praise and blame in Ireland, see Henry 1979–1980:122 (black and white poetry, satire vs. praise); Robinson 1912:102, 106. Diodorus Siculus (5.31.2) writes of Celtic bards that, "These men, singing with instruments similar to lyres, praise [*humnousin*] some, but they abuse [*blasphēmousi*] others" (εἰσὶ δὲ παρ' αὐτοῖς καὶ ποιηταὶ μελῶν, οὓς βάρδους ὀνομάζουσιν. οὗτοι δὲ μετ' ὀργάνων ταῖς λύραις ὁμοίων ᾄδοντες οὓς μὲν ὑμνοῦσιν, οὓς δὲ βλασφημοῦσι).

[153] Meroney 1949–1950:222.

[154] *neim laidhe*: Meroney 1949–1950:105 (#27), 107 (#58). Meroney compares the phrase *neim-tenga* 'poison-tongue' (118); see also O'hO'gain 1979:51–52. An Old Irish fragment refers to "a bag of poison on the tongues of poets," ibid. 52; Stokes and Meyer 1900 1:272, *uath n[e]ime for tengthaib na filed*. There is a poet named Bricriu Poisontongue (*Nemthenga*), see "Bricriu's Feast," Henderson 1899; Stokes 1905:13n1; Chadwick and Chadwick 1932 1:49.

[155] Meroney 1949–1950:118 (#50). The brew that induces poetic inspiration in *The Tale of Gwion Bach* (Ford 1977:163) is potent poison except for the three poetic drops.

We have already met the ominous satirist-warrior Dubthach Chafertongue, almost schizophrenic in his division between gentleness and savagery. After the description of the poet, which includes the metaphor of a spear dipped in poison, Mebd exclaims, "By our conscience, the description is venomous!" Cu Roi answers: "Venomous is he whose description it is."[156] As in Greece, the poet is the lethal gift, the *dosis* of poison; he causes wars and strife,[157] kills with blame, destroys honor, and is a revolting leper. Yet he also is sacred,[158] has priestly functions,[159] has martial functions, and is indispensable to the king. Watkins writes, "For the patron, the *rí . . . molad, clú, blad, ainm* [praise], were a moral necessity . . . and the poet alone could celebrate this fame, and make known [*noíd*] the name of his patron. A 'king without poets' was proverbial in Ireland for 'nothing'." But "The patron in his turn was obligated to maintain the poet munificently, often to the detriment of his own wealth."[160]

And, as in the case of the vile-looking leper, the poet can act as a savior figure.[161] However repulsive the experience may be, one must still kiss the poetic leper.

---

[156] *"Dar ar cubus is nemnech in tuarascbáil," ar Medb. "Is nemnech cách 'sa tuarascbáil," ar Cú Ruí.*

[157] See especially Bricriu Poisontongue's role in "Bricriu's Feast," Henderson 1899.

[158] See on prophecy above; Robinson 1912:122–123, for the inviolability of the poet's person; cf. the Indo-European poet as inviolate herald, Caerwyn Williams 1972:107. The cognate for Greek *kērux* (Dor. *kārux*) 'herald' is Vedic *kārú* 'singer, poet'. See also Dillon 1973:4–5 (on royal staff); Meroney, 1949–1950:128 (poet's wand); Hesiod *Theogony* 30–31 (cf. West's notes), see above, ch. 6.

[159] Cf. Mac Cana 1968:181 (the poet blesses the king at inauguration and receives his garment); Ní Chatháin 1979–1980:207; Dillon 1947:262 (the earliest *fili* corresponds to the Hindu brahman); Caerwyn Williams 1972:98–102; Thurneysen 1921:69–71; Maier 1989:26. For the poet's role as sanctioner of law, see above, this chapter. See also below, ch. 19 (Odin's poets are priests); and above, ch. 8 (Sappho).

[160] Watkins 1976:271 and 1995. See also Caerwyn Williams 1972; Dillon 1973; and above on Sappho as praise poet, ch. 8.

[161] See Ó hÓgáin 1985:236 for positive aspects of the poet in Irish traditions—poet as "protector of the community," who banishes sickness, ghosts, curses rats, and is the enemy of landlords and oppressors. Ó hÓgáin remarks on "the moral basis of anger" in poets who satirize: "He stands fair and square within the circle of righteousness" (1985:246). Ó hÓgáin is chiefly working from later folklore, but see the discussion of moral Irish poets at the beginning of this chapter.

18

The Stakes of the Poet: Starkaðr/Suibhne

IN 1942, THE INDO-EUROPEANIST GEORGES DUMÉZIL published *Horace et les Curiaces*, in which he treated the battle-fury of the Indo-European warrior.[1] *Aspects de la fonction guerrière chez les Indo-Européens* (1956) was his first book-length examination of the warrior from a comparative Indo-European perspective; in this book he discussed for the first time the striking theme of the three sins of the warrior—in which the warrior, though bound by ties of loyalty to his king and people, commits a flagrant offense against each of society's three classes or "functions"—and compared the Scandinavian hero Starkaðr to Heracles in Greece and Indra in India. He revised this book substantially to produce *Heur et malheur du guerrier* in 1968, another treatment of Starkaðr, Heracles, and Indra. Finally, in 1971, he wrote, as the first part of the second volume of *Mythe et épopée*, "*L'enjeu du jeu des dieux—un héros*,"[2] his culminating treatment of the hero-warrior—here, Starkaðr and Heracles are once more dealt with, though at greater length, while in India, Indra is replaced by the evil Śiśupāla of the *Mahābhārata*. Here the warrior is seen as the "stakes" in a game played by the gods—in the case of Starkaðr, by Odin and Thor, who, toward the beginning of his career, weave his fate in a series of blessings (from Odin) and offsetting curses (from Thor).

---

[1] On Dumézil, see Littleton 1982; Puhvel 1987; Mallory 1989. Dumézil developed the theory that embedded in myths, rituals, formulae, and epics in the Indo-European traditions were references to three social "functions": first, priest-sovereign; second, warrior; and third, herder-cultivator. Thus we have a kind a social structuralism influenced by Durkheim. Often these "functions" have complex (and often prickly) interrelationships, and interdependencies. For instance, both kings and warriors are dependent on the herder-cultivators for food. The first and third functions rely on the warrior when the tribe is menaced by outsiders. But the warrior is difficult to control, and sometimes is an internal menace to the rest of society, see below. In Dumézil's view, by comparing similar themes in myths from different Indo-European countries, we can work back to genetic Proto-Indo-European myth.

[2] Translated as *The Stakes of the Warrior* (1983).

These treatments of the warrior have been among Dumézil's most impressive works.[3] The comparison of Starkaðr and Śiśupāla is especially convincing, as both warriors are generals devoted to specific kings and king-ship, who are pruned of monstrous supernumerary appendages by inimical gods (Kṛṣṇa in Śiśupāla's case, Thor in Starkaðr's case), who commit grave sins against the king (as part of the canonical sins against the functions), and who die by beheading, bestowing a sort of immortality as they die (and, in Śiśupāla's case, obtaining a sort of immortality—his essence flows into Kṛṣṇa, and he continues to live through the god who has just killed him). The third member of this martial triptych, Heracles, is not as neat a comparison, though Dumézil makes a reasonable case for him. Like Starkaðr, he is bandied about by the gods, one persecuting him (Hera), the other helping him (Athena, backed by Zeus); he commits a version of the required functional sins.[4] As in the case of the other two warriors, Heracles has a paradoxical link with the divinity who persecutes him, Hera: she nurses him while he is a baby and he derives his name from her; later, in Olympus after his "death" and deification, he will be adopted by Hera as her son and will marry her daughter. Analyzing the persecuting god theme purely from a Greek perspective, Burkert has formu-lated the pattern: continuity in cult will accompany opposition in myth.[5] (But, in the case of Heracles, we have continuity within the myth itself, for Hera nurses the exposed baby-hero. However, this theme of maternal nurturing is turned into a symbol for enmity, for Heracles bites her breast.)

Gregory Nagy, in *The Best of the Achaeans*, treats the theme of ambiva-lent enmity between god and hero in the myths of Aesop and Archilochus. In the case of Aesop, he is persecuted by Apollo, who arranges his death, while he is supported by the Muses. Archilochus is killed (in battle) by an Apolline "Crow," but Apollo then instructs the "Crow" to honor the dead poet with cult. Nagy suggests that the background for this ambivalent enmity may be found in Indo-European myth, in the paradigm of the warrior studied by Dumézil in *Stakes*.[6]

This may be a valuable line of inquiry, since Archilochus, though a poet, is preeminently a warrior, and a *therapōn* of Ares. Other poets and scapegoat

---

[3] According to Littleton, *Aspects* "must indeed be ranked among Dumézil's most significant publi-cations" (1982:127). See Puhvel, "The Warrior at Stake," in Puhvel 2002:30–38, which summa-rizes Dumézil's accomplishment in pursuing the warrior theme, but warns of the dangers of over-imposing the three sins pattern.

[4] Diodorus Siculus 4.9.6, 4.10.1; *Etymologicum Magnum* p. 435, 10ff., cf. Photius *Library* p. 147b, 16ff.

[5] See Burkert 1975; cf. above, ch. 16 (Apollo kills Achilles).

[6] Nagy 1979:303.

figures (Tyrtaeus, Alcaeus, Androgeus, Codrus, Aglauros) also have strong war associations. And, on the other hand, Starkaðr is a famous poet, the preeminent skald of his tradition. Dumézil treats Starkaðr's poetic vocation, but only as a comparative note in relation to Heracles—not a strong comparison, since Heracles is not known for his poetic gifts, though he had some association with music and the Muses.

However, David Cohen has proposed a Celtic warrior who fits the *Stakes* pattern—the mad tree-dwelling wanderer Suibhne Geilt. Suibhne is, for our purposes, a particularly attractive comparison because he, like Starkaðr, is a famous poet. If Suibhne is a valid parallel, we may conclude that the poetic aspect of the warrior may be important to the genetic paradigm; before, with only Heracles as a comparand, the case was not as strong. (Śiśupāla, like Heracles, has little or no reputation as a poet, though he was verbally abusive.)

We may then examine Starkaðr and Suibhne more closely, paying special attention to their poetic vocations, looking for continuities with the themes we have been examining in Greece and Ireland.

Starkaðr: Sacrificer, Sacrifice, Satirist

Starkaðr is the best, extraordinary in many categories. He had an "incredible preeminence of spirit and body."[7] "Nature had equipped him with a super-human physique and spiritual endowments to match, so that men believed that in bravery he was second to none."[8] He was remarkable "for his unusual size, famous for his courage and his artistry in composing songs [or spells]."[9] Like Aesop and numerous other Greek poets, he was ugly and animalistic in appearance:

> Hlæja rekkar,
> er mik séa,
> ljótan skolt,

---

[7] Saxo Grammaticus (died ca. 1204), *History of the Danes* VI.151; 170, Fisher translation = Holder ed., 182: *ob incredibilem corporis animique prestanciam.* Translation in Fisher and Davidson 1979 vol. 1, including the first nine books of the *History of the Danes.* Translations of Saxo in this chapter are from Fisher, unless otherwise noted. The Latin text is from Holder 1886, or from an online version from the Danish Royal Library, http://www.kb.dk/elib/lit/dan/saxo/lat/or.dsr/index.htm.

[8] Ibid. *Siquidem excellentius humano habitu corpus a natura sortitus, ita id animi magnitudine aequabat, ut nulli mortalium virtute cedere putaretur.*

[9] VI.152; 171=184: *inusitata prius granditate conspicuum, non solum animi fortitudine, sed etiam condendorum carminum pericia.*

langa trjónu,
hár úlfgrátt,
hangar tjálgur,
hrjúfan háls,
húð jótraða.

"Warriors laugh who see me," he complains, "with ugly muzzle, long snout, wolf-grey hair and hanging paws, rough neck and rugged hide."[10] Nevertheless, he had a saving, culture hero aspect, was "a man regularly at the side of the distressed, one who often happily intervened to rescue people in desperate straits."[11] Thus he is a remarkable hero in every way, extraordinary in size, courage, generosity; and also extraordinary in his skill in *carmina*, whether that is translated "songs" or "spells." Hatherus, Starkaðr's final executioner, addresses him as "adept composer of native poetry ... fluent bard [*uates*] of a Danish muse."[12] In the *Skáldatal* (*List of Poets*), Starkaðr is the first poet mentioned, the oldest of the poets.[13]

Starkaðr receives his poetic gifts from Odin, in the curious consecration scene in which Odin and Thor award him his good and bad fates. The last three fate themes are battle success (Odin), balanced by a wound in every combat (Thor); the gift of poetry (*skáldskap*) and "improvisation"[14] (Odin), balanced by inability to remember his poetry (Thor); a strong tie to the highborn (Odin), balanced by hatred of the common people (Thor).[15] Thus, his gifts of poetry and war prowess are parallel.[16]

In Starkaðr's history, there are frequent occasions when he uses his poetry; the link between warrior and poet is not obscure, for Starkaðr is an aggressive satirist. His verbal attack often accompanies physical attack.

[10] *Gautrekssaga*, see Turville-Petre 1964:206. Translation thanks to Randall Gordon, who remarks that the literal translation makes the wolf persona very obvious. For the poet as wolf (as in the case of Alcaeus, ch. 9) i.e. outsider, see Kershaw 2000:133–179. Another notable theme surfaces in this passage: ugliness making the poet the victim of mockery (as in the case of Hipponax, ch. 4). Cf. Pálsson and Edwards 1968:41.

[11] VI.162; p. 179=194: ... *qui indigentibus adesse et tristes plerumque casus felici interventu redimere soleat.*

[12] VIII.226; p. 249=271: *patrias solitus scriptare poeses ... Danicae vates promptissime Musae.*

[13] Turville-Petre 1964:212, cf. Clover 1980:452.

[14] *Óðinn mælti: "Ek gef honum skáldskap, svá at hann / skal eigi seinna yrkja en mæla."* Pálsson and Edwards (1968:39) translate, "I give him the art of poetry, so that he shall compose verses as fast as he can speak."

[15] *Gautrekssaga* ch. 7, pp. 28–31, cf. Dumézil 1983:14–15. For Starkaðr as an Odin or Thor hero, see Turville-Petre 1964:326 (de Vries vs. Dumézil), 205–211; Polomé 1990.

[16] Thor's last three curses form a trifunctional pattern, if poetry is linked to the first function: war, poetry, common people.

Starkaðr, incognito, witnesses a goldsmith's lecherous advances toward a princess; when he "had drunk his fill of rage . . . he could not restrain his arm any longer" (*tantum hauserat irae, ut ulterius cohibendae manus impatiens*), so unsheathes his sword and delivers a blow to the smith's buttock. "After Starkaðr had looked all round and noticed that the household were grieved at the recent defeat of their master, he took care to enlarge the wounded man's dishonour with insults and began to taunt him." [17]

A long poem follows, in which Starkaðr reproaches the princess, and attacks the smith for daring to approach a highborn woman. The story ends with the abusive poet turning immediately to his warrior aspects: "After saying these things, Starkaðr, who obtained no less delight from his speech than from action, sought out Haldan again, and embraced soldiery in the closest intimacy [with him], and never shrank from fighting wars, so that he tortured his soul, withdrawn from luxuries, by a continual wielding of weapons." [18]

Thus verbal attack (in poetic form) and physical attack are strictly parallel, and Starkaðr derives as much pleasure from causing shame in the verbal attack as he does from striking the smith. Both attacks are the result of righteous rage; when the rage has reached its boiling point, it finds expression in verbal and physical aggression. The resulting poem is in the tradition of sexual blame linked with class contempt; its savagery reminds one of Juvenal.[19] The incident is a striking exemplification of the earlier three fates: we have Starkaðr the warrior, Starkaðr the poet, and Starkaðr the enemy of the lower classes.

---

[17] VI.158; 176–177= 191, trans. Fisher, *Cumque Starcatherus circumspectam undique familiam recenti hospitis iactura indoluisse cognosceret, ignominiam saucii invectivis exaggerandam curavit insultandoque sic coepit.*

[18] Ibid. 179, my trans., *His dictis, Starcatherus, non minorem ex voce quam opere voluptatem sortitus, Haldanum repetit eiusque militiam promixa familiaritate complexus numquam bellorum exercitio abstitit, ita ut abstractum deliciis animum continua armorum intentione torqueret.*

[19] Some have seen the influence of Horace and Juvenal in Saxo, and particularly in the poems Saxo has Starkaðr recite (see Fisher and Davidson 1979 2:106n89, 135n81). Was Saxo drawing on Roman models because they were comparable to poetic traditions connected with Starkaðr, or did he simply apply Juvenal and Horace to a poet with a general reputation for abusiveness? In Starkaðr's long poem on the miseries of old age, comparable to Juvenal's tenth satire, there are no close verbal echoes, as Fisher notes. Davidson 1981:39 admits the classical influence in Saxo, but writes that his heroes "were, after all, breathing a northern air, with their feet firmly set on Danish soil, in a region which had remained outside the domination of Rome." Speaking specifically of Starkaðr's poetry, she writes that Saxo has "combined the use of language . . . in the classical manner with the rich traditions of his own background and the verbal skills of the North" (1981:50). Friis-Jensen 1981b, speaks of that poem spoken by Starkaðr "rising from a fruitful combination of Nordic and Latin tradition." See also Gudnason 1981:79–93, esp. 85, on Starkaðr (with useful bibliography).

Another incident again shows rage and shame, seething within him, explode into verbal and physical aggression. The scene is, typically, a banqueting scene, where a man's honor is so often defined by seating,[20] and where food defines the host's morals. In this banquet, everything that could possibly happen to humiliate and enrage the visiting hero takes place. While in Sweden, he hears that his old friend Frothi, King of Denmark, has been deceitfully deposed, and that his son Ingel, the new king, far from punishing the deposing party, is friendly with them. Outraged, Starkaðr returns immediately to Denmark; on the way, he carries coals with which, he tells passers by, he will form a keen edge to Ingel's dull brains—a bit of preliminary verbal abuse.[21]

When Starkaðr arrives at the castle, the king is hunting, and the hero sits down in his accustomed place of honor at a feast. But the king's wife, not recognizing him dressed in muddy rags, tells him in insulting terms to leave his place lest he dirty the cushions, and not to try to sit with his betters. Starkaðr, by virtue of his astounding self-control, takes this rebuke in silence. But he must give vent to the rage seething inside him, so goes to a deserted part of the castle and hurls himself against a wall—"he flung his body against the stout walls with such a crash that the timbers shook violently and the building was almost brought down in ruins."[22]

Thus the situation has been set up for defensive satirical attack. Even though Ingel returns home, recognizes the aged warrior, rebukes his wife, and she tries to win Starkaðr's favor back, he will not forget the snub[23] and takes a horrible vengeance—she afterwards sees the banqueting table "stained with the blood of her brothers" (*loca . . . fratrum suorum cladibus cruentata conspiceret*). Ingel induces Starkaðr to sit at the banqueting table and tries to mollify him with exquisitely cooked culinary delicacies. But Starkaðr steels himself against these temptations, for "he had no wish to allow his celebrity as a warrior to be impaired by the enticements of an orgy."[24] In Dumézilian tems, he shows the need for the warrior class to separate itself from the joys of consumption perhaps representative of the third function. The bad king is here defined as one who has allowed himself to be influenced too much by the third function.

The old warrior manages to find some "smoky, rancid food" that is more to his (moral) taste.[25] The queen further alienates the warrior by offering him

---

[20] Cf. O'Leary 1984.

[21] Cf. Fisher 1979 2:105n81.

[22] VI.166; 184=200: *adeo ipsa parietum robora demissi corporis impulsu contudit, ut tectum ruina paene eximia tignorum trepidatione submitteret.*

[23] VI.168; 185=202.

[24] VI.167; 185=201: *ne bellicam claritatem convivalibus illecebris absumendam permitteret.*

[25] *fumidoque ac randidulo cibo.* The theme is immorality expressed by excessive cookery—Starkaðr

her own hair circlet to wear; the warrior is not about to submit to wearing such an effeminate article, and "wisely" throws it back in her face. Then the irascible warrior throws a bone at a flautist the queen has instructed to play to try to soften him.[26] King Ingel, meanwhile, has succumbed to the degenerate foreign (Saxon) food. "With mouth agape after an orgy of stuffing himself Ingel would emit in crude belches the fumes from his last bout of hoggery."[27]

The scene is set for Starkaðr's rebuke, the Lay of Ingellus,[28] an abusive satirical poem defining moral kingship. This directly follows an expression of Starkaðr's pent-up fury—seeing the murderers of the king, "he betrayed in his wild stare the vast rage [*furoris magnitudinem*] this engendered . . . the unmasked savagery [*aperta . . . seuicia*] of his glances bore witness to the secret tempest within his heart."[29] This monstrous rage is expressed, not by an immediate physical attack, but by poetry. The long poem is interrupted only by a doublet of the queen's earlier chaplet-gift incident. Starkaðr, "disgusted, flung it insultingly back in her face and once more sang in a loud voice" (*Quo Starcatherus quam turpissime in os offerentis cum indignatione reiecto, clara rursum voce recinuit*). The physical violence and poetic violence are exactly parallel.

In the first verse of the poem the sexual implications of the chaplet are made explicit: "Please take away that womanish gift . . . A hero never puts on chaplets suited only to love-making" (*Amove, quaeso, muliebre donum . . . Infulas nemo Venerem decentes / fortis adoptat*). The poem continues in lines that use sexual imagery to attack the degenerate food of the evening.

> Uxor Ingelli levis ac petulca
> Theutonum ritus celebrare gestit,
> instruit luxus et adulterinas
> praeparat escas.

---

particularly disapproves of meat that has been both roasted and boiled (VI.167; 185=201; VI.169; 186=204). The question of Juvenalian influence must again be considered. But food and sexuality are standard targets at which blame is directed. If Ingel is immoral, his food will define him.

[26] The effeminacy of such music is emphasized; all of the warrior's temptations, food, clothing, and music are defined by effeminacy.

[27] VI.170; 187=204: *quod nimiae saturitatis usu oscitans partam edendo crapulam foeda ructatione exhalaret*.

[28] VI.170ff.; p. 180ff.; cf. Friis-Jensen 1981b.

[29] VI.168: *Videns autem Starcatherus eos, qui Frothonem oppresserant, in summa regis dignatione versari, concepti furoris magnitudinem acerrimo oculorum habitu prodidit internosque motus externo oris indicio patefecit, occultam animi procellam aperta luminum saevitia testatus.* For the "war fury" of the Indo-European warrior, see on Cuchulainn in ch. 17. All these warriors had a dark, demonic side. I have not yet seen Frédéric Blaive, *Impius Bellator: Le Mythe Indo-Européen du Guerrier Impie* (1996), but see a review by Miller 2001b.

> The wife of Ingel, skittish and wanton,
> joys to practice Teuton rites,
> devises orgies and
> prepares adulterate foods.
>
> VI.173; 189 = 207

The poem, not to miss a standard blame topos, intra-sexual tension, lingers on the queen: "a loathsome female, heedless of decency, priestess of vice."[30]

The violent abuse is intensely moral, a call to repentance: Ingel is "entombed in vice [*uicio sepultus*]." "Why, you sluggard," rebukes the poet, "do you worship feasting, softer than harlots, lean back your belly?"[31] The reason for the poet's presence is: "To smite . . . corruption [*uicium ferire*]."[32] The poem also defines good kingship in its descriptions of Frotho, Ingel's father.

There is an important emphasis on posture as a defensive satirist: on Starkaðr's reception he was viciously mocked:

> Aulici risu populi lacessor
> advenae digno vacuus receptu,
> aspero carpor sale, dum loquaci
> mordeor ausu.
>
> I am baited by the titters of this courtly throng,
> denied the welcome a stranger deserves,
> rent with their thorny wit and gnawed by
> presumptuous gibing.
>
> VI.171; 188 = 205

Thus the satirist is mocked, and retaliates with interest. The theme of inhospitality is also explicitly brought to the fore.

Starkaðr's potent abusive paraenesis (Ingel's guardian's "urgent exhortations," *monitus sui incitamento*) does not fail in its purpose.[33] The king's courage and integrity, which had been in "exile," return. He draws his sword and attacks his father's murderers, whom he had previously been feasting: "Speedily he carved them to pieces and bathed the table-ceremonies in blood."[34] Ingel's

---

[30] VI.173; 190 = 208.13–14: *neglegens morum vitiique cultrix, / femina turpis.*

[31] VI.172; 188 = 206.1–2: *Quid dapem deses colis otioque / mollior scortis stomachum reclinas?* Cf. ibid., lines 23–24: "the joys of an obese belly" (*obesi gaudia uentris*).

[32] VI.172; 188–206.

[33] Starkaðr is, as Dumézil notes in dealing with this episode, "imperiously and didactically, a true educator" (1983:38).

[34] VI.178; 194 = 213: *His namque continuo trucidatis, sacra mensae sanguine involvit.*

newfound good character "replenished the goblets with blood instead of wine."[35] Thus we have a curious double inversion of the sacrality of the feast and guest-friendship: since a good man is feasting evil men, he is justified in defiling the sacrality of the host's table. A darkly moral sacrificial scene is the result, an inverted sacrament.

Starkaðr accompanies the violence of his words with the violence of his arm, helping Ingel in his slaughter, and displays "outstanding bravery himself" (*fortitudinem . . . in se plenissimam*) in killing the evil men. The poet and the warrior are precisely in harmony.

The combination of verbal and physical attack is, indeed, a conscious modus operandi for the hero: "He believed that opponents should be spurned with words first, weapons afterwards."[36] His penchant for verbal abuse is shown in one of the more comically grotesque incidents in his history. After he has been cut nearly to pieces by nine brothers who had challenged a royal friend, Helgi,[37] for whom Starkaðr serves as a champion, he is offered help by a succession of characters who offend his highly developed aristocratic snobbery—a bailiff, a man who had married a maidservant, and a female mill slave.[38] But he refuses their help as he lies dying with his entrails falling out of his body. He "preferred the torture of his agonizing wounds before the ministrations of those in low walks of life."[39] After refusing their aid, he verbally abuses them. Rejecting a bailiff partially because "he made jeering language his business" (*scurrilitatis officia sectaretur*), ironically, "he was not content with rejecting him but crushed him with abuse."[40] Thus the theme of satirical violence is combined with the theme of satirist attacking satirist.

---

[35] VI.178; 194 = 213: *cruore quam mero calices imbuens.*

[36] VI.163; 181 = 196: *. . . aduersarios prius dictis quam armis contemnendos putabat.* One can compare this military blame with military paraenesis; see the nine brothers who bark at Starkaðr like dogs and "were animating one another for the fight [with Starkaðr] by mutual encouragement." See following note.

[37] And he, true to form, has attacked them verbally before dispatching them with physical violence. The treatment of these brothers is striking—they are portrayed as a pack of dogs, a canine *Männerbund* (see previous note, for their mutual military paraenesis). Starkaðr seems to find their berserker-type madness degraded (cf. Fisher 1979 2:105n73): VI.162; 180 = 195.

[38] Curiously, though, he finally accepts help from a farmer's son, and he praises the farmer's life as honest labor. Thus the warrior's attitude toward the lower class may be complex—just as he has an ambivalence toward kingship (he kills two kings, but is their passionate champion and defender), he also has an ambivalence toward the third function. He disapproves of their excesses of sexuality and eating, which would tend to sap a warrior's strength, make him unfit and unprepared for battle, but will allow for the necessity of the food producer within certain limits.

[39] *vulnerum acerbitate cruciari quam sordidae condicionis hominum ministerio uti praeoptans.*

[40] VI.164; 182=197: *spernere non contentus etiam convicio proculcavit.*

Starkaðr's enmity with the lower classes is further documented in the following passages: when Starkaðr is near death, a peasant mockingly asks him for one of his two swords: Starkaðr runs him through (VIII.224; 247 = 268). Once again, Starkaðr is goaded by mockery to violence. Boasting of his deeds, he recalls how he was attacked by common people who had smithed their own weapons: "Here I first learnt what power is contained in the implements of anvils and how much spirit lies in the common people."[41] The poet associates the inimical common people with smithery. Earlier (VI.160; 178 = 193) he had levelled a verbal attack on smiths, after he had attacked the lecherous gold-smith (*auri faber*) physically; yet there is still an ambivalence, for smiths who make weapons—whom the warrior obviously must have close ties with—are morally viable ("in my view, they are superior who forge swords and spears for the battles of men," *Me iudice praestant, qui gladios et tela viris ad proelia cudunt*). It is only the smith inclined toward luxury, jewelry, and wealth that the stern warrior disapproves of. Starkaðr has a definite anti-aesthetic bias, poet through he may be—he disapproves of the plastic arts here; at the feast of Ingel he attacked the musician.

This ambivalence only points up the complexity of the Indo-European warrior type. As Dumézil and Puhvel have pointed out, the conflict between Odin and Thor over Starkaðr, though it has extrafunctional resonances (Odin as a problematic first function figure, Thor as a problematic second),[42] is primarily an intrafunctional conflict—the dark "destructive" warrior versus the light "constructive" warrior (Puhvel prefers "demonic" versus "culture god" terminology). Starkaðr's internal ambivalence is most acutely expressed after he murders King Olo for a bribe as Olo takes a bath—a cowardly act that runs against everything Starkaðr has ever preached in his loftily moral blame poetry. "Later he was stung with shame and remorse; his grief over the felony he had committed was so bitter that, if any mention were made of it, he could not restrain his tears. When he came to his senses, his conscience blushed at the enormity of his guilt."[43] To atone for his murder, he kills those who had bribed him to do it! This guilt paradoxically turns his crime almost into a witness for his loyalty to the idea of kingship, for Olo had been a bad king.

---

[41] VIII.227; 250 = 272: *Hic primum didici, quid ferramenta valerent incudis, quantumve animi popularibus esset.*

[42] Aside from the question of how functional gods may be applied to Starkaðr, here we face the problem of Germanic functional slippage, see Puhvel 1987:191–192.

[43] VIII.221; 244 = 265: *Postmodum paenitentia ac pudore perculsus, tanta animi acerbitate commissum facinus luxit, ut, si mentionem eius incidere contigisset, a lacrimis temperare non posset. Adeo culpae atrocitatem resipiscens animus erubescebat.*

Starkaðr's first sin against royalty, the execution of Vikar, has a curious relationship with his immediately preceding poetic consecration by Odin and the agonistic fate-allotting of Odin and Thor. After Starkaðr receives all his blessings from Odin, including poetry, the god demands that Starkaðr "send" him king Vikar. The god gives the warrior the death weapon, a spear that will appear to be a reed; Starkaðr deceives the king into submitting to a mock sacrifice. A gallows made of a tree and calf intestine is prepared; the king submits; Starkaðr pierces him with the spear, the intestine becomes withy, and the warrior addresses Vikar: "Now I give you to Odin." The king dies after being swept by a branch into the tree.[44]

As Dumézil notes, this sacrifice is beneficial to all concerned, Odin, Vikar, and Starkaðr. Vikar receives an honorable death, is received into the presence of Odin, the warrior's paradise. The god has called a devoted servant into his presence. Starkaðr, in turn, has faithfully followed the commands of a god from whom he had just received great favors; he has helped a friend and king receive a happy afterlife. Yet the sacrifice is still a crime, for Starkaðr feels guilt after perpetrating it:

> Skylda ek Víkar
> í viði hávum
> Geirþjófsbana
> goðum of signa;
> lagða ek geiri
> gram til hjarta,
> þat er mér harmast
> handaverka.

"I was made to dedicate Vikar (the killer of Geirthjof) to the gods high up in the tree. I thrust with a spear into the king's heart: no act of mine has brought me such pain."[45] It is one of the sins Thor has cursed him with, and Starkaðr blames that god for forcing him to commit the crime: "I was forced without glory to do evil."[46] "From this deed Starkaðr became much despised by the people, and was exiled from Hördaland."[47] Here we have the theme of exile, though it has nothing obvious to do with poetry. Instead he is exiled for deceitful regicide,

---

[44] Pálsson and Edwards 1968:40. Saxo has a slightly different, less precise and convincing, version of Vikar's execution, VI.152–153; 170=184.

[45] Trans. Pálsson and Edwards 1968:41.

[46] *Gautrekssaga*, stanzas 31, 32, cf. Dumézil 1983:28. *hlaut ek óhróðigr / illt at vinna.*

[47] *Af þessu verki varð Starkað mjök / óþokkaðr af alþýðu, ok af þessu verki varð hann fyrst / landflótti af Hörðalandi.*

a god-ordered sacrifice.[48] He is exiled as sacrificer. But the sacrifice has a relationship to the giving of poetry. Not only is poetry one of the gifts that obligates Starkaðr to perform the regicide, but there is an even tighter link in the myth of Odin's poetic consecration through hanging on a tree.

In the "Rune Poem" section of the *Hávamál*, Odin gains secret rune wisdom, poetic skill, by hanging on the world tree, Yggdrasil, for nine days, wounded by a spear. In this case, he is both the sacrificer and sacrificed one:

> Veit ek at ek hekk
> vindga meiði á
> nætr allar níu
> geiri undaðr
> ok gefinn Óðni
> sjálfr sjálfum mér . . .
>
> . . . nýsta ek niðr
> nam ek upp rúnar
> œpandi nam
> fell ek aptr þaðan
>
> Fimbulljóð níu
> nam ek af inum frægja syni
> Bölþórs Bestlu föður
> ok ek drykk of gat
> ins dýra mjaðar
> ausinn Óðreri
>
> Þá nam ek frævask
> ok fróðr vera
> ok vaxa ok vel hafask
> orð mér af orði
> orðs leitaði
> verk mér af verki
> verks leitaði
>
> I know that I hung
> on the windswept tree
> for nine full nights,

---

[48] For the ambiguity of sacrifice, which is at the same time paradigmatically sacred and at the same time an act of profane violence, cf. Burkert: "Sacrament and sacrilege merge in every act of sacral killing" (1985:81, cf. 57, 58).

wounded with a spear,
and given to Óthinn,
myself to myself . . .

I peered downward,
I grasped the runes,
screeching I grasped them;
I fell back from there.

I learned nine mighty songs
from the famous son
of Bölthórn, father of Bestla,[49]
and I got a drink of the precious mead,
I was sprinkled with Ótherir.[50]

Then I began to grow
and gain in insight, to wax also in wisdom:
one verse [orð] led on to another verse,
one poem [verk] led on to the other poem.

Hávamál, Stanzas 138–141[51]

The poem goes on to describe Odin's knowledge in magical spells, writing, reading, painting runes, understanding, asking, offering, supplicating, and sacrificing.

The parallel with the death of Vikar is discussed by E. O. G. Turville-Petre and Lee Hollander.[52] Vikar's death replicates the sacrifice by which Odin gained poetic knowledge, a sacrifice carried out on a world tree. As Turville-Petre interprets, the god gains knowledge by dying, visiting the world of the dead, and returning (which bring the Odyssean catabasis immediately to mind, though Odysseus does not explicitly die).[53] For the link to Starkaðr's poetic

---

[49] See Turville-Petre 1964:49.

[50] See Chadwick and Chadwick 1932 1:620.

[51] Cf. verses 144 and following. Trans. Turville-Petre 1964:42, except for the last verse, which is from Hollander 1962:36, slightly modified. Turville-Petre, in the last two lines, speaks of words and deeds, not verses and poems. See also below, ch. 19, on Odin's consecrations.

[52] Hollander 1962:36n67; Turville-Petre 1964:44–50. Cf. Puhvel 1987:194, who emphasizes shamanic aspects of this sacrifice/consecration.

[53] The classic problem in Norse myth, the degree of Christian influence, must also be considered here. One could also think of Prometheus, as a hanging, suffering demigod. However, Turville-Petre concludes that all of the elements of the Norse account are authentically Scandinavian; even if they were influenced by the New Testament or Greek myth, the theme of poetic consecration is entirely absent from the crucifixion or Aeschylus' *Prometheus Bound*.

consecration to be even stronger, one would expect for him to be the sacrifice, the hanging, spear-pierced victim; instead, he is the sacrificer. But curiously, Odin is also the sacrificer in his own sacrificial poetic consecration. Perhaps Starkaðr and Vikar are both doubles of Odin. Thus the god, through himself, sacrifices himself to himself. Poetic knowledge is somehow connected to this mortal mechanism for sacralization.

Donald Ward has analyzed the sacrifice of Vikar as an attestation of the threefold death theme,[54] in which each aspect of a death corresponds to one of the functions: hanging is characteristic of first function; a blow by a weapon is characteristic of second function; drowning is characteristic of third function (all of which may vary from story to story). Thus, in the sacrifice of Vikar, we have the hanging and the spear blow; Ward suggests that the drowning was in the original version of the tale, but was weakened to falling from a stump. Ward does not compare Odin's parallel hanging/consecration, in which the god also hangs and is wounded by a spear, but this parallel is so obvious as to be implicit. If we can interpret these two sacrifices as decadent versions of the threefold death theme—and their very closeness might argue against such an interpretation, though not necessarily, as one version might be modified to follow the other—we have, first, a picture of Odin giving Starkaðr a three-fold gift, a triple lifespan, in which he will commit three functional sins, then requiring that a royal victim be executed by a trifunctional death. Starkaðr's execution of the trifunctional death against a king is his sin against the first function. In the second case, a first-function god sacrifices himself to himself by the threefold death, and as a result gains poetic knowledge. In both cases, poetic knowledge depends on the trifunctional death of a first-function figure. Perhaps the complex interplay between king-priest and the entire scope of society is suggested. There is one significant difference between the two accounts; in the first, the warrior sacrificing the king becomes the poet; in the second, the sacrificed king becomes the poet. Yet in the first case, the warrior receives his poetry from a first-function god by killing a first-function figure.

This analysis only hints at the complexity of the situation, which is augmented by the problematic nature of Germanic myth in Indo-European studies.

The sacrificial ideology in Starkaðr's death, which Dumézil has analyzed skillfully, may be relevant here. The warrior, having committed his last *facinus*, grows very old; in addition, depressed over his killing of Olo, he voluntarily decides to die. He disdains a peaceful death, seeks a death more in keeping

---

[54] Ward 1970.

with his martial spirit.[55] After a few encounters with commoners (whom he almost absentmindedly does away with), he encounters Hatherus, the son of one of Olo's murderers—whom Starkaðr had recently murdered. Hatherus is Starkaðr's perfect executioner—high born, with a solid motive for killing him; the aged warrior even throws in his blood money to tempt him. After some verbal, poetic sparring, Hatherus agrees to the execution. Starkaðr tells the youth that if he will leap between his head and trunk he will gain invulnerability. (Saxo is quite ambivalent about the meaning of this offer—"It is uncertain whether he said this to instruct his murderer or to punish him.")[56] Starkaðr extends his neck, and Hatherus beheads him, though he decides not to jump between head and body. Starkaðr's head "snapped at the soil with its teeth as it hit the ground, the fury of the dying jaws indicating his savage temper."[57] The old warrior is finally dead.

As Jan De Vries notes, this is a sacrifice: "The decrepit old man extends his head to the youth, as a sacrificial victim, *pronam cervicem applicuit*, and Hatherus has only to strike."[58] The identity of Hatherus makes this more interesting, for the youth is connected with Höthr, the god of blind warrior's fate, a very Odinic god. Thus, "it is Odin himself, the divine Höthr, who recalls Starkaðr to him at the end of his life,"[59] just as earlier Starkaðr, obeying Odin, had helped the god call King Vikar to him.

The motif of passing between head and trunk for invulnerability is given a negative interpretation by Saxo, though he admits to not knowing whether negative or positive interpretation is right. Dumézil argues convincingly that the positive interpretation must be right, for Starkaðr has no enmity toward his highborn executioner, and has, except for the three fated *facinora*, been a model of military decorum throughout his life. Starkaðr was offering him immortality. On a theological level, man-Starkaðr dealing with Höthr-god, "this would be literally a transfusion of the hero into the god."[60] "A gift and also a fusing, a union."[61] Odin calls the hero back; he coalesces with Odin, obtains a warrior's redemption.

---

[55] VIII.223–224; 247=268. Dying through illness was regarded as dishonorable by warriors, Saxo explains. The volition is explicit: "*voluntarium . . . exitum . . . proprio . . . arbitrio.*"

[56] VIII.228: *Quod utrum instruendi percussoris gratia an puniendi dixerit, incertum est.*

[57] *Quod corpori avulsum impactumque terrae glaebam morsu carpsisse fertur, ferocitatem animi moribundi oris atrocitate declarans.*

[58] Quoted in Dumézil 1983:48.

[59] De Vries, quoted in Dumézil 1983:48.

[60] Dumézil 1983:49.

[61] Dumézil 1983:46.

Thus, as in the case of Vikar's death, Odin is seen in every character: Odin calls the Odinic Starkaðr to himself through the Odinic Höthr.[62] Odin executes Odin to himself. The poet-warrior meets his sacrificial fate, sacrificed to the poet-warrior god, fusing with him. There is a definite relationship with the execution of Vikar. Interestingly, though, Starkaðr's death is not threefold—it is a simple warrior's death by weapon—Starkaðr remains a warrior to the end. (And in fact, there is a variant account of his death in which he is killed in battle. His head is chopped off, but his body continues to fight![63])

In conclusion, Starkaðr is the best (at war, at poetry); ugly; a wandering, wolflike warrior-poet, wedding physical and verbal aggression; given to violent, nearly uncontrollable rages; sporadically criminal, and suffering intense guilt as a result. He receives a poetic consecration; is a moral satirist; functions by the psychological mechanism of defensive satire, fighting back at inhospitable hosts; acts as general to a king, and is a *therapōn*, servant, representative of the king. He is exiled once, not for his poetry, but for his enmity to the common people. His death is engineered by an ambiguously friendly god. He acts as priest and victim for the god at different times of his career. Thus, a central figure in the Indo-European mythology of the warrior is a poet, and not only a poet, but a savagely eloquent satirist.

The echoes of Greece are worth considering: ugly poet; poet as wanderer; poet as wolf; poet as warrior; defensive satire connected with inhospitality; poet as criminal; consecration theme; morally justified satirist; poet as general to the king (Aesop, Tyrtaeus); poet as victim of ambiguously friendly god. Such parallels may be typological, and still be valuable on that level, but it is also possible that the Greek traditions are reflexes of an Indo-European heritage.[64]

Suibhne: Warrior, Poet, Madman

In some ways, Suibhne is quite different from Starkaðr. He is a writer of delicate nature poetry; a bizarre madman who "flies" in great hops and roosts in trees. He does not write violent invective; when his poetry turns to blame, it is sadly accusing in tone.[65] Yet in other ways, Suibhne is directly comparable to

---

[62] Note the theophorous name: Stark(h)athr 'Strong as god', like Heracles, cf. Puhvel 1987:247, 250. Thus Starkaðr is priest, victim, and god at the same time. Cf. ch. 19, on poet-priests of Odin.

[63] *Poetic Edda*, "Helgakviða Hundingsbana" II (Stanza 20–21) as cited in Polomé 1990:270.

[64] For further on Starkaðr, see Polomé 1990 and Miller 1991 (both on the duality of the hero, divided between loyalty to functions one and two).

[65] He is forgivably peevish toward Mongan, the herd who has speared him by mistake, O'Keefe 1913:147–151; all subsequent citations of *Buile Suibhne* will refer to the O'Keefe edition by

the Danish hero: he commits a reasonable set of the trifunctional sins; he is a king-supporter; most importantly, for our present purposes, he is a prominent warrior-hero who is also a prominent early poet in the Irish legendary literary tradition.

Suibhne is (before his madness) the best warrior—he volunteers to face the fearsome Oilill Cedach in combat, and leaves him headless[66]—"When there was a fight or a tussle / I was a match for thirty," he boasts.[67] Loingseachan, his foster brother, calls him a splendid warrior and a noble champion, and refers to his savage, wound-dealing sword.[68]

Suibhne also has kingly aspects, a problem not entirely resolved. We read of a sovereignty that Suibhne had given up (45); he states, "In my auspicious kingship / I was a good, great king" (27).[69] This kingly aspect would seem to at least dilute Suibhne's credentials as warrior and reduce his value as a comparand to Starkaðr. In fact, Joseph Nagy interprets Suibhne as a king primarily.[70] However, O'Keefe, who notes that there is no historical king Suibhne in the king lists, conjectures that Suibhne was a regent during Congal's absence. "Suibhne is called king, but the word is used loosely in the annals; the designation of lord may have more closely represented the position."[71] If Suibhne is king, he is an underking to Congal, whose summons he follows at a moment's notice, dropping the pressing duties of cleric persecution he was engaged in at the time (5). He also confronts Oilill in response to an invitation by Congal (113). In this loyalty to a king, he is comparable to Starkaðr and Śiśupāla (who is also an "underking").[72] Heracles is also an underking.[73]

Before his madness, Suibhne is a general, again like Starkaðr and Śiśupāla, and when wandering he misses the military camp: "Ten hundred and ten warriors, that was my host at Druim Fraoch . . . Gloomy is my night to-night

---

page number. There are also elements of misogynist blame in his poetry, see J. Nagy 1982–1983:57n76; however, Suibhne's relationships with women are very ambivalent, as Nagy shows. One must also bear in mind that the lampoons of Irish blame poetry are often so subtle that only the initiated can perceive them, cf. Ward 1973:136; Robinson 1912:106 (white, black, and speckled satire).

[66] He boasts of this in a poem, O'Keefe 1913:113–115. See also 11.

[67] 113: *áit ina mbíodh treas nó troid / robsam comhlann do thríochaid.*

[68] 57, 59, 54.

[69] 27: *ar mo ríghe raith / robsam rígh maith mór.* Cf. 3, 145.

[70] See 1982–1983:59n84. Cf. 3, 145.

[71] xxxi, cf. Cohen 1977:115–116.

[72] See Dumézil 1983:59, 54, 57.

[73] *Odyssey* xxi 25; Rose 1959:211: "The real Herakles was indeed a lord of Mycenaean times, but a vassal of the greater lord of Argos or of Mycenae."

/ without serving-man, without camp" (37).[74] This would seem to bring him closer into the "Stakes" orbit than even Cohen has argued. The kingship aspects, if not dominant, still remain, however. Perhaps the functions of king and warrior always intersect somewhat (warrior-kings are common in Ireland); as Puhvel notes, "Royalty appears to originate in the warrior class (cf. Vedic *rājanyà-*, and Indra as king)."[75] Whether Suibhne is a kingly warrior or a warrior-king, his warrior aspects are pronounced enough to make him a close parallel to Starkaðr and Śiśupāla.

After a series of offenses against the cleric Ronan, including the murder of Ronan's foster son by a spear (the sacral first-function sin), the warrior is cursed by the saint to live a life of nakedness and birdlike, subhuman flight, wandering for years throughout Ireland, and then to die by the same kind of spear thrust he had inflicted on Ronan's foster son. As a result, when he is fighting in the battle of Mag Rath, the clamor of war reaches a peak and the din drives Suibhne mad; he flees the battle (his second-function crime). His life of madness and misery—wandering, naked, "flying" about, living in trees, fleeing from other men—begins. It is interrupted only briefly by two lapses into sanity. Paradoxically, it is only now that Suibhne becomes a poet.

This is perhaps the central theme of Suibhne's life—the utter misery of his wandering outcast existence. It is expressed frequently in his poetry:

> Mór múich a ttá-sa anocht,
> rotreaghd mo chorp an gháoth ghlan,
> toll mo throighthiu, glas mo ghrúadh,
> a Dhé mhóir, atá a dhúal damh.

> . . . anocht robhretait mo bhoill
> i nglaic chroinn i nGáille ghlúair.

> Rofhuilnges mór ttreas gan tlás
> ó rofhás clúmh ar mo chorp,
> ar gach n-oidhche is ar gach ló
> as mó sa mhó fhuilghim d'olc.

---

[74] *Deichneamhar is deich cét laoch / rob é mo shlúagh ag Druim Fraoch . . . Múichnidhe mh'aghaidh anocht / gan giolla is gan longphort.*

[75] 1987:242; and though the king later became detached from a purely militarist focus, the military aspect always remained. We may compare Yudhiṣṭhira, Mitraic king, who takes part in battle, though his brothers Bhīma and Arjuna are military specialists. See Dumézil, who discusses the weapons of all five Pāṇḍava brothers, including Yudhiṣṭhira and other sovereign figures in Indo-European myth (1968 1:99–100). Even if weapons define sovereignty, they are still weapons of war. See also Oguibenine 1978, and below, this chapter.

Romchráidh sioc, síon nach súairc,
romthuairg snechta ar Sléibh mhic Sin,
anocht romgeóghain an ghaéth
gan fraech Ghlenna Bolcáin bil.

Utmhall mh'imirce in gach íath . . .

Dúairc an bhetha bheith gan teach,
as truagh an bhetha, a Chríosd chain . . .

Tuisledh do bharraibh chraobh ccríon,
imthecht aitin, gníom gan gháoi,
seachna daoine, cumann cúan,
coimhrith re damh rúadh dar raéi.

Feis oidhche gan chlúimh a ccoill
i mullach croinn dosaigh dhlúith,
gan coisteacht re guth ná glór,
a mhic Dé, is mór an mhúich.

I am in great grief tonight,
the pure wind has pierced my body,
wounded are my feet, my cheek is wan,
O great God! it is my due.

. . . to-night my limbs are racked
in the fork of a tree in pleasant Gaille.

I have borne many a fight without cowardice
since feathers have grown on my body;
each night and each day
more and more do I endure ill.

Frost and foul storm have wrung my heart,
snow has beaten on me on Sliabh mic Sin;
to-night the wind has wounded me,
without the heather of happy Glen Bolcain.

Unsettled is my faring through each land . . .
Wretched is the life of one homeless,
Sad is the life, O gentle Christ! . . .

Stumbling from withered tree-tops,
faring through furze—deed without falsehood—

> shunning mankind, keeping company with wolves,
> racing with the red stag over the field.
>
> Sleeping of nights without feathers in a wood
> in the top of a thick, bushy tree,
> without hearing voice or speech;
> O Son of God, great is the misery![76]

"I am the most discontented and unhappy creature in the world," says the unfortunate poet.[77] Thus Suibhne is an outcast/exile par excellence. He cannot tolerate the company of men for fear they will kill him or imprison him.[78]

In leaving the company of men, he enters the fellowship of animals. As we have seen in the poem quoted above, he is explicitly ornithic—flying, roosting in trees, even growing feathers.[79] Like Alcaeus, he lives with wolves; as a wanderer, he finds the howling of wolves melodious.[80]

Yet Suibhne, having become subhuman, also becomes suprahuman, for as a mad, outcast wanderer he is also a poet,[81] a prophet, and a saint, entirely sacral. Misery and degradation are a requirement, as it were, for gaining sacral inspiration. Joseph Nagy acutely observes that Suibhne hates his animalistic haunts, the forest, the wilderness, open to wind and snow, and this defines his existential misery; yet his story is full of sensitive nature poetry, praising the beauty of extra-urban, extra-human, animal-filled nature.[82]

Suibhne's poetic persona is obvious throughout his story, which is frequently interrupted by his poems. He was greatly prized as a poet in the later Irish tradition, as was Starkaðr in his tradition, for a tenth-century Irish law tract tells us that one of the triumphs of the battle of Mag Rath was Suibhne's turning mad. Yet the battle was not a triumph simply because

---

[76] Trans. adapted from O'Keefe 1913:119–120.

[77] 133: *uair as meisi dúil as anshádhaile & anshocra.* Cf. 25–29, 125–127, 135.

[78] See 133.

[79] Cf. 13. See J. Nagy 1982:50, for further references and discussion. Nagy treats the theme as shamanic; for further on Suibhne and shamanism, see Benesch 1961. For shamanism in Indo-European culture, Closs 1968. See above, ch. 16, on poet as prophet/shaman.

[80] See p. 153; Kershaw 2000:133–143. Cf. ch. 9 (Alcaeus); ch. 19, on Odinic berserkers.

[81] Suibhne's poems are scattered throughout his story. Like Starkaðr, he will break into verse periodically, often in moments of crisis.

[82] "While many of the Suibhne poems are laments about life in the wilderness, others are virtual paeans to his wild existence in isolated places" (J. Nagy 1982–1983:51, see O'Keefe 1913:63–83). Suibhne even praises the watercress and strong wind that elsewhere cause him special agony, p. 71.

Suibhne turned mad; it was a triumph because his madness caused him to recite stories and poems.[83]

Suibhne's prophetic aspects include supernatural knowledge and knowledge of future events, specifically of how his death will take place.[84] When St. Moling asks him how he knows the prayer hour has come in Rome, he replies, "Knowledge comes to me from my Lord / each morn and each eve" (139).[85]

Suibhne, originally demonic,[86] has become a saint by the end of his story. St. Moling castigates the swineherd who has killed him: "Woe to him who has slain by dint of his strength / the king, the saint, the saintly madman."[87] He has been "without reproach" since his madness (149). The end of Suibhne's life is filled with motifs of sacralization and redemption. When he first comes to Teach Moling, St. Moling welcomes him with joy, and enjoins him to visit him each night to tell him of his experiences—a tacit acknowledgment that his experiences as a madman are edifying and praiseworthy to the Christian saint.[88] After Suibhne has been assaulted by the swineherd, it is prophesied repeatedly that the poet will attain heaven,[89] and his story ends when, after having been lifted from a "death-swoon" by Moling's handclasp, and after being brought by him to the church, he touches the doorpost, dies in the

---

[83] See O'Keefe 1913:xvi–xvii; cf. J. Nagy 1982–1983:44n3. In Tom Stoppard's *Travesties*, James Joyce rebukes a Dadaist by remarking that without Homer Troy would now be nothing but dust and broken pots (1975:62). Much of Suibhne's poetry is agonic—e.g. 101, 134–135, 137–141. In this last passage, Suibhne trades couplets with St. Moling to make up quatrains; their competitive, riddling nature is clear. Often Moling asks questions, which the poet answers; often his answers "cap" the saint's, as is shown by their frequent use of comparatives: "More delightful . . . more wearisome . . . more grievous."). The poetic dialogue is explicitly mantic, for in it Suibhne displays supernatural knowledge, predicts his own death, and commends Moling's prophetic gifts.

[84] 141; cf. J. Nagy 1982–1983:45n7. For further on the mantic nature of *geilt*, see Chadwick 1942; for Suibhne's prophetic nature, see 110.

[85] *Fios tig dhamh óm Thigerna / gach madain 's gach nóin.*

[86] Perhaps he is portrayed as demonic because of the sectarian (Christian) coloring of the received Suibhne tale, just as the Śiśupāla tradition comes to us only with sectarian overlay, making him entirely demonic, too (Puhvel 1987:250, 253). On the other hand, Starkaðr has his pronounced demonic aspects. One detail that might point to a more positive coloring in the original Śiśupāla tradition is his name, which can mean 'protector of the small' (Dumézil 1983:57)—paralleling Starkaðr's and Heracles' soteric aspects; Heracles' role as culture hero, destroyer of destructive monsters, is well known. However, Śiśupāla can also be interpreted as 'small-lord', a Sivaistic epithet, "Junior Śiva" (Puhvel 1987:247).

[87] 144: *mairg domharb a los a neirt / an rígh, an náomh, an náomhgheilt.*

[88] 143. He later, after Suibhne's death-swoon, recalls the joy and pleasure Suibhne's association gave him (155). Suibhne's life in nature, outside of human intercourse, has obvious monastic overtones. Much of his nature poetry has close parallels in Irish medieval poetry praising the isolated monastic life.

[89] 145, 147, 151 (twice).

doorway—an extraordinarily liminal death[90]—and his spirit immediately flees to heaven. The transformation of this bellicose cleric tormentor into a cleric-guided, heavenly soul is no less striking, perhaps, that its obvious Indo-European parallel—the transformation of the demonic Śiśupāla into the substance of Kṛṣṇa.[91]

The physical means of Suibhne's death—he is killed by a swineherd,[92] Mongan, whose wife feeds Suibhne milk from an indentation in manure, after the swineherd has been falsely led to believe that Suibhne has committed adultery with her[93]—offers a parallel to the death of Hesiod. Both poets are killed where they had accepted hospitality, after wandering far from home; both are murdered because of a false accusation of sexual wrongdoing with a woman of the household. The murderers both die prematurely as a result.[94]

Another parallel is the theme of the double death, attested in the legends of Aesop and Hesiod. After Suibhne's extended, almost operatic, death scene, ending with a long poem, he experiences a "death-swoon" (*táimhnéll*)[95] and Moling and the clerics all place a stone on Suibhne's tomb. Moling recites a lament full of praise for the poet. Then he calls on God:

> Masa chead le re Rígh na reann
> éirigh agus imthigh leam,

---

[90] This death in a door emphasizes the theme of death as passage, a liminal rather than terminal experience. Cf. J. Nagy's "Liminality and Knowledge in Irish Tradition," 1981–1982. Comparable is the death-swoon, see Eliade, 1964:33ff., for death and resurrection as a shamanic theme. The death-swoon would be part of an initiatory, liminal experience. Nagy interprets Suibhne as a sacral man (king) who experiences a different, less social kind of sacrality (shamanic madness) as an "end in itself." For my view of Suibhne as an underlord, see above. He is also associated with asacral, violent, cleric-persecuting, warmongering (Ronan had tried to make peace between kings, and Suibhne had intentionally flouted the saint's ban on bloodshed). Thus there is a simpler symmetry in the story: evil, warrior-king, enmity with a saint; wandering, subhuman, asocial, mantic madness; death, reconciliation and salvation, friendship with a saint. The middle state is truly liminal, a state of passage, for Suibhne looks back in misery on his glory days as a warrior, yet his poetic/mantic aspects point him forward to his final meeting with Moling.

[91] See below.

[92] In light of the importance placed on the warrior's executioner in the cases of Starkaðr (an Odin double), and Śiśupāla (the warrior's opposite, the righteous Kṛṣṇa), one may consider the possibility that Mongan as executioner has some connection with the mystical stature of the swineherd in Ireland, see Ni Chatháin 1979–1980. Thus, Suibhne would be killed by a shamanic figure; Mongan is already a member of Moling's household. The "friendly" "god" is behind Suibhne's death. In some traditions, Suibhne's killer suffered the threefold death, see above.

[93] 143–145.

[94] See 151, 147. Mongan's life is literally shortened in Moling's prophecy—a safely clerical equivalent to murder. Hesiod's murderers undergo sacrificial execution—see above, ch. 6.

[95] 154.

> tucc dhamh, a chridhe, in do lámh
> ón lighe agus ón leachtán.
>
> If it be the will of the King of the stars,
> arise and come with me,
> give me, O heart, thy hand
> from the grave and from the tomb!"

Then Suibhne rose out of his "swoon" (*niull*, from *néll*)," only to die for the final time moments later as he touches a church (157–158).

It is not absolutely clear that the "death-swoon" is a real death, though many details suggest that it is—the association with a tomb, the funeral lament, the call of Moling for the poet to give him his hand "from the grave and from the tomb."

This double death could be simply a narrational doublet; but it may also be interpreted as a shamanic motif. The shaman, undergoing initiation, often had to die symbolically, through some sort of sickness. This is often a swoon: "In general . . . the shaman's symbolic death is suggested by the long fainting spells and lethargic sleep of the candidate."[96] Suibhne's double death is a close parallel to this; Hesiod's double death, we have seen, has also been interpreted in a shamanic context.[97]

Another important aspect of the Suibhne tradition is its association with the theme of the threefold death we have seen in the Starkaðr saga. While Suibhne does not die by the threefold death, the threefold death is prominent in stories related to the Suibhne legend.[98]

Thus Suibhne is, like Starkaðr, a famous warrior-champion-general for a king; he is also a famous early poet. Like Starkaðr he was a wanderer, uncouth;

---

[96] Eliade 1964:53. See also ibid., pp. 33–66; Benesch 1961:317–318, who compares Suibhne's death to the burial of a shaman, not the initiation.

[97] Cohen 1977:118 admits that his case would be stronger if there were an actual sexual sin, not just an accusation, in this crime against the third function. "There is no totally convincing means to explain away this discrepancy." If there were a variant tradition of Starkaðr being guilty of sexual sin, as in the case of Hesiod, one could explain this equivocal theme. (For variant traditions in Suibhne's life, cf. e.g. the tradition that has him killed in the battle of Mag Rath, see Cohen 1977:116.) See above, ch. 3 (Archilochus); ch. 17, the poet DonnBo killed in battle, and the various poetic victims of Cuchulainn.

[98] In St. Moling legends, Suibhne's murderer suffers the threefold death, see Ward 1970:136–137; in the Wild Man of the Wood stories, of which Suibhne's legend is an example, the hero often dies by the threefold death, see Cohen 1977:120. Suibhne's death by spear is possibly a remnant of an original threefold death tradition. On the other hand, we may note the strong parallel with our other warriors in Suibhne's death by weapon only; Starkaðr and Śiśupāla also die by means of weapons alone, fitting warriors' deaths. (Heracles, as often, is anomalous in this group, dying by fire and poison.)

unlike him, he does not specialize in invective, and his poetic aspect is clearly separated from his warlike aspect. He is a remarkable example of our central theme: the poet as exile, outcast. As soon as Suibhne becomes mad, he flees all social intercourse and lives with animals, as an animal, in the wilds. There his poetic manticism is balanced by his utter misery, or perhaps is produced by it.

Śiśupāla as Satirist

Though Śiśupāla is not overtly a poet, his close parallels to Starkaðr and Suibhne invite an examination of his story for poetic or satirical, verbally abusive aspects. Such a search is quickly rewarded, for the *Mahābhārata*[99] portrays him as engaging in a long, intricately abusive speech before his death. Though Śiśupāla is not a poet *strictu sensu*, he is skilled at verbal attack, and his blame offers close parallels to the poetic aspects of Starkaðr especially. In both their cases, physical violence is matched by verbal violence;[100] and in both their cases, their abuse is an attack on those who have, in their opinions, downgraded royalty.

Śiśupāla, after his early career, including ninety-nine crimes, of which five are recognizably functional, is invited to the anointing of Yudhiṣṭhira, along with all the kings of the world. Yudhiṣṭhira, on Bhīṣma's advice, offers the most honorable guest gift to Kṛṣṇa, who is not a king. At this juncture, Śiśupāla "berated Bhīṣma and the King Dharma in the assembly and went on to insult Vasudeva [Kṛṣṇa]."[101] Ironically, in defending kingship, Śiśupāla attacks the true universal king, Yudhiṣṭhira; this is in keeping with his demonic nature. Starkaðr is diametrically opposite, if pursuing the same theme; the good warrior, he upholds true kings and kingship, except in his fated criminal lapses, in which he is a serial regicide. David Cohen insightfully proposes that the prelunatic Suibhne is defending royal prerogatives as he tries to keep Ronan from encroaching on royal land.[102] If so, he is an exact parallel

---

[99] *Mahābhārata*, book 2, The Book of the Assembly Hall, 33–42; van Buitenen 1975 2:93–104. Subsequent references to the *Mahābhārata* will be to van Buitenen's edition.

[100] Śiśupāla is described as "berserk in battle" (89). See *Mahābhārata* 2.31.14: *śiśupālo mahāvīryaḥ saha putreṇa bhārata / āgacchat pāṇḍaveyasya yajñaṁ saṁgrāmadurmadaḥ* (Śiśupāla of great gallantry, and berserk in battle, came with his son, O Bhārata, to the sacrifice of the Pāṇḍaveya). The violence of his words nearly leads the kings at Yudhiṣṭhira's coronation to a violent riot, 103. See above, ch. 17 on "war fury" in Ireland.

[101] Van Buitenen 1975: 93, *Mahābhārata* 2.33.32: *sa upālabhya bhīṣmaṁ ca dharmarājaṁ ca saṁsadi / apākṣipad vāsudevaṁ cedirājo mahābalaḥ*. Dumézil notes the parallel with Irish feast strifes over points of honor; cf. Starkaðr's slighting reception at the feast of Ingellus, see above.

[102] Cohen 1977:121.

to Śiśupāla in his demonic support of kingship. Starkaðr's violent support of kingship in the feast of Ingellus, causing hospitality to dissolve into a feast of blood, is perhaps not far off from this demonic pattern.

Śiśupāla's speech runs through the gamut of blame themes: the offending parties are stupid[103] and religious transgressors—Kṛṣṇa is a cow killer (98 [2.38.16]); Bhīṣma ignores the Law (99 [2.38.21]); the goose of a fable he tells is hypocritical and commits an unholy crime (99 [2.38.37,40]). Śiśupāla uses typical animal similes for abuse, as when he compares Janādana to a dog eating a sacrificial offering [94 [2.34.19]); he compares Bhīṣma to the scavenging *bhūlinga* bird (98 [2.38.17], 102 [2.41.18–19], compare the fable, 99 [2.38.29–40]); he uses sexual slurs (Bhīṣma's celibacy is a lie that he maintains because he is either inept or impotent [99 [2.38.24–25]); like Starkaðr, he emphasizes his victim's effeminacy (100 [2.39.8]).

Also like Starkaðr, he is an enemy of the lower classes, and this is a key theme of his blame; the whole point of his speech is that honor has gone incorrectly to a man of inferior caste. Kṛṣṇa is "a vicious serf" (103 [2.42.4]);[104] Śiśupāla praises King Jarāsaṃdha for refusing to fight with Kṛṣṇa, "saying he was no more than a serf," (99 [2.39.1]);[105] he is a mere herdsman (102 [2.41.17]).

In the fable Śiśupāla uses to attack Bhīṣma (99), the birds bring food to a law-preaching goose, and leave their eggs for him to guard; when the birds find that the goose has been eating the eggs, they band together to kill him. This is a strangely Aesopic motif, the abusive animal fable in the last speech before death, accusing and threatening the object of the blame. Everything is inverted though; the blamer is evil, accusing falsely; the victim of the attack is righteous.

The violence of Śiśupāla's verbal attack hits its targets; Bhīma is thrown into a war rage, and is restrained with difficulty by Bhīṣma (100 [2.39.10–15]). Just as Śiśupāla's fable had predicted the kings' collective killing of Bhīṣma, the kings become filled with fury, and threaten to kill Bhīṣma like a sacrificial animal, or by burning. (103 [2.41.29]). Thus Śiśupāla's last speech is military paraenesis used on behalf of the ideology of kingship.

---

[103] P. 93, *Mahābhārata* 2.34.3. *bālā yūyaṃ na jānīdhvaṃ dharmaḥ sūkṣmo hi pāṇḍavāḥ.* "You are children, you don't know! For the Law is subtle, Pāṇḍavas!"

[104] *ye tvāṃ dāsam arājānaṃ bālyād arcanti durmatim / anarham arhavat kṛṣṇa vadhyās ta iti me matiḥ.* (In their folly they honored you, a vicious serf, not a king, as though you had earned the honor, Kṛṣṇa. Yes I hold I must kill them!).

[105] *śiśupāla uvāca / sa me bahumato rājā jarāsaṃdho mahābalaḥ / yo 'nena yuddhaṃ neyeṣa dāso 'yam iti saṃyuge.* (Śiśupāla said: Highly did I esteem him, the powerful King Jarāsaṃdha, who refused to give battle to this one, saying he was no more than a serf).

At this point, Bhīṣma calls upon the kings to duel with Kṛṣṇa, and hot-blooded, aggressive (103 [2.42.1]) Śiśupāla takes up the challenge, not knowing that he has committed his one hundredth crime and is vulnerable to his enemy. But the time for the physical combat has not yet come—another stage in the verbal duel must take place. Vasudeva, eagerly accepting Śiśupāla's challenge, takes the opportunity to revile the demonic warrior, listing his many crimes.

The effect on the kings is immediate; in a curious reversal, they turn against Śiśupāla and begin to revile him (104 [2.42.16–17]). Śiśupāla is unconcerned, bursts into laughter, and jeers at them. He accuses Kṛṣṇa of having married a defiled woman; while he has barely begun this final attack, even as he speaks, violent words escalate into violent acts: Kṛṣṇa throws his discus and slices off his opponent's head—an argument that proves entirely persuasive. There follows the mystical scene in which Śiśupāla's body gives forth a "sublime radiance" that enters into Kṛṣṇa:

> tathā bruvata evāsya bhagavān madhusūdanaḥ
> vyapāharac chiraḥ kruddhaś cakreṇāmitrakarṣaṇaḥ
> sa papāta mahābāhur vajrāhata ivācalaḥ
> tataś cedipater dehāt tejo 'gryaṁ dadṛśur nṛpāḥ
> utpatantaṁ mahārāja gaganād iva bhāskaram
> tataḥ kamalapatrākṣaṁ kṛṣṇaṁ lokanamaskṛtam
> vavande tat tadā tejo viveśa ca narādhipa
> tad adbhutam amanyanta dṛṣṭvā sarve mahīkṣitaḥ
> yad viveśa mahābāhuṁ tat tejaḥ puruṣottamam
> anabhre pravavarṣa dyauḥ papāta jvalitāśaniḥ
> kṛṣṇena nihate caidye cacāla ca vasuṁdharā

He was still speaking when the blessed Madhusūdana, scourge of his enemies, irately cut off his head with his discus. The strong-armed king fell like a tree that is struck by a thunderbolt. Thereupon the kings watched a sublime radiance rise forth from the body of the king of the Cedis, which, great king, was like the sun rising up from the sky; and that radiance greeted lotus-eyed Kṛṣṇa, honored by the world, and entered him, O king. When they saw that, all the kings deemed it a miracle that that radiance entered the strong-armed man, that greatest of men. In a cloudless sky heaven rained forth and blazing lightning struck and the earth trembled, when Kṛṣṇa slew the Caidya.

Mahābhārata 104 (2.42.22)

There are numerous remarkable elements in this account—especially the verbal violence paralleling the physical violence, producing war madness, berserker behavior. The conflict of blame between Bhīṣma and Kṛṣṇa on the one hand and Śiśupāla on the other is also notable; the execution of Śiśupāla by weapon seems merely an extension of verbal violence, a tool of the verbal violence. Most interesting, though, is the final isolation of the blame poet, after an unpredictably swift peripety, when all the kings turn against him and revile him. He who had the power nearly to make another man a sacrifice is suddenly himself the center of collective hostility and will be beheaded in a moment. It is his power to make another a victim that has made him a victim. He undergoes a typically ambiguous death, for our hero type: killed by his divine enemy, he flows into the god, and receives salvation.

Śiśupāla as master of violence-generating invective, deployed in support of kingship, is particularly close to Starkaðr as poet, and thus enables us to view Śiśupāla as a blame poet, and a valuable parallel to Starkaðr and Suibhne.

Heracles

We should look briefly at Heracles, the third leg of Dumézil's triptych. Discussion of Greek myth in the context of Dumézil's trifunctional comparative analysis is complicated by "the problem that was Greece," as C. Scott Littleton puts it.[106] The inherited Indo-European traditions in archaic Greece were complicated by Greece's intercultural complexity (including much influence from the Near East, Crete, and Asia Minor) and its creativity, by the brilliance of its poets, who had a tendency to shape myth to their own individual purposes. As Puhvel puts it, the Greek pantheon is more remarkable for its originality than for its preservation.[107]

Nevertheless, Greek is fully an Indo-European language, and there is certainly a strong strain of Indo-European tradition in Greek myth and religion. Greece was never the center of Dumézil's analysis; nevertheless, he did not neglect it, as his treatment of Heracles shows. Indo-Europeanists have continued to analyze its wealth of myth and epic.[108]

Heracles has a deity who persecutes and then helps deify him, Hera.[109] Her persecution of the hero starts early; while he is still in the womb, she delays

---

[106] Littleton 1980.

[107] Puhvel 1987:129.

[108] See Strutynski 1980; Puhvel 1987:126–143; Dumézil 1994:209–286; Sergent 1998; Miller 2001.

[109] Diodorus Siculus 4.39.2–3; Homer *Odyssey* xi 601–626; Hesiod *Theogony* 950–955; Pindar *Nemean Odes* 10.18.

his birth so that Eurystheus rules over him (*Iliad* XIX 95–125). Then when Heracles is in swaddling clothes, the malevolent goddess sends monstrous snakes to murder him, a story attested as early as Pindar *Nemean Odes* 1.33–72: "but the queen of the gods in her heart's anger sent two snakes against him straightway."[110] The infant hero throttles them, of course.

As a result of Eurystheus' Hera-engineered rule, Heracles must humiliate himself and serve him. The goddess then causes Heracles to go mad and kill his wife and children, which produces a defilement that forces him to undergo the labors.[111] In the labors themselves, she is instrumental in trying to endanger him, for she nurtures the monsters Heracles must face. Hesiod writes, "And again she [Echidna] bore a third [child], the evil-minded Hydra of Lerna, whom the goddess, white-armed Hera nourished, being angry beyond measure with the mighty Heracles."[112] She also nurtures the invulnerable Nemean Lion.[113]

For Heracles' ties with Hera, we first have his name.[114] As a baby Heracles was nursed by Hera, despite her enmity.[115] After his apotheosis, Hesiod writes,

καὶ] θάνε καί ῥ' Ἀΐδ[αο πολύστονον ἵκε]το δῶμα.
νῦν δ' ἤδη θεός ἐστι, κακῶν δ' ἐξήλυθε πάντων,
ζώει δ' ἔνθά περ ἄλλοι Ὀλύμπια δώματ' ἔχοντες
<u>ἀθάνατος</u> καὶ ἄγηρος, ἔχων καλλ[ίσ]φυρον Ἥβην,
παῖδα Διὸς μεγάλοιο καὶ Ἥρης χρυσοπεδίλου·
τὸν πρὶν μέν ῥ' ἤχθηρε θεὰ λευκώλενος Ἥρη
ἔκ τε θεῶν μακάρων ἔκ τε θνητῶν ἀνθρώ[πων,
νῦν δ' ἤδη πεφίληκε, <u>τίει</u> δέ μιν ἔξοχον ἄλλ[ων
ἀθανάτων μετά γ' αὐτὸν ἐρισθενέα Κρ[ο]νίωνα.

And he died and went down into the <much-groaning> house of Hades. But now he is a god, and he has escaped all evils. And he lives in the same place as others having homes on Olympos, immortal

---

[110] Trans. Lattimore, ἀλλὰ θεῶν βασίλεα / σπερχθεῖσα θυμῷ πέμπε δράκοντας ἄφαρ.

[111] See Euripides, *Heracles Crazed*.

[112] Hesiod *Theogony* 313–315, trans. Evelyn-White, τὸ τρίτον Ὕδρην αὖτις ἐγείνατο λυγρὰ ἰδυῖαν / Λερναίην, ἣν θρέψε θεὰ λευκώλενος Ἥρη / ἄπλητον κοτέουσα βίη Ἡρακληείη.

[113] Hesiod *Theogony* 328–332; Bacchylides 9.6–9.

[114] See Pindar fr. 291, Apollodorus 2.4.12 (the Delphic sibyl renames Heracles); scholion on the *Iliad* XIV 324; Diodorus Siculus 4.10.1. Pötscher 1971 (who suggests a chronological division of Hera's enmity and friendship for Heracles); Davidson 1980; Cook 1906, which is unconvincing for Heracles as husband of Hera, but valuable for surveying the close ties between the two deities. For enmity between hero and goddess, see p. 371.

[115] Lycophron 38–39, 1327–1328; "Eratosthenes" *Constellations* 44; Hyginus *Astronomy* 2.43; Pausanias 9.25.2; Diodorus Siculus 4.9.6. Evidence from art shows that this theme predated the Hellenistic era, Gantz 1993:378.

[*athanatos*] and ageless, having fair-ankled Hebe, daughter of great Zeus and golden-sandled Hera. Before, the white-armed Hera hated him above all the other gods and mortals, but now she loves him, and honors [*tiei*] him above all the other gods after mighty Kronion himself.

Fr. 25.25–33 M-W[116]

Just as Heracles seems to fit as the Indo-European warrior to a certain extent, but not neatly, so he only fits problematically as poet. Heracles is definitely a singer, *aoidos*, a *mousikos anēr*.[117] Yet he is not a thoroughgoing poet, like Starkaðr or Suibhne. His poetic aspects are merely a component in his all-around heroic persona, just as the warrior Achilles will take time out to play the lyre on occasion. Starkaðr, on the other hand, is given to savage satire that parallels, and often leads to, his warlike aggressiveness, and is known as a famous poet; Suibhne is primarily a poet. Archilochus, primarily a poet and warrior, is a much closer parallel to the Starkaðr/Suibhne poetic warrior type. And a closer parallel to Heracles as poet is Cuchulainn or Lugh, who, though they are primarily warriors, have strong poetic aspects.

However, the fact that both Heracles and Achilles, the two most prominent heroes of the Greeks, were to some extent poets, may have more than incidental importance. Perhaps Heracles made into an *aoidos*, albeit a violent *aoidos*, and Achilles (whose personality is dominated by his wrath, his *mēnis*) singing to himself, may be the atrophied remnants of an earlier, stronger tradition of the poetic warrior. In addition, some have interpreted Odysseus the storyteller as a poet.[118] The Greek hero as, in part, poet is perhaps more central to the Greek tradition that has been realized in the past.

Four Heroes

We may now analyze our four heroes, from a poetic perspective, and see how they add up. All of the figures are famous warriors, and commit a version of the trifunctional sins; they are all buffeted like pawns by friendly and inimical

---

[116] Trans. Gantz 1993:461.

[117] See above, ch. 16.

[118] Starting with Eumaeus, *Odyssey* xvii 514, 518–521. Cf. Nagy 1979:234; Bergren 1982:44, 57–58; Segal 1994. If we accept Odysseus as a kind of storytelling poet, he becomes the wandering poet who is denied hospitality as the hosts, especially Antinous, offer him inadequate food and insult him, Nagy 1979:232. Odysseus blames Antinous, and violent retribution comes to the satirist, in the form of a thrown footstool. The inhospitable hosts pay a horrible price.

gods—moreover, by gods ambiguously inimical and friendly.[119] Śiśupāla receives deification through the weapon of his enemy, Kṛṣṇa, who had earlier ridded him of monstrous supernumerary limbs; Starkaðr receives a similar treatment of congenital monstrosity from the inimical Thor, who accounts for all his evil fate. Suibhne also is shorn of his violent proclivities and given his sacral manticism by his "divine" enemy, St. Ronan. Heracles also has a persecuting tutelary deity, Hera.

Suibhne and Starkaðr are overt, versifying, famous poets. Śiśupāla is a "blame poet" in theme; Heracles is a poet, if something of a dilettante. Starkaðr and Śiśupāla are specialists in invective; Suibhne's poetry has its blame aspects.

Starkaðr and Suibhne are revolting in appearance; they are both lonesome wanderers; they are both associated with the wolf—this lupine association expresses both their grizzled ugliness and outcast, wandering temperaments, as well as associations with the *Männerbund*, perhaps. Starkaðr and Suibhne both express powerfully the misery of wandering in their poetry. Heracles also was a wanderer.

The themes of the poetry of Starkaðr, Suibhne, and Śiśupāla closely parallel each other. Starkaðr and Śiśupāla both employ violent invective and praise in support of kingship. This supports their functions as ambiguous king supporters, a function shared by Suibhne. All three are also generals in armies, warrior underkings for higher kings in the cases of Suibhne and Śiśupāla. Both Starkaðr and Suibhne act as champions for kings in combat situations.

A related poetic theme, hatred of common man, is found strongly expressed in the invective of Starkaðr and Śiśupāla. The common people drive Starkaðr into exile on occasion. Starkaðr and Suibhne also share misogyny as a poetic theme.

Madness is a characteristic of poets: all four of our figures suffer forms of lunacy, often connected with poetry. Starkaðr has frequent rages bordering on madness, rages leading both to violent poetry and violent deeds. Śiśupāla's rage is quite similar; he expresses fury through invective, and incites others to violence with it. Heracles has frequent bouts of violent insanity (one directed against his music teacher, Linus, whom he kills with a lyre). Suibhne's madness, in contrast, is mantic, a characteristic of his liminal state on the way to redemption, partaking of both humiliation and holiness. However, he was also given to violent rages before his liminal manticism.

Suibhne would seem to be our only overtly mantic poet. However, the theme of divine poetic consecration creates the mantic poet, and Starkaðr

---

[119] See Dumézil 1983:135–144, cf. Puhvel 1987:244–255.

receives his poetic consecration from Odin, as Suibhne receives his consecration (an ambiguous "curse" that makes him both a miserable outcast and sacral) from his "bright god," St. Ronan. Both these poets are given to violent rage, and have mantic aspects, though in opposite proportions. Heracles' association with the Muses may have aspects of poetic consecration. At the moment of death, Suibhne, Śiśupāla, and Starkaðr grow close to their poetic aspects as they deliver long final speeches. Suibhne's and Starkaðr's are intertwined with poetry; Śiśupāla's includes an insulting animal fable.

As Puhvel has noted, Starkaðr is perhaps the most archaic figure in this pattern, as he shares important binary isothemes with each of the other two primary figures.[120] My poetic analysis has developed along the same lines: Starkaðr has strong poetic connections with both Suibhne and Śiśupāla, who in turn are fairly dissimilar to each other. The Germanic hero is closest to Suibhne: both are famous poets, both are wanderers, and express it in their poetry, both are wolflike, both are uncouth in appearance, both receive a divine poetic consecration, both are champion warriors, and generals for kings.

Yet the Starkaðr–Śiśupāla connection is more close than one would expect, considering that Śiśupāla has no reputation as a poet. Both are violent abusive verbalists, masters of invective; they both attack enemies of kingship, those of lower caste, in their invective; their poetic madness expresses their rage and causes violence. Both are generals for kings.

The Suibhne–Śiśupāla axis is not strong. Their strongest common trait is their dominantly demonic nature, and this may derive from the hostile sectarian environment in which their stories have been preserved. However, they were both generals for kings, underkings themselves.

Heracles does not link strongly with anyone, though he was a general (of sorts), warrior (of sorts), and a poet (of sorts). He was also a wanderer, and a savior figure, as was Starkaðr. He also had a persecuting/protective deity, Hera.

Thus we have, perhaps, an archetype, a poet-warrior given to violent rages and violent poetry, in some ways a liminal manticist, a general of kings and a supporter of kingship in poetry and life. A weary, lonesome wanderer; inspired by a god in poetry and life, and persecuted by another god (who, however, helps civilize him); a noble warrior figure who yet commits execrable crimes against the range of society, especially against the king he so fanati-

---

[120] 1987:251.

cally supports, and who is finally killed by the god who inspired his poetry and civilized him. He delivers a final dramatic speech before death.

There are significant parallels here to our theme of legendary Greek poet as scapegoat and warrior, protected and persecuted by ambiguously malevolent/benevolent gods. This similarity is strengthened by the fact that Starkaðr and Suibhne are famous poets in their own right, and that Starkaðr and Śiśupāla are masters of violent invective, Śiśupāla even employing a blame-oriented animal fable in a last speech. All of these "poets," incidentally, are outcasts, all examples of the poet as exile or scapegoat, each in his own unique way.

The Warrior-Poet

We may briefly probe some of the implications of the warrior-poet that have been examined. First, why is this odd warrior figure, always latently demonic, always grotesque and violent, also such a pronounced poet? Conversely stated, why is the poet associated so strongly with the most violent level of society?[121]

The central figure, Starkaðr, perhaps supplies the clearest answer to the question, for his story gives us a striking picture of a hero driven by aggressive impulses. This aggression finds expression in violent speech and violent acts; often the violent speech prepares the way for physical violence.[122] Thus, in a society in which war was a dominant aspect of existence, poetry had to serve a precise functional purpose: military paraenesis—or rather, the paraenesis of violence. And as violence was dependent on a special kind of war madness, so poetry also was dependent on madness (of course, the word "mantic" is related to "mania").

The ambiguities of warrior and poet are also related—just as society often cannot tolerate the violence of the warrior in times of peace (thus the conflict of the warrior with the farmer and pastoralist, even with the king), so it is hard to tolerate the violence of the blame poet. As the Irish myths show, it is most useful to have satirical poets in wartime; but if a king's poets turn their verbal weapons against him, the poet cannot be tolerated. Either the king must abdicate, or the poet must be exiled or killed.

[121] For other warrior heroes who were also poets, such as the skald Egil, Gunnlaugr Serpent-Tongue, or Finn, see Miller 2000:232–238, 251–254. Some skalds were anti-monarchical, 235, 252–253, though one could argue that abuse of a bad king supports the insitution of just monarchy.

[122] For the combination of verbal and physical attack in epic, see Miller 2000:234–236.

One wonders if poetry is characteristically linked with the second function, considering its strong associations with the archetypal Indo-European warrior. One might suggest that the blame poet, the Archilochus, the wielder of verbal weapons, is peculiarly suited to war, while the praise poet, the Pindar, might be applicable to other levels, aspects of society. However, as we have previously noted, there probably is no such thing as a pure praise or blame poet. Archilochus can write military paraenesis and love poetry; Sappho can write iambics.

Starkaðr mixes venomous blame of the slothful, vice-burdened king with praise of good kings, good kingship. A good deal of the warrior's poetry is devoted to kingship; thus it plays a part in the intricate interplay between the classes of society. In the same way, in Dumézil's studies of praise and blame in Rome and Ireland, poetry seems to emanate from the third function, the farmers and herdsmen, but is directed toward controlling the quality of kingship. If the land is unfruitful, the king must be blamed. The poet here represents the populous lower classes, a first tool of democracy, as it were. The poet, as prophet and priest, can also be associated with the first function, the class of magico-religious sovereignty. There is a small, but interesting, dossier of kings who are also poets. The persistent association of Odin with poetry is worth noting, for he is somewhat of a first-function figure, though with warlike leanings.[123]

Finally there is the question of how the study of Starkaðr, Suibhne, and the others sheds light on our original question, why the poet is seen as a *pharmakos*. One avenue of approach to the subject is the tendency for these warrior-poet heroes to act as champions in battle—sometimes generals for overkings, but sometimes literally substitutes for the king in dangerous battle—thus, *therapōn*, servant, the ritual substitute for the king. Perhaps the king was originally the best warrior—an extension of the strongest man of the tribe, the leader of the pack, as it were. Anthony Snodgrass writes: "The kings of Sparta were called not only 'kings', but also by the old title 'war-lord' or 'commander' (*archagetas*) . . . The original and most important raison d'être of Greek kingship had been for the king to lead the tribe and (where he survived

---

[123] See Dumézil 1973:32–37. As Puhvel notes, Odin "does not 'embody' martial ecstasy, he dispenses it . . . an orchestrator of conflict rather than a combatant" (1987:193). Thus we have the warrior Starkaðr influencing kings, and the king of gods and men influencing the warrior class. The king's control of the warrior is a crucial element of his power, as Latin American politics, with its democratic governments often overthrown by military strong men, still shows. One thinks of Agamemnon, the Greek overking, stalking the Greek battle lines in the *Iliad*, dispensing military praise and blame to ensure optimum fighting efficiency, see above, ch. 17, Lugh exhorting his troops. For kings as poets, see below, ch. 19, Odin as king and poet.

in existence long enough) the state in warfare."[124] There is also evidence that the archaic Indo-European king (Latin *rēx*, Sanskrit *rājā*, Irish *rī*, *rīg* [genitive]) originally came from the warrior class (as Indra, the warrior, became king of the gods), and the "best warrior" became king—originally in times of crisis, such as invasions. Later the "best warrior" became the permanent leader. Even later, the king became more associated with ruling and priestly functions, with war only one of his responsibilities.[125]

Eventually the warrior, the specialist in violence, became the king's substitute. The warrior would have to have almost a supernatural loyalty to the king; but, if he had any intelligence, he would always feel ambivalent about his role, as he had to undergo the danger of violent death on another's behalf.

This suggests Burkert's scenario for the scapegoat, though not exactly. Burkert envisions a herd of animals dogged by predators, who are forced to exclude one of their weakest, youngest, or lamest members so they can survive.[126] A war is a threatening disaster like plague, and Burkert gives numerous example of scapegoats given up in times of war. Soldiers sent out to battle are, as it were, scapegoats sent to die to uphold society, to defend the king. They do have a tendency to be young; but they also have a tendency to be strong, unlike Burkert's scapegoats. Society and the king are sending out the best, the strongest to face the threatening predators.

One remembers the role played by Aesop when Croesus besieges Samos. He is the best in the city, but when the Croesus threatens the destruction of the city unless they give up Aesop, they are first willing to sacrifice him, then they they become unwilling; but Aesop voluntarily goes, and persuades the king to spare the city. Thus a city threatened by the disaster of war seeks to give up their best citizen, not their worst. There is ample ambiguity here, though, as anyone considered expendable can also be considered the worst in society's eyes. Aesop the best riddle warrior is also the worst in terms of physical ugliness.

In addition, the best warrior might also be the most skillful in weaponry, and even the shrewdest, trickiest fighter. There is evidence in the following cognates that the Indo-European ruler was related to the intelligent, skilled craftsman: Latin *faber* 'adept'; Old Church Slavic *dobrŭ* '*agathos*'; Armenian *darbin* 'smith'; Hittite *tabarna*- < **dhobhro-no*- 'ruler'. The PIE word is perhaps **dhabhronos*.[127] Some have posited a second type of warrior, the trickster, the

---

[124] Snodgrass 1980:98, 97.

[125] See Winn 1995:130–131; Puhvel 1987:242–243; Dillon 1946–1947:260.

[126] 1979:71.

[127] Eichner 1975:81; Puhvel 1989:360. For the poet as craftsman in the archaic Greek and Indo-

intellectual, as a contrast to the warror given to violent furies, Odysseus as opposed to Achilles.[128]

This pattern—sending out the warrior, strongest, most possessed, cleverest, to face the enemy—would explain the warrior as scapegoat, ritual substitute. The poet, then, could be selected because, as we have seen, the aggression and madness of the blame poet is related to the aggression and madness of the warrior in archaic cultures. The verbal weaponry is parallel to the physical weaponry. The warrior must be a specialist in the madness that makes him invincible in battle; this exaltation is linked with poetry; in fact, is often produced by it.[129] Thus the poet is a crucial figure, as is the warrior; in fact, he often is the warrior. In the case of Aesop, as in that of Starkaðr, the poet-warrior is a key stakes in the games of society and the gods.

European traditions, see Nagy 1979:297–300; Durante 1971–1974 II:170. Thus Odysseus *polutropos*, as storyteller/creative artist/poet, shrewd, tricky warrior, and ruler has special interest. For smiths in epic legend, Miller 2000:260–266.

[128] Dumézil 1968:50 examines a pattern in which there are complementary pairs of warriors, one more violent than the other: Slugger and Runner (Wind), Force and Quickness. See also Miller 2000:280–281.

[129] See above, ch. 11 (Tyrtaeus's poetry creates "divine fury" [*enthousiasmos*] in young Spartan soldiers approaching war); ch. 17, on Dubthach Chafertongue.

19

The Sacrificed Poet: Germanic Myths

A S WAS PREVIOUSLY SHOWN, Starkaðr is the Odinic hero par excellence; he is given his poetic consecration by Odin, as well as his martial consecration; he is killed by an Odinic god. Odin, like Starkaðr, is closely associated both with war[1] and with poetry.[2] A number of myths cluster around the theme of Odin as poet, consecration myths showing how the god received his poetic wisdom, and the theme of the sacrificed poet is found in these myths (though sometimes the sacrifice is only partial). Thus a brief look at the poetic Odin and his consecrations will be valuable. Odin is a complex god; for the Dumézilian, he has associations in the first and second functions, possibly due to functional slippage; he is both the beneficent ruling father god and a maleficent Rudraic god (and here we might have first and second function duality again, for Rudra can be located in the dark aspect of the warrior caste).[3] It would be impossible to solve these problems or simplify Odin in this short chapter, but both aspects of Odin's persona, dark and light, will be examined here.

The *Ynglingasaga* tells us, of Odin:

Mælti hann alt hendingum svá sem nú er þat kveðit, er skáldskapr heitir. Hann ok hofgoðar hans heita ljóðasmiðir, þvíat sú íþrótt hófsk af þeim í Norðrlöndum. Óðinn kunni svá gera, at í orrostu urðu óvinir hans blindir eða daufir eða óttafullir, en vápn þeira bitu eigi heldr en vendir, en hans menn fóru brynjulausir ok váru galnir sem hundar eða vargar, bitu í skjöldu sína, váru sterkir sem birnir eða griðungar. Þeir drápu mannfólkit en hvártki eldr né járn orti á þá. Það er kallaðr berserksgangr.

---

[1] See Turville-Petre 1964:50; Dumézil 1973a:29; Kershaw 2000 passim; Miller 2000:313 (the death of warriors on the battlefield is a sacrifice to Odin).

[2] See Turville-Petre 1964:35–41; Dumézil 1973a:29; Kershaw 2000:77.

[3] See Dumézil 1983:87, with bibliography; Puhvel 1987:200.

All he spoke was in rimes, as is now the case in what is called skald-ship. He and his temple priests are called songsmiths, because that art began with them in the northern lands.[4] Óthin was able to cause his enemies to be blind or deaf or fearful in battle, and he could cause their swords to cut no better than wands. His own men went to battle without coats of mail and acted like mad dogs or wolves. They bit their shields and were strong as bears or bulls. They killed people, and neither fire nor iron affected them. This is called berserker rage.

Ynglingasaga ch. 6[5]

This collocation of skaldship and war madness is no accident; war madness and poetic madness are closely related, as we have seen in the case of Starkaðr (and Tyrtaeus). Thus Odin was pictured as actually singing damaging song-spells against opposing military forces, and protecting his own troops by runes. In the *Hávamál*, he uses rune magic for the following ends: stanza 148: he dulls the swords of his foes; stanza 150: he stays their spears; stanzas 156, 158: he protects his friends in battle; stanza 160: he brings victory.[6] One expects that his songs also caused berserker rage among his troops.[7]

Odin's mastery of magic is connected with his gift for poetry. After a description of Odin's many sources of occult knowledge (Mímir's head, hanged men, ravens), the *Ynglingasaga* tells us that "By these means he became very wise in his lore. And all these skills he taught with those runes and songs which are called magic songs [charms]. For this reason the Aesir are called Workers of Magic."[8] He used words to control the forces of nature, fire, wind, the sea, and guardians of buried treasure.[9]

---

[4] An explicit attestation of the theme of poet as priest; see above, ch. 17, final paragraph; ch. 18, Starkaðr's death.

[5] Trans. from Dumézil 1973a:28.

[6] Cf. De Vries 1956 2:73; see above, ch. 17, on poetic possession and war fury. In the *Iliad*, Apollo "bewitched" (*ethelxe*) the Greeks' hearts in their breasts as they are routed (XV 321–322); cf. Janko 1992 *ad loc.*

[7] For discussions of Odin's connections with the berserker phenomenon, see De Vries 1956 2:97; Puhvel 1987:196. Puhvel mentions the term for an outlaw berserker type, *vargr í véum* 'temple robber', but literally 'wolf in sanctuary'. Clandestine murder was called *morðvargr*, lit. 'murder wolf', *Grágás*, an old Icelandic law code, 1.23. We are reminded of Aesop as temple robber, Alcaeus and Suibhne in the wolf thickets (ch. 9; ch. 18); cf. Gerstein 1972; Kershaw 2000:42–67. See ch. 17 above, on the *furor heroicus* of Cuchulainn.

[8] *Ynglingasaga* ch. 7; trans. from Dumézil 1973a:28. *Af þessum hlutum varð hann stórliga fróðr. Allar þessar íþróttir kendi hann með rúnum ok ljóðum þeim, er galdrar heita. Fyrir því eru Æsir kallaðir galdrasmiðir.*

[9] *Ynglingasaga* ch. 7.

Odin's skill with poetry and war is linked to the fact that he is a specialist in madness—and poetry was seen as a form of ecstatic intoxication, as we shall see. His name, etymologically linked with the Latin *uātēs* 'prophet, poet', as well as with the Irish *fáith* 'prophet', means 'rage, fury, possessed'. Old Norse *Óðinn* is from Proto-Germanic **Wōðanaz*, in turn from **Wātónos* and the adjective **wātós*; related words are Old Norse *óðr*, German *Wut* 'rage, possession, fury'; Gothic *wōths*, 'possessed'. Wodan is glossed by Adam of Bremen as *furor*, '[martial] madness'. Though Adam explicitly refers to the furor as military, a cognate word in English shows that Odin's madness also has a poetic application: Old English *wōð* 'chant'—presumably, madness-induced or madness-inducing song.[10] It is curious that a god should be "possessed" (by a higher god?), a "prophet" as it were. Apollo is prophet of Zeus,[11] but there a lesser god broadcasts the will of a higher god, while Odin heads his own pantheon.

Thus Odin, the war god, the magician, the poet, is "consecrated" with poetic wisdom. There are numerous attestations of this theme in Odinic mythology, all of them involving poetic sacrifice. The simplest of them is the story of Mímir's well. Mímir had a well under a root of Yggdrasil, the world tree.[12] Mímir is a wisdom figure because he drinks from this well.[13] Odin went there and asked for a drink of the well, but was refused unless he left an eye as a pledge. The *Völuspá* shows that the springwater is seen as mead:

> alt veit ek, Óðinn!
> hvar þú auga falt:
> í inum mœra
> Mímis brunni;
> drekkr mjöð Mímir
> morgin hverjan
> af veði Valföðrs
> Vituð ér enn eða hvat?

> Well know I, Ygg [Odin],   where thy eye is hidden:

---

[10] See Puhvel 1987:193; Dumézil 1973a:36–37; Chadwick 1952; Chadwick and Chadwick 1932 1:620; Haugen 1983:6; Watkins 1995:117–118. On Adam of Bremen, De Vries 1956 2:94n1. Cf. shamanic ecstasy, induced by song or dance, below, this chapter; also ch. 3 (Archilochus); ch. 16 (Greek shamanism and poetry).

[11] See *Hymn to Apollo* 132; Jebb 1912:24; Burkert 1985:148.

[12] Mímir = 'memory', see Fleck 1971:393; Dumézil 1959a:228n101a; Haugen 1983:13. Cf. the Muses' connection with Mnemosyne 'memory', their mother, Hesiod *Theogony* 53–54, 915–917; *Homeric Hymn to Hermes*, 429–430; Detienne 1996:41–42; ch. 2 (Aesop and the statue of Mnemosyne).

[13] *Gylfaginning* 15, in *Prose Edda*, Young 1973:43. *hann er fullr af vísindum, fyrir því at hann drekkr ór brunninum.* Text in Lorenz 1984; Jónsson 1954.

> in the wondrous well of Mímir;
> each morn Mímir his mead doth drink
> out of Fjolnir's [Odin's] pledge: know ye further, or how?

Völuspá 28[14]

Thus, poetic knowledge can come only at a price, the sacrifice of an eye, dismemberment. The theme of poetic knowledge as intoxication and madness is also here, for the water is mead.[15]

In addition, we have the story, referred to in the previous chapter, of Odin hanging for nine days, "wounded with a spear," apparently dead, as a result of which he receives magical and poetic wisdom, learning "nine mighty songs from the famous son of Bölthórn, father of Bestla,[16] and drinking "precious mead."[17] Verse leads to verse, poem to poem. Thus, according to the interpretation discussed earlier, Odin gains his poetic knowledge by dying, visiting the world of the dead, and then returning to life.[18] Our main theme, the death of the poet, is here again. It is the death, the ultimate marginalization, of the god that brings about his mastery of poetic knowledge. A related consecration theme has Odin receive his knowledge from dead men—thus he is *hangaguð* 'god of the hanged men'.[19] Even though Odin gets wisdom from his hanging, this is still linked with his drinking mead—poetry again is intoxication, madness.

---

[14] Trans. from Hollander 1962:6. For the equation of eye with spring in Indo-European and Semitic lexicography, see Puhvel 1987:194n1; cf. Fleck 1971:399n199.

[15] For one-eyed figures in Indo-European myth, see Dumézil 1974. The Greek Muses are also associated with springs, Hesiod *Theogony* 1–4. The idea might be prophetic powers given by drinking water from sacred springs. See above, ch. 16, the Muses and the Castalian spring.

[16] This seems to be a reference to an Odinic consecration we know little about, in which he receives knowledge from a giant. Cf. the *Lay of Vafthrudnir*, in which Odin engages in a wisdom contest with the giant, "The Mighty in Riddles." Haugen discusses the theme of Odin's receiving knowledge from a Sibyl (1983:13). Clearly, the source of Odin's poetic, numinous knowledge was an obsessive theme in Germanic myth.

[17] See chapter 18, Starkathr's execution of Vikar compared to Odin's death/consecration. Also, van Hamel 1932, for Irish parallels; Fleck 1971. For interpretation, see Turville-Petre 1964:323: Pipping sees shamanism here; Ström emphasizes the theme of wisdom from world of death. Fleck (1981) opposes a shamanic interpretation, arguing that one must judge shamanism against a complete shamanic complex, and that the whole complex is not present in Odin mythology, cf. Haugen 1983:20. However, there are important shamanic themes that are recognizable even outside of the totality of the shamanic complex, and one need not find the whole dossier before one can use the word "shamanic." Cf. Buchholz 1971:19; H. Chadwick 1899.

[18] Another main avenue of interpretation is that the hanging was an initiation (cf. Turville-Petre 1964:50n50); but Turville-Petre notes that symbolic death was always an aspect of initiation, so the two interpretations are not exclusive. A major article by Fleck interprets Odin's hanging as the inverted hanging given to sacrificial victims who are to be drained of their blood (1971:126).

[19] See *Hávamál* st. 157; Hollander 1962:39n89; Turville-Petre 1964:43. Cf. Fleck 1971:130n61.

In an important interpretation, Jere Fleck correlates the Mímir's well consecration, and the Kvasir consecration, still to be discussed, to the hanging. He sees it as Odin's accession to fatherhood of his pantheon, sacred kingship, and outlines its trifunctional character. To become the sacred king, the god must take responsibility for all three functions. The second function (war) is represented by secular kingship—a statement that Fleck does not adequately document, though we have mentioned the significance of the possible origination of secular kingship in the warrior class. The third function is represented by sexual imagery in the hanging scene—the phallic Yggdrasil between male heaven and female earth; Odin's blood from his wound drops as *sperma* to fill Mímir's well and fertilize the earth below. This is a *hieros gamos* that brings about Odin's ritual rebirth, and has relations to cyclic cosmogony.[20]

Fleck's theory is strongest in his correlation of the different consecrations, which are obviously but enigmatically related; but it is weakest in his assignment of aspects of Odin's hanging to a Dumézilian framework. Secular kingship is still more closely connected to the first function than to the second, and the phallic interpretations seem strained. However, the triple-death theme discussed in chapter 18 might fit neatly into Fleck's theory; the wound from a weapon (spear, perhaps) is a more convincing tie to the second function; the well, which Fleck ties closely to the hanging scene, is unproblematically related to the third function.

The next consecration, Odin between the fires in the *Grímnismál*, is quite similar to the hanging story; in fact it is parallel, as Fleck notes.[21] After a heavenly quarrel, in which Odin's wife, Frigg, accuses a favorite of Odin, Geirröd, king of the Goths, of torturing his guests out of stinginess, Odin resolves to travel incognito to Geirröd and vindicate him. He arrives at the king's court in a dark mantle, calling himself "The Masked One," Grimnir. Geirröd has been made wary by a messenger from Frigg, who has told him that a magician is coming to bewitch him. When Odin refuses to state his business, the suspicious Geirröd tortures the god, placing him between two fires for eight nights. Agnar, Geirröd's youngest son, is the only one who takes pity on the guest; offering him drink, he criticizes his father for letting this wanderer be tormented without cause. The torture of the fire heats Odin into knowledge and he sings the metrical contents of the *Grímnismál*. He describes the mansions of the gods, the world tree, and ends with a list of his names, including this stanza:

---

[20] Fleck 1971:400–403. Cf. Talley 1974.
[21] Fleck 1981:61.

Saðr ok Svipall
ok Sanngetall,
Herteitr ok Hnikarr,
Bileygr, Báleygr,
Bölverkr, Fjölnir,
Grímr ok Grímnir,
Glapsviðr ok Fjölsviðr;

Truthful, Changeable, Truth-getter,
Battle-happy, Overthrower,
Death-worker, Many-shaped, One-Eyed, Fire-eyed,
Lore-master, Masked, and Deceitful.

Grímnismál stanza 47[22]

The ambiguity of Odin as poet—both truthful and deceitful—reminds one of Hesiod's Muses. And this is a double consecration scene: Odin has received knowledge as a result of his fiery suspension, and begins to pass it on as soon as Agnar befriends him. As he finishes his song, he unveils his chief name to Geirröð and prophesies the king's death. The ruler draws his sword to loose the divinity but falls on it accidentally, and Agnar succeeds to the kingship. According to Fleck's interpretation, Odin's transferral of "numinous knowledge" to the youngest son has fitted him for his regal calling.[23] Thus a poetic consecration of a god leads to a royal consecration of his king—a remarkable, and rare, attestation of the theme of king as poet-prophet. Here again Odin is hanged, tortured, and fasts for eight days; at the end of which time he receives poetic knowledge. The heating motif has led commentators to see parallels in the Indian *tapas*,[24] where we also find the pattern: asceticism, hanging, heat, numinous knowledge, throne. For our purposes, the important theme of Odin's near death or death, partial sacrifice, followed by reception of poetic knowledge, is here. But equally intriguing is the theme of the stingy host receiving the wandering poet-guest; far from treating the poet hospitably, he tortures him, and pays the price for his misdeed. His youngest son is defined as good by his hospitality to and pity for the guest (and his pity and hospitality show that Geirröð is to be blamed, even though Frigg has compounded the difficulty of his test by making him suspicious). Combined with the hospitality motif is the story of the disguised god testing the mortal, and the theme of regal succession.

---

[22] Trans. Haugen 1983:12.
[23] Fleck 1970; cf. Haugen 1983:9–10.
[24] See Fleck 1971:131–136, with further bibliography.

Our next consecration story, the myth of Kvasir, is the classic mead-poetry myth in the literature, and a central Germanic and Indo-European myth also, one of the key myths reflecting the ideological assimilation of the third function (here the Vanir, whom Dumézil associates with the third function) into the trifunctional societal totality (here represented by the Aesir, whom Dumézil associates with the sovereignty and warrior functions).[25]

> Ok enn mælti Ægir: "Hvaðan af hefir hafizt sú íþrótt, er þér kallið skáldskap?"
>
> Bragi svarar: "Þat váru upphöf til þess, at goðin höfðu ósætt við þat fólk, er Vanir heita. En þeir lögðu með sér friðstefnu ok settu grið á þá lund, at þeir gengu hvárirtveggju til eins kers ok spýttu í hráka sínum. En at skilnaði þá tóku goðin ok vildu eigi láta týnast þat griðamark ok sköpuðu þar ór mann. Sá heitir Kvasir. Hann er svá vitr, at engi spyrr hann þeira hluta, er eigi kann hann órlausn. Hann fór víða um heim at kenna mönnum frœði . . .

Aegir asked again: "Where did the accomplishment known as poetry come from?"

Bragi answered: The beginning of it was the gods were at war with the people known as the Vanir and they arranged for a peace-meeting between them and made a truce in this way: they both went up to a crock and spat into it. When they were going away, the gods took the truce token and would not allow it to be lost, and made of it a man. He was called Kvasir. He is so wise that nobody asks him any question he is unable to answer. He travelled far and wide over the world to teach men wisdom . . .

Skáldskaparmál ch. 5, in *Prose Edda*[26]

Kvasir, the embodiment of poetry, is accordingly "an onomastic personification of an intoxicating drink, which recalls the *kvas* of the Slavs,"[27] a drink made of squashed vegetables, fermented by spittle. As Dumézil notes, "we are here dealing with a ceremonial or communal drink, sanctioning the agreement between two social groups," thus requiring "the spittle of all concerned." Apparently there is a communal feast involved.[28]

---

[25] See Van Hamel 1934; further bibliography in Turville-Petre 1964:323.

[26] See Young 1954:100.

[27] Dumézil 1973a:21; De Vries 1956 2:67–72. Cf. also Norwegian *kvase*, Danish *kvase*, English *quash*; Turville-Petre 1964:40n36.

[28] Cf. Benveniste for the German guilds, *conuiuia*, which are "a means of reconciliation (1973:60–61). Once the crime is over and paid for, an alliance becomes established and we return to the

Thus poetry is the sign ("token") of the assimilation of the third function to the first two.[29] He is a micro-being for the mechanism of unified society: he contains the spit of every god. The poet, perhaps because he is the medium for communication, the medium of intrafunctional exchange and understanding, can be thus the representative of the unified society.

This intoxication-man of reconciliation, the token of all society, is understandably omniscient; he travels throughout the world acting as a culture hero for men and is also something of a riddle master: "nobody asks him any question he is unable to answer."

But in his travels he runs afoul of two murderous dwarves, Fjalar and Galar, after accepting an invitation to feast with them. "These called him aside for a word in private and killed him . . ."[30] Thus we have once again the guest-friend situation, the defiled feast, the murder by trickery. Androgeos, Aesop, and Hesiod were thus killed by their hosts, by trickery, far from home. This situation is clearly elemental to the Indo-European mind, expressive of profound evil.

Most important for our central theme is the central datum: the poetry man must be killed. Only his death will unleash the power of intoxicating inspiration, possession, and knowledge. The poet is the emblem of unified society; only the poet's death can infuse inspiration, wisdom, and poetry into the group. Though the death is a temporary setback to the furtherance of poetic knowledge, it will in the end only serve to disseminate it more widely.

The dwarves let Kvasir's blood run into three vessels; they then mix honey into it, "and it became the mead which makes whoever drinks of it a poet or scholar" (*ok varð þar af mjöðr sá, er hverr, er af drekkr, verðr skáld eða fræðamaðr*). Thus poetry was called "the blood of Kvasir" (*Kvasis dreyri*) in skaldic poetry.[31] When one drinks the mead of inspiration, one drinks the death of Kvasir, as it were. The creative processes—sacral, prophetic possession—are dependent on a primeval sacrifice.[32]

---

notion of the guild." Benveniste notes that a "sacred banquet" is at the very center of the notion of the guild. Thus Kvasir represents the sacral feast of reconciliation, not just a simple intoxicant.

[29] And in a variant text in the *Ynglingasaga* (4, see Dumézil 1973a:9), Kvasir is explicitly a member of the Vanir, a third-function figure, but he is introduced into the two higher functions as a hostage, thus becoming a member of the Aesir. We find him acting as one of the Aesir in an episode in the *Prose Edda*, Young 1954:85, where he is even called the wisest of all the Aesir. Thus Kvasir is a member of both the Vanir and Aesir, the mediator between the two.

[30] *ok þá er hann kom at heimboði til nökkurra, Fjalars ok Galars, þá kölluðu þeir hann með sér á einmæli ok drápu hann . . .*

[31] See Turville-Petre 1964:39.

[32] Fleck shows the actual ritual realities behind this motif, for Germanic hanged victims were bled, and the blood retained in containers, 1971:127n45.

The dwarves, as they continue to pursue their murderous inclinations, drown a giant, Gilling, and when they are threatened by the giant's son, Suttung, they offer the mead as *weregild*, ransom, which brings about a reconciliation. Even after his death, Kvasir is acting as a mediating, conciliating force. Odin later sleeps with Suttung's daughter, the guardian of the mead, drinks the three crocks of poetry-mead, and escapes from Suttung's house in the form of an eagle. Suttung also transforms into an eagle shape and pursues Odin, but the god reaches Asgard and regurgitates the mead into crocks (though letting some spill to the ground before he reaches his destination); hereafter it has been drunk by the Aesir and by poets.

Overarching this story is the theme of poetic inspiration as intoxication, which we have seen especially in Irish myth, but also in Greece. Odin is the first to drink the mead; he then dispenses it, acting as the prophet of Kvasir, as it were. He shares the ecstatic wisdom of the sacrificed, reconciled unity of the functions to gods and poets. This ecstatic drunkenness is of course quite different from modern, secularized drunkenness: "In Scandinavia the ecstatic states produced by alcohol and poetry are holy, taking their place in ritual and even bringing men into communion with the gods," writes Turville-Petre.[33]

A parallel myth from India provides an enlightening contrast. The general body of gods, headed by Indra (the story reflects Epic, not Vedic, theology) refuses to allow the Nasatya twins (classic third function gods) access to the Soma sacrifice, as the twins are not proper gods. The situation escalates into open conflict. The Nasatya have an ascetic ally who creates for them a monster, "Drunkenness" (Mada), who threatens to destroy the world. The gods cannot conquer such a monster, and they allow the Nasatya to enter their company. The ascetic, aided by the gods, cuts up "Drunkenness" into four pieces: drink, women, gambling, and hunting.[34]

---

[33] Turville-Petre 1964:40n38, see further bibliography listed there. Also, Eliade 1964:221, for shamanic intoxication through mushrooms. Donald Ward suggests that there may be ancient connotations in the fact that grain alcohol is referred to as *spiritus*. However, cf. ecstatic techniques in which the supernatural being "whispers in the ear" of the shaman, "in the same way in which 'birds' inspire the epic bards." "Magico-religious music" and dancing induce the trance. Mushroom intoxication, by comparison, appears to be "late and derivative . . . a mechanical and corrupt method of reproducing 'ecstasy,'" Eliade 1964:222–223, see also 416, 477, 493. Perhaps drunkenness is only a metaphor for poetic/prophetic possession. Gabriel Garcia Marquez, in the Paris Review interviews, tells of being constantly asked if he wrote *A Hundred Years of Solitude* on hallucinogens, but responds that such questioners know nothing of the creative process, which requires full, unimpaired concentration and good health (Plimpton 1984:329).

[34] *Mahābhārata* 3(33)123–125; van Buitenen 1973 2:460–462.

The correspondences with the Scandinavian myth are clear, and nothing substantial needs to be added to Dumézil's analysis.[35] There is a war of classes, first and second versus the third. Intoxication, given concrete, bodily form, is associated with the unification. After the reconciliation, intoxication is killed, divided into discrete parts, and its influence continues among men and gods. For our purposes, we note that there is no mention of poetry here. In fact, as Dumézil notes, the Indic intoxication is negative—used as a weapon against the main gods, it threatens to destroy the world; its four dismembered parts are negative influences—enticing, but habit-forming, destructive. However, if we can associate the Indic intoxication with poetry through comparative analysis, the myth may point up the destructive possibilities of the art; certainly the two myths together point up the ambiguity of intoxication. The Indic intoxication has a strong martial orientation; we see the third function using drunkenness as a weapon in war. In Scandinavia, though, intoxication is poetry, magic, wisdom, and power (Kvasir is wisest of the Aesir).

However, positive aspects of Indic intoxication can be found in the phenomenon of Soma and myths associated with it. "Soma is said to stimulate the voice, and to be the leader of poets. Those who drink it become immortal and know the gods."[36] We should remember that allowing Nasatya to partake of the Soma sacrifice is the goal of the whole Mada myth. In one myth, Indra, assisted by an eagle (or falcon), or in the form of an eagle, steals soma/ambrosia, prized because it gives immortality, from demonic guardians. Thus, this aspect of the Kvasir story, the positive, magical side of drunkenness, guarded by demonic creatures and stolen from them, has an Indic parallel.[37]

A final Odin-consecration theme is found in the *Ynglingasaga* variant tradition of the war of Aesir and Vanir.[38] The two sides send hostages to each other; the Vanir send Kvasir, "the cleverest among them," to the Aesir. There is no mention of a subsequent death. (And the *Prose Edda* has him, still alive, acting as the wisest of the Vanir in the myth of vengeance taken upon Loki.)

However, the theme of poetic knowledge through sacrificial dismemberment surfaces in the other side of the story, the hostages sent from the Aesir to the Vanir: Hoenir, a large, handsome chieftainlike "man," and Mímir, a wisdom figure. Hoenir is described; then "together with him the Aesir sent one called

---

[35] Dumézil 1973a:22–25.

[36] Turville-Petre 1964:41. See O'Flaherty 1981:119–138.

[37] *Rig Veda* 4.26–27, in O'Flaherty 1981:128–131; *Kāṭhaka Saṃhitā* 37.14a; in O'Flaherty 1975:280–281, further references on p. 337. See discussion of the soma (*amṛta*) / poetic mead parallels in Fleck 1971:404–405.

[38] *Ynglingasaga* 4; trans. in Dumézil 1973a:8–10.

Mímir, a very wise man; and the Vanir in return sent the one who was the cleverest among them. His name was Kvasir."[39] This may be an exchange of poets. It is certainly an exchange of the wisest, it seems, and wisdom usually equates with poetry in these stories, as the omniscience of Kvasir shows.

The Vanir, feeling cheated in the exchange (as Hoenir is quite dense, receiving guidance from Mímir as to what he should say), behead Mímir and send the head back to the Aesir. Odin, however, preserves the head with herbs and brings it to life with charms, "giving it magic power so that it would answer him and tell him many occult things."[40] Thus Mímir, a wisdom figure (and we have seen such figures are poets or sources of poetry), is a hostage, a guest, and is killed treacherously by those who have promised his safety. Dismembered, his head ends up in Odin's possession and supplies him with knowledge (= poetry). Again, the poet effects reconciliation between the functions; his death brings about poetic knowledge.[41]

Another example of the theme of torture of the poet is found in the expulsion, imprisonment, and torture of a satirist, the god Loki, recounted in the *Lokasenna*.[42] Loki's nature is extremely problematic—sometimes he can have a sympathetic trickster side, but he is usually demonic.[43] Here Loki is the satirist, but the dark satirist, a creature of evil; his very malevolence causes him to tell the truth unsparingly. This evil satire is the first of many parallels with Irish poets in this story.

The scene is a feast;[44] all the gods (with the exception of Thor) are gathered in the hall of Aegir. They admire their host's servants, so Loki kills one of them, seemingly because he simply resents the idea of praise. The gods,

---

[39] *Með honum sendu Æsir þann, er Mímir hét, inn vitrasti maðr, en Vanir fengu þar í mót þann, er spakastr var í þeira flokki. Sá hét Kvasir.*

[40] *Þá tóku þeir Mími ok hálshjoggu ok sendu höfuðit Ásum. Óðinn tók höfuðit ok smurði urtum þeim, er eigi mátti fúna, ok kvað þar yfir galdra ok magnaði svá, at þat mælti við hann ok sagði honum marga leynda hluti.* The *Poetic Edda* has two other references to the wisdom of Mímir's head, *Völuspá*, st. 45, and *Sigrdrífumál*, st. 16. For the mantic severed head in Greece and Ireland, see above, ch. 16 (Orpheus).

[41] Cf. Dumézil 1959a:224–230, on the relationship of Mímir and Hoenir; Dumézil 1948:111–121.

[42] However, some (notably Ström) have interpreted Loki as an Odinic hypostasis, see Turville-Petre 1964:324. For interpretation of the *Lokasenna*, see Dumézil 1959a:112–113. Ström and others interpret the poem as a late, Christian attack on the heathen gods; Dumézil argues that a consistent element of heathen myth is a tolerant view of the gods' "human" failings.

[43] "More ink has been spilt on Loki than on any other figure in Norse myth. This, in itself, is enough to show how little scholars agree, and how far we are from understanding him," writes Turville-Petre (1964:324), who summarizes interpretation of the figure. As Loki shows, the trickster figure and the demonic figure are not mutually exclusive.

[44] Cf. Haugen 1983:16–18, 23n18 for the feast of the gods as an Indo-European motif. See also Dumézil's first book, *Le festin d'Immortalité*, 1924:11–15, 51–60.

outraged, drive the murderer from the feast, into the woods. This is the first expulsion, in which Loki is expelled not as a poet, but simply as a murderer.

Loki returns, but before entering the feast, he tells Aegir's other servant: "brawls and bickering I bring the gods, their ale I shall mix with evil."[45] Thus the poet, as in Ireland, causes strife. Entering the feast hall, Loki asks for a place at the banquet table. Though Bragi denies him, Odin relents, fearing Loki's lewd words. He orders Vithar to rise so "the Father of the Wolf" (*úlfs föður*) may take his seat. The slanderous god joins the feast. Bragi offers Loki a sword, horse, and arm ring if he will not satirize him,[46] and then adds a threat. Loki, unfazed, describes Bragi's cowardice in battle.

There follows a long dialogue in which Loki slanders all of the gods in turn, to their bitter chagrin; his satire is divided between martial and sexual blame. The gods are womanish; the goddesses are promiscuous; most practice perversions and incest; scatological references are frequent. Loki boasts of his adulterous conquests, in particular a rendezvous with Sif, Thor's wife. At this point, Thor arrives on the scene; Loki proceeds to oppose him with words, but Thor threatens to kill the satirist, and Loki, admitting that Thor's hammer is the only thing he fears, leaves the banquet with a curse: the gods will never again brew for a banquet, and the banquet hall will burn. Thus Loki is expelled from the banquet of the gods a second time, this time as a poet. The poet's verbal weapons bow before the brute force of real weapons, just as Cuchulainn's spears prevailed against malevolent satirists.

Possibly the curse was fulfilled,[47] and Loki hides. When he is caught, the gods

> Hann var bundinn með þörmum sonar síns Vála ... Skaði tók eitrorm ok festi upp yfir annlit Loka; draup þar ór eitr. Sigyn kona Loka sat þar ok helt munnlaug undir eitrit. En er munnlaugin var full, bar hón út eitrit; en meðan draup eitrit á Loka. Þá kippðist hann svá hart við, at þaðan af skalf jörð öll; þat eru nú kallaðir landsskjálftar.

> bound him with the guts of his son Nari ... Skathi took a venomous serpent and hung it about Loki's face so that its poison dripped on him. Loki's wife Sigyn sat by him and held a bowl under the poison,

---

[45] St. 3, trans. in Hollander 1962:91. *jöll ok áfu / færi ek ása sonum, / ok blend ek þeim svá meini mjöð.* See above, ch. 17. The very power of the satirist is what causes his or her exile.

[46] An exact parallel to the Irish motif, see above, ch. 17 (the men of Leinster offer jewelry to Aithirne to stay away and not satirize them; also, king Eochaid gives Aithirne his eye).

[47] As Hollander suggests (1962:103n58).

and she carried it out whenever it was full; but meanwhile the poison dripped on Loki. Then he writhed so fearfully that all the earth shook: men call this "earthquakes" nowadays.

Prose ending of *Lokasenna*[48]

Thus the satirist is, as it were, society's poison, the most evil. He is expelled, once for murder, once for slander. But after he is captured by the gods, he is bound and tortured by drops of poison that cause him monstrous writhings. Just as the exiling poet is exiled, or the murderous poet is executed, so the poisonous poet is poisoned.

These myths raise a number of intriguing questions. First of all, Starkaðr seems unambiguously a warrior-poet—although chiefly a warrior, he is also a famous poet. We have seen, in Greece, Ireland, and Scandinavia, poetry residing strongly in the warrior function. In Odin's myths, though, poetry seems allied to his first-function aspects—Odin as priest and king—and his omniscience seems clearly linked to his capacity for ruling.[49] Poetry is linked to magic, and we need only mention the importance of the "magical sovereign" in Dumézil's mythical theory.[50] However, as we have seen, Odin does use his occult poetic knowledge for martial purposes, as the Irish poets did. Like Starkaðr, he is something of a warrior-poet.[51] This may be a result of Scandinavian functional slippage, though.

And the figure of Kvasir is originally a clear-cut third-function figure (in one tradition), though he ends up as a member of the Aesir, and thus a symbol of the totality of the functions. Since Kvasir ends up in the belly of Odin, who dispenses him to gods and men, perhaps this represents the king's ability to orchestrate and reconcile the functions.[52] But the king is dependent on poetry,

---

[48] Trans. Hollander 1962:103. This same story of Loki's imprisonment and torture is found in the *Prose Edda*, see Young 1954:85, but there the gods are taking vengeance for the death of Baldr. For the poison theme, cf. above, ch. 17, "The Poisonous Poet."

[49] See the two articles by Fleck, 1981 and 1970, on the "knowledge-criterion" for sacred kingship. Thus, as it were, one had to be a poet-prophet to become king. For knowledge and poetry in Hesiod's consecration, see above, ch. 6. For the dependence of the ruler on poetry and poets, see Duban 1980; Roth 1976.

[50] See Dumézil 1977 for Dumézil's nearly final thoughts on Indo-European sovereign gods. For Varuna as king, see 74; on his magic, 64–65. Cf. the section on Odin, "*Oðinn roi et magicien*," 189–196.

[51] We may note that Indra is a key imbiber of Soma, which inspires him to war fury; see *Rig Veda* 9.113.1, "Let Indra the killer of Vr̥ta drink Soma in Śaryaṇāvat, gathering his strength within himself, to do a great heroic deed. O drop of Soma, flow for Indra," trans. O'Flaherty, *śaryaṇāvati somamindraḥ pibatu vr̥trahā / balaṃ dadhāna ātmani kariṣyan vīryaṃ mahadindrāyendo pari srava.*

[52] See Dumézil 1959b:408, 412; 1973b:38–42; Lincoln 1975b:131n39, with further bibliography. The

the poet, and the sacrifice of the poet as the orchestrating medium. The question of the association of the poet with the three levels of Indo-European society remains unresolved; the poet may simply be a transfunctional phenomenon. However, associations with the warrior level are very strong.

Another aspect of these myths deserves comment. We started by looking at putatively historical stories of exiled or executed poets, though obviously mythical or folkloric motifs were combined with the narratives. Then we found, in the stories of Marsyas and other mythical poets, overtly mythical stories that had many of the same themes; Aesop and Socrates were even viewed as Marsyas figures. Then in examining the theme of the poet's ambiguously protective and inimical gods, we evaluated Indo-European epic, Starkaðr and Suibhne, as possibly related to the theme, applied to heroes who were full-fledged poets as well as warriors. Now, behind Starkaðr, we find the theme of the killed and expelled poets applied to the divine level. Gods are behind mythical heroes; mythical, superhuman heroes are behind revered historical figures. The mythical theme lives on in increasingly secular trappings, ending up as "history."

To take the myths back a further step: Eliade's thesis, that myths of beginnings, creation, and first fathers lie behind all myth and all sacrality, was taken by him to great lengths,[53] but can still be useful when used as one of a number of important thematic tools. Here we merely note that a myth of the unification of the three functions is a myth of the beginnings of society, and the death of a divine poet is associated with it. Also, the tree Odin hangs on is Yggdrasil, the cosmic tree; in another consecration myth, he drinks from a well lying under the same tree. The cosmic tree implies beginnings.[54] Yggdrasil is called Mīmameiðr 'Mímir's tree',[55] so Mímir, one of Odin's sources of wisdom, is closely linked to the tree. If Fleck's interpretation of the Odinic hanging is correct, all of these myths may be connected, and the myth relates overtly to the Germanic myths of destruction and renewal, Ragnarok and its aftermath.

Thus myths of the sacrifice of a primeval man perhaps lie behind the Odinic myths of sacrificed poet. In Germanic myth, we have the myth of the

---

king "contains" priests, warriors, and commoners in his body. For sacred kingship in Germany, Fleck 1981 and 1970. Cf. Jean Cocteau's film, *Le Sang d' un poète*; Dubuisson 1978.

[53] Eliade's most central thematic books are *The Sacred and the Profane* (1959) and *The Myth of the Eternal Return, or Cosmos and History* (1971).

[54] For tree as cosmic symbol, see Eliade 1963b:265–330; 1959:147–151. On Yggdrasil, Eliade 1963b:265, 276–277; De Vries 1956 2:380–383.

[55] Puhvel 1987:218; Fleck 1971:386.

giant Ymir, killed and dismembered to create the world. Puhvel, starting from Roman myth, has discussed an Indo-European cosmology involving the sacrifice of a "twin" (Ymir, Yamá, Remus, Púruṣa, Gayomart) by a "man" (Mannus, Mánu, Rōmulus).[56] Just as the deaths of Kvasir and Mímir were associated with the unification of the three classes to form a totality of society, the primordial twin sacrifice is linked to the formation of society in its three functions: "Remus had to die as part of the act of creation which led to the birth of the three Roman 'tribes' (Ramnes, Luceres, Tities) and the accession of Romulus to his role as first king."[57] In the same way, the brahmins, kṣatriyas, vaiśyas, and śūdras come from the sacrificed body of Puruṣa,[58] and three Germanic tribes derive from the Twin and the Man.[59]

By this interpretation, the killing of the poet may reflect the death of the sacred being needed to consecrate a cosmic beginning.[60] The poet's sacrality and ability to mediate between the functions make this possible.

The usefulness of the mediating poet is shown by a final myth associated with the cosmic tree. "A squirrel called Ratatosk [Gnaw-tooth] springs up and down the ash tree and conveys words of abuse exchanged between the eagle [who sits at the top of Yggdrasil[61]] and Niðhögg [the serpent that gnaws at the root of Yggdrasil[62]]."[63] The squirrelly satirist is thus invaluable in the cosmic scheme of things, mediating between the highest and lowest points in the world tree. The poet does the same on a societal level, mediating between the "highest" and "lowest" functions, though the mediation is not always welcome.

---

[56] See Puhvel 1975, summarized in Puhvel 1987:284–290. For different interpretations of the Romulus-Remus myth, see Bremmer and Horsfall 1987:34–38; Bannon 1997:158–173.

[57] Puhvel 1987:288; 1975:155; Propertius 4.1.31. Cf. Burkert 1962a:366–367. For exhaustive examination of the theme of the sacrificed brother, see the work of Heino Gehrts, discussed by Ward 1982b. In the pattern studied by Gehrts, the king's brother, who is killed, often in battle, endows the surviving brother with redoubled powers of kingship and battle prowess. See also Gehrts 1967:262–282. Cf. below, ch. 27, the warrior as double of the king in African ritual.

[58] *Rig Veda* 10.90; cf. bibliography in O'Flaherty 1975:314.

[59] Puhvel 1975:308.

[60] Just as Remus's death is "an essential consecrational act for the good of the new urban creation" (Puhvel 1975:149).

[61] Cf. De Vries 1956 2:380–381; Dumézil 1973a:143n11; 141.

[62] Cf. Dumézil 1973a:144.

[63] *Gylfaginning* 16, *Prose Edda*, Young 1954:45, *Íkorni sá, er heitir Ratatoskr, renn upp ok niðr eftir askinum ok berr öfundarorð milli arnarins ok Níðhöggs.*

Part Three

ROME

20

"Wounded by Tooth that Drew Blood": The Beginnings of Satire in Rome

S*ATURA QUIDEM TOTA NOSTRA EST*," wrote Quintilian. "Satire is entirely ours [Roman]."[1] Thus blame in verse, of a certain type, was a characteristically Roman genre, despite some influence from Hellenistic Greek poetry.[2] Cicero, in the *Tusculan Disputations*, tells us that "Cato, that most authoritative author, said in the *Origins* that our ancestors had this custom at feasts, that they would sing to the flute, one after another, the praises and braveries of outstanding men, as they were reclining," but soon after this he speaks of "poems made for the injury of someone else" in archaic Rome. "The Twelve Tables show that songs used to be written already at that time, because they made it illegal for a song to be written to injure someone else."[3] Valerius Maximus adds this important passage:

> Maiores natu in conuiuiis ad tibias egregia superiorum opera carmine comprehensa pangebant, quo ad ea imitanda iuuentutem alacriorem redderent. Quid hoc splendidius, quid etiam utilius certamine? ... Quas Athenas, quam scholam, quae alienigena studia huic domesticae disciplinae praetulerim? Inde oriebantur Camilli, Scipiones, Fabricii, Marcelli, Fabii.

---

[1] Quintilian 10.1.93. Of course, Quintilian was well aware of the Greek satiric tradition. He was using the word in a limited, technical sense, of a certain Roman satirical genre, the *satura*. However, there was a strain of satire that was characteristically Latin. See Coffey 1976:3–23; Knoche 1975:3–16; Hendrickson 1927.

[2] See Knoche 1975:4–5 for a discussion of the Greek element in Roman satire.

[3] Trans. Warmington, revised, *Grauissimus auctor in Originibus dixit Cato, morem apud maiores hunc epularum fuisse, ut deinceps, qui accubarent, canerent ad tibiam clarorum virorum laudes atque virtutes ... XII tabulae declarant, condi iam tum solitum esse carmen, quod ne liceret fieri ad alterius iniuriam, lege sanxerunt* (*Tusculan Disputations* 4.2); cf. Hendrickson 1925:125; Duff 1960:54; Cicero *Brutus* 19.75; Varro, quoted by Nonius Marcellus, p. 76, *assa uoce pro sola*.

Our ancestors, in feasts, accompanied by flutes, would compose poetry on the outstanding deeds of distinguished men, by which they would make the youth more eager to imitate those works. What is more splendid than this, what indeed more useful in battle? ... What Athens, what school, what foreign studies shall I prefer to this native custom? From this arose the Camilli, the Scipiones, the Fabricii, the Marcelli, the Fabii.

Valerius Maximus 2.1.10, my trans.

Thus narrative poetry, as martial paraenesis, is central to archaic Roman culture; it also seemingly has an aspect of ancestor worship in it.

Though this passage speaks only of praise, martial blame would have been an inextricable component of the poetry, as we have seen in the martial paraenesis of the Iliadic Agamemnon and in Tyrtaeus.[4] We find comparable praise and blame expressed in Roman funeral ritual: according to Pliny, the Romans kept wax portraits of their illustrious ancestors around the house, along with accompanying spoils of battle, pedigrees, archives, and statues—"so that the houses continued to triumph eternally even after they had changed masters." But a specific purpose of all this praise of deeds of ancestors was martial blame: "This was a powerful stimulus, when the walls each day reproached an unwarlike owner for having thus intruded upon the triumphs of another."[5] Polybius describes the Roman funeral, where men wore these masks in procession, and where the funeral orator recaps all of the illustrious deeds of the deceased's ancestors.[6] So we see that praise, blame, and cult of martial ancestors linked together.

The laws of the Twelve Tables, referred to above, show the power of blame in early Rome: *Qui malum carmen incantassit* ... ([He or she] who has chanted an evil song ... [will be punished]).[7] Elsewhere, Cicero quotes the Twelve Tables as saying, *si quis occentauisset* ([He or she] who has sung a satire against someone [will be punished], Cicero *On the Republic* 4.10.12). Some scholars believe that this is a variant reading for the same law, and that *occentassit* should be the correct reading; others believe that the word *occentassit* is connected with a

---

[4] See above, ch. 11; ch. 17 (poet as warrior section).

[5] Pliny *Natural History* 35.2; trans. from Lewis and Reinhold 1966 1:483, *triumphabantque etiam dominis mutatis aeternae domus. erat haec stimulatio ingens, exprobrantibus tectis cotidie inbellem dominum intrare in alienum triumphum.*

[6] Polybius 6.53.1–54.2.

[7] Pliny *Natural History* 28.2.17; possible variant reading, *incantassit: occentassit.* See Ernout 1966:119; Marmorale 1950:53, with bibliography; Pugliese 1941:22ff. (further bibliography); Momigliano 1942; Fraenkel 1925; Usener 1901; Warmington 1936:474.

different law or a different section of the law. In any case, this word places the offense in the realm of personal attack, slander, and verbal abuse. Festus explains: "Our ancestors used to say 'he has sung an abusive song' [*occentassit*] for what we say now, 'he has made a *convicium*,' because it is done openly and with a certain clamor, so that it can be heard at a great distance. Which is held to be shameful, because it is not thought to be done without cause."[8]

With *incantassit*, we have more of an occult context: the connection will be with *incantatio* 'incantation, enchantment'. However, it would be a mistake to separate satirical destructive language from magico-religious destructive language too completely, as often curses used abusive language. This kind of attempted separation can result from imposing neat modern categories—magic and religion versus literature—on the archaic mind. James Boykin Rives writes, "we should see 'magic' and 'slander' not as exclusive alternatives, but as points on the same spectrum."[9]

The punishment for breaking this law was capital, as supporting texts show us. Cicero writes:

> Nostrae contra duodecim tabulae cum perpaucas res capite sanxissent, in his hanc quoque sanciendam putauerunt, si quis <u>occentauisset</u> siue <u>carmen</u> condidisset, quod <u>infamiam</u> faceret <u>flagitium</u>ue alteri. Praeclare; iudiciis enim magistratuum, disceptationibus legitimis propositam uitam, non <u>poetarum ingeniis</u> habere debemus, nec <u>probrum</u> audire nisi ea lege ut respondere liceat et iudicio defendere.

> Though our Twelve Tables attached the penalty of death only to a very few offenses, yet among these few this was one: if any man should have sung a satire against someone [*occentauisset*], or have composed a satire [*carmen*] calculated to bring infamy [*infamiam*] or disgrace [*flagitium*] on another person.[10] Wisely decreed. For it is

---

[8] Festus 190 (p. 181 Müller), *'Occentassit' antiqui dicebant, quod nunc convicium fecerit dicimus, quod id clare, et cum quodam canore fit, ut procul exaudiri possit. quod turpe habetus, quia non sine causa fieri putatur.* The emphasis on the justice of the satire is a familiar theme. OLD defines *convicium* as 'angry noise, clamor, uproar; insulting talk, abuse, reproof, mockery ...' See Ernout 1966:119; Marmorale 1950:53, with bibliography; Pugliese 1941:22ff. (further bibliography); Momigliano 1942; Fraenkel 1925; Usener 1901; Warmington 1936:474; Lewis and Crawford 1996:677–679 (in a thorough reconstruction of the Twelve Tables with their most important testimonia); Rives 2002.

[9] Rives 2002:285, cf. Momigliano 1942:120. For the curse containing elements of abuse, see Watson 1991; for blame, curse, and spell, ch. 17, above, on Lugh in battle, and on the *glám díchenn*.

[10] Some critics regard the second clause as Cicero's explanation of *si quis occentauisset*. Rives 2002:282–283, following Fraenkel, suggests that the second clause was part of the original law,

273

by the decisions of magistrates, and by a well-informed justice, that our lives ought to be judged, and not by the flighty fancies of poets [*poetarum ingeniis*]; neither ought we to be exposed to hear calumnies [*probrum*], save where we have the liberty of replying, and defending ourselves before an adequate tribunal.

> Cicero *On the Republic* 4.10.12, *ap.* Augustine *City of God* 2.9[11]

Considering the role of invective in Cicero's career and death, this is a highly ironic passage; he assumes that a system of justice will be just.

Horace (*Epistles* 2.1.139–155) offers a useful historical outline of Roman blame:

> Agricolae prisci, fortes paruoque beati,
> condita post frumenta leuantes tempore festo
> corpus et ipsum animum spe finis dura ferentem,
> cum sociis operum et pueris et coniuge fida
> Tellurem porco, Siluanum lacte piabant,
> floribus et uino Genium memorem breuis aeui.
> Fescennina per hunc inuenta licentia morem
> uersibus alternis opprobria rustica fudit,
> libertasque recurrentis accepta per annos
> lusit amabiliter, donec iam saeuus apertam
> in rabiem coepit uerti iocus et per honestas
> ire domos impune minax. Doluere cruento
> dente lacessiti, fuit intactis quoque cura
> condicione super communi; quin etiam lex
> poenaque lata, malo quae nollet carmine quemquam
> describi: uertere modum, formidine fustis
> ad bene dicendum delectandumque redacti.

The farmers of old, a sturdy folk with simple wealth, when, after harvesting the grain, they sought relief at holiday time for the body, as well as for the soul, which bore its toils in hope of the end,

---

which contained three clauses. Lewis and Crawford reconstruct this law (VIII, 1) as *qui malum carmen incantassit . . . <quive> occentassit carmen<ve> cond<issit> . . .*

[11] Trans. Dods, adapted. Some critics regard this as a restatement of the Pliny passage; others see two different laws, one against sorcery, one against slander. See Momigliano 1942:121. Other statements on capital punishment for slander: Horace *Epistles* 2.1.154 (see below in text); Scholiast ("Cornutus") *ad* Persius *Satires* 1.123, *cautum est ut fustibus feriretur qui publice invehebatur* ("It was laid down that, if anyone was found to be uttering a slander in public, he should be clubbed to death"), trans. in Warmington 1938:475, adapted.

together with slaves and faithful wife, partners of their labors, used to propitiate Earth with swine, Silvanus with milk, and the Genius who is ever mindful of the shortness of life with flowers and wine. Through this custom came into use Fescennine licence [*Fescennina licentia*],[12] which in alternate verse poured forth rustic taunts [*opprobria rustica*]; and the freedom, welcomed each returning year, was innocently gay, till jest, now growing cruel [*saevus*], turned to open frenzy [*apertam in rabiem*] and stalked amid the homes of honest folk, fearless in its threatening [*impune minax*].[13] They who were bitten by tooth that drew blood [*cruento dente lacessiti*] were stung to the quick, and even those untouched felt concern for the common cause; and at last a law was carried with a penalty, forbidding the portayal of any abusive strain [*malo carmine*]. Men changed their tune, and terror of the cudgel [*formidine fustis*] led them back to good and gracious forms of speech. (trans. Fairclough, adapted)

According to Horace, then, Roman blame thus started from light-hearted ritual abuse at harvest festivals; this became more and more abusive and political, and was turned against the aristocracy. Society, even those who were not attacked, saw it as a major problem, and the Twelve Tables law was passed against it, after which poets had to be more civil and even entertaining.

Like many historical outlines, this one is suspect. Certainly, these "eras" shaded into one another; violent personal abuse surely coexisted with ritual abuse from times immemorial.[14] And "damaging" poetry postdated the law of the Twelve Tables, as our examples of exiled Roman poets will show. But even if this is not a strictly chronological schematic outline, all of the poetic phenomena described in it probably existed. It is valuable as a witness to the cultural situation that brought about the perceived need for punitive poetic legislation, the Twelve Tables laws. These laws, of course, explicitly suggest the trial of the poet and his punishment, execution by clubs. Horace portrays the satirical poets unsympathetically; yet their crime was attacking the aristocracy (*honestas ... domos*), perhaps as representatives of the lower classes.

---

[12] See Brink 1982:191 for Fescennine abuse.

[13] For the sense of *honestas ... domos*, see Brink 1982:194.

[14] Archilochus is the first great abusive poet of Greece, and his family was associated with the worship of Demeter, which had a large element of ritual abuse. Perhaps familiarity with ritual abuse would equip a poet for abuse of wider application. There is also an element of ritual abuse in Sappho (the *epithalamia*), see app. A below. Fescennines were used in marriages and triumphs, to avert evil—Adams 1982:4; Duff 1960:59. Cf. the ritual mockery in the Nonae Capratinae, Plutarch *Camillus* 29; Bremmer and Horsfall 1987:82.

Someone who had less identification with upper classes might view the satirists more sympathetically. The fact that an aristocratic satirist like Lucilius could go unscathed legally[15] may show that this law, like many laws, prosecuted selectively, legislated against the politically oppressed.[16]

While abuse and blame were not always expressed metrically, they were always an important part of Roman society, even under the emperors. "Rome, said Cicero, was a *maledica civitas*; slander was a national pastime." The full Ciceronian passage is worth quoting: "[Caelius had not departed from the right way] How do we know? There were no expenses, no financial loss, no borrowing. But there was gossip. How many are there who can escape that, especially in such a slanderous state?"[17] The virulence of Cicero's oratorical abuse, a keynote of his most prominent speeches, from the *For Roscius Amerinus* to the *Catilines*, the *For Caelius*, the *Verrines* and *Philippics*, was one of the sources of his popularity, legal effectiveness, and political power.[18]

Thus, poetic/verbal abuse was a well-attested phenomenon in ancient Rome. And the companion theme, the exiled or executed poet, is attested at the beginnings of Rome's literary history, in Naevius, and continues through the Empire, with such a poet as Ovid, and into Silver Latin, with Juvenal.

---

[15] See Wiseman 1985:132, a valuable discussion of the sanctions against slander in Rome.

[16] For further on this passage, see Braund 2004:413–414.

[17] Wiseman 1985:134; Cicero *For Caelius* 38: *Quid signi? Nulli sumptus, nulla iactura, nulla versura. At fuit fama. Quotus quisque istam effugere potest praesertim in tam maledica civitate?*

[18] See below, ch. 22. For surveys of Roman blame, see Koster 1980; Opelt 1969, a collection of texts; Elliott 1960:100–129; Ward 1973:131.

21

Naevius: *Dabunt malum Metelli Naevio poetae*

WE FIND THE THEME of the exiled Roman poet first in the life of Naevius (ca. 270–199 BC), Rome's first writer of plays with Roman subjects, and writer of the first Roman epic with Roman subject matter, *The Punic War*. The scant details of his life, with their story of satirical freedom and political repression, have been thoroughly debated.[1] I tend to place some credence in the historicity of the traditions, though if they are not historical, they have an equal interest, if a different meaning.

Naevius began to present plays in Rome in about 235 BC.[2] Though he wrote tragedies adapted from Greek originals and historical plays, his métier must have been comedy, for he wrote a great number of them (thirty-four, as compared to seven tragedies). The fragments of these are full of satire and political needling. A youthful indiscretion of Scipio Africanus is referred to in one fragment:

> Etiam qui res magnas manu saepe gessit gloriose,
> cuius facta viva nunc vigent, qui apud gentes solus praestat,
> eum suus pater cum palliod unod ab amica abduxit.

> Even that man whose hand did often accomplish mighty
>   exploits gloriously,
> Whose deeds wane not but live on to this day,
> the one outstanding man in all the world—
> That man, with a single mantle, his own father dragged from
>   a lady-love's arms.

> Gellius 7.8.5, trans. Warmington, adapted[3]

---

[1] The most important testimonia on Naevius' life are conveniently collected in Jocelyn 1969. For his poetry, see Büchner 1982:20–40, and Marmorale 1950.

[2] Gellius 17.21.44.

[3] See also Marmorale 1950:226, 99; Jocelyn 1969:38–39; Cicero *On Oratory* 2.249.

This passage is an elegant combination of praise and blame—the praise sets up the satirical punchline, which entirely deflates it.

According to one testimony, Naevius "wounded" many with his plays. Gellius speaks of "his misdemeanors, and . . . the insolence of his utterances with which he had wounded [*laeserat*] many in the past," and of "constant slander and abuse [*maledicentiam et probra*] uttered against leading men of the state in the manner of Greek poets."[4]

Naevius' most famous targets were the Metelli, whom he attacked with a celebrated line: *Fato Metelli Romae fiunt consules*: "By chance the Metelli become consuls at Rome."[5] Robert Elliott ascribes importance to the fact that the objects of the satirist's attack were named in this verse; thus it fits into his account of name magic in archaic satire, a virulent form of malevolent spell, a curse.[6] Such a powerful form of "magic" would have turned against the poet; it was so powerful, whether for magical reasons or for more mundane reasons of intolerable embarrassment in a culture concerned with saving face, that the politically powerful targets would not endure it. Paradoxically, as we have seen, such power often brings about the poet's exile.

The Ciceronian commentator who preserves this fragment describes the line as "spoken in a witty and spiteful way" (*dictum facete et contumeliose*). Caesius Bassus adds that "the Metelli . . . were several times exasperated [*lacessiti*, literally, 'wounded'] by him [Naevius] in verse."[7] The current Metellus consul, "angered" (*iratus*), answered in an ominous catalectic Saturnian: *Dabunt malum Metelli Naevio poetae*. "The Metelli will hurt the poet Naevius."[8] Caesius Bassus reports that the verse was posted in a public place.[9]

---

[4] Gellius 3.3.15 (Jocelyn 1969:37) The full passage, part of which is translated and discussed below: *Sicuti de Naevio quoque accepimus fabulas eum in carcere duas scripsisse, Hariolum et Leontem, cum ob assiduam maledicentiam et probra in principes civitatis de Graecorum poetarum more dicta in vincula Romae a triumviris coniectus esset. Unde post a tribunis plebis exemptus est, cum in his quas supra dixi fabulis delicta sua et petulantias dictorum quibus multos ante laeserat diluisset.* For Naevius' "wounding," cf. Horace Epistle 2.1.150–151.

[5] "Asconius" *ad* Cicero Verrines 1.10.29 (Marmorale 1950:254, 66; Jocelyn 1969:42). For interpretation of the ambiguous *fato* 'chance' (Frank) or 'evil' (Frank) or the Stoic 'fatal necessity' (Wissowa, Zumpf) or 'oracular prediction' (Marx), see Frank 1927:105–106. Frank believes that Naevius' *fato* combined an ablatival sense, 'by fate' and a double dative: 'for an evil', with intentional ambiguity (108).

[6] Elliott 1960:123, 122–129. For naming in poetry, see below, ch. 22 (Cicero); ch. 23 (Ovid); ch. 26 (Juvenal); above, ch. 17 (on Dub's "sea-spell"; on the *glám dicenn* as satire/spell).

[7] Keil 1857 6.266 (Jocelyn 1969:42), my trans. *Sed ex omnibus istis qui sunt asperrimi . . . optumus est quem Metelli proposuerunt de Naevio, aliquotiens ab eo uersu lacessiti: 'malum . . .* etc.

[8] "Asconius." Cf. references in Warmington 1936:154; Frank 1927.

[9] Keil 1857 6.266. Cf. Jocelyn 1969:43n106.

Accordingly, the poet "was thrown into chains by the *triumviri*."[10] Plautus, a contemporary of Naevius, probably referred to his imprisonment in *Miles Gloriosus* (211–212), "I have heard that the face of a foreign[11] poet is columned, and two guards always watch him at all hours."[12] Tenney Frank suggests that Naevius was the victim of "strict censorship . . . applied temporarily by some praetor . . . The Metelli were supporting Scipio's invasion of Africa to end the war. Scipio was vigorously opposed by the older conservative nobles and Naevius was writing in the interest of the latter. The younger group were ready to resort to extreme measures to remove the offensive satirist."[13] If this scenario is correct, we have a situation similar to that of Aristophanes: a conservative poet attacking a more militaristic political faction. One wonders if Naevius attacked war directly, as did Aristophanes.

Our judgment of how serious a punishment this was will vary according to whether we consider Naevius a Roman citizen. H. D. Jocelyn considers him "a migrant from Capua" with "the private rights of Roman citizenship, but where public life was concerned even his right to vote was circumscribed, if it existed at all." According to H. J. Rose, however, the very fact of the punishment itself argues that the poet was not a citizen; J. Wight Duff argues from the poet's name, common in Rome, that he was.[14] And Frank remarks on the severity of the punishment if Naevius was guilty only of verbal attacks, however scurrilous; many later Roman satirists escaped political reprisal; Lucilius is a good example.[15] If Naevius was a Roman citizen, this punishment was considerable.[16]

According to Gellius, the poet wrote two apologetic plays in prison, which effected his release. "We have received also concerning Naevius that he wrote two plays in prison, *Hariolus* and *The Lion*." "He was freed by the tribune of the plebs when in the plays I mentioned above, he atoned for his misdeeds and the insolence of his utterances, by which he had wounded many previously."[17] But he was nevertheless exiled. Jerome writes, "he was driven from Rome by

---

[10] Gellius 3.3.15. See Marmorale 1950:104–105.

[11] Probably from a Greek standpoint.

[12] *Nam os columnatum poetae esse indaudiui barbaro, / Quoi bini custodes semper totis horis occubant.* See Marmorale 1950:112ff.; Jocelyn 1969:34–37. For the *os columnatum*, see Jocelyn 1969:36.

[13] Frank 1927:110n17.

[14] Jocelyn 1969:34, cf. 33n15 (Gellius 1.24.2); Rose 1960b:26n29; Duff 1960:93n5, with further references. See also Marmorale 1950:21–26.

[15] Frank 1927:109.

[16] Jocelyn 1969.

[17] Gellius 3.3.15, my trans.; Jocelyn 1969:37; Marmorale 1950:124–134.

a faction of the nobles and especially the Metelli."[18] He died in Utica, Africa, around 201 BC.[19]

So we have such familiar themes as conflict of satirist with political leaders; imprisonment of poet; his exile. The death in exile adds a piquant touch to the story.

How historical is this tale? Jocelyn concludes that it contains some elements of truth, but also has contradictory details that undermine its credibility. A. Momigliano, after arguing for slander as a capital crime in the Twelve Tables, takes this as a likely key for understanding Naevius' story.[20] The two certain points in the poet's story, for him, are the imprisonment and death at Utica, which he thinks are most likely connected (by an exile).

But even if the story of Naevius's punishment and exile were entirely fictitious, it would be valuable as an example of how it was felt desirable to fit satirical poets into the mold of the victim—imprisoned and exiled. If it is historical, of course, it shows once again how the satirical poet can become a victim in history as well as myth.

A few relevant ancillary themes show up in Naevius's *vita*, especially in relation to war. Naevius fought in the First Punic War.[21] So, as was the case in Greece, we find the archaic poet with satirical leanings serving as a soldier.

The subject matter of Naevius' magnum opus was, of course, the same war. This epic, *The Punic War*, started with explanations of the ancient roots of the strife of Rome and Carthage. Such a theme creates a bridge between Naevius the satirist and Naevius the soldier and military poet, for the mythological beginnings of strife are basic to the outlook of the archaic blame poet.[22]

---

[18] *pulsus Roma factione nobilium ac praecipue Metelli.* Jerome *Chronological Tables*, year 1816 (from Abraham) = 201 BC; Jocelyn 1969:41; Marmorale 1950:132.

[19] See Jerome, ibid.; Marmorale 1950:31; Duff 1960:94.

[20] Momigliano 1942. As do Lewis and Crawford 1996:679.

[21] Varro *ap.* Gellius 17.21.45 (Marmorale 1950:233): "Naevius, according to . . . M. Varro . . . served as a soldier in the first Punic war and asserts that very fact himself in the Song which he wrote on that war" (*M. Varro . . . stipendia fecisse ait (Naevium) bello Poenico primo, idque ipsum Naevium dicere in eo Carmine quod de eodem bello scripset*). An introduction to this epic can be found in Feeney 1991:108–112.

[22] Nagy 1979:127–141, 213–221, 309–316; Hunt 1981:31–32; and above, ch. 17 (poets Aithirne and Laidchenn as causes of strife and war). Cf. the importance of *Mōmos* 'Blame' in the mythological beginnings of the Trojan War (*Cypria* fr. 1, in Allen 1919 5:117; West 2003b:80): "For they say that the earth, burdened by an overabundance of men, and since there was no piety among men, asked Zeus to be relieved of the weight. Zeus with no delay first brought about the Theban war, through which he dispatched very many men. Later, once again, he took Momos as his advisor, whom Homer calls the plan of Zeus, since Zeus was prepared at that time to destroy all men by thunderbolts and cataclysms. Momos hindered this, but suggested to him Thetis' marriage to a mortal and the begetting of a fair daughter [Helen],

The similarities to the *Aeneid* are obvious; the influence this poem had on Virgil has often been discussed.[23]

One of Naevius' *fabulae praetextae*, the *Clastidium*, had a martial theme. Its hero was M. Claudius Marcellus, a victor in 222 BC and winner of the *spolia opima* from the Gallic chieftain Virdumarus.[24] The one fragment we possess from *Clastidium* is standard praise, referring to the eternal glory of the warrior: "Back to his native land, happy in life never dying" (*Vita insepulta laetus in patriam redux*). It is probable that we will never find a pure praise poet or a pure blame poet. Even in Archilochus we find praise, and even in Sappho and Pindar we find blame.[25] The archaic poet will love his friends and hate his enemies; in poetic terms, this is praise and blame.

Thus Naevius, the satirist, exiled by a powerful political faction for his poetry, was a soldier and wrote on martial themes.

We know little about the death of Naevius, beyond the datum that he was believed to have died at Utica. But we do have the epitaph he supposedly wrote for himself. In it we find a familiar and fitting theme:

> Immortales mortales si foret fas flere
> flerent divae Camenae Naevium poetam.
> Itaque postquamst Orchi traditus thesauro,
> obliti sunt Romae loquier lingua latina.

> If it were lawful for the immortals to weep for mortals,
> The divine Muses would lament the poet Naevius.

---

from both of which war came about for the Hellenes and barbarians" (φασὶ γὰρ τὴν γῆν βαρουμένην ὑπ' ἀνθρώπων πολυπληθίας, μηδεμιᾶς ἀνθρώπων οὔσης εὐσεβείας, αἰτῆσαι τὸν Δία κουφισθῆναι τοῦ ἄχθους· τὸν δὲ Δία πρῶτον μὲν εὐθὺς ποιῆσαι Θηβαικὸν πόλεμον, δι' οὗ πολλοὺς πάνυ ἀπώλεσεν· ὕστερον δὲ πάλιν συμβούλῳ τῷ Μώμῳ χρησάμενος, ἣν Διὸς βουλὴν Ὅμηρός φησιν, ἐπειδὴ οἷός τε ἦν κεραυνοῖς ἢ κατακλυσμοῖς πάντας διαφθείρειν. ὅπερ τοῦ Μώμου κωλύσαντος, ὑποθεμένου δὲ αὐτῷ τὴν Θέτιδος θνητογαμίαν καὶ θυγατέρος καλῆς γένναν, ἐξ ὧν ἀμφοτέρων πόλεμος Ἕλλησι τε καὶ βαρβάροις ἐγένετο).

For *mōmos* as blame diction, in fact, "blame" in binary opposition to "praise" (*epaineō*), see Nagy 1979:223–224. For the overburdened earth as an Indo-European mythical theme, see Dumézil 1968:31–257; De Jong 1985:397–400. For the personified "Strife" (*Eris*) as cause of the Trojan War, bringing about the Judgment of Paris from an otherwise peaceful marriage feast, see Proclus *Chrestomathy* 1, in Allen 1919 5:102; Apollodorus *Library*, Epitome 3.3 (with further references in Frazer 1921); Nagy 1979:218–219. For satire and the beginnings of war, cf. Aristophanes *Acharnians* 509–556 on the beginnings of the Peloponnesian war.

[23] See e.g. Duff 1960:97–98; Warmington 1936:xvii; Luck 1983; Terzaghi 1929; Wigodsky 1972. Ennius was also influenced by Naevius' poem, Cicero *Brutus* 75–76.

[24] Varro *On the Latin Language* 7.107; 9.78; Jocelyn 1969:34; Duff 1960:95; Marmorale 1950:202.

[25] See on Pindar in ch. 3 (Archilochus).

Chapter Twenty-One

> And so, after he was delivered to the treasure vault of Orchus,
> They forgot how to speak the Latin language at Rome.
>
> Gellius 1.24.2[26]

This poet-soldier envisions himself as worthy of lamentation by the Muses, like Achilles; so his life ends with a theme closely tied to hero cult in Greece.

---

[26] Gellius 1.24.2 = Marmorale 1950:261, my trans. Earlier, Naevius had addressed the Muses in the beginning of his epic: "You daughters nine of Jupiter, harmonious sisters," *Novem Iovis concordes filiae sorores.*" (Caesius Bassus *ap.* Keil 1857 6.265.10; Marmorale 1950:233). Cf. the beginning of Livius' *Odyssey* (Gellius 18.9.5): "Tell me, Muse, of the cunning man . . ." (*Virum mihi, Camena, insece versutum*). See also Latacz 1976. See above, ch. 16, the Muses lamenting Achilles' death.

22

Cicero *Maledicus*, Cicero *Exul*

THIS CHAPTER WILL REGARD CICERO AS A POET in a nontechnical sense, an
artist projecting the archaic categories of praise and blame in his verbal
medium, oratory, and will examine how "aggressive" elements in his
speeches contributed to his exiles and death.

Oratory, even if it is not metrical, is closely linked to poetry. When it was
no longer customary to write editorials in poetry, as Solon did, politicians
became poets in prose, as it were, continuing the archaic Greek traditions
of praise and blame.[1] The poet and orator were closely associated. Aristotle
wrote, "It was naturally the poets who first set the movement going . . . it was
because poets seemed to win fame through their fine language when their
thoughts were simple enough, that the language of oratorical prose at first
took a poetical colour."[2] Cicero could write, "For the poet is extremely close
[*finitimus*] to the orator, a little more confined by meter, freer however in his
choice of words, his partner [*socius*] certainly in using many kinds of figura-
tive language, and nearly the same."[3] Already by the time of Aristotle, praise
(*epainesis*) and blame (*psogos*) were a central part of oratorical theory.[4]

---

[1] Juvenal admired Cicero's abusive art (the second *Philippic* is "divine and of outstanding fame,"
10.125, *conspicuae divina Philippica famae*), and many of the traditional invective *topoi* used by
Cicero are found in Juvenal e.g. *luxuria*: Cicero *For Roscius* 75 cf. Juvenal 6.292–297; drunken-
ness, Cicero *Against Piso* 22, cf. Juvenal 6.314; see Merrill 1975:2–3, 15, 121, 153, 169. Cf. Winkler
(1988), who sees mockery, but admiration, in Juvenal's treatment of the orator. The tradition
extended back to a comic poet, Plautus, cf. Merrill 1975:2, 18n5; Geffcken 1973.
  For praise and blame in the Greco-Roman world, see Dumézil 1943; "Census," in
Dumézil 1969:103–124; Ward 1973:130, 135; ch. 2 (Aesop).

[2] *Rhetoric* 3.1, 1404a (trans. Roberts): Ἤρξαντο μὲν οὖν κινῆσαι τὸ πρῶτον, ὥσπερ πέφυκεν, οἱ
ποιηταί . . . Ἐπεὶ δ' οἱ ποιηταί, λέγοντες εὐήθη, διὰ τὴν λέξιν ἐδόκουν πορίσασθαι τήνδε τὴν
δόξαν, διὰ τοῦτο ποιητικὴ πρώτη ἐγένετο λέξις . . .

[3] *On Oratory* 1.69–70: Est enim *finitimus* oratori poeta, numeris astrictior paulo, verborum autem licentia
liberior, multis vero ornandi generibus *socius*, ac paene par.

[4] Aristotle *Rhetoric* 1.3.10–37 (1358b), 1.9 (1366a–1367b). See also Plato *Phaedrus* 267c–d; Hinks
1936; Usher 1999:62–63. After Demosthenes delivered his devastating oratorical attack on

Gorgias, the rhetorician and sophist, was reputed to be the student of Empedocles, the philosopher, prophet, and poet.[5] But, for Diogenes, Empedocles is already a *rhētōr*.[6] Gorgias spoke of the power of the word, "the incantatory power which by its witchery enchants, persuades, and changes the souls of men."[7] Thus, just as the dividing line between philosopher, magician, and sophist is not easy to draw, the line between poet and orator is not clearly marked either. Though they have obvious differences, they share much in common.

Roman oratory, like Greek oratory, had a substantial component of invective. Rome was a "*maledica civitas*," according to Cicero.[8] Ronald Syme writes, "The law-courts were an avenue for political advancement through prosecution, a battle-ground for private enmities and political feuds, a theatre for oratory. The best of arguments was personal abuse."[9] N. W. Merrill, in a valuable discussion of invective in Rome, asserts that "attacking the morality and behavior of one's opponent became the standard method of winning a case." He adds, perhaps unnecessarily, "This concept is totally alien to modern legal procedure."[10]

As Merrill and others have shown, the invective, however extreme it seems to us now, was often accepted in a good-humored way.[11] The *topoi* were stereotyped and conventional; the most a skillful orator could do would be to give them new vividness by his oratorical brilliance, as did Cicero. If one attacked an opponent, this was *accusatio*; if one was attacked, the abuse was a *maledictum*.[12] The attacks were expected, and sometimes seem almost friendly. However, Antony's response to Cicero's *Philippics* shows that oratorical invective could sting deeply. Oratorical invective could pass from the conventional to bitter attack.

Aeschines, the latter chose to leave Athens, Plutarch *Demosthenes* 24.2 (857). For Demosthenes' invective, see Rowe 1968 and 1966; Usher 1999:227–285. Demosthenes produced his masterpiece, perhaps, of invective, *De Corona*, only after Aeschines had attacked his reputation in the *Against Ctesiphon*; thus, it was viewed (by the author) as defensive satire.

[5] See Diogenes Laertius 8.58 (DK 82 A3); Olympiodorus in *Gorgias* 6.17 N. (A10); *Suda* s.v. Gorgias (A2); cf. Isocrates *Antidosis* 268 (Empedocles and Parmenides are "sophists," and Gorgias is listed with them).

[6] Diogenes Laertius 8.58 (DK 82 A3). For Empedocles as poet, see Lucretius 1.731.

[7] *Encomium of Helen* 10 (trans. Dodds 1959:8): ἡ δύναμις τῆς ἐπωιδῆς ἔθελξε καὶ ἔπεισε καὶ μετέστησεν αὐτὴν γοητείαι. See DK 82 B11; Entralgo 1970:32–107.

[8] See above, ch. 20; *For Caelius* 38.

[9] Syme 1939:149–152; also "The Uses of Invective," in Jerome 1962; Nisbet 1961:192–197; Williams 1970:606; Fowler 1909:106–107.

[10] Merrill 1975:30.

[11] See Merrill 1975:39–42.

[12] Merrill 1975:33–34; Cicero *For Caelius* 6.

Anthony Corbeill, in an important book on Roman invective, argues that invective was based on important values and "biases" in Roman society, and in turn, "helped shape the ethical standards current during the politically convulsive period of the late Republic." Thus it exercised "real powers of persuasion." Invective and the laughter it produced often were used to "exclude" the political opponent as despicable and non-Roman.[13] Thus invective has a distinct ethical flavor. "The orator reserves his contempt for the evil citizen; invective provides a kind of supplement to normal legal proceedings."[14] Thomas N. Mitchell highlights the themes of *frugalitas* and moderation as opposed to *luxuria* and subservience to *libido*—viewed politically, these attributes support or harm the republic—as supplying the material for Cicero's rhetoric of praise and blame.[15]

Thus, in Rome, as in Greece, praise (*laus*) and blame (*vituperatio*) became a defined aspect of oratorical theory.[16] The archaic categories continued to exercise power in the politics of Republican Rome.

In such an environment, where invective was so powerful, it is not surprising that actual poets, such as Naevius, and later Ovid and Juvenal, should offend political leaders and be punished by exile. In the case of Cicero, as a dominant practitioner of traditional Roman invective, we find the same mechanisms of punishment and exclusion in place. The orator gains power, to a large extent, through his ability to attack verbally, to defend his client by abusing the client's enemy. Oratory was Cicero's main path to political power, and invective and satirical language were central aspects of Roman oratory. As Merrill and Syme state, attacking one's opponent was the standard method of winning a case.

On the other hand, many other factors contributed to Cicero's success, obviously: artistic "positive" language in his oratory, skillful political and legal maneuvering, shrewd alliances, pre-existing family connections, a polit-

---

[13] Corbeill 1996:5. As I will argue, it is the orator's power to "exclude" his enemy that leaves him open to the counterattack of force. Cf. Corbeill 1996:19.

[14] Corbeill 1996:19; for the ethics of seemingly extreme satirists, see ch. 3 (Archilochus), ch. 4 (Hipponax) and app. B.

[15] Mitchell 1991:41–42.

[16] Cicero *On Rhetorical Invention* 2.177–178 (trans. Hubbell, adapted): "Praises and vituperations will be derived from the topics that are employed with respect to the attributes of persons . . ." (*Laudes autem et vituperationes ex eis locis sumentur qui loci personis sunt attributi . . .*); *On Oratory* 2.349 (trans. Sutton): "these topics of praise and blame we shall frequently have occasion to employ in every class of law-suit" (*his locis et laudandi et vituperandi saepe nobis est utendum in omni genere causarum*). Cicero *On Oratory* 2.182; "Cicero" *Rhetoric To Herennius* 3.10–15; Quintilian *Training in Oratory* 3.4.1–10. Merrill 1975:5; Corbeill 1996:16; Craig 2004:188–190.

ical situation favorable to his advancement, and luck. Yet at all times in his career there is a close synergy of oratory and politics. In times of great crisis, he would deliver speeches to hurt his enemies and praise his own allies and causes. The *Catilines* and *Philippics* are obvious examples. Cicero's speeches in the senate and elsewhere had an enormous impact, serving a function similar to that of political advertising, editorializing, newspapers, and magazines today. Mitchell, despite his extensive survey of Cicero's family connections and his early political alliances, writes that he was a "*novus homo* whose main hope for political distinction lay in eloquence."[17]

But, as we have seen, the greater the power through artistic invective, the greater the danger to the practitioner, who is often exiled and executed. If Cicero fits this pattern, he is particularly valuable because his life is so well documented; here we are dealing substantially with history (which is not the case with many exiled poets). Though, of course, some legendary material might still be attracted to such a heroic figure, our extensive documentation allows us to control it more precisely.

The paradigm for Cicero as exiled poet is dependent on an understanding of the importance of Roman law pleading for political advancement: (1) Cicero, as a new man, was not from one of the prominent Roman families. He could not gain political success through his family and political connections alone.[18] (2) Cicero's oratory was the main factor in elevating him. Aside from oratory's value in politics generally, Cicero, as Rome's dominant orator, gained political favors and alliances by defending his allies and attacking his allies' enemies (that is, to defend Roscius, he had to attack Chrysogonus. Praise and blame are inextricably intertwined). (3) The nature of the Roman law courts, as described by Syme, cannot be emphasized enough. You made political progress by means of prosecuting in the courts, where battles involving private and political feuds were conducted. Personal attacks were far more effectual than appeals to evidence. Oratory as sword to wield against enemies— "personal abuse"—is here given central emphasis. Invective is a key element of oratory, since we are dealing with "prosecution," "enmities," and "feuds" (in Syme's words). To repeat Merrill, "Attacking the morality and behavior of one's opponent became the standard method of winning a case." Christopher Craig tempers this judgment only to the extent of affirming that invective was an important tool both in the law courts and in the senate; but invective had more impact in the law courts if it was based on truth.[19]

---

[17] Mitchell 1979: 44. Cf. also Habicht 1990.

[18] See Mitchell 1979:44.

[19] Craig 2004, cf. Riggsby 1997:248, who argues against Syme et al. that law courts were generally

Though Cicero wrote some poetry,[20] his artistic blame is primarily found in his prose speeches, which, as has been noted, were replete with inventive and artistic verbal humor and abuse.[21] Plutarch recounts an incident in which the consul Cicero, in a law case, made fun of the absurd paradoxes of the Stoics to undercut his opposing lawyer, the Stoic Murena; when the audience laughed loudly, Murena remarked acidly, "What a funny man we have, my friends, for consul." Plutarch comments, "Cicero was naturally prone to laughter and fond of jesting." However, he was also "often carried away by his love of jesting into scurrility [*bōmolokhon*] and when, to gain his ends in his cases, he treated matters worthy of serious attention with ironical mirth and pleasantry he was careless of propriety."[22]

The wit and venom of his invective were an important part of the oratorical fireworks that made his speeches so entertaining, popular, and successful. Cicero's success in winning the Roscius case, which he did in a great part by attacking Chrysogonus, ensured that he was never without law cases afterwards.[23]

Cicero's invective, wielded in the law court, could destroy a powerful, if corrupt, political career, as in the case of Verres, who was forced to endure exile in Massilia after Cicero's devastating courtroom performance against him, just as Demosthenes had forced Aeschines out of Athens through his invective.

Of course, Verres fled before Cicero had delivered all of the Verrine orations, but Cicero did prosecute for a full day, which was enough. It has been suggested that it was Cicero's evidence, not his oratory, that made the prosecu-

---

oriented toward judgments based on truth. However, he writes, "In invective, truth is largely irrelevant."

[20] See Plutarch *Cicero* 2.3 (861); Townend 1965:109–134; Spaeth 1931.

[21] For Cicero's invective, satire, and humor, see Macrobius *Saturnalia* 11.3; Cicero *On Oratory* 1.17; 2.217–290; *On Rhetorical Invention* 1.16–22; 100–105; "Cicero" *Rhetoric To Herrenius* 2.47–49; 3.10–15; Koster 1980:134–145; also pt. 3A; Opelt 1969:40–57, in which the Cicero section is the largest section for any one author; Haury 1955, esp. 106–109; Merrill 1975, "Cicero and Early Roman Invective"—an excellent thesis, which concludes that Cicero always used traditional *topoi* in his invective, but used them with enormous skill; Delacy 1941. See also, Nisbet 1965, esp. 65–67; Corbeill 1996; Craig 2004; Volpe 1977:311–312; Geffcken 1973; Austin 1960; Nisbet 1961:192–195; Watson 1970 (unconvincing); Wooten 1983:73–86; Solmsen 1938:542–546; Sollmann 1960:51–53, 55–58; De Saint-Denis 1958; Canter 1936; Grant 1924:131–139; Dunkle 1967; Hands 1962.

[22] *Demosthenes & Cicero Compared* 1.4–5, 886 (trans. Perrin): Κικέρων δὲ πολλαχοῦ τῷ σκωπτικῷ πρὸς τὸ βωμολόχον ἐκφερόμενος, καὶ πράγματα σπουδῆς ἄξια γέλωτι καὶ παιδιᾷ κατειρωνευόμενος ἐν ταῖς δίκαις εἰς τὸ χρειῶδες, ἠφείδει τοῦ πρέποντος ... "ὡς γελοῖον ὦ ἄνδρες ἔχομεν ὕπατον." δοκεῖ δὲ καὶ γέλωτος οἰκεῖος ὁ Κικέρων γεγονέναι καὶ φιλοσκώπτης.

[23] *Brutus* 312; see below.

tion so devastating, but that would be an oversimplification. It was the combi-
nation of "evidence," cross-examination of witnesses, and Cicero's powerful
oratory that caused Verres to flee. As has been shown above, Roman courts
were more oriented toward oratory than toward evidence in the modern
sense, though evidence was a factor. D. Stockton writes of the central impor-
tance of Cicero's oratorical skill, with its satirical bent, on that first day of trial.
More than speedy legal maneuvering was necessary to win the trial: "Clarity of
exposition . . . mastery of a . . . maze of detail, and all crowned by all the arts of
public persuasion—cajolery, irony, sarcasm, the sly hint, the rolling thunder of
justified reprobation, the neat joke . . . often just the sheer music of the spoken
word: these too were needed, and . . . dazzled contemporary Rome."

Stockton reasonably supposes that much of this early examination of
witnesses is preserved in the *actio secunda* of the Verrines. After this case,
"Cicero thus became Rome's foremost advocate."[24] In much the same way,
Cicero's remarkable sustained attack on Catiline, the *First Catiline*, forced the
conspirator out the senate hall and out of Rome.[25]

As has been repeatedly noted, such power is always dangerous for the
person who wields it, and in the changing fortunes of Roman politics, Cicero
endured a series of exiles; he was even singled out for assassination by the
Catiline conspirators. After he successfully defended Roscius of Ameria in 79
BC, largely by attacking Chrysogonus, a powerful freedman of Sulla,[26] he spent
the next two years in Athens and Rhodes—perhaps his first exile, though he
departed Rome ostensibly for his health and education. Plutarch tells us that
Sulla had merely used Chrysogonus in the Roscius murder, and that Cicero
left Rome because he indeed feared Sulla after winning the Roscius case. He
"undertook the defence of Roscius, won his cause, and men admired him for
it; but fearing Sulla he made a journey to Greece, after spreading a report that
his health needed attention."[27] In 77 the orator returned to Rome; his "health
had improved," after Sulla had died in 78.

Scholars are divided as to which story to believe, Plutarch's or Cicero's.
Erich Gruen rejects Plutarch, presenting a carefully argued case. His main argu-

---

[24] Stockton 1971:47–48. Cf. Scullard 1959:98.

[25] Cicero *Against Catiline* 2.1; Plutarch *Cicero* 16.3–4 (868); Scullard 1959:113.

[26] Cicero mentions the shock that was felt by the prosecuting cousins when he actually mentioned
the freedman's name, *For Roscius* 60. For mockery of the real wrongdoers in the case, see Sihler
1914: 51. Cf. Elliott 1960:123, 122–129; and above, ch. 21.

[27] Plutarch *Cicero* 3 (862b–c): ἀναδεξάμενος οὖν τὴν συνηγορίαν καὶ κατορθώσας ἐθαυμάσθη,
δεδιὼς δὲ τὸν Σύλλαν ἀπεδήμησεν εἰς τὴν Ἑλλάδα, διασπείρας λόγον ὡς τοῦ σώματος αὐτῷ
θεραπείας δεομένου.

ment is chronological (the interval between the *For Roscius*, in 80, and Cicero's departure from Rome, in 79). However, it is entirely possible that it took some months for Cicero's situation to become increasingly dangerous, after the first major offense of the Roscius case, and that it took time for him and his friends to learn of his danger. In addition, it is possible that the combination of the Roscius case and the case of the woman of Arretium, in which Cicero again criticized Sulla indirectly, might have caused Sulla's real or imagined wrath. Thus, Plutarch's interpretation is not certain, but is at least a possibility that should be taken seriously. The chronology of Cicero's return also fits in neatly with the Plutarch story.[28]

Cicero's second exile took place in 58, when Clodius, acting with the support of the First Triumvirate, and after frequent verbal attacks on the orator,[29] passed a law calling for the exile of anyone who had executed a citizen without trial (as Cicero had done during the Catiline conspiracy).[30] Cicero left Rome in humiliation and agony, deserted by the Pompey he had so loyally supported, but who was now, as part of the First Triumvirate, involved in Caesarian and Clodian alliances. After Cicero had left Rome, the malevolent Clodius passed a law stating that he could be killed with impunity within four hundred miles of Rome, and the orator's residence in Rome and properties outside the city were soon sacked and destroyed.

The torture of exile for the urban dweller of antiquity is shown by Cicero's constant thoughts of suicide during the exile. He was "a kind of image of a dead man, a breathing corpse."[31] It was reported that Cicero's mind was "becoming unhinged with grief."[32] He wrote to his wife from Brundisium: "Would that I had been less eager to live! . . . if however, these ills can never be removed, I assure you, my dearest, that my desire is to see you as soon as

---

[28] Cicero also pleads health reasons in *Brutus* 313–314. Gruen 1968:149–178, cf. Mitchell 1979:93n1. Schur (1962:216) accepts Plutarch here, cf. Bucheit 1975:570.

[29] *On the Responses of the Haruspices* 17; *On His House* 76 (*in isto tuo maledicto*).

[30] See Nisbet 1961:ix–xiv; Shackleton Bailey 1965–1968 2:227–232; Herescu 1961, who contrasts Cicero's actual exiles with a psychic exile during Caesar's ascendancy; Seager 1965; Cremaschi 1944; Gahan 1985, esp. 145n1; Grasmück 1977, and 1978:110–126; Habicht 1990:47; Mitchell 1991:132–157; Stroh 2004, with further literature.

[31] *Letters to his Brother, Quintus* 1.3.1, *quamdam effigiem spirantis mortui*. See also Cicero *Letters to Atticus* 3.7–21; *Letters to his Brother, Quintus* 1.4; Plutarch Cicero 32.5 (877b): "he led a disheartened and excessively mournful existence for the most part" (ἀθυμῶν καὶ περίλυπος διῆγε τὰ πολλά). Cf. Stockton 1971:190; Sihler 1914:208–209. The exile was an "intolerable wound," Nisbet 1965:64. For Cicero's exile as a death, see Claassen 1996:574–575, 1999:107. For exile generally as death, see Doblhofer 1987:166–178; 57; and below, ch. 23 (Ovid's misery in exile), ch. 25 (Seneca's exile poetry). For Cicero's psychological state, Briot 1968.

[32] *Letters to Atticus* 3.13.2, *mentis errore ex dolore adfici*.

possible and die in your arms."[33] If his life helps his children, he will live, even if life is unbearable.[34] "No practical wisdom or mere erudition either is strong enough to endure so great a grief."[35] However, as R. G. M. Nisbet notes, Cicero was able to view his exile as a "voluntary martyrdom";[36] the "voluntary motif" is an important recurring theme in the ideology of poetic victims.[37]

Cicero waited in Macedonia until he was recalled as a result of the belated efforts of Pompey and his friend Milo. After his return, his first speech, *After his Return: To the Senate*, lacerated the consuls, Gabinius and Piso, who had allowed his exile:[38] "The dominant note is a veritable paroxysm of hatred . . . This bottomless depth of rancor, of hatred, of revenge, uttered without any moderation, is the soul and spirit of [*After his Return*] . . . We shiver at this fury."[39] Soon Cicero would lash out at a favorite target, Clodius, in the *On His House*.[40]

So closely was a Roman's happiness bound up with residence in Rome that Cicero viewed his Cilician governorship (51–50 BC) as a painful exile, and was constantly thirsty for political news from Rome.[41]

After Julius Caesar's assassination in 44 BC, the stage was set for Cicero's final, fatal series of invective speeches, the *Philippics*. Cicero was inevitably aligned with the Republican party, the assassins, and opposed the Caesarian leader, Antony. In mid-44 Cicero had contemplated a visit to Greece, but turned back when it appeared that his presence would be necessary for the struggle of the senate against the dictatorial powers of Antony.[42] After he entered

---

[33] *Letters to His Friends* 14.4.1 (trans. Williams): *quod utinam minus vitae cupidi fuissemus! . . . si haec mala fixa sunt, ego vero te quam primum, mea vita, cupio videre et in tuo complexu emori.*

[34] *Letters to His Friends* 14.4.5.

[35] *Letters to his Brother, Quintus* 1.3.5 (trans. Sihler): *neque enim tantum virium habet ulla aut prudentia aut doctrina ut tantum dolorem possit sustinere.*

[36] Nisbet 1965:64; Nisbet discusses the important passage in *For Sestius* (45, cf. *On his House* 63–64; 98–99; *Against Piso* 21), in which Cicero sees himself as a passenger on a ship menaced by pirates; when the pirates demand Cicero, his friends refuse to surrender him, but Cicero is willing to give himself up for the good of his companions. This self-sacrificial motif had great mythical power, for it crops up again in Cicero's death (see below); earlier it had defined the deaths of Aesop (see above, ch. 2; cf. G 92–100) and Socrates (see above, ch. 15). Paradoxically, even when the victim is forced into exile or execution, he departs or dies "willingly." For the voluntary ideology in sacrifice, see Burkert 1983:4, cf. Petronius fr. 1.

[37] For further on the experience of Cicero's exile, see Doblhofer 1987:73–75.

[38] See *After His Return: To the Senate* 10–18; this blame of his exilers is balanced by a section of praise extended to Cicero's supporters, 18–23. Cf. *Letters to Atticus* 4.1.4.

[39] Sihler 1914:216.

[40] See Stroh 2004.

[41] Cf. Herescu 1961:139; Sihler 1914:271.

[42] *Letters to Atticus* 16.7.1–2.

Rome to cheering crowds, Antony called a meeting of the senate, in which he planned to pass legislation calling for honors devoted to the deified Caesar. Cicero refused to attend, pleading fatigue.[43] Antony responded by attacking Cicero violently in the senate, threatening to tear down his house—"this indeed was said much too wrathfully, and with great fury."[44] Cicero responded, in a senate meeting on September 2, with the first *Philippic*—significantly, it is a defensive document; Antony had attacked the orator unreasonably; Cicero retaliates only in response.

This speech was still somewhat restrained in tone; but the verbal hostilities would escalate. Antony called a meeting of the senate for September 19; he came to it *"agmine quadrato"* (with battle-line in order),[45] and delivered a violent tirade against Cicero, vividly described by the orator: "He seemed to all to be, in his usual fashion, rather spewing than speaking . . . He poured all his drunken frenzy on my single head . . . but I cast him, belching and full of nausea, into the toils of Caesar Octavianus."[46]

Cicero, again put on the defensive, then composed one of his masterpieces of invective, the second *Philippic*, which was probably distributed as a pamphlet in December after being circulated among Cicero's friends.[47] In its first half (2–17) Cicero answered Antony's attacks against himself; in the second half, he delivered an exhaustive *vituperatio* against Antony's character.[48] The rest of the *Philippics* followed, by which Cicero succeeded in turning the senate against Antony and keeping him from Rome, thus showing once again how the "satirist" has the power to "exile" his enemy. Plutarch writes: "He raised a successful faction against Antony, drove him [*exekrouse*] out of the city, and sent out the two consuls, Hirtius and Pansa, to wage war upon him."[49]

---

[43] *Philippics* 1.5–6; 2.43.

[44] *Philippics* 1.5: *Nimis iracunde hoc quidem et valde intemperanter.*

[45] *Philippics* 5.7.

[46] *Letters to His Friends* 12.2.1, 12.25.4 (trans. Ker): *itaque omnibus est visus, ut ad te antea scripsi, vomere suo more, non dicere . . . omnemque suum vinulentum furorem in me unum effunderet . . . quem ego ructantem et nauseantem conieci in Caesaris Octaviani plagas.* Cf. *Philippics* 2.1 (*me maledictis lacessisti*); 3.33; 5.19–20: Antony "vomited a speech" against Cicero "from his most filthy mouth" (*orationem ex ore impurissimo evomuit*). For defensive characterization of one's verbal attacker as expelling verbal filth, cf. Aristophanes *Acharnians* 377ff. For the motif of Antony actually vomiting, see *Philippics* 2.63, 76, 84, 104; Merrill 1975:120–121.

[47] *Letters to Atticus* 16.11. See Holmes 1928:198, and Stockton 1971:298n56 for the dating of this speech's appearance.

[48] Cf. Wooten 1983:53–54; Sussman 1994.

[49] *Cicero* 45.3 (884) (trans. Perrin): τὸν μὲν Ἀντώνιον ἐξέκρουσε καὶ κατεστασίασε, καὶ πολεμήσοντας αὐτῷ τοὺς δύο ὑπάτους, Ἵρτιον καὶ Πάνσαν, ἐξέπεμψε . . .

Political and military considerations were of course intertwined with Cicero's oratory.[50] One could argue, against Plutarch, that Antony left Rome (soon after November 28) merely to deal with Decimus Brutus in Gaul. However, Cicero's oratory was an important factor in Antony's discomfiture toward the end of his consular year. Cicero's first *Philippic* had struck an important blow against Antony's prestige and influence in the senate; and in the third and fourth *Philippics*, delivered in the senate and forum on December 20, Cicero branded Antony an outlaw. The senate gave Cicero most of his requests after the fifth *Philippic*, delivered on January 1 when Antony was no longer consul; but they balked at a complete break with Antony, and instead tried to negotiate with him. However, the two new consuls, Hirtius and Pansa, would eventually lead an army against Antony, which was Cicero's main objective. Antony had in effect become an outlaw, a *hostis* of the senate, to a large extent through Cicero's oratorical and political efforts. Unfortunately for Cicero, though the consuls won a major battle, they did not succeed in killing Antony.[51] And Cicero's own exile would follow quickly.

When Octavian formed the Second Triumvirate with Antony, Cicero's days were numbered. Though Octavian reportedly at first tried to save the orator whom he had not long since called "Father," he acceded to Antony, and Cicero was soon proscribed by the man against whom he had been marshaling his invective.[52]

The sources for Cicero's death have been collected and commented upon by Homeyer.[53] Plutarch, primarily followed here, is the fullest and most important account.[54] On the point of sailing from Italy at Circaeum, the orator hesitated, tortured by indecision. Perhaps the sea was too rough to sail on; perhaps he was too ill to sail; perhaps he had not totally given up trust in Octavian. He actually started a journey back to Rome, then returned to the coast, at Astura.

From here he sailed to Caieta, where he owned some lands. Perhaps he preferred to die in Italy; Livy, in a pretty embellishment, has him say, "Let

---

[50] For a sympathetic political analysis of Cicero's position at this time, see Mitchell 1991:300–311.

[51] Third *Philippic* 24; 11; 27; *Letters to His Friends* 10.28.1. On the occasion of the third and fourth *Philippics*, see *Letters to His Friends* 10.28.2.

[52] Plutarch *Cicero* 46.2–3 (884); Mitchell 1991:319–323.

[53] Homeyer 1977. The ancient sources can be found on p. 56n1; see especially Plutarch *Cicero* 46–49 (884–886); *Brutus* 27.6; *Antony* 20; Appian *Civil Wars* 4.19.73; 4.20.81; Dio Cassius 47.8.3; Livy *ap.* Seneca Rhetor *Persuasive Discourses* 6.17. Homeyer shows that, as might be expected, the sources are contradictory and embellished by folkloric details. See also Homeyer 1971; Buechner 1958; Egger 1958; and treatments in such standard works as Syme 1939:192; Gelzer 1939, esp. 1087–1088; Stockton 1971:332; Sihler 1914:462.

[54] See Homeyer 1977: 57–68.

me die in my own country which I have often saved."[55] He retired to a private house; changing his mind once more, he was being carried to the sea when Antony's soldiers found and executed him. The final death had the voluntary motif, for Cicero "stretched forth his neck out of the litter."[56] The Judas of the piece carried out the sentence, Popillius Laenas, whom Cicero had defended.[57] According to Appian, it was a horrible death, for Laenas "struck and cut through his neck three times because of his inexperience." This is may be ahistorical, a secondary accretion that increases the brutality of the murderers and the suffering of the sacrificial hero-victim.[58]

Cicero's head and hands (because they had written the *Philippics*) were taken to Rome and displayed on the rostrum. Dio tells us that Antony's wife, Fulvia, after holding the head in her lap and mocking it, stuck a pin into its tongue. Invective warfare is felt so passionately that it is carried on even after death, as the full details of the account show:

ὡς δ' οὖν καὶ ἡ τοῦ Κικέρωνός ποτε ἐκομίσθη σφίσι (φεύγων γὰρ καὶ καταληφθεὶς ἐσφάγη), ὁ μὲν Ἀντώνιος πολλὰ αὐτῷ καὶ δυσχερῆ ἐξονειδίσας ἔπειτ' ἐκέλευσεν αὐτὴν ἐκφανέστερον τῶν ἄλλων ἐν τῷ βήματι προτεθῆναι, ἵν' ὅθεν κατ' αὐτοῦ δημηγορῶν ἠκούετο, ἐνταῦθα μετὰ τῆς χειρὸς τῆς δεξιᾶς, ὥσπερ ἀπετέτμητο, ὁρῷτο· ἡ δὲ δὴ Φουλουία ἔς τε τὰς χεῖρας αὐτὴν πρὶν ἀποκομισθῆναι ἐδέξατο, καὶ ἐμπικραναμένη οἱ καὶ ἐμπτύσασα ἐπί τε τὰ γόνατα ἐπέθηκε, καὶ τὸ στόμα αὐτῆς διανοίξασα τήν τε γλῶσσαν ἐξείλκυσε καὶ ταῖς βελόναις αἷς ἐς τὴν κεφαλὴν ἐχρῆτο κατεκέντησε, πολλὰ ἅμα καὶ μιαρὰ προσεπισκώπτουσα.

When, however, the head of Cicero also was brought to them one day (he had been overtaken and slain in flight), Antony uttered many bitter reproaches, and then ordered it to be exposed on the rostra more prominently than the rest, in order that it might be seen in the very place where Cicero had so often been heard declaiming against him, together with his right hand, just as it had been cut off.

[55] Livy *ap.* Seneca Rhetor *Persuasive Discourses* 6.17: *"moriar" inquit "in patria saepe servata."* This is probably unhistorical. Buechner (1958) argues unconvincingly that Cicero decided to die so that his influence would continue on, even if the Republic had died. Cf. following note.
[56] Plutarch *Cicero* 48.4–5 (885): ἐσφάγη δὲ τὸν τράχηλον ἐκ τοῦ φορείου προτείνας.
[57] Thus Seneca Rhetor *Persuasive Discourses* 6.20; Appian *Civil Wars* 4.20.77; Dio Cassius 47.11.12 (who, with Plutarch among others, mentions that Cicero had defended him against a charge of patricide—perhaps an ironic ornamentation, for the *pater patriae* to be killed by a patricide, see Homeyer 1977:66). Plutarch, however, has Herennius kill the orator, cf. Homeyer 1977:65–66.
[58] See Homeyer 1977:68–80, esp. 70n33.

And Fulvia took the head into her hands before it was removed, and after abusing it spitefully and spitting upon it, set it on her knees, opened the mouth, and pulled out the tongue, which she pierced with the pins that she used for her hair, at the same time uttering many brutal jests.

Cassius Dio 47.8.3–4[59]

Thus the man who had caused just exile and execution for others had received the equivalent reward unjustly from a political strongman. Plutarch adds a telling detail; when Romans saw the orator's head and hand on the rostrum, "they thought they saw there, not the face of Cicero, but an image of the soul of Antony."[60] The juridical death of the "poet" has paradoxically enshrined the criminality of the lawless politician forever.

To summarize: Cicero was the most powerful wielder of invective of his generation. It was largely by means of this legal and political abuse that he pursued his brilliant career, making his name by attacking Chrysogonus and Verres. Satire is often the weapon of the comparatively socially disadvantaged; Cicero, from nonaristocratic background, became consul, a *novus homo*, to a great extent as a result of it. Just as satirists could cause the exile or death of their victims, so Cicero's invective caused Catiline, Verres, and perhaps Antony[61] to leave Rome. On the other hand, Cicero's attack on Chrysogonus perhaps resulted in his own exile; and his attack on Antony resulted in his departure from Rome, and the most permanent exile, execution. So history seems to copy the earlier legends of satirists killing or exiling their satirical victims and being exiled and executed in turn; but this can only be because the legends reflect authentic, and persistent, social structures.

---

[59] Trans. Cary. This story is probably another fictional detail emphasizing further the monstrousness of Cicero's persecutors, cf. Gelzer 1939:1088; Homeyer 1977:82n64. For the theme of the mutilation of the poet's tongue, cf. Plutarch *On Exile* 16 (606B); Seneca *On Anger* 3.17, where Lysimachus removes a man's tongue, eyes, ears, and nose to punish a chance bit of verbal mockery; ch. 17 (poet Teig Dall O'Higgin's tongue cut out); epilogue. For Fulvia, cf. Plutarch *Antony* 10.5 (920c–d); Babcock 1965.

[60] Plutarch *Cicero* 49.1 (885): οὐ τὸ Κικέρωνος ὁρᾶν πρόσωπον οἰομένοις, ἀλλὰ τῆς Ἀντωνίου ψυχῆς εἰκόνα.

[61] According to Plutarch, see above. At the very least, Cicero's oratory was a central force in turning the senate against Antony and making him a hostis, an 'enemy, outlaw' of Rome.

23

Ovid: Practicing the *Studium Fatale*

PERHAPS THE MOST FAMOUS POETIC EXILE in Latin literature is Ovid's. He was
the first major poet-victim of the repressive powers of the *imperator*;
as he was the most popular living poet,[1] this banishment served notice
that freedom of poetic expression would be severely curtailed in the Augustan
regime. This had been prefigured in the cases of Labienus and Cassius Severus.
Labienus was an abusive orator who opposed the Augustan order; he was pros-
ecuted, and all his writings were burned.[2] Cassius Severus, another prominent
orator, had published *famosi libelli* 'scandalous pamphlets' jibing at prominent
aristocratic men and women. He was condemned by the senate (probably in
12 BC) and banished to Crete.[3] Thus, as Syme writes, "freedom of speech was
curbed and subverted under the pretext of social harmony."[4] And one could be
prosecuted for more than just invective directed against the aristocracy: any
attack on ruler or government could be prosecuted. Even historians had to be
careful about praising the Republican past, as the case of Cremutius Cordus
shows.[5]

Ovid was exiled by Augustus in late autumn, AD 8.[6] Augustus had come to
power in 31 BC; Ovid, who stayed aloof from the emperor's "minister of propa-
ganda," Maecenas, was aligned instead with Messalla and his group (including
Ovid's closest poetic friend, Tibullus).[7] Ovid published the first *Amores* perhaps

---

[1] See *Tristia* 2.519–520; Fränkel 1945:45, 259, 72. For further on Ovid's exile, see Owen 1924, who
assembles the evidence for the exile from Ovid's own poems; Thibault 1964; Fairweather 1987;
Holleman 1971; Wiedemann 1975; Goold 1983; Gahan 1985; Grasmück 1978:135–137; Claassen
1999.

[2] Seneca *Controversies* X, praef. 4–10; Syme 1978:212–213.

[3] Tacitus *Annals* 1.72.3. *Annals* 4.21.3, cf. Syme 1978:213.

[4] Syme 1978:214, 229.

[5] Tacitus *Annals* 4.61.

[6] Cf. Syme 1978:214.

[7] *Amores* 3.9. For the Messalla connection and its possible impact on the exile, cf. Thibault
1964:89–99; see also Wheeler 1925.

in 20 BC; the *Heroides*, letters from famous women to absent husbands or lovers, came between this and the next edition of the *Amores*; this was published immediately before the *Art of Love* (first two books), which appeared in 1 BC or after. The *Metamorphoses* and *Fasti* were written from AD 2 to the exile; the *Metamorphoses* had not received its final revision when Ovid left Rome.[8]

Meanwhile, in 18 and 17 BC, Augustus had passed the *lex Iulia de adulteriis* (which made adultery a public crime) and the *lex Iulia de maritandis ordinibus* (which nearly made bachelorhood a public crime). Obviously, Ovid's love elegies did not fit neatly into the spirit of Augustus' moral reforms; the *Art of Love*, a how-to book on the illicit affair, is almost a blatant invitation to disregard the reforms. It is easy to see the reasons for the conflict that was gradually taking shape, and from which the poet would later suffer.[9] But perhaps the lack of precedent for a poet receiving major punishment made Ovid ignore the danger his poems might cause him.

Thus, Ovid's exile is, in general, by no means inexplicable; there are, however, aspects of it that remain enigmatic to this day. A key text is *Tristia* 2.207–244:

> perdiderunt cum me duo crimina, <u>carmen</u> et <u>error</u>
>   alterius facti <u>culpa</u> silenda mihi:
> nam non sum tanti, renovem ut tua vulnera, Caesar
>   quem nimio plus est indoluisse semel.
> altera pars superest, qua <u>turpi carmine</u> factus
>   arguor obsceni doctor adulterii.
>   * * *
> at si, quod mallem, vacuum tibi forte fuisset,
>   nullum legisses crimen in Arte mea.
> illa quidem fateor frontis non esse severae
>   scripta, nec a tanto principe digna legi:
> non tamen idcirco legum contraria iussis
>   sunt ea Romanas erudiuntque nurus.

Though two crimes, a poem [*carmen*] and a blunder [*error*], have brought me ruin, of my fault [*culpa*] in the one I must keep silent, for my worth is not such that I may reopen your wounds, O Caesar;

---

[8] Cf. Kenney 1982:855.

[9] Cf. Syme, "In sharp contrast to Virgil and Horace, the writers of elegiac verse eschew national and patriotic attitudes; they are averse from extolling governmental achievements in war and peace" (1978:188). Something more than indifference can be found in Ovid, though: "malicious frivolity or even muted defiance" (190). See also, Stroh 1979.

it is more than enough that you should have been pained once. The other remains: the charge that by an obscene poem [*turpi carmine*] I have taught foul adultery ... [Ovid explains why a great emperor should be too busy to read the poet's trifling poems] ... Yet if ... you had happened to have the leisure, you would have read no crime in my "Art." That poem, I admit, has no serious mien, it is not worthy to be read by so great a prince; but not for that reason is it opposed to the commandments of the law nor does it offer teaching to the daughters of Rome. (trans. Wheeler, adapted)

By Ovid's account, then, he was exiled for a "poem" and a "mistake." This would seem simple enough, though the *error* is not specified. But then one wonders which was the more important *crimen*. Peter Green argues that participation in a political scandal of some sort was the reason for the exile, and that the mention of Ovid's poetry was mere window dressing, a *prophasis* for the real crime.[10] While such an interpretation is possible, much evidence argues against it.[11] In the passage quoted above, Ovid calls his political offence an *error*, a very mild word, hardly enough to cause the harsh sentence of exile. Elsewhere, he says it should be called *culpa*, not a *facinus*.[12]

In one passage, Cupid, speaking to the poet, implies that of the two *crimina*, the *error* injured the poet more,[13] but other Ovidian data contradicts this. One passage explicitly says that poetry was the chief cause of the exile. Ovid, speaking to the Muses, writes: "By your leave, nine sisters, would I say it: you are the chief cause of my exile" (*pace, novem, vestra liceat dixisse, sorores: / vos estis nostrae maxima causa fugae*).[14] This would be, according to Green, diversionary, but it seems excessively diversionary.

In the two passages already cited, it is worth noting that the poem is always mentioned first. And in the first passage, after a brief mention of the *error*, Ovid spends the rest of the (long) poem protesting that his poem was not

---

[10] Green 1982.

[11] Green's statement that, "of the three main theories [for Ovid's exile] ... two can be dismissed out of hand: ... only a political solution to the problem is acceptable" seems overly doctrinaire (1982:209).

[12] *Letters from Pontus* 1.6.25.

[13] *Letters from Pontus* 3.3.65–76 (trans. Wheeler, modified): "There resides no crime in your 'Art'. As I defend you on this score, would I could on the rest! You know there is another thing that has injured you more." (*Artibus et nullum crimen inesse tuis. / utque hoc, sic utinam defendere cetera possem! / scis aliud, quod te laeserit, esse, magis*).

[14] *Tristia* 5.12.45–50. See also *Tristia* 1.1.67, 113; 2.2, 2.10, 2.495, 3.3.73, 3.7.9; *Ibis* 5, *Letters from the Pontus* 2.7.47; 2.10.15; 3.3.46; 3.5.4; 4.2.32; 4.13.41.

a crime. This would lead one to entertain the possibility that the *error* could be diversionary camouflage.

Green's most convincing argument is "the irrational delay between publication and punishment; there is no reason why Augustus should have waited so long to strike . . . and then to have struck, *on that basis,* so improbably hard."[15] However, Green fails to allow time for publishing and dissemination—not a quick process before the printing press, obviously—and for the fact of Ovid's continuing popularity. As Ovid's popularity grew, it would become more and more offensive to the emperor, and, in his mind, more pernicious.

It is also significant that the *Art of Love* was removed from public libraries at the time of the exile, not a common occurrence.[16] Augustus and Ovid, working in tandem, would seem to be carrying out an extremely elaborate diversion if Ovid was not exiled to a significant degree for his poetry.

Yet one should not ignore the *error.* J. C. Thibault suggests that the two *crimina* were related.[17] Syme ends his treatment of the exile by concluding that "the '*carmen*' and the '*error*' are in a tight nexus. Neither charge was good enough without the other." Yet he also inclines toward the *Art of Love* as the most important cause, "the root and cause of enduring resentment."[18] I conclude, then, that Ovid's *Art of Love* was a major cause, perhaps the major cause, for the poet's exile.[19]

We are then left with a picture that resonates in familiar ways. Augustus sees the Roman people diminishing through lack of marriage and propagation; it is, as it were, a plague on the country. (One thinks of the beginning of the *Oedipus Rex*, where all of the productivity of the country has been struck down. Cows will not calve; fields will not produce; women will not bear children, 25–27.) Legislation is passed to combat this, with not entirely satisfactory results. On top of this Ovid publishes the *Art of Love*, explaining to the Roman how to go about breaking Augustus' laws. Ovid, the most popular poet of his day, is seen by Augustus as a cause of the plague of infertility; the *peripsēma* is expelled from the commonwealth to ward off the plague. Syme has an good summary:

> [There is] . . . the anger and resentment of the septuagenarian despot. Augustus can never have liked a man who spurned the

---

[15] Green 1982:203.

[16] *Tristia* 3.1.65ff.; *Letters from Pontus* 1.1.5ff.

[17] 1964:31.

[18] 1978:222, cf. 219, on the false dichotomy of politics and morals.

[19] Cf. Bretzigheimer 1991:71, with further bibliography on this point.

career of honours and continued to be proud of his secession. Ovid should have entered the Senate as quaestor in the salubrious season of the *Leges Iuliae*, perhaps to rise high as a loyal representative of old Italy. Instead, something noxious and odious: a declared and defiant '*praeceptor amoris*.'[20]

"Something noxious and odious" must be expelled to cleanse the state.

Archilochus too was evidently punished for obscene, sexual poetry.[21] Yet Archilochus, according to cult legend, was in reality pious, acting as prophet for the god, Dionysus. So too Ovid, the seemingly gay, secular mocker of the gods, was still quite interested in the concept of the poet as prophet, holy— even if, for him, this may have been just a metaphor for secular realities. J. K. Newman writes, "If we were to go by mere statistics, we should conclude that Ovid was the most ardent supporter of the *vates*-concept (cf. his eighteen uses in the *Amores* by contrast with the *Georgics* or *Odes*)." Newman thinks that Ovid marks a degeneration of the *vates*-concept, but one suspects that he merely disapproves of Ovid.[22]

In the *Amores* (3.9.17–18), we read, "Yes, we bards [*vates*] are called sacred [*sacri*], and the care of the gods; there are those who even think we have the god [*numen*] within."[23] In this same poem, the Tibullus elegy, when Ovid was as serious as he seemingly ever gets, he mourns that death can "profane [*profanat*]" "every sacred thing [*omne sacrum*]" (that is, Tibullus). In *Amores* 3.8.23–24, Ovid writes that he is the "unstained priest [*purus sacerdos*]" of Apollo and the Muses. Sacred *vates*, poet-prophet, pure priest, possessing *numen*: Ovid's concept of the poet, of himself, certainly exploits sacral diction and imagery. Thus he is "pure," holy, clean; but to Augustus, "noxious and odious," a typically ambiguous poet.[24]

There is even a consecration scene, with Cupid, not the Muses, as the inspirer; Ovid, seeking to write epic, is shot by Cupid's arrow:

> "quod" que "canas, <u>uates</u>, accipe" dixit "opus."
> me miserum! certas habuit puer ille sagittas.
> > uror, et in uacuo pectore regnat Amor.
> > sex mihi surgat opus numeris, in quinque residat;

---

[20] 1978:221.

[21] See above, ch. 3.

[22] Newman 1967:52, 51. See also Jocelyn 1995:23nn18, 19.

[23] *at <u>sacri vates</u> et divum cura vocamur; / sunt etiam qui nos <u>numen</u> habere putent.*

[24] Cf. *Tristia* 4.10.18–19; ibid., lines 41–42, 55–56, 129, 39–40; *Amores* 2.1.38; *Art of Love* 1.25–30 (Ovid as "prophet" of Venus).

Chapter Twenty-Three

"Singer" [*uates*], he said, "here, take that which will be the subject
of your song!" Ah, wretched me! Sure were the arrows that boy had.
I am on fire, and in my formerly vacant heart Love reigns. In six
numbers let my work rise, and sink again in five.

Amores 1.1.24–27[25]

This passages touches on the theme in the legendary Homer tradition of the
poet as persecuted by his inspiring god:[26] Cupid is *saeve puer*, "cruel boy,"
(*Amores* 1.1.5); he is *ferus* 'savage', his arrow wounds, pierces violently, and
brands (*Art of Love* 1.9); in *Metamorphoses* 1.45, his wrath is again cruel.

In *Tristia* 5.12.45–68, Ovid addresses bitter words to his inspiring Muses—
they caused his exile; he wishes he had burned the *Art of Love*. Poetry is "the
death-dealing pursuit" (*studium fatale*, 51). Still, he cannot stop writing poetry,
even if he burns what he writes (59–62).

Ovid recognized that his very pre-eminence brought about his exile.
In the *Remedies for Love*, he wrote that some had attacked his love poetry as
proterua 'wanton' (362). But he did not care, as long as he was sung in all the
world; Homer too was attacked. "What is highest is Envy's mark: winds sweep
the summits, and thunderbolts sped by Jove's right hand seek out the heights.
. . . Burst yourself, greedy Envy! My fame is great already, it will be greater
still."[27] Thus the scapegoat is the best, and at the same time, the intolerable
worst.

So Ovid was exiled,[28] and his departure apparently was accompanied by
a "wave of public dislike."[29] Thus the community that had accepted Ovid as
the best gathered to expel him as worst. The poet lived the last years of his
life in a miserable town on the Black Sea. There he wrote our largest and most
influential classical corpus of exile poetry, the *Tristia*, whose title expresses the
misery of exile in the ancient world, and the *Letters from Pontus*.[30] Exile poetry

---

[25] Trans. Showerman, adapted. Cf. *Amores* 2.1.38; 2.18.1–18; *Art of Love* 1.25–31.

[26] See above, ch. 5.

[27] *Remedies* 369–370, 389: *Summa petit liuor: perflant altissima venti, / summa petunt dextra fulmina missa Iouis. . . . rumpere, Liuor edax: magnum iam nomen habemus; / maius erit . . .*

[28] For further bibliography on the reasons for the exile, see Thibault 1964; a small update in Nagle 1980:7; cf. Bretzigheimer 1991.

[29] See Green 1982:209.

[30] For Ovid's misery, cf. Fränkel 1945:261; see also Nagle 1980; Richmond 1995. Froesch interprets Ovid as the "European Prototype of '*der verbannte Poet*,'" see Nagle 1980:7n18. For exile as death, see, representative of many examples, *Tristia* 1.2.45–75, 3.3; *From the Pontus* 4.16; *Ibis* 16. For Ovid's exile poetry, Froesch 1976; Nagle 1980; Evans 1983; Doblhofer 1987; Bretzigheimer 1991; Richmond 1995; Claassen 1996; Forbis 1997; Claassen 1999. For the exile as death, further in Nagle 1980:23–32, Doblhofer 1987:170–171, and Claassen 1996:577–578. Ovid virtually founded

is another point of contact between Archilochus and the Roman poet. Jo-Marie Claassen, in an important book on exile poetry, argues that Ovid consistently mythologized his experiences as an exile, both by heightening the miseries and isolation of his surroundings in Tomus, and by portraying himself as "*Ovidius heros*," "a lonely, long-suffering survivor in a malevolent, mythical world."[31] When he arrives in the Pontic area he experiences shattering physical and pyschological symptoms—or so his poems lead us to believe—that have occasioned modern psychiatric diagnoses.

Certainly the most curious of Ovid's exilic poems is the *Ibis*, a curse poem modeled on Callimachus' poem of the same name.[32] In its obscurity and malevolence, it is quite unlike anything else the poet ever wrote. Ovid targets an unnamed person who has done the poet grievous wrong, and runs through a long catalogue of the horrifying things that could happen to him, if he does not repent. Prominent among these dooms is Ovid's threat to actually call his target by name, a powerful threat in curse or satirical tradition.[33] The poem certainly is a curiosity; interpreters are divided as to whether it is merely a wooden exercise in Hellenistic ingenuity, or whether it reflects authentic hatred. In addition, the *Ibis* is a valuable source for information on the *pharmakos* and on previous exiled poets; thus Ovid stands directly in the Hipponactian tradition, the exiled poet who curses his satiric target by assimilating him to the *pharmakos*.[34]

---

the conventions of exile poetry, one of whose basic themes is "the metaphor of exile as death," writes Claassen. "Death is his [Ovid's] theme from first to last" (Claassen 1996:583). However, Claassen sees a vision of immortality following the depression of exile. See ch. 22 above (Cicero); ch. 25 below (Seneca).

[31] Claassen 1999:198.

[32] See Watson 1991:113–129; Claassen 1999:142–146.

[33] On the power of the name in blame, see above, ch. 14 (Aristophanes); ch. 21 (Naevius); ch. 22 (Cicero).

[34] *Ibis* seems too vitriolic to have Augustus as its target (though he is an obvious possibility), and too intense to be directed at a friend who has neglected Ovid in exile (another theory). Perhaps it was directed at an official who was instrumental in keeping the poet exiled. See Claassen 1999:142, Elliott 1960:126–128.

24

Phaedrus: Another Fabulist

I N PHAEDRUS, we meet once again, in miniature format, the direct Aesopic line of tradition: Aesop, Archilochus, Socrates; fables, offense of the powerful, punishment. Phaedrus, an Augustan freedman of Thracian birth, versified (like Socrates) and Latinized Aesop's fables; but he added some fables of his own, which reflected somewhat the current sociopolitical scene, and included an occasional combative response to a critic.[1] The sinister Sejanus, Tiberius' prefect of the Praetorian Guard, the man responsible for the execution of numerous nobles, took offense at these Greek beast tales, perceiving veiled criticism in them. Phaedrus' prologue to his third book tells us all we know about the situation:

> Nunc, fabularum cur sit inventum genus,
> brevi docebo. servitus obnoxia,
> quia quae volebat non audebat dicere,
> affectus proprios in <u>fabellas</u> translulit,
> calumniamque <u>fictis</u> elusit <u>iocis</u>.
> ego illius pro semita feci viam,
> et cogitavi plura quam reliquerat,
> in <u>calamitatem</u> deligens quaedam meam.
> quodsi accusator alius Seiano foret,
> si testis alius, iudex alius denique,
> dignum faterer esse me tantis malis,
> nec his dolorem delenirem remediis.
> suspicione si quis errabit sua,
> et, rapiens ad se quod erit commune omnium,
> stulte nudabit animi conscientiam,
> huic excusatum me velim nihilo minus.

---

[1] For responses to detractors, see 4.7; 3.prol.23; 4.prol.15; 4.22; Perry 1965:lxxv.

neque enim notare singulos mens est mihi,
verum ipsam vitam et mores hominum ostendere.

Now I will explain briefly why the type of thing called fable was invented. The slave, being liable to punishment for any offence, since he dared not say outright what he wished to say, projected his personal sentiments into fables [*fabellas*] and escaped censure under the guise of jesting with made-up stories [*fictis . . . iocis*].[2] Where Aesop made a footpath, I have built a highway, and have thought up more subjects that he left behind; although some of the subjects I chose led to disaster [*calamitatem*] for me. But if anyone other than Sejanus were the prosecutor, or anyone else the chief witness, or indeed if anyone other than Sejanus were the judge, then I should confess that I deserve my troubles, great as they are, and should not now be soothing my grief with such remedies as this. If anyone hereafter shall be deceived by his own suspicions, and, by rashly appropriating to himself the moral that belongs to all alike, shall expose his own bad conscience, none the less I hope that he will pardon me. For in fact it is not my intention to brand individuals, but to display life itself and the ways of men and women.

Prologue to III, lines 33–50[3]

Thus Sejanus felt that some of the fables in the first two books of Phaedrus referred to him in a derogatory way; he judged the fabulist summarily, acting as prosecutor, witness, and judge; and he leveled a punishment. All we know about the punishment is that it was great, a disaster, *calamitas*, and painful; that Phaedrus was still enduring it when he wrote his third book; and that he wrote to lessen the pain. These would all fit exile perfectly, and Alice Brenot suggests that the punishment probably was exile; exile is also the first punishment that Duff lists as a possibility. Phaedrus may very possibly have been an exiled fabulist; whether or not he was exiled, he was certainly punished severely. (Duff also mentions as possibilities imprisonment or "even a return to slavery.")[4]

---

[2] See above, ch. 3 (Archilochus, the fable of the fox and eagle, with notes); ch. 2 (Aesop as slave and animal fabulist); West 1984:107–108; cf. Meuli 1954:65.

[3] Trans. Perry. Cf. above, ch. 3 (Archilochus, the fable of the fox and eagle). The Negro tales of Joel Chandler Harris are comparable: animal stories that show the plight of the black man in a white society, see Rubin, Jr. 1981.

[4] Brenot 1924:x; Duff 1960:115. Perry 1965:lxxv, suggests that Phaedrus's books could have been banned and destroyed, but this would not seem to measure up to the painful calamity the poet is still enduring as he writes the Book three prologue.

Phaedrus represents himself as being treated unfairly by Sejanus, as if he had nowhere had Sejanus in mind when he wrote his first two books, and Sejanus' guilty conscience caused him to apply some passages to himself. However, there are passages in the first two books that are critical of informers and miscarriages of justice in law courts,[5] and one may even see Sejanus in the fable of the jackdaw in peacock feathers.[6] "At any rate, for the emperor's minister Sejanus there was decidedly unpalatable reading in the first two books."[7] Perhaps Phaedrus was more of a conscious and focused satirist than he admits.

In the same passage in which Phaedrus says he is not attacking specific people, but human generalities, he says, at the beginning of the quoted passage, that the fable came about so slaves could criticize their social betters elliptically without being punished, an intriguing account of the birth of the fable in class struggle. Working from such a rationale, criticisms of Sejanus in his first two books would not be so unlikely. One comes to look at this minor poet, this versifier of Aesop, with new respect—this former slave who published satire critiquing the most powerful and murderous man in a repressive society. He was not an unworthy inheritor, in his humble way, of the Aesopic-Socratic tradition. "For one of his humble status Phaedrus is singularly outspoken," writes F. R. D. Goodyear.[8]

A number of other aspects of Phaedrus deserve at least brief examination. His satire was didactic, not just amusing; it upheld honesty and justice.[9] If his detractors criticize him for his principles, we have a situation where the righteous blame poet strikes out at a corrupt society.[10]

The theme of expulsion of a scapegoat appears in his fables. One of Phaedrus' non-Aesopic, Roman "fables," "Pompey and his Soldier," is almost a tour de force of the scapegoat theme in a Roman military setting. This story serves as the central text for a stimulating article by Cristiano Grottanelli.[11] In this fable, there is in the camp of Pompey the Great a notoriously effeminate homosexual soldier who is nevertheless of very sturdy build. When he steals the general's mules along with precious metals and jewels, and is caught and

---

[5] 1.1; 1.15; cf. Goodyear 1982:625; Duff 1960:114.

[6] *Fable* 1.3, a little drama of expulsion. The vainly dressed up jackdaw, trying to associate with a crowd of peacocks, is stripped of his peacock feathers, pecked, and expelled. Returning to his own jackdaws, he is expelled from their company also.

[7] Duff 1960:114. Cf. de Lorenzi 1955:5.

[8] Goodyear 1982:625.

[9] IV.2.1–4; III. epil. 29–35; cf. Duff 1960:115.

[10] Duff 1960:112–113.

[11] Grottanelli 1983. See also a lively interpretation in Henderson 2001:131–150.

accused, he brazenly denies with an oath that he has had any involvement in the theft. "Then Pompey, being a man of simple honesty, orders this disgrace to the camp [*dedecus castrorum*] to be driven away [*propelli*]."[12] Later a huge champion of an opposing army proposes single combat with any soldier in the Roman army, but the foremost Roman warriors mutter in cowardice. However, the effeminate thief—"a catamite in bearing but a Mars in prowess" (*cinaedus habitu sed Mars uiribus*)—approaches Pompey and asks, "in a delicate voice" (*uoce molli*), if he can fight the opposing champion. Pompey is enraged that the catamite would trifle with him in such a desperate situation, and once again he orders the soldier to be expelled (*eici . . . imperat*). However, a senior advisor recommends that the catamite would not be such a bad choice for champion, because he "would be no great loss" (*in quo iactura levis est*), while a valiant man might be defeated and lost to the army. Pompey accedes to this counsel, and the effeminate soldier becomes champion of the Romans. He promptly decapitates the enemy champion and "returns as conqueror" (*victorque rediit*). Pompey gives him a crown (*corona*), but swears by the same oath that the soldier had sworn that the soldier was certainly the thief of the mules and valuables.

Thus, in this story, we have the warrior as scapegoat—continually banished, and finally sent virtually as a sacrificial offering to the enemy champion, because he is not worth anything at all. The scapegoat is entirely ambiguous; super-manly (in stature) and sub-manly (effeminate in gait and speech); a thief and a liar, yet most courageous of all the soldiers, and skillful in hand-to-hand combat; judged the worst of the Romans, he yet receives the crown of victory from the general. As Grotanelli notes, he is blamed even as he is crowned.[13] The scapegoat as champion recalls Starkaðr and Suibhne as well as the Irish fool Tamun. The deformed worst excluded because he is worthless—who yet becomes the best soldier—replicates the story of Tyrtaeus.

---

[12] Perotti's appendix, 10.12–13 (trans. Perry, modified): *tum uir animi simplicis / id dedecus castrorum propelli iubet.* Perry's translation of *propelli* 'to be sent on his way', seems too weak for the word, which has a sense of driving, pushing, hurling (see *OLD* s.v.). Grotanelli notes that typical punishment for such offenses (thievery, perjury, sexual offenses, all of which are covered by our hero) in the Roman army included stoning and beating with rods (1983:130). Expelled from the camp, one was protectionless, like a dead man.

[13] Grotanelli 1983:129.

25

Seneca, Petronius, and Lucan: Neronian Victims

O F THREE MAJOR REPRESENTATIVES of "Menippean" satire, Varro, Seneca, and Petronius, two met their deaths at the hand of Nero, as did Lucan, another prominent poet. In addition, it is possible that Persius was poisoned by Nero; he died of stomach sickness, always suspect in the imperial age. He was friendly with the Nero opposition party among the Stoics; some have thought that the portrait of Midas (1.119–121) was aimed at Nero.[1] Though these are not exiled or executed poets in the grand tradition, they are still case studies of poets practicing the *studium fatale*.

Seneca

One does not immediately think of Seneca as a satirist; he is known primarily as a philosopher, tragic dramatist, and politician.[2] However, his *Apocolocyntosis*, the "Pumpkinification" of the emperor Claudius, puts him directly in the tradition of Menippean satire in its mixture of prose and verse; the Menippean genre also provides a link to Seneca as philosopher, for Menippus wrote from a philosophical, Cynic perspective.[3]

---

[1] See Dilke 1972, esp. p. 74; Herrmann 1963; the Stoic Cornutus censored the satires after Persius' death. On Menippean satire, see below. On Lucan, see Suetonius *The Life of Lucan*; Tacitus *Annals* 15.49.

[2] Some authors, faced with this contradiction, have tried to disassociate him from authorship of the *Pumpkinification*, see Duff 1936:91n19.

[3] Menippus, cynic, who lived in the first half of the third century BC, originated the *spoudogeloion* style (cf. Strabo 16.2.29 [759]), in which serious, philosophical views were expressed in a thoroughgoing comic way. He influenced Lucian and Meleager of Gadara. See Diogenes Laertius 6.99–101; Lucian *Menippus*. The Stoics traced a philosophical lineage to Socrates through the Cynics (Zeno—Crates—Diogenes—Antisthenes—Socrates). Seneca was a close friend of Demetrius, a Cynic. For Menippean satire, see Helm 1931; Sullivan 1968:89–90; Coffey 1976:162; Relihan 1993.

Though the *Pumpkinification* may seem a shallow, if amusing and skillful, lampoon, and very safe satire in its mockery of a dead,[4] limping, lisping, pedantic, somewhat pathetic, and eminently satirizable emperor,[5] it was yet "an implicit satire on the whole idea of apotheosis."[6] For our purposes, we note that it is a drama of exclusion—the hero is given trial by the gods for membership in heaven, and is driven from their company as unworthy (after an influential speech by the divine Augustus). Claudius is cast out of heaven, passes by earth, and is tried again in Hades, where he is humiliated to the level of slave, and a slave moreover owned by a Greek freedman. Such themes as exclusion of the lame Thersites *pharmakos*, and peripety from king to slave, are familiar and striking. This is purely in the Hipponactian tradition (continued by Ovid and Phaedrus) of attacking your satirical target by assimilating him to the *pharmakos*.

Seneca was both exiled and executed (by Claudius and Nero, respectively); and a third emperor Gaius Caligula, jealous of his oratorical skill, had once condemned him to death. ("Seneca . . . who was superior in wisdom to all the Romans of his day and many others as well, came near being destroyed, though he had neither done any wrong nor had the appearance of doing so, but merely because he pleaded a case well in the senate while the emperor was present.")[7] So the *Pumpkinification* is in reality retaliatory; Claudius excluded the philosopher, so he excludes the dead emperor from postmortem bliss—as it were, denies him hero cult. Actually, Claudius' notorious wife, Messalina, was apparently the moving force in the exile,[8] though it took place under the emperor's authority. Technically, the senate gave Seneca his sentence, the death penalty, and Claudius softened it to exile.[9] But Seneca blamed the emperor: "He was thought to hate Claudius because of the pain of the injustice done him."[10] The orator was accused of having an adulterous affair with

---

[4] Duff notes that the *Apocolocyntosis* is very different from the flattery Seneca had earlier offered Claudius, 1936:95.

[5] It is possible that Nero suggested the satire to Seneca, Duff 1936:96.

[6] Duff 1936:93.

[7] Cassius Dio 59.19 (trans. Foster): ὁ δὲ δὴ Σενέκας . . . ὁ πάντας μὲν τοὺς καθ᾽ ἑαυτὸν Ῥωμαίους πολλοὺς δὲ καὶ ἄλλους σοφίᾳ ὑπεράρας, διεφθάρη παρ᾽ ὀλίγον μήτ᾽ ἀδικήσας τι μήτε δόξας, ὅτι δίκην τινὰ ἐν τῷ συνεδρίῳ παρόντος αὐτοῦ καλῶς εἶπε. Caligula orders his execution, but rescinds the decree when a woman tells him Seneca will soon die of consumption. Cf. Griffin 1976:53.

[8] According to Cassius Dio 60.8.5; cf. Griffin, who thinks Dio's accusation is plausible (1974:9). Seneca was "the innocent victim" of Messalina.

[9] *To Polybius, On Consolation* 13.2.

[10] Tacitus *Annals* 12.8: *infensus Claudio dolore iniuriae credebatur.* Cf. *Annals* 13.42 (trans. Grant): "'Seneca hates Claudius' friends,' said Suillius. 'For under Claudius he was most deservedly

Julia Livilla, the sister of Gaius Caligula, and was exiled to Corsica.[11] There he wrote the two books of consolation, reflecting more or less obliquely on his plight, and epigrams describing the misery of his exile, thus adding to our long tradition of exile poetry in the classical tradition.[12] Lines from an epigram on Corsica are typical:

> Non panis, non haustus aquae, non ultimus ignis:
> hic sola haec duo sunt, exsul et exsilium.

> Here there is no bread, no drawing of water, no final fire:
> here there are only two things, the exiled man and exile.

Seneca *Epigram* 3

The exiled man is a living corpse.[13] The intensity of the philosopher's hatred of exile is remarkable, especially considering his earlier Stoic writings on the subject. "I may become an exile," he had written earlier. "I will act like a native of the place where I am sent."[14] Ferguson points this out in a decidedly unsympathetic treatment of the philosopher.[15] Ferguson may be underestimating the depressive impact of exile; Cicero, earlier, had been nearly suicidal in exile.[16] Euripides wrote, "What is the loss of a country? A great ill? The greatest; and no words can do it justice."[17]

Seneca stayed in Corsica for some eight years, until Claudius' newer wife, Agrippina, had him recalled, and he was made tutor to Agrippina's son, the young Nero. A period of great political influence for Seneca followed, especially when Nero, still too young to fully take the reins of government, acceded to the throne in AD 54, and Seneca acted as imperial advisor. But eventually Nero began to rule more independently, began his famous series of murders,

---

exiled!'" (*Senecam increpans infensum amicis Claudii, sub quo iustissimum exilium pertulisset*). Cf. Seneca *On Benefits* 4.32.3; Ferguson 1972:8.

[11] It seems unlikely that the charge was true, though "Seneca's sexual life was suspect," as Ferguson remarks (1972:8). Griffin presents evidence that the two consolations would be ludicrous if Seneca had been guilty (1976:60–61); both Ferguson and Griffin mention the frequency of the adultery charge as a device to get rid of political enemies.

[12] For Seneca's exilic epigrams, see Prato 1964; Herrmann 1955. They are not certainly authentic.

[13] For Seneca's exile as a death, see Claassen 1996:586–587.

[14] *Exul fiam; ibi me natum putabo, quo mittar. Moral Epistles* 24.17, trans. in Ferguson 1972:8.

[15] Ferguson 1972:8.

[16] See above, ch. 22; cf. ch. 23 (Ovid's misery in exile).

[17] *Phoenician Women* 388f., quoted in Plutarch *On Exile* 2 (599E), trans. De Lacy, τί τὸ στέρεσθαι πατρίδος; ἦ κακὸν μέγα; / μέγιστον· ἔργῳ δ' ἐστὶ μεῖζον ἢ λόγῳ. Cf. Gahan 1985; Grasmück 1978:138–140; Doblhofer 1987:173, for the exile as death theme in Seneca. Further on Seneca's exile, Kamp 1934.

and listened to unscrupulous advisors who disparaged the philosopher. When Seneca's ally and protector, Burrus, the prefect of the praetorian guard, died in 62, the philosopher saw that his power had evaporated. Donating his property to Nero, he retired to read and write philosophy (Tacitus *Annals* 14.49). Tension between Nero and Seneca was partly artistic; Nero's bad counselors reported to the emperor that Seneca made fun of the emperor's singing (Tacitus *Annals* 14.49).

After Seneca's retirement, Nero tried, and failed, to kill him by poison, but later implicated him, evidently unjustly, in the Pisonian conspiracy.[18] The philosopher was sentenced to death, and committed suicide at Nero's order.

In Tacitus' long description of Seneca's death, parallels with Socrates' death are plentiful. Seneca rebukes the tears of his followers; he impassively carries out the sentence, committing suicide almost willingly; he even takes hemlock when his bleeding cuts (in arms, ankles, and knees) prove ineffectual (though his lack of blood circulation blocks the poison from taking effect).[19] He finally has to suffocate in a vapor bath. At all times during the suicide he discourses eloquently and stoically, and he even dictates an extensive text (probably on the soul, Miriam Griffin surmises) after opening his veins. He offers a libation, to Jupiter Liberator (evidently a reference to the liberation of the soul in death) and exhorts his friends to live by his philosophical teachings.[20] Thus Socrates'—and Aesop's—death continued to live on, replicated in different settings. Seneca's death, in turn, was later copied by Thrasea.[21]

Petronius

Petronius Arbiter's death was less philosophical, but no less distinctive. After having become an intimate of Nero, an arbiter of his decadence and luxury ("to the blasé emperor nothing was smart or elegant unless Petronius had given it his approval"),[22] he incurred the jealousy of another imperial favorite,

---

[18] Tacitus *Annals* 14.49, 15.58–62. Seneca was a friend of Piso; whatever his knowledge of the conspiracy, he certainly was not a ringleader. The unsympathetic Ferguson argues that he was not involved (1972:11).

[19] Tacitus, or Seneca, explicitly bows to Socrates: "Poison, such as was formerly used to execute State criminals at Athens," trans. Grant, *Annals* 15.64: *venenum quo damnati publico Atheniensium iudicio extinguerentur.*

[20] Tacitus *Annals* 15.63. See Griffin 1976, who treats most of these Socratic parallels. Seneca had frequently celebrated Socrates' death, see Griffin 1976:373n2.

[21] See Tacitus *Annals* 16.34–35; cf. Griffin 1974:29.

[22] Tacitus *Annals* 16.18 (trans. Grant): *dum nihil amoenum et molle adfluentia putat, nisi quod ei Petronius adprobavisset.*

Tigellinus (because he was "a more expert hedonist," *scientia voluptatum potiorem*) and received a trumped-up death sentence from the emperor not long after the Pisonian conspiracy. Like Seneca, he quickly cut his veins, but bandaged and opened them in a long, drawn-out death, during which he dined and discoursed with friends and listened to recitations of "light lyrics and frivolous poems,"[23] not Platonic dialogues on the soul. As a final will and testament to Nero, he chronicled all the emperor's sexual indiscretions and sent the document to the tyrant: a long catalogue of sexual blame, directed against a king, in the Aesopic and Socratic tradition of just accusation at the point of death.

Thus our two Menippean satirists were executed unjustly by stark political force, and died, in their contrasting styles, quite "willingly," once the death sentence had been given.

As we have seen in the cases of Hipponax and Aristophanes, often satirists are themselves fascinated by the *pharmakos*, even as they are themselves assimilated to its pattern.[24] So it is notable that the standard evidence on the scapegoat in Marseilles is Petronius fr. 1. It is likely that the narrator of the *Satyricon* is assimilated to the *pharmakos* at Marseilles, after he has committed some crime, perhaps temple robbery (133.3, lines 7–8). There may have been a plague and a public expulsion.[25]

Bremmer notes that Petronius is the only Latin writer to use the word *pharmacus*.[26] We also find the following in the *Satyricon*: "Some of the people who were walking in the colonnades threw stones at Eumolpus as he recited. But he recognized this tribute to his genius, covered his head, and fled out of the temple. I was afraid that he would also call me a poet" (*Ex is, qui in porticibus spatiabantur, lapides in Eumolpum recitantem miserunt. At ille, qui plausum ingenii sui nouerat, operuit caput extraque templum profugit. Timui ego, ne me poetam uocaret*, 90). Lurking behind this comic scene is the theme of the stoning of a poet. Eumolpus is also thrown out of the baths for reciting poetry, so we have the archaic Indo-European theme of poetic expulsion, in comic form (90.1; 92.6).

---

[23] Tacitus *Annals* 16.19 (trans. Grant): *levia carmina et facilis versus*. For Petronius' death, cf. Rankin 1971:2.

[24] See above, ch. 4 (Hipponax).

[25] For a reconstruction of the novel's beginning and discussion of fr. 1, see Sullivan 1968:40–41.

[26] *Satyricon* 107; Bremmer 1983b:300n8.

Lucan

Lucan, on the other hand, was an actual conspirator, "almost the ringleader"[27] in the Pisonian conspiracy. But his motivations for joining the plot were artistic, not political, curiously enough. He had started his political career with a eulogy of Nero;[28] he was later recalled from Athens by the emperor and became one of his intimates. But artistic jealousy divided the poet and his poet-emperor. The envious Nero left a reading by Lucan, calling a meeting of the senate on the spur of the moment "with no other motive than to throw cold water on the performance." From then on Lucan "did not refrain from words and hostility to the prince, which are still notorious."[29] Tacitus (*Annals* 15.49) confirms this antagonism, though he speaks in more general terms: "The wrongs perpetrated against him inflamed Lucan, because Nero, vain in his competitiveness, continually repressed the fame of his [Lucan's] poems, and had kept him from publicizing them."[30] Though Lucan is known primarily as an epic poet, he was also a satirist, for at this juncture "he also tongue-lashed [*gravissime proscidit*] not only the emperor, but also his most powerful friends in a scurrilous poem [*famoso carmine*]."[31] The unsuccessful assassination plot followed; thus the weapon of satire was followed by the plan for using actual weapons.

The conspiracy was discovered and conspirators started implicating each other. Lucan was arrested, and sentenced to death.[32] He died, as had Seneca and Petronius, by bleeding to death. As he felt his strength leaving him, he remembered a wounded soldier in his *Civil War* who had died in the same way, and he recited the passage as he slowly faded into unconsciousness.

Nero, oddly enough, was also a satirist. His poetic vocation helped stoke the Pisonian conspiracy, bringing two men into it, Lucan and Afranius Quintianus, this last a notoriously dissolute character "who had been insulted

---

[27] Suetonius *Life of Lucan: paene signifer.*

[28] Suetonius *Life of Lucan.*

[29] Suetonius *Life of Lucan* (trans. Rolfe): *Revocatus Athenis a Nerone cohortique amicorum additus atque etiam quaestura honoratus, non tamen permansit in gratia: si quidem aegre ferens, <quod se> recitante subito ac nulla nisi refrigerandi sui causa indicto senatu recessisset, neque verbis adversus principem neque factis excitantibus post haec temperavit.* Suetonius retells a scurrilous anecdote in which the defecating Lucan mocks a line of Nero's poetry (ibid.).

[30] My trans. *Lucanum propriae causae accendebant, quod famam carminum eius premebat Nero prohibueratque ostentare, vanus adsimulatione.*

[31] Suetonius *Life of Lucan* (trans. Rolfe): *Sed et famoso carmine cum ipsum, tum potentissimos amicorum gravissime proscidit.*

[32] Tacitus adds that he informed on his mother before death (*Annals* 15.64), but this seems a vindictive embellishment.

by Nero in an offensive poem [*probroso carmine*], and desired revenge."[33] Nero also wrote a satire, "The One-Eyed Man," directed against Claudius Pollio.[34] When Galba and the Spanish provinces rebelled against Nero, he responded by ridiculing the revolt's leaders "in verses set to wanton music [*iocularia . . . carmina lasciveque modulata*]" (Suetonius *Nero* 42.).

Nero was executed as a bad political leader, but J. P. Sullivan argues that one of the primary reasons that Nero became such a bad political leader was because he spent so much time in artistic pursuits.[35] His devotion to his own poetry almost amounted to an obsession.[36] His conflict with Lucan shows that his poetic ambitions helped bring about Lucan's assassination plot. And the emphasis Nero put on his poetry and singing shows that his executions of Seneca, Petronius, and Lucan might easily have been caused in part by poetic jealousy. "The trepidation and anxiety with which he took part in the contests, his keen rivalry of his opponents and his awe of the judges, can hardly be credited . . . he used to show respect to them [his rivals] and try to gain their favour, while he slandered them behind their backs, sometimes assailed them with abuse when he met them, and even bribed those who were especially proficient."[37] It is an Alexandrian intrigue of rival poets given nightmarish dimensions by the fact that one of the rival poets possesses unlimited power, and is also losing his grip on reality.

On the other hand, Nero's response to lampoons directed at him was comparatively mild. However, he did exile an actor, Datus, for satirical allusion; a Cynic philosopher, Isidorus, who had satirized him (Suetonius *Nero* 29); another philosopher, L. Annaeus Cornutus, who had criticized Nero's literary ambitions (Dio 62.29.2); and a poet, Antistius Sosianus, who had written "offensive poems" (*carminibus probrosis*) about the emperor (evidently, the original sentence was capital) (Tacitus *Annals* 16.14; 21). Antistius won his return to Rome by informing on a fellow exile. In addition, Fabricius Veiento, a minor writer who had published an offensive satire on senators and priests, was also exiled.[38]

---

[33] Tacitus *Annals* 15.49 (trans. Grant): *a Nerone probroso carmine diffamatus contumeliam ultum ibat.*

[34] Suetonius *Domitian* 1; cf. Duff 1936:96.

[35] Sullivan 1985:23.

[36] For Nero and his poetry, see Suetonius *Nero* 12, 20–25, 41, 52, 53; Tacitus *Annals* 13.3; 14.16; 15.33–35, 39 (Nero sings as Rome burns); 16.4–5.

[37] Suetonius *Nero* 23 (trans. Rolfe): *Quam autem trepide anxieque certaverit, quanta adversariorum aemulatione, quo metu iudicum, vix credi potest. Adversarios . . . observare, captare, infamare secreto, nonnumquam ex occursu maledictis incessere ac, si qui arte praecellerent, conrumpere etiam solebat.*

[38] See Sullivan 1985:34–35. On all of these, see Sullivan 1985:154, who follows Suetonius in portraying Nero as relatively unrepressive.

When the military rebellion had spread and Nero's support even at Rome had evaporated, he began to prepare for death. At this point, he delivered one of his most famous sayings: *Qualis artifex pereo!* (What an artist the world is losing!).[39] Soon, to avoid a threatened torturous execution, he committed suicide. So one more satirist, albeit an extraordinarily powerful, mediocre (at least according to Tacitus *Annals* 14.14), and mentally unbalanced satirist, met his death.

.

---

[39] Suetonius *Nero* 49, trans. Rolfe.

26

Juvenal: The Burning Poet

I T IS FITTING that we should end our survey with Juvenal, for his savagery and artistry mark a culmination of Roman satire. For Gilbert Highet, "The Roman Juvenal was the greatest satiric poet who ever lived."[1] Though bitterness and venom characterize Juvenal's poetry,[2] its intent was highly moral and didactic; the good satirist reproves and teaches.[3] In Juvenal we find many of the standard themes of blame: like Starkaðr, he rages against old age;[4] the misery of poverty is a constant theme;[5] like Starkaðr, he excoriates the lower classes and foreigners rising above their proper level.[6] Satire 6 is a massive misogynistic manifesto, Juvenal's longest satire, and, many think, his masterpiece; Satire 1 starts out with the theme of poet satirizing poet. The archaic theme of poet satirizing his stingy patron is found in the fifth satire.[7]

Thus, it is entirely appropriate that a persistent tradition of embittered exile should be attached to the *vita* of the poet. Even if he was not exiled— and, just as in the case of Naevius, some scholars deny that the exile ever took place[8]—such a story would be a necessary topos in the life story of a dominant satirist. The exile is not explicitly attested in the satires; Sidonius, born in AD 430, clearly refers to an exile that may be Juvenal's, but he does not mention Juvenal by name. After mentioning Ovid, he refers to another poet, who "later,

---

[1] Highet 1961:2.

[2] Cf. *Satire* 1, esp. line 45, where his "fevered soul burns with wrath" (*siccum iecur ardeat ira*). Anderson 1964; Braund 1988.

[3] See Highet 1961:163.

[4] 10.188–288.

[5] *Satire* 7, on poverty of the literary life; 3.152–153; *Satire* 5; for many more references, see Highet 1961:359.

[6] 4.32; 1.24–30.

[7] See above, ch. 2 (Aesop and the Delphians); ch. 7 (Simonides).

[8] Notably Strack 1880; cf. Wilson 1903:xvi–xvii; Hild 1884; Vahlen 1923:181–201; further bibliography in Strack 1880:33; and in Wilson 1903. Courtney suggests that because Juvenal's writings were long out of fashion, "nothing was known about his life when he again came into fashion, and resort was made to inference and fabrication" (1980:9).

in a similar disaster, blown by a gust from the noisy public, was banished by an irritated actor."[9] The sixth-century Byzantine chronicler John Malalas is our first explicit attestation for the exile. He wrote:

ὁ δὲ αὐτὸς βασιλεὺς Δομετιανὸς ἐφίλει τὸν ὀρχηστὴν τοῦ πρασίνου μέρους τῆς Ῥώμης, τὸν λεγόμενον Πάριδα. περὶ οὗ καὶ ἐλοιδορεῖτο ἀπὸ τῆς συγκλήτου Ῥώμης καὶ Ἰουβεναλίου τοῦ ποιητοῦ τοῦ Ῥωμαίου, ὡς χαίρων εἰς τὸ πράσινον. ὅστις βασιλεὺς ἐξώρισε τὸν αὐτὸν Ἰουβενάλιον τὸν ποιητὴν ἐν Πενταπόλει ἐπὶ τὴν Λιβύην, τὸν δὲ ὀρχηστὴν πλουτίσας ἔπεμψεν ἐν Ἀντιοχείᾳ τῇ μεγάλῃ ἐπὶ τὸ οἰκεῖν αὐτὸν ἔξω τῆς πόλεως.

The emperor Domitian loved the dancer known as Paris from the Green faction in Rome; he was reproached for this by the Senate at Rome and by the Roman poet Juvenal, for favoring the Green faction. The emperor banished the poet Juvenal to Pentapolis in Libya, but enriched the dancer and sent him to Antioch the Great to live there, outside the city.

John Malalas *Chronicles* 10.49[10]

Aside from this one reference, only the *vitae* attached to the scholiasts and manuscripts, contradictory and unfactual as they often are, attest explicitly to the poet's exile. Trying to piece together a historically convincing Juvenalian exile from the scholiast lives is a problematic task; however, a rough consensus can be obtained.[11] Following is the most common version of the *Vita*:

D. Iunius Iuuenalis, libertini locupletis incertum est filius an alumnus, ad mediam fere aetatem declamauit animi magis causa quam quod se scholae aut foro praepararet. deinde paucorum uersuum satura non absurde composita in Paridem pantomimum poetamque eius semestribus militiolis tumentem genus scripturae industriose excoluit; et tamen diu ne modico quidem auditorio quicquam committere ausus est. mox magna frequentia tantoque successu bis aut ter auditus est, ut ea quoque quae prima fecerat inferciret nouis scriptis . . . erat tum in deliciis aulae histrio multique fautorum eius cottidie prouehebantur. uenit ergo Iuuenalis in suspicionem, quasi tempora figurate notasset, ac statim per honorem

[9] Sidonius Apollinaris *Poems* 9.271–273: . . . *qui consimili deinde casu / ad volgi tenuem strepentis auram / irati fuit histrionis exul* (trans. Highet 1961:23), cf. Courtney 1980:6.
[10] Text in Dürr 1888:20. Translation Jeffreys et al. 1986:139.
[11] See Dürr 1888:22–30. I will use Dürr's system of numbering when referring to the lives.

militiae quamquam octogenarius urbe summotus est missusque
ad praefecturam cohortis in extremam partem Aegypti tendentis.
id supplicii genus placuit, ut leui atque ioculari delicto par esset.
uerum intra breuissimum tempus angore et taedio periit.

Junius Juvenalis, the son or adopted son (this is not established)
of a rich freedman, was a declaimer until about middle age, more
as a hobby than because he was preparing himself for a career as
a professional declaimer or barrister. Then he composed a satire
of a few verses, quite wittily, against the pantomime dancer Paris
and his librettist, who was vain because of trivial six-month mili-
tary appointments, and proceeded to devote himself to this style of
writing. Yet for a long time he did not venture to entrust anything
even to quite a small audience. Subsequently he gave readings a
few times to packed audiences with such success that he inserted
into his later writings his first composition also [*Satire* 7.90–92 is
quoted]. At that time there was an actor who was a court favourite,
and many of his fans were being promoted daily. Therefore Juvenal
came under suspicion of making indirect attacks on the times, and,
although in his eighties, he was removed from Rome by a military
appointment and sent to take command of a cohort on its way to the
remotest part of Egypt. This kind of punishment was decided upon
so that it might match his trivial and humorous offence. However
within a very short time he died because of vexation and disgust.

Vita Ia[12]

There are many variations. Most of the lives have the poet exiled to Egypt;
however, two send him to Britain.[13] Seven lives have him exiled by Nero (a
chronological difficulty, to say the least, as Juvenal was born (perhaps) around
AD 60, and Nero became emperor in 54); four have him exiled by Domitian.[14]
He usually dies in exile, though in two lives (Ib and IIIb) he dies in Rome after
the exile. One (IIIb) also has the charming detail, patently unfactual, that he
returned to Rome and found that Martial was no longer there—so he died of
"sadness and vexation" (*tristitia et angore* instead of the more usual *angore et
taedio*). Another life (IIa) has him die when he learns why Domitian exiled him;
another has him die because he missed Rome's games and festivals (IIIc). The

---

[12] Trans. Courtney 1980:6, text in Clausen 1959:179; Dürr 1888:22.
[13] *Vita* IV; scholiast, codex Bibl. reg. 1.
[14] See Strack 1990:27.

emperor sometimes exiles Juvenal with the intent of killing him: "enraged because of this [Juvenal's satirical lines on Paris], when he could find no other occasion for contriving Juvenal's death, he made him, under the pretext of an honor, military prefect against the Scots, who were making war against the Romans, so that Juvenal would be killed there."[15] Thus the theme of exile and execution is combined; as we have noted, exile is always a form of death. (Many prefer death to exile, as in the cases of Socrates and Cicero.)[16]

The exile is always a military appointment, but it is always a pretext for getting rid of the poet: we find such phrases as *sub obtentu*, *sub praetextu*, and *sub specie* used. It is worth noting that apparently the emperor needed a pretext; in fact, two lives make it explicit: "he did not dare to punish a man of such great prestige publicly."[17] The poet is a force to be reckoned with, even by an emperor. But the poet is conquered by pure political power, as often happens.

Virtually all of the lives agree that the specific cause of the exile was verse addressed against Paris, a pantomime in favor with the emperor,[18] accusing the *histrio* of having power to distribute military appointments. This short epigram theoretically was later incorporated into *Satire* 7 (lines 90–92). The emperor suspects that Juvenal "had criticized the times,"[19] and the exile follows. The detail remains, but variants surround it. In Ia, Juvenal satirizes Paris and his "*poeta*," librettist. In one scholiast (IIa), Paris buys the verses and sings them as his own. However, in IIb Juvenal merely attacks the vice and luxury of Rome, said to be at a record low point of degradation. *Vita* V speaks of Paris's hatred for the poet; Codex Barberinus is uncertain whether the hatred of the poet or the emperor caused the exile. (*Incertum profecto id Paridis pantomimi odio . . . an ipsius imperatoris offensa factum sit.*) In IIb, Paris is the worst kind of informer (*delator . . . pessimus*), and uses his influence to have Juvenal shipped away.

As E. Courtney notes, we have a mixture "fantastical elements" with elements that have some degree of plausibility.[20] It is impossible to separate fact from fiction with certainty. Highet, however, accepts the historicity of the

---

[15] *Vita* IV, my trans. *qua ex re commotus, nulla alia occasione reperta struendae mortis in Iuvenalem, sub honoris pretextu fecit eum praefectum militis contra Scotos, qui bellum conta Romanos moverant, ut ibi interficeretur Iuvenalis. Vita* IIa also hints that Domitian was seeking his death; cf. IV cod. Omnib.: *hoc modo poetae mortis instruendae opportunitatem invenit* ("In this way he found a means for bringing about the poet's death," my trans.).

[16] See above, ch. 15; also chs. 22; 25.

[17] *Vita* IIa: *cum tantae auctoritatis virum publice punire non auderet . . .* Cf. IIc.

[18] Or his lover, according to John Malalas.

[19] E.g. *Vita* IIb: *quod iste sua tempora notasset, fecit eum exulare.*

[20] Courtney 1980:7.

exile story, reconstructing a historical life thus: Juvenal was quite well-to-do, well educated, and started a military career, but was not promoted. Though he curried the favor of Roman nobles, he saw the unworthy promoted while he languished. Thus he wrote a satire on the topic of unworthy advancement, mentioning Paris, dead in disgrace some nine years. In Highet's view, "The suspicious Domitian took this as a covert attack on the probity of his administration, and exiled Juvenal to Egypt [not under the pretext of a military appointment], confiscating all his considerable property."[21] The poet returns to Rome eventually, and experiences the humiliating life of a poverty-stricken client. His embittered satires are now written, under Trajan and Hadrian. The poet comes into a modest sum of money, and ends his days less embittered than he might have been, though the keynote of his writing is still a savage contempt for humanity.

If the exile is historical, and the poet was exiled by Domitian (or Trajan) to Egypt, then we would also have the exile theme in Juvenal's poetry, for satire fifteen attacks the customs of Egypt.[22]

In *Satire* 1.149–157, Juvenal reveals an important aspect of his satire: he will satirize by name only those who have died. Satirizing the living is too dangerous, as he had come to know, possibly, from harsh experience:

> omne in praecipiti vitium stetit. utere velis,
> totos pande sinus. . . .
> . . . cuius non audeo dicere nomen?
> quid refert dictis ignoscat Mucius an non?
> pone Tigillinum, taeda lucebis in illa
> qua stantes ardent qui fixo gutture fumant
> et latum media sulcum deducit harena.

All vice is at its acme; up with your sails and shake out every stitch of canvas! . . . [Lucilius says] "What man is there that I dare not name? What matters it whether Mucius forgives my word or not?"

But just describe Tigellinus [the favorite of Nero] and you will blaze amid those faggots in which men, with their throats tightly gripped, stand and burn and smoke, and you trace a broad furrow through the middle of the arena.[23]

---

[21] Highet 1937:506.

[22] Cf. Highet 1961:151–152. The centerpiece of satire fifteen is a revolting account of feudal omophagia.

[23] Trans. Ramsay. Variant readings: *gutture /pectore; deducit / deducis.* These lines are problematic in their details, though the main image and thought are clear enough.

Thus if the poet satirizes by name, he will be publicly burned, as were early Christians, accused by Nero of arson.[24] The Christians were scapegoated for the great fire in AD 64;[25] the truthful satirist will be killed just like these unfortunate sufferers. We remember that one unparalleled statement has the Greek *pharmakos* killed by fire.[26] The image of the burning poet is a symbol of imperial repression that lives on in the poetry of one more exiled poet— whether Juvenal was exiled in historical or mythical reality.[27]

[24] Cf. Green 1967:192n26, on the *tunica molesta* 'shirt of pitch'.

[25] Tacitus *Annals* 15.44.

[26] "Finally they burnt him with fire" (τέλος πυρὶ κατέκαιον, Tzetzes *Chiliades* 5.737). Cf. Bremmer 1983b:317; Gebhard 1926:3, with bibliography. Some scholars have accepted this detail, but most have been skeptical of it.

[27] On the tightening of Roman censorship under emperor and imperial bureaucracy, see Highet 1961:55; Sullivan 1985:153.

Part Four

CONCLUSIONS

27

Transformations of Myth:
The Poet, Society, and the Sacred

THIS SURVEY ENDS WITH ROME, since in Rome we have entered history, for the most part. All of our Roman poets are certainly historical. Much of the Greek material, on the other hand, is clearly legendary or mythical.[1] Greece and Rome allow us to see a number of stages in the transition from myth to history (or perhaps, to historicized myth).

1. Overt myths telling of conflicts between divine and semidivine figures (for example, Marsyas and Apollo).

2. *Vitae* of poets who perhaps never existed (Aesop) that are constructed from some of the same mythical themes; gods are still dramatis personae (the Muses; Apollo). However, the poet is definitely human.

3. *Vitae* of poets who are historical, but whose *vitae* are embellished with overtly mythical material (Archilochus, meeting the Muses).

4. *Vitae* of historical figures whose lives are embellished with subtly mythical material (Socrates assimilated to Marsyas and Aesop, still associated with Delphi). Here the divine apparatus has been minimized or expressed in a secondary way.

5. Finally, the historical figure like Alcaeus whose life follows the pattern, expressed previously in myth, of the excluded blame poet. While we meet such figures in Greece, nearly all of the Roman poets in chapters 20–26 fit in this category.

So, as has been noted, we should be skeptical of the historicity of the *vitae*, but we might also be skeptical of their fictional "mythicality"—seem-

---

[1] In the context of this discussion I am using a fairly standard definition of myth, as traditional story, often supernatural. In other contexts, one might emphasize other definitions or aspects of myth. A sampling of introductory treatments of myth: Eliade 1963a; Detienne 1986; Puhvel 1987; Edmunds 1990; Graf 1993; Buxton 1994; Bremmer 1987; Gantz 1993; Calame 2003.

ingly mythical, folkloric elements may not be pure fiction. Perhaps there was an Aesop; perhaps the Delphians refused him room and board; perhaps he made a public nuisance of himself; perhaps he was brought to trial, and goaded his captors into an extreme punishment. A man like Diogenes could easily goad an unsympathetic court into voting an exile. From all accounts, an Aesop (if he existed) or Archilochus might have been equally capable of this.

So we are left with a skepticism that turns back against itself. Was Juvenal exiled, or was that story the creation of enthusiastic scholiasts who had to fit the great satirist to the mythical pattern?—which is certainly a possibility. Or did his actual life fit the mythical pattern because the mythical pattern itself reflects social realities? This seems equally possible. Was Tyrtaeus an obscure, mild-mannered poet who lived an uneventful life, or was he really the lame Athenian given to the Spartans as a joke, who became a successful general? One is skeptical of such a neat folktale, but perhaps a historical figure lies behind the story, and perhaps the story has some validity. We do know that the Spartans "imported" poets. If the neatness was not there, something somehow related to that story may have nevertheless happened.

It is striking that Platonic Socrates versified Aesop and composed a hymn to Apollo while he awaited death; perhaps these are a brilliant student's inventions, graceful literary mirrorings of the mythical realities inherent in Socrates' execution. But then one remembers that Seneca apparently modeled his death on Socrates' (only to have Thrasea copy his own death); perhaps the historical Socrates did think of himself as the new Aesop. Or perhaps the Platonic death of Socrates is largely myth; then a myth has passed into history (Seneca's death, historical, was modeled on the myth, replicates pure myth). So refractions of myth scatter influentially throughout history.

It is also striking that the Roman versifier of Aesop offended with his didactic, just satire, and was severely punished by an oppressive political leader—perhaps by exile.

This survey, then, would agree with theorists such as Durkheim that myth and folklore often encapsulate historical, social realities. They are not just fanciful neuroses, or a disease of language, or naïve nature speculations. At the same time, of course, myth can supplant history. A great poet's audience, his or her disciples, later commentators would apply a preexistent standard heroic life to her or him, in whole or in part—poets must be consecrated by the gods, they must be the best, yet they must suffer expulsion, perhaps die unjustly far from home. The myth, minus the explicit divine apparatus, is based on society's treatment of past poets. History will continue to replicate the myth.

If myth can reflect persistent social patterns, people see their contemporary realities in terms of past history, which, if one goes back far enough, is sacral history. And history does replicate itself. Aesop died once (perhaps only in story) at Delphi; a successor died in 399 BC Athens; and another fabulist suffered again at the hands of Sejanus and Nero.

If we go back even further, we find, behind Aesop and Archilochus and Heracles—warrior-poets tormented by ambivalently inimical gods and helped by others—the archetype formed by Starkaðr and Suibhne, the warrior-poet of Indo-European epic, sacrificing and sacrificed, harried and saved by tutelary and pernicious deities. And behind Starkaðr, the Odinic hero, we have Odin, god of mantic poetic possession and berserker war fury, gaining poetic knowledge by sacrificing himself to himself, suffering a primeval triple death on the world tree to ensure cyclical continuity for the earth.

Aesop, Tyrtaeus, and Archilochus, Starkaðr and Suibhne all combine strong poetic and martial aspects (often they are both the best warriors and best poets in their respective traditions);[2] all are exiled, excluded, or sacrificed; and all are watched over or destroyed by divine, ambivalent patrons (who have given them poetry as a divine gift, a gift that is itself ambivalent).

Thus in the investigation of the meaning of the exiled or executed poet, the satirist excluded from society by king or political leaders, the association with war will often play an important part. It is significant that two of the most influential scapegoat theorists of our generation, Burkert and Girard, have both brought the scenario of military disaster firmly into their interpretations of the *pharmakos*. The scapegoat, in myth, is often a means of warding off threatening enemies and destruction by war. Yet, though these two theorists have recognized the importance of war in these stories and rituals, still their treatments do not seem to fit the victimized warrior-poets in this study precisely, perhaps because they have underemphasized the tendency of the scapegoat to be the best—the strongest (warrior), the most intelligent (poet), the most possessed, frenzied (both). He can be *therapōn*, an authentically effective servant, of king and society. A brief look at Burkert and Girard will shed insight on the excluded warrior-poet, but it will also permit an assessment of the strengths and limitations of their perspectives.[3]

In *Structure and History in Greek Mythology and Ritual*, Burkert closes a masterly examination of the *pharmakos* with a summary of interpretations; he then adds his own—as is usual for him, a behavioral analogy from prehis-

---

[2] There is even the interesting tradition, discussed above in ch. 15, of Socrates as "best warrior."
[3] This continues the discussion of Burkert found at the end of ch. 18.

tory—almost from prehumanoid evolution.[4] He isolates two patterns, one of which has the aggressive community lash out at the outsider, the one who is different. But this pattern is minimized, for group aggression plays little or no part in the rituals Burkert has examined in his chapter. A more prominent pattern is that of the voluntary scapegoat adorned by the people before he or she departs from the community. Here Burkert imagines the "unritual- ized" behavior behind the ritual: the group (of men or apes) is surrounded by predators. The anxiety of the chased group ceases and turns to relief when a marginal group member—someone who is lame, sick, young, or an outsider—is caught by the predators (though what an outsider is doing with the group, or why it lags behind is not explained, unless the group intentionally sends it to the rear). The lame or outsider member has brought salvation to the group. To relieve traumatic guilt at this injustice, the victim is thought of as the worst, offscourings; or as the best; or as a combination of the two. It is comforting, but not factual, to think that the scapegoat goes voluntarily to death.

This is an attractive, original scenario, and in many points fits our present pattern. In stories of scapegoat poets, the theme of "voluntary" death is often found: the lives of Starkaðr, Aesop, Socrates, Cicero, and Seneca all have a form of it.[5] The theory explains neatly the exclusion of the lame, sick, or young, the deformed *pharmakos*.

However, other details do not fit quite as well, especially details connected with the "exclusion of the best" theme. In actuality, by Burkert's account, the best would never be excluded, and the excluded one would never really be willing to die. The guilty, if anxiety-cleansed, group thinks of the scapegoat as "voluntary" and as "the best" to assuage their guilt and trauma.

Yet, while the "voluntary" victim would soothe the guilt of the commu- nity, how would the "best" victim lessen it? (Also, if the predator kills the lame and sick, does it not just kill the laggard? There would be no conscious exclu- sion on the part of the group—no choosing, adorning of victim. The victim is simply slow.)

In the case of Aesop at Delphi, the pattern seems nearly opposite: a morally corrupt group excluding their intellectual better. This is a standard pattern, more like Burkert's first pattern. Aesop's exclusion as filth is actually society's self-exclusion from any kind of justification.

A modification of Burkert's prehistoric scenario would lessen the problem somewhat: we have the group cornered by a predator or predators. The group

---

[4] Burkert 1979:71.
[5] Cf. Kees Bolle's treatment of freedom in sacrifice (1983:61–63).

chooses its strongest individual or individuals, and sends him or them forth to kill the predators. Sometimes the champion dies; if he survives, he becomes the tribal leader.

And there would be an intellectual aspect to the best also, for the person who is intelligent enough to wield a weapon cleverly or outsmart a predator (by noose, trap, and so on) would survive the confrontation more consistently than even a stronger rival who was less intelligent. However, this champion would still be subjected to considerable danger, and when he came to realize that his role was not safe to perform time after time, he would send a servant, a substitute, a military specialist, the king's general—to represent him. Thus Starkaðr, Śiśupāla, Suibhne, Aesop, and Phaedrus' catamite.

Burkert collects a number of stories involving the scapegoat that present the war scenario. Codrus, whose country, Attica, is threatened by the Dorian invasion, saves it by going out to meet the enemy.[6] P. Decius Mus performs the *devotio*, dedicating himself and the enemy forces to death, then throws himself recklessly into enemy lines; his presence at first spreads panic among the enemy, but when he falls, "from that moment there was no doubt that the Latin cohorts were thrown into complete confusion and had emptied the battlefield to scatter far and wide in flight."[7] In the *devotio*, while the general devotes himself in legend, and Macrobius can say, "Dictators and generals only can perform *devotio*,"[8] in practice the general could, and generally would, call on a lesser soldier to be devoted (Livy 8.10.11). Bremmer observes that Decius and other generals who devoted themselves were legendary, not historical, and that there is a similar contrast between legendary regal scapegoats and practical lowly scapegoats in Greece.[9] This suggests a curious pattern: the general is *therapōn* of the king; but the general chooses his own *therapōn*. Thus, Achilles is *therapōn* of Agamemnon, but in turn sends Patroclus to be his *therapōn* in battle. In fact, the *Iliad* might be seen as a drama of *therapōn* relationships gone perverse. Achilles withdraws from his relationship with Agamemnon; and Patroclus becomes Achilles' double almost against Achilles' will; after Patroclus dies, Achilles reassumes his proper *therapōn* relationship, but at the cost of his eventual death.

---

[6] Burkert 1979:62. Codrus is a king, but also a warrior, see 1979:170n13; see above, ch. 1.

[7] Livy 8.9.12 (trans. Radice): *inde iam haud dubie consternatae cohortes Latinorum fugam ac uastitatem late fecerunt.* Burkert 1979:63. Gehrts begins *Das Märchen und das Opfer* with an analysis of Decius' *devotio* (1967:9–19).

[8] *Saturnalia* 3.9.9: *dictatores imperatoresque soli possunt devovere.*

[9] Bremmer 1983b:304n37.

In Hittite ritual, a plague is averted by sending an adorned, crowned ram to the enemy.[10] There is a similar ritual in India.[11] Thus, a scapegoat is not just expelled; he is sent to destroy the enemy. Cnopus makes war against the "Cretan" Erythrae in Asia Minor. An oracle instructs him to take a Thessalian priestess as his general;[12] when she arrives, she has a bull adorned and given a drug. This turns the bull mad,[13] and he runs to the enemy, who sacrifice him and are themselves driven mad; so Cnopus can conquer them easily.

When an army from Miletus and Erythrae invades Naxos, Polycrite, left in a sanctuary of Apollo, falls into the enemy's hands and becomes the lover of the enemy general. She gains military information, passes it on to her people, and averts destruction. The destruction of the invaders takes place during the Thargelia. Polycrite, "chosen out of many" is "stoned" with clothes in her home town when she returns; then she receives hero cult.[14]

An important example that Burkert does not discuss is the Roman scapegoat, Mamurius Veturius, who is in many respects parallel to the Greek *pharmakos*. On the last day of the year, Mamurius is led in a procession through Rome, beaten by rods, and driven out of the city. His name means "the old Mars," and he is beaten by the Salii, the dancing priests of Mars; thus he is associated with the Roman god of war. And there apparently was a tradition that the original Mamurius was driven from Rome to the Roman enemies, the Oscans.[15] He was driven out because he, a metalsmith, had kept back the best

---

[10] ANET 347; Burkert 1979:60–61. The importance of Asia Minor in the figures we have studied (Hipponax, Aesop, Marsyas) is worth noting. See above, ch. 1, on Codrus; ch. 17, on DoDera and Patroclus.

[11] *Kausika Sutra* 14, 22f.; Oldenberg 1923:496ff.; Frazer 1911 pt. VI, 9:192f.; Burkert 1979:60n7 (further bibliography), 10.

[12] For the theme of the oracle demanding an unlikely general in wartime, see above, on Tyrtaeus, ch. 11.

[13] Perhaps symbolic of the warrior's battle fury.

[14] Parthenius 9 = Andriscus FGH 500 F 1; Plutarch *On the Virtues of Women* (254b–f); Aristotle fr. 559; Burkert 1979:72–73. There seems to be a connection with the Roman story of Tarpeia, which however is inverted, see Livy 1.11; Dionysius of Halicarnassus *Roman Antiquities* 2.38–40; Plutarch *Romulus* 17; Propertius 4.4; Burkert 1979:76–77. Interestingly, there is a variant in which Tarpeia is the enemy's daughter, captured by Romulus (Plutarch *Romulus* 17); this would be closer to Polycrite. For another dangerous female war gift, cf. Gullveig ('Gold Drunk'), "sent by the Vanir to corrupt the Aesir" (Puhvel 1987:211), comparable perhaps both to Tarpeia, but also to Mada, who represents drunkenness and female sexuality (see above, ch. 19, on Kvasir's mead).

[15] See Joannes Lydus *On the Months* 3.29; 4.36; Roscher 1884–1937 s.v. Mamurius; Frazer 1911 9:229–231. For Mamurius being driven to the Oscans, see Propertius 4.2.61–64, where the expelled Mamurius is in Oscan, enemy, territory; see Roscher and Frazer 1911 9:231n1. If Mamurius is expelled to the inimical Oscans, it would lead us to interpret the ritual as associated with war, not as a fertility rite with the old-year king departing (as Frazer interprets it). Then we would not need to explain Mars as a god of "fertility" in connection with Mamurius, as does Frazer;

shield, and the gods had sent misfortune to the people in return. It would be appropriate if the misfortune sent to the people was an Oscan invasion; it is not named.[16]

The pattern that emerges is that one army threatens another, causing anxiety. The scapegoat, the fatal gift, is sent to the enemy, bringing them destruction.

Phaedrus' fable is comparable. The enemy champion causes great anxiety; the despised and asocial catamite is expelled the third time (after he volunteers to fight), but this time as a champion, perhaps to die. Pompey and his counselors cynically consider him expendable. He returns triumphant, having brought disaster to the enemy, and is crowned.[17] Protesilaus, as he dies, brings about the first step of the destruction of Troy. Though an oracle had proclaimed that the first Greek to touch Trojan land would die, Protesilaus is the first to jump ashore (the voluntary motif again, in some versions of the story) when the Greek ships arrive to wage the Trojan war; he is immediately killed by an unidentified Trojan or by Hector. As a reward for serving as this first victim in the war, he is given an especially high barrow at Elaius and inside it he is honored as in a temple.[18]

Thus society is ambivalent in its attitudes toward warriors; they are considered expendable, and sent to danger; when they return victorious, they are crowned, are accounted the best. Significantly, the warrior volunteers— but such volition does not seem forced, as his type is willing to take risks (the pronounced anti-social tendencies in his personality, as when Phaedrus' champion steals the general's property, would seem to fit this type of personality). Thus, Suibhne, Starkaðr, Śiśupāla (and Aesop), general-champions, *therapontes* for the king, fit closely into this scenario.

---

the god's connection with the rite as a god of war becomes natural. However, Mamurius' connection with the calendrical crisis at the end of the year is still present. Perhaps this crisis was seen as a martial crisis. We remember that supposedly, on the first day of the Thargelia, Troy was sacked, the battles of Marathon and Plataea took place, and Alexander defeated Darius; see above, ch. 15 (Socrates).

[16] See Gebhard 1926:77–78, with further bibliography.

[17] See above, ch. 24. For the use of champions in battle, see the battle of the Horatii and Curiatii in the conflict of Rome and Alba Longa (Livy 1.24–26), cf. Dumézil 1942. It is significant that the surviving Horatius is a classic example of murderous battle fury; he kills his sister in a rage immediately following the battle, and must undergo purification to be reintegrated into Roman society. Cf. above, ch. 17, on warrior-poet Dubthach Chafertongue; ch. 1—Androgeus is sent against the bull of Marathon to be killed.

[18] See *Iliad* II 701; *Cypria* fr. 17 (Allen 1919 5:123; West 2003b:76); Herodotus 9.116; *Palatine Anthology* 7.385; Hyginus *Fables* 103 (here, the oracle is common knowledge); Gantz 1993:592-593. Protesilaus also receives a brief resurrection.

Yet they are primarily regarded as warriors; one must relate their poetic vocations to this phenomenon. As has been shown, satirists especially are specialists in aggression, mechanisms of physical and verbal attack; they are specialists in the madness that unleashes aggression, verbal and physical. But they are also clever, and thus suited for championship of the group against the less intelligent carnivore or enemy champion (one remembers the small David felling the monstrous Goliath with a cast of the sling). Thus Odysseus *polutropos*, Aesop as cleverest of all, consummate riddle-warrior, will serve well as champions for society and the king.

Such a scenario for poet-warrior as scapegoat may perhaps underemphasize the other aspect of the *pharmakos'* ambiguity—his leastness. Yet, the ambiguity of the warrior in society is inescapable—he is seen as least, expendable—Phaedrus' catamite is a criminal, anti-social. This does not solve the problem completely, for a lame warrior is not fitted for battle (unless his lameness has caused him to develop his wits abnormally to outsmart an opponent).

Vernant's demand for the essential ambiguity of the scapegoat is worth considering in this connection. The *pharmakos* is higher than man, divine, and less than man, animalistic, and thus suited for mediation, liminal sacrality. Without leaving the military scenario completely—for the champion is mediator, entering into the middle space, the no man's land between two armies— we may turn to the Germanic traditions on poet as mediator: between man and god, between different elements of society. His ambiguity, his leastness, suits him for this position, for he can travel from the least to the greatest. Thus the prophet must move between evil man and holy god, equally at home on both levels of communication. The poet must move between the common people, the least, and the king, the greatest, the first and third functions; between king and warrior. The squirrel Ratatosk runs from bottom of the world tree to the top, exchanging invective between root-serpent and tree-top eagle. The poet must be the least, but ascend the heights.[19]

Aglauros is a significant figure, both best (royal, young) and marginal (a woman).[20] Nevertheless, when Athens is at war, she wins the battle for them (by oracle-prescribed symbolic method: she throws herself off the cliff of the Acropolis, a *pharmakos* death). Afterward, there is a shrine to her where

---

[19] However, cf. Starkaðr's enmity with common people. Still, there is some ambiguity in that relationship, as Starkaðr approves of weapon smiths and honest farmers; Starkaðr also has very ambiguous relations with the king. Yet perhaps the enmity is a crucial element of the poet's involvement with a person or class; his critique helps and improves (as when his satirical attack reclaims Ingel from decadent kingship).

[20] For Aglauros, see ch. 1.

she died, where ephebes take their oath in connection with entering military service, leaving the city to defend Athens on her borders. Her death is a charter for warriors leaving the city to face death.

Girard has been an influential interpreter of the scapegoat; his most widely known book, *Violence and the Sacred*,[21] is stimulating, enlightening, annoying, and difficult by turns. Yet Girard offers insight into elements of the poet-as-scapegoat complex. His view is that sacrifice, in particular the sacrifice of the scapegoat, came about as a psychic mechanism to stop the violence of vengeful feuding. This symbolic act of violence, which defines the sacred, has the power to deflect destructive impulses onto a harmless object—a marginal member of society, a person who is lame, a slave, an outsider, a criminal; or onto an animal. Thus, when a well-developed law system is instituted in a society, in which a murderer is punished for his own crime and in which the victim's family will not take the law into their own hands, sacrifice, and the sacred, will become unnecessary and fall into disuse. Thus, our present society lacks sacrifice, and it also lacks an understanding and experience of archaic sacrality. We also have not faced the extent to which the sacred is generated by violence, though in an attempt to stem violence. The sacrifice was then originally a ritual murder, which soon made use of the surrogate victim. A member of a tribe kills a man from another tribe; the other tribe mobilizes for war. The first tribe does not want to give up an important chief in recompense, to satisfy the opposing tribe; so a surrogate, a marginal, entirely innocent man or woman is sacrificed instead. This detail, which at first seems entirely unjust and unlikely, is supported by precise anthropological parallels. The Chukchi Indians, for example, when a member of their tribe has committed a murder against a member of another tribe, kill not the offender, but a member of his family.[22]

To reduce a closely argued book to a paragraph will obviously oversimplify. Nevertheless, one possible objection to Girard's theory is that it seems to deny the presence of the sacred where a workable law system is present. Though Girard points out the decline of sacrifice in a society that has a comparatively modern law system (Greece, Rome),[23] he does not explain how thoroughly steeped in sacrifice Greek and Roman religion apparently still were.[24] Further, in limiting the sacred to sacrifice, he underemphasizes the multiplicity of religious phenomena, which may be more widely defined as commu-

---

[21] Girard 1977, see also 1987b, 1986, and 1987a.
[22] Girard 1977:25.
[23] Girard 1977:18.
[24] Cf. Burkert 1983:9.

nication between god and man, of which sacrifice is one important aspect.[25] The work of Hubert and Mauss establishes an interpretation of sacrifice as a means of communication between god and man (in which the sacrificer is changed); Detienne and Vernant have pursued an important interpretation of sacrifice as mediation.

However, if Girard's thesis is seen as a contributing theory rather than an all-encompassing explanation, it offers valuable insights into the nature of sacrifice and the scapegoat. Like Burkert, Girard places the scapegoat in the martial sphere.[26] Thus, Aesop saves Samos from invasion by offering himself as the victim to the overpowering besieger, Croesus. Tamun the fool is sent as representative-victim to face Cuchulainn.[27] The poet as champion for the king in battle is the relevant theme.

In Girard's description of an African ritual, the scapegoat is a warrior chosen by the king:

> At the height of the battle between the warriors and the king, the king withdraws once more to his enclosure. He reemerges armed with a gourd, which he hurls at the shields of his assailants. After this attack, the groups disband. H. Kuper's native informants told him that in time of war, any warrior struck by the royal gourd would forfeit his life. In the light of this information, the anthropologist suggests that we look upon the warrior whom the king singles out to be struck by the gourd as a sort of national scapegoat. This amounts to seeing him as a double for the king, a man who symbolically dies in his place.[28]

It is significant that the warrior scapegoat is sacrificed only during war.

The Germanic myths of the sacrificed poet offer material very susceptible to a Girardian interpretation. While Kvasir is not killed to effect reconciliation in the war of the Aesir and Vanir, he is nevertheless a poet who is the living emblem of that reconciliation, and his death perpetuates the beneficial effects of that reconciliation in the ability of Odin to rule the totality of society with

---

[25] As a counterbalance, one may compare a good phenomenology of religion, such as van der Leeuw's *Religion in Essence and Manifestation* (1967). Cf. also Jensen 1963, who argues that human sacrifice is universally a characteristic of the cults of relatively advanced agricultural peoples.

[26] Which again highlights the importance of the warrior-hero studied by Dumézil in his series of treatments of Starkaðr et al.

[27] Girard notes the importance of the fool as double of the king (1977:12); cf., for the holy fool, 253. Tamun, though, is killed without effecting a peace between armies, see above, ch. 17.

[28] Girard 1977:111. The concept of warrior-victim as double of the king again suggests Gehrts's work, see Gehrts 1967, Ward 1982b and above ch. 19.

the requisite omniscience. Furthermore, in a parallel drama of human sacrifice, Kvasir's blood-mead effects peace between the murderous dwarves who have killed him and the family of the giant they later drown. Here the magical value of the dead poet-being is explicit *weregild*; by it, peace is effected between enemies. And the death of Kvasir also unites the three levels of society, since Odin's kingly knowledge comes from it.

In the variant account of the Aesir and Vanir conflict, the figure of Mímir serves the Kvasir function. He is sent, the wisest of the Aesir, as a hostage, with Hoenir, to the Vanir.[29] However, the Vanir feel cheated because Hoenir is apparently not actually intelligent by himself. The logical thing to do would be to kill Hoenir, and perhaps reopen hostilities with the Aesir. But the Vanir kill Mímir instead (no explanation is given) and send the head to the Aesir; Odin uses it as a source of knowledge so he can rule the combined functions. There is no mention of further Aesir–Vanir hostility.

Again, the death of a poet figure produces knowledge that allows the king of the gods to rule all of society. But the story also reminds one vividly of Girard's insistence on an innocent victim as scapegoat;[30] the person who is guilty of committing the offense is never killed. Hoenir lives; Mímir is sacrificed. Hostilities end.[31]

A number of isolated themes have relevance to Girard. He too looks carefully at the theme of the voluntariness of the scapegoat.[32] He discusses a pattern in which the scapegoat is excluded by derision;[33] it can be killed by words;[34] it can be a sexual transgressor.[35] Prophetic inspiration can often be part of the sacrificial "crisis,"[36] as can madness.[37] There is much in Girard on the ambiguity of the scapegoat, as he is both king and monster;[38] which recalls Aesop as a portent and monstrosity, *teras* and *ainigma*.[39]

---

[29] One would ordinarily think of Odin as the wisest—thus it is tempting to see Kvasir/Mímir as representatives of Odin. Notice that Odin drinks Kvasir in the previous myth to gain his knowledge.

[30] 1977:25, 257.

[31] According to Plutarch *Cicero* 49 (885), when Antony saw Cicero's head and hands, he cried out that the proscriptions would be terminated immediately.

[32] 1977:27, cf. Girard 1986:63ff.; see above, ch. 2, Aesop's "voluntary" death.

[33] 1977:254; cf. 44 (tragedy as stichomythia, protagonists trading insults, until the final violence), 98 (verbal violence is a preface to sacrifice; a ritualization of the conflict that sacrifice ends).

[34] 1977:98.

[35] 1977:98.

[36] 1977:133, 159. "During the sacrificial crisis, all men are endowed with the spirit of prophecy."

[37] 1977:154.

[38] See 1977:252.

[39] 1977:251; ch. 2.

The oddity of the sacrality of the blame poet whose mockery and abuse is feared has been noted earlier; but Girard shows that a person can be sacred because he or she is violent.[40] The scapegoat embodies violence. One thinks of the Irish poet, Séafra O'Donnchú, who had given up poetry, was satirized, and who responded in a paroxysm of rage-induced satire; or Dubthach Chafertongue, the half-crazed warrior-satirist whose lance drips poison and who is himself poisonous; or Archilochus and Hipponax, attacked unjustly, driving their enemies to death. The combination of poet and warrior has an archaic logic, as does the tendency for the poet-warrior to undergo the mechanism for sacralization.[41]

---

[40] See 1977:257.

[41] There is much more in Girard that would repay detailed study, but this short treatment shows the richness of his book, and that the data we have surveyed on the excluded, sacrificed poet have relevance to his theory.

Epilogue

THE PROCESS LEADING FROM "MYTH" TO "HISTORY"—though such terms cannot be strictly distinguished at all times, as history can function on a sacral level, and myth is always perceived by believers as history—can be seen as a process of secularization. The poet is an omniscient god; then a superhuman hero tied closely, in both a positive and negative way, to the same god;[1] then the prophet-poet consecrated by god in revelation and sacrificed to him; then a man vaguely inspired, vaguely mad; then a man who uses the convention of divine inspiration in his poetry (as does the irreverent Ovid). The sacred has weakened into a poetic convention; one prays for inspiration at the beginning of an epic poem, even if one is, like Lucretius, an Epicurean, whose belief in literal gods is nonexistent.

Yet, as Eliade has shown, though sacred myth may be overtly gone, it is often only disguised, camouflaged.[2] The structures will continue to endure, and have profound mythological meaning as structures, even if they appear to the outsider as empty. The sacral may continue in the persona of the poet—the mantic aspects of his inspiration, his moralizing tendency, his scathing denunciation of evil and injustice, his tendency to be repressed by corrupt society and its leaders.[3]

A friend studying journalism in Latin America and Russia told me in the 1980s that in Mexico some forty journalists had been violently killed in recent years. Manuel Buendía, a distinguished journalist, was assassinated, and the government did not inquire seriously into the reason for the murder.[4] Ariel Dorfman, a prominent Chilean novelist and journalist, went into exile when Pinochet came to power in 1973, and has been able to return

---

[1] On the process of epicization of mythology, see Puhvel 1987:39.

[2] Eliade 1963a:162–195.

[3] Cf. Burnett for a defence of the possibility of literal contemporary poetic inspiration (1987:156). For poetry and the sacred, see van der Leeuw 1963 ch. 3.

[4] See Rading 1984:180.

only infrequently.[5] The Sandinistas closed down *La Prensa*, their only opposition newspaper in Nicaragua, and imprisoned key *Prensa* journalists. The Argentine publisher, Jacobo Timerman, was imprisoned and tortured during the 1977 war in Argentina; unlike many others, he escaped execution, then fled to Israel, where he wrote *Prisoner Without a Name, Cell Without a Number*.[6] In Colombia, journalists are continually menaced by drug lords who are in many ways stronger than the regular government.

For Russia, we need only mention Solzhenitsyn, forced out of Russia; Joseph Brodsky, who received the 1988 Nobel Prize for Literature, is another Russian exile. Numerous poets, such as Gumilov, Majakovski, Mandelstam,[7] were driven to suicide by Lenin and Stalin. Sakharov has been exiled to Gorki.[8] Pasternak's companion, Olga Ivinskayn, was imprisoned and tortured to exert pressure on the author; when *Dr. Zhivago* won the Nobel Prize, the author initially accepted it, but renounced the prize when he was threatened with exile. At a mass meeting, a Soviet official compared Pasternak to a pig "who fouled the spot where he ate and cast filth on those by whose labor he lives and breathes,"[9] an interesting modern example of the marginalization of the poet in a meeting of the people.

Thus repression of free speech and marginalization of the writer/poet is still a reality in our modern world. To return to the ancient world briefly, we remember Lysimachus, one of Alexander's successors, and king of Thrace, who punished a former friend, Telesphorus, because he had mocked the king's wife in a symposium. He had Telesphorus' eyes removed, his tongue cut out, and his ears and nose cut off. Then he imprisoned him in a cage and displayed him to visitors. "Thus I deal with those who harm me," he tells the visiting philosopher, Theodorus.[10] According to Seneca, Telesphorus wallowed in his own dung, developing callouses on his hands and knees, and sores from rubbing. Thus this satirist became, according to Seneca, a *monstrum*—unlike a human being; yet, "he who inflicted [these punishments] was still less like

---

[5] Ariel Dorfman, "Pinochet Meets the Press," *Los Angeles Times*, Nov. 12, 1987, Pt. II, p. 7.

[6] Timerman 1981.

[7] The very poet cited by Burnett as a modern poet receiving inspiration from outside himself, see above, this chapter. André Chenier under Robespierre also comes to mind in this connection. See generally Rubenstein 1980.

[8] Rubenstein 1980:271.

[9] Rubenstein 1980:11–12.

[10] Plutarch *On Exile* 16 (606B), trans. De Lacy, "οὕτως ἐγὼ διατίθημι τοὺς κακῶς με ποιοῦντας." Theodorus is unimpressed: "Who cares if I rot above or below ground?" he replies ("τί δὲ Θεοδώρῳ μέλει," ἔφη, "πότερον ὑπὲρ γῆς ἢ ὑπὸ γῆς σήπεται;"). Theodorus is himself an exiled philosopher (ibid.).

one."[11] We can take some comfort in the expectation that truth-seeking poets, novelists, and journalists today will be remembered and honored as they were in archaic Greece, Rome, and Europe; and that the brutality of repressive politicians will continue to contribute to the honor of the men and women they have killed, imprisoned, tortured, or exiled.

---

[11] Seneca *On Anger* 3.17: . . . *factusque poena sua monstrum misericordiam quoque amiserat. Tamen, cum dissimillimus esset homini qui illa patiebatur, dissimilior erat qui faciebat.* See also Athenaeus 14.616c.

Appendix A
Poetry, Aggression, Ritual

W ALTER BURKERT HAS PIONEERED an analysis of ancient Greek ritual that sees its roots in aggression, in biological impulses than can be observed in animals—Konrad Lorenz was especially fascinated by geese.[1] In the survey of poets in previous chapters, themes and poetic phenomena that related to ritualized aggression have formed a background for archaic poetry (in particular, Archilochus, our first lyric poet; Homer and Hesiod are shadowy, probably non-historical or quasi-historical figures). A key passage from Burkert deserves full quotation:

Aggressive behavior evokes a highly attentive, excited response. Pretended aggression thus plays a special role in ritual communication. Raising one's hands, waving branches, wielding weapons and torches, stamping the feet while turning from attack to flight, folding the hands or lifting them in supplication, kneeling and prostration: all these are repeated and exaggerated as a demonstration whereby the individual proclaims his membership and place in the community. A rhythm develops from repetition, and auditory signals accompanying the gestures give rise to music and dance. These, too, are primordial forms of human solidarity, but they cannot hide the fact that they grew out of aggressive tensions, with their noise and beating, attack and flight . . . in ethology, even laughter is thought to originate in an aggressive display of teeth. Gestures of disgust or "purification" are not far removed from the impulses of aggression and destruction. Some of these ritual gestures can be traced with certainty to the primates, from waving

---

[1] Burkert 1983:23–24; Lorenz 1966. A most interesting essay is Gerard Neuman's "How We Became (In)human" (1987). Critiques of Lorenz can be found in Montagu 1973, introductory essays in Maple and Matheson 1973.

branches and rhythmic drumming to phallic display and raising the hand in supplication.[2]

Parallels with poets and poems we have examined will be obvious:

1. Satire and laughter are obviously related; and laughter, perhaps, originated in "aggressive display of teeth." Satire is, in a way, such a display; and we remember numerous comparisons of satirical poetry to fangs. Pindar, in his reference to Archilochus, writes that he, Pindar, on the other hand, will "flee the violent bite of evil speech."[3] Horace speaks of satirical victims "wounded by this blood-drawing fang."[4] In his sixth *Epode*, the same poet warns that if attacked, he will "bite back."[5] The poet Nede describes his profession as "piercing flesh." Meroney describes the curse/satire *glám dícind* as "an action of fangs."[6]

2. "A rhythm develops from repetition, and auditory signals accompanying the gestures give rise to music and dance." Greek poetry was originally closely connected with music and dance: Homer was sung, and in Sappho's day, lyric was still tightly connected with music. Of course, the chorus tradition, extending from the choral lyric to dramatic chorus, never lost its musical and dancing aspects. Even poetry that lost its musical adjunct kept its metrical, rhythmic nature.

3. "Aggressive tensions, with their noise and beating, attack and flight." Once again, one thinks of the haunting rhythmic nature of poetry.[7]

4. "Attack and flight." Satirical poetry was often explicitly attack, but more often the poet portrayed it as counterattack.[8]

5. "Phallic display." One thinks immediately of Archilochus, who offended through his obscene, probably phallic poetry. When he is punished, his tormentors "[became weak] in the genitals." The closest parallel to this story is a myth in which the Athenians, after dishonoring Dionysus, suffer a plague "in the genitals." They institute phallic cult to Dionysus to gain an alleviation of the curse.[9] Comedy, of course, possibly originated in phallic cult. Aristotle writes that comedy "originated in improvisation . . .

---

[2] Burkert 1983:24.

[3] *Pythian Odes* 2.53: δάκος ἀδινὸν κακαγοριᾶν.

[4] *Epistles* II 1.150–151: *cruento dente lacessiti.*

[5] *me remorsurum.* See below, app. B.

[6] See above, ch. 17.

[7] On drumming, see Eibl-Eibesfeldt 1971:27.

[8] See esp. app. B below; also, above, ch. 3 (Archilochus); ch. 4 (Hipponax); ch. 22 (Cicero).

[9] See above, ch. 3 (Archilochus); Fehling 1974:7–18.

from the prelude to the phallic songs which still survive as institutions in many cities."[10] Semus describes a procession of hymn-singing *phallophoroi* 'phallus bearers' into the theater; there, they would "run forward and jeer [*etōthazon*] at any one they picked out."[11]

6. "Gestures of disgust. " Satirical poetry can often be a verbal "gesture of disgust."

7. "Gestures of . . . purification. " We think of the association of *pharmakos* and purification. Expelling the scapegoat purifies the city. The poet, when he expels an enemy through poetry, is a purifier; and his enemy, expelling the poet, thinks of himself as purifier. There is ambiguity, depending on whom one considers just, the poet or his enemy. And there is ambiguity in the purifying nature of the expelled dirt; in human terms, the human "dirt" can be heroic in his or her departure. But in any event, these phenomena are "not far removed from the impulses of aggression and destruction."

In addition, as we have seen, Greco-Roman ritual included overtly satirical elements. The cult of Demeter in particular was connected with ritual abuse. A famous example is the *gephurismos* in the Eleusinian mysteries, the mockery of prominent citizens in a procession as they passed over a bridge.[12] Another Eleusinian connection to ritual abuse is Iambe, who coaxes the grieving Demeter into laughter through her jests. Demeter grieves for her stolen daughter,

πρίν γ᾽ ὅτε δὴ χλεύῃς μιν Ἰάμβη κέδν᾽ εἰδυῖα
πολλὰ παρασκώπτουσ᾽ ἐτρέψατο πότνιαν ἁγνὴν
μειδῆσαι γελάσαι τε καὶ ἵλαον σχεῖν θυμόν.

---

[10] Aristotle *Poetics* 4.14 (1449a10), trans. Fyfe. For the phallus in Old Comedy, see Pickard-Cambridge 1988:220–223 and 1962:133, 137, 147, cf. 228–240. Even if comedy did not derive from phallic cult, as in Aristotle's view, it certainly had a close connection with phallic cult. Cf. Giangrande 1963. F. M. Cornford (1968:110–111) proposes that only the abusive aspect of comedy derived from phallic cult (not its structure), because this was always connected with ritual abuse (which sometimes functions as a good luck, fertility charm). According to Herodotus (2.49), Melampus, the seer who died in the riddle contest, introduced to Greece "the name of Dionysus and his sacrifice and the procession of the phallus." Cf. above, ch. 16, on Melampus. G. Else prefers the manuscripts' *phaul(l)iká* to *phalliká*, which is found in most editions (1957:163). However, undoubted phallic processions in Aristophanes *Acharnians* 241–279 and Semus (see next note) incline one toward the phallic reading; and cf. Giangrande 1963:4n1. See above, ch. 14 (Aristophanes); Adrados 1975:2.

[11] Semus at Athenaeus 14.621f–622d: εἶτα προτρέχοντες ἐτώθαζον οὓς προέλοιντο.

[12] Hesychius s.v. *gephuris*—*gephuristai*; Strabo 9.400; Mylonas 1961:256; Rosen 1988c:25.

341

Until when with jokes, the wise Iambe, greatly mocking, turned the
holy mistress to smile and laugh and have a cheerful soul.

Hymn to Demeter 202–204[13]

One immediately thinks of the word *iambos*, the meter of satirical poets, a
word often used with the meaning 'satire'. In the case of Iambe's kind mockery,
laughter may be a symbol of death and rebirth.

Archaic Greek poetry was, in turn, often closely connected with cult. We
remember that Paros is listed immediately after Eleusis as a cult center for
Demeter in the Homeric *Hymn to Demeter* (491), and that Archilochus' family
had a connection with the cult of Demeter.[14] The *Etymologicum Magnum* tells
us that comedy [*kōmōidia*] received its name from the fact that it was first
performed among the villages [*kōmas*] in the festivals of Dionysus and of
Demeter.[15] It is striking that Archilochus had ties with both cults. West notes
that the etymology of *iambos* is uncertain, but the word has obvious ties to
dithurambos, *thriambos*, and *ithumbos*, all associated with Dionysian cult.
"*Dithurambos* and *thriambos* are titles of Dionysus and also songs in his honor,"
writes West. The *ithumbos* was a "dance performed at a Dionysiac festival"
(Pollux 4.104) and also a poem "for joking and laughter" or "a long and some-
what sinister song" (Hesychius).[16]

The scholiastic accounts of the origins of comedy link it with farmers,
those who would be involved with agricultural work, the cultivation of
Demeter's gifts. Carlos Miralles and Jaume Pòrtulas link the tendency for
poetic initiations to take place in agricultural or pastoral settings (Hesiod,
Archilochus; compare Aeschylus, Epimenides) with agricultural ritual.[17]

Fescennine abuse offers a Roman parallel. Once again, farmers are
involved, and there is ritual offered to a Demeter-like figure, "Earth-mother
Tellus"; there is also a sacrifice of a pig, which reminds us again of Demeter
and Eleusis.[18] Horace wrote:

---

[13] My trans. Cf. Richardson 1974 *ad loc.*, 213–217, with numerous examples, and, for *aischrologia*,
p. 213; Conon *Narratives* 49, cf. parallels in Henrichs 1987:258n11; 270n20. See also Rusten
1977:157–161; Cornford 1968:276; Adams 1982:4–5; Olender 1985; O'Higgins 2001; Collins
2004:225–230. See above, ch. 3, for Iambe, hanged women, and for Charila at Delphi.

[14] See above, ch. 3; cf. Richardson 1974, at *Hymn to Demeter* 491.

[15] See Koster 1975:68. This is admittedly only one of several explanations for the name. Cf. the
Dionysian phallic element in the origins of comedy, see above, this chapter.

[16] West 1974:23, 36–37. Hesychius s.v. *ithumbos*: ποιήματα ἦν ἐπὶ χλεύῃ καὶ γέλωτι συγκείμενα.
καὶ ᾠδὴ μακρὰ καὶ ὑπόσκαιος.

[17] Koster 1975:11–12, cf. 70, 86. Miralles and Pòrtulas 1988:36; 1983:61–80.

[18] Cf. Burkert 1983:256–264. On Tellus, the Earth, and a close associate of Ceres, Growth, see Ovid
Fasti 1.671–674; Altheim 1931:108–129. Lydus *On the Months* 4.49 translates Tellus with *Dēmētēr*.

The farmers of old, a sturdy folk with simple wealth, when, after harvesting the grain, they sought relief at holiday time for the body, as well as for the soul, which bore its toils in hope of the end, together with slaves and faithful wife, partners of their labors, used to propitiate Earth with swine, Silvanus with milk, and the Genius who is ever mindful of the shortness of life with flowers and wine. Through this custom came into use Fescennine licence [*Fescennina licentia*],[19] which in alternate verse poured forth rustic taunts [*opprobria rustica*]; and the freedom, welcomed each returning year, was innocently gay, till jest, now growing cruel [*saevus*], turned to open frenzy [*apertam in rabiem*] and stalked amid the homes of honest folk, fearless in its threatening [*impune minax*].[20] They who were bitten by tooth that drew blood [*cruento dente lacessiti*] were stung to the quick, and even those untouched felt concern for the common cause; and at last a law was carried with a penalty, forbidding the portayal of any abusive strain [*malo carmine*]. Men changed their tune, and terror of the cudgel [*formidine fustis*] led them back to good and gracious forms of speech.

Horace *Epistles* 2.1.139–155, trans. Fairclough, adapted[21]

Fescennine abuse is "discovered through this festival"; as one wonders why, some possibilities come to mind. Perhaps there was a celebratory atmosphere and the abuse was meant in the spirit of pure fun, which seems to be Horace's view. Another explanation could be that festivals offered a sacred time in which one could criticize openly because there would be extreme religious sanctions on violence during the festival (*impune minax*).[22] This would allow the lower classes to criticize the upper classes without being punished, as Horace suggests, for it is the "respectable houses" who are upset at the satirical, ritual attack (presumably from those involved in agricultural ritual), and who have the power to pass a law against it. Thus, the feasts of Dionysus and Demeter might have become tools for the more "democratic" movements (including small farmers) as opposed to the ascendant oligarchies (in the cities). There is some evidence that Dionysiac cult did have democratic connections. Dodds writes that the Dionysiac religion "probably made its original appeal mainly

---

[19] See Brink 1982:191, for Fescennine abuse.
[20] For the sense of *honestas ... domos*, see Brink 1982:194.
[21] Latin text above, in ch. 20.
[22] Cf. Lysias fr. 53 Thalheim; Isocrates 8.14; Plato *Laws* 934d–6b; Aristotle *Politics* 1336b3–23; Halliwell 1991a and 1991b:292–296.

to people who had no citizen rights in the aristocratic 'gentile state' and were excluded from the older cults associated with the great families."[23]

Perhaps controlled aggression is brought into a happy, relaxed harvest festival so as to neutralize aggression. Or perhaps this controlled aggression helped participants "let off steam" before the new beginning of a new time period, such as a new year, as in Carnival.[24]

The Nonae Capratinae offers an example of ritualized abuse shading into ritualized fighting. "The handmaidens, in gay attire, run about jesting and joking with the men they meet. They have a mock battle, too, with one another, implying that they once took a hand in the struggle with the Latins."[25] Another detail in the Horace passage that suggests the aggressive, fighting aspect of this ritual abuse is the alternation of verses, which, as we have seen, are often competitive in nature.[26] One would expect friendly insults, one capping the other.

Thus, satire, the cult of Demeter/Dionysus, and ritualized elements of aggression formed a shadowy backdrop to the cult history of Archilochus that included a verbal phallic offense connected with Dionysiac cult, a trial and punishment of the poet, possibly exile, and punishment of society (impo-

---

[23] Dodds 1953:128. Cf. Aristotle *Politics* 6.4 1319b; Plutarch *On Love of Wealth* 8 (527d); Herodotus 1.23–24; Burkert 1985:291; Thomson 1968:141; 1946:120, 151–154; How and Wells 1928 2:344. Cf. the tradition that Aesop was a slave who used fables so as to escape punishment from his masters when he criticized them, see above, ch. 3, ch. 24 (Phaedrus) and the scholiastic account of the origins of comedy, above, this chapter; according to these texts, farmers sang with faces disguised so that they could criticize city dwellers freely.

[24] For Carnival, see Burke 1978:178–204. "Perhaps the mocking of outsiders (Jews at the Roman Carnival, peasants in that of Nuremberg) was, among other things, a dramatic expression of community solidarity" (200). Jews were pelted with mud and stones at Carnival as they raced through Rome (187), cf. Mamurius, ch. 27—on the last day of the old year, he is led in a procession through Rome, is beaten by the priests of Mars, the Salii, and then driven from the city. Violent death was common during Carnival (188), and public execution was ritualized (197). Ritual is used as social control, and even anti-hierarchical ritual preserves hierarchy (201). But sometimes "the wine barrel blew its top" (203). One thinks of Aristophanes brought to trial by Cleon, even though freedom of verbal attack was protected by festival license. "It may well have been that some of those excluded from power saw Carnival as an opportunity to make their views known and so to bring about change" (203). Cf. Bremmer and Horsfall 1987:82n29.

[25] Plutarch *Camillus* 33.6 (trans. Perrin): ἔπειτα κεκοσμημέναι λαμπρῶς αἱ θεραπαινίδες περίασι παίζουσι διὰ σκωμμάτων εἰς τοὺς ἀπαντῶντας. γίνεται δὲ καὶ μάχη τις αὐταῖς πρὸς ἀλλήλας, ὡς καὶ τότε τοῦ πρὸς τοὺς Λατίνους ἀγῶνος συνεπιλαμβανομέναις. See Bremmer and Horsfall 1987:76 (bibliography). Cf. Graf 1985:310.

[26] Clearchus, at Athenaeus 10.457c–e; Collins 2004:225–235. Griffith 1990:188 writes that "it is hardly an exaggeration to say that most Greek poetry, from the time of Homer and Hesiod to that of Euripides, was composed for performance in an explicitly or implicitly agonistic context." See above, ch. 2 (Aesop as riddle warrior); ch. 6 (Hesiod); ch. 17 (the poetic *agōn* in Ireland).

tence), ending in cult honors to Archilochus as favorite of Dionysus. The narrative mechanism that is the central focus of this book, which excludes the just poet unjustly, has important connections with this archaic nexus. Archilochus, the poet-scapegoat, is something of a priest, and a specialist in aggression. Perhaps the sin of the Parian burghers was to disallow the controlled aggression found in ritual abuse.

Appendix B
Aggression and the Defensive Topos: Archilochus, Callimachus, Horace

THUS FAR, I HAVE FOCUSED on the lives of the poets, with only occasional supportive reference to the poet's poetry. The subject of this chapter will be a theme that has been considered in passing, aggression and the defensive stance as an apologetic for satirical attack,[1] as it is reflected in poetry. This topos, extending from Archilochus to Callimachus to Horace,[2] allows the poets to portray themselves as victims; thus, as they attack, they are moral, administering justice. Satirical poets are not scurrilous, inherently negative; they are, in fact, positive, lashing out at evil. The moral satirist is almost by definition a victim.

Here the theme of poet as victim is in the poet's poetry, not just in the biographical tradition. The stories of the persecuted poets, whatever their source, exist in a tight nexus with the poets' creations.

Archilochus

A classic statement of the satirical apologetic is found in Archilochus 223W/167T, in which the poet is a cicada having its wing pulled by a callous human. Lucian, in his *The Liar* 1,[3] addresses a man who has humiliated him by criticizing a literary mistake he supposedly made:

τὸ δὲ τοῦ Ἀρχιλόχου ἐκεῖνο ἤδη σοι λέγω, ὅτι τέττιγα τοῦ πτεροῦ συνείληφας, εἴπερ τινὰ ποιητὴν ἰάμβων ἀκούεις Ἀρχίλοχον, Πάριον τὸ γένος, ἄνδρα κομιδῇ ἐλεύθερον καὶ παρρησίᾳ συνόντα, μηδὲν ὀκνοῦντα ὀνειδίζειν, εἰ καὶ ὅτι μάλιστα λυπήσειν ἔμελλε τοὺς

---

[1] Cf. Pulkkinen 1987; Ulrich 1973.
[2] This is a selection of especially striking texts; there are many other examples of the same theme in Greek and Roman literature, cf. Dickie 1981:193–195; Watson 2003:252.
[3] Cf. Lasserre 1950:29–31.

περιπετεῖς ἐσομένους τῇ χολῇ τῶν ἰάμβων αὐτοῦ. ἐκεῖνος τοίνυν πρός τινος τῶν τοιούτων ἀκούσας κακῶς τέττιγα ἔφη τὸν ἄνδρα εἰληφέναι τοῦ πτεροῦ, εἰκάζων ἑαυτὸν τῷ τέττιγι ὁ Ἀρχίλοχος φύσει μὲν λάλῳ ὄντι καὶ ἄνευ τινὸς ἀνάγκης, ὁπόταν δὲ καὶ τοῦ πτεροῦ ληφθῇ, γεγωνότερον βοῶντι. "Καὶ σὺ δή" ἔφη, "ὦ κακόδαιμον ἄνθρωπε, τί βουλόμενος ποιητὴν λάλον <u>παροξύνεις</u> ἐπὶ σεαυτὸν αἰτίας ζητοῦντα καὶ ὑποθέσεις τοῖς ἰάμβοις;"

And the phrase of Archilochus—I apply it to you now—that you have seized[4] a cicada by the wing, if indeed you have heard of a certain poet of iambs, Archilochus, of Parian stock, a man absolutely free and given to outspokenness, not hesitating to insult even if he was going to inflict extreme pain on those who were going to incur the wrath of his iambs. Therefore, he, being slandered by one of those sort, said the man had seized a cicada by the wing, Archilochus likening himself to the cicada, which is talkative by nature, even without any compulsion, and also, whenever it is seized by the wing, crying out with a louder voice. "And indeed," he said, "O ill-starred man, why do you wish to provoke [*paroxuneis*] a talkative poet, who seeks causes and pretexts for iambs against you?"

Thus the unnamed antagonist slandered Archilochus. Archilochus is forced to resort to iambs to attack the slanderer in response. The aggressor has forced the issue—as it were, he is asking for the iambs. The original attack is likened to a man taking a cicada by the wing, which makes the insect cry out louder. This metaphor has a rich range of resonances, characterizing as it does both the slanderer and the poet. The slanderer is the type of person who would take a beautiful insect by the wing, a most delicate part of its body. He is viewed as callous, even malignant, torturing a very much smaller, less powerful creature for his own amusement.

The poet, on the other hand, is the cicada. As we have noted he is small, comparatively defenseless on a physical plane; he is a continual singer, as Lucian notes—"talkative by nature, even without any compulsion." This is an important aspect of Archilochus' apologetic, for the torturer knows that the cicada sings continually, is good at it; the slanderer should have had respect for his art. In other words, Archilochus' slanderer probably knew Archilochus was a poet, but despised the art and powers of the satirist. This adds to the culpability of the victimizer and the innocence of the poet.

---

[4] Cf. Diels 1988:279.

Furthermore, the cicada is an effective symbol for the poet as creator of beauty—the cicada was proverbial for its lovely singing, as is well documented. One of our earliest references to the *tettix* is the well-known passage in Hesiod's *Works and Days* (582–584):

> Ἦμος δὲ σκόλυμός τ' ἀνθεῖ καὶ ἠχέτα <u>τέττιξ</u>
> δενδρέῳ ἐφεζόμενος λιγυρὴν καταχεύετ' <u>ἀοιδὴν</u>
> πυκνὸν ὑπὸ πτερύγων, θέρεος καματώδεος ὥρῃ...

> [Summer is the season]... when the thistle flowers, and the
>   resounding cicada [*tettix*],
> sitting on a tree, pours down its clear song [*aoidēn*]
> continuously from beneath its wings, in the season of tiring
>   heat.[5]

Thus the poet is a creator of beauty, an innocent defenseless creature, who is being tortured by an arrogant, powerful enemy. The poet is the victim, the beautifully singing insect being mangled. He fights back only in self defense; and his counterattack, satire, is the powerful weapon of the oppressed, a weapon of justice.[6]

Archilochus also used animal fable to attack Lycambes, in the "Lycambes epode" (172–181W).[7] The satirical apologetic is a focal point of this fable (Aesop *Fable* 1 Perry, quoted before 172W). In Aesop's version of it, the fox and the eagle make a treaty (emphasized by Archilochus, *xuneōniēn / emeixan*, 174W) of friendship. However, the eagle tramples on it, and feeds the fox's children to his own. The fox, which cannot reach its enemy of the air, is reduced to cursing him. The eagle carries a burning piece of sacrificial meat to its nest, accidentally sets the nest on fire (thanks also to a sudden gust of wind), and burns his children. They drop out of the nest, and the fox eats them in front of his enemy—exactly symmetrical justice, if a repulsive image for modern sensibilities.[8] The eagle is more powerful and prestigious than the fox, which makes his original act all the more despicable. In Aesop's fable, the fox is weaker, the victim, and aggressive verbalizing is the only defense of the oppressed: "Because of which, standing far off, she [the fox] cursed her enemy, which is the only thing left to those who are powerless and weak" (διόπερ

---

[5] Cf. *Iliad* III 152, the cicada emits a "delicate (literally, 'lily-like') song" (ὄπα λειριόεσσαν); Hesiod *Shield of Heracles* 393; Simonides 173–174; Plato *Phaedrus* 262d; and Boedeker 1984:81–83.

[6] See above, ch. 3.

[7] For background on this poem, see Lasserre 1950:28–109; Treu 1959:230–37; West 1982:30–32; Hendrickson 1925a:155–157; above, ch. 3.

[8] This detail is not in the Archilochus version.

πόρρωθεν στᾶσα, ὃ μόνον τοῖς ἀδυνάτοις καὶ ἀσθενέσιν ὑπολείπεται, τῷ ἐχθρῷ κατηρᾶτο).

We have only a few fragments of the Archilochean treatment of the fable, but one of them seems to be a quotation from that curse. It is not at all the kind of curse one might expect from the Archilochus of evil reputation; instead, it is theological, an appeal to Zeus, to justice.[9]

> ὦ Ζεῦ, πάτερ Ζεῦ, σὸν μὲν οὐρανοῦ κράτος
> σὺ δ' ἔργ' ἐπ' ἀνθρώπων ὁρᾶις
> λεωργὰ καὶ θεμιστά, σοὶ δὲ θηρίων
> ὕβρις τε καὶ δίκη μέλει.

> O Zeus, father Zeus, who rules heaven,
>   you look upon the deeds of men,
> both evil and lawful; you are
>   concerned for outrage and justice [even among the] beasts.

Archilochus 177W

This is not the Archilochus who arbitrarily fattens himself on hatreds (Pindar *Pythian Odes* 2.55); it is instead a hapless victim who appeals to god for justice, and punishes, perhaps, in Zeus' name, almost as an earthly representative of the god. He views his poetic task almost as a theological imperative.[10]

We also find the satirical apologetic in Hipponax 115W.[11] Here we find a powerful example of extreme abuse, perhaps the most virulent blame poetry in archaic Greece. At first glance, the poet seems the aggressor, and is making his target a victim. But at the end of the fragment as we have it, we find that the invective is buttressed by the same satirical apologetic that we have found in Archilochus' poetry:

> ταῦτ' ἐθέλοιμ' ἂν ἰδεῖν,
> ὅς μ' ἠδίκησε, λ[ὰ]ξ δ' ἐπ' ὁρκίοις ἔβη,
> τὸ πρὶν ἑταῖρος [ἐ]ών.

> I would love to see these things,
> [since] he wronged me [*ēdikēse*], and he trampled on our oaths
>   [*orkiois*],
> though previously he was a comrade.

Hipponax 115W

---

[9] The curse is a formal, ritualistic phenomenon, including invocation of god, see above, ch. 9 (Alcaeus). For the importance of *dikē* 'justice' in the ethics of the curse, Watson 1991:38–42.

[10] For an interpretation of 181W that follows these lines, see West 1982:30–32.

[11] See above, ch. 4.

Hipponax curses his enemy, but only because his enemy, once a trusted friend, has done the poet a serious injustice, breaking solemn oaths. For the Greeks, there was a deep religious dimension to oath breaking. Jon D. Mikalson writes, "The violation of an oath was an impious act of the type which the gods were thought to punish . . . The individual often specified in a curse the punishment which should afflict him if he violated his oath."[12] The poet's only recourse is bitterly abusive verse, this poem, which is something of a curse. The poet, who at first glance appears to be making a victim of an enemy, sees himself as the actual weak, primary victim, and is satirizing and cursing only in self-defence.[13]

Callimachus

Callimachus might seem to offer a vivid contrast to the bitter abuse of Archilochus and Hipponax. He is urbane, scholarly; as a Hellenistic Alexandrian, he is in many ways writing in a different intellectual universe than that of the two early satirists. Yet an essential aspect of Callimachus' sophistication was his absorption and use of earlier poets; he was influenced by Archilochus, and Hipponax was a favorite, as any reader of his *Iambs* knows. Some have explained this relationship in purely formal, technical terms: Callimachus was attracted to the originality of Hipponax's diction, his meters, his learning, his concentration on lyric rather than epic. But if Callimachus did not have sympathy for some aspect of Hipponax's central themes, one would be hard pressed to explain his resurrection of the iambist in the important, programmatic *Iamb* 1.[14]

In one of the Alexandrian poet's most famous poems, the introduction to the *Aetia*, we find the satirical apologetic emphasized, and applied to a literary quarrel. Callimachus attacks the "Telchines," mischievous hobgoblins, his rival poets, who have abused him because of his refusal to write epic;[15] now he abuses them in self-defence (lines 1–5):

Οἶδ' ὅτ]ι μοι Τελχῖνες ἐπιτρύζουσιν ἀοιδῇ
νήιδες οἳ Μούσης οὐκ ἐγένοντο φίλοι,

---

[12] Mikalson 1983:31–38, 35.

[13] Cf. Alcaeus 129V, lines 22–24, 13–16; above, ch. 9.

[14] See above, ch. 4 (Hipponax); Dickie 1981:196; Hughes 1997. For Archilochus' influence on Callimachus, see Bühler 1964.

[15] For the actual poet and critics Callimachus had in mind, see the Florentine scholium, Pfeiffer 1949:3; cf. Lesky 1966:710–711; Watson 1991:129. Cameron 1995 is a skeptic, believing there was no specific target for this abuse.

εἵνεκεν οὐχ ἓν ἄεισμα διηνεκὲς ἢ βασιλ[η . . .
. . .]ας ἐν πολλαῖς ἤνυσα χιλιάσιν
ἢ . . .]ους ἥρωας . . .

I know that] the Telkhines mutter against my song,
who are ignorant and are not friends of the Muse,
because I didn't accomplish one continuous song
of many thousand lines [singing of] kings . . . and heroes . . .

Callimachus proceeds to explain that quality, not quantity, makes great poetry, and that often the smaller is the more beautiful (16, 24). Furthermore, he sings "among those who love the clear voice of the cicada, and not the tumult of asses" (τεττίγω]ν ἐνὶ τοῖς γὰρ ἀείδομεν οἳ λιγὺν ἦχον /. . . θ]όρυβον δ' οὐκ ἐφίλησαν ὄνων, 29–30).[16] Here we have the Archilochean motif of the poet as cicada, adapted to Callimachus' literary-critical argument, and in a poem that is rhetorically structured as a defence and counterattack. The image of the poet surrounded by malevolent beings, Telchines, is the base conception here, and suggests elemental realities; on a human level, stoning, a collective punishment that involves a community singling out an especially despised scapegoat; and, on a more primeval level, the animal cornered by a pack of predators.

A similar rhetorical stance is found in the ending of the *Hymn to Apollo* (105–113). In this famous passage, Envy states that it will not praise a singer who does not even sing as broadly as the sea; Apollo strikes or banishes Envy with his foot and replies that a big river like the Euphrates is full of mud and refuse. We have attack and defence leading to counterattack once again, applied to practitioners of different kinds of poetry.[17]

Thus this familiar defensive stance in key programmatic Callimachean texts is an adept application of archaic, Archilochean technique toward Hellenistic literary polemic. In addition, Callimachus' extended satirical poem, the *Ibis*, which Ovid used as a model for his own *Ibis*, compares its target to a bird who pollutes constantly.[18] Probably the satirical apologetic was at work here too, if Ovid's work adequately reflects its model.[19]

---

[16] For Trypanis's reading *tettigō]n*, see Trypanis 1958:8.

[17] Cf. scholion *ad loc.* 2.106/T37. For the apologetic nature of this passage, and its influence especially in Rome, see Wimmer 1960:59–70. For introductions to problems in this poem: Köhnken 1981; Williams 1978:86–92.

[18] Strabo 17.823. Apollonius may have been the target of the *Ibis*, see Watson 1991:129. Two ancient testimonia do support the identification. Cameron (1995) tends to see no specific target for the poem. See further Watson:1991:121–129.

[19] For the defensive nature of Ovid's *Ibis*, see 9–20, 29–30.

It is curious to see this rhetorical strategy—that allowed Archilochus to write poetry that would drive those who had once been close friends to the point of suicide (in legend, at least)—applied in an Alexandrian aesthetic.[20] It shows us how much archaic Greece and the Hellenistic tradition had in common, and how different they were. Before Callimachus turned his satirical aggression against his opponents, he had to feel attacked, by numerous envious critical hobgoblins; he was a literary isolate as it were, a literary victim receiving aggression unjustly before he returned it justly (and elegantly).

Horace

Rome continued the Hellenistic literary traditions of Callimachus. Like Callimachus, Horace turned to Archilochus and Hipponax for inspiration, and his book of *Epodes* includes poems of surprising savagery, seemingly uncharacteristic of the urbane, gently witty Horace.[21] Some have explained the occasional violence and crudity in these poems by suggesting that the *Epodes* may be close reworkings of Archilochus or Hipponax. But though there may be some adaptation of these poets here,[22] Horace's own voice is also present; in his other work, he was consistently a satirist, obviously in the *Satires*, often even in the *Odes*.[23]

The sixth *Epode* is almost a manifesto for the satirist's defensive apologetic:[24]

> Quid immerentis hospites vexas, canis,
>   ignavus adversum lupos?
> quin huc inanis verte, si potes, minas
>   et me remorsurum pete.
> nam qualis aut Molossus aut fulvus Lacon,

---

[20] Though curiously, in the scholiastic tradition, we find an account of Callimachus killing an enemy through poetry, see above, ch. 4.

[21] Schmidt 1978 offers a valuable treatment of these three writers, though Schmidt perhaps overemphasizes Archilochus' helplessness. See also Wistrand 1964 and Koenen 1977. For the *Epodes* generally, see now Watson's massive commentary (2003) and Mankin 1995.

[22] See Watson 2003:506; 1991:58 (cf. *Epode* 10). For further on the curse in Horace, see Watson 1991:242.

[23] He was indebted to Archilochus and Hipponax, though he "transmuted" his iambic heritage, partially by softening (Watson 2003:6). "Almost every feature" of the problematically coarse *Epodes* 8 and 12, discussed below, can be paralleled in Archilochus and Hipponax (Watson 2003:8).

[24] For the programmatic nature of this poem, see Olivier 1917:67–77; Bucheit 1961; and Schmidt 1977; Dickie 1981:195–196. Watson, 2003:256, disagrees.

amica vis pastoribus,
agam per altas aure sublata nives,
 quaecumque praecedet fera;
tu, cum timenda voce complesti nemus,
 proiectum odararis cibum.
cave, cave: namque in malos asperrimus
 parata tollo cornua,
qualis Lycambae spretus infido gener
 aut acer hostis Bupalo.
an, si quis atro dente me petiverit,
 inultus ut flebo puer?

Why, dog, do you harass innocent
 strangers,[25] a coward against wolves?
Why not turn your empty threats here, if you are able,
 and attack me, who will bite you back.
For like a Molossian or a tawny Laconian,
 a strong friend to shepherds,
I will go through the deep snows with my ears raised,
 whatever wild animal will go before;
you, when you have filled the forest with your fearful voice,
 sniff at the food thrown at you.
Beware, beware, for I, most harsh toward evil men,
 raise my horns in readiness,
just as the spurned would-be son-in-law did to faithless Lycambes
 or the bitter enemy of Bupalus did to him.
Or if anyone attacks me with venomous[26] tooth,
 will I cry like a child, and not take revenge?

Like Archilochus, Horace turns to animal imagery, which is used skillfully to characterize the poet and his enemy. The bad dog is aggressive, and attacks those who are innocent [*immerentis*]; it is very loud—line 1 is probably a reference to barking; we have "threats" in line 3; in line 9, his fearful voice fills the forest. But if he meets a real challenge, wolves, he is a coward. The good dog, the poet, is, on the other hand, strong, faithful to his masters the shepherds; a fearless defender against wild animals, heroically wading through deep snow with his ears perked up. And if the bad dog attacks him, he will bite back

---

[25] On *hospites*, cf. Bucheit 1961:521.
[26] Lit., 'black'. Watson (2003:265) interprets this as referring to malice.

(*me remorsurum*).[27] This is the defensive apologetic for literary violence in its pure form. The poet does not begin the hostilities; he only bites in return—in defense, as punishment.[28]

Dropping the metaphor in line 11, the poet is "most harsh toward wicked men" (*in malos asperrimus*). His attack is directed only at those who are evil; the satirist is repaying the balance, a person with a powerful weapon for good. Some argue for a limited tooth-for-tooth interpretation of this passage, but I would argue that Lindsay Watson's interpretation of the poet as sheepdog argues for the more general ethical interpretation here.[29] The whole poem brilliantly characterizes the poet's enemy as cowardly, loud, and inhospitable, while the sheepdog is loyal, determined, and courageous. David Mankin denigrates the idea of iambic poet as "crusader,"[30] but the image of a loyal sheepdog protecting the sheep as he wards off predators with his ears alert, running through thick snow, is precisely a heroic image.[31]

Taking up animal metaphor again, the poet is a man with a sharp weapon, a bull with horns prepared for action. And the final lines characterize the enemy as a poisonous snake; if the poet is bitten, he warns, he will not go unavenged. He uses verbal weaponry only when he has been attacked; twice Horace uses biting imagery as he portrays the poet as victim; he is bitten by a dog, and by a poisonous snake. Given such provocation, he is forced to resort to satire, like Archilochus' cicada having its wing pulled by a callous tormentor. It is striking that, as we have seen, the satirist's art is often compared to the bite of an animal or a poisonous attack; however, here we see the satirist is merely responding justly to such attacks, even if he is responding in kind.

A straightforward expression of the idea is found in Horace's second book of *Satires*:

> . . . sed hic stilus haud petet ultro
> quemquam animantem et me veluti custodiet ensis
> vagina tectus: quem cur destringere coner
> tutus ab infestis latronibus? o pater et rex

---

[27] For other examples of the satirist as dog, see Watson 2003:252, 258.

[28] For a treatment of this metaphor, see Watson 1983:156–159. Watson makes the important point that, in attacking the dog's sheep, the enemy has attacked the dog himself, see 158n7. For further explanation of the "authorial canine" as sheepdog, not hunter (the usual interpretation), see Watson 2003:259–260.

[29] For *malus* as *improbus*, the general ethical interpretation, see Dickie 1981:197–198, and literature cited by Watson in 2003:262, though Watson disagrees.

[30] Mankin 1995:141.

[31] Cf. the "murderous thieves" in Horace's *Satire* 1 of Book Two, see below. For the poet of *Epode* 6 as hero, Dickie 1981:200, who contrasts the "noble" and "ignoble" dogs.

Iuppiter, ut pereat positum robigine telum
nec quisquam noceat cupido mihi pacis! at ille,
qui me conmorit—melius non tangere, clamo—
flebit et insignis tota cantabitur urbe.

But unprovoked, this pen will not attack
any living soul, and will protect me like a sword
covered by a scabbard: why would I try to unsheathe it
if I were safe from murderous thieves? O father and king
Jupiter, may that weapon be laid aside and perish with rust,
neither may anyone harm me, when I desire peace! but he
who shall trouble me—better not to touch, I cry out—,
will weep and, infamous, will be sung throughout the city.

Satire 1:39–46

Two problematic poems, *Epodes* 8 and 12, puzzlingly extreme, obscene attacks on an older woman, a former lover, both use the satirical apologetic, which may help us understand them better, despite their unpleasantly misogynous overtones.[32] In both, the poet is responding to an earlier attack, in which the lover disparaged his manhood publicly. The eighth *Epode* describes in repulsive detail the physical attributes of an aging woman, but only because she has accused the poet of aging, losing his sexual prowess. Horace—or Horace's Greek model—is angered by her hypocrisy.

Rogare longo putidam te saeculo,
    viris quid enervet meas,
cum sit tibi dens ater et rugis vetus
    frontem senectus exaret

For you, rotten with your long life, to ask
    what weakens my powers,
when your teeth are black, and old age
    furrows your face with wrinkles!

Epode 12 quotes the actual words the woman uses to attack the poet's masculinity:

qui sudor vietis et quam malus undique membris
    crescit odor . . .

---

[32] Fraenkel writes, "*Epodes* VIII and XII, with all their polish, are repulsive" (1957:58). Cf. Grassmann 1966:87 nn. 147–148; 47. For abuse of old women, see Davies 1985:39.

> vel mea cum saevis agitat fastidia verbis:
> "Inachia langues minus ac me;
> Inachiam ter nocte potes, mihi semper ad unum
>   mollis opus. pereat male quae te
> Lesbia quaerenti taurum monstravit inertem.
>   cum mihi Cous adesset Amyntas . . ."

> What sweat, and what a foul odor rises everywhere
>   from her withered limbs . . .
> she even attacks my fastidiousness with savage words:
>   "With Inachia you are less feeble than with me;
> you are able [to service] Inachia three times a night, with me
>   you are always
>   soft after one effort. May Lesbia come to a bad end, who
> offered you, so sluggish, to me, when I was asking for a bull,
>   when Coan Amyntas was available to me . . . "

The target of this epode, then, has attacked the poet's virility, has compared him insultingly with a more capable bedmate. Who was right in this particular quarrel—whether the poet attacked the woman with more or less justification—is immaterial for the present discussion, and certainly unanswerable in any case; for our present purposes, it is enough to recognize that the poet takes pains to show that he has been attacked; his satire, aggressive as it is, has a defensive cast to it. From his perspective, it was provoked, and is a just response.

Poet as Victim

This very selective survey shows that the satirist taking the defensive rhetorical stance is a theme that extends through the Greco-Roman poetic tradition. An essential aspect of this theme is the victimization of the poet (by the poet's lights). Archilochus is the helpless cicada held callously by the wing; Hipponax has seen the oaths he swore with a friend trampled underfoot; Callimachus' poetry has been attacked by tasteless, vindictive literary rivals; Horace is bitten by dog and poisonous serpent. Satirists, in programmatic poems expressing the reasons for their satire, view themselves as victims; they must see themselves as victims, or their invective cannot exist, given a moral perspective. And the defensive apologetic shows how important the moral perspective is to the satirist.

Thus, the theme of poet as victim is not just in legends or stories that are possibly nonhistorical, but is also in the poet's poetry. Lefkowitz would argue that scholiasts may have taken these passages as starting points, and fabricated stories of exile and adverse trial from them. This certainly happened at times. Legends of poets also were produced by oral tradition long before they were written down. Such legends served as charter myths for the poetic profession, for the poet in the social matrix of ancient Greece (with heroized poets and warnings against inhospitable society embedded in the tales, and a theology for inspired poets' apparent failures). Ritual sources for some legends should also be taken into account. All of these factors interrelated with each other.

But these phenomena should not prevent us from considering another cause-and-effect relationship, and ask what caused the victimization theme to appear in the poet's poetry. Certainly, a thoroughgoing application of the biographical fallacy should be rejected. An artist can seem quite different from the art he or she creates. On the other hand, it is absurd to see the poets living their actual lives as completely divorced, emotionally, from what they write. Poets write on themes they are concerned with emotionally, aesthetically, humanely. In the case of Archilochus, even if he did not undergo all that later legend ascribed to him, he evidently did feel like a victim, attacked unjustly, at some point. And one cannot rule out the historical possibility that society will occasionally exile, execute, or punish poets because their poetry is offensive, as the lives of Alcaeus, Socrates, and Ovid richly show.

Appendix C
Themes

Pharmakos themes

1. *Ritual pollution.*

   1a. *Crime of hero.* Pharmakos. Aesop (imputed). Archilochus (imputed). Hesiod (imputed or actual). Socrates (imputed).

      1a1. *Criminal impiety.* Aesop. Socrates (imputed)

         1a1a. *Theft of sacred things.* Pharmakos. Aesop (imputed).

         1a1b. *Parricide.* Oedipus.

         1a1c. *Incest.* Oedipus.

      1a2. *Sexual.* Oedipus. (Archilochus). (Sappho). Hesiod (actual and imputed).

      1a3. *Murder.* Oedipus. Athlete heroes. Heracles.

      1a4. *Offensive verbalizing, anti-social or obscene.* Aesop. Archilochus. Socrates.

   1b. *Crime against hero.* Androgeus, Aesop. Archilochus. Hesiod. Socrates. Homer.

      1b1. *Inhospitality.* Androgeus. Aesop. Hesiod. Homer.

      1b2. *Murder.* Androgeus. Aesop. Hesiod. Ibycus. Stesichorus.

      1b3. *Deceit.*

         1b3a. *False accusation.* Aesop. Hesiod. Socrates.

         1b3b. *Ambush.* Androgeus. Hesiod.

      1b4. *Broken vow or communal oaths.* Archilochus. Hipponax. Sappho. Alcaeus. Heracles.

2. *Communal disaster.*

   2a. *Communal disaster causes hero's expulsion or death*, e.g. "plague of shame." Androgeus. Aesop (at Samos). Oedipus.

     2a1. *Plague.* Oedipus.

     2a2. *Famine.* Oedipus.

     2a3. *War.* Aesop (Samos). Aglauros. Codrus. Tyrtaeus.

     2a4. *Psychological plague* ("plague of shame," destructive verbalizing). Aesop. Archilochus. Socrates.

   2b. *Communal disaster caused by hero's death or expulsion.* Androgeus. Aesop. Archilochus. Hesiod.

     2b1. *Plague.* Aesop. Archilochus. Hesiod.

     2b2. *Famine.*

     2b3. *War.* Aesop.

3. *Oracle, often prescribing remedy for disaster.* Androgeus. Aesop. Archilochus. Hesiod

4. *The Worst.* Ritual *pharmakos.* Cf. Codrus in disguise.

   4a. *Poverty.* Archilochus. Homer. Tyrtaeus.

     4a1. *Beggar.* Homer.

     4a2. *Poor or scanty food.* Hipponax.

   4b. *Slave.* Aesop. Archilochus (slave parentage). Phaedrus.

   4c. *Criminal* (see 1a–1b above). Aesop (imputed). Hesiod (imputed).

   4d. *Ugly/deformed.* Aesop. Hipponax. Sappho. Simonides. Tyrtaeus. Aeschylus. Euripides. Socrates. Marsyas. Thersites.

   4e. *Foreigner.* Androgeus. Aesop. Hesiod.

   4f. *Poison imagery.* Archilochus. Hipponax. Socrates.

   4g. *Animalistic.* Aesop. Socrates. Marsyas.

5. *The Best.*

   5a. *Sacred.* See 23. Aesop. Archilochus. Sappho. Hesiod. Homer. Socrates.

   5b. *Salvation, salvation imagery.* Aesop (Samos).

   5c. *Victorious.* Androgeus. Aesop (in riddle contest). Hesiod (in riddle/ poetry contest). Tyrtaeus (in war).

5d. *Athlete.* Androgeus.

5e. *Royal.* Androgeus. Codrus. Aglauros.

5f. *Wisest.* Aesop. Archilochus. Socrates.

6. *Peripety.* Androgeus. Codrus. Aesop. Socrates. Oedipus.

7. *Trial, unjust. Adverse judgment by public meeting.* Aesop. Archilochus. Homer. Aeschylus. Euripides. Socrates. Marsyas.

8. *Voluntary (exile or death).*

8a. *Ambivalent volition.* Aesop. Socrates. Cicero.

9. *Procession.* Aesop?

9a. *Blows. Pharmakos.* Hipponax.

10. *Expulsion.*

10a. *Exile.* Archilochus. Hipponax. Homer. Sappho. Alcaeus. Theognis. Aeschylus. (Euripides?) Naevius. Cicero. Ovid. (Phaedrus?) Juvenal.

10b. *Death in distant country.* Aesop. Hesiod. Ibycus. Homer. Theognis? Euripides.

11. *Death* (cf. 1f). Aesop. Hesiod. Seneca. Petronius. Lucan.

11a. *Stoning. Pharmakos.* Aesop. Hipponax. Aristophanes (theme in poetry).

11b. *Thrown from cliff. Pharmakos.* Aesop. Sappho. (Oedipus.)

11c. *Poisoning.* Socrates.

11d. *By sword or knife.* Androgeus. Hesiod. Cicero.

11e. *Hanging.* Charila. Iambe. See *vitae* of Archilochus and Hesiod.

11f. *Unjust.* Androgeus. Aesop. Hesiod.

12. *Sacrifice.* Aesop.

12a. *Death at a cult site.* Aesop. Sappho. Homer. Hesiod. Aeschylus. Euripides. Orpheus.

13. *Hero cult.* Androgeus. Codrus. Aglauros. Aesop. Archilochus. Hesiod. Homer. Sappho. Theognis? Tyrtaeus? Aeschylus. Euripides. Socrates. Orpheus.

13a. *Immortality of hero.* Aesop (cf. 23d).

13b. *Bones transfer.* Hesiod.

13c. *Tomb struck by lightning.* Euripides.

Legendary scapegoat themes

14. *Royal.* Euripides. See 5e.

15. *Youth, virgin, as scapegoat.* Aglauros. Euripides.

16. *Evil eye.* Polykrite. Aesop.

17. *Fatal, saving gift.* Codrus. Polykrite. Aesop. Socrates. Cf. 4f.

18. *Divine persecutor-patron.* Aesop. Homer. Hesiod. Socrates. Ovid. Marsyas. Thamyris.

Athlete–hero, related to above themes (see 5c–d)

19. *Madness of hero.* Sappho. Tyrtaeus. Aeschylus. Heracles.

20. *Murderer.* (See 1a3, 1b2.)

21. *Imprisonment.* Aesop. Socrates. Naevius. Phaedrus?

Themes of Poets, related to above themes

22. *Blame poet as hero/poetry/satirical themes.* (See 1a4, 2a4.) Aesop. Archilochus. Hipponax. Sappho. Alcaeus. Theognis. Euripides. Aristophanes. Socrates. Callimachus. Naevius. Cicero. Ovid. Phaedrus. Juvenal.

22a. *Killing through blame.* Aesop. Archilochus. Hipponax. Callimachus.

22a1. *Hanging.* Archilochus. Hipponax. Hesiod. Alcaeus.

22b. *Exiling through blame.* Alcaeus. Demosthenes. Cicero.

22c. *Animal fables used for blame.* Aesop. Archilochus. Hesiod. Socrates. Phaedrus.

22d. *Artist satirizing artist.* Hipponax. Sappho. Aristophanes. Callimachus.

22e. *Curse as theme.* Aesop. Archilochus. Hipponax. Homer. (Sappho.) Alcaeus. Theognis. Aristophanes. Socrates. Callimachus. Ovid. Horace.

22f. *Defensive topos.* Archilochus. Hipponax. Alcaeus. Callimachus. Horace.

23. *Poet is sacred, superhuman.* (see 5a above)

23a. *Consecration of poet* (often by theophany, with physical gift). Aesop. Archilochus. Hipponax? Homer. Hesiod. Stesichorus. Aeschylus. Callimachus. Socrates. Naevius. Marsyas.

23b. *Association with Muses.* Aesop. Archilochus. Hesiod. Homer.

23c. *Animal helper.* Hesiod. Arion. Ibycus.

23d. *Resurrection.* Androgeus. Oedipus. Aesop. Hesiod. Epimenides.

23e. *Immortality through poetry.* (Cf. 13a.) Archilochus. Sappho. Homer. Naevius.

24. *Conflict with political leaders.* Aesop. Archilochus. Hipponax. Homer. Hesiod. Alcaeus. Theognis. Euripides. Aristophanes. Socrates. Naevius. Cicero. Ovid. Juvenal.

25. *Agōn, contest.* (See 5c, victorious; 7, trial, unjust.)

25a. *Riddle-poetry contest.* Oedipus. Aesop. Homer. Hesiod. Aeschylus.

25b. *Music contest.* Marsyas. Thamyris. Pan.

25c. *Poetry or drama contest.* Aeschylus.

26. *Poet as soldier.* (See 2a and 2b.) Aesop. Archilochus. Alcaeus. Theognis. Tyrtaeus. Aeschylus. Socrates. Naevius. (Achilles, Heracles: soldier as poet.)

26a. *Martial paraenesis as poetic theme.* Archilochus. Alcaeus. Theognis. Tyrtaeus. Solon.

27. *Exile as poetic theme.* (Archilochus.) (Hesiod.) Alcaeus. Theognis. Cicero. Ovid. Seneca.

28. *Wolf imagery, linked to exile.* Hero. Alcaeus.

Bibliography

Adams, J. 1982. *The Latin Sexual Vocabulary.* London.

Adrados, F. R. 1975. *Festival, Comedy, and Tragedy.* Leiden.

——. 1979. "The 'Life of Aesop' and the Origins of the Novel in Antiquity." *Quaderni Urbinati di Cultura Classica,* n.s. 1:93–112.

Adrados, F., ed. 1984. *La Fable.* Entretiens Fondation Hardt XXX. Vandoeuvres-Genève.

Allen, T. W. 1919. *Homeri Opera.* 5 vols. 2nd ed. Oxford.

Aloni, A. 1981. *Le Muse di Archiloco.* Copenhagen.

Altheim, F. 1931. *Terra Mater.* RVV 22.2. Giessen.

Ancient Laws of Ireland. 1865–1901. 6 vols. Dublin.

Anderson, W. S. 1964. "Anger in Juvenal and Seneca." *California Publications in Classical Philology* 19:127–196.

Andrewes, A. 1956. *The Greek Tyrants.* London.

Anhalt, E. K. 1993. *Solon the Singer: Politics and Poetics.* Lanham, MD.

Antonaccio, C. 1993. "The Archaeology of Ancestors." In Dougherty and Kurke 1993:46–72.

Antonaccio, C. 1995. *An Archaeology of Ancestors: Tomb Cult and Hero Cult in Early Greece.* Lanham, MD.

Ardizzoni, A. 1960. "Calliamaco 'Ipponatteo.'" *AFLC* 28:3–16.

Arrighetti, G. 1964. *Satiro, Vita di Euripide.* Studi Classici e Orientali 13. Pisa.

——. 1981. "Il misoginismo di Esiodo." In *Misoginia e maschilismo in Greciae e in roma.* 27–48. Genoa.

Arrowsmith, W., trans. 1969. *Aristophanes, Three Comedies.* Ann Arbor.

Atkinson, J. E. 1992. "Curbing the Comedians." *Classical Quarterly* 42:56–64.

Austin, R. G., ed. 1960. *Pro M. Caelio Oratio.* 3rd ed. Oxford. (Orig. pub. 1952.)

Babcock, C. L. 1965. "The Early Career of Fulvia." *American Journal of Philology* 86:1–32.

Bannon, C. 1997. *The Brothers of Romulus.* Princeton.

Barkan, I. 1979. *Capital Punishment in Ancient Athens*. New York. Printed with John Lofberg, *Sycophancy in Athens*. (Orig. pub. 1936.)

Bates, W. 1897. "The Date of Tyrtaeus." *Transactions and Proceedings of the American Philological Association* 28:xlii–xlv.

Bauer, O. 1963. "Sapphos Verbannung." *Gymnasium* 70:1–10.

Beaulieu, M.-C. 2004. "L'héroïsation du poète Hésiode en Grèce ancienne." *Kernos* 17:103–117.

Bell, J. M. 1978. "Κίμβιξ καὶ σοφός: Simonides in the Anecdotal Tradition." *Quaderni Urbinati di Cultura Classica* 28:29–86.

Benedetto, V. 1982. "Sulla biografia di Saffo." *Studi Classici Orientali* 32:217–230.

Benedict, R. 1946. *The Chrysanthemum and the Sword*. New York.

Benesch, B. 1961. "Spuren von Schamanismus in der Sage 'Buile Suibhne.'" *Zeitschrift für celtische Philologie* 28:309–334.

Benveniste, E. 1973. *Indo-European Language and Society*. Trans. E. Palmer. London. = *Le Vocabulaire des institutions indo-européennes*. Paris, 1969.

Bergin, O. 1912–1913. "Bardic Poetry." *Journal of the Ivernian Society* 5:153–166; 203–219 = *Irish Bardic Poetry* 3–22. Dublin, 1970.

Bergren, A. 1982. "Sacred Apostrophe: Re-presentation and Imitation in the Homeric Hymns." *Arethusa* 15:83–108.

———. 1983. "Odyssean Temporality: Many (Re)Turns." In Rubino 1983:38–73.

Berve, H. 1967. *Die Tyrannis bei den Griechen*. Munich.

Best, R. I., Bergin, O., and O'Brien, M. A., eds. 1954–1983. *The Book of Leinster, formerly Lebar na Núachongbála*. 6 vols. Dublin.

Bie, O. 1884–1937. "Musen." In Roscher 1884–1937 2.2:3238–3295.

Birch, C. M. 1955. "Traditions of the Life of Aesop." Diss. Washington University. St. Louis.

Blaive, F. 1996. *Impius Bellator. Le Mythe Indo-Européen du Guerrier Impie*. Arras.

Bloomfield, M., and Dunn, C. 1989. *The Role of the Poet in Early Societies*. Cambridge.

Blumenthal, A. von. 1948. "Tyrtaios." RE, 2nd ser., 7A 1941–1956.

Boedeker, D. 1984. *Descent From Heaven, Images of Dew in Greek Poetry and Religion*. Chico, CA.

———. "Hero Cult and Politics in Herodotus: The Bones of Orestes." In Dougherty and Kurke 1993:164–177.

Boehringer, D. 2001. *Heroenkulte in Griechenland von der geometrischen bis zur klassischen Zeit. Attika, Argolis, Messenien*. Klio Beih., Neue Folge, 3. Berlin.

Bohringer, F. 1979. "Cultes d'athlètes en Grèce classique: Propos politiques, discours mythiques." *Revue des Études Anciennes* 81:5–18.

Bolle, K. 1983. "A World of Sacrifice." *History of Religions* 23:37–63.

Bolton, J. D. P. 1962. *Aristeas of Proconnesus*. Oxford.

Boruhovi, V. 1981. "Zur Geschichte des sozialpolitischen Kampfes auf Lesbos (Ende des 7; Anfang des 6. Jh v. Chr.)." *Klio* 63:247–259.

Bowra, C. M. 1960. *Early Greek Elegists*. New York.

———. "Arion and the Dolphin." *Museum Helveticum* 20:121–134.

Boyancé, P. 1937. *Le culte des muses chez les philosophes grecs: Etudes d'histoire et de psychologie religieuses*. Paris.

Braund, S. H. 1988. *Beyond Anger*. Cambridge.

Braund, S. M. 2004. *"Libertas* or *Licentia?* Freedom and Criticism in Roman Satire." In Sluiter and Rosen 2004:409–428.

Breatnach, L. 1980. *"Tochmarc Luaine ocus Aided Athairne."* *Celtica* 13:1–31.

———, ed. 1987. *Uraicecht Na Ríar: The Poetic Grades in Early Irish Law*. Dublin.

———. 1996. "Poets and Poetry." In *Progress in Medieval Irish Studies* (ed. K. McCone and K. Simms), 65–77. Maynooth.

Breitenstein, T. 1971. *Hesiode et Archiloque*. Odense.

Brelich, A. 1949/1950. "Osservazioni sulle 'esclusioni rituali.'" *Studi e Materiali di Storia delle Religioni* 22:16–21.

———. 1958. *Gli eroi greci*. Rome.

———. 1961. *Guerre, agoni e culti nella Grecia Arcaica*. Bonn.

Bremer, J. M., van Erp Taalman Kip, A. M., Slings, S. R. 1987. *Some Recently Found Greek Poems: Text and Commentary*. Leiden.

Bremmer, J. 1978. "Heroes, Rituals and the Trojan War." *Studio Storico Religiosi* 2:5–38.

———. 1982. "The Suodales of Poplios Valesios." *Zeitschrift für Papyrologie und Epigraphik* 47:133–147.

———. 1980. "Medon, the Case of the Bodily Blemished King." In Piccaluga 1980:67–76.

———. 1983a. *The Early Greek Concept of the Soul*. Princeton.

———. 1983b. "Scapegoat Rituals in Ancient Greece." *Harvard Studies in Classical Philology* 87:299–320.

———, ed. 1987. *Interpretations of Greek Mythology*. London.

———. 1990. "Adolescents, Symposion, and Pederasty." In *Sympotica, a Symposium on the Symposion* (ed. O. Murray) 135–148. Oxford.

Bremmer, J., and Horsfall, N. M. 1987. *Roman Myth and Mythography*. London.

Brenk, F. E. 1975. "Interesting Bedfellows at the End of the *Apology*." *Classical Bulletin* 51:44–46.

Brenot, A. 1924. *Phèdre*. Paris.

Bretzigheimer, G. 1991. *"Exul ludens*. Zur Rolle von relegans und relegatus in Ovids *Tristien*." *Gymnasium* 98:39–77.

Brickhouse, T., and Smith, N. 1989. *Socrates on Trial*. Oxford.

Brink, C. O. 1982. *Horace on Poetry: Epistles Book II: The letters to Augustus and Florus*. Cambridge.

Briot, P. 1968. "Sur l'exil de Cicéron." *Latomus* 27:406–414.

Bromwich, R., trans. 1961. *Trioedd Ynys Prydein: the Welsh Triads*. Cardiff.

———. 1967. *Tradition and Innovation in the Poetry of Dafydd ap Gwilym*. Cardiff.

Brown, C. 1988. "Hipponax and Iambe." *Hermes* 116:478–481.

Bucheit, V. 1961. "Horazens programmatische Epode." *Gymnasium* 68:520–526.

———. 1975. "Ciceros Kritik an Sulla in der Rede für Roscius aus America." *Historia* 24:570–591.

Buchholz, P. 1971. "Shamanism—the Testimony of Old Icelandic Literary Tradition." *Medieval Scandinavia* 4:7–20.

Büchner, C., ed. 1982. *Fragmenta Poetarum Latinorum Epicorum et Lyricorum Praeter Ennium et Lucilium*. Leipzig.

Buechner, K. 1958. "Ciceros Tod." *Historisches Jahrbuch* 77:5–20.

Bühler, W. 1964. "Archilochos und Kallimachos." In Pouilloux et al. 1964:223–253.

Burke, P. 1978. *Popular Culture in Modern Europe*. London.

Burkert, W. 1962a. "Caesar und Romulus-Quirinus." *Historia* 11:356–376.

———. 1962b. "*Goēs*. Zum griechischen 'Schamanismus.'" *Rheinisches Museum für classische Philologie* 105:36–55.

———. 1966. "Greek Tragedy and Sacrificial Ritual." *Greek, Roman, and Byzantine Studies* 7:87–121.

———. 1972. *Lore and Science in Ancient Pythagoreanism*. Trans. Edwin L. Minar, Jr. Cambridge, MA. = *Weisheit und Wissenschaft. Studien zu Pythagoras, Philolaos und Platon*. Nuremberg, 1962.

———. 1975. "Apellai und Apollon." *Rheinisches Museum für classische Philologie* 118:1–21.

———. 1979. *Structure and History in Greek Mythology*. Berkeley.

———. 1983. *Homo Necans: The Anthropology of Ancient Greek Sacrificial Ritual and Myth*. Trans. P. Bing. Berkeley. = *Homo Necans: Interpretationen altgriechischer Opferriten und Mythen*. Religionseschichtliche Versuche und Vorarbeiten 32. Berlin, 1972.

———. 1985. *Greek Religion*. Trans. J. Raffan. Cambridge, MA. = *Griechische Religion der archaischen und klassischen Epoche*. Stuttgart, 1977.

———. 1992. *The Orientalizing Revolution: Near Eastern Influence on Greek Culture in the Early Archaic Age*. Trans. M. E. Pinder and W. Burkert. Cambridge, MA. = *Die Orientalisierende Epoche in der griechischen Religion und Literatur*. Heidelberg, 1984.

———. 2004. *Babylon Memphis Persepolis: Eastern Contexts of Greek Culture.* Cambridge, MA. = *Da Omero ai magli: La tradizione orientale nella cultura greca.* Venice, 1999.

Burnet, J. 1911. *Plato's Phaedo.* Oxford.

———. 1924. *Plato's Euthyphro, Apology of Socrates, and Crito.* Oxford.

Burnett, A. P. 1983. *Three Archaic Poets, Archilochus, Alcaeus, Sappho.* London.

———. 1987. Review of *Poetry into Drama: Early Tragedy and the Greek Poetic Tradition* by John Herington. *Classical Philology* 82:156.

Burzacchini, G. 1976. "Alc. 130b Voigt, Hor. Carm. I 22." *Quaderni Urbinati di Cultura Classica* 22:39–58.

———. 1986. "Some Further Observations on Alcaeus fr. 130B Voigt." *Papers of the Liverpool Latin Seminar V (1985)* (ed. F. Cairns) 373–382. Liverpool.

Buxton, R. A. 1980. "Blindness and Limit: Sophokles and the Logic of Myth." *Journal of Hellenic Studies* 100:22–37.

———. 1987. "Wolves and Werewolves in Greek Thought." In Bremmer 1987:60–79.

———. 1994. *Imaginary Greece: The Contexts of Mythology.* Cambridge.

Caerwyn Williams, J. E. 1972. *The Court Poet in Medieval Ireland.* Proceedings of the British Academy 57. Oxford.

Cairns, D. L. 1993. *Aidōs: The Psychology and Ethics of Honour and Shame in Ancient Greek Literature.* Oxford.

Calame, C. 1977. *Les choeurs de jeunes filles en Grèce archaïque.* Rome. = *Choruses of Young Women in Ancient Greece: Their Morphology, Religious Role, and Social Function.* Trans. D. Collins and J. Orion. Lanham, MD, 1997.

———. 1996. "Montagne des Muses et Mouseia: La consécration des *Travaux* et l'héroïsation d'Hesiode." In *La Montagne des Muses* (ed. A. Hurst and A. Schachter) 43–56. Geneva.

———. 2003. *Myth and History in Ancient Greece : The symbolic creation of a colony.* Trans. D. W. Berman. Princeton. = *Mythe et histoire dans l'antiquité grecque: la création symbolique d'une colonie.* Lausanne, 1996.

Cameron, A. 1995. *Callimachus and His Critics.* Princeton.

Campbell, D. A. 1967. *Greek Lyric Poetry.* New York.

———, ed. 1982. *Greek Lyric I.* LCL 142. Cambridge, MA.

———. 1983. *The Golden Lyre: The Themes of the Greek Lyric.* London.

———, ed. 1991. *Greek Lyric III: Stesichorus, Ibycus, Simonides & Others.* LCL 476. Cambridge, MA.

Cantarella, R., ed. 1949. *Aristofane, Le Commedie.* 5 vols. Milan.

Carafides, J. L. 1971. "The Last Words of Socrates." *Platon* 23:229–232.

Carawan, E. M. 1990. "The Five Talents Cleon Coughed Up." *Classical Quarterly* 40:137–147.

Carey, C. 1986. "Archilochus and Lycambes." *Classical Quarterly* 36:60–67.

———. 1994. "Comic Ridicule and Democracy." In *Ritual, Finance, Politics: Athenian Democratic Accounts Presented to David Lewis* (ed. R. Osborne and S. Hornblower) 69–83. Oxford.

Carney, J. 1959. "Cath Maige Muccrime." In Dillon 1959:152–166.

———. 1967. *The Irish Bardic Poet: A study in the relationship of poet and patron as exemplified in the persons of the poet, Eochaidh Ó hEoghusa (O'Hussey) and his various patrons, mainly members of the Maguire family of Fermanagh.* Dublin.

Carr, A. D. 1973. "The World of Dafydd ap Gwilym." *Poetry Wales* 8:3–16.

Canter, H. V. 1936. "Irony in the Orations of Cicero." *American Journal of Philology* 57:457–464.

Cerri, G. 1968. "La terminologia sociopolitica di Teognide." *Quaderni Urbinati di Cultura Classica* 6:7–32.

Chadwick, H. 1899. *The Cult of Othin.* London.

Chadwick, H. M., and Chadwick, N. 1932–1940. *The Growth of Literature.* 3 vols. Cambridge.

Chadwick, N. 1934. "Imbas Forosnai." *Scottish Gaelic Studies* 4:97–135.

———. 1942. "Geilt." *Scottish Gaelic Studies* 5:131.

———. 1952. *Poetry and Prophecy.* Cambridge.

Chatháin, P. N. 1979–1980. "Swineherds, Seers, and Druids." *Studia Celtica* 14/15:200–211.

Choite, T., and Latacz, J. 1981. "Zum Gegenwärtigen Stand der 'Thalysien-Deutung.'" *WürzJahr* (n.f.) 7:85–95.

Chroust, A.-H. 1957. *Socrates, Man and Myth: The Two Socratic Apologies of Xenophon.* London.

Claassen, J-M. 1994. "'Ovid's Exile: Is the Secret Out Yet?' A review of R. Verdière, *Le secret du voltigeur d'amour, ou, Le mystère de la relégation d'Ovide* (Brussels 1992). *Scholia* 3:107–111.

———. 1996. "Exile, Death and Immortality: Voices from the Grave." *Latomus* 55:571–590.

———. 1999. *Displaced Persons: The Literature of Exile from Cicero to Boethius.* London.

Clader, L. 1976. *Helen, the Evolution from Divine to Heroic in Greek Epic Tradition.* Leiden.

Clausen, W. V. 1959. *A. Persi Flacci et D. Iunii Juvenalis Saturae.* Oxford.

Clay, D. 1972. "Socrates' Mulishness and Heroism." *Phronesis* 17:53–60.

———. 2000. *Platonic Questions: Dialogues with the Silent Philosopher.* University Park, PA.

———. 2004. *Archilochos Heros: The Cult of Poets in the Greek Polis.* Hellenic Studies 6. Washington DC.

Closs, A. 1968. "Der Schamanismus bei den Indoeuropäern." In *Studien zur Sprachwissenschaft und Kulturkunde, Gedenkschrift für Wilhelm Brandenstein* (ed. M. Mayrhofer) 289–302. Innsbruck.

Clover, C. J. 1980. "The Germanic Context of the Unferþ Episode." *Speculum* 55:444–468.

Cobb-Stevens, V. 1985. "Opposites, Reversals, and Ambiguities: The Unsettled World of Theognis." In Figueira and Nagy 1985:159–175.

Cobb-Stevens, V., Figueira, T., and Nagy, G. 1985. "Introduction." In Figueira and Nagy 1985:1–8.

Coffey, M. 1976. *Roman Satire.* London.

Cohen, D. 1977. "Suibhne Geilt." *Celtica* 12:113–124.

Coldstream, J. N. 1976. "Hero-Cults in the Age of Homer." *Journal of Hellenic Studies* 96:8–17.

Collins, D. 2004. *Master of the Game: Competition and Performance in Greek Poetry.* Hellenic Studies 7. Washington DC.

Colombo, I. C. 1977. "Heros Achilleus-Theòs Apollon." In *Il Mito Greco, Atti del Convegno Internazionale Urbino 1973* (ed. B. Gentili and G. Paioni) 231–269. Rome.

Compton, T. M. 1990. "The Trial of the Satirist: Poetic Vitae (Aesop, Archilochus, Homer) as Background for Plato's *Apology.*" *American Journal of Philology* 111:330–347.

Comyn, D. and Dineen, P.S., eds. 1908. *Geoffrey Keating's Foras Feasa air Eirinn, History of Ireland.* 3 vols. ITS 4, 8, 9. London. Available online at CELT, Corpus of Electronic Texts, http://celt.ucc.ie/index.html.

Coman, J. 1938. "Orphee, civilisateur de l'humanite." *Zalmoxis* 1:130–176.

Connellan, O., ed. 1860. *Imtheacht na Tromdhaimhe or Proceedings of the Great Bardic Institution.* Transactions of the Ossianic Society 5. Dublin.

Connolly, A. 1998. "Was Sophocles Heroised as Dexion?" *Journal of Hellenic Studies* 118:1–21.

Cook, A. B. 1906. "Who Was the Wife of Zeus?" *Classical Review* 20:365–378, 416–419.

Cook, R. M. 1948. "Notes on the Homeric Epigram to the Potters." *Classical Review* 62:55–57.

———. 1951. "The Homeric Epigram to the Potters." *Classical Review* 65:9.

Corbeill, Anthony. 1996. *Controlling Laughter: Political Humor in the Late Roman Republic.* Princeton.

Cornford, F. M. 1952. *Principium Sapientiae. The Origins of Greek Philosophical Thought.* Cambridge.

———. 1968. *The Origins of Attic Comedy.* Gloucester, MA.

Courtney, E. 1980. *A Commentary on the Satires of Juvenal.* London.

Craig, C. 2004. "Audience Expectations, Invective, and Proof." In *Cicero the Advocate* (ed. J. Powell and J. Paterson) 187–214. Oxford.

Cremaschi, C. 1944. "Sull' atteggiamento di Cicerone di fronte all' esilio." *Aevum* 18:133–168.

Cross, R. 1970. *Socrates, the Man and His Mission.* Freeport, NY.

Cross, T. P., Slover, C. H., and Dunn, C., eds. 1969. *Ancient Irish Tales.* New York.

Csapo, E. 2003. "The Dolphins of Dionysus." In Csapo and Miller 2003:69–99.

Csapo, E. and Miller, M. C., eds. 2003. *Poetry, Theory, Praxis. The Social Life of Myth, Word and Image in Ancient Greece: Essays in Honour of William J. Slater.* Oxford.

Culianu, I. P. 1980. "*Iatroi kai Manteis,* Sulle Strutture Dell'Estatismo Greco." *Studio Storico Religiosi* 4:287–303.

Cumont, F. 1949. *Lux Perpetua.* Paris.

Dahlmann, H. 1948. "*Vates.*" *Philologus* 97:346.

Daly, L. W. 1961. *Aesop without Morals.* New York.

Damon, P. 1974. *The Cults of the Epic Heroes and the Evidence of Epic Poetry.* Center for Hermeneutical Studies in Hellenistic and Modern Culture, Colloquy 9, ed. W. Wuellner. Berkeley.

D'Armes, E., and Hulley, K. 1946. "The Oresteia-Story in the *Odyssey.*" *Transactions and Proceedings of the American Philological Association* 77:207–213

Daux, G. 1942. "Sur quelques passages du '*Banquet*' de Platon." *Revue des études grecques* 55:236–272.

Davidson, H. 1981. "Wit and Eloquence in the Courts of Saxo's Early Kings." In Friis-Jensen 1981a:39–52.

———. 1983. "Insults and Riddles in the Edda Poems." In Glendinning and Bessason 1983:25–46.

Davidson, O. M. 1980. "Indo-European Dimensions of Herakles in *Iliad* 19.95–133." *Arethusa* 13:197–202.

Davies, M. I. 1969. "Thoughts on the *Oresteia* before Aischylos." *Bulletin de correspondance Hellénique* 93:214–260.

Davies, M. 1981. "Archilochus and Hipponax in a Scholium on Ovid's *Ibis.*" *Prometheus* 7:123–124.

———. 1985. "Conventional Topics of Invective in Alcaeus." *Prometheus* 11:31–39.

———, ed. 1991. *Poetarum Melicorum Graecorum Fragmenta, vol. I. Alcman Stesichorus Ibycus.* Oxford.

Degani, E. 1983. *Hipponactis Testimonia et Fragmenta.* Leipzig.

———. 1984. *Studi su Ipponatte.* Bari.

———. 1988. "Giambo e commedia." In *La Polis e il suo teatro II* (ed. Eugenio Corsini) 157–179. Padua.

———. 1993. "Aristofane e la tradizine dell'invettiva personale in Grecia." In *Aristophane, Entretiens sur L'Antiquite Classique XXXVIII* (ed. J. M. Bremer and E. W. Handley) 1–36. Vandoeuvres-Genève.

De Jong, J. W. 1985. "The Over-Burdened Earth in India and Greece." *Journal of the American Oriental Society* 105:397–400.

Delacy, P. 1941. "Cicero's Invective Against Piso." *Transactions and Proceedings of the American Philological Association* 72:49–58.

Delatte, A. 1934. *Les Conceptions de l'Enthousiasme chez les Philosophes Présocratiques.* Paris.

de la Vega, J. S. L. 1952. "Sobre la etimologia de *lussa.*" *Emerita* 20:32–41.

de la Torre, E. Suarez. 1987. "Hiponacte comico." *Emerita* 55:113–139.

Delcourt, M. 1933. "Les Biographies Anciennes d'Euripide." *L'Antiquité Classique* 2:271–290.

Delgado, J. F. 1986. *Los oraculos y Hesiodo. Poesia oral mantica y gnomica griegas.* Caceres.

de Lorenzi, A. 1955. *Fedro.* Florence.

Den Boer, W. 1954. *Laconian Studies.* Amsterdam.

Derenne, E. 1930. *Les procès d'impiété intentes aux philosophes à Athènes au Vme et au IVme siècle avant J.C.* Liège.

Derrida, J. 1981. *Dissemination.* Trans. B. Johnson. Chicago. = *La dissémination.* Paris, 1972.

De Saint-Denis, E. 1958. "Le plus spirituel des discours cicéroniens, le *Pro Caelio.*" *L'Information littéraire* 10:105–113.

de Smedt, C., and de Backer, J., eds. 1888. *Acta Sanctorum Hiberniae.* Edinburgh.

Detienne, M. 1957. "La légende pythagoricienne d'Hélène." *Revue de l'Histoire des Religions* 152:129–152.

———. 1973. *Les maîtres de vérité dans la Grèce archaïque.* 2nd ed. Paris. (Orig. pub. 1967.) = *The Masters of Truth in Archaic Greece.* Trans. J. Lloyd. New York, 1996.

———. 1986. *The Creation of Greek Mythology.* Trans. M. Cook. Chicago. = *L'Invention de la mythologie.* Paris, 1981.

Deubner, L. 1932. *Attische Feste.* Berlin.

Devereux, G. 1987. "Thamyris and the Muses." *American Journal of Philology* 108:199–201.

De Vries, J. 1956. *Altgermanische Religionsgeschichte.* 2 vols. Berlin.

———. 1958. "L'aspect magique de la religion Celtique." *Ogam* 10:273–284.

DeVries, K. 2000. "The Nearly Other: The Attic Vision of Phrygians and Lydians." In *Not the Classical Ideal: Athens and the Construction of the Other in Greek Art* (ed. Beth Cohen) 338–363. Leiden.

Dickie, M. 1981. "The Disavowal of *Invidia* in Roman Iamb and Satire." In *Proceedings of the Liverpool Latin Seminar* (ed. F. Cairns) 183–208. Liverpool.

Diels, H. 1988. "Atacta." *Hermes* 23:279–288.

Dietrich, B. C. 1961. "A Rite of Swinging during the Anthesteria." *Hermes* 89:36–50.

Dijk, G.-J. van. 1995. "The Fables in the Greek *Life of Aesop.*" *Reinardus* 8:131–150.

Dilke, O. A. W. "Lucan's Political Views and the Caesars." In Dudley 1972:62–82.

Dillery, J. 1999. "Aesop, Isis and the Heliconian Muses." *Classical Philology* 94:268–280.

Dillon, M., ed. 1946. "The Yew of Disputing Sons." *Ériu* 14:154–165.

———. 1946–1947. "The Hindu Act of Truth in Celtic Tradition." *Modern Philology* 44:137–140.

———. 1947. "The Archaism of the Irish Tradition." *Proceedings of the British Academy* 33:246–247.

———. 1948. *Early Irish Literature.* Chicago.

———, ed. 1959. *Irish Sagas.* Dublin.

———, 1973. "The Consecration of Irish Kings." *Celtica* 10:4–5.

Dinneen, P., trans. 1900. *The Poems of Egan O'Rahilly.* ITS 3. Dublin.

Doblhofer, E. 1987. *Exil und Emigration: Zum Erlebnis der Heimatferne in der römischen Literatur.* Darmstadt.

Dodds, E. R. 1951. *The Greeks and the Irrational.* Berkeley.

———, ed. 1953. *Euripides, Bacchae.* 2nd ed. Oxford. (Orig. pub. 1944.)

———, ed. 1959. *Plato, Gorgias.* Oxford.

Dorey, T. A., ed. 1965. *Cicero.* New York.

Dougherty, C. and Kurke, L., eds. 1993. *Cultural Poetics in Archaic Greece: Cult, Performance, Politics.* Cambridge.

Dovatus, A. 1972. "Theognis von Megara und sein soziales Ideal." *Klio* 54:77–89.

Dover, K. J. 1966. "Aristophanes' Speech in Plato's Symposium." *Journal of Hellenic Studies* 86:41–50.

———. 1972. *Aristophanic Comedy.* Berkeley.

———. 1975. *Greek Popular Morality in the Time of Plato and Aristotle.* Oxford.

———. 1976. "The Freedom of the Intellectual in Greek Society." *Talanta* 7:24–54.

———. 1978. *Greek Homosexuality.* New York.

———. 1980. *Plato, Symposium.* Cambridge.

Duban, J. M. 1980. "Poets and Kings in the *Theogony* Invocation." *Quaderni Urbinati di Cultura Classica*, n.s., 4:7–21.

Dubuisson, D. 1978. "Le roi indo-européen et la synthèse des trois fonctions." *Annales d'histoire économique et sociale* 33:21–34.

Dudley, D. R., ed. 1972. *Neronians and Flavians, Silver Latin 1.* London.

Dué, C., and Nagy, G. 2004. "Illuminating the Classics with the Heroes of Philostratus." In *Philostratus's Heroikos: Religion and Cultural Identity in the Third Century C.E.* (ed. E. B. Aitken and J. K. B. Maclean) 49–74. Leiden.

Duff, J. W. 1960. *A Literary History of Rome, From the Origins to the Close of the Golden Age.* 3rd ed. London. (Orig. pub. 1909).

———. 1960. *A Literary History of Rome in the Silver Age.* 2nd ed. New York. (Orig. pub. 1927.)

———. 1936. *Roman Satire, Its Outlook on Social Life.* Sather Classical Lectures 12. Berkeley.

Dumézil, G. 1924. *Le festin d'Immortalité.* Paris.

———. 1940. "La tradition druidique et l'écriture: Le Vivant et le Mort." *Revue de l'Histoire des Religions* 122:125–133.

———. 1942. *Horace et les Curiaces.* Collection "Les Mythes Romains," vol. 1. Paris.

———. 1943. *Servius et la Fortune: Essai sur la fonction sociale de louange et de blâme et sur les éléments indo-européens du cens romain.* Paris. (Updated in Dumézil 1969.)

———. 1948. *Mitra-Varuna: Essai sur deux représentations indo-européennes de la souveraineté.* 2nd ed. Paris. (Orig. pub. 1940.) = *Mitra-Varuna : An Essay on Two Indo-European Representations of Sovereignty.* Trans. D. Coltman. New York, 1988.

———. 1949. *L'Heritage indo-européen à Rome: Introduction aux séries "Jupiter, Mars, Quirinus" et "Les mythes romains."* Paris.

———. 1959. *Loki.* Trans. I. Köck. Darmstadt.

———. 1959b. "Le *rex* et les *flāmines maiores.*" In *La Regalità sacra: Contributi al tema dell'VIII Congresso internazionale di storia delle religioni, Roma, aprile 1955* (Studies in the History of Religions 4) 407–417. Leiden.

———. 1968, 1971, 1973. *Mythe et épopée.* 3 vols. 1: *L'idéologie des trois fonctions dans les épopées des peuples indo-européens.* 2: *Un héros, un sorcier, un roi.* 3: *Histoires romaines.* Paris.

———. 1969. *Idées romaines.* Paris.

———. 1970a. *Archaic Roman Religion.* Trans. P. Krapp. Chicago. = *La religion romaine archaïque, avec un appendice sur la religion des Étrusques.* Paris, 1966.

———. 1970b. *The Destiny of the Warrior.* Trans. A. Hiltebeitel. Chicago. = *Heur et malheur du guerrier: Aspects mythiques de la fonction guerrière chez les Indo-Europée.* Paris, 1969.

———. 1973a. *Gods of the Ancient Northmen.* Trans. and ed. by E. Haugen. Berkeley. = *Les dieux des germains: Essai sur la formation de la religion scandinave.* Paris, 1959.

———. 1973b. *The Destiny of a King.* Trans. A. Hiltebeitel. Chicago. (= Vol. 2, pt. 3 of *Mythe et épopée.*)

———. 1974. "'Le Borgne' and 'Le Manchot': The state of the problem." In Larson et al. 1974:17–28.

———. 1977. *Les dieux souverains des Indo-Européens.* Paris.

———. 1983. *The Stakes of the Warrior.* Trans. D. Weeks. Berkeley. = "L'enjeu du jeu des dieux—un héros." (= Vol. 2, pt. 1 of *Mythe et épopée.*)

———. 1985. *Heur et malheur du guerrier: Aspects mythiques de la fonction guerrière chez les Indo-Européens.* 2nd ed. Paris. (Orig. pub. 1969.)

———. 1994. *Le Roman des Jumeaux et autres essais. Vingt-cinq esquisses de mythologie (76-100).* Ed. J. Grisward. Paris.

Dundes, A. 1980. "Wet and Dry, the Evil Eyes." In *Interpreting Folklore* (ed. A. Dundes) 93–133. Bloomington, IN.

Dunkle, R. 1967. "The Greek Tyrant and Roman Political Invective." *Transactions and Proceedings of the American Philological Association* 98:151–171.

Dürr, J. 1888. *Das Leben Juvenals.* Ulm. Texts from this book available online at www.geocities.com/athens/oracle/7207/victimtest.html.

Durante, M. 1957. "Il nome di Omero." *Rendiconti della Classe di Scienze morali, storiche e filologiche dell'Accademia dei Lincei,* 8th ser., 12:94–111.

———. 1958. "*Epea pteroenta.* La parola come 'cammino'." *Rendiconti della Classe di Scienze morali, storiche e filologiche dell'Accademia dei Lincei,* 8th ser., 13:3–14.

———. 1962. "Ricerche sulla preistoria della lingua poetica greca l'epiteto." *Rendiconti della Classe di Scienze morali, storiche e filologiche dell'Accademia dei Lincei,* 8th ser., 17:25–43.

———. 1971–1974. *Sulla preistoria della tradizione poetica greca.* 2 vols. Incunabula Greca 50, 64. Rome.

Dyer, L., ed. 1976. *Plato, Apology of Socrates and Crito.* Rev. T. Seymour. New Rochelle, NY. (Orig. pub. 1885.)

Easterling, P. E. 1985. "Greek Poetry and Greek Religion." In Easterling and Muir 1985:34–49.

Easterling, P. E., and Knox, B. M. W., eds. 1985. *Greek Literature. (The Cambridge History of Classical Literature I.)* Cambridge.

Easterling, P. E., and Muir, J. V., eds. 1985. *Greek Religion and Society.* Cambridge.

Edmonds, J. M. 1927. *Lyra Graeca.* 3 vols. LCL 142–144. Cambridge, MA.

———. 1931. *Greek Elegy and Iambus.* 2 vols. LCL 258–259. Cambridge, MA.

Edmunds, L. 1980. "Aristophanes' *Acharnians.*" *Yale Classical Studies* 26:1–42.

———. 1981. "The Cults and the Legend of Oedipus." *Harvard Studies in Classical Philology* 85:221–238.

———. 1985α. "The Genre of Theognidean Poetry." In Figueira and Nagy 1985:96–111.

———. 1985b. "Aristophanes' Socrates." *Proceedings of the Boston Area Colloquium in Ancient Philosophy* 1:209–230. Lanham, MD.

———. 1987. *Cleon, Knights, and Aristophanes' Politics.* Lanham, MD.

———, ed. 1990. *Approaches to Greek Myth.* Baltimore, MD.

———. 2001. "Callimachus *Iamb* 4: From Performance to Writing." In *Iambic Ideas: Essays on a Poetic Tradition from Archaic Greece to the Late Roman Empire* (ed. A. Cavarzere, A. Aloni, and A. Barchiesi) 77–98. Lanham, MD.

Egger, G. 1958. "*De Ciceronis extremo itinere.*" *Latinitas* 6:203–207.

Eibl-Eibesfeldt, I. 1971. *Love and Hate: On the Natural History of Basic Behaviour Patterns.* Trans. G. Strachan. London. = *Liebe und Hass. Zur Naturgeschichte elementarer Verhaltensweisen.* Munich, 1970.

Eichner, H. 1975. "Die Vorgeschichte des hethitischen Verbalsystems." In *Flexion und Wortbildung* (ed. Helmut Rix) 71–103. Wiesbaden.

Eitrem, S. 1977. *Opferritus und Voropfer der Griechen und Römer.* Hildesheim. (Orig. pub. 1915.)

Ekroth, G. 2002. *The Sacrificial Rituals of Greek Hero-cults in the Archaic to the Early Hellenistic Periods.* Kernos Supplement 12. Liège.

Eliade, M. 1959. *The Sacred and the Profane: The Nature of Religion.* Trans. W. Trask. New York. = *Das Heilige und das Profane: vom Wesen des Religiösen.* Hamburg, 1957.

———. 1961. "Recent Works on Shamanism." *History of Religions* 1:152–186.

———. 1963a. *Myth and Reality.* Trans. W. Trask. New York. = *Aspects du mythe.* Paris, 1963.

———. 1963b. *Patterns in Comparative Religion.* Trans. R. Sheed. Cleveland. = *Traité d'histoire des religions.* Paris, 1949.

———. 1964. *Shamanism: Archaic Techniques of Ecstasy.* Trans. W. Trask. Princeton. = *Le Chamanisme et le techniques archaïques de l'exstase.* Paris, 1951.

———. 1968. "Notes on the Symbolism of the Arrow." In *Religions in Antiquity* (ed. J. Neusner) 463–475. Leiden.

———. 1971. *The Myth of the Eternal Return, or Cosmos and History*. Trans. W. Trask. Princeton. = *Le mythe de l'éternel retour; archétypes et répétition*. Paris, 1949.

———. 1972. *Zalmoxis, the Vanishing God*. Chicago.

———. 1975. *Rites and Symbols of Initiation: the Mysteries of Birth and Rebirth*. Trans. W. R. Trask. New York. = *Naissances mystiques; essai sur quelques types d'initiation*. Paris, 1959.

Elliott, R. C. 1960. *The Power of Satire: Magic, Ritual, Art*. Princeton.

Ellis, R., ed. 1881. *P. Ovidii Nasonis Ibis; ex novis codicibus edidit, scholia vetera commentarium cum prolegomenis, appendice, indice addidit*. Oxford.

Else, G. 1957. *Aristotle's Poetic: the Argument*. Cambridge, MA.

Entralgo, P. L. 1970. *The Therapy of the Word in Classical Antiquity*. Ed. and trans. L. J. Rather and J. M. Sharp. New Haven. = *La Curación por la Palabra en la Antigüedad Clásica*. Madrid, 1958.

Erbse, H. 1954. "Socrates im Schatten des Aristophanischen 'Wolken.'" *Hermes* 82:385–420.

Ernout, A. 1949. "*Iussa*." *Revue de Philologie* 23:154–156.

———. 1966. *Recueil de Textes Latins Archaïques*. Paris.

Escher-Bürkli, J. 1894. "Achilleus." RE 1.221–245.

Evans, H. 1983. *Publica Carmina, Ovid's Books from Exile*. Lincoln, NE.

Evelyn-White, H. G. 1917. "The Heliconian Prelude to the *Theogony*." *Classical Review* 31:157–158.

———. 1936. *Hesiod, the Homeric Hymns and Homerica*. LCL 57. Rev. ed. Cambridge, MA. 1st ed. 1914 Cambridge, MA.

Fairweather, J. 1973. "The Death of Heraclitus." *Greek, Roman, and Byzantine Studies* 14:233–239.

———. 1974. "Fiction in the Biographies of Ancient Writers." *Ancient Society* 5:231–275.

———. 1987. "Ovid's Autobiographical Poem *Tristia* 4.10." *Classical Quarterly* 37:181–196.

Falter, O. 1934. *Der Dichter und sein Gott bei den Griechen und Römern*. Würzburg.

Faraone, C. 1992. *Talismans and Trojan Horses: Guardian Statues in Ancient Greek Myth and Ritual*. Oxford.

———. 2001. "A Collection of Curses against Kilns (Homeric Epigram 13.7–23)." In *Antiquity and Humanity: Essays on Ancient Religion and Philosophy Presented to Hans Dieter Betz on his 70th Birthday* (ed. A. Y. Collins and M. M. Mitchell) 435–450. Tübingen.

———. 2004a. "Hipponax Fragment 128W: Epic Parody or Expulsive Incantation?" *Classical Antiquity* 23:209–245.

———. 2004b. "Orpheus' Final Performance: Necromancy and a Singing Head on Lesbos." *Studi Italiani di Filologia Classica* 97:5–27.

Farnell, L. R. 1896–1909. *Cults of the Greek States*. 5 vols. Oxford.

———. 1921. *Greek Hero Cults and Ideas of Immortality*. Oxford.

Faust, M. 1969. "Metaphorische Schimpfwörter." *Indogermanische Forschungen* 74:69–125.

———. 1970. "Die künstlerische Verwendung von *kuōn* 'Hund' in den homerischen Epen." *Glotta* 48:8–31.

Feeney, D. C. 1991. *The Gods in Epic*. Oxford.

Fehling, D. 1974. *Ethologische Überlegungen auf den Gebiet der Altertumskunde.* Zetemata 61. Munich.

Ferguson, A. S. 1913. "The Impiety of Socrates." *Classical Review* 7:157–175.

Ferguson, J. 1972. "Seneca the Man." In Dudley 1972:1–23.

———. 1980. *Callimachus*. Boston.

Ferrari, F., Bonelli, G., and Sandrolini, G., eds. 2002. *Romanzo di Esopo.* Introduzione e Testo Critico a Cura di F. Ferrari. Traduzione e Note di G. Bonelli e G. Sandrolini, 2nd ed. Milan.

Ferrari, W. 1940. "Due note su *hagnos.*" *Studi Italiani di Filologia Classica* 17:33–53.

Figueira, T. and Nagy, G., eds. 1985. *Theognis of Megara, Poetry and the Polis.* Baltimore. Available online at http://www.chs.harvard.edu/chs_pubs/ epubs.html.

Figueira, T. 1985. "Chronological Table: Archaic Megara, 800–500 B.C." In Figueira and Nagy 1985:261–304.

———. 1999. "The Evolution of the Messenian Identity." In *Sparta: New Perspectives* (ed. S. Hodkinson and A. Powell) 211–243. London.

Fileni, M. G. 1983. "Sull' idea di tiranno nella cultura greca italica." *Quaderni Urbinati di Cultura Classica* 43:29–35.

Finkelpearl, E. 2003. "Lucius and Aesop Gain a Voice: Apuleius *Met.* 11.1–2 and *Vita Aesopi 7.*" In *The Ancient Novel and Beyond*. Menemosyne Supplement 241 (ed. S. Panayotakis, M. Zimmermnan, and W. Keulen) 37–52. Leiden.

Finley, M. 1973. *Democracy, Ancient and Modern*. London.

———. 1977. *Aspects of Antiquity*. 2nd ed. Harmondsworth. (Orig. pub. 1968.)

———. 1978. *The World of Odysseus*. Rev. ed. New York. (Orig. pub. 1954.)

Fisher, P., trans. and Davidson, H. 1979. *The History of the Danes: Saxo Grammaticus.* 2 vols. Vol. 1, by Fisher, is translation; vol. 2, by Davidson and Fisher, is commentary. Cambridge.

Fisher, R. 1997. "The Lore of the Staff in Indo-European Tradition." In *Studies in Honor of Jaan Puhvel, Part One, Ancient Languages and Philology* (ed. D. Disterheft, M. Huld, and J. Greppin) 49–70. Washington DC.

Flacelière, R. 1965. *Daily Life in Greece at the Time of Pericles.* Trans. P. Green. London. = *La vie quotidienne en Grèce au siècle de Périclès.* Paris, 1959.

Fleck, J. 1970. "*Konr-Ottarr-Geirröðr*: A Knowledge Criterion for Succession to the Germanic Sacred Kingship." *Scandinavian Studies* 42:39–49.

———. 1971. "Oðinn's Self-Sacrifice—A New Interpretation." *Scandinavian Studies* 43:119–142; 385–413.

———. 1981. "The 'Knowledge-Criterion' in the *Grimnismál*: The Case against 'Shamanism.'" *Arkiv för Nordisk Filologi* 86:49–65.

Flower, R. 1947. *The Irish Tradition.* Oxford.

Foley, H. P. 1985. *Ritual Irony (Poetry and Sacrifice in Euripides).* Ithaca, NY.

———. 1993. "Oedipus as *Pharmakos*." In *Nomodeiktes: Greek Studies in Honor of Martin Ostwald* (ed. R. M. Rosen and J. Farrell) 525–538. Ann Arbor.

———, ed. 1994. *The Homeric Hymn to Demeter: translation, commentary, and interpretive essays.* Princeton.

Foley, J. M. 1998. "Individual Poet and Epic Tradition: Homer as Legendary Singer." *Arethusa* 31:149–178.

Fontenrose, J. 1959. *Python: A Study of Delphic Myth and its Origins.* Berkeley.

———. 1968. "The Athlete as Hero." *California Studies in Classical Antiquity* 1:73–104.

———. 1978. *The Delphic Oracle.* Berkeley.

Forbis, E. P. 1997. "Voice and Voicelessness in Ovid's Exile Poetry." In *Studies in Latin Literature and Roman History VIII*, Collection Latomus 239 (ed. C. Deroux) 245–267. Brussels.

Ford, A. 2002. *The Origins of Criticism: Literary Culture and Poetic Theory in Classical Greece.* Princeton.

Ford, P., trans. and ed. 1977. *The Mabinogi and Other Medieval Welsh Tales.* Berkeley.

———. 1990. "The Blind, the Dumb, and the Ugly: Aspects of Poets and their Craft in Early Ireland and Wales." *Cambridge Medieval Celtic Studies* 19:27–40.

Fowler, W. W. 1909. *Social Life at Rome in the Age of Cicero.* New York.

Fraenkel, E. 1925. Review of F. Beckmann, *Zauberei und Recht in Roms Frühzeit. Gnomon* 1:185–200 = *Kleine Beiträge zur klassischen Philologie* 2:400ff. 1964.

———. 1957. *Horace.* Oxford.

Fraenkel, H. 1975. *Early Greek Poetry and Philosophy.* Trans. M. Hadas and J. Willis.

Oxford. = *Dichtung und Philosophie des fruehen Griechentums: Eine Geschichte der griechischen Literatur von Homer bis Pindar.* New York, 1951.

———. 1945. *Ovid: A Poet Between Two Worlds.* Sather Classical Lecture 18. Berkeley.

Franco, C. 1986. "Euripide e gli Ateniesi." In *La Polis e il suo Teatro* (ed. E. Corsini) 149–184. Padua.

Frank, T. 1927. "Naevius and Free Speech." *American Journal of Philology* 48:105–110.

Frazer, J. G. 1911–1936. *The Golden Bough: A Study in Magic and Religion.* 3rd ed., 13 vols. London. (Orig. pub. 1890.)

———, ed. 1913. *Pausanias, Description of Greece.* 2nd ed., 6 vols. London. (Orig. pub. 1898.)

———, ed. 1921. *Apollodorus, The Library.* 2 vols. LCL 121–122. Cambridge, MA.

Freiert, W. 1991. "Orpheus: A Fugue on the Polis." In *Myth and the Polis* (ed. D. Pozzi and J. Wickersham) 32–48. Ithaca, NY.

Friedländer, P. 1969. *Plato.* 2nd ed. Trans. H. Meyerhoff. Princeton. = *Platon.* 2 vols. Berlin, 1928–1930.

Friedrich, P. 1973. "Defilement and Honor in the Iliad." *Journal of Indo-European Studies* 1:115–126.

Friis-Jensen, K., ed. 1981a. *Saxo Grammaticus, A Medieval Author Between Norse and Latin Culture.* Copenhagen.

———. 1981b. "The Lay of Ingellus and its Classical Models." In Friis-Jensen 1981a:65–77.

Frisch, H. 1942. *The Constitution of the Athenians.* Copenhagen.

Froesch, H. 1976. *Ovid als Dichter des Exils.* Bonn.

Frontisi-Ducroux, F. 1986. *L' Cithera du Achilles: Essai sur la poétique de l'Iliade.* Rome.

Frye, N. 1957. *Anatomy of Criticism.* Princeton.

Fuqua, C. 1981. "Tyrtaeus and the Cult of Heroes." *Greek, Roman, and Byzantine Studies* 22:215–226.

Fürtwangler, A. 1884–1937. "Apollon." In Roscher 1884–1937 1.1:422–468.

Gabathuler, M. 1937. *Hellenistische Epigramme auf Dichter.* Basel.

Gager, J. 1992. *Curse Tablets and Binding Spells from the Ancient World.* Oxford.

Gahan, J. 1985. "Seneca, Ovid, and Exile." *Classical World* 78:145–147.

Gallavotti, C. 1970. "Aiace e Pittaco nel carme di Alceo." *Bollettino del Comitato per la Preparazione dell'Edizione nazionale dei Classici greci e latini,* n.s., 18:3–29.

Gantz, Timothy. 1993. *Early Greek Myth: A Guide to Literary and Artistic Sources.* Baltimore.

Gariepy, R., Jr. 1978. "Recent Scholarship on Ovid, 1958–68." In *The Classical World Bibliography of Roman Drama and Poetry and Ancient Fiction* (ed. W. Donlan) 184–185. New York.

Garland, R. 1995. *The Eye of the Beholder.* Ithaca, NY.

Gärtner, H. 1978. "Zoilos (Homeromastix)." *RE Suppl.* 15:1531–1554.

Gaster, T. 1981. *Myth, Legend, and Custom in the Old Testament: A comparative study with chapters from Sir James G. Frazer's Folklore in the Old Testament.* 2 vols. Gloucester, MA. (Orig. pub. 1969.)

Gebhard, V. 1926. "Die Pharmakoi in Ionien und die Sybacchoi in Athen." Diss. Amberg.

Geffcken, K. 1973. *Comedy in the Pro Caelio.* Leiden.

Gehrts, H. 1967. *Das Märchen und das Opfer: Untersuchungen zum europäischen Brüdermärchen.* Bonn.

Gelzer, M. 1939. "Cicero als Politiker." In RE, ser. 2, 7.1:827–1091.

Gelzer, T. 1970. "Aristophanes." *RE Suppl.* 12 (1970):1392–1569.

Gennep, A. van. 1960. *The Rites of Passage.* Chicago. = *Les rites de passage: étude systématique des rites de la porte et du seuil, de l'hospitalité, de l'adoption, de la grossesse et de l'accouchement, de la naissance, de l'enfance, de la puberté, de l'initiation, de l'ordination, du couronnement des fiançailles et du mariage, des funérailles, des saisons, etc.* Paris, 1909.

Gentili, B. and Prato, C., eds. 1979–1985. *Poetarum elegiacorum testimonia et fragmenta.* 2 vols. Leipzig.

Gentili, B. 1988. *Poetry and Its Public in Ancient Greece: From Homer to the Fifth Century.* Trans. A. Th. Cole. Baltimore. = *Poesia e pubblico nella Grecia antica: Da Omero al V secolo.* Rome, 1984.

Gerber, D. E. 1995. "Archilochus Fr. 30 Tarditi." In *Studia classica Iohanni Tarditi oblata,* vol. 1 (ed. L. Belloni, G. Milanesi, A. Porro). Milan.

———. 1999. *Greek Elegiac Poetry: From the Seventh to the Fifth Centuries BC.* LCL 258. Cambridge, MA.

———. 1999b. *Greek Iambic Poetry: From the Seventh to the Fifth Centuries BC.* LCL 259. Cambridge, MA.

Gernet, L. 1981. *Anthopology of Ancient Greece.* Trans. J. Hamilton and B. Nagy. Baltimore. = *Anthropologie de la Grèce antique.* Paris, 1968.

Gershenson, D. E. 1991. *Apollo the Wolf-God.* Journal of Indo-European Studies Monographs Number 8. McLean, VA.

Gerstein, M. R. 1972. "*Warg:* the Outlaw as Werwolf in Germanic Myth." Ph.D. diss., UCLA.

———. 1974. "The Outlaw as Werwolf." In Larson et al. 1974:131–156.

Giangrande, G. 1963. "The Origin of Attic Comedy." *Eranos* 61:1–24.

Giarratano, C. 1906. "Tirteo e i suoi Carmi." *Atti di Accademia di archeologia lettere e belle arti* 24:105–129.

Gigon, O. 1947. *Sokrates, Sein Bild in Dichtung und Geschichte.* Bern.

Gil, L. 1967. *Los Antiguos y la "Inspiration" Poetica.* Madrid.

Gill, C. 1973. "The Death of Socrates." *Classical Review* 67:25–28.

Gilula, D. 2000. "Hermippus and his catalogue of goods (fr. 63)." In Harvey and Wilkins 2000:75–90.

Girard, R. 1977. *Violence and the Sacred.* Trans. P. Gregory. Baltimore. = *La violence et le sacré.* Paris, 1972.

———. 1986. *The Scapegoat.* Trans. Y. Freccero. Baltimore. = *Bouc émissaire.* Paris, 1982.

———. 1987a. "Generative Scapegoating." In *Violent Origins* (ed. R. G. Hamerton-Kelly) 73–105. Stanford.

———. 1987b. *Things Hidden since the Foundation of the World.* Trans. S. Bann and M. Metteer. London. = *Des choses cachées depuis la fondation du monde.* Paris, 1978.

Glendinning, R. and Bessason, H., eds. 1983. *Edda, A Collection of Essays.* Manitoba.

Gonda, J. 1950. *Notes on Brahman.* Utrecht.

Goodyear, F. R. D. 1982. "Minor Poetry." In CHCL 2:624–632.

Goold, G. P. 1983. "The Cause of Ovid's Exile." *Illinois Classical Studies* 8:94–107.

Goossens, R. 1962. *Euripide et Athènes.* Brussels.

Gow, A. F. S. 1965. *Theocritus.* Cambridge.

Graf, F. 1985. *Nordionische Kulte.* Rome.

———. 1987. "Orpheus: A Poet Among Men." In Bremmer 1987:80–106.

———. 1993. *Greek Mythology: An Introduction.* Trans. T. Marier. Baltimore. = *Griechische Mythologie: Eine Einführung.* Munich, 1985.

Graham, A. J. 2001. *Collected Papers on Greek Colonization.* Mnemosyne Supplement 214. Leiden.

Grant, M. A. 1924. *Ancient Rhetorical Theories of the Laughable.* University of Wisconsin Studes in Language and Literature 21. Madison, WI.

Gras, M. 1984. "Cité grecque et lapidation." In *Du châtiment dans la cité: supplices corporels et peine de mort dans le monde antique: table ronde,* 75–89. Rome.

Grasmück, E. L. 1977. "Ciceros Verbannung aus Rom." In *Bonner Festgabe Johannes Straub zum 65. Geburtstag am 18. Oktober 1977* (ed. A. Lippold and N. Himmelmann) 165–177. Bonn.

———. 1978. *Exilium: Untersuchungen zur Verbannung in der Antike.* Paderborn.

Grassmann, V. 1966. *Die erotischen Epoden des Horaz.* Munich.

Gratwick, A. S. 1982. "Ennius' *Annales.*" In Kenney and Clausen 1982:60–77.

Gray, E., ed. 1982. *Cath Maige Tuired: The Second Battle of Mag Tuired*. ITS 52. Dublin.

Green, P. 1967. *Juvenal, the Sixteen Satires*. New York.

———. 1982. "*Carmen et error*: *prophasis* and *aitia* in the matter of Ovid's exile." *Classical Antiquity* 1:202–220.

Greenhalgh, P. 1982. "The Homeric *THERAPON* and *OPAON* and their Historical Implications." *Bulletin of the Institute of Classical Studies* 29:81–90.

Griffin, M. 1974. "'*Imago Vitae Suae*.'" In *Seneca* (ed. C. D. N. Costa) 1–38. London.

———. 1976. *Seneca, A Philosopher in Politics*. Oxford.

Griffith, M. 1990. "Contest and Contradiction in Early Greek Poetry." In *Cabinet of the Muses: Essays on Classical and Comparative Literature in Honor of Thomas G. Rosenmeyer* (ed. M. Griffith and D. Mastonarde) 185–207. Atlanta.

Griffith, R. D. 1990. "The Humiliation of Oedipus in Sophocles' *Oedipus Tyrannus*." *Sileno* 16:97–106.

———. 1993. "Oedipus *Pharmakos*? Alleged Scapegoating in Sophocles' *Oedipus the King*." *Phoenix* 47:95–114.

Grottanelli, C. 1983. "Tricksters, Scapegoats, Champions, Saviors." *History of Religions* 23:117–139.

Gruen, E. 1968. *Roman Politics and the Criminal Courts*. Cambridge, MA.

Gruffydd, R. G. 1979/80. "The Early Court Poetry of South West Wales." *Studia Celtica* 14/15: 95–105.

Gudnason, B. "The Icelandic Sources of Saxo Grammaticus." In Friis-Jensen 1981a:79–93.

Guépin, J.-P. 1968. *The Tragic Paradox: Myth and Ritual in Greek Tragedy*. Amsterdam.

Gulermovich Epstein, A. 1997. "The Morrígan and the Valkyries." In *Studies in Honor of Jaan Puhvel, Part Two, Mythology and Religion* (ed. J. Greppin and E. C. Polomé) 119–150. Washington DC.

Gummere, F. B. 1901. *The Beginnings of Poetry*. New York.

Gurney, O. R. 1977. *Some Aspects of Hittite Religion*. Oxford.

Guyonvarćh, C. J. 1964, 1965. "Notes d'Étymologie et Lexicographie gaulises et celtiques XX." *Ogam* 16:427–446 and *Ogam* 17:143–166.

Gwynn, E. J. 1940/1942. "An Old Irish Tract on the Privileges and Responsibilities of Poets." *Ériu* 13:1–60, 220–236.

Habicht, C. 1990. *Cicero the Politician*. Baltimore.

Hack, R. K. 1929. "Homer and the Cult of Heroes." *Transactions and Proceedings of the American Philological Association* 60: 57–74.

Hackforth, R. 1955. *Plato's Phaedo*. Cambridge.

Hallberg, P. 1962. *The Icelandic Saga*. Trans. P. Schach. Lincoln, NE.

Halliday, W. R. 1967. *Greek Divination, A Study of Its Methods and Principles*. Chicago. (Orig. pub. 1913.)

Halliwell, S. 1984a. "Ancient Interpretation of *kōmōidein onomasti* in Aristophanes." *Classical Quarterly* 34:86–87.

———. 1984b. "Aristophanic Satire." *Yearbook of English Studies* 14:6–20.

———. 1991a. "Comic Satire and Freedom of Speech in Classical Athens." *Journal of Hellenic Studies* 111:48–70.

———. 1991b. "The Uses of Laughter in Greek Culture." *Classical Quarterly* 41:279–296.

———. 2004. "Aischrology, Shame, and Comedy." In Sluiter and Rosen 2004:115–144.

Hambly, W. D. 1925. *The History of Tattooing and its Significance*. London.

Hamilton, E., and Cairns, H., eds. 1961. *The Collected Dialogues of Plato*. Princeton.

Hammond, N. G. L., and Scullard, H. H., eds. 1970. *The Oxford Classical Dictionary*. 2nd ed. Oxford. (Orig. pub. 1949.)

Hands, A. 1962. "Humor and Vanity in Cicero." In *Studies in Cicero* (ed. J. Ferguson) 115–125. Rome.

Hansen, W. F. 1978. "The Homeric Epics and Oral Poetry." In *Heroic Epic and Saga* (ed. F. J. Oinas) 7–26. Bloomington, IN.

———. 1998. *Anthology of Greek Popular Literature*. Bloomington, IN.

Harriott, R. 1985. *Aristophanes, Poet and Dramatist*. London.

Harrison, E. 1902. *Studies in Theognis*. Cambridge.

Harrison, J. 1888. "Some Fragments of a Vase Presumably by Euphronios." *Journal of Hellenic Studies* 9:143–146.

———. 1922. *Prolegomena to the Study of Greek Religion*. 3rd ed. Cambridge. (Orig. pub. 1903.)

Harvey, D., and Wilkins, J. 2000. *The Rivals of Aristophanes. Studies in Athenian Old Comedy*. London.

Haslam, M., ed. 1986. *The Oxyrhynchus Papyri* vol. 53. London.

———. 1992. Review of Papathomopoulos, *Aesopus Revisitatus* and Ὁ Βίος τοῦ Αἰσώπου. Ἡ Παραλλαγὴ G. *The Classical Review* 42:188–189.

Haugen, E. 1983. "The Edda as Ritual." In Glendinning and Bessason 1983:3–24.

Haury, A. 1955. *L'Ironie et l'humour chez Cicéron*. Leiden.

Hägg, R., ed. 1999. *Ancient Greek Hero Cult : Proceedings of the Fifth International Seminar on Ancient Greek Cult, organized by the Department of Classical Archaeology and Ancient History, Göteborg University, 21-23 April 1995*. Stockholm.

Hägg, T. 1997. "A Professor and his Slave: Conventions and Values in the *Life of Aesop.*" In *Conventional Values of the Hellenistic Greeks* (ed. P. Bilde et al.) 177–203. Aarhus.

Heath, M. 1987. *Political Comedy in Aristophanes.* Göttingen.

Hedreen, G. 1991. "The Cult of Achilles in the Euxine." *Hesperia* 60:313–330.

———. 1992. *Silens in Attic Black-figure Vase-painting: Myth and Performance.* Ann Arbor.

Heintze, H. von. 1966. *Das Bildnis der Sappho.* Mainz.

Helm, R. 1931. "Menippus." In RE 15.1:888–893.

Heldmann, K. 1982. *Die Niederlage Homers im Dichterwettstreit mit Hesiod.* Göttingen.

Henderson, G. 1899. *Fled Bricend: The Feast of Briciu.* Irish Texts Society. Dublin. Available online at CELT Corpus of Electronic Texts, http://www.ucc.ie/celt/irllist.html" http://www.ucc.ie/celt/irllist.html.

Henderson, J. 1975. *The Maculate Muse: Obscene Language in Attic Comedy.* New Haven.

———. 1990. "The *Demos* and Comic Competition." In Winkler and Zeitlin 1990:271–313.

Henderson, J. 2001. *Telling Tales on Caesar: Roman Stories from Phaedrus.* Oxford.

Hendrickson, G. L. 1925a. "Archilochus and Catullus." *Classical Philology* 20:155–157.

———. 1925b. "Archilochus and the Victims of his Iambics." *American Journal of Philology* 46:101–127.

———. 1927. "*Satura Tota Nostra Est.*" *Classical Philology* 22:46–60. Repr. in 1971. *Satire: Modern Essays in Criticism* (ed. R. Paulson) 37–51. Englewood Cliffs, NJ.

Hennessy, W. M. 1870. "The Ancient Irish Goddess of War." *Revue Celtique* 1:32–57.

Hennessy, W., trans. and ed. 1889. *Mesca Ulad: or, The Intoxication of the Ultonians.* Dublin.

Henrichs, A. 1984. "Male Intruders among the Maenads. The So-Called Male Celebrant." In *Mnemai. Classical Studies in memory of Karl K. Hulley* (ed. H. D. Evjen) 69–91. Chico, CA.

———. 1987. "Three Approaches to Greek Mythology." In Bremmer 1987:242–278.

Henry, P. L. 1979/1980. "The Caldron of Poesy." *Studia Celtica* 14/15:114–128.

———. 1982. "*Furor Heroicus.*" *Zeitschrift für celtische Philologie* 39:235–242.

Herescu, N. I. 1961. "Les trois exils de Cicéron." In *Atti del I Congresso Internazionale di Studi Ciceroniani, aprile 1959,* 2 vols. (no editor) 1:137–156. Rome.

Herrmann, L. 1955. *Douze poèmes d'exil de Sénèque.* Col. Latomus 22. Brussels.

———. 1963. "Néron et la mort de Perse." *Latomus* 22:236–239.

Hester, D. A. 1984. "The Banishment of Oedipus." *Antichthon* 18:13–23.

Higgins, W. E. 1977. *Xenophon the Athenian.* Albany, NY.

Highet, G. 1937. "The Life of Juvenal." *Transactions and Proceedings of the American Philological Association* 68:480–506.

———. 1961. *Juvenal the Satirist.* Oxford.

Hild, J. A. 1884. *Juvénal, Notes biographiques.* Paris.

Hinks, D. A. G. 1936. "*Tria Genera Causarum.*" *Classical Quarterly* 30:170–176.

Hirzel, R. 1909. "Die Strafe der Steinigung." *Abhandlung der Koeniglich Saechsischen Gesellschaft der Wissenschaften, phil.-hist. Kl.*, 27:224–266.

Hoffmann, F. 1965. "Die Beziehungen zwischen Kunst und Krankheit im Werke Thomas Manns." *Academia, Nouvelle Revue Luxembourgeoise* 3:253–285.

Holzberg, N., ed. 1992a. *Der Äsop-Roman: Motivgeschichte und Erzählstruktur.* Tübingen.

———. 1992b. "Der Äsop-Roman." In Holzberg 1992a:33–75.

———. 1999. "The Fabulist, the Scholars, and the Discourse: Aesop Studies Today." *International Journal of the Classical Tradition* 6:236–242.

———. 2002. *The Ancient Fable: An Introduction.* Trans. by C. Jackson-Holzberg. Bloomington, IN = *Die antike Fabel: eine Einführung.* Darmstadt, 1993. (2nd Germ. ed. in 2001.)

Hornblower, S., and Spawforth, A. 1996. *The Oxford Classical Dictionary.* 3rd ed. Oxford.

Houbaux, J. 1923. "Le Plongeon Rituel." *Musée Belge* 27:1–81.

Höfer, O. 1884–1937. "Pharmakos." In Roscher 1884–1937 3.2276–2284.

Holder, A., ed. 1886. *Saxonis Grammatici Gesta Danorum.* Strassburg.

Hollander, L., trans. 1962. *The Poetic Edda*, 2nd ed. Austin, TX. (Orig. pub. 1928.)

Holleman, A. W. 1971. "Ovid and Politics." *Historia* (Wiesbaden) 20:458–466.

Holmes, T. R. 1928. *The Architect of the Roman Republic.* Oxford.

Homeyer, H. 1971. "Ciceros Tod im Urteil der Nachwelt." *Das Altertum* 17:165–174.

———. 1977. "Die Quellen zu Ciceros Tod." *Helikon* 17:56–96.

Hommel, H. 1980. *Der Gott Achilleus.* Heidelburg.

Honko, L., ed. 1990. *Religion, Myth, and Folklore in the World's Epics: The Kalevala and its Predecessors.* Berlin.

Hooker, G. T. W. 1960. "The Topography of the *Frogs.*" *Journal of Hellenic Studies* 80:112–117.

Hooker, J. T. 1988. "The Cults of Achilles." *Rheinisches Museum für classische Philologie* 131:1–7.

Hopkins, K. 1993. "Novel Evidence for Roman Slavery." *Past & Present* 138:3–27.

How, W. W., and Wells, J. 1928. *A Commentary on Herodotus.* 2 vols. Oxford. (Orig. pub. 1912.)

Hudson-Williams, T. 1910. *Elegies of Theognis.* London.

Huizinga, J. 1955. *Homo Ludens: A Study Of The Play-Element In Culture.* Boston.

Hughes, B. 1997. "Callimachus, Hipponax and the Personality of the Iambographer." *Materiali e discussioni per l'analisi dei testi classici* 37:205–216.

Hughes, D. 1991. *Human Sacrifice in Ancient Greece.* London.

Hunt, R. 1981. "Satiric Elements in Hesiod's Works and Days." *Helios* 8:29–40.

Hutchinson, G. O., ed. 1985. *Aeschylus, Septem Contra Thebas.* Oxford.

Huxley, G. L. 1962. *Early Sparta.* London.

———. 1966. *The Early Ionians.* London.

———. 1969. *Greek Epic Poetry from Eumelos to Panyassis.* London.

Irwin, E. 1998. "Biography, fiction and the Archilochean *ainos.*" *Journal of Hellenic Studies* 118:177–183.

Jackson, S. 1994. "Callimachus, Ister and a Scapegoat." *Liverpool Classical Monthly* 19:132–135.

Jacoby, F. 1904. *Das Marmor Parium.* Berlin.

———. 1918. "Studien zu den ältern griechischen Elegikern." *Hermes* 53:1–44.

———. 1933. "Homerisches I. Der Bios und die Person." *Hermes* 68:1–50. = 1961. *Kleine Schriften* I 1–53. Berlin.

Jaeger, W. 1966. "Tyrtaeus on True *Arete.*" In *Five Essays,* trans. A. Fiske, 103–42. Montreal. = "Tyrtaios. Über die wahre *ARETH.*" In *Scripta Minora* II, 75–99. Rome, 1960. (Orig. pub. 1932.)

———. 1945. *Paideia: the Ideals of Greek Culture.* Trans. G. Highet. New York. = *Paideia: Die Formung des griechischen Menschen.* 3 vols. Berlin, 1934–1959.

James, E. O. 1955. *The Nature and Function of Priesthood.* London.

Janko, R. 1982. *Homer, Hesiod and the Hymns: Diachronic Development in Epic Diction.* Cambridge.

———. 1992. *The Iliad: A Commentary.* Vol. IV: books 13–16. Cambridge.

Jeanmaire, H. 1939. *Couroi et Couretes.* Lille.

Jebb, R., ed. 1893–1900. *Sophocles: The Plays and Fragments.* 3rd ed. Cambridge.

———, ed. 1912. *The Oedipus Tyrannus of Sophocles.* Cambridge.

Jedrkiewicz, S. 1989. *Sapere e paradosso nell'antichità: Esopo e la favola.* Filologia e Critica 60. Rome.

Jeffreys, E., Jeffreys, M., Scott, R. et al., trans. 1986. *The Chronicle of John Malalas.* Byzantina Australiensia 4. Melbourne.

Jensen, A. 1963. *Myth and Cult Among Primitive Peoples.* Chicago. = *Mythos und*

Kult bei Naturvölkern, religionswissenschaftliche Betrachtungen. Wiesbaden, 1951.

———. 1966. *Die getötete Gottheit: Weltbild einer frühen Kultur.* Stuttgart.

Jerome, T. S. 1962. *Aspects of the Study of Roman History.* New York.

Jocelyn, H. D. 1969. "The poet Cn. Naevius, P. Cornelius Scipio, and R. Caecilius Metellus." *Antichthon* 3:32–47.

Jónsson, G., ed. 1954. *Edda. Snorra Sturlusonar.* Reykjavik.

Joynt, M., ed. 1931. *Tromdámh Guaire.* Medieval and Modern Irish Series 2. Dublin.

Jullian, C. 1902. "De la Littérature Poétique des Gaulois." *Revue Archéologique* 40:304–327.

Kakridis, J. Th. 1983. "Ζυm ἀγὼν Ὁμήρου καὶ Ἡσιόδου." In *Festschrift für Robert Muth* (ed. P. Haendel and W. Meid) 189–192. Innsbruck.

Kambylis, A. 1963. "Zur 'Dichterweihe' des Archilochus." *Hermes* 91:129–150.

———. 1965. *Die Dichterweihe und ihre Symbolik.* Heidelberg.

Kamp, H. W. 1934. "Concerning Seneca's Exile." *Classical Journal* 30:101–108.

Kassel, R. and Austin, C. 1983–. *Poetae Comici Graeci.* Multi-volumed; publication ongoing. Berlin.

Katz, J. and Volk, K. 2000. "'Mere Bellies'? A New Look at *Theogony* 26–28." *Journal of Hellenic Studies* 120:122–131.

Kearns, E. 1989. *The Heroes of Attica.* Bulletin of the Institute of Classical Studies Supplement 57. 1989. London.

———. 1990. "Saving the City." In *The Greek City from Homer to Alexander* (ed. O. Murray and S. Price) 323–346. Oxford.

Keel, O. 1977. *Vögel als Boten.* Freiburg.

Keil, H. 1857–1880. *Grammatici Latini.* 7 vols. Leipzig.

Keller, O., ed. 1967. *Pseudoacronis, scholia in Horatium vetustiora.* Stuttgart.

Kenney, E. J., and Clausen, W. V., eds. 1982. *Latin Literature.* (*The Cambridge History of Classical Literature*, vol. 2.) Cambridge.

———. 1970. "Ovid." In OCD 763–764.

———. 1982. In CHCL II 855.

Kerényi, K. 1945. "*Heros Iatros.* Über Wandlungen und Symbole des ärztlichen Genius in Griechenland." *Eranos-Jahrbuch* 12:33–54.

———. 1959. *The Heroes of the Greeks.* Trans. H. J. Rose. London.

———. 1974. *The Gods of the Greeks.* Trans. N. Cameron. London. (Orig. pub. 1951.)

Kershaw, K. 2000. *The One-eyed God: Odin and the (Indo-)Germanic Männerbünde.* Journal of Indo-European Studies, Monograph No. 36. Washington DC.

Killeen, J. F. 1973. "Sappho, fr. 111." *Classical Quarterly* 23:197.

King, H. 1983. "Bound to Bleed: Artemis and Greek Women." In *Images of Women in Antiquity* (ed. A. Cameron and A. Kuhrt) 118–124. London.

King, K. C. 1987. *Achilles: Paradigms of the War Hero from Homer to the Middle Ages.* Berkeley.

Kinsella, T., trans. 1969. *The Tain.* Oxford.

Kircher, K. 1910. *Die sakrale Bedeutung des Weines im Altertum.* Giessen.

Kirk, G. S. 1962. *The Songs of Homer.* Cambridge.

Kirkwood, G. M. 1961. "The Authorship of the Strasbourg Epodes." *Transactions and Proceedings of the American Philological Association* 92:267–282.

———. 1984. "Blame and Envy in the Pindaric Epinician." In *Greek Poetry and Philosophy: Studies in Honour of Leonard Woodbury* (ed. Douglas E. Gerber) 169–183. Chico, CA.

Kittredge, G. L. 1916. *A Study of Gawain and the Green Knight.* Cambridge, MA.

Knoche, U. 1975. *Roman Satire.* Trans. E. S. Ramage. Bloomington, IN. = *Die römische Satire.* Berlin, 1949.

Knox, A. D. ed. 1929. *Herodes, Cercidas, and the Greek Choliambic Poets.* LCL 225. Cambridge, MA. Printed with J. M. Edmonds, ed., *The Characters of Theophrastus.*

Koch, C. 1960. *Religio.* Nuremberg.

Koenen, L. 1977. "Horaz, Catull und Hipponax." *Zeitschrift für Papyrologie und Epigraphik* 26:73–93.

Koller, H. 1963. *Musik und Dichtung im altern Griechenland.* Bern.

Köhnken, A. 1981. "Apollo's Retort to Envy's Criticism." *American Journal of Philology* 102:411–422.

Konstantakos, K. M. 2003. "Riddles, Philosophers and Fishers: Aesop and the θαλάσσιον πρόβατον (*Vita Aesopi* W 24, G 47)." *Eranos* 101:94–113.

Kontoleon, N. M. 1964. "Archilochus und Paros." In Pouilloux et al. 1964:37–73.

Körte, A. 1921. "Komödie (griechische)." RE 11:1207–1275.

Koster, S. 1980. *Die Invektive in der griechischen und römischen Literatur.* Meisenheim am Glan.

Koster, W. J. W., Wilson, N. G. et al., eds. 1969, 1975–. *Scholia in Aristophanem Part 1, Prolegomena de Comoedia, Scholia in Acharnenses, Equites, Nubes.* Fasc. 1a, *Prolegomena de Comoedia* (ed. W. J. W. Koster, 1975). Fasc. 1b, *Scholia in Aristophanis Archarnenses* (ed. N. G. Wilson, 1975). Fasc. II, *Scholia Vetera in Aristophanis Equites* (ed. D. M. Jones, 1969), *Scholia Triciliniana in Aristophanis Equites* (ed. N. G. Wilson, 1969). *Scholia in Aves* (ed. D. Holwerda, 1991). Groningen.

Kotsidu, H. 1991. *Die musischen Agone der Panathenäen in archaischer und klassischer Zeit.* Munich.

Kraus, W. 1985. *Aristophanes' politische Komödien*. Vienna.

Kroymann, J. 1937. *Sparta und Messenien*. Berlin.

Kugel, J. L., ed. 1990. *Poetry and Prophecy: The Beginnings of a Literary Tradition*. Myth and Poetics No. 4. Ithaca, NY.

Kuhnert, E. 1884–1937. "Satyros und Silenos." In Roscher 1884–1937 4.444–531.

Kuiper, F. B. J. 1960. "The Ancient Aryan Verbal Contest." *Indo-Iranian Journal* 4:217–281.

Kurke, L. 1991. *The Traffic in Praise: Pindar and the Poetics of Social Economy*. Ithaca, NY.

———. 1993. "The Economy of *Kudos*." In Dougherty and Kurke 1993:131–163.

———. 2003. "Aesop and the Contestation of Delphic Authority." In *The Culture Within Ancient Greek Culture* (ed. C. Dougherty and L. Kurke) 77–100. Cambridge.

Kümmel, H. M. 1967. *Ersatzrituale für den hethischen König*. Studien zu den Boğazköy-Texten 3. Wiesbaden.

La Penna. A. 1957. *Publi Ovidi Nasonis Ibis*. Florence.

Larson, G., Littleton, C. S., and Puhvel, J., eds. 1974. *Myth in Indo-European Antiquity*. Berkeley and Los Angeles.

Larson, J. 1995. *Greek Heroine Cults*. Wisconsin Studies in Classics. Madison, WI.

Lasserre, F. 1950. *Les Épodes d'Archiloque*. Paris.

———. 1984. "La fable en Grece dans la poesie." In Adrados 1984:61–105.

Lasserre, F. and André Bonnard. 1968. *Archiloque. Fragments*. 2nd ed. Paris. (Orig. pub. 1958.)

Latacz, J. 1976. "Zum Musenfragment des Naevius." *Würzburger Jahrbücher für die Altertumswissenschaft*, N.F., 2:119–134.

Latte, K. 1946. "Hesiods Dichterweihe." *Antike und Abendland* 2:152–163.

———. 1947. "Zu den neuen Alkaiosbruchstücken (P. Ox. 18, 2165)." *Museum Helveticum* 4:141–146.

Lattimore, S. 1988. "The Nature of Early Greek Victor Statues." In *Coroebos Triumphs* (ed. Susan Bandy) 245–256. San Diego, CA.

Leeuw, G. van der. 1963. *Sacred and Profane Beauty; the Holy in Art*. Trans. D. Green. New York. = *Wegen en granzen*. Amsterdam, 1932.

———. 1967. *Religion in Essence and Manifestation*. Trans. J. Turner. Gloucester, MA. (orig. pub. 1938.) = *Phänomenologie der Religion*. Tübingen, 1933.

Lefkowitz, M. L. 1976. "Fictions in Literary Biography: The New Poem and the Archilochus Legend." *Arethusa* 9:181–189.

———. 1981. *The Lives of the Poets*. Baltimore.

———. 1984. "Aristophanes and Other Historians of the Fifth-Century Theater." *Hermes* 112:143–153.

———. 1987. "Was Euripides an Atheist?" *Studi italiani di filologia classica* 5:159–161.

Lefkowitz, M., and Lloyd-Jones, H. 1987. *"lukaikhmiais."* *Zeitschrift für Papyrologie und Epigraphik* 68:9–10.

Lesky, A. 1966. *A History of Greek Literature.* Trans. J. Willis and C. de Heer. New York. = *Geschichte der griechischen Literatur.* Bern, 1957/1958.

Leutsch, E., and Schneidewin, F., eds. 1958–1961. *Corpus Paroemiographorum Graecorum.* 3 vols. Hildesheim. (Orig. pub. 1887.)

Leutsch, E., and Schneidewin, F., eds. 1961. *Corpus Paroemiographorum Graecorum: supplementum.* Hildesheim.

Levine, D. 2002. "Poetic Justice: Homer's Death in the Ancient Biographical Tradition." *Classical Journal* 98:141–160.

Lewis, A. D. E., and Crawford, M. H. 1996. In *Roman Statutes,* 2 vols. (ed. M. H. Crawford) 2:555–721.

Lewis, I. M. 1971. *Ecstatic Religion. An Anthropological Study of Spirit Possession and Shamanism.* Harmondsworth.

Lewis, N., and Reinhold, M. 1966. *Roman Civilization, Sourcebooks, Vol. 1: The Republic.* New York.

Lilja, S. 1979. "Animal Imagery in Greek Comedy." *Arctos* 13:85–90.

Lincoln, B. 1975a. "Homeric *lússa,* 'Wolfish Rage.'" *Indogermanische Forschungen* 80:98–105.

———. 1977. "Death and Resurrection in Indo-European Thought." *Indo-European Studies* 5:47–64.

Lindow, J. 1975. "Riddles, Kennings, and the Complexity of Skaldic Poetry." *Scandinavian Studies* 4:311–327.

Linforth, I. 1919. *Solon the Athenian.* Berkeley.

———. 1941. *The Arts of Orpheus.* Berkeley.

Lissarrague, F. 1990. "Why Satyrs Are Good to Represent." In Winkler and Zeitlin 1990:228–236.

———. 2000. "Aesop, Between Man and Beast: Ancient Portraits and Illustrations." In *Not the Classical Ideal: Athens and the Construction of the Other in Greek Art* (ed. B. Cohen) 132–149. Leiden.

Littleton, C. S. 1970. "Some Possible Indo-European Themes in the '*Iliad*'." In Puhvel 1970:229–246.

———. 1980. "The Problem That was Greece: Some Observations on the Greek Tradition from the Standpoint of the New Comparative Mythology." *Arethusa* 13:141–159.

———. 1982. *The New Comparative Mythology,* 3rd. ed. Berkeley.

Lloyd, G. E. R. 1979. *Magic, Reason, and Experience.* Cambridge.

Lloyd-Jones, Hugh. 1968. "The Cologne Fragment of Alcaeus." *Greek, Roman, and Byzantine Studies* 9:125–139.

———. 1990. "Honour and Shame in Ancient Greek Culture." In *Greek Comedy, Hellenistic Literature, Greek Religion, and Miscellanea: the Academic Papers of Sir Hugh Lloyd Jones*, 253–280. Oxford.

Lloyd-Jones, J. 1948. "The Court Poets of the Welsh Princes." *Proceedings of the British Academy* 34:167–197.

Löffler, I. 1963. *Die Melampodie: Versuch einer Rekonstruktion des Inhalts.* Meisenheim am Glan.

Loomis, R. M., trans. 1982. *Dafydd ap Gwilym, The Poems.* Binghamton, NY.

Loraux, N. 1984. "Le corps etrangle." In *Du châtiment dans la cité: supplices corporels et peine de mort dans le monde antique :table ronde.* 195–218. Rome.

———. 1985. "Socrate, Platon, Herakles: Sur un Paradigme Heroïque du Philosophe." In *Histoire et Structure, A la Memoire de Victor Goldschmidt* (ed. J. Brunschwig, C. Imbert, and A. Roger) 93–105. Paris.

———. 1987a. *Tragic Ways of Killing a Woman*, trans. A. Forster. Cambridge, MA. = *Façons tragiques de tuer une femme.* Paris, 1985.

———. 1987b. "Voir dans le noir." *Le champ visuel* 35:219–230.

Lord, A. B. 1960. *The Singer of Tales.* Cambridge, MA.

Lorenz, Gottfried, trans. and ed. 1984. *Snorri Sturluson, Gylfaginning.* Darmstadt.

Lorenz, K. 1966. *On Aggression.* New York.

Lowe, J. 2000. "Kicking over the Traces: The Instability of Cú Chulainn." *Studia Celtica* 34:119–130.

Lowenstam, S. 1981. *The Death of Patroklos, A Study in Typology.* Königstein.

Luck, G. 1983. "Naevius and Virgil." *Illinois Classical Studies* 8:267–275.

Luginbill, R. D. 2002. "Tyrtaeus 12 West: Come Join the Spartan Army." *Classical Quarterly* 52:405–414.

Luppe, W. 2000. "The Rivalry between Aristophanes and Kratinos." In Harvey and Wilkins 2000:15–20.

Maas, P. 1929. "Stesichoros." In *RE*, 2nd ser., 3.2:2458–2462.

Macan, R.W. 1897. "A Note on the Date of Tyrtaeus, and the Messenian War." *Classical Review* 11:10–12.

Mac Airt, S., ed. 1944. *Leabhar Branach: the Book of the O'Byrnes.* Dublin.

———. 1958. "Filidecht and Coimgne." *Ériu* 18:139–152.

Macalister, R. A. S., and MacNeill, J. 1916. *Leabhar Gabhála, The Book of Conquests of Ireland.* Dublin.

Macalister, R. A. S., trans. 1938–1956. *Lebor Gabhála Érenn: The Book of the Taking of Ireland.* 5 vols. ITS 34, 35, 39, 41, 44. Dublin.

Mac Cana, P. 1968. "An 'Archaism' in Irish Poetic Tradition." *Celtica* 8:174–181.

Bibliography

Maclean, J. K. B., and Aitken, E. B., trans. and eds. 2001. *Heroikos, Flavius Philostratus.* Atlanta.

Maehler, H. 1963. *Die Auffassung des Dichterberuf im frühen Griechentum bis zur Zeit Pindars.* Göttingen.

Mainoldi, C. 1984. *L'Image du loup et du chien dans la Grece ancienne d'Homere a Platon.* Paris.

Mair, A. W., trans. 1960. *Callimachus, Hymns and Epigrams.* Cambridge, MA.

Mallory, J. P. 1989. *In Search of the Indo-Europeans.* London.

Manieri, F. 1972. "Saffo: Appunti di metodologia generale per un approccio psichiatrico." *Quaderni Urbinati di Cultura Classica* 14:46–64.

Mankin, D. 1995. *Horace Epodes.* Cambridge.

Maple, T., and Matheson, D., eds. 1973. *Aggression, Hostility and Violence, Nature or Nurture?* New York.

Markwald, G. 1986. *Die Homerischen Epigramme.* Königstein.

Marmorale, E. V. 1950. *Naevius Poeta: Introduzione biobibliografica, testo dei frammenti e commento,* 2nd ed. Firenze.

Marquardt, P. 1982. "Hesiod's Ambiguous View of Woman." *Classical Philology* 77:283–291.

Martin, R. 1983. *Healing, Sacrifice and Battle, Amechania and Related Concepts in Early Greek Poetry.* Innsbruck.

———. 1993. "The Seven Sages as Performers of Wisdom." In Dougherty and Kurke 1993:108–128.

Masson, O. 1949. "Sur un papyrus d'Hipponax, III. Les allusions au *pharmakos* dans le fragment P. Oxy XVIII 2176–8." *Revue des études grecques* 62:311–319.

———. 1951. "Encore les 'Epodes des Strasbourg.'" *Revue des études grecques* 64:427–442.

———. 1962. *Les Fragments du Poete Hipponax.* Paris.

Mattes, J. 1970. *Der Wahnsinn im griechischen Mythos und in der Dicthung bis zum Drama des fünften Jahrhunderts.* Heidelberg.

McCone, K. R. 1984. "*Aided Cheltchair maic Uthechair:* Hounds, Heroes and Hospitallers in Early Irish Myth and Story." *Ériu* 35:1–30.

———. 1985. "OIr. *Olc, Luch-* and IE **wl̥k(w)os, *lúk(w)os* 'Wolf'." *Ériu* 36:171–176.

———. 1986. "Werewolves, Cyclopes, Diberga, and Fianna: Juvenile Delinquency in Early Ireland." *Cambridge Medieval Celtic Studies* 12:1–22.

———. 1987. "Hund, Wolf und Krieger bei den Indogermanen." In *Studien zum indogermanischen Wortschatz* (ed. W. Meid) 111–154. Innsbruck.

———. 1989. "A Tale of Two Ditties: Poet and Satirist in *Cath Maige Tuired.*" In *Sages, Saints and Storytellers. Celtic Studies in honour of Professor James*

Carney, Maynooth Monographs 2 (ed. D. Ó Corráin, L. Breatnach, and K. McCone) 122–143. Maynooth.

McGinty, P. 1978. "Dionysos's Revenge and the Validation of the Hellenic World-View." *Harvard Theological Review* 71:77–94.

MacDowell, D. 1971. *Aristophanes, Wasps*. Oxford.

MacKay, K. J. 1959. "Hesiod's Rejuvenation." *Classical Review* 53 (9 n.s.):1–5.

McEvelley, T. 1978. "Sappho, Fragment Thirty-one. The face behind the mask." *Phoenix* 32:1–18.

Maier, B. 1989. "Sacral Kingship in Pre-Christian Ireland." *Zeitschrift für Religions- und Geistesgeschichte* 41:12–32.

Mead, M. 1937. *Cooperation and Competition among Primitive Peoples*. New York.

Meid, W. 1974. "Dichtkunst, Rechtspflege und Medizin im Alten Irland." In *Antiquitates Indogermanicae Gedenkschrift für Hermann Güntert* (ed. M. Mayrhofer et al.) 21–34. Innsbruck.

Meijer, P. A. 1981. "Philosophers, Intellectuals and Religion in Hellas." In *Faith, Hope and Worship* (ed. H. S. Versnel) 216–262. Leiden.

Melia, D. F. 1979. "Some Remarks on the Affinities of Medieval Irish Saga." *Acta Antiqua Academia Scientiarum Hungaricae* 27:255–261.

Mendelsohn, D. 1992. "Συγκεραυνόω: Dithyrambic Language and Dionysiac Cult." *Classical Journal* 87:105–124.

Mercier, V. 1962. *The Irish Comic Tradition*. Oxford.

Meridier, L. 1925. *Euripide I*. Paris.

Merkle, S. 1992. "Die Fabel von Frosch und Maus. Zur Funktion der λόγοι im Delphi-Teil des Äsop-Romans." In Holzberg 1992a:110–128.

Meroney, H. 1949–1950. "Studies in Early Irish Satire." *Journal of Celtic Studies* 1:199–226; 2:59–130.

Merrill, N. W. 1975. "Cicero and Early Roman Invective." Diss. University of Cincinnati.

Meuli, K. 1935. "Scythica." *Hermes* 70:121–176.

———. 1954. "Herkunft und Wesen der Fabel." *Schweizer Archiv für Volkskunde* 50:65–93.

Meyer, K., ed. 1892. *Aislinge Meic Conglinne, The Vision of MacConglinne*. London. Available online at "http://www.yorku.ca/inpar/macconglinne_meyer.pdf". Irish text available online at CELT Corpus of Electronic Texts, "http://www.ucc.ie/celt/irllist.html"

———, ed. 1900. "How King Neill of the Nine Hostages was Slain [*Orcuin Néill Nóigíallaig*]." *Otia Merseiana* 2:84–92. Cf. online, http://www.ancienttexts.org/library/celtic/ctexts/niall.html.

———. 1906. *Contributions to Irish Lexicography*. Halle.

Bibliography

———, ed. 1912. *Sanas Cormaic. An Old-Irish Glossary compiled by Cormac úa Cuilennáin, King-Bishop of Cashel in the 10th century. Edited from the copy in the Yellow Book of Lecan.* In *Anecdota from Irish Manuscripts.* Vol. 4. Halle.

Meyer, K., and Nutt, A. eds. 1972. *The Voyage of Bran, Son of Febal, to the Land of the Living. An Old Irish Saga.* 2 vols. New York. (Orig. pub. 1895–1897.)

Mikalson, J. D. 1983. *Athenian Popular Religion.* Chapel Hill, NC.

———. 2003. *Herodotus and Religion in the Persian Wars.* Chapel Hill, NC.

Miller, D. A. 1977. "A Note on Aegisthus as 'Hero'." *Arethusa* 10:259–268.

Miller, D. 1991. "Two Warriors and Two Swords: The Legacy of Starkað." *Journal of Indo-European Studies* 19:309–323.

———. 2000. *The Epic Hero.* Baltimore.

———. 2001. "*Trifunctionalia Rediviva*: A Note on Some Greek Possibilities." *Journal of Indo-European Studies* 29:173–184.

———. 2001b. Review of Frédéric Blaive. *Impius Bellator. Le Mythe Indo-Européen du Guerrier Impie* (1996, Arras). *Journal of Indo-European Studies* 29:508–511.

Milne, M. 1965. "Appendix III: The Poem Entitled 'Kiln.'" In *The Techniques of Painted Attic Poetry* (ed. J. V. Noble) 102–113. New York.

Miralles, C., and Pòrtulas, J. 1983. *Archilochus and the Iambic Poetry.* Rome.

Miralles, C., and Pòrtulas, J. 1988. *The Poetry of Hipponax.* Rome.

Mitchell, T. N. 1979. *Cicero: the Ascending Years.* New Haven.

———. 1991. *Cicero: the Senior Statesman.* New Haven.

Molyneux, J. H. 1971. "Simonides and the Dioscuri." *Phoenix* 25:197–205.

———. 1992. *Simonides: A Historical Study.* Wauconda, IL.

Momigliano, A. 1942. "Review of Laura Robinson, *Freedom of Speech in the Roman Republic.*" *Journal of Roman Studies* 32:120–124.

———. 1971. *The Development of Greek Biography.* Cambridge, MA.

Montagu, A., ed. 1973. *Man and Aggression.* Oxford.

Montuori, M. 1981. *Socrates, Physiology of a Myth.* Trans. J. and M. Langdale. Amsterdam. = *Socrate: fisiologia di un mito.* Firenze, 1974.

Morganwg, I., ed., and Probert, W., trans. 1977. *The Triads of Britain.* London.

Moulton, C. 1981. *Aristophanic Poetry.* Göttingen.

Müller, C. W. 1985. "Die Archilochoslegende." *Rheinisches Museum für classische Philologie* 128:99–151.

Murphy, G. 1940. "Bards and Filidh." *Éigse* 2:200–207.

———. 1948. *Glimpses of Gaelic Ireland.* Dublin.

———. 1966. "Saga and Myth in Ancient Ireland." In *Early Irish Literature* (ed. E. Knott and G. Murphy) 97–144. New York.

Murray, G. 1913. *Euripides and his Age.* New York.

———. 1933. *Aristophanes*. Oxford.

———. 1934. *The Rise of the Greek Epic*, 4th ed. Oxford. (Orig. pub. 1907.)

———. 1940. *Aeschylus, the Creator of Tragedy*. Oxford.

Murray, P. 1981. "Poetic Inspiration in Early Greece." *Journal of Hellenic Studies* 101:87–100.

———. 1983. "Homer and the Bard." In *Aspects of the Epic*. (ed. T. Winnifrith, P. Murray, and K. Grandsen) 1–15. New York.

Murray, P., and Wilson, P., eds. 2004. *Music and the Muses: The Culture of Mousikē in the Classical Athenian City*. Oxford.

Murray, R. D. 1965. "Theognis, 341–50." *Transactions and Proceedings of the American Philological Association* 96:277–281.

Mylonas, G. E. 1961. *Eleusis and the Eleusinian Mysteries*. Princeton.

Naafs-Wilstra, M. C. 1987. "Indo-European 'Dichtersprache' in Sappho and Alcaeus." *Journal of Indo-European Studies* 15:273–283.

Nagle, B. 1980. *The Poetics of Exile*. Bruxelles.

Nagy, G. 1973. "Phaethon, Sappho's Phaon, and the White Rock of Leukas." *Harvard Studies in Classical Philology* 77:137–177. (Cf. Nagy 1990a:223–262.)

———. 1974. *Comparative Studies in Greek and Indic Meter*. Cambridge, MA.

———. 1976. "*Iambos*: Typologies of Invective and Praise." *Arethusa* 9:191–205.

———. 1979. *The Best of the Achaeans*. Baltimore. Available online at http://www. press.jhu.edu/books/nagy/.

———. 1982. "Hesiod." In *Ancient Writers: Greece and Rome* (ed. T. J. Luce) 43–73. New York.

———. 1982b. "Theognis of Megara: The Poet as Seer, Pilot, and Revenant." *Arethusa* 15:109–128.

———. 1983. "On the Death of Sarpedon." In Rubino 1983:189–217 = Nagy 1990:122–142.

———. 1985. "Theognis and Megara: A Poet's Vision of His City." In Figureira and Nagy 1985:22–81.

———. 1990a. *Greek Mythology and Poetics*. Ithaca, NY.

———. 1990b. *Pindar's Homer: The Lyric Possession of an Epic Past*. Baltimore. 2nd ed. 1994, paperback. Available online at http://www.press.jhu.edu/ books/nagy/.

———. 1996. *Poetry as Performance: Homer and Beyond*. Cambridge.

———. 2002. *Plato's Rhapsody and Homer's Music*. Hellenic Studies 1. Cambridge, MA.

Nagy, J. 1981. "The Deceptive Gift in Greek Mythology." *Arethusa* 14:191–204.

———. 1981–1982. "Liminality and Knowledge in Irish Tradition." *Studia Celtica* 16/17:135–143.

———. 1982–1983. "Wisdom of the Geilt." *Éigse* 19:44–60.

———. 1984. "Heroic Destines in the Macgnímrada of Finn and Cú Chulainn." *Zeitschrift für celtische Philologie* 40:23–39.

———. 1985. *The Wisdom of the Outlaw*. Berkeley.

———. 1990. "Hierarchy, Heroes, and Heads, Indo-European Structures in Greek Myth." In Edmunds 1990:199–238.

Nancy, C. 1983. "*Pharmakon sōtērias*: Le mecanisme du sacrifice humaine chez Euripide." In *Théâtre et spectacle dans l'antiquité* (= *Actes Colloque Strasbourg 5-7 Nov. 1981*) 17–30. Leiden.

Nestle, W. 1898. "Die Legenden vom Tode des Euripides." *Philologus* 57:134–149.

Neuman, G. 1987. "How We Became (In)human." In *Origins of Human Aggression* (ed. G. Neuman) 78–104. New York.

Newman, J. K. 1967. *The Concept of Vates in Augustan Poetry*. Brussels.

Ní Chatháin, P. 1979/1980. "Swineherds, Seers, and Druids." *Studia Celtica* 14/15:200–211.

Niese, B. 1891. "Die ältere Geschichte Messeniens." *Hermes* 26:1–32.

Nilsson, M. P. 1967–1974. *Geschichte der Griechischen Religion*. 3rd ed., 2 vols. Munich. (Orig. pub. 1941–50.)

———. 1972. *Greek Folk Religion*. Philadelphia. (Orig. pub. 1940.)

———. 1906. *Griechische Feste von religiöses Bedeutung mit Ausschluss der attischen*. Berlin.

Nisbet, R. G. M., ed. 1961. *M. Tulli Ciceronis in L. Calpurnium Pisonem Oratio*. Oxford.

———. 1965. "The Speeches." In Dorey 1965:47–79.

Notopoulos, J. 1952 (Nov. 17). "The Warrior as an Oral Poet: A Case History." *Classical Weekly* 46:17–19.

Nussbaum, M. 1980. "Aristophanes and Socrates on Learning and Practical Wisdom." *Yale Classical Studies* 26:43–97.

Oates, W. J. 1932. *The Influence of Simonides of Ceos Upon Horace*. Princeton.

O'Connor-Visser, E. 1987. *Aspects of Human Sacrifice in the Tragedies of Euripides*. Amsterdam.

O'Curry, E. 1873. *On the Manners and Customs of the Ancient Irish*. 3 vols. London.

O'Daly, A. 1852. *The Tribes of Ireland*. Trans. J. Mangan, with an introduction by J. O'Donovan. Dublin.

O Daly, Máirín, ed. 1962. "*Lānellach Tigi Rīch 7 Ruirech*." *Ériu* 19:81–86.

———, ed. 1975. *Cath Maige Mucrama: The Battle of Mag Mucrama*. ITS 50 Dublin.

Ó Duilearga, S. 1961. "*Cnuasach Andeas*." *Béaloideas* 29:107–108.

O'Donovan, J. 1846. "Covenant Between Mageoghegan and the Fox, with brief historical Notices of the two Families." In *The Miscellany of the Irish Archaeological Society* 1:179–197.

———, trans. 1856. *Annals of the Kingdom of Ireland, by the Four Masters, from the earliest period to the year 1616.* 2nd ed. 7 vols. Dublin. (Orig. pub. 1848.) Available online at CELT Corpus of Electronic Texts, http://www.ucc.ie/celt/irllist.html.

O'Flaherty, Wendy, trans. 1975. *Hindu Myths.* New York.

———, trans. 1981. *The Rig Veda.* New York.

Ogden, D. 1997. *The Crooked Kings of Ancient Greece.* London.

———. 2004. *Aristomenes of Messene: Legends of Sparta's Nemesis.* Swansea, Wales.

O'Grady, S., ed. 1857. *Account of the Pursuit of Diarmuid O'Duibhne and Grainne* . . . Publications of Ossianic Society 3. Dublin.

———, ed. and trans. 1970. *Silva Gadelica (I–XXXI): A collection of tales in Irish with extracts illustrating persons and places.* 2 vols. New York. (Orig. pub. 1892.)

Oguibenine, B. 1978. "Complément à l'image du guerrier indo-européen." *Journal Asiatique* 266:257–290.

O'Higgins, D. M. 2001. "Women's Cultic Joking and Mockery: Some Perspectives." In *Making Silence Speak: Women's Voices in Greek Literature and Society* (ed. A. Lardinois and L. McClure) 137–160. Princeton.

O' hO'gáin, D. 1979. "The Visionary Voice: A Survey of Popular Attitudes to Poetry in Irish Tradition." *Irish University Review* 9:44–61.

———. 1985. *The Hero in Irish Folk History.* Dublin.

O'Keefe, J. G. 1911. "Mac Dá Cherda and Cummaine Foda." *Ériu* 5:18–44.

———, trans. 1913. *Buile Suibhne.* ITS 12. London. English and Irish texts available online at CELT, http://celt.ucc.ie/index.html.

Okin, L. 1985. "Sources for the History of Archaic Megara." In Figueira and Nagy 1985:9–21.

Oldenberg, H. 1923. *Die Religion des Veda.* Stuttgart.

O'Leary, P. 1984. "Contention at Feasts in Early Irish Literature." *Éigse* 20:115–127.

———. 1991. "Jeers and Judgments: Laughter in Early Irish Literature." *Cambridge Medieval Celtic Studies* 22:15–30.

Olender, M. 1985. "Aspects de Baubō." *Revue de l'Histoire des Religions* 202:3–55.

= 1990. "Aspects of Baubo" in *Before Sexuality* (ed. D. Halperin, J. Winkler, and F. Zeitlin) 83–113. Princeton.

Olivier, F. 1917. *Les Epodes d'Horace.* Lausanne.

Olson, S. D. 2002. *Aristophanes Acharnians.* Oxford.

Oost, S. I. 1973. "The Megara of Theagenes and Theognis." *Classical Philology* 68:188–196.

Bibliography

Opelt, I. 1969. *Vom Spott der Römer*. Munich.

O'Rahilly, C., ed. 1967. *Táin Bó Cúalnge from the Book of Leinster*. ITS 49. Dublin.

——, ed. 1976. *Táin Bó Cúailnge, Recension 1*. Dublin.

O'Rahilly, T. F. 1922. "Irish Poets, Historians, and Judges in English Documents." *Proceedings of the Royal Irish Academy* 36:86–101.

——. 1946. *Early Irish History and Mythology*. Dublin.

O'Reilly, E. 1820. *Transactions of Iberno-Celtic Society for 1820, Containing a Chronological Account of Nearly Four Hundred Irish Writers . . .* Dublin.

O'Sullivan, N. 1992. *Alcidamas, Aristophanes and the Beginnings of Greek Stylistic Theory*. Hermes Einzelschriften Heft 60. Stuttgart.

Otto, W. F. 1955. *Die Gestalt und das Sein*. Düsseldorf-Köln. 365–398 = "Tyrtaios und die Unsterblichkeit des Ruhmes."*Geistige Überlieferung, Jahrbuch* (1942) 2:66–95.

Owen, S. G. 1924. *Tristium, Liber Secundus*. Oxford.

Page, D. 1955. *Sappho and Alcaeus*. Oxford.

——. 1962. *Poetae Melici Graeci; Alcmanis, Stesichori, Ibyci, Anacreontis, Simonidis, Corinnae, poetarum minorum reliquias, carmina popularia et convivialia quaeque adespota feruntur*. Oxford.

——. 1972. *Aeschyli, Septem Quae Supersunt Tragoedias*. Oxford.

Paley, F. A. 1872. *Euripides 1*. 2nd ed. Cambridge. (Orig. pub. 1857–1860.)

Pálsson, H., and Edwards, P., trans. 1968. *Gautrek's Saga And Other Medieval Tales*. New York.

Papademetriou, J. Th. 1997. *Aesop as an Archetypal Hero*. Studies and Research 39. Athens.

Papathomopoulos, M., ed. and trans. 1991. Ὁ Βίος τοῦ Αἰσώπου. Ἡ Παραλλαγὴ G. Κριτικὴ ἔκδοση μὲ εἰσαγωγὴ καὶ μετάφραση. 2nd ed. Joannina. (Orig. pub. 1990.)

——, ed. and trans. 1999. Ὁ Βίος τοῦ Αἰσώπου. Ἡ Παραλλαγή W. Editio Princeps. Εἰσαγωγή—Κείμενο—Μετάφραση—Σχόλια. Athens.

Parke. H. W. 1933. *Greek Mercenary Soldiers*. Oxford.

Parker, H. 1996. "Sappho Schoolmistress." In *Re-Reading Sappho: Reception and Transmission*, Classics in Contemporary Thought 3 (ed. E. Greene) 146–183. Berkeley.

Parker, R. 1983. *Miasma, Pollution and Purification in Early Greek Religion*. Oxford.

Parry, T. 1952. *Gwaith Dafydd ap Gwilym*. Caerdydd.

Pascal, E. 1985. "Muses Olympiennes et Muses Héliconiennes dans la *Théogonie* d'Hésiode." In *Actes du Troisième Congrès International sur la Beotie Antique (Montreal-Quebec, 31.x.1979 - 4.xi.1979)* (ed. J. M. Fossey and H. Giroux) 111–117. Amsterdam.

Pauly, A., Wissowa, G., and Kroll, W., eds. 1893–. *Real-Encyclopädie der klassischen Altertumswissenschaft.* Stuttgart.

Pearson, A. C., ed. 1957. *Sophoclis Fabulae.* Oxford.

Pearson, L. 1962. "The Pseudo-History of Messenia and its Authors." *Historia* 11:397–426.

Pease, A. S. 1907. "Notes on Stoning among the Greeks and Romans." *Transactions and Proceedings of the American Philological Association* 38:5–18.

———, ed. 1955. *Ciceronis, De Natura Deorum.* Cambridge, MA.

———, ed. 1963. *M. Tulli Ciceronis, De Divinatione.* Darmstadt.

Penglase, C. 1994. *Greek Myths and Mesopotamia: Parallels and Influence in the Homeric Hymns and Hesiod.* London.

Peppmüller, R. 1895. "Über das vierte Homerische Epigramm." *Jahrbücher für classische Philologie* 151:433–441.

Peristiany, J., ed. 1966. *Honour and Shame: the Values of Mediterranean Society.* Chicago.

Perry, B. 1936. *Studies in the Text History of the Life and Fables of Aesop.* Haverford, PA.

———. 1952. *Aesopica: A Series of Text Relating to Aesop or Ascribed to Him or Closely Connected with the Literary Tradition That Bears His Name,* vol. 1 (vol. 2 never published). Urbana, IL.

———, ed. 1965. *Babrius and Phaedrus.* LCL 436. Cambridge, MA.

Pfeffer, F. 1976. *Studien zur Mantik in der Philosophie der Antike.* Meisenheim am Glan.

Pfeiffer, R., ed. 1949, 1953. *Callimachus.* 2 vols. Oxford.

———. 1968. *History of Classical Scholarship from the Beginnings to the End of the Hellenistic Age.* Oxford.

Pfister, F. 1909–1912. *Der Reliquienkult im Altertum.* Giessen.

Picard, C. 1922. *Ephese et Claros.* Paris.

Piccaluga, G., ed. 1980. *Perennitas. Studi in onore di Angelo Brelich.* Rome.

Piccolomini, E. 1888. "Sulla morte favolosa di Eschilo, Sofocle, Euripide, Cratino, Eupoli." *Annali delle Università Toscane* 18:95–132.

Pickard-Cambridge, A. W. 1962. *Dithyramb, Tragedy and Comedy,* 2nd ed., rev. T. B. L. Webster. Oxford . (Orig. pub. 1927.)

———. 1988. *The Dramatic Festivals of Athens.* 2nd ed. Oxford. (Orig. pub. 1953.)

Platthy, J. 1985. *The Mythical Poets of Greece.* Washington DC.

Plescia, J. 1970. *The Oath and Perjury in Ancient Greece.* Tallahassee, FL.

Plimpton, G. 1984. *Writers at Work.* 6th series. New York.

Podlecki, A. J. 1969. "Three Greek Soldier-poets, Archilochus, Alcaeus, Solon." *Classical World* 63:73–81.

Bibliography

———. 1974. "Archilochus and Apollo." *Phoenix* 28:1–17.

———. 1984. *Early Greek Poets and Their Times.* Vancouver.

Politzer, H. 1961. "The 'Break-Through': Thomas Mann and the Deeper Meaning of Disease." *Ciba-Symposium* 9:36–43.

Polomé, E. C. 1990. "Starkað: Oðinn- or Þórr-Hero." In Reichert and Zimmermann 1990:267–286.

Pòrtulas, J. 1983[1985]. "Para leer a Safo." *Argos* 7:59–75.

Pötscher, W. 1971. "Der Name des Herakles." *Emerita* 39:169–184.

Pouilloux, J. et al. 1964. *Archiloque; sept exposés et discussions par Vandœuvres-Genève, 26 août-3 septembre 1963.* Geneva.

Powell, J. 1925. *Collectanea Alexandrina.* Oxford.

Prato, C. 1955. *Euripide nella critica di Aristofane.* Galatina.

———. 1964. *Gli epigrammi attribuiti a L. Anneo Seneca.* 2nd ed. Rome. (Orig. pub. 1955.)

Pritchard, J. B., ed. 1974. *Ancient Near Eastern Texts Relating to the Old Testament.* 3d ed., with supplement. Princeton.

Pritchett, W. K. 1979. *The Greek State at War: Religion.* Vol. 3 of 5 vols. Berkeley.

Privitera, G. A. 1969. "Il commento del peri hupsous al fr. 31 L.P. di Saffo." *Quaderni Urbinati di Cultura Classica* 7:26–35.

Proietti, G. 1987. *Xenophon's Sparta.* Leiden.

Przyluski, J. 1940. "Les confréries de loups-garous dans les sociétés indo-euro-péennes." *Revue de l'Histoire des Religions* 121:128–145.

Pugliese, G. 1941. *Studi sul l'"iniuria."* Milan.

Puhvel, J., ed. 1970. *Myth and Law Among the Indo-Europeans.* Berkeley.

———. 1975. "Remus et frater." *History of Religions* 15:146–157. Also in Puhvel 1981:300–311.

———. 1976. "Asklepios Unmasked." *The Pharos of Alpha Omega Alpha* 39:20–22.

———. 1980. "The Indo-European Strain in Greek Myth." In *Panhellenica: Essays in Ancient History and Historiography In Honor of Truesdell S. Brown* (ed. S. M. Burstein and L. Okin) 25–30. Lawrence, KA.

———. 1981. *Analecta Indoeuropaea.* Innsbruck.

———. 1983. "Introduction" to Dumézil 1983:xiii–xiv.

———. 1986. "Who Were the Hittite *hurkilas pesnes?*" In *O-o-pe-ro-si: Festschrift für Ernst Risch* (ed. A. Etter) 151–155. Berlin.

———. 1987. *Comparative Mythology.* Baltimore.

———. 1989. "Hittite Regal Titles: Hattic or Indo-European?" *Journal of Indo-European Studies* 17:351–361.

———. 2002. *Epilecta Indoeuropaea: Opuscula Selecta Annis 1978-2001 Excusa Imprimis ad Res Anatolicas Attinentia.* Innsbruck.

Pulkkinen, L. 1987. "Offensive and Defensive Aggression in Humans." *Aggressive Behavior* 13:197–212.

Pulleyn, S. 1997. *Prayer in Greek Religion*. Oxford.

Radin, P. 1927. *Primitive Man as Philosopher*. New York.

Radt, S. 1985. *Tragicorum Graecorum Fragmenta*. Vol. 3, *Aeschylus*. Göttingen.

Randolph, M. C. 1941. "Celtic Smiths and Satirists: Partners in Sorcery." *Journal of English Literary History* 8:184–197.

———. 1942. "Female Satirists of Ancient Ireland." *Southern Folklore Quarterly* 6:75–87.

Rankin, H. D. 1971. *Petronius the Artist*. The Hague.

———. 1974. "Archilochus was No Magician." *Eos* 19:5–21.

———. 1977. *Archilochus of Paros*. Park Ridge, NJ.

Ranulf, S. 1933. *Jealousy of the Gods and Criminal Law at Athens*. London.

Rawson, E. 1969. *The Spartan Tradition in European Thought*. Oxford.

Rees, A. and Rees, B. 1967. *Celtic Heritage*. London.

Reichert, H., and Zimmermann, G., eds. 1990. *Helden und Heldensage: Otto Gschwantler zum 60. Geburtstag*. Vienna.

Reinhard, J. R. and Hull, V. E. 1936. "Bran and Sceolang." *Speculum* 11:42–58.

Relihan, J. C. 1993. *Ancient Menippean Satire*. Baltimore.

Rhys, J. 1979. *Lectures on the Origin and Growth of Religion as illustrated by Celtic heathendom*. Hibbert Lectures, 1886. New York. (Repr. of 3rd ed., 1898.) (Orig. pub. 1888.)

Richardson, L., Jr., ed. 1977. *Propertius, Elegies I–IV*. Norman, OK.

Richardson, N. J. 1974. *The Homeric Hymn to Demeter*. Oxford.

———. 1981. "The Contest of Homer and Hesiod and Alcidamas' *Mouseion*." *Classical Quarterly*, n.s., 31:1–10.

Richmond, J. 1995. "The Latter Days of a Love Poet: Ovid in Exile." *Classics Ireland* 2. Consulted online at http://www.ucd.ie/classics/95/Richmond95.html.

Richter, G. M. A. 1965. *Portraits of the Greeks*. 3 vols. London.

Riggsby, A. M. 1997. "Did the Romans Believe in their Verdicts?" *Rhetorica* 15:235–251.

Rives, James Boykin. 2002. "Magic in the XII Tables Revisited." *Classical Quarterly* n.s. 52:270–290.

Rivier, A. 1967. "Observations sur Sappho 1, 19 sq." *Revue des études grecques* 80:84–92 = *Etudes de littérature grecque*, 235–242. Geneva, 1975.

Robert, Carl. 1920, 1921, 1926. *Die Griechische Heldensage*. 3 vols. Berlin. This is Bd. II of Ludwig Preller and Carl Robert, *Griechische Mythologie*, 4th ed., 2 Bands, 4 volumes. 1894-1926. (Orig. pub. 1854.)

Bibliography

Robertson, M. 1985. "Greek Art and Religion." In Easterling and Muir 1985:155–190.

Robertson, N. 1988. "Melanthus, Codrus, Neleus, Caucon: Ritual Myth as Athenian History." *Greek, Roman, and Byzantine Studies* 29:201–261.

———. 2003. "Aesop's Encounter with Isis and the Muses, and the Origins of the 'Life of Aesop.'" In Csapo and Miller 2003:247–266.

Robinson, F. N. 1912. "Satirists and Enchanters in Early Irish Literature." In *Studies in the History of Religions. Presented to Crawford H. Toy* (ed. D. G. Lyon and G. F. Moore) 95–130. New York. Repr. in *Satire: Modern Essays in Criticism* (ed. R. Paulson) 1–36. Englewood Cliffs, NJ, 1971.

Rocchi, M. 1980. "La Lira di Achilleus (Hom. *Il.* IX 186)." *Studio Storico Religiosi* 4:259–268.

———. 1985. "Persona reale o persona poetica? L'interpretazione dell' 'io' nella lirica greca arcaica." *Quaderni Urbinati di Cultura Classica*, n.s., 19 (o.s. 48):131–144.

Rohde, E. 1925. *Psyche: The Cult of Souls and Belief in Immortality among the Greeks.* 8th ed. Trans. W. Hillis. 2 vols. London. = *Psyche: Seelencult und Unsterblichkeitsglaube der Griechen.* Freiburg, 1894.

Roscher, W. H., ed. 1884–1937. *Ausführliches Lexikon der griechischen und römischen Mythologie.* 6 vols. Leipzig.

———. 1884–1937. "Mars," in Roscher 1884–1937 2.2:2385–2438.

Rose, H. J. 1959. *A Handbook of Greek Mythology.* New York.

———. 1960a. *A Handbook of Greek Literature.* New York.

———. 1960b. *A Handbook of Latin Literature.* New York.

Rosen, R. 1988a. "Hipponax and His Enemies in Ovid's *Ibis.*" *Classical Quarterly* 38:291–296.

———. 1988b. "Hipponax, Boupalos, and the Conventions of *Psogos.*" *Transactions and Proceedings of the American Philological Association* 143:29–41.

———. 1988c. *Old Comedy and the Iambographic Tradition.* Atlanta.

———. 1988d. "A Poetic Initiation Scene in Hipponax?" *American Journal of Philology* 109:174–179.

Rosenbloom, D. 2002. "From *Ponēros* to *Pharmakos*: Theater, Social Drama, and Revolution in Athens, 428–404 BCE." *Classical Antiquity* 21:283–346.

Rosenmeyer, P. 1992. *The Poetics of Imitation: Anacreon and the Anacreontic Tradition.* Cambridge.

Rösler, W. 1980. *Dichter und Gruppe: Eine Untersuchung zu den Bedingungen und zur historischen Funktion früher griechischer Lyrik am beispiel Alkaios.* Munich.

Roth, C. P. 1976. "Kings and Muses in Hesiod's *Theogony*." *Transactions and Proceedings of the American Philological Association* 106:331–338.

Rothwell, K. S., Jr. 1995. "Aristophanes' *Wasps* and the Sociopolitics of Aesop's Fables." *Classical Journal* 93:233–254.

Rotolo, V. 1980. "Il rito della *Boulimou exelasis*." In *Philias charin. Miscellanea di studi classici in onore di Eugenio Manni* (ed. M. J. Fontana, M. T. Piraino, and F. P. Rizzo) 1947–1961. Rome.

Roussel, P. 1922. "Le thème du sacrifice volontaire dans la tragédie d'Euripide." *Revue Belge de Philologie et d' Histoire* 1:225–240.

Rowe, G. 1966. "The Portrait of Aeschines in the Oration *On the Crown*." *Transactions and Proceedings of the American Philological Association* 97:397–406.

———. 1968. "Demosthenes' First *Philippic*: The Satiric Mode." *Transactions and Proceedings of the American Philological Association* 99:361–374.

Rowland, I. 1980. "*Hieros Aner*: An Interpretation the 'Holy Man' in Classical Greece." Diss. Bryn Mawr College.

Rubin, L., Jr. 1981. "Uncle Remus and the Ubiquitous Rabbit." In *Critical Essays on Joel Chandler Harris* (ed. R. B. Bickley, Jr.) 158–173. Boston.

Rubino, C., and Shelmerdine, C., eds. 1983. *Approaches to Homer*. Austin, TX.

Rubenstein, J. 1980. *Soviet Dissidents*. Boston.

Rudhardt, J. 1960. "La définition du délit d'impiété d'après la législation attique." *Museum Helveticum* 17:87–105.

———. 1970. "Les mythes grecs relatifs à l'instauration du sacrifice." *Museum Helveticum* 27:1–15.

Runes, M. 1926. "Geschichte des Wortes vates." In *Festschrift für ... Paul Kretschmer* (1926) 202–216. Vienna.

Russell, P. 1988. "The Sounds of Silence: the Growth of Cormac's Glossary." *Cambridge Medieval Celtic Studies* 15:1–30.

Rusten, J. S. 1977. "*Wasps* 1360–69: Philokleon's TWTHASMOS." *Harvard Studies in Classical Philology* 81:157–161.

Sauvé, J. L. 1970. "The Divine Victim: Aspects of Human Sacrifice in Viking Scandinavia and Vedic India." In Puhvel 1970:173–192.

Schadewaldt, W. 1936. "Aischylos' Achilleis." *Hermes* 71:25–69.

———, ed. and trans. 1959a. *Legende von Homer dem fahrenden Sänger*. Zurich.

———. 1959b. *Von Homers Welt und Werk*. Stuttgart.

Schauer, M. and Merkle, S. 1992. "Äsop und Sokrates." In Holzberg 1992a:85–96.

Scheinberg, S. 1979. "The Bee Maidens of the Homeric Hymn to Hermes." *Harvard Studies in Classical Philology* 83:1–28.

Schmid, W. 1948. "Das Sokratesbild der Wolken." *Philologus* 97:209–228.

Schmidt, E. A. 1977. "*Amica vis pastoribus.* Der Jambiker Horaz in seinem Epodenbuch." *Gymnasium* 84:401–423.

————. 1978. "Archilochos, Kallimachos, Horaz. Jambischer Geist in drei Epochen." *Wiener Humanistische Blätter* 20:1–17.

Schmitt, J. 1921. *Freiwilliger Opfertod bei Euripides.* Giessen.

————. 1927. "Lykabas." RE vol. 13.2, col. 2228.

Schmitt, R. 1967. *Dichtung und Dichtersprache in indogermanischer Zeit.* Wiesbaden.

Schönberger, K. J. 1912. "Kaminos." *Wochenschrift für klassische Philologie* 29:781–783.

Schultz, W. 1909–1912. *Rätsel aus dem hellenischen Kulturkreise.* Leipzig.

Schur, W. 1962. *Das Zeitalter des Marius und Sulla.* (*Klio*, Beiheft XLVI). Wiesbaden.

Schwartz, E. 1899. "Tyrtaios." *Hermes* 34:428–468.

————. 1937. "Die messenische Geschichte bei Pausanias." *Philologus* 92:19–46.

————. 1956. *Gesammelte Schriften* II. Berlin. Includes Schwartz 1937.

Schwenn, F. 1915. *Die Menschenopfer bei den Griechen und Römern.* Religionsgeschichtl. Versuche und Vorarbeiten. Giessen.

Scodel, R. 1980. "Hesiod Redivivus." *Greek, Roman, and Byzantine Studies* 21:301–320.

Scullard, H. H. 1959. *From Gracchi to Nero: A History of Rome from 133 B.C. to A.D. 68.* New York. (5th ed., 1982)

Seaford, Richard, ed. 1984. *Euripides, Cyclops.* Oxford.

————. 1994. *Reciprocity and Ritual: Homer and Tragedy in the Developing City-State.* Oxford.

Seager, R. 1965. "Clodius, Pompeius, and the Exile of Cicero." *Latomus* 24:519–531.

Sealey, R. 1957. "From Phemios to Ion." *Revue des études grecques* 70: 312–355.

See, K. von, ed. *Europäische Heldendichtung.* Darmstadt.

Segal, C. 1974. "Eros and Incantation." *Arethusa* 7:139–160.

————. 1981. *Tragedy and Civilization.* Cambridge, MA.

————. 1994. *Singers, Heroes and Gods in the Odyssey.* Ithaca, NY.

Seibert, J. 1979. *Die Politischen Flüchtlinge und Verbanneten in der Griechischen Geschichte.* 2 vols. Darmstadt.

Sergent, B. 1998. *Les trois fonctions indo-européennes en Grèce ancienne I: de Mycènes aux tragiques.* Paris.

Shackleton Bailey, D. R. 1965–1968. *Cicero's Letters to Atticus.* 6 vols. Cambridge.

Sharpe, R. 1979. "Hiberno-Latin *Laicus*, Irish *Láech* and the Devil's Men." *Ériu* 30:75–92.

Sihler, E. G. 1914. *Cicero of Arpinum.* New Haven.

Skutsch, O. 1985. *The Annals of Quintus Ennius.* Oxford.

Slater, W. J. 1972. "Simonides' House." *Phoenix* 26:232–240.

Sluiter, I. and Rosen, R. M., eds. 2004. *Free Speech in Classical Antiquity.* Mnemosyne Supplement 254. Brill.

Snell, B. 1953. *The Discovery of the Mind in Greek Philosophy and Literature.* Trans. T. G. Rosenmeyer. New York. = *Die Entdeckung des Geistes: Studien zur Entstehung des europäischen Denkens bei den Griechen.* Hamburg, 1946.

———. 1961. *Poetry and Society: The Role of Poetry in Ancient Greece.* Bloomington, IN.

Snodgrass, A. 1980. *Archaic Greece: The Age of Experiment.* London.

Snyder, J. M. 1997. *Lesbian Desire in the Lyrics of Sappho.* New York.

Sokolowski, F. 1969. *Lois sacrées des cités grecques.* Paris.

Sollmann, M. A. 1960. "Cicero's Sense of Humor (*de Or.* and *Att.*)." *Classical Bulletin* 36:51–58.

Solmsen, F. 1938. "Cicero's First Speeches: A Rhetorical Analysis." *Transactions and Proceedings of the American Philological Association* 61:542–556.

Solmsen, F., Merkelbach, R., and West, M. L., eds. 1983. *Hesiodi Theogonia Opera et Dies Scutum. Fragmenta Selecta.* 2nd ed. Oxford. (Orig. pub. 1970.)

Sommerstein, A., ed. and trans. 1980. *Acharnians.* Warminster.

———, ed. and trans. 1983. *Wasps.* Warminster.

———. 1986. "The Decree of Syrakosios." *Classical Quarterly* 36:101–108.

———. 2004. "Harassing the Satirist: The Alleged Attempts to Prosecute Aristophanes." In Sluiter and Rosen 2004:145–174.

Somville, P. 1984. "Le Dauphin dans le Religion Grecque." *Revue de l'Histoire des Religions* 201:3–24.

Sourvinou-Inwood, C. 1990. "The Cup Bologna PU 273: A Reading." *Metis* 5:137–153.

Spaeth, J. W. 1931. "Cicero the Poet." *Classical Journal* 26:500–515.

Spenser, E. 1810. *View of the State of Ireland.* Dublin.

Sperduti, A. 1950. "The Divine Nature of Poetry in Antiquity." *Transactions and Proceedings of the American Philological Association* 81:209–240.

Stark, R. 1953. "Socratisches in den 'Vogeln' des Aristophanes." *Rheinisches Museum für classische Philologie* 96:77–89.

Steffen, V. 1954. "De Aristophane a Cleone in ius vocato." *Eos* 47.1:7–21.

Steiner, D. T. 1995. "Stoning and Sight: A Structural Equivalence in Greek Mythology." *California Studies in Classical Antiquity* 14:193–211.

Stern, J. 1991. "Scapegoat Narratives in Herodotus." *Hermes* 119:304–311.

Stern, L. C. 1910. "Davydd ab Gwilym, ein walisische Minnesänger." In *Zeitschrift für Celtische Philologie* 7:1–265.

Steuart, E. M. 1921. "The Earliest Narrative Poetry of Rome." *Classical Quarterly* 15:31–37.

Stevens, P. T. 1956. "Euripides and the Athenians." *Journal of Hellenic Studies* 76:87–94.

Stockton, D. 1971. *Cicero: A Political Biography.* Oxford.

Stokes, W. 1862. *Three Irish Glossaries.* London.

———, trans. 1887. "The Siege of Howth." *Revue Celtique* 8:47–64. Available online at www.geocities.com/athens/oracle/7207/victimtest.html.

———, ed. 1891. "The Second Battle of Moytura." *Revue Celtique* 12:52–130, 306–308. Available online at CELT, http://celt.ucc.ie/index.html.

———, ed. 1892. "The Battle of Mag Mucrime." *Revue Celtique* 13:434–436. Available online at http://www.ancienttexts.org/library/celtic/ctexts/mucrama.html.

———. 1893. "On the Bodleian Fragment of Cormac's Glossary." *Transactions of the Philological Society* 1891–1893:149–206.

———, trans. 1894–1895. "The Prose Tales in the Rennes Dindsenchas." *Revue Celtique* 15:272–336, 418–484; 16:31–83, 135–167, 269–312.

———. 1899–1900. "The Bodleian Amra Choluimb Chille, appendix." *Revue Celtique* 20:31–55, 132–183, 248–289, 400–437; 21:133–136.

———, trans. 1901. "The Destruction of Dá Derga's Hostel." *Revue Celtique* 22:9–61, 165–215, 282–329, 390–437. Available online at The Medieval Source Book, http://www.fordham.edu/halsall/source/1100derga.html and http://www.bartleby.com/49/3/. Irish text available online at CELT, http://celt.ucc.ie/index.html.

———, trans. 1903a. "The Battle of Allen." *Revue Celtique* 24:41–70. Available online at www.geocities.com/athens/oracle/7207/victimtest.html.

———, trans. 1903b. "The Wooing of Luaine and Death of Athirne." *Revue Celtique* 24:270–287. Available online at http://www.geocities.com/patrickbrown40/luaine.htm.

———, trans. 1905. "Colloquy of the Two Sages." *Revue Celtique* 26:4–64. Available online at Celtic Literature Collective, http://www.ancienttexts.org/library/celtic/ctexts/irish.html.

Stokes, W., and Meyer, K., eds. 1900. *Archiv für celtische Lexikographie.* 3 vols. Halle.

Stokes, W., and Windisch, E. 1887. "Táin bó Regamna." In *Irische Texte*, 2nd ser., 2:24. Available online at CELT, http://celt.ucc.ie/index.html. Translation available at Irish Literature Collective, http://www.ancienttexts.org/library/celtic/ctexts/irish.html.

Stoppard, T. 1975. *Travesties.* London.

Storey, I. 1995. "*Wasps* 1284–91 and the Portrait of Kleon in *Wasps.*" *Scholia* 4:3–23. Accessed online at http://www.otago.ac.nz/classics/scholia/index.html.

———, 1998. "Poets, Politicians and Perverts: Personal Humour in Aristophanes." *Classics Ireland* 5. Accessed online at www.ucd.ie/classics/98/Storey98html.

Strack, C. 1880. *De Juvenalis exilio.* Frankfurt.

Stroh, W. 1979. "Ovids Liebeskunst und die Ehegesetze des Augustus." *Gymnasium* 86:323–351.

Stroh, W. 2004. "*De Domo Sua*: Legal Problem and Structure." In *Cicero the Advocate* (ed. J. Powell and J. Paterson) 313–370. Oxford.

Strutynski, U. 1980. "Ares: A Reflex of the Indo-European War God?" *Arethusa* 13:217–231.

Sullivan, J. P. 1968. *The Satyricon of Petronius.* London.

———. 1985. *Literature and Politics in the Age of Nero.* Ithaca, NY.

Sullivan, J. 2001. "A Note on The Death of Socrates." *Classical Quarterly* n.s. 51:608–610.

Sussman, L. A. 1994. "Antony as a *Miles Gloriosus* in Cicero's *Second Philippic.*" *Scholia* 3:53–83. Available online at http://www.otago.ac.nz/classics/scholia/index.html.

Sutton, D. F. 1988. "Dicaeopolis as Aristophanes, Aristophanes as Dicaeopolis." *Liverpool Classical Monthly* 13:105–108.

Svenbro, J. 1976. *La parole et le marbre: Aux origines de la poétique grecque.* Lund.

Syme, R. 1939. *The Roman Revolution.* Oxford.

———. 1978. *History in Ovid.* Oxford.

Szegedy-Maszak, A. 1978. "Legends of the Greek Lawgivers." *Greek, Roman, and Byzantine Studies* 17:199–209.

Talley, J. E. 1974. "Runes, Mandrakes, and Gallows." In Larson et al. 1974:157–168.

Tarditi, G. 1969. "L'asebeia di Aiace e quella di Pittaco." *Quaderni Urbinati di Cultura Classica* 8:86–96.

Tarditi, I. 1968. *Archilochus.* Rome.

Terzaghi, N. 1929. *Studi sull'antica poesia Latina.* Rome.

Thalmann, W. G. 1988. "Thersites: Comedy, Scapegoats, and Heroic Ideology in the *Iliad.*" *Transactions and Proceedings of the American Philological Association* 118:1–28.

Thibault, J. C. 1964. *The Mystery of Ovid's Exile*. Berkeley.

Thieme, P. 1968. "Die Wurzel vat." In *Indogermanische Dichtersprache* (ed. R. Schmitt) 187–203. Darmstadt.

Thomas, K. 1971. *Religion and the Decline of Magic*. New York.

Thompson, S. 1955. *Motif-Index of Folk Literature: A Classification of Narrative Elements in Folktales, Ballads, Myths, Fables, Mediaeval Romances, Exempla, Fabliaux, Jest-books, and Local Legends*. Rev. ed. Bloomington, IN. (Orig. pub. 1932–1936.)

Thomson, G. 1968. *Aeschylus and Athens*. 3rd ed. London. (2nd ed., 1946; 1st ed., 1941.)

Thurneysen, R. 1891. "Mittelirische Verslehren." In *Irische Texte: mit Übersetzunger und Wörterbuch* (ed. W. Stokes and E. Windisch), 3rd ser., 1:1–182. Leipzig.

———. 1921. *Die irische Helden- und Königsage bis zum siebzehnten Jahrhundert*. Halle.

Tigerstedt, E. N. 1965–1978. *The Legend of Sparta in Classical Antiquity*. 3 vols. Stockholm.

———. 1970. "*Furor Poeticus*: Poetic Inspiration in Greek Literature before Democritus and Plato." *Journal of the History of Ideas* 31:163–178.

Tischler, J. 1993. *Hethitisches Etymologishes Glossar*. Teil III, Lieferung 9, T, D/2. Innsbruck.

Todd, J. H., ed. and trans. 1848. *Leabhar Breathnach Annso Sis. The Irish Version of the Historia Britonum of Nennius*. Irish Archaeological Society 11. Dublin.

Toepffer, J. 1888. "Thargeliengebräuche." *Rheinisches Museum für classische Philologie* 43:142–145.

———. 1893. "Androgeos." RE 1:2143–2145.

———. 1889. *Attische Genealogie*. Berlin.

Townend, G. B. 1965. "The Poems." In Dorey 1965:109–134.

Tracy, H. L. 1937. "Plato as Satirist." *Classical Journal* 33:153–162.

Treu, M. 1959. *Archilochos, Griechisch und Deutsch herausgegeben*. Munich.

Trever, A. A. 1925. "The Intimate Relation Between Economic and Political Conditions in History, as Illustrated in Ancient Megara." *Classical Philology* 20:115–132.

Trumpf, J. 1973. "Über das Trinken in der Poesie des Alkaios." *Zeitschrift für Papyrologie und Epigraphik* 12:139–160.

Trypanis, C. A., trans. 1958. *Callimachus, Aetia, Iambi, Hecale and Other Fragments*. LCL 421. Cambridge, MA.

Tsagarakis, O. 1979. "Some Neglected Aspects of Love in Sappho's Fr. 31LP." *Rheinisches Museum für classische Philologie* 22:97–118.

———. 1986. "Broken Hearts and the Social Circumstances in Sappho's Poetry." *Rheinisches Museum für classische Philologie* 129:1–17.

Tsantsanoglou, K. 2003. "Archilochus Fighting in Thasos. Frr. 93a + 94 from the Sosthenes Inscription." *Hellenika* 53:235–255.

Tucker, J. A. 1987. "Ritual Insults for Gluttony and Laziness in Greek Poetic Initiations. *Theogony* 26 and its Echoes." Diss. Univ. of Michigan.

Turville-Petre, E. O. G. 1964. *Myth and Religion of the North.* New York.

Ulrich, R. 1973. "Pain as a Cause of Aggression." In *Aggression, Hostility and Violence, Nature or Nurture?* (ed. T. Maple and D. Matheson) 152–181. New York.

Usener, H. 1901. "Italische Volksjustiz." *Rheinisches Museum für classische Philologie* 56:1–28 = *Kleine Schriften* 4.356–382. Leipzig, 1912.

Usher, S. 1999. *Greek Oratory: Tradition and Originality.* Oxford.

Utley, F. L. 1944. *The Crooked Rib.* Columbus, OH.

Vahlen, J. 1923. "Juvenal und Paris." *Gesammelte philologische Schriften 2.* Leipzig.

van Brock, N. 1959. "Substitution rituelle." *Revue Hittite et Asianique* 65:117–146.

van Buitenen, J. A. B., trans. and ed. 1973, 1975, 1978. *The Mahābhārata.* 3 vols. (including books 1–5). Chicago.

van den Bruwaene, M., ed. 1970. *Ciceron, De Natura Deorum.* 3 vols. Brussels.

van Hamel, Anton Gerard. 1932–1933. "Óðinn hanging on the Tree." *Acta Philologica Scandinavica* 7:260–288.

———. 1934. "The Mastering of the Mead." In *Studia Germanica Tillägnade Ernst Albin Kock* 76–85. Lund.

van Leeuwen, J. 1888. "De Aristophane Peregrino." *Mnemosyne,* n.s., 16:263–288.

Van Unnik, W. C. 1962. "A Formula Describing Prophecy." *New Testament Studies* 9:86–94.

Vendryes, J. 1913. Review of F. N. Robinson's "Satirists and Enchanters in Early Irish Literature." *Revue Celtique* 34:94–96.

———. 1987. *Lexique Etymologique de L'Irlandais Ancien: Lettre C.* Paris.

Vernant, J.-P.. 1981. "Ambiguity and Reversal: On the Enigmatic Structure of Oedipus Rex." In *Tragedy and Myth in Ancient Greece* (ed. J.-P. Vernant and P. Vidal-Naquet, translated by J. Lloyd), 87–119. New Jersey. = *Greek Tragedy, Modern Essays in Criticism* (ed. E. Segal) 189–209. New York, 1983.

———. 1983. *Myth and Thought Among the Greeks.* London. Esp. 75–106, "Mythical Aspects of Memory."

Verrall, A. W. 1896. "Tyrtaeus: A Graeco-Roman Tradition." *Classical Review* 10:269–277.

———. 1897. "The Date of Tyrtaeus." *Classical Review* 11:185–190.

Vickers, B. 1973. *Towards Greek Tragedy: Drama, Myth and Society.* London.

Vickery, J. B. 1972. *The Scapegoat: Ritual and Literature*. Boston.

Visser, M. 1982. "Worship Your Enemy." *Harvard Theological Review* 75:403–428.

Vogel, M. 1964. "Der Schlauch des Marsyas." *Rheinisches Museum für classische Philologie*, N.F., 107:34–56.

Voight, E.-M., ed. 1971. *Sappho et Alcaeus: Fragmenta*. Amsterdam.

Volpe, M. 1977. "The Persuasive Force of Humor. Cicero's Defense of Caelius." *Quarterly Journal of Speech* 63:311–323.

von Arnim, H. 1913. *Supplementum Euripideum*. Bonn.

Vox, O. 1977. "Ipponatte fr. 41W, una parodia oscena." *Quaderni Urbinati di Cultura Classica* 26:87–89.

Vürtheim, J. 1919. *Stesichoros' Fragmente und Biographie*. Leiden.

Wade-Gery, H. T. 1952. *The Poet of the Iliad*. Cambridge.

Wagner, H. 1970. "Studies in the Origins of Early Celtic Civilization. II. Irish *fáth*, Welsh *gwawd*, Old Icelandic *óðr* 'Poetry' and the Germanic God Wotan/Óðinn." *Zeitschrift für celtische Philologie* 31:46–57.

Walcot, P. 1957. "The Problem of the Prooemium of Hesiod's Theogony." *Symbolae Osloenses* 33:37–47.

Wallace, P. W. 1985. "The Tomb of Hesiod and the Treasury of Minyas at Orchomenos." In *Actes du troisième congrès international sur la Beotie antique, Montreal-Quebec* (ed. J. M. Fossey and H. Giroux) 165–179. Amsterdam.

Walsh, P. 1933. *Gleanings from Irish Manuscripts*. 2nd ed. Dublin. (Orig. pub. 1918.)

Ward, D. 1968. *The Divine Twins: An Indo-European Myth in Germanic Tradition*. Berkeley.

———. 1970. "The Threefold Death: An Indo-European Trifunctional Sacrifice?" In Puhvel 1970:123–142.

———. 1973. "On the Poets and Poetry of the Indo-Europeans." *Indo-European Studies* 1:127–144.

———. 1982a. "Honor and Shame in the Middle Ages: An Open Letter to Lutz Röhrich." In *Jahrbuch Für Volksliedforschung* (Festschrift Lutz Röhrich) 1–16. Berlin.

———. 1982b. "Review of H. Gehrts, *Ramayana: Brüder und Braut im Märchen-Epos*." *Canadian Review of Comparative Literature* 9:253–255.

Warmington, E. H., trans. 1936. *Remains of Old Latin*, vol. 2. Cambridge, MA.

———, trans. 1938. *Remains of Old Latin*, vol. 3. Cambridge, MA.

Watkins, C. 1963. "Indo-European Metrics and Archaic Irish Verse." *Celtica* 6:215–249.

———. 1976. "The Etymology of Irish *duan*." *Celtica* 11:270–277.

———. 1982. "Aspects of Indo-European Poetics." In *The Indo-Europeans in the Fourth and Third Millennia* (ed. E. C. Polomé) 104–120. Ann Arbor.

———. 1995. *How to Kill a Dragon: Aspects of Indo-European Poetics*. Oxford.

Watson, L. 1983. "The Iambist as Sheep-Dog: Horace, *Epode* VI 7–8." *Mnemosyne* 36:156–159.

———. 1991. *Arae: The Curse Poetry of Antiquity*. Leeds.

———. 2003. *A Commentary on Horace's Epodes*. Oxford.

Watson, W. L. 1970. "The Surname as Brickbat in Cicero's Speeches." *Classical Journal* 66:55–58.

Wehrli, F. 1967–1969. *Die Schule des Aristoteles, Texte und Commentare*. 2nd ed. 10 vols. Basel. (Orig. pub. 1944–1959.)

———. 1969. *Phainias von Eresos, Chamaileon, Praxiphanes*. Vol. 9 of Wehrli 1967–1969. Basel.

Weil, H. 1900. *Etudes sur l'antiquite grecque*. Paris.

Weiler, I. 1974. *Der Agon im Mythos*. Darmstadt.

Welsford, E. 1936. *The Fool, His Social and Literary History*. New York.

West, M. L. 1966. *Hesiod: Theogony*. Edited with prolegomena and commentary. Oxford.

———. 1967. "The Contest of Homer and Hesiod." *Classical Quarterly*, n.s., 17:433–451.

———. 1971. "Stesichorus." *Classical Quarterly* 21:302–314.

———. 1973. "Greek Poetry 2000–700 B.C." *Classical Quarterly* 67:179–192.

———. 1973b. "Indo-European Meter." *Glotta* 51:161–187.

———. 1974. *Studies in Greek Elegy and Iambus*. Berlin.

———. 1975. *Immortal Helen*. Inaugural lecture, Bedford College, University of London. London.

———. 1978. *Hesiod: Works and Days*. Edited with prolegomena and commentary. Oxford.

———. 1982. "Archilochus's Fox and Eagle: More Echoes in Later Poetry." *Zeitschrift für Papyrologie und Epigraphik* 45:30–32.

———. 1983. *The Orphic Poems*. Oxford.

———. 1984. "The Ascription of Fables to Aesop in Archaic and Classical Greece." In Adrados 1984:105–136.

———. 1985a. "Archilochus: New Fragments and Readings." *Zeitschrift für Papyrologie und Epigraphik* 61:10–13.

———. 1985b. Review of Robert Parker, *Miasma* in *Classical Review* 35:94.

———. 1989. *Iambi et Elegi Graeci*. 2nd ed., enlarged and revised. Oxford.

———. 1996. "Riddles." In Hornblower and Spawforth 1996:1317.

———. 1997. *The East Face of Helicon: West Asiatic Elements in Greek Poetry and Myth*. Oxford.

———. 1999. "The Invention of Homer." *Classical Quarterly* 49:364–382.

———, ed. and trans. 2003. *Homeric Hymns; Homeric Apocrypha; Lives of Homer.* LCL 496. Cambridge, MA.

———, ed. and trans. 2003b. *Greek Epic Fragments: From the Seventh to the Fifth Centuries BC.* LCL 497. Cambridge, MA.

West, S. 1966. Review of Arrighetti 1964 in *Gnomon* 38:546–550.

Westermann, A. 1845. *Biographoi, Vitarum Scriptores Graeci Minores.* Brunswick. Repr. 1964. Amsterdam.

Wheeler, A. L. 1925. "Topics from the Life of Ovid." *American Journal of Philology* 46:1–28.

Whitman, C. 1964. *Aristophanes and the Comic Hero.* Cambridge, MA.

Wiechers, A. 1961. *Aesop in Delphi.* Meisenheim am Glam.

Wiedemann, T. 1975. "The Political Background of *Tristia* 2." *Classical Quarterly* 25:264–271.

Wigodsky, M. 1972. *Vergil and Early Latin Poetry.* Hermes-Einzelschriften 24. Wiesbaden.

Wilamowitz-Moellendorff, U. von. 1893. *De Tribus Carminibus Latinis.* Göttingen.

———. 1900. *Der Textgeschichte der griechischen Lyriker.* Berlin.

———. 1914. *Aeschyli Tragoediae.* Berlin.

———. 1916a. *Die Ilias und Homer.* Berlin.

———. 1916b. *Vitae Homeri et Hesiodi.* Bonn.

———. 1956. *Sappho und Simonides.* Berlin.

———. 1958. *Aeschylus.* Berlin.

Williams, F. 1971. "A Theophany in Theocritus." *Classical Quarterly* n.s. 21:137–145.

———. 1978. *Callimachus, Hymn to Apollo: A Commentary.* Oxford.

Williams, G. W. 1970. "Libel and Slander in Rome." In OCD 606.

Wilson, H. L. 1903. *Juvenal.* Boston.

Wimmer, W. 1960. *Kallimachos in Rom.* Wiesbaden.

Windisch, E. 1905. *Die altirische Heldensage Táin Bó Cúalnge nach dem Buch von Leinster.* Leipzig.

Winkler, J. J. 1985. *Auctor & Actor: A Narratological Reading of Apuleius's Golden Ass.* Berkeley.

Winkler, J., and Zeitlin, F., eds. 1990. *Nothing To Do With Dionysos? Athenian Drama in its Social Context.* Princeton.

Winkler, M. 1988. "Juvenal's Attitude Toward Ciceronian Poetry and Rhetoric." *Rheinisches Museum für classische Philologie* 131:84–97.

Winn, S. M. M. 1995. *Heaven, Heroes, and Happiness: The Indo-European Roots Of Western Ideology.* Lanham, MD.

Wiseman, T. P. 1985. *Catullus and his World: A Reappraisal.* Cambridge.

Wistrand, E. 1964. "Archilochus and Horace." In Pouilloux et al. 1964:255–287.

Wolters, P. 1903. "*ELAPHOSTIKTOS.*" *Hermes* 38:265–273.

Wooten, C. 1983. *Cicero's Philippics and their Demosthenic Model.* Chapel Hill, NC.

Wroth, W. 1975–1983. *Catalogue of the Greek Coins of Troas, Aeolis, and Lesbos,* vol. 17 of *A Catalogue of the Greek Coins in the British Museum.* Repr. Bologna. (Orig. pub. 1873–1929.)

Wünsch, R. 1912. *Antike Fluchtafeln.* Bonn.

Young, J., ed. and trans. 1954. *The Prose Edda of Snorri Sturluson; Tales from Norse Mythology.* Berkeley.

Zeller, E. 1962. *Socrates and the Socratic Schools.* Trans. O. Reichel, excerpted from *Die Philosophie der Griechen.* New York. = *Die Philosophie der Griechen: Eine Untersuchung über Charakter, Gang und Hauptmomente ihrer Entwicklung.* Tübingen, 1844–1852.

Online Bibliography

Classics

The Perseus Digital Library has most basic Greek and Roman authors in Greek, Latin and English. http://www.perseus.tufts.edu/.

Greek lyric poets: A sampling of texts can be found online at Bibliotheca Augustana, at http://www.fh-augsburg.de/~harsch/augusta.html#la.

For Latin authors, see also Corpus Scriptorum Latinorum at http://www.forumromanum.org/literature/index.html.

Old Ireland

CELT, Corpus of Electronic Texts. http://www.celt.ucc.ie/index.html. Many texts in Old Irish and English.

Celtic Literature Collective: http://www.ancienttexts.org/library/celtic/ctexts/home.html.

For individual texts, see entries above.

Old Germanic

The Gautreksaga: can be found at Zoe Borovksy's Norse saga page, http://www.server.fhp.uoregon.edu/Norse/.

The Heimskringla can be found at OMACL, The Online Medieval and Classical Library, http://sunsite.berkeley.edu/OMACL/.

Bibliography

The Poetic Edda: The Normannii Thiud & Reik site, has the Benjamin Thorpe translation, and facing Old Norse. http://www.normannii.org/ guilds_lore/lore/poetic/index.htm. Text also at TITUS, Thesaurus Indogermanischer Text- und Sprachmaterialien, http://titus.uni-frankfurt.de/texte/etcs/germ/anord/edda/edda.htm. Text from http://etext.old.no/Bugge/voluspa/, the Sophus Bugge edition.

The Prose Edda: The Arthur Gilchrist Brodeur translation of the *Prose Edda* (1916) can be found at the Internet Sacred Text Archive site, http:// www.sacred-texts.com/neu/pre/.

Saxo Grammaticus, *History of the Danes*. Online version available from the Danish Royal Library, http://www.kb.dk/elib/lit/dan/saxo/lat/or.dsr/ index.htm. A translation by Oliver Elton is available at Berkeley's Online Medieval and Classical Library, http://sunsite.berkeley.edu/OMACL/.

The Ynglingasaga: The Samuel Laing translation of *the Ynglingasaga* (part of the *Heimskringla* by Snorri Sturlson) can be found online at the Internet Sacred Text Archive site, http://www.sacred-texts.com/neu/heim/ index.htm.

Sanskrit

The Mahābhārata. The entire *Mahābhārata*, in the English translation by Kisari Mohari Ganguli, available at the Internet Sacred Text Archive, http:// www.sacred-texts.com/hin/maha/index.htm. Sanskrit texts at www. sanskrit.gde.to/mirrors/mahabharata/ or http://www.sub.uni-goettingen.de/ebene_1/fiindolo/gretil/1_sanskr/2_epic/mbh/sas/ mahabharata.htm.

Indo-European generally

See TITUS, Thesaurus Indogermanischer Text- und Sprachmaterialien, at http://titus.uni-frankfurt.de/indexe.htm.

Testimonia

Testimonia related to this book (including the scholiast lives of Juvenal as well as texts relating to the Greek pharmakos, Androgeus, Codrus, and Aglauros) are available online at www.geocities.com/athens/ oracle/7207/victimtest.html.

Index

This book was composed by Ivy Livingston
and manufactured by Victor Graphics, Baltimore, MD

The typeface is Gentium, designed by Victor Gaultney
and distributed by SIL International